THE VINTAGE BOOK OF INDIAN WRITING 1947–1997

Salman Rushdie is the author of ten books. His work has been published in thirty languages. Elizabeth West is a freelance editor.

BY SALMAN RUSHDIE

Fiction

Grimus

Midnight's Children

Shame

The Satanic Verses

Haroun and the Sea of Stories

East, West

The Moor's Last Sigh

Non-Fiction

The Jaguar Smile:
A Nicaraguan Journey

Imaginary Homelands

'The Wizard of Oz'

THE VINTAGE BOOK OF INDIAN WRITING 1947–1997

edited by

SALMAN RUSHDIE
and
ELIZABETH WEST

$\mathcal{V}$

VINTAGE

First published in Great Britain by
Vintage, 1997

Vintage
Random House, 20 Vauxhall Bridge Road, London SW1V 2SA

Random House Australia (Pty) Limited
20 Alfred Street, Milsons Point, Sydney,
New South Wales 2061, Australia

Random House New Zealand Limited
18 Poland Road, Glenfield,
Auckland 10, New Zealand

Random House South Africa (Pty) Limited
Endulini, 5A Jubilee Road, Parktown 2193, South Africa

Random House UK Limited Reg. No. 954009

A CIP catalogue record for this book
is available from the British Library

ISBN 0099731010

Papers used by Random House UK Ltd are natural, recyclable
products made from wood grown in sustainable forests. The
manufacturing processes conform to the environmental
regulations of the country of origin

Set in 10½/12 Sabon by SX Composing DTP, Rayleigh, Essex
Printed and bound in Great Britain by
Cox & Wyman, Reading, Berkshire

A VINTAGE ORIGINAL

CONTENTS

INTRODUCTION

I once gave a reading to a gathering of university students in Delhi and when I'd finished a young woman put up her hand. 'Mr Rushdie, I read through your novel, *Midnight's Children*,' she said. 'It is a very long book, but never mind, I read it through. And the question I want to ask you is this: fundamentally, what's your point?'

Before I could attempt an answer, she spoke again. 'Oh, I know what you're going to say. You're going to say that the whole effort – from cover to cover – that is the point of the exercise. Isn't that what you were going to say?'

'Something like that, perhaps . . .' I got out.

She snorted. 'It won't do.'

'Please,' I begged, 'do I have to have just one point?'

'Fundamentally,' she said, with impressive firmness, 'yes.'

So here, once again, is a very long book; and though it is not a novel, but an anthology selected from the best Indian writing of the half-century since the country's independence, still one could easily say of the work contained in these pages that the whole collective effort, from cover to cover, is the point of the exercise. Fifty years of work, by four generations of writers, is impossible to summarise, especially when it hails from that huge crowd of a country (close to a billion people at the last count), that vast, metamorphic, continent-sized culture that feels, to Indians and visitors alike, like a non-stop assault on the senses, the emotions, the imagination and the spirit. Put India in the Atlantic Ocean and it would reach from Europe to America; put India and China together and you've got almost half the population of the world. It's high time Indian literature got itself noticed, and it's started happening. New writers seem to emerge every few weeks. Their work is as multiform as the place, and readers who care about the vitality of literature will find at least some of these voices saying something they want to hear. However, my Delhi interrogator may be pleased to hear that this large and various survey turns out to be making, fundamentally, just one – perhaps rather surprising – point.

This is it: the prose writing – both fiction and non-fiction – created in this period by Indian writers *working in English*, is proving to be a stronger and more important body of work than most of what has been produced in the 16 'official languages' of India, the so-called 'vernacular languages', during the same time; and, indeed, this new, and still burgeoning, 'Indo-Anglian' literature represents perhaps the most valuable contribution India has yet made to the world of books.

It is a large claim, and while it may be easy for Western readers to accept it (after all, few non-English-language Indian writers, other than the Nobel laureate Tagore, have ever made much of an impact on world literature), it runs counter to much of the received critical wisdom within India itself. It is also not a claim which, when we set out on the enormous and rewarding task of doing the reading for this book, we ever expected to make. The task we set ourselves was simply to make the best possible selection from what is presently available in the English language, including, obviously, work in translation. To our considerable astonishment, only one translated text – S.H. Manto's masterpiece, the short story *Toba Tek Singh* – made the final cut.

Two qualifications should be made at once. First: there has long been a genuine problem of translation in India – not only into English but between the vernacular languages – and it is possible that good writers have been excluded by reason of their translators' inadequacies rather than their own. Nowadays, however, such bodies as the Indian Sahitya Akademi and UNESCO – as well as Indian publishers themselves – have been putting their resources into the creation of better translations, and the problem, while not eradicated, is certainly much diminished. And second: while it was impossible, for reasons of space, to include a representative selection of modern Indian poetry, it was evident to us that the rich poetic traditions of India continued to flourish in many of the sub-continent's languages, whereas the English-language poets, with a few distinguished exceptions (Arun Kolatkar, A.K. Ramanujan, Jayanta Mahapatra, to name just three), did not match the quality of their counterparts in prose.

Those who wish to argue with the conclusion we have drawn may suspect that we did not read enough. But we have read as widely and deeply as we could. Others may feel that, as one of the editors is English and the other a practising English-language writer of Indian origin, we are simply betraying our own cultural and linguistic prejudices, or defending our turf, or – even worse – gracelessly blowing our own trumpet. It is of course true that any anthology worth its salt will reflect the judgements and tastes of its editors. I can only say that our tastes are pretty catholic and our minds, I hope, have been open. We have made our choices, and stand by them.

(As to the inclusion here of my own work, the decision was taken with some unease; but *Midnight's Children* is undeniably a part of the story of these fifty years, and we decided, in the end, that leaving it out would be a weirder decision than putting it in. After its publication, incidentally, I learned that the idea of a long saga-novel about a child born at the exact moment of independence – midnight, August 14-15, 1947 – had occurred to other writers, too. A Goan poet showed me the first chapter of an abandoned novel in which the 'midnight child' was born not in Bombay, but in Goa. And as I travelled round India, I heard of at least two other aborted projects, one in Bengali, the other in Kannada, with pretty similar themes. I just had the good fortune to finish my book first.)

The lack of first-rate writing in translation can only be a matter for regret. However, to speak more positively, it is a delight to be able to showcase the quality of a growing collective *œuvre* whose status has long been argued over, but which has, in the last twenty years or so, begun to merit a place alongside the most flourishing literatures in the world.

For some, English-language Indian writing will never be more than a post-colonial anomaly, the bastard child of Empire, sired on India by the departing British; its continuing use of the old colonial tongue is seen as a fatal flaw that renders it forever inauthentic. 'Indo-Anglian' literature evokes, in these critics, the kind of prejudiced reaction shown by some Indians towards the country's community of 'Anglo-Indians' – that is, Eurasians.

In the half-century since Jawaharlal Nehru spoke, in English, the great 'freedom at midnight' speech that marked the moment of independence, the role of English itself has often been disputed in India. Attempts in India's continental shelf of languages to coin medical, scientific, technological and everyday neologisms to replace the commonly used English words sometimes succeeded, but more often comically failed. And when the Marxist government of the state of Bengal announced in the mid-1980s that the supposedly élitist, colonialist teaching of English would be discontinued in government-run primary schools, many on the left denounced the decision itself as élitist, as it would deprive the masses of the many economic and social advantages of speaking the world's language; only the affluent private-school élite would henceforth have that privilege. A well-known Calcutta graffito complained: *My son won't learn English. Your son won't learn English. But Jyoti Basu* [the Chief Minister] *will send his son abroad to learn English*. One man's ghetto of privilege is another's road to freedom.

Like the Greek god Dionysos, who was dismembered and afterwards reassembled – and who, according to the myths, was one of India's earliest conquerors – Indian writing in English has been called 'twice-born' (by the critic Meenakshi Mukherjee) to suggest its double parentage. While I am, I must admit, attracted to the Dionysiac resonances of this supposedly double birth, it seems to me to rest on the false premise that English, having arrived from outside India, is and must necessarily remain an alien there. But my own mother-tongue, Urdu, the camp-argot of the country's earlier Muslim conquerors, became a naturalised sub-continental language long ago; and by now that has happened to English, too. English has become an Indian language. Its colonial origins mean that, like Urdu and unlike all other Indian languages, it has no regional base; but in all other ways, it has emphatically come to stay.

(In many parts of South India, people will prefer to converse with visiting North Indians in English rather than Hindi, which feels, ironically, more like a colonial language to speakers of Tamil, Kannada or Malayalam than does English, which has acquired, in the South, an aura of *lingua franca* cultural neutrality. The new Silicon Valley-style boom in computer technology that is transforming the economies of Bangalore and Madras has made English, in those cities, an even more important language than before.)

Indian English, sometimes unattractively called 'Hinglish', is not 'English' English, to be sure, any more than Irish or American or Caribbean English is. And it is a part of the achievement of the writers in this volume to have found literary voices as distinctively Indian, and also as suitable for any and all of the purposes of art, as those other Englishes forged in Ireland, Africa, the West Indies and the United States.

However, Indian critical assaults on this new literature continue. Its practitioners are denigrated for being too upper-middle-class; for lacking diversity in their choice of themes and techniques; for being less popular in India than outside India; for possessing inflated reputations on account of the international power of the English language, and of the ability of Western critics and publishers to impose their cultural standards on the East; for living, in many cases, outside India; for being deracinated to the point that their work lacks the spiritual dimension essential for a 'true' understanding of the soul of India; for being insufficiently grounded in the ancient literary traditions of India; for being the literary equivalent of MTV culture, of globalising Coca-Colonisation; even, I'm sorry to report, for suffering from a condition that one sprightly recent commentator, Pankaj Mishra, calls 'Rushdie-itis . . . [a] condition that has claimed Rushdie himself in his later works'.

It is interesting that so few of these criticisms are literary in the pure sense of the word. For the most part they do not deal with language, voice, psychological or social insight, imagination or talent. Rather, they are about class, power and belief. There is a whiff of political correctness about them: the ironical proposition that India's best writing since independence may have been done in the language of the departed imperialists is simply too much for some folks to bear. It ought not to be true, and so must not be permitted to be true. (That many of the attacks on English-language Indian writing are made in English by writers who are themselves members of the college-educated, English-speaking élite is a further irony.)

Let us quickly concede what must be conceded. It is true that most of these writers come from the educated classes of India; but in a country still bedevilled by high illiteracy levels, how could it be otherwise? It does not follow, however – unless one holds to a rigid, class-war view of the world – that writers with the privilege of a good education will automatically write novels that seek only to portray the lives of the bourgeoisie. It is true that there tends to be a bias towards metropolitan and cosmopolitan fiction, but, as this volume will demonstrate, there has been, during this half-century, a genuine attempt to encompass as many Indian realities as possible, rural as well as urban, sacred as well as profane. This is also, let us remember, a young literature. It is still pushing out the frontiers of the possible.

The point about the power of the English language, and of the Western publishing and critical fraternities, also contains some truth. Perhaps it does seem, to some 'home' commentators, that a canon is being foisted on them from outside. The perspective from the West is rather different. Here, what seems to be the case is that Western publishers and critics have been growing gradually more and more excited by the voices emerging from India; in England at least, British writers are often chastised by reviewers for their lack of Indian-style ambition and verve. It feels as if the East is imposing itself on the West, rather than the other way around. And, yes, English is the most powerful medium of communication in the world; should we not then rejoice at these artists' mastery of it, and at their growing influence? To criticise writers for their success at 'breaking out' is no more than parochialism (and parochialism is perhaps the main vice of the vernacular literatures). One important dimension of literature is that it is a means of holding a conversation with the world. These writers are ensuring that India, or rather, Indian voices (for they are too good to fall into the trap of writing *nationalistically*), will henceforth be confident, indispensable participants in that literary conversation.

Granted, many of these writers do have homes outside India. Graham Greene, Anthony Burgess, James Joyce, Samuel Beckett, Ernest Hemingway, Gertrude Stein, Doris Lessing, Mavis Gallant, James Baldwin, Henry James, Gabriel García Márquez, Mario Vargas Llosa, Jorge Luis Borges, Vladimir Nabokov, Muriel Spark, were or are wanderers, too. Muriel Spark, accepting the British Literature Prize for a lifetime's achievement in March 1997, went so far as to say that travel to other countries was essential for all writers. *Literature has little or nothing to do with a writer's home address.*

The question of religious faith, both as a subject and an approach to a subject, is clearly important when we speak of a country as bursting with devotions as India; but it is surely excessive to use it, as does one leading academic, the redoubtable Professor C.D. Narasimhaiah, as a touchstone, so that Mulk Raj Anand is praised for his 'daring' merely because, as a leftist writer, he allows a character to be moved by deep faith, while Arun Kolatkar's poetry is denigrated for 'throwing away tradition and creating a vacuum' and so 'losing relevance', because in *Jejuri*, a cycle of poems about a visit to a temple town, he sceptically likens the stone gods in the temples to the stones on the hillsides nearby ('and every other stone/is god or his cousin'). I hope readers of this anthology will agree that many of the writers gathered here have profound knowledge of the 'soul of India'; many have deeply spiritual concerns, while others are radically secular, but the need to engage with, to make a reckoning with, India's religious self is everywhere to be found.

In the end, the writing gathered here will either justify, or fail to justify, our claims for it. What is unquestionable is that the cheapening of artistic response implied by the allegations of deracination and Westernisation is notably absent from these writers' work. As to the claims of excessive Rushdie-itis, I can't deny that I've on occasion felt something of the sort myself. On the whole, however, it seems to be a short-lived virus, and those whom it affects soon shake it off and find their own, true voices.

In my own case, and I suspect in the case of every writer in this volume as well, knowing and loving the Indian languages in which I was raised has remained of vital importance. As an individual, Hindi-Urdu, the 'Hindustani' of North India, remains an essential aspect of my sense of self; as a writer, I have been partly formed by the presence, in my head, of that other music, the rhythms, patterns and habits of thought and metaphor of my Indian tongues. What I am saying is that there is not, need not be, should not be, an adversarial relationship between English-language literature and the other literatures of India. We drink from the same well. India, that inexhaustible horn of plenty, nourishes us all.

Ironically, the century before independence contains many vernacular-language writers who would merit a place in any anthology: Bankim Chandra Chatterjee, Rabindranath Tagore, Dr Muhammad Iqbal, Mirza Ghalib, Bibhutibhushan Banerjee (the author of *Pather Panchali*, on which Satyajit Ray based his celebrated Apu Trilogy of films), and Premchand, the prolific (and therefore rather variable) Hindi author of, among many others, the famous novel of rural life, *Godaan*, or *The Gift of a Cow*. Those who wish to seek out their leading present-day successors should try, for example, O.V. Vijayan (Malayalam), Suryakant Tripathi Nirala (Hindi), Nirmal Verma (Hindi), U.R. Ananthamurthy (Kannada), Suresh Joshi (Gujarati), Amrita Pritam (Punjabi), Qurratulain Haider (Urdu), or Ismat Chughtai (Urdu), and make their own assessments.

The first Indian novel in English was a dud. *Rajmohan's Wife* (1864) is a poor melodramatic thing. The writer,

Bankim, reverted to Bengali and immediately achieved great renown. For seventy years or so there was no English-language fiction of any quality. It was the generation of independence, 'midnight's parents', one might call them, who were the true architects of this new tradition (Jawaharlal Nehru himself was a fine writer). Of these, Mulk Raj Anand was influenced by both Joyce and Marx but most of all, perhaps, by the teachings of Mahatma Gandhi. Raja Rao, a scholarly Sanskritist, wrote determinedly of the need to make an Indian English for himself, but even his much-praised portrait of village life, *Kanthapura*, seems dated, its approach at once grandiloquent and archaic. The autobiographer Nirad C. Chaudhuri has been, throughout his long life, an erudite, contrary and mischievous presence. His view, if I may paraphrase and summarise it, is that India has no culture of its own, and that whatever we now call Indian culture was brought in from outside by the successive waves of conquerors. This view, polemically and brilliantly expressed, has not endeared him to many of his fellow-Indians. That he has always swum so strongly against the current has not, however, prevented *The Autobiography of an Unknown Indian* from being recognised as the masterpiece it is.

The most significant writers of this first generation, R.K. Narayan and G.V. Desani, have had opposite careers. Narayan's books fill a good-sized shelf; Desani is the author of a single work of fiction, *All About H. Hatterr*, and that singleton volume is already fifty years old. Desani is almost unknown, while R.K. Narayan is, of course, a figure of world stature, for his creation of the imaginary town of Malgudi, so lovingly made that it has become more vividly real to us than most real places. (But Narayan's realism is leavened by touches of legend; the river Sarayu, on whose shores the town sits, is one of the great rivers of Hindu mythology. It is as if William Faulkner had set his Yoknapatawpha County on the banks of the Styx.)

Narayan shows us, over and over again, the quarrel between traditional, static India on the one hand, and modernity and progress on the other; represented, in many of his stories and novels, by a confrontation between a 'wimp' and a 'bully' – *The Painter of Signs* and his aggressive beloved with her birth control campaign; *The Vendor of Sweets* and the emancipated American daughter-in-law with the absurd 'novel writing machine'; the mild-mannered printer and the extrovert taxidermist in *The Man-Eater of Malgudi*. In his gentle, lightly funny art, he goes to the heart of the Indian condition, and beyond it, into the human condition itself.

The writer I have placed alongside Narayan, G.V. Desani, has fallen so far from favour that the extraordinary *All About H. Hatterr* is presently out of print everywhere, even in India. Milan Kundera once said that all modern literature descends from either Richardson's *Clarissa* or Sterne's *Tristram Shandy*, and if Narayan is India's Richardson then Desani is his Shandean other. *Hatterr*'s dazzling, puzzling, leaping prose is the first genuine effort to go beyond the Englishness of the English language. His central figure, 'fifty-fifty of the species', the half-breed as unabashed anti-hero, leaps and capers behind many of the texts in this book. Hard to imagine I. Allan Sealy's *Trotter-Nama* without Desani. My own writing, too, learned a trick or two from him.

The beauty of Nayantara Sahgal's memoir *Prison and Chocolate Cake* (extracted here) is paralleled by the liveliness and grace of her fiction; while Kamala Markandaya's *Nectar in a Sieve* is a justly renowned study of village life.

Ved Mehta is represented here by a part of *Vedi*, his memoir of a blind boyhood that describes cruelties and kindness with equal dispassion and great affect. (More recently, Firdaus Kanga, in his autobiographical fiction, has also transcended physical affliction with high style and genuine comic brio.)

Ruth Prawer Jhabvala has written so many fine short stories that it has been hard to choose just one. As a writer, she is sometimes under-rated in India because, I think, the voice of the rootless intellectual (so quintessentially her voice) is such an unfamiliar one in that country where people's self-definitions are so rooted in their regional identities. That Ruth Prawer Jhabvala has a second career as an award-winning screen-writer is well known. But not many people realise that India's greatest film director, the late Satyajit Ray, was also an accomplished author of short stories. His father edited a famous Bengali children's magazine, *Sandesh* and Ray's biting little fables, such as our selection, *Big Bill*, are made more potent by their childlike charm.

Anita Desai is one of India's major living authors. Her novel *In Custody*, perhaps her best to date, finely uses English to depict the decay of another language, Urdu, and the high literary culture which lived in it. Here the poet, the last, boozing, decrepit custodian of the dying tradition, is (in a reversal of Narayan) the 'bully'; and the novel's central character, the poet's young admirer Deven, is the 'wimp'. The dying past, the old world, Desai tells us, can be as much of a burden as the awkward, sometimes wrong-headed present. Her story in this anthology, *Games at Twilight*, is, like the Ved Mehta memoir, exceptional for the acuteness, poignancy and unsentimental humour with which the world of childhood is entered, and revealed.

One of the most important voices in the story of modern literature, V.S. Naipaul, is regrettably absent from this book, not by our choice, but by his own. His three non-fiction books on India, *An Area of Darkness*, *A Wounded Civilisation* and *India: A Million Mutinies Now* are key texts, and not only because of the hackles they have raised. Many Indian critics have taken issue with the harshness of his responses. Some have fair-mindedly conceded that he does attack things worth attacking. 'I'm anti-Naipaul when I visit the West,' one leading South Indian novelist told me, 'but I'm often pro-Naipaul back home.'

Some of Naipaul's targets, like – this is from *A Wounded Civilisation* – the intermediate-technology institute that invents 'reaping boots' (with blades attached) for Indian peasants to use to harvest grain, merit the full weight of his scorn. At other times he appears merely supercilious. India, his migrant ancestors' lost paradise, cannot stop disappointing him. By the third volume of the series, however, he seems more cheerful about the country's condition. He speaks approvingly of the emergence of 'a central will, a central intellect, a national idea', and disarmingly, even movingly, confesses to the atavistic edginess of mood in which he had made his first trip almost 30 years earlier: 'The India of my fantasy and heart was something lost and irrecoverable . . . On that first journey, I was a fearful traveller.'

In *An Area of Darkness*, Naipaul's comments on Indian writers elicit in this reader a characteristic mixture of agreement and dissent. When he writes,

> . . . the feeling is widespread that, whatever English might have done for Tolstoy, it can never do justice to the Indian language writers. This is possible; what I read of them in translation did not encourage me to read more. Premchand . . . turned out to be a minor fabulist . . . Other writers quickly fatigued me with their assertion that poverty was sad, that death was sad . . . many of the 'modern' short stories were only refurbished folk tales . . .

then he is expressing, in his emphatic, unafraid way, what I have also felt. (Though I think more highly of Premchand than he.) When he goes on to say,

> The novel is part of that Western concern with the condition of men, a response to the here and now. In India thoughtful men have preferred to turn their backs on the here and now and to satisfy what President Radhakrishnan calls 'the basic human hunger for the unseen'. It is not a good qualification for the writing and reading of novels,

then I can go only some of the way with him. It is true that many learned Indians go in for a sonorously impenetrable form of critico-mysticism. I once heard an Indian writer of some renown, and much interest in India's ancient wisdoms, expounding his theory of what one might call Motionism. 'Consider Water,' he advised us. 'Water without Motion is – what? Is a lake. Very well. Now, Water plus Motion is – what? Is a river. You see? The Water is still the same Water. Only Motion has been added. By the same token,' he continued, making a breathtaking intellectual leap, 'Language is Silence, to which Motion has been added.'

(A fine Indian poet, who was sitting beside me in the great

man's audience, murmured in my ear: 'Bowel without Motion is – what? Is constipation! Bowel plus Motion is – what? Is shit!')

So I agree with Naipaul that mysticism is bad for novelists. But in the India I know, for every obfuscating Motionist, there is a debunking Bowelist whispering in one's ear. For every unworldly seeker for the ancient wisdoms of the East, there is a clear-eyed witness responding to the here and now in precisely that fashion which Naipaul inaccurately calls uniquely Western. And when Naipaul concludes by saying that in the aftermath of the 'abortive' Indo-British encounter, India is little more than a very Naipaulian community of mimic men – that the country's artistic life has stagnated, 'the creative urge' has 'failed', that 'Shiva has ceased to dance' – then I fear we part company altogether. *An Area of Darkness* was written as long ago as 1964, a mere 17 years after independence, and a little early for an obituary notice. The growing quality of Indian writing in English may yet change his mind.

In the 1980s and 1990s, the flow of that good writing has become a flood. Bapsi Sidhwa is technically Pakistani, but this anthology has no need of Partitions, particularly as Sidhwa's novel *Ice-Candy-Man* (retitled *Cracking India* in the US), extracted here, is one of the finest responses to the horror of the division of the subcontinent. Gita Mehta's *A River Sutra* is an important attempt by a thoroughly modern Indian to make her reckoning with the Hindu culture from which she emerged. Padma Perera, Anjana Appachana and Githa Hariharan, less well-known than Sidhwa and Mehta, confirm the quality of contemporary writing by Indian women.

A number of different styles of work are evolving: the Stendhalian realism of a writer like Rohinton Mistry, the equally naturalistic but lighter, more readily charming prose of Vikram Seth (there is, admittedly, a kind of perversity in invoking lightness in the context of a book boasting as much sheer avoirdupois as *A Suitable Boy*), and the elegant social observation of Upamanyu Chatterjee can be set against the more flamboyant manner of Vikram Chandra, the linguistic play of I. Allan Sealy and Shashi Tharoor and the touches of fabulism in Mukul Kesavan. Amitav Ghosh's most impressive achievement to date is the non-fiction study of India and Egypt, *In an Antique Land*. It may be (or it may not) that his greatest strength will turn out to be as an essayist of this sort. Sara Suleri, whose memoir *Meatless Days* is, like Bapsi Sidhwa's *Ice-Candy-Man*, a visitor from across the Pakistani frontier, is a non-fiction writer of immense originality and grace. And Amit Chaudhuri's languorous, elliptic, beautiful prose is impressively impossible to place in any category at all.

Most encouragingly, yet another talented generation has begun to emerge. The Keralan writer Arundhati Roy has arrived to the accompaniment of a loud fanfare. Her novel, *The God of Small Things*, is full of ambition and sparkle, and written in a highly wrought and utterly personal style. Equally impressive, are the débuts of two other first novelists. Ardashir Vakil's *Beach Boy* and Kiran Desai's *Strange Happenings in the Guava Orchard* are, in their very unalike ways, highly original books. The Vakil book is sharp, funny and fast; the Kiran Desai, lush and intensely imagined. Kiran Desai is the daughter of Anita: her arrival establishes the first dynasty of modern Indian fiction. But she is very much her own writer, the newest of all these voices, and welcome proof that India's encounter with the English language, far from proving abortive, continues to give birth to new children, endowed with lavish gifts.

The map of the world, in the standard Mercator projection, is not kind to India, making it look substantially smaller than, say, Greenland. On the map of world literature, too, India has been undersized for too long. This anthology celebrates the writers who are ensuring that, fifty years after India's independence, that age of obscurity is coming to an end.

Salman Rushdie
March 1997

THE VINTAGE BOOK OF INDIAN WRITING 1947–1997

Jawaharlal Nehru

TRYST WITH DESTINY

Speech delivered in the Constituent Assembly, New Delhi, 14 August 1947, on the eve of the attainment of Independence

LONG YEARS AGO we made a tryst with destiny, and now the time comes when we shall redeem our pledge, not wholly or in full measure, but very substantially. At the stroke of the midnight hour, when the world sleeps, India will awake to life and freedom. A moment comes, which comes but rarely in history, when we step out from the old to the new, when an age ends, and when the soul of a nation, long suppressed, finds utterance. It is fitting that at this solemn moment we take the pledge of dedication to the service of India and her people and to the still larger cause of humanity.

At the dawn of history India started on her unending quest, and trackless centuries are filled with her striving and the grandeur of her success and her failures. Through good and ill fortune alike she has never lost sight of that quest or forgotten the ideals which gave her strength. We end today a period of ill fortune and India discovers herself again. The achievement we celebrate today is but a step, an opening of opportunity, to the greater triumphs and achievements that await us. Are we brave enough and wise enough to grasp this opportunity and accept the challenge of the future?

Freedom and power bring responsibility. The responsibility rests upon this Assembly, a sovereign body representing the sovereign people of India. Before the birth of freedom we have endured all the pains of labour and our hearts are heavy with the memory of this sorrow. Some of those pains continue even now. Nevertheless, the past is over and it is the future that beckons to us now.

That future is not one of ease or resting but of incessant striving so that we may fulfil the pledges we have so often taken and the one we shall take today. The service of India means the service of the millions who suffer. It means the ending of poverty and ignorance and disease and inequality of opportunity. The ambition of the greatest man of our generation has been to wipe every tear from every eye. That may be beyond us, but as long as there are tears and suffering, so long our work will not be over.

And so we have to labour and to work, and work hard, to give reality to our dreams. Those dreams are for India, but they are also for the world, for all the nations and peoples are too closely knit together today for any one of them to imagine that it can live apart. Peace has been said to be indivisible; so is freedom, so is prosperity now, and so also is disaster in this One World that can no longer be split into isolated fragments.

To the people of India, whose representatives we are, we make an appeal to join us with faith and confidence in this great adventure. This is no time for petty and destructive criticism, no time for ill will or blaming others. We have to build the noble mansion of free India where all her children may dwell.

Nayantara Sahgal

WITH PRIDE AND PREJUDICE

THE END OF the Christmas vacation brought our departure from the United States still closer, and once again I was shadowed by doubt. India would not be the home I had left behind, for Papu would not be there. I was going back to a free India. The struggle into which I had been born and during which I had grown up was over at last, but it had torn my country in two, and it had taken my father with it.

Never again would I see him walking on the dew-wet grass of early morning, as he had loved to do, a brown Kashmir shawl thrown over his white, khadi-clad figure. Never again would I be able to talk to him of books and music, of stars and trees and people, of the thousand things he had taught me to understand. Never again would I be with him in the pine-scented air of Khali, watching the sunsets on the snow-topped mountain peaks or hearing him sing as he worked in the garden.

It was ironic that he had had to go, my gallant, laughter-loving father, to whom life was adventure, a day-to-day challenge accepted with zest and enthusiasm. His was not the dreary world of politics and prisons to which he had chosen to be confined. He had called himself a 'proud pagan'. He should have been free and untrammelled, left to think and write creatively, to fulfil his vast talent for living. An independent India could deservedly have flaunted his scholarly genius, hailed him as an ambassador of her culture to foreign

Extract from the memoir *Prison and Chocolate Cake*.

lands. But a subject India had chosen him to serve among her martyrs, and a prison, the grey symbol of all that was opposed to his nature, had claimed him in the end. For me, India would be empty without him, every familiar place echoing his gay voice, mirroring his smile. I wanted to run back through time into the security of his presence and his wisdom, cancelling the years that had taken him from me, but I had to go forward. Lekha had already gone back to India, and Rita had been there at the time of Papu's death and after. For me, the lonely ordeal still remained.

Bitterness filled me that he had had to die, till I remembered that bitterness had been his most scorned enemy. He had sent us away so that we would grow up free from it, strong and proud, 'children of the light', as he had said. To bow before it now would be to deny all he had lived for and the purpose for which he had died.

On hearing the news of Papu's death, Gandhiji had sent a beautiful message to my mother:

People will come to condole with you, but I shall not sorrow for you. How dare I pity you? One does not sorrow for the daughter of a courageous father, the sister of a courageous brother, the wife of a courageous husband. You will find your courage within yourself.

And Mummie had found that courage, left alone though she was, with Mamu* in prison, unable to reach her, and no strength but her own on which to rely. I had her example before me.

To which home would I return? The only place that was home to me was locked, for no one lived there any more. Anand Bhawan was a house full of ghosts and memories. Mamu was in Delhi; Mummie was India's Ambassador to Moscow. I would, of course, go to Delhi and live with Mamu, but Delhi was just a name to me, a city where I had never been and which I could never think of as home.

*The author's uncle, Jawaharlal Nehru.

As I thought about going home, I gradually became more accustomed to the idea. So much had happened since I had come to America, and now Mamu was Prime Minister, the first Prime Minister of an independent India! I repeated it over and over again to myself in wonder and awe, not quite believing it. It was a distant, dazzling title. It spelled victory after a long, hard, sad battle. But to me it had no reality. What had reality was Jawaharlal Nehru, the Mamu I had played with, and known, and loved. He was infinitely more inspiring than the Prime Minister of India. And suddenly I was eager and impatient to be with him again. I had been the ardent little hero-worshipper, trudging solidly behind him in the make-believe processions of our games. Now I was ready to walk beside him towards whatever future the building of a New India would involve.

On a dark October evening in 1947 my plane landed at Delhi's Palam airport. I had spent a few days in Bombay on my arrival from the United States, so I had had a brief glimpse of free India. Meeting acquaintances of the family after several years, I had felt at a loss to cope with their barrage of questions, which invariably related to political events that had taken place in the country during my absence. In India independence was news, the Partition was news, and nothing short of an invasion from Mars could have diverted attention from these topics.

A crusty old gentleman whom I met at a party vented his criticism of the new Government on me. 'What I want to know,' he blustered, 'is what does Jawaharlal think he's doing? Everybody who co-operated with the British Raj should be locked up. Start with a clean slate, that's what I say. All this compromise – bah!'

He gave me a black scowl, and I hastened to reassure him that everything would work out all right.

'Think so, do you? Such optimism can only be ascribed either to extreme youth or total ignorance of current affairs.

In your case, both. Nevertheless, young woman,' he continued, unappeased by my meek acceptance of his rebuke, 'you give Jawaharlal my message.'

I promised to do so. But no sooner had I slid warily out of the corner into which he had propelled me than I found myself face to face with another irate person, this time one who held me personally responsible for the partition of India and all its consequent ills.

'Business has gone to pot,' he asserted angrily, helping himself to a handful of salted nuts.

'Oh, has it?' I murmured apologetically.

'Take a look around you – housing shortages, food shortages, too many people everywhere,' he harangued.

I glanced around the tastefully decorated apartment, with the foaming sea framed in one open window, the beautifully groomed guests, and the turbaned bearers decorously winding in and out among them with trays of drinks and hot snacks.

'And what is the Government doing about it, I ask you,' my tormentor persisted.

'I really couldn't say,' I replied helplessly. 'You see, I just arrived in India yesterday.'

He was not the least interested in my pathetic appeal to logic.

'Well, *I'll* tell you. Z-e-r-o,' he boomed theatrically.

'How interesting,' I muttered, unthinking, vainly seeking an escape.

'Interesting?' he exploded. 'It's outrageous!'

The righteous indignation in his tone roused me to a new perception. Looking about me at that roomful of self-appointed critics, I suddenly felt a glow of happiness. It was unquestionably a free country, where men could grumble and grouse about the Government. Why should they not when it was theirs to do with as they chose? This was no land where the opposition spoke in whispers.

As I stepped down from the plane at Palam a few evenings later, I was filled with a mixture of excitement and apprehension. Indi was waiting for me with her son, a serious-faced little boy of three, with beautiful, dark, expressive eyes and incredibly long, curling lashes like his mother's. He was Rajiva, who had been born while I was in America. We drove home through clean, quiet, tree-lined roads, and home, I discovered, was a modest, two-storey house at the corner of one such road. The October air was growing chilly as we left the car, and I was glad I had on a heavy winter coat, my last purchase before leaving New York.

Indi took me to her room to show me ten-month-old Sanjaya, her younger son, in deep, sweet slumber in his cot. His plump, dimpled fists and soft, brown curls gave him the look of a cherub in an Italian painting.

'Just imagine,' I said to Indi foolishly, 'they hadn't even been thought of when I went away.'

Here I was with two little nephews whom I had never seen before, in an unfamiliar house and a strange city. It was not at all like the homecoming I had pictured. It was not Anand Bhawan with all its loved and well-remembered haunts. And then suddenly Hari danced in, breaking the spell of strangeness, and I felt as though I had just come home on vacation from Woodstock. If I had grown older and taller in the four and a half years that had gone by, Hari did not appear to have changed at all. He was just as diminutive, just as rotund, and just as bubbling with breezy nonsense as on the day of his release from prison, when he had tumbled blithely out of the tonga in the portico of Anand Bhawan. He embraced me fondly and pranced up the stairs ahead of me to show me to my room.

'I have put cigarettes in your room,' he announced with pride.

I did not dare show my surprise at his modernity lest his feelings might be hurt.

'Oh, thank you, Hari, but I don't smoke,' I said.

'You're a good girl,' he said, beaming.

'Where's Mamu?' I inquired impatiently.

'He came home from a Cabinet meeting a little while ago, and now he is having his bath.'

Indi had told me we were to dine at Government House, so

I hurried into my bath. I wanted to be in Mamu's room before he came out.

He emerged from his dressing-room looking immaculate in a black *achkan* with a red rosebud tucked into a buttonhole. He looked more tired than I had ever seen him before, but as I jumped up from the bed to kiss him, his delighted smile of welcome swept the tiredness from his face. For no reason at all I wanted to cry. Now that he was here I felt I had really come home.

'What d'you mean by growing so tall?' he demanded.

'Oh, it's not me; it's these high heels I've got on,' I sniffled unashamedly.

'Those combined with American milk, no doubt,' he smiled. 'Well, darling, Her Excellency will be getting agitated about you. We had better send her a cable to let her know you arrived safely.'

He drew my arm through his and we went into his office across the hall to send the cable. Mummie, who was Ambassador to Moscow, was at that time leading India's delegation to the United Nations. I had left her in New York a week earlier.

A little while later, Indi, Mamu, and I got into the car to go to Government House and I sat holding Mamu's hand while he pointed out the shadowy outlines of Delhi's Secretariat buildings. I thought Delhi resembled Washington, DC, and told Mamu so. Only, I thought to myself, Washington is more familiar to me than Delhi. And what is strangest of all is this drive through the night to have dinner with the Governor General of India and his lady. Subject India had been governed by a British viceroy whose policies were dictated by Britain. During her first year of freedom, the Government of India was headed by a Governor General who, though British, worked in co-operation with an Indian Prime Minister and his Cabinet.

For the first time I regretted not having been in India to watch the chain of events that had led up to this unbelievable phenomenon. Faced with it abruptly in this fashion, I could hardly grasp its significance. I felt a little like Rip van Winkle, who woke up from a deep sleep to find that a new king reigned. Not a very long while had passed since the days of jail-going, but what changes had taken place! I found I had arrived in time for the last act of the drama of India's struggle for freedom. The India I had known as a child would now be a chapter in a history book, the yellowing pages of old newspapers, and the conversation of the people who reminisced about it.

We were the only guests at dinner, and as we waited in one of the huge drawing-rooms, I glanced around at the ornate, high-ceilinged room with its solid furniture, its large paintings in their heavy gold frames, at the crystal chandeliers, which tinkled in the mild breeze from the garden, and I wondered at all the magnificence that the British rulers of India had carved out for themselves. But before I had had time to dwell on it, a trim aide-de-camp had sprung to soldierly attention to announce the Earl and Countess Mountbatten. I saw two tall, attractive people enter the room, and my first impression was what a regal-looking pair they made, and how well the splendour of the room became them. No sooner were they beside us, however, than a subtle transformation took place. They were no longer the Governor General and his lady, the last of a haughty procession of viceroys and vicereines who had governed India for two hundred years. They were a host and hostess of infinite charm. Mamu and Indi were calling them by their first names, and the four of them were joking like old friends.

I recalled Mummie's remark before I left New York that the Mountbattens were unlike any former occupants of Government House in their disregard of its Imperial tradition. They had dropped in to see Mamu informally one evening and had eaten strawberry ice-cream out on the lawn. They had inaugurated the custom of throwing open the grounds of House once a week to the general public. Government House had previously been the exclusive preserve of the British community and those Indians who had chosen to associate themselves with British rule. It was unheard of that all and sundry should be permitted to stroll within its precincts. The movements of a viceroy had likewise been hedged about by rigid protocol. A viceroy could no more eat ice-cream on a private lawn at a moment's notice than could the King of England. Yet tradition and protocol had been nonchalantly set aside by two people eager to be India's friends and not her rulers.

Charm is a byword among the Nehrus. They have been blessed with more than their sparkling share of it, and I had seen it exercised consciously and unconsciously by them on crowds and on individuals. As a family they had few rivals in the field. Yet here was charm to match theirs. It wove through the Mountbattens' conversation a quality of warmth and sympathy, making them instantly likeable.

'This is my young niece, just back from America,' Mamu introduced me. 'She has been studying at Wellesley College.'

'Wellesley?' repeated Lord Mountbatten. 'Isn't that somewhere near Harvard University? Is it affiliated to Harvard by any chance?'

'Only socially,' I replied without thinking, and grew hot with embarrassment at the burst of laughter which greeted my remark.

I grew more self-conscious as I noticed that both Indi and Lady Mountbatten were dressed in sober colours, while I was in a bright turquoise-coloured sari, which gleamed blue-green like a butterfly's wing in the soft light. It was the only uncrumpled sari I had been able to find in my suitcase, but I was more appropriately attired for a ball than for a quiet dinner.

Dinner was announced, and we went into another high-ceilinged room where a small round table laid for five made a brave attempt to hold its own amid formal surroundings. After the comparatively slow, slurred American speech I had become accustomed to hearing, I had to be very attentive in order to follow the clipped accents around me. I was so engrossed in the conversation that I did not realise that dessert had been placed before us and that our host and hostess, Mamu and Indi had risen to their feet to toast the King. Never before having dined at Government House, I had no idea that this was customary procedure. Hurriedly I groped for my shoes under the table and, not finding them quickly enough, I sprang up in my bare feet, feeling very foolish.

Lady Mountbatten remarked casually when we were seated: 'I always have to remember to slip on my shoes in time for the toast. I have a dreadful habit of taking them off when I sit down at table. Once I was taken completely unawares at an official banquet and it was most awkward.'

Inwardly I thanked her for the tact with which she had smoothed over my *faux pas*, but when I went to bed that night it was with the uncomfortable feeling that I had not distinguished myself in the social graces.

For a long time I looked at Delhi as a stranger might, alive to the newness of it, but without the stranger's detachment, for everything I saw and heard affected me deeply. Here I wanted to be part of the surging activity I saw all around me, not merely a spectator. I had come from the academic seclusion of college, where all learning was contained in books. I had had a glimpse of the 'outside world' too, a select world of highly polished diplomats and statesmen, a milieu of brilliant discussion and debate, the whole fascinating design of the United Nations. But for me that, too, had been in the nature of an intellectual exercise. It had been the verbal sparring of one scissor-sharp brain against another. In the prosperous setting of New York it had been dispute about problems in faraway places. Whatever battles of wits may have gone on in the debating-rooms of the United Nations, the life of New York City had rolled on undisturbed. In Delhi there was a battle of another kind altogether, one involving the whole human being, his mind, his physical welfare, and his emotions, or perhaps I thought so because I was an Indian myself and eager to contribute to it my own small share in some way. I spoke to Mamu about it, complaining to him about my lack of any specific talent.

'How old are you, Taru?' he asked me.

'Twenty,' I replied.

'Well,' he said, smiling, 'I shouldn't worry too much if I were you. There is time ahead of you to make decisions. When I was your age I was still a student. There is so much that is new for you to get used to. Why not take this opportunity to look around?'

'I wonder if I shall ever do anything worthwhile,' I said discontentedly.

Mamu looked up from his desk in surprise. It was late at night, and I had as usual come to his office to distract him, so that he would be forced to leave his work and go to bed. My ruse never worked, but I persisted.

'Do you feel so pessimistic about yourself?' he asked. 'I had no idea of that. Personally, I like you enormously and I have no doubt that you will do a great deal that is worthwhile. But there is no hurrying these things, you know.'

In the end I found that the most obvious and natural occupation for me was to try and make Mamu's house a home for him. When Indi went to Lucknow, I was left alone to do what I could for Mamu's comfort.

Mamu had made his discovery of India by travelling the length and breadth of the country over a period of many years, by re-creating her past in his imagination and building upon it his vision of her future. I discovered India in a different way, through him, watching day by day his conversion of that vision into a living reality. I watched some demon of energy at work within him which scorned rest, some fathomless well of compassion which found time and inspiration when there appeared to be none. And through these qualities he functioned like an army of men instead of an individual. I thought of Sir Galahad's lovely lines: 'My strength is as the strength of ten, because my heart is pure,' and of how well they applied to Mamu. There is a confining sound about the label of Prime Minister, as there is, for that matter, about any label. It suggests specific duties. In Mamu the human being seemed always ascendant to the label. He was a sensitive person passionately devoted to certain humane ideals before he was anything else. To me he resembled a knight in quest of the Grail, or an artist dedicated to the completion of his task, much more than he did a prime minister. On the night of 14 August, the eve of India's independence, Mamu had begun his broadcast to the nation with the eloquent words: 'Long years ago we made a tryst with destiny, and now the time comes when we shall redeem our pledge . . . At the stroke of the midnight hour, when the world sleeps, India will awake to life and freedom . . .' It was as if he had taken upon himself the entire burden of the new freedom and the entire responsibility, fiercely and proudly borne, of India's treading the path of the Mahatma's teachings and no other.

To each person his country signifies something in particular, some outstanding idea or attribute that makes him especially proud to be what he is. It may be the place where he spent his happy childhood, it may be his country's constitution, or some admirable trait of his countrymen which has made them rise above their troubles. The marine whom I had met on the boat going to America in 1943 had said he was fighting the war for apple pie à la mode. It was his way of expressing what his country meant to him. My country was for me inextricably bound up with my uncle's ideal of it. I had sensed this as a child. Now I was convinced of it. His was the India with which I wanted to associate myself, and in which I wanted to live.

The day was dominated by Mamu's programme. In the morning, crowds of homeless refugees, the legacy of the Partition, swarmed around the house, seeking to voice their complaints to him. Every European must have seen just such hopeless, hungry faces during and after the war, but I had never seen any, for I had been in the safe haven of America. Listening to them was the first item on Mamu's schedule. Lunch was usually a late and hurried meal. There were frequently people waiting to see Mamu even during that short interval, and quite often they stayed on to eat, so that Indi and I would at times have to wind up with omelets in the kitchen. This, at least, was not very different from the old days at Anand Bhawan.

At night the light shone in Mamu's office till long past midnight, while more files and papers awaited him on his bedside table. One night I was reading in bed when, seeing my lamp on when he left his office, Mamu came into my room.

'Here we are in the same house, and yet I hardly see you.' He spoke tiredly, and his face was drawn. 'There are so many things I want to talk to you about, darling, now that you have come back – but when? Personal matters have to wait. There is so much work to do and so little time.'

I thought back to the day when I had cried out to Papu: 'There are so many things I want to talk to you about.' And another day when Lekha, Rita, and I had asked Mamu in the library at Anand Bhawan: 'When will things be normal?' I knew now that there had been more time in the past for family matters than there would be in the future and that 'normal living' was no nearer to us.

Mamu smiled and momentarily his fatigue vanished. 'You might come along with me when I go to see Bapu tomorrow. You haven't been to him since your return.'

It was as if going to see Bapu was the solution to his dilemma of time and his weariness, as if the presence of Bapu would in itself answer questions and heal wounds.

The following day I accompanied Mamu on his daily visit to Birla House, where Gandhiji was staying. We went to a room at the end of a corridor, where he was seated on a mat on the floor, with a number of people around him. I took my shoes off at the door, and on entering touched Bapu's feet. I felt a smart slap on my cheek as he pulled me down beside him, and I heard his chuckle, so infectious that it brought smiles to the faces of the others in the room, as grown-ups smile at a child's spontaneous peal of laughter.

'So!' he said in Hindi, his eyes twinkling. 'You have come home! What are you going to do now? Not too grown up to talk to me about it, I hope.'

Gandhiji had recently seen his countrymen engaged in bitter fighting against one another, ignoring the lesson of non-violence he had sought to teach them, for the Partition had brought much tragedy and bloodshed in its wake. Yet in spite of his profound hurt and disappointment, he had not forgotten the little girl who had gone away to America. Despite the many demands made daily on him for guidance, he showed an interest in her future.

'I want to talk to you, Bapu,' I said earnestly, 'when you are not too busy.'

'Busy? I am never too busy. Let me know when you are coming.'

In the clamour that was Delhi in 1947 Bapu remained a sanctuary of calm thought. During the riots that had broken out in some parts of India both before and after the Partition, he had, whenever he could, gone fearlessly among the rioters exhorting them to give up their madness. Yet though he had been in the turmoil and danger, he had somehow remained unperturbed by it. Now he was back in Delhi, holding prayer meetings in the garden of Birla House every evening. As before, *bhajans* and hymns were sung at these gatherings and passages were read from the *Bhagavad-Gita*, followed by talks by him.

To those who listened, they were unlike any talks they had heard before, for Bapu thought out loud rather than spoke with the desire to have any effect on his audience. Gandhiji was not a politician. He was not afraid to change his mind or to contradict himself if he believed he had made a mistake. He was not ashamed to proclaim that his religion was his guide. And, as always, his concern was with the suffering of his fellow-men and how he could best alleviate it. Independence had come to India, but no one in India could have been less impressed by it than the man who had made its achievement possible for his country. It had never been his chief concern. His preoccupation had been with morality. So while Indian statesmen drew up elaborate plans for the country's development and welfare, Bapu's quiet voice was content to preach his moral code: that right means must be employed to attain right ends, that nothing great and good can be built up on a soiled foundation.

A number of foreign visitors used to attend those prayer meetings, and I wondered what they thought of the unimpressive-looking, sparsely clad little man who seemed to charm such adoration out of the people around him. Did they treat what they saw as an interesting phenomenon but one that could not possibly happen in England, or America, or

Holland, or wherever they happened to hail from? What did it all mean to them, I wondered. My own reaction was awe mingled with reverence. Could it be true that a man could talk of love and truth and goodness, and apply these religious terms to politics, and not be laughed at? Could it be true that such sentiments could actually guide a nation's policy? Yet in India all these things were true. I felt wonderfully elated that I was an Indian and that to be an Indian in Gandhi's India would for ever be associated with this eminently sane way of thinking.

On a lovely January afternoon Indi, Rajiva, and I went to see Bapu. Masi and Padmasi, Mrs Naidu's daughter, who had come to Delhi for a few days, went with us. We found him in the garden enjoying a sunbath. The cold weather was well under way, making a treat of sunshine, and the garden was a mass of flowers, for in Delhi winter is the season of flowers. Rajiva chased butterflies on the lawn while we sat in basket chairs around the low wooden *takht* on which Bapu was seated. He was in a carefree mood, and we spent a happy hour with him, teasing him for taking such excellent care of himself and availing himself of vitamin D whenever he had the chance.

As we were leaving him he remarked: 'It is good you came to see me today, because the next time you see me will be in a crowd.'

We looked at each other nonplussed. Wasn't Bapu always in a crowd? It was hardly necessary for him to mention the fact; we took it for granted. His casual remark gave us no premonition that we would never again see him alive. The next time would indeed be in a crowd, the gigantic mourning throng through which his funeral procession would make its way. There in the sun-dappled afternoon had Bapu prophesied his approaching death?

Delhi was people in agony after a cruel Partition, but it was also a vital new capital waking to life. Tourists from abroad flocked to the city, and the diplomatic corps expanded rapidly. The world was curious about this India of Gandhi,

curious about the manner in which she had achieved her freedom, and still more curious to see whether such a policy could
continue. Mamu's residence, 17 York Road, became India's
10 Downing Street, White House, and Kremlin rolled into
one. Breathlessly I rushed about the house in a vain attempt
to keep up with Mamu's appointments and visitors. Dr
Shahriar, Indonesia's then Foreign Minister at Djakarta,
whom I had met earlier in New York in more leisurely circumstances and who was staying with us, gave me an amused
look from his armchair in the drawing-room.

'So the tempo is different from New York,' he twinkled.
'You find it faster here!'

At 17 York Road I met some of the first diplomatic representatives to free India.

Mme Novikov, the wife of the Russian Ambassador, shivered as she huddled closer to the electric heater the first time
she and her husband came to dinner. The doors leading to the
veranda had been closed and the curtains drawn, but she
could not bring herself to take off her fur coat.

'But surely, madame,' I said, 'the cold here can't affect you
so much when you are used to the Moscow winter.'

'That is quite a different matter,' she laughed. 'There our
houses are centrally heated, and indoors it is quite pleasant.
This Delhi winter is terrible. One cannot get warm.'

Mrs Win, the Burmese Ambassador's wife, could endure
the cold no better. In her light, summery Burmese clothes she
did not look at all suitably equipped to face Delhi's draughty
weather. She and her husband had come to dinner by
themselves one night; afterwards, seeing Mamu and the
Ambassador in low-toned conversation on the sofa, I invited
Mrs Win to my bedroom upstairs. I made her comfortable in
an armchair with a blanket tucked around her, and there we
sat cosily while the Indo-Burmese situation was discussed
below. She spoke scarcely any English and I spoke no
Burmese, but that did not prevent us from stumblingly and
laughingly making friends.

I went with Indi one morning to call on Mrs Grady, the
American Ambassador's wife. We found her in her drawing-

room attending to some electric-light fixtures. She had already met Mummie, and welcomed me with open arms.

'Mr Singh!' she called, beckoning delightedly to the tall Sikh electrician across the room. 'Come here and meet the daughter of our beloved across the seas!'

If this unorthodox introduction took Mr Singh unawares and left him completely in the dark as to my identity, he showed no sign of it, but politely said: '*Namaste*' ('How do you do?'), and went back to his work.

'Now you must treat this Embassy like home. After all, you belong to us too, you know,' said Mrs Grady in her warm, spontaneous way, and then, suddenly: 'Darling, you must knit for us.'

I gathered that her second 'us' referred to one of the several homes for displaced persons in the city. Mrs Grady was a generous, large-hearted person who espoused the cause of everyone in distress.

'I should love to,' I offered, and went home armed with several skeins of green wool.

Will anyone ever understand the reason why Gandhiji was shot, or, for that matter, Christ crucified or Socrates condemned to death? Can madness of this sort have been dictated by sanity? Can it have had any meaning except to make those who lived after them bitterly repent the crimes of their fellow-human beings? Who stood to gain by Gandhiji's death? Not the assassin, because he was caught, tried, and eventually hanged. Not the enemies of Gandhiji's teachings, because his death threw the searchlight on his message more powerfully than ever before. In his lifetime he had been called a saint. His martyrdom crowned him with an even more glorious immortality. To ask the reason why he was killed is to probe a mystery that has no beginning. The whys of history are seldom answered.

Indi and I were having tea at home on the evening of 30 January 1948, when we were summoned to Birla House by an urgent telephone call saying that Gandhiji had been shot on his way to a prayer meeting. Shock numbed us to all sensation as we got into the car and hurried to him; the others, his relatives and followers gathered around his body in his room at Birla House, seemed to be affected the same way. There was silence in the room as Gandhiji breathed his last.

Mamu received the news at a meeting and arrived at the scene soon after us. I do not think that as he strode into the room, tense with anxiety at the news he had been given, he realised that Gandhiji had passed away. I do not think he believed that Gandhiji could die so suddenly, so wordlessly, leaving him alone at the time when he needed advice and help more than ever before. The group of people in the room who had stood aside to let Mamu stride in watched without a sound as he knelt beside the beloved body and forgot himself in his grief for a brief moment. But what had happened was too colossal a phenomenon to permit the luxury of grief. When Mamu rose to his feet, he had regained complete self-control, and through the ordeal of loneliness and personal loss which was to follow in the days to come he was never again to show a vestige of it. Those who could bear to look at his face during those days saw a strained white mask through which only the eyes revealed stark anguish.

Word of the assassination had leaped through Delhi like a flame fanned by wind, for soon dumb, stricken hordes of men and women had collected like sentinels around Birla House, and out of every window one could see a brown blur of faces. They did not make a sound, and an unnatural silence reigned. It was as if the earth and time stood still for those few minutes. That was in the beginning, when they were too stunned to speak. Later they clamoured wildly, shouting, crying, and jostling one another in a stampede to break into the house. They became a little calmer when it was announced that they would be allowed to file past Gandhiji's body and see it before the funeral on the following day. Some officials were in favour of embalming the body so that it would be preserved for at least a few days and people from all over India might have the opportunity to pay their last respects to it before it was cremated. But Gandhiji, foreseeing the possibility of some such occurrence, had always said that he did not wish his body to be preserved after his death for any reason at all.

It is significant that when one is faced with the shock of a loved one's death, one's first question is not: 'Where has he gone? What has become of him?' This thought dawns later with the pain. But first one whimpers: 'What will become of me now that he has left me?' This was surely the question uppermost in the hearts of the mourning multitudes, for their expressions were those of lost children. It was the question in many of our hearts as we sat, still shocked, still unbelieving, listening to Mamu's broadcast telling the people of India that their Bapu was no more.

Into that climate of fear and uncertainty Mrs Naidu came the next morning from the UP, where she was Governor. Her face was haggard and her eyes glassy with unshed tears, but her spirit was as indomitable as ever.

'What is all the snivelling about?' she demanded harshly. 'Would you rather he had died of decrepit old age or indigestion? This was the only death great enough for him.'

Gandhiji's funeral was to take place the day after his death, and hours in advance people lined the route his procession was to follow, for it had been announced over the radio by Mamu. It was a route that would require innumerable arrangements, and Mamu and others had sat up nearly all night to make them. In the morning we were told that there would be a few conveyances for those among us who felt they could not walk the entire distance.

Padmasi spoke for us all when she said simply: 'We will walk. It is the last time we shall be walking with Bapu.'

It was an agonising walk. For all the thousands who silently watched the procession go by, many thousands more frantically besieged the open truck carrying the flower-wreathed body, weeping bitterly, trying once again to touch Bapu's feet. It was impossible to take even a short step forward without being crushed from all sides. The procession left Birla House in the morning. It was evening when it reached the cremation ground, a distance of about three miles.

I realised as we inched our way along with difficulty that I was in the midst of something more than a grieving multitude. This was even more than the funeral procession of India's most beloved leader. I was among human beings for whom walking with Bapu had had a profound significance, for they had walked with him over the rough and smooth of much of India's recent history. They could not now resign themselves to the fact that he who had led them over many arduous paths was never going to walk with them again. Bapu's slight figure had walked, staff in hand, over a large part of India. To walk is to make slow progress. It is to think with clarity and to notice with heightened awareness all that is around you, from the small insects that cross your path to the horizon in the distance. To walk is the way of the pilgrim, and for Bapu every walk had been a pilgrimage, the dedication of the body in preparation for the spirit's sacrifice. It was no accident that he had chosen to walk. To walk, moreover, was often the only way open to the average Indian. It required no vehicle but his own body and cost him nothing but his energy. Gandhiji took this simple necessity and sublimated it, as he took so much that was obvious and commonplace and translated it into a joyful effort.

As the flames of the funeral pyre consumed Bapu's body, we sat around it at some distance on the ground. Members of the diplomatic corps were there, and in front of them all the Earl and Countess Mountbatten, seated cross-legged on the ground like the rest of us. Gandhiji had inspired heartfelt homage from the people whose Government had so often made a prisoner of him.

Some days after the funeral a special train took Gandhiji's ashes to Allahabad, where, in accordance with Hindu practice, they were to be immersed in the Ganges. Mamu and other members of the family, together with the Mountbattens, were to fly to Allahabad to receive the train, and I was among those privileged to travel on it. The compartment containing the ashes was flower-bedecked and fragrant. The people in it, Gandhiji's relatives and the close followers who had served him all his life, sang *bhajans* most of the way. There was no weeping any more, for his presence seemed to be among them

21

amid the flowers, the songs, and the verses from the *Gita* which he had loved best. At every station huge lamenting crowds filled the platform and at times tried to storm the compartment containing the urn of ashes. And so, amid song and prayer and the homage of millions of his countrymen, the train reached Allahabad. It was a city that had seen the performance of the last rites of many members of my family; it seemed fitting that Bapu's ashes, too, should be brought here, for he had ruled their lives.

The ashes were immersed in the Ganges, where a mammoth crowd had gathered on the bank, and afterwards we all went back to Delhi. From that time onwards it seemed to me that Mamu's devotion to his work was almost religious in nature, though he did not like the word 'religion' and did not consider that it could ever apply to him. His face took on a spiritual transparency, like that of a monk. So must an apostle of Jesus have looked after his Master's crucifixion, and so must he have taken upon himself the burden of the cross.

Back in Delhi I felt at sea. It was true that I had not worked with Gandhiji, gone to prison at his call, or made any sacrifice for my country's sake. That had been the work of a different generation. My sisters and I, and other young people like me, had been merely onlookers. But still I felt at sea, and I think the reason was that my feeling of loss went deeper than consciousness. It was as if the continuity of a long process begun before my birth had suddenly snapped like a dry twig, leaving me entirely without a sense of direction. I had grown up within a magic circle, which now had melted away, leaving me unprotected.

With an effort I roused myself from my imaginings. Was I, after all, going to relegate my childhood and all that it represented to the realm of a dream I had dreamed? Were my values so fragile – had Bapu lived and died for nothing? – that I could so easily lose courage when he was no longer there? Millions of people would have been ordinary folk, living their humdrum lives unperturbed but for him. He had come to disturb them profoundly, to jolt them out of indifference, to awaken them to one another's suffering, and in so doing to make them reach for the stars. Those stars still beckoned luminously. Bapu's ashes had been scattered over the Ganges, but what if he had gone? We were still there, young, strong, and proud, to bear his banner before us. Who among us dared lose heart when there was this work to be done? The curtain had hung down over a great drama, but another one was about to begin. Gandhi was dead, but his India would live on in his children.

Saadat Hasan Manto

TOBA TEK SINGH

A COUPLE OF YEARS after the Partition of the country, it occurred to the respective governments of India and Pakistan that inmates of lunatic asylums, like prisoners, should also be exchanged. Muslim lunatics in India should be transferred to Pakistan and Hindu and Sikh lunatics in Pakistani asylums should be sent to India.

Whether this was a reasonable or an unreasonable idea is difficult to say. One thing, however, is clear. It took many conferences of important officials from the two sides to come to this decision. Final details, like the date of actual exchange, were carefully worked out. Muslim lunatics whose families were still residing in India were to be left undisturbed, the rest moved to the border for the exchange. The situation in Pakistan was slightly different, since almost the entire population of Hindus and Sikhs had already migrated to India. The question of keeping non-Muslim lunatics in Pakistan did not, therefore, arise.

While it is not known what the reaction in India was, when the news reached the Lahore lunatic asylum, it immediately became the subject of heated discussion. One Muslim lunatic, a regular reader of the fire-eating daily newspaper *Zamindar*, when asked what Pakistan was, replied after deep reflection: 'The name of a place in India where cut-throat razors are manufactured.'

This profound observation was received with visible satisfaction.

A Sikh lunatic asked another Sikh: 'Sardarji, why are we

being sent to India? We don't even know the language they speak in that country.'

The man smiled: 'I know the language of the *Hindostoras*. These devils always strut about as if they were the lords of the earth.'

One day a Muslim lunatic, while taking his bath, raised the slogan '*Pakistan Zindabad*' with such enthusiasm that he lost his footing and was later found lying on the floor unconscious.

Not all inmates were mad. Some were perfectly normal, except that they were murderers. To spare them the hangman's noose, their families had managed to get them committed after bribing officials down the line. They probably had a vague idea why India was being divided and what Pakistan was, but, as for the present situation, they were equally clueless.

Newspapers were no help either, and the asylum guards were ignorant, if not illiterate. Nor was there anything to be learnt by eavesdropping on their conversations. Some said there was this man by the name Mohamed Ali Jinnah, or the Quaid-e-Azam, who had set up a separate country for Muslims, called Pakistan.

As to where Pakistan was located, the inmates knew nothing. That was why both the mad and the partially mad were unable to decide whether they were now in India or in Pakistan. If they were in India, where on earth was Pakistan? And if they were in Pakistan, then how come that until only the other day it was India?

One inmate had got so badly caught up in this India–Pakistan–Pakistan–India rigmarole that one day, while sweeping the floor, he dropped everything, climbed the nearest tree and installed himself on a branch, from which vantage point he spoke for two hours on the delicate problem of India and Pakistan. The guards asked him to get down; instead he went a branch higher, and when threatened with punishment, declared: 'I wish to live neither in India nor in Pakistan. I wish to live in this tree.'

When he was finally persuaded to come down, he began

embracing his Sikh and Hindu friends, tears running down his cheeks, fully convinced that they were about to leave him and go to India.

A Muslim radio engineer, who had an MSc degree, and never mixed with anyone, given as he was to taking long walks by himself all day, was so affected by the current debate that one day he took all his clothes off, gave the bundle to one of the attendants and ran into the garden stark naked.

A Muslim lunatic from Chaniot, who used to be one of the most devoted workers of the All India Muslim League, and obsessed with bathing himself fifteen or sixteen times a day, had suddenly stopped doing that and announced – his name was Mohamed Ali – that he was Quaid-e-Azam Mohamed Ali Jinnah. This had led a Sikh inmate to declare himself Master Tara Singh, the leader of the Sikhs. Apprehending serious communal trouble, the authorities declared them dangerous, and shut them up in separate cells.

There was a young Hindu lawyer from Lahore who had gone off his head after an unhappy love affair. When told that Amritsar was to become a part of India, he went into a depression because his beloved lived in Amritsar, something he had not forgotten even in his madness. That day he abused every major and minor Hindu and Muslim leader who had cut India into two, turning his beloved into an Indian and him into a Pakistani.

When news of the exchange reached the asylum, his friends offered him congratulations, because he was now to be sent to India, the country of his beloved. However, he declared that he had no intention of leaving Lahore, because his practice would not flourish in Amritsar.

There were two Anglo-Indian lunatics in the European ward. When told that the British had decided to go home after granting independence to India, they went into a state of deep shock and were seen conferring with each other in whispers the entire afternoon. They were worried about their changed status after independence. Would there be a European ward or would it be abolished? Would breakfast continue to be served or would they have to subsist on bloody Indian chapati?

There was another inmate, a Sikh, who had been confined for the last fifteen years. Whenever he spoke, it was the same mysterious gibberish: *'Uper the gur gur the annexe the bay dhayana the mung the dal of the laltain.'* Guards said he had not slept a wink in fifteen years. Occasionally, he could be observed leaning against a wall, but the rest of the time, he was always to be found standing. Because of this, his legs were permanently swollen, something that did not appear to bother him. Recently, he had started to listen carefully to discussions about the forthcoming exchange of Indian and Pakistani lunatics. When asked his opinion, he observed solemnly: *'Uper the gur gur the annexe the bay dhayana the mung the dal of the Government of Pakistan.'*

Of late, however, the Government of Pakistan had been replaced by the Government of Toba Tek Singh, a small town in the Punjab which was his home. He had also begun inquiring where Toba Tek Singh was to go. However, nobody was quite sure whether it was in India or Pakistan.

Those who had tried to solve this mystery had become utterly confused when told that Sialkot, which used to be in India, was now in Pakistan. It was anybody's guess what was going to happen to Lahore, which was currently in Pakistan, but could slide into India any moment. It was also possible that the entire subcontinent of India might become Pakistan. And who could say if both India and Pakistan might not entirely vanish from the map of the world one day?

The old man's hair was almost gone, and what little was left had become a part of the beard, giving him a strange, even frightening, appearance. However, he was a harmless fellow and had never been known to get into fights. Older attendants at the asylum said that he was a fairly prosperous landlord from Toba Tek Singh, who had quite suddenly gone mad. His family had brought him in, bound and fettered. That was fifteen years ago.

Once a month, he used to have visitors, but since the start of communal troubles in the Punjab, they had stopped coming. His real name was Bishan Singh, but everybody called him Toba Tek Singh. He lived in a kind of limbo, having no idea what day of the week it was, or month, or how many years had passed since his confinement. However, he had developed a sixth sense about the day of the visit, when he used to bathe himself, soap his body, oil and comb his hair and put on clean clothes. He never said a word during these meetings, except occasional outbursts of *'Uper the gur gur the annexe the bay dhayana the mung the dal of the laltain.'*

When he was first confined, he had left an infant daughter behind, now a pretty young girl of fifteen. She would come occasionally, and sit in front of him with tears rolling down her cheeks. In the strange world that he inhabited, hers was just another face.

Since the start of this India–Pakistan caboodle, he had got into the habit of asking fellow inmates where exactly Toba Tek Singh was, without receiving a satisfactory answer, because nobody knew. The visits had also suddenly stopped. He was increasingly restless, but, more than that, curious. The sixth sense, which used to alert him to the day of the visit, had also atrophied.

He missed his family, the gifts they used to bring and the concern with which they used to speak to him. He was sure they would have told him whether Toba Tek Singh was in India or Pakistan. He also had a feeling that they came from Toba Tek Singh, where he used to have his home.

One of the inmates had declared himself God. Bishan Singh asked him one day if Toba Tek Singh was in India or Pakistan. The man chuckled: 'Neither in India nor in Pakistan, because, so far, we have issued no orders in this respect.'

Bishan Singh begged 'God' to issue the necessary orders, so that his problem could be solved, but he was disappointed, as 'God' appeared to be preoccupied with more pressing matters. Finally, he told him angrily: *'Uper the gur gur the annexe the mung the dal of Guruji da Khalsa and Guruji ki fateh . . . jo boley so nihal sat sri akal.'*

What he wanted to say was: 'You don't answer my prayers because you are a Muslim God. Had you been a Sikh God, you would have been more of a sport.'

A few days before the exchange was to take place, one of

28

Bishan Singh's Muslim friends from Toba Tek Singh came to see him – the first time in fifteen years. Bishan Singh looked at him once and turned away, until a guard said to him: 'This is your old friend Fazal Din. He has come all the way to meet you.'

Bishan Singh looked at Fazal Din and began to mumble something. Fazal Din placed his hand on his friend's shoulder and said: 'I have been meaning to come for some time to bring you the news. All your family is well and has gone to India safely. I did what I could to help. Your daughter Roop Kaur . . .' – he hesitated – 'She is safe too . . . in India.'

Bishan Singh kept quiet. Fazal Din continued: 'Your family wanted me to make sure you were well. Soon you will be moving to India. What can I say, except that you should remember me to bhai Balbir Singh, bhai Vadhawa Singh and bahain Amrit Kaur. Tell bhai Bibir Singh that Fazal Din is well by the grace of God. The two brown buffaloes he left behind are well too. Both of them gave birth to calves, but, unfortunately, one of them died after six days. Say I think of them often and to write to me if there is anything I can do.'

Then he added: 'Here, I brought you some rice crispies from home.'

Bishan Singh took the gift and handed it to one of the guards. 'Where is Toba Tek Singh?' he asked.

'Where? Why, it is where it has always been.'

'In India or in Pakistan?'

'In India . . . no, in Pakistan.'

Without saying another word, Bishan Singh walked away, murmuring: *'Uper the gur gur the annexe the be dhyana the mung the dal of the Pakistan and Hindustan dur fittey moun.'*

Meanwhile, exchange arrangements were rapidly getting finalised. Lists of lunatics from the two sides had been exchanged between the governments, and the date of transfer fixed.

On a cold winter evening, buses full of Hindu and Sikh lunatics, accompanied by armed police and officials, began moving out of the Lahore asylum towards Wagah, the dividing line between India and Pakistan. Senior officials from the two sides in charge of exchange arrangements met, signed documents and the transfer got under way.

It was quite a job getting the men out of the buses and handing them over to officials. Some just refused to leave. Those who were persuaded to do so began to run pell-mell in every direction. Some were stark naked. All efforts to get them to cover themselves had failed because they couldn't be kept from tearing off their garments. Some were shouting abuse or singing. Others were weeping bitterly. Many fights broke out.

In short, complete confusion prevailed. Female lunatics were also being exchanged and they were even noisier. It was bitterly cold.

Most of the inmates appeared to be dead set against the entire operation. They simply could not understand why they were being forcibly removed, thrown into buses and driven to this strange place. There were slogans of '*Pakistan Zindabad*' and '*Pakistan Murdabad*', followed by fights.

When Bishan Singh was brought out and asked to give his name so that it could be recorded in a register, he asked the official behind the desk: 'Where is Toba Tek Singh? In India or Pakistan?'

'Pakistan,' he answered with a vulgar laugh.

Bishan Singh tried to run, but was overpowered by the Pakistani guards who tried to push him across the dividing line towards India. However, he wouldn't move. 'This is Toba Tek Singh,' he announced. '*Uper the gur gur the annexe the be dyhana mung the dal of Toba Tek Singh and Pakistan.*'

Many efforts were made to explain to him that Toba Tek Singh had already been moved to India, or would be moved immediately, but it had no effect on Bishan Singh. The guards even tried force, but soon gave up.

There he stood in no man's land on his swollen legs like a colossus.

Since he was a harmless old man, no further attempt was made to push him into India. He was allowed to stand where he wanted, while the exchange continued. The night wore on.

Just before sunrise, Bishan Singh, the man who had stood on his legs for fifteen years, screamed and as officials from the two sides rushed towards him, he collapsed to the ground.

There, behind barbed wire, on one side, lay India and behind more barbed wire, on the other side, lay Pakistan. In between, on a bit of earth which had no name, lay Toba Tek Singh.

G. V. Desani

ALL ABOUT H. HATTERR

THE NAME IS H. Hatterr, and I am continuing . . .

Biologically, I am fifty-fifty of the species.

One of my parents was a European, Christian-by-faith merchant merman (seaman). From which part of the Continent? Wish I could tell you. The other was an Oriental, a Malay Peninsula-resident lady, a steady non-voyaging, non-Christian human (no mermaid). From which part of the Peninsula? Couldn't tell you either.

Barely a year after my baptism, in white, pure and holy, I was taken from Penang (Malay P.) to India (east). It was there, that my old man kicked the bucket rather in a hurry. The via media? Chronic malaria and pneumonia-plus.

Whereupon, a local litigation for my possession ensued.

The odds were all in favour of the India-resident Dundee-born Scott, who was in the jute.

He believed himself a good European, and a pious Kirk o' Scotland perisher, whose right-divine Scotch blud mission it was to rescue the baptised mite me, from any illiterate non-pi heathen influence. She didn't have a chance, my poor ma, and the court gave him the possession award.

I don't know what happened to her. Maybe, she lives. Who cares?

Rejoicing at the just conclusion of the dictates of his conscience, and armed with the legal interpretation of the testament left by my post mortem seaman parent, willing I be

Extract from the novel *All about H. Hatterr*.

brought up Christian, and the court custody award, the jute
factor had me adopted by an English Missionary Society, as
one of their many Oriental and mixed-Oriental orphan-
wards. And, thus it was that I became a sahib by adoption, the
Christian lingo (English) being my second vernacular from
orphan-adoption age onwards.

The E. M. Society looked after me till the age of fourteen or
thereabouts.

It was then that I found the constant childhood preoccupation with the whereabouts of my mother unbearable: the religious routine unsuited to my temperament, the evangelical
stuff beyond my ken, and Rev the Head (of the Society's
school), MA, DLitt, DD, also CBE, ex-Eton and Cantab
(Moths, Grates, and Home Civ), Proctor par excellence, Feller
of the Royal Geographical, Astronomical and Asiatic
Societies (and a *writer*!), too much of an intellectual stimula-
tion for my particular orphan constitution.

(The sort of loco parentis who'd shower on you a penny,
and warn you not to squander it on women, *and* wine, *and*
song!)

'Help others! Help others!' he used to say. Knowing that
the most deserving party needing help was self, I decided to
chuck the school, get out into the open spaces of India, seek
my lebensraum, and win my bread and curry all on my own.

And one warm Indian autumn night, I bolted as planned,
having pinched for voluntary study, an English dictionary, the
Rev the Head's own-authored the 'Latin Self-Taught' and the
'French Self-Taught', the Missionary Society's school stereoscope complete with slides (my second love after my mother),
and sufficient Missionary funds lifted from the Head's pocket
to see me through life.

From that day onwards, my education became free, and my
own business. I fought off the hard-clinging feeling of my
motherlessness. I educated myself. I studied the daily press,
picked up tips from the stray Indian street-dog, as well as the
finest Preceptor-Sage available in the land. I assumed the
style-name H. Hatterr ('*H*') for the nom de plume
'*Hindustaaniwalla*', and '*Hatterr*', the nom de guerre inspired

by Rev the Head's too-large-for-him-hat), and, by and by (autobiographical *I*, which see), I went completely Indian to *an extent few pure non-Indian blood sahib fellers have done*.

I have learnt from the school of *Life*; all the lessons, the sweet, the bitter, and the middling messy. I am debtor both to the Greeks and the Barbarians. And, pardon, figuratively speaking, I have had higher education, too. I have been the personal disciple of the illustrious grey-beards, the Sages of *Calcutta*, *Rangoon*, *Madras*, *Bombay*, and the right Honourable the Sage of *Delhi*, the wholly Worshipful of *Mogalsarai*, and his naked Majesty Number One, the Sage of *All-India* himself!

And – in a manner of speaking – I have had a lesson from one 'Ell See (which, see).

Only a few years ago, Master Keeper, I was sitting in my humble belle-vue-no-view, cul-de-sack-the-tenant, a landlady's Up-and-do-'em opportunity apartment-joint in India.

On the walls were hanging many home-framed photogravures of well-known passenger boats of the mail lines; and, on the top of the only shelf, a stuffed crocodile, the six foot of which, yours humbly once shot in the Baluchistan borders.

Outside the window, in the Street of Dyers and Cleaners (a mean street and no boulevard), the annual Spring-season fair was going on.

Indian kiddies, Hindu tots, Muslim cubs, were riding on roundabouts, some mounted on papier mâché horses, laughing and shouting; others, on a centrifugal Chairoplane, swinging round and round, dingle-dangle, till the urchins were a'most, a'most horizontal, instead of vertical! There were bright-capped youths, too; enjoying themselves as minors, imps and youngsters alone can, and a man was trying hard to interest 'em in coloured lemonade, and Cantonese catherine-wheels, bawling his wares in a chronic-laryngitis sotto-voce.

It was a dam' fine day: and the atmosphere, warm champagne sun, oh, absolutely belles-lettres!

The earth was blotto with the growth of willow, peach, mango-blossom, and flower. Every ugly thing, and smell, was in incognito, as fragrance and freshness.

Being prone, this typical spring-time dash and vivacity, played an exulting phantasmagoria note on the inner-man. Medically speaking, the happy circumstances vibrated my ductless glands, and fused into me a wibble-wobble *Whoa, Jamieson*! fillip-and-flair to *live, live*!

Electrified, and half-consciously, not quite knowing what I was doing, I opened my money-box and, smiling, viewed my meagre savings.

Then, all in a huff, I suffered an overpowering Hereford and Angus bull-power impulse, *Now* or *never*!

Yet, I could not quite make up my mind.

After a brief pause, I dished out a *rupee* from my pocket, and tossed the coin in the room-atmosphere.

Heads I go West in the cheapest gross-registered-tons tramp ship I could find, tails I remain out East yet.

And, exactly three days after that law of gravitation(al) return of the coin to me, I bought me the IIIrd class, and got into a train, which was about to push off, all in a flurry-hurry, rub-a-dub, rub-a-dub! towards the blue-green sea-extension, which separates India from the Western shores.

My Indian pal Banerrji was there. He had tears in his eyes as he was saying adieu with rose and jasmine garlands. I was receiving the same, with the best feelings, and my *topee* off.

'No need, old feller, no need at all,' I was reassuring him. 'Don't worry, Banerrji. This is the opportunity I have been waiting for all my life. Romance, adventure, success, old friend! I shall not forget to contact Nuffield. Everything will be fine! No botherum!'

And I stepped aside, to let pass the coolie-porter. He was unloading my sole belongings: the American fur coat (the Benjamin), my smoked-cane trunk, and the Missionary Society's stereoscope, complete with five hundred slides: views of Florence, Naples, Venice, Paris, Pompeii, Rome, the Vatican, the English Lake District, the Scottish Highlands, and the London West-End.

'Woof, woof, woof,' she said. Then iron and steel, wheels began to clatter, clattering clatter clatter, shush, shush! the engine's puffing-chocking cough, the last locomotive shriek-and-wheeze, the guard's whistle, the final salaams to my pal, and we were *off!*

Slicing a mango with my scout knife, as the train gained momentum, and the clatter-clatter calmed, merging into a smooth tempo, the daddle-daddle, I felt like California here I come!

Within four weeks of that toss with Fate, and farewell to India (my adopted land), ship ahoy, first anchor Durban, Suid Afrika! I reached the Liverpool docks.

Damme, as unexpected a hole as I ever unexpected!

There was no transparent amber and cider sunshine-glow, which I had accustomed myself into imagining as a perpetual God's gift aura over England from stolen peeps into Rev the Head's privately owned Our Lovely Homeland type of sunny Devon-Cornwall illustrated-in-tri-colour publication (and confirmed by the Society's stereoscope). No: instead, by Pitt ('88) and Gladstone ('86)! lightning, clang o' doom, thunder, and Glasgow fury!

But, despite this unpleasant Lancs incident, in spite of the fact that the anti-climax was too much of a sedative for my physique, and made me feel as if I was facing the very Whistling Percy and Sighing Sarah, both rolled into one substantial cannon-ball, somehow, willynilly, I felt sore glad!

And, why not?

All my life I wanted to come: come to the Western shores, to my old man's Continent, to the Poet-Bard's adored Eldorado, to England, the God's own country, that seat of Mars, that damme paradise; to Rev the Head's mother and fatherland, to the Englishman's Home, his Castle, his garden, fact's, the feller's true alma mammy, and apple-orchard.

And, now, I had arrived!

The realisation made me feel humble, and, OHMS *posthaste*, thank Almighty for same!

Forgetting all reserve, forsaking all Do-as-Romans-do etiquette, and in full view of Liverpool's sardonically inclined docker population, and the vastly jocosed ship's sailor-company, I greeted the soil, both in the true English and the Eastern fashion.

I took off my tropical-lid, the solar-*topee*, in sincere salutation, and next, without a waterproof, in my white drill shorts, I knelt on the mud-beds of the old country, the soft depths of its textilopolis County Palatine, aye, Keeper, luv, the blessed wet earth of Liverpool, in a thousand salaams!

The name is H. Hatterr, once more, and greetings and a good morrow to you!

That all is my background: the past, Master Keeper.

As to the present . . .

You are kindly referred to the incident relating to the feller who dug up a pyramid in order to catch a glimpse of five flee-ing mice, scouting away from him: and the supposition as to the two tired elephants who decided to sit upon one's anatomy, and the worth of one's feelings about the circum-stances.

And I am the feller, the same feller, who salaamed the earth of your country, the same what has written this book.

I have written the work for one good reason: to shield myself from further blows of Fate, and to ensure me against drifting from isolation to utter eclipse, and, perhaps, depriva-tion of grub.

Because, friend, I have had a miff with Fate, for things are not what I thought they were, what they seemed they were, and what might-have-been I wish they were!

I write rigmarole English, staining your goodly godly tongue, maybe; but, friend, I forsook my Form, School and Head, while you stuck to yours: learning reading, 'riting, and 'rithmetic.

And, if I am in your way, in your Street, in this earth of majesty, this other Eden, this demi-paradise, this precious stone set in the silver sea, this blessed plot, this earth, this England, among this happy breed of men, and wouldn't avaunt, trudge, be gone; and, if, by the Bard o' Avon (Henry the Eighth), sir, I desire you to do me right and justice, for I am a most poor man and a stranger, having here no judge indifferent, nor no more assurance of equal friendship and proceeding; it is not because I wish to be in your way, not because this folio has any piety, poise, or worth; not because I seek a clown's abandon, nor, I swear, the rewards of a mountebank, truly; not because I crave the gain of an unmerited prize, or wealth, or riches, or honour, or more, or less; but, because, by the Lord God of hosts, the Holy, who made you of the happy breed and I of the stricken, He alone knowing the aught of making mortal things, I am *lonely*!

'In the empire of a Maharaja,' expounded the Sage of *Calcutta* to the disciple, 'there once lived a potter, his name Ali Bee, who was stratagem personified. He owned an exceeding fluent parakeet, called Ahmed. One day, the Maharaja-Emperor was engaged utmost privately in clinging to his chamber-maid. While he was acting imperially, and was past-gone in a state of the eagerest insurgent impatience, for the speedy satisfaction of his amorous and soul-consuming fervour, for the said chamber-maid, suddenly, through the curtained-off window, lo, shame! a Voice entered the regal chamber. In a shrill, incredible tone, the Voice cried "*Stop, donkey!*" Whereupon, the Maharaja stopped. He discontinued endearing the maid, and came to grief.'

'Why?'

'Because, O fool,' replied the Sage impatiently, 'passion-blind humans crave privacy. They abhor interruption!'

'I comprehend. Continue.'

'The Maharaja forsook his couch, and proceeded to the window, with utmost dispatch, to seek and punish the one who had wantonly spied on him. There was no one present, lo, except an ultra symmetrical dove of exceeding beauty! On sighting the laced turban, the comely bird, shame! flew away, excessively frightened. Whereupon, attend, the Emperor considered the Voice as Sky-speech: otherwise, no wise human, but as talk issuing from the gods to earthly wrong-doers. He nevertheless wanted to know which god had issued him the admonition.'

'Who among the palace residents uttered the untimely rebuke, O *Calcutta*?'

'Attend. For ten years, the Maharaja-Emperor consulted astrologers and soothsayers to fix the identity of the Voice. Desperate, he took an oath. He offered half his empire, and, also, his Empress in marriage, to the one who could solve the riddle of the Sky-speech. The potter solved it, behold!'

'But, how, O precious? This is enterprise indeed! How did he become half-Emperor, and the husband of his king's queen?'

'Attend. After bribing the Home Minister handsomely, he secured an audience with the Emperor. Submitted the potter Ali Bee, "O august Maharaja! the utterer of rebuke to your Highness was my cage-bird talking-bird Ahmed (patronymic, Abdullah). I miss him, alas! On the day thy Mightiness wast brought to grief, list, O king! and her Grace the chosen maid likewise, a vicious hawk pounced upon my pet. But, Ahmed was housed in a cage! Finding his entry therein un-easy, the villainous hawk stole Ahmed, *along* with the cage. The brute bird was in flight, I vow! carrying off Ahmed, in the cage, and it was my quality parakeet who enunciated '*Stop, donkey!*' Ahmed was imitative, and meant no disrespect to you, sir King! Whilst thou, O unspeakably exalted Highness! wert searching the skies for the source, the hawk had flown aloft, past thy vision!" "O subject potter!" replied the intensely vexed Emperor, thereupon, "I wish thee to Satan, and commit thy illustrious sons to hell! For bringing up thy accursed bird I desire thee in a dungeon, and thy dear begotten progeny in the ghostland! Ah, me! But if I could go back on my oath! Son of thy beetle-like father! O ill-bred Ali Bee! I accord thee, alas, the dignity of half-Emperor for the sake of my oath! Mayst thou, O half-Honourable! spend many an unhappy day with my beloved wife! My salaams, kinglet!"'

'I submit, O mountain of intellectuality!' said the disciple, 'her Excellency the chamber-maid too was most relieved to hear of the domestic solution made possible by the acute potter's stratagem?'

'The moral of the tale, fool, is not the chamber-maid. But, rather, as follows. To gain their heart's desire, man and beast make belligerent illusions to bewilder one another. Even as the Maharaja-Emperor was confused by the potter, Ali Bee. For, know, disciple, it was *not* the bird Ahmed who had brought the Emperor to grief. It was the Empress! Her Highness, who was an adept in ventriloquism, spoke the words of discretion, unseen, and through a bamboo tube. A wise man, therefore, must master the craft of dispelling credible illusions. He should be *suspicious*. The moral is, "Be suspicious!"'

'I suspect that is exceeding true,' commented the disciple, reassuringly.

End of Instruction I.

PRESUMPTION NO. 1

AN INTERNATIONAL SCHOOL OF THOUGHT (MINUS A HEAD-MASTER-ELECT) IS ANTITHESIS.

'Antithesis' is my parlance for the fellers who always oppose. They hate mankind.

They maintain, that, human nature is rotten to the core!

I am often tempted to agree with the school, and join the classes of hate.

Why so tempted?

I will deal out the answer in the following.

First about a loose immoral woman, next about so-called friends and playmates, thirdly, about a depraved man, in this autobiographical, I shall attempt to illustrate the ethical basis of the antithesis school.

The incidents take place in India.

I was exceeding hard-up of cash: actually, in debts.

And, it is amazing, how, out of the Orient, the shortage of cash gets mixed up with romance and females somehow!

In this England, they say, if a fellah is broke, females, as a matter of course, forsake.

Stands to reason.

Whereas, out in the East, they attach themselves!

Damme, this is the Oriental scene for you!

Every feller I knew out East, whenever he was down and out, had to answer a literal habeas corpus call from the female side!

The member of the specie, who had a crush on me, was the *dhobin*: viz., my Indian washerwoman.

'Damme, Banerrji,' I confided in my pal, 'I am in a hell of a trouble!'

'Is in the morning the pharoah's spirit really troubled, as the Good Book says? I am deeply sorry.'

'Damme, old feller, you don't understand! I am in a hell of a mess. A woman is enamoured of me!'

'I don't mind, Mr H. Hatterr. Good luck to her. Whereas, I deplore and deprecate sensual love, I am wholeheartedly for romance. Is her name Priscilla, or is it Daphne? Is it a boy and girl affair? I am anxious to know if you could concur with the bard Walt Whitman, and sing to her, As I lay my head in your lap, camerado? In other words, do you reciprocate her kind regards?'

'I loathe the very sight of her. I have told her so.'

'Undaunted? She has my sympathy. On her part, excuse me, it might be a genuine Darby and Joan feeling. If so, Mr Robert Bridges rightly protests, Quit in a single kiss?'

'Damme, Banerrji, a woman of her age ought to know better! I place her nearer sixty than fifty.'

'Does she suffer from a morbid fascination of the male-sex anatomy? Is she an *Elephant*?'

'Kindly explain that interrogation, old feller. I have lived a sheltered life.'

'Well, Mr H. Hatterr,' said my pal, 'as an Indian, and a Hindu student-gentleman, I am deeply attached to the ancient classics. According to the sages, all women can be summed up and recognised under four species. In other words, the *Lotus*, the *Art*, the *Sea-Shell*, and the *Elephant*. These are the four sorts of Woman. The *Lotus-woman* is A1 vintage. She has a face as pleasing as the moon. She is lovely as a yellow lily. She launches a thousand ships, as Mr Marlow says. Her complexion is fine, and her eyes are beautiful, with red corners. In fact, the lady is worth washing in asses' milk. She is dainty, like a rose petal. She eats little, and sleeps lightly . . .'

'Thanks for the enlightenment. You know what a heavy sleeper my wife is, don't you? And she is no rose petal either.'

'I am gradually coming to her, Mr H. Hatterr. Let me now sound you on the *Art-woman*. She is middle height, her body has the scent of honey, and she is a light sleeper as well. The *Sea-Shell*, on the other hand, is hard-hearted, fault-finding, and she prefers scarlet colour to any other. Her sleep is also disturbed. Lastly, may I refer you to the *Elephant-woman*? Excuse me, I don't like her. She has male contours. She is narrow of the hip, broad of the shoulder, and her voice is tenor. She is short, stout, and a glutton. Her walk has no lithe grace of a serpent. Instead, she rolls her hips. She sleeps very soundly, and perspires a great deal.'

'Thank you! My perspiring and hip-rolling wife thanks you! Where I come from, man, we recognise only *two* kinds of Woman. The good and the rotten. This one is rotten.'

'I am deeply perturbed to learn that you mix yourself with rotten women! Talmud says . . .'

'Half a minute. Did you say, I mix with 'em? She is my *dhobin*, isn't she? Used to come in the wife's absence to collect dirty linen. I owed her two months' laundry bills. As the result, she tried to be personal, being indecent, and so on. Damme, Banerrji, I can't stand virilism in females! Last week, she decided to collect her bill by carrying on with me. These are the bare facts . . .'

'I am sorry, but I *must* interrupt. I have previously heard you describe this lilac domino as a flower of her class, and the best *dhobin* in the district. Were you trying to gild the lily, or were your motives ecclesiastical?'

'My motives were charitable.'

'I apologise. Once again, I am humbled by your noble nature, H. H. There is no Tammany Hall talk about you. I compare you to Henry Cornelius Agrippa von Nettesheim. Like him, excuse me, you are better suited to holy orders.'

'Thanks. When the woman made advances to me, I pointed out to her that this could not go on. Not on your life! I was at her mercy all the same, damme, old feller, the bills! I was reluctantly compelled to put her in good humour with a sundry kiss or two.'

'Well might I exclaim with Samuel XIII, 19, Absalom, my son, my son! I can see you confer kisses on her, and I can visualise her reflex. Out of Christian charity, yet unawares, by your lip-salute, you were actually fanning her passion for you to the pitch of "*Cossack, charge!*" I deeply regret that this took place.'

'You are right, Banerrji, absolutely right! I am ashamed to relate what followed. Feeling encouraged, like you said, "*Cossack, charge!*" the woman acted as if it was a backstairs affair! She tried to remove her reach-me-downs in my presence!'

'Truly, a Job's Comforter! If I may say, a May–December clandeste love! Did you return her Judas kiss?'

'I removed her from the bed-sitter, old feller! I spoke to her in the pointed vernacular. "Snake," I said to her, Banerrji, "Snake, go! Disgrace to thy ill-fated father! Reptile! Go, go, go!"'

'Ah, Hebe, Venus, Aphrodite!'

'Kindly explain the exclamatories, old feller.'

'I apologise for my emotion. As the Bard says, Lay on, Macduff. Please continue, Mr H. Hatterr.'

'Well, she went, shedding a flash of lightning from the orbit of her eye. Not a soft look, but the flames to singe one!'

'These are extremely poetic words. They show that you are deeply moved. But after his Worship's show comes the Council's dirt-cart. What are you going to do now, please?'

'Hell, Banerrji, I don't mind saying I am scared of her. You should have seen the Indian version of the dirty look she gave me! Do you think a private interview with her will do any good?'

'You talk such innocent omnibus-wisdom, enough to have

my monkey up! You are swapping horses amid-ships. Sometimes, it is better to pay the piper a penny to play and two pennies to leave off! No private interviews, please. I am advancing you her bill-money, pay the woman, and seek another *dhobin*.'

I called on the woman.

I knocked at her door.

She banged the door in my face.

She refused to take the money due to her!

The next step the party took was downright singular!

She went to my club.

Damme, to a feller's club!

The Secretary tried to disperse her, but failed.

She remained on the premises, squatting on the green lawn, and wept loudly!

Facing the sundry sahibs and memsahibs, poised at 'em at an angle of forty-five degrees, the woman pulled her hair, tore up her clothes, and wailed, 'O my mothers-and-fathers! I am a poor woman! I am starving! My children are starving! H. Hatterr sahib owes me money! He owes me money!'

Damme, damme, damme!

Wham!

Fellers out East do away with themselves following such foul exhibitions against them!

The sahibs, who had reluctantly heard her poignant sorrow, were dumbfounded!

Right through the curry-courses, not a feller could cough up a single word, except such sundry expressions of pain as, 'The fellow is a cad, sir!' 'Gad, the man deserves a birching!'

While commenting in this derogatory vein was going on behind my back, the Club Secretary, Harcourt Pankhurst-Sykes, summoned an extraordinary general meeting.

And the agenda alleged that I, H. Hatterr, fellow-member of the Club, was letting down my brother sahibs!

As a member of the Club, I owed on drinks, same as any other feller.

Black on white, and I was bound to honour the chits.

Yet, the Secretary held that too against me!

In the light of the exhibition made by the *dhobin*, extreme loss of confidence in my integrity prevailed in the Club.

At the extraordinary meeting, thank God, ideals came to my rescue.

I avoided all mention of the *dhobin*.

I never gave away a woman, not even a *dhobin!*

And I spoke at the meeting concisely.

'If you censure me,' I said to the fellers, 'I won't disguise the fact that it would be a blow to my prestige. If the Club is so dam' keen on members' financial status quo, the Club should advance me a loan. I am forthwith applying to you for same. Otherwise, damme, Harcourt Pankhurst-Sykes, you can't touch me! Hands off, I say! Can't nail me to the barn-door for nothing! Otherwise, damme, I shall see the whole bunch of you in hell first! You can't hold lucre same as honour! Mark my words, damme, all of you!'

After being kept waiting for nearly four hours – during which time the extraordinary meeting were dealing with the liquor contractor, the scavenger's wage-increase application, every blasted thing but my matter – I was unanimously declared a defaulter, black-balled, and *struck off!*

Hell, did you ever!

I hadn't for a moment imagined that they would do that to me, swine fever to 'em! and all because of a *dhobin!*

When I heard the committee-decision, the earth beneath my feet felt like being pulled away by a supernatural sub-agent!

Till this happened, I don't mind admitting, that I had regarded life ahead as a bed of roses: and thorns absent.

I ate the finest chilli-hot curries in the land, did a good square job of it, remained a sahib, and, life on the whole had been fine.

I walked back from the Club, alone, and when in the digs, wept without restraint.

Banerrji called in soon after.

I told the feller I didn't wish to breathe no more. I meant to do the Dutch act to myself that very evening.

'Mr H. Hatterr,' said my brother, upset to his foundations, 'I have already heard that you have been mercilessly kicked out. I came to appeal, please, do not contemplate the drastic action! Life is sacred. No man may destroy same. Excuse me, but my heart bleeds for you! May I, therefore, make a present to you of this parcel of an all-in-one pantie-vest? It has just come from Bond Street of dear England. It is delightfully snug, made in Huddersfield, forming no wrinkles. Its colour is a charming peach, with a stylish elastic round the waist and the knees. Also, it has got gay little le-dandy motifs in lazy-daisy stitch, and will make a perfect foundation garment for you in the coming severe winter. Originally, I had ordered the parcel for my own use. But, please accept it with my kindest regards.'

This spontaneous gesture from a true friend, the gift of a valuable garment, and made out of pure love, braced me up both spiritually and mentally.

'Banerrji,' I said, accepting the pantie, my eyes still red from the previous orgy of grief, 'don't worry, old feller. I won't take the drastic step. To hell with the sahibs! Not an *anna*-piece for the drink chits! Not a ruddy chip! Damme, I will go Indian! Live like you fellers, your neighbourhood, and no dam' fears! Go to flannel dances! No fancy rags for me! The sahibs have kicked me. But for that kick, mark me, I will return ten, till the seats of their pants wear out!'

And, by all the pits of the Punjab countryside, I tried to do so!

I went completely Indian, and kicked out of the house the only sahib who came to condole!

The chap was the hearty sort, respected no institutions, and had made me wink off my real origin. He had got me into the Club under false pretences, as an Indian-born, pure Anglo-Saxon breed. Consequence, used to flirt with the wife as his natural due!

To celebrate the bust-up with the feller, and, to spite the Club, I gave Banerrji the exclusive news-item for his uncle's fortnightly journal: *Ex-member of the Sahib Club kicks a member out of the house! Mr Haakon K. Olsen, prominent Norwegian grid-bias battery manufacturer, defies Thou shalt not covet thy neighbour's wife commandment! Involved in the eternal triangle! Alleged found making love to the ex-member's wife!*

Thereupon, a social highlight by the name of A. Arnot-Smith, OBE, came to see me.

Said A-Smith, 'It is the climate, old chap. Fellows can't help loving other fellows' wives. Gad, no need to kick up a row! Think of the Club, man! You are running down a fellow-European by allowing trash like this to be published in vernacular rags. Jerry Olsen's a scout. We don't wish to take notice, but if you want to prosecute the paper, the Club would render financial aid. It will all be confidential, of course. I strongly advise legal action.'

I threw A. Arnot-Smith out of the house, and wished his ancestors to a hotting up in Flames.

I told Banerrji of the facts.

'Do not let Mr Albion Arnot-Smith, OBE, persecute you,' said my brother, 'you may regard yourself as merely human. It is rightly said, *omnia Minervæ homo!*'

'What does it mean?'

'It is Latin, please. Nevertheless, I am saying, now that you have openly turned Indian, you don't have to depend on any OBE of the sahib community for kind regards. You are going to be independent. As my best friend, you shall have a job too. I have arranged for an appointment for you. You meet tomorrow Mr Chari-Charier, the Indian extreme-wing gentleman. He will give you a journalistic job on his daily without question. He is a great friend of the underdog. Mr Chari-Charier himself was struck off from the All Souls' College, Oxford. He has a very high regard for struck-off gentlemen.'

The next day I called on Chari-Charier.

The feller created a tremendous impression on me at first sight.

He was intense. He had hold. The sort of a feller who didn't glance, but hypno-stared: didn't knock, but smashed in: didn't fish in a river, but drained it off . . .

Journalistic appetite, animal magnetism, and sardonique were written all over him.

Sitting on an immense chair, he was wearing a red turban

over khaki knickers, and was very point-blank.

'My dear man,' said Chari-Charier to me, point-blank, 'you probably know that my paper the *Bazaar* will give anybody a job who has been thrown out of the Sahib Club. But the *Bazaar* insists on efficiency. I insist on efficiency. I am giving you the very responsible post of a suburban reporter. You bring in the stuff, and we shall write it up for you. All I ask in return is, efficiency. If I find any nonsense, you will be dismissed. I like to make this clear to avoid any misunderstanding afterwards. I am sure we understand each other. Good day, and shut the door behind you, my dear man.'

I was then interviewed by the assistant editor.

He had an assignment for me, all ready.

'Here is the address of a great man,' he said, giving me a slip of paper. 'He is very wise, and has written a commentary on Panini's Sanskrit Grammar. The work has been noticed in Europe and America for its great scholarship. He lives as a recluse, and is known as the Sage of the Wilderness. I want you to interview him. Find out why is he practising severe austerities. Bring me some local colour to help me write him up. The editor would like you to deliver him the stuff this evening. Good luck!'

I started out of the office to interview the suburban Sage.

It was a dam' hot day.

After a long ride in the tram, I marched nearly four miles in the blazing sun.

Tropical sun produces extreme thirst.

My taste in drinks is not inferior, but the heat, and the availability of what was available, made me give in.

I stopped at the wayside bamboo stalls, and had five or six glasses of *todii*.

Though, duly fermented, it is a dam' potent stuff, with a kick of a fighting Barcelona bull attached, it is the true beer of the tropics.

Having the drink for the first time in my life, physically, it made me more thirsty: and, mentally, it brought on me a feeling of *extreme humility*!

After some more walking, and the last additional glass of

todii, away from nowhere, I sighted the Sage's hut.

His disciple received me solemnly, without uttering a word.

But for his loin-cloth, he was entirely nude.

I could not help noticing his stomach, the largest, damme, I had yet seen!

Thereon – as the Eastern mystic has held that there is no difference between flesh and *ash* – he had rubbed much of the latter.

Maybe, because I was tired, maybe, it was the *todii* effect telling on me, but as soon as I saw that man's stomach, a tremendous feeling of awe overpowered me.

I wanted to go down on my knees, impromptu-like, salaam like hell, beat a tom-tom, and worship the feller's tummy, as if it were a demi-god!

He led me into the hut, meanwhile, affording me no time to make a sincere obeisance to his abdomen, like I wanted to so much.

Inside, surrounded by swarms of mosquitoes, which were making a sharp, Indian pipe-like sound, I saw, squatting on the floor, a very tall man.

He was lean, ash-bathed, his hair matted, and he had a long beard.

His eyes were closed in meditation.

On seeing his venerable countenance, I hastened to touch his feet with my forehead.

With due regard to the feeling of utter humility and awe which was upon me, I considered myself lucky to have the dust off his feet on my forehead!

'O Sage of the Wilderness,' I said presently, in the vernacular, to that countenance devoid of all expression, 'I am a newspaper reporter. Interview me. Please, master, utter a few words of wisdom, and, through your humble, comfort the reading class. Earn merit from thy act of piety, O adorned with ash!'

He sighed, and opened his eyes.

When I saw deep into those tar-black eyes of his, I felt so humble, you have my word.

His face was the most contented I had yet seen out East.

49

And I wanted to cry on his shoulder, lie prone at his feet in abject adoration, and tell him all about my troubles: about my unhappy birth and after, about my constant search for my mother, about giving the old lady everything she should want, about the Club, about my great ambition to win the world's admiration by a startling daring deed, about establishing H. Hatterr dynasty, my own kids, oh, everything!

'My son,' said the Sage of the Wilderness to me in a benign whisper, meanwhile, and overlooking my emotion, 'extend thy palm.'

I extended my palm.

The Sage then raised his hand, and from the swarm of mosquitoes flying nearest him, he caught a handful.

Emptying the buzzing things on my palm, he said, 'Throw away these items of life outside the hut, my son, or, altern, if you wish charity, give them to my disciple to consume.'

I was dumbfounded, having never seen such anticlimax behaviour!

I held the mosquitoes tight in my fist, and ran outside like hell.

I released them there, a good many having been choked from sheer want of ozone.

And I returned to the hut.

Said the Sage to me, after the incident, in an excessively soft voice, 'Thou art laudably intelligent, O nephew! A fool would have ventured the minute creatures to my disciple, and caused him stomach-ache. I am glad upon thee. Thou art pleasant. We shall have a meal together. Hast brought the eatables?'

I remembered too late, alas, the wholesome Indian custom of never going to see a holy man empty-handed.

However, the disciple approached me.

I could not help disliking the feller!

Though the feeling of terror, apropos his stomach, was still upon me, I hated him for his over-anxiety to touch me.

Nevertheless, I gave him the lucre he was silently seeking.

While the feller was away buying the eatables, the Sage closed his eyes, and seemed lost in contemplation.

After some time, the disciples returned with rice, salt,

greens and onions.

He walked into the hut with the bundle, and mutely signalled me to wait outside the hut, so as not to disturb the
Sage's meditation.

Yonder, under a palm, he made a fire, and began curry-
cooking.

I was sitting on a hot brick, leaning against the thatched
wall of the hut, to get as much of the shadow as I could.

The sun was scorching!

Sundry thoughts began to occupy my mind, in the interim.

'Damme, maybe,' I said to myself in a boozologue solilo-
quy, 'I am in the presence of one of the greatest living men! I
have heard stories of occult-clairvoyant sages making a pen-
niless feller equal to H. Ford in riches! And all that, by merely
blessing a feller! Maybe, this godly man will be gracious to
me! Has he, or has he not, singled me out for the merit of pro-
viding him with a meal?'

I must have dropped off with such notions.

It was long after the sun had crossed the meridian, that the
disciple woke me up.

I was heavy with a terrific hangover, a brick in the head
larger than any yielded by any peg in the Eastern Club-
history, but, as the disciple beckoned me, I entered the hut,
and joined-in in the meal.

The Sage had little, barely enough to keep the body alive.

I had a bucket of water, and less than my share of rice.

The disciple went into the attack, however, in a big way,
gorging, and doing himself proud.

The meal over, the Sage looked at me so solicitously,
enough to make me break my heart from sorrow, for the love
of his saintly person!

And, he said to me, 'Canst thou, my nephew, spare me thy
trousers, thy jacket, thy shirt, thy shoes, thy cuff-links, thy
watch, every accessory thou hast on thy person? Speak, if
thou wilt.'

Before I could say by what old how, the disciple
approached me spontaneously, with a dirty towel in his hand,
bearing the orange textile-imprint of India's *G. I. P.* Railway,

fully expecting of me a posthaste denuding!

I gave the feller the filthy look he had so richly deserved!

Yet, when I turned around, and saw the Sage, my ready-anger became love!

'Yes, master, yes!' I heard myself say, responding with sizeable emotion. 'I will do anything at thy bidding! Command me, Sage, and I will give my life for you! Though I am non-Indian, I am well versed in the classics. Know, the ways of saints and sages are known to this unworthy! In thy occult inquiry, I affirm, is hidden a deep meaning! I shall act as thou wisheth! Whisper to me, for thy bidding is command!'

The disciple signalled me, and I began to strip without further ado.

In a few minutes, I stood there naked, wearing the dirty Railway towel, and minus my belongings, even my reporter's notebook.

Yet, somehow, I felt glad to oblige!

I could not say why!

If the medical profession insists on an explanation, maybe, this perversion of values was due to *todii*; perhaps, it was the excess of the beer vitamin; but, like I said, I was only too happy to oblige.

I made a pyramid of my trousers, shirt, jacket and all. And, wearing the dirty towel as a loin-object, I did a dam' unique thing.

I began to dance around the clothes, the said pyramid, playing whooping-Indians.

I made signs with my fingers to assure myself that I was wearing feathers, and then went round and round the pile of clothes, dancing, making tremolando sounds with my lips and palms, laughing, shouting, barking, and yelling war cries, *Cooee! Tee-he! Ra, ra, ra! Moo-oo! Chirrup! Yee-hoo!* and, thrum-strum, doing my beat, bowing low to the pile when I completed the circle, and on again, gobbling and snorting!

Damme, did you ever such a *How!*

I never had a normal kind of a boy's life, and what *tamasha!* – what fun!

The Sage and the disciple watched this exhibition with

mute unconcern, absolutely unmoved.

Then I stopped.

The mood of utter humility overcame me again, and I sat down ashamed, feeling like a schoolboy, who had misbehaved himself somewhat!

The fun over, the disciple was collecting the pyramid.

The Sage then turned to him, and gave him, in an undertone, you have my word as a sportsman, *absolutely* correct measurements of my clothes, the inside leg, the collar size, the waistline, the foot-size, everything!

The amazing accuracy of the measurements was what unhinged me utterly!

It seemed occult!

Then the disciple signalled me out of the hut, himself leading.

Once in the open air, having inhaled some oxygen, and spared of the hypnotising pipe-like insect-music, the correct perspective of the situation dawned on me for a bit.

And I turned to the disciple, and said to the feller, with a fair measure of assertion, like my old sahib self, 'Hey, you! I cannot go back to the office in this outfit! I am a journalist on an assignment, man! Let me have my clothes back! Come on, I want my trousers, *Jaldi!* hurry!'

Thereupon, another singular thing happened!

The big stomach, acting silently as before, sprang on me, like a panther from a dark delta, and pushed me away a few feet, literally, threw me out in the open space!

In a moment, I was out, surprised beyond all calculus, and wiping with my palms the dust which had lodged itself into my armpits, the axillae, as the result of the fall.

Amazing, the degree of the lack of self-confidence which ensues minus one's clothes! Undress a king, a dictator, or a president of a nation, give him a dirty rag bearing the name of his railway transport to wear, and let him walk down the high street. He will instinctively act more like a hunted rat, than a king, dictator or president of men!

I waited at a good distance from the hut for a while.

The disciple came out, once or twice, for this or that convenience, and he ignored me utterly.

As if I wasn't there.

Though temperamentally I am not physical, yet, I am not yeller.

But the loss of my clothes had robbed me of all self-assertion, and I could not very well risk a skirmish with the feller.

Not possessing any option, I walked up to the yonder palm, collected some ash from the dying fire, and rubbed it liberally over my body and face.

Feeling satisfied that I could pass for a holy man, I made for the city.

The long walk from the suburb to the city was what tested my mettle to the utmost!

By the time I reached Chawk Alladin, the city's centre thoroughfare, adding to my dam' serious predicament, I had a party of admiring minstrels after me, making easy capital with song and dance!

As I was supposed to be an absolute recluse, not even possessing a pocket, I could not help myself, though I was jolly keen on making a spot of easy ready by having a go at a little harmless begging!

Nearer the office, I felt obliged to disengage myself from the minstrels somehow.

A quick about turn, and I ran like hell.

In a jiffy, I found myself in Chari-Charier's editorial sanctuary.

The sardonic feller was there, on night duty, editing, still at it.

He absolutely ignored the change in my appearance.

Damme, after all, I had left respectably dressed, and had returned to the office, face and body polished with ash, and wearing a towel bearing the colourful words, *Great Indian Peninsular Railway* on my bottom!

'Shut the door behind you, my dear man. Where is the interview?' the feller addressed himself to me, point-blank.

'Spare me a pair of trousers first, Mr Chari-Charier, do you mind?' I said, ignoring his animal magnetism.

He sent the office boy to fetch some jute knickers.

'Now, my dear man,' spoke the feller, indifferently eyeing my ash-coated face, 'I know all my reporters smell of *todii* after a visit to the suburban palms. I am not interested. I am not interested if you fellows booze away your money on drink. What I want to know is, have you brought me the interview?'

'No.'

'No?'

'Sorry.'

'You are sorry, my dear man? I am sorry. I am sorry for *you*! And for the six reporters whom I have dismissed for misbehaviour on this very assignment. Every reporter I have assigned to the job,' continued Chari-Charier, a shade more sardonic and bitter, 'every reporter I have assigned on this interview has chosen to loiter in the city wearing a dirty towel! And now you! I advise you to leave reporting alone. I shall miss you. Goodbye, my dear man.'

As I shut the door behind me, I wondered, why? Seven fellers stripped, and sacked, as the result of being put on an admittedly difficult suburban assignment!

And I was one of the septet!

This fact got me vastly interested in that particular suburb.

The next day, and the next, and the following, I called on the Sage.

The disciple would eye me askance, and mutely signify his displeasure at seeing me again. He refused to lead me to the Sage.

But, I literally sat an Indian *dharna* outside the feller's hut: *viz.*, hang about till appeased.

Then the Sage sent for me.

'Thou art persistent, O non-Indian,' he said, approvingly, though his countenance was as expressionless, and voice as low, as hithertofore. 'I shall reward thee for thy perseverance. Thy reward shall not be in cash, nor in kind. I shall reward thee by answering three questions. Ask what thou wilt.'

He sprang a surprise on me!

I had merely called to collect my goods, and no questions asked.

'Question one,' I said, giving in, after a brief hesitation, 'wilt thou return my belongings, O son of thy mother? I now return thee, herewith, thy Railway towel. Wilt thou reciprocate?'

And, the Sage quoth the answer in the negative!

'I am greatly mystified!' I said, recovering from the shock he dealt me. 'With thy permission, question two. Answer me, son of thy matchless mother, what is the prime motive of thy existence? Question three, what does it all mean? A man's clothes! Do you belong to a sect of the worshippers of the male reproductive organs as divine symbols? Do you consider a *darshan* and an auspicious look at male creative organs meritorious? Why have you stripped six of my brother reporters of their clothes?'

The Sage, he spake, 'I shall take thee into a confidence, nephew, for, I declare, thou art a man of business. Thy intelligence is good. This man is not my disciple. He is my younger brother.'

'Excuse wearying interruption, son of thy father,' I butted in, 'is he dumb? Why doesn't he talk?'

'He is not dumb,' quoth the ash-coat, in the same characteristic hush-hush tone, and his face as expressionless as ever. 'He is monetary. And he can read and write! He contemplates business enterprises all day. That is why he observes silence. We were both in the second-hand goods and clothes business in Lucknow city, and were widely known as Ranjhee Bros. & Co., Tailors and Furriers. At first, we were a confirming house for imported second-hand overcoats. In the first week after establishing, we booked indents to the value of twenty bales! But, despite this initial fortunate turnover, owing to the fierce competition prevailing in the trade, we could not win profits. My brother contemplated over this dire situation, and, as the consequence, we moved to this city. We still continue to be in business.'

'You do?'

'Yes, friend. But our method of collecting stock is the one witnessed by you. It is devised by my brother. He pays nothing, rejoice, absolutely nothing, for our stock in trade, meaning, the second-hand goods and clothes. He invests not an *anna*, yet we collect the full sale proceeds through our broker, working on the basis of a mere four and a half per cent option and free meals! We issue no invoices! My brother makes parasites earn for him! A man can work only in the day, but the industrious parasites are buzzing night and day, making wealth for us! Behold, I am the Sage, and I have callers other than blood-sucking insects. Even such as thou, O equal to the first-born of my wife!'

Thereat, damme, I had an irresistible desire to hit the Sage on the head with a handy poker.

I controlled feelings, however.

'Son of a thug,' I said to the feller, giving him a bit of my fifty-fifty Oriental mind. 'Monstrosity! Disgrace to *mahatmas*! Thy mother the daughter of a vendor of the forbidden meat! Thy grandfather a wasp! Dog-sired! Wouldst thou permit a grace, and allow this utter unworthy, a concession question? Enlighten this slave-of-thine on this fourth issue now. How came you to be known as the honourable author of a learned commentary?'

The Sage, he spake . . .

'My brother and I chanced upon a second-hand household goods deal in Muttra, nephew. A widow's property. My brother's business intelligence is good. In the material we purchased from the widow, he chanced upon an exercise book of no worth. But he brought it with him from Muttra city to this city. It was mingling with ash in this hut, till a pundit came to honour me. On sighting the exercise book, lo! the learned one wept with delight at the contents. I was silent, and my brother mutely signalled him agreement that I had composed the works. Thereupon, for an offering, a publishing works company of Benares printed it.'

Duly enlightened, I gave it to him in the celebrated vernacular.

'I spit at thy beard! I spill dust at thee! I shall expose thee and they crafty brother! Son of a merciless cheetah! Tyrant! Pathos-promoter! Unspeakable materialist! Shame upon Hindus! Refund! I bid thee, refund! Be forthright, and refund!

I seek of thee the sale-proceeds of all my belongings, and thy accursed broker's four and a half per cent option!'

Thereupon, the silent contemplative disciple screamed, as if suddenly wasp-stung!

After screaming – at the mere mention of a dead loss! – this culpable friar hovered towards me like a wild elephant's trunk, with the intent to pounce on me, and mete out violence as previously.

Realising that I was a gentleman, and no jungleman, I acted quick, threw up the sponge, and saved myself from walking Spanish at the feller's bidding.

I gave in, before the feller could be physical.

'It is the climate, Sages,' I said, OHMS *posthaste*, 'let bygones be bygones.'

'Correctly spoken, friend,' commented the Sage calmly from the yonder nook, still whispering. 'I confided unto thee our commercial secret, for our mutual satisfaction. We have an immediate vacancy for a broker, as our previous connection has been imprisoned this morning. Know, nephew, he was policed for a deed unconnected with our particular enterprise. He was a victim of greed, the ugly demon. And we seek a new broker. We are good principals, and thy perseverance is exceeding commendable!'

In the interim, meanwhile . . .

A deputation of suburban town councillors arrived in the hut, led by their mayor.

His Worship was begging the Sage to open an orphanage, or, if inconvenient to his Holiness, to grant the undertaking his blessings.

The Sage heard the appeal.

Then I saw him close his eyes, open his eyes, raise his hand, and from the nearest swarm of mosquitoes buzzing around his matted head, catch a handful.

Emptying the same in the mayor's palm, he quoth, hush-hush, *'Throw away these items of life outside the hut, my son, or, altern, if you wish charity, give them to my disciple to consume.'*

Damme, a mayor!

I was seized by an extreme spur-of-the-moment dejection, and walked out of the hut, unable to bear the sight of a city father arsing about the town, dressed exclusively in stolen railway property.

As to the *Presumption* contained in this monograph . . .

Damme, do you call this fair play?

If that feller was a Sage, I am a crab!

He catches mosquitoes! He has a vacancy for a broker! He is a good principal! He was a confirming house! His brother contemplates business deals! He doesn't issue any invoices! He makes mosquitoes pay! His tout has been policed this morning! Greed is an ugly thing! He knows the correct measurements of a feller's clothes and shoes at sight!

Of all the dirty Svengalis!

I have known chaps who would, by way of mitigation, put this down to the climate.

Arnot-Smith (pronounced it, R-*No*! Smith)!

If a chap is broke and down-under, isn't it jolly well the business of his Club to pull him through?

What the hell is a Club for?

A Club is an assembly of souls, kindred spirits, friendly bodies, rising and falling together, in good fortune, and in misfortune, simultaneous: actually, it should be one body politic outside the home.

And if it were, that would be real *shikar* and fox-hunting for you!

Otherwise, hell, the entire clubbing instinct is mere falconry!

And, as to that female . . .

What is a true crush, if not instalments of pain, a continuous willing self-sacrifice, a gradual death of one, so that love might remain green, and the beloved alone flourish?

If that dam' *dhobin* prima buffa was a lover, once again, I am a crab!

I assess, the world is made up of the two contrasting kinds: the Hitters (fellers who hit others without scruple or reserve), and the ruddy crabs, at the other end of the line. And, there are two sorts of contrasting ruddy crabs. The first sort, after being hit below the belt, behaves like a cat who has swallowed a poisoned rat, bouncing like hell to cough out the stuff, restore internal order and tranquillity, and turning Hitter, *never* allows the same to happen again. The second-class ruddy crab *bears up*, does not hit back, and having got a kick on the bottom, hangs about, cadging, complaining, invoking divine aid; just expecting compensation – money, tit bits, *anything!*

Not quite knowing my sort, and conjecturing over the quandary, the other day, I was walking down the High in Oxford.

I saw an intellectual sahib feller in the street.

And for no reason at all, rummy, I wanted to use my cuticle scissors on him, and clip off his grey locks!

Then kick the feller in the pants, and knock off his beret!

For no dam' reason, and *without malice*, I wanted to assault him, and to act in the retributive!

Which observation sums up the *antithesis* school: it is, above all, *retributive*! *compensatory*!

This desire for retributing, though without malice, satisfies the fellers who have had a mean deal from life.

Nirad C. Chaudhuri

MY BIRTHPLACE

KISHORGANJ, MY BIRTHPLACE, I have called a country town, but this description, I am afraid, will call up wholly wrong associations. The place had nothing of the English country town about it, if I am to judge by the illustrations I have seen and the descriptions I have read, these being my only sources of knowledge about England, since I have never been there, nor in fact anywhere outside my own country. Kishorganj was only a normal specimen of its class – one among a score of collections of tin-and-mat huts or sheds, comprising courts, offices, schools, shops and residential dwellings, which British administration had raised up in the green and brown spaces of East Bengal. It had come into existence as a municipal township in the sixties of the last century and was, in the terminology of British local government in India, a subdivisional headquarters, which meant that it was an administrative unit next to the principal town of the district where the Collector resided.

I shall presently have something to say of the moral quality of our urban existence. But, to begin with, let me give some idea of its physical aspect. Had there been aeroplanes in our boyhood the town would have had the same appearance to our eyes, when looked at from a height, say, of five hundred feet, as a patch of white and brown mushrooms in the grass below must have to a little bird perched on a tree. The white corrugated-iron roofs were indeed too hard for the surround-

Extract from *The Autobiography of an Unknown Indian*.

ing landscape, but this unattractive material had in my childhood just begun to oust the thatch. The brown mat walls,
however, matched with the trees and the soil. Altogether, the
town did not mark too hard a blotch on the soft countryside.
Besides, the huts were flimsy. They creaked at almost every
wind, and one strong cyclone was enough to obliterate the
distinction between country and town. I myself, arriving
home one dark night from Calcutta after the great cyclone of
1919, had very great difficulty in finding the town among the
fallen trees.

THE RIVER AND THE RAINS

The town had grown around and along a visible thread, a
three-stranded thread, which was formed by a little river with
two roads running along its two banks. We inherited the tradition that the river once had its day, but what we saw was
only its impoverished old age. Except during the rains, when
it was full to the brim and shining across its whole breadth of
some two hundred yards between one road-bound bank and
another, it was an emaciated channel where the water never
was more than waist-deep and in most places only knee-deep.
But we loved the stream. To compare small things with great,
it was our Nile. Our town was the gift of the river. We drank
its water, although this water never allowed us to see the sides
or the bottom of the tumbler unless fetched very early in the
morning. We bathed in the river, paddled in it, and when we
got dry after our bathe we looked fairer than we really were
with a coat of fine white sand. Sometimes we even glinted in
the sun, thanks to the presence in the sand of minute specks
of mica. The cows and elephants of the town also bathed in
the river but, as a rule, only after we had had our turn and
never alongside us. Often we ran after our cow when the servant took her down for a wash. We took up the water in our
folded hands and, sniffing it, found it charged with the acrid
smell of cattle. We also looked on with delight when the elephant of Joyka, a near neighbour of ours, waded majestically
into the river and disported herself in it. She had a young com-

panion, not her own calf though, who also came with her on occasions and had his bathe in the river.

If we loved the river where it permitted even those of us who did not swim to take inconceivable liberties with it, we worshipped it where it was deep, and there were such spots. Just as an old family fallen on poverty happens to keep a few pieces of valuable antique furniture, so our decayed river had, every two or three miles of its course, a large pool where the water was deep, dark, still, and cool. There was one such pool within the town about half a mile from our house, just behind the excise depot and the Government treasury. It was an oval expanse of water where we often went to bathe and swim. At our strokes the water broke into white streaks resembling crushed ice, and we could never dive deep enough to touch the bottom. Once we took a sounding. Even quite close to the bank the water was twenty feet or a little more. The place was the home of the big and fierce-looking but silvery chital fish which at times nibbled at us. We were told by our elders, I cannot say whether truthfully or with the sole object of keeping us out of mischief, that in the middle of the pool these creatures attacked human beings in shoals. On the far bank stood thick clumps of very tall bamboo with a border of scrub near the water, and almost exactly opposite our ghat a sandy lane opened out like a funnel. Down this path peasant women with earthen pitchers appeared off and on out of the dark jungle, walked into the water and bent over it, filling their gurgling vessels. We could always see the gurgling although we could not hear it. After they had filled their pitchers the peasant women went away.

Brick buildings were such rarities in our parts that one dilapidated pile to be seen from the ghat about half a mile to the west made a deep impression on us. It was a half-ruined mosque, standing on a terrace jutting well forward into the bed of the river. Its outlines always stood out against the sky, and against the sunset they were etched more distinctly still.

The contrast between the general poverty and the few surviving heirlooms of our river vanished for about four months every year. During the monsoon season it filled out, became swift, or at all events moving, and permitted navigation all the way through. After the first few showers the narrow water-course would begin to gain on the low meadows and mud-flats on either side and reach out towards its old and higher permanent banks. Little by little the water rose and became muddy as well as full of life. The first crowd to hold revels in it were the frogs. We heard their croaking throughout the day and throughout the night. Then arrived the leeches, which frightened us not so much by sticking to our shins, arms and backs as by the threat, imagined by us, of creeping into the body cavities, of whose existence and vulnerability children seem to be so acutely and painfully conscious. At the next stage of the rise of the river came larger parties of peasants from the hamlets surrounding the town. They came with bamboo fishing cages and small fishing nets fixed to bamboo poles slung on their arms. They had flat and wide-brimmed leaf hats on the head, but nothing beyond the thinnest of modesty clouts below the belt. They ran into the water with loud shouts, scattered into small parties, and plunged and rose and shoved in search of fish. They came in this manner every day until the water became too deep for fishing by this method.

Last of all came the boats which were the sight of the season we loved best. Every year they came like migratory birds, in twos and threes for the first few days and then in larger numbers. Some chose to be moored in unsociable isolation, some even midstream, but the majority preferred the appointed mooring-places, and lay huddled together. When the boat traffic got into its stride these places looked like small plantations of bamboo shorn of leaf, for the usual method of making these boats fast was to tie them by the bows to the bamboo poles with which they were propelled, after driving the poles deep into the muddy bottom of the river. In most cases the boats also had oars and masts, but the first were folded away for use in really deep water, while the masts were laid flat on the mat-and-bamboo roofs, since in the wooded areas about our town there never was enough wind to make sailing possible. Punting was the normal method of propulsion of these boats.

They were all country boats, having the outlines and general shape of the model boats found in the tombs of the Middle Kingdom of Egypt. But they could be classed by function like modern steamers and by power of propulsion like the ancient galleys. The tramps had no roof and carried poor people, market produce, or even fish, according to chance or expediency. The others stuck fastidiously to their line, the passenger boats to passengers and the cargo boats to cargoes, each being exclusive in its way. They were always kept spick-and-span, for, as the boatmen were in the habit of saying, 'The fortunes of boat and wench alike depend on the make-up.' Even the smell of burning paddy-husk which always hung about them (owing to the braziers being kept perpetually burning to feed the *hookah*) was clean and astringent. In respect of power the boats were graded according to the number of boatmen they had. The smallest had only one boatman and were called 'single-handers'. The next class with two men passed as 'double-handers', and the largest boats used for passenger traffic were the 'three-handers'. Ordinarily we travelled in these. They were our triremes.

During the day the boats were a pretty and friendly sight. At night they became something more, mysterious. They themselves could be seen only as blurred masses, for their little kerosene lamps could never break up the nearly solid darkness around them, but the reflections of these lamps seemed to set the fringes of the river on fire. When the water was still, there appeared to be an illumination going on two or three feet below the surface of the water, and with breezes and ripples swaying ladders, spirals and festoons of amber-coloured light made their appearance. I was sorry to hear that thousands and thousands of these boats had been ruthlessly destroyed at the time of the Japanese invasion scare of 1942.

A less companionable vessel also visited us occasionally. One of the annual or biennial visitors was the budgerow of Mr Stapleton, the Inspector of Schools. As the house-boat stood moored a little stand-offishly, we, the boys, gaped at it in wonder. It seemed to be a palace in comparison not only with the other boats but also with our houses. But in spite of its beautiful lines, its red, white and green paint, and its essentially aquatic presence it was not, now that I recall the picture after more than forty years, quite in keeping with the surroundings.

A more congruous pageant was provided for us on one day of August or September, on which took place the grand boat race of the year. Scores of racing boats came for the occasion. They were open, narrow, and long boats, brightly painted on the sides with red, yellow, blue, green, and white floral or geometrical patterns, and with tigers, leopards, peacocks or dolphin heads on the bows and sterns. The crews, varying between ten and thirty men, sat in two rows, oars in hand. These oars too were painted, but they were not fixed like ordinary oars to the sides of the boats. They were small and carried in hand by the men, who alternately struck the gunwhales with them to beat time to their boat-song and plunged them into the water. We gazed bewitched at the boats as they darted past us one after another to the accompaniment of a tremendous chorus, and we trembled with suspense when the fantastic *Ootar* boat, which looked more like a rainbow floating upside down in the water than a boat, came gliding with its apparent disequilibrium in the path of the shooting racers. We thought it would turn turtle and go down. But of course it did not.

We watched the race from land as it was not considered safe for small children to venture out in a boat for fear of collisions. Once, however, we went out in a boat, although not at Kishorganj but near our ancestral village, where the waters were broader. While the boats raced in the gleaming midstream we dawdled in the darker backwaters, looking on the race and at the same time luxuriously trailing our hands and feet in water. We not only stroked both the kinds of water lily, the red and the white, which were to be found on our side, but also tore up their succulent stalks, which dripped cool threads of water. It is a strange and in some ways a most revealing experience for a terrestrial creature like man to get into intimate tactile relationship with the weeds and plants of water.

If the picture on the river during the rainy season at

Kishorganj was the Deluge and the Ark made homely, gregarious and sociable, we were no less steeped in the spirit of water on land. Everything was wet to the marrow of the bone. Neither we nor our clothes were ever properly dry. When we were not slushy we were damp. The bark of the trees became so sodden that it seemed we could tear it up in handfuls like moss. We could not walk from the hut which was our bed- and living-room to the hut which was our kitchen and dining-room except on a line of bricks laid at intervals of about two feet or on a gangway made of bamboos, and the meals were more often than not held up by unseasonable showers. Little rills were running off the road cutting miniature ravines in its side. Our servants were always wet, and their brown skins were always shining.

The tremendous drenching power of the rain was brought home to us by the dripping coming and going of our father and of our visitors, but above all by the sight of the birds. The ludicrously pitiable appearance of the crows in the rainy season is so notorious that the phrase 'bedraggled crow' has become the figurative synonym in the Bengali language for an untidy and dishevelled person. Apart from crows I once had a glimpse of drenched birds which has sunk ineffaceably into my memory because at the time it struck something like terror into my mind. A tall and slender betel-nut palm had been brought down by a rainstorm. Among its leaves was a nest and in the nest a pair of pied mynas, dead and stiff. Their feathers had been clotted by rain into hard and thorny quills and these quills stood up thorn-like on the ghastly white skin.

But one of the most attractive and engaging sights of the season was to be seen in the inner courtyard of our house, when there was a heavy downpour. The rain came down in what looked like closely packed formations of enormously long pencils of glass and hit the bare ground. At first the pencils only pitted the sandy soil, but as soon as some water had collected all around they began to bounce off the surface of water and pop up and down in the form of minuscule puppets. Every square inch of ground seemed to receive one of the little things, and our water-logged yard was broken up into a pattern which was not only mobile but dizzily in motion. As we sat on the veranda, myriads of tiny watery marionettes, each with an expanding circlet of water at its feet, gave us such a dancing display as we had never dreamt of seeing in actual life. It often went on for the best part of an hour but had a trick of stopping suddenly. No magic wand could make elves vanish more quickly. The crystalline throng was brushed off even before the rustle of rain ceased in our ears.

Another curious sight of the season was a palmyra, fan-palm, or toddy-palm, as it is variously called, standing in water midway between the two permanent banks of the river, exactly in front of our house. These trees normally grow on high ground, and there were seven of them in a straight line on the western side of the front lawn of our house. There was also one on the low meadow before it which once was the bed of the river and in our time became flooded in the monsoon season. How the palm had grown in that situation was a mystery, for during its childhood it must have been totally submerged for three or four months every year for many years. But there was no doubt that it had survived the unnatural experience. In our childhood it was a full-grown tree, with the lower seven or eight feet of its shaft under water during the rainy months. The spectacle did not strike me as unusual until I had revolved it over in my mind a good many years later. As children we took the palm's presence in the water for granted as part and parcel of the landscape to which we were born.

THE PROCESS OF THE SEASONS

From all that has been written so far the reader must be forming the notion that ours was a water-sprite's existence. It was not, except for about four months in the year. A revolution took place between mid-October and mid-November, which was like passing from Shakespeare's sea dirge to Webster's land dirge. If, as Charles Lamb has said, the first was of the water watery, the second, as Lamb has equally said, was of the earth earthy. Generally, by the middle of October the water was going down and ugly grey mud-flats coming up. These took about two or three weeks to be covered again with grass. By that time the road before our house had also dried up, hardened, and decomposed again, completing the half-cycle from ankle-deep mud to ankle-deep dust. We held this soft deep dust in great affection. It offered not simply the childish delight of being able to make dust castles, but something more profound. We felt the same contempt for those who walked on this road in shoes, missing so much and so much, as Mrs Cornford has recorded for the fat white woman who walked through the fields in gloves. The best part of the pleasure of walking was to feel one's bare feet sinking in the dust, just as the keenest edge of the joy of kicking, that activity so natural in children and so essential for them, was in raising dust as high as the head. One of the reasons why as boys we looked down upon and disliked the *other bank*, as we always called the half of the town on the southern bank of the river, was that its main road was metalled; of course not metalled in the proper sense but given a foundation of smashed bricks, with the only result (so far as we could see) that pieces of brick with sharp edges and corners were showing all over the road surface. Our bare feet, when not cut or bruised by them, became sore if we had to walk on that road. Our road on the contrary was so sensitive that we could always tell which way people had gone by looking at the footprints. There never was any time of the day and night when the road did not show footmarks. But they pointed differently at different times. At midday, after the great litigious crowd had gone towards the courts, the toes all pointed westward, and in the early morning eastward. In addition, in every section of the road coinciding with each house-front, there were one or more bigger depressions, showing where the pariah dog or dogs belonging or voluntarily attaching themselves to that particular house had slept the night before.

Another sign of the transition from the wet to the dry season was to be seen in the immense number of jute-stem stacks standing on every field and lawn. After the bark which yields the fibre had been stripped off, the stems of the jute plant were dried and put to a variety of uses. Consisting of a white pith-like substance and being light, brittle, and inflammable, they were used for lighting fire; and being tall and rigid at the same time they were made into screens, partitions and the like with a stiffening of bamboo. Every household bought the year's supply at the end of the wet season, but before being put away the stems were given a thorough airing and drying. So they stood everywhere in white stacks eight to ten feet high, spread out at the bottom and tied at the top, and bearing some resemblance to the wigwams of Red Indians. We made narrow doors into them by pushing away some of the stems and hid within, either in the course of hide-and-seek or for sheer mischief.

Generally we got punished for this, not by our parents though, but by a more appropriate agency. These stacks were full of hairy caterpillars, and more often than not we emerged out of them with blisters on the most sensitive parts of our bare bodies. These creatures were the plague of our lives almost throughout the year. We usually could spot the bigger and the more fiery ones, but the smaller greyish things passed unnoticed and caused us excruciating tortures. The only remedy we knew of was to smear ourselves with a mixture of mustard oil and slaked lime, which although frequently put on us was considered by us to be as bad as, if not worse than, the disease.

The ordinary ants did not give us much trouble except that by giving us swollen lips they almost always betrayed us to our mother when we had stolen sugar from the store-room. But there was one species of big and poisonous red ants living in trees which gave us a mortal fright whenever we saw them. A salutary respect for them prevented our keeping the magpie robin which was the best songster we had, because this bird had to be fed on the larvae of the dreaded red ant. Yet we saw them but occasionally. A more persistent nuisance was the centipedes. There were many species of them, some big, brown and poisonous, but these too were comparatively rare. The commonest was the small lacquer-red species which curled itself up into a tight ring as soon as touched. When it was in that state we could pull it to pieces more easily than straighten it out. These centipedes were so common that the very first riddle we were asked and learned was about them. It ran:

> There's a creature red in tint,
> Struck like rupees at the mint;
> His shanks number ninety-nine:
> I trow on him you chaps dine.

At first we were totally baffled by this conundrum. But when once we were told its meaning we always gleefully shouted 'Centipede, centipede', whenever the question was put to us. It was this vermin and not snakes which we feared most when we lay in the grass or hay or straw. The general belief was that they crept into the ears and finally made their way into the brain causing all kinds of mental disorders. 'To have a centipede in the head' was the equivalent in our parts to saying that a person was crazy or had inexplicable fads and crotchets. The expression was used jocularly, but it must have had its source in a primitive conviction which even grown-up men could not wholly shake off and women and children certainly had not. Our ears were always examined for centipedes after we had rolled or lain for some time in grass.

Towards the middle of November we celebrated the formal passing of the wet season and the coming of the cold by lighting bonfires. For ourselves we wished good to come and evil to depart, and for the flies, mosquitoes and other insects the most humiliating discomfiture. Then we witnessed a succession of happenings which revealed to us the inexorable process of the seasons. First of all, the municipal workmen cleaned up the ditch which ran from one end of the town to the other separating all the houses from the road. This ditch had to be spanned in every case by a small bridge, made in some instances of brick but more generally of bamboo and beaten earth. The weeds which had grown in it during the rains were torn up and then the sides and the bottom scraped till the soft brown earth stood exposed. The drain, about three feet wide and only slightly less in depth, was never filthy, for it carried nothing but rain water. We always crept along it in our games, and after the annual cleaning it was our favourite resort.

A similar weeding was given to our grounds, and, as at this time large droves of swine were passing through the town in their journeys from their monsoon quarters to their winter quarters (we had no precise idea where they were), we requested the swineherds to bring their animals into our grounds and get them to dig up and destroy the bulbous arum plants which had grown so plentifully during the rains. We did not, however, allow the pigs to plough up our inner court-yard. This square of some forty feet by as many feet was entrusted to a special workman who tore up every blade of grass individually. It was *de rigueur* in every self-respecting household to keep the inner yard free of grass. To have even short stubbles of green showing there was as improper among us as it is to wear two-day-old stubbles of beard in English society.

About the same time one or two women were requisitioned to recondition our earthen floors. All our huts were built on platforms of beaten earth, about three feet high, the tops of which, without any kind of additional covering, constituted our floors. These floors were rubbed every morning with fresh mud and water in order to keep them firm and clean, and the sides too were given the same treatment almost every day. But during the monsoon the sides could not receive the same attention, if any at all, and so, at the end of the rains, they became rough, peeled, and in extreme cases even pot-holed. Ordinarily the senior servant or even my mother did this daily smearing, for it called for considerable skill and practice if the whole place was not to be made utterly messy. But my mother could hardly be expected to carry out the extensive renova-tion and the senior servant was a busy man, having to see to cooking and the meals. Accordingly, professional 'mud-smearers' were sent for and they saw the job neatly through for a few annas.

These floors of ours call for some explanation but certainly no apologies. Although in our childhood, so far as the houses of the gentlefolk were concerned, mud floors were to be found only in our district and in one or two adjacent ones, we were carrying on a venerable tradition once established all over Bengal and very solidly. In later life, I read an old Bengali tract written to promote the cause of 'female education', which unconsciously provided a mud floor for a royal palace. The pamphlet was written and published in 1822 and has thus a just claim to be called a Bengali incunabulum. Its writer was concerned with citing instances of female literacy from ancient Bengali history and chose no less an example than that of the daughter-in-law of the famous king of Bengal, Vallala Sena, and wife of the last independent Hindu king of Bengal, Lakshmana Sena. Lakshmana Sena as heir apparent, the story ran, had been sent on some expedition by his father and separated from his wife, and one rainy day the love-lorn princess could repress her anguish no more. So, while smearing with water and mud the place where the king, her father-in-law, was to have his midday meal, she forgot herself completely and scratched a few lines of verse on the mud floor. The quatrain was in Sanskrit, but here is a rough translation:

> Rumbling cloud and rustling rain,
> Peacock's call: the same thing say –
> Lord of Love shall crown this day,
> Or Lord of Death shall end the pain.

The princess forgot to rub out the lines, and when the king came in to dine he read the verses and immediately understood the situation. He sent for his son and united the unhappy pair.

That was decisive enough in its day to prove that the last Hindu queen of Bengal knew her three R's, but to me, when I read the passage, the most valuable point was the historical justification the polemist had provided in it for our mud floors. What old Bengali tradition considered good enough for the palace of Vallala Sena was good enough, if not too good, for us. Incidentally, I found many Bengali ladies, including my mother, given to the habit of scratching on the mud floor. I never saw my mother scratching any poetry but I often saw her drawing very fine little designs of florets, peacock heads, elephants, or horses on the mud floor with her nails or with a bamboo pin, when she was abstracted either from vexation or some other mental preoccupation. We, the children, however, were never allowed to tamper with the floor, which, to tell the truth, if given a free hand, we would fain have dug up like the wolf in Webster's poem.

To conclude the story of the pigs, occasionally they and their men encamped on the low meadow before our house. I particularly remember one big camp, in which there were women and children as well as men and, of course, the pigs, and which was pitched so elaborately that it had bamboo screens all around it. I have no recollection why the party stayed in the town but I have a vague feeling that it remained for about a week and did some business with the sweepers of the town, who took this occasion to replenish their piggeries. Despite the severest warning against going anywhere near the unclean animals we felt the profoundest interest in the sucking-pigs which were carried in bamboo baskets and were perpetually squealing. We were always hanging about the camp, and when a particularly shrill chorus of squeals reached our ears we threw ourselves with desperation on the screen in order to peer and find out what was happening inside. The word went round that the sucking-pigs were being killed and roasted. Thus, even without knowing anything about Charles Lamb's Chinese boy or Mrs Beeton's recipe for roasting sucking-pigs, we were taking the road which led to the first and through the first to the second.

There was another encamping we very much looked forward to seeing in the cold season, but which, throughout the years of my childhood spent at Kishorganj, I saw only twice. It was the encampment of the gypsies. We looked upon them with fascination and fear not only because extra police were posted to keep an eye on their comings and goings, but even more because it was reported to us that they caught and ate the malodorous animal which was almost legendary with us and which in our dialect was given a name which indiscriminately meant the civet as well as the polecat. And one day I saw with my own eyes a gypsy coming in with a hairy animal, swinging it by a striped tail, and flinging the furry bundle on the ground before his tent.

There was another thing in the gypsy camp which perhaps we admired even more, certainly not less. It was the ass. Asses are not native to East Bengal, nor are they kept or used there as domestic animals, so we never had a sight of asses before the gypsies brought them to our town for the first time. They were a delight to child and adult alike, and no okapi even could cause greater sensation. Their braying was listened to with even greater pleasure, and we should not have been surprised if like the oryx of legend the asses had stood in mystical ecstasy before the rising sun and sneezed. I have read that when the Hyksos brought the horse into Egypt, the Egyptians, previously unfamiliar with that noble animal, gave it the name – Ass of the East. We were disposed to call the ass the Horse of the West.

Many years afterwards my friend Tridib Chaudhuri confirmed to me this fact of general ignorance of the ass in East Bengal with a most interesting anecdote. One day, when I casually mentioned to him that we in East Bengal had no asses, he immediately remarked that he had been given conclusive proof of that unfamiliarity when he was in Deoli detention camp in Rajputana as a political prisoner. That was the camp where, between 1932 and 1937, some hundreds of Bengali young men had been kept in detention without trial for suspected complicity in terrorist activities. The first day Tridib Chaudhuri arrived there some previously arrived fellow-prisoners, who were from East Bengal, told him that at night they could hear the roaring of the lions at Kotah, kept in the menagerie of the Maharao, a famous Rajput prince.

My friend was naturally surprised, for Kotah was fifty-four miles away. But his new friends promised to wake him up at night and make him hear the lions. A little after midnight the tired young man was shaken to wakefulness and his companions whispered: 'There, listen!' Tridib Chaudhuri, whose home was in West Bengal, was stupefied at first, then he cried out, 'Why, it's only an ass braying.' For this remark, taken as an unseasonable flippancy, he got only icy looks to begin with; had he not been a newcomer things would have gone very much farther. But the next morning brought his vindication. While he was walking with his companions near the edge of the camp, which was on a hill, he saw down below the hut of a *dhobi* or washerman, with a number of asses grazing near by. As good fortune would have it, just at that moment one of the animals began to bray, and the enigma of the Kotah lions was finally solved.

That reminds me of our general ignorance about animals. Anything with a feline look and dashes of yellow and black in it was, and still is, a tiger of some sort or other. With inexplicable perversity we persisted in calling the common hare found at Kishorganj 'spotted deer'. In the fine zoological gardens of Calcutta not the least part of the entertainment is provided by the visitors with their imaginative wealth of observations. Listening with an appearance of unconcern, I have heard all kinds of names applied to the puma and the jaguar and all sorts of mythical attributes set down to the credit of the brown bear, the orang, and the hippopotamus. But the story which deserves to be classical is about a father and son and a zebra, and was told to me by another friend. The little boy was standing before the zebra enclosure and he asked his father what the animals were. The father replied that they were African tigers. The boy, who apparently had more wits than he was born with, protested: 'But, father, they look like horses.' The father began to scold the boy, when my friend, unable to bear it any longer, intervened: 'Sir,' he said, 'why are you scolding the boy? You must be familiar with the shape of that animal, although it has not got exactly your colouration.' The father got more angry still and moved away growling that he was not going to be insulted before his son.

Another outstanding experience of the cold season was a folk-ritual which was performed every day for one whole month from the middle of January to the middle of February. It was a ritual for little girls, but it was very elaborate and if one was to draw the fullest benefit out of it, it had to be performed for twelve years in succession. Therefore the girls began quite early in life, even at the age of three or four, so that they might see a substantial portion through before they were married off. But of course one could not speak of standards of performance before they had done it for some six or seven years, because the designs which had to be executed required skill in drawing. About twelve feet square or even more of the inner courtyard had to be covered with figures of the sun and the moon, floral decorations of various sorts, and big circles which had to be truly drawn. The palette was similar to that used by the Cromagnon man – dull red, black, and white, with only a greater preponderance of white. The actual colouring material used was, however, simpler than that of later palaeolithic society, namely, brick dust instead of red peroxide of iron, charcoal dust instead of pyrolusite, and rice powder for white. The girls took the powders in handfuls, closed their fists, and released the colours through the hole formed by the curled little finger, regulating the flow by tightening or loosening their grip. It was wonderful to see how quickly they filled up the space. The sun was a staring face about two feet in diameter, the moon slightly smaller. The first was laid out mainly in red and black, producing a fiery effect, while the moon was for the most part in rice powder which very successfully brought out its blanched appearance. The floral decorations were of course *motifs* on which Bengali women had practised no one knows for how many generations, and they came out as quickly and neatly as if they were being done from stencils.

Two girls of the house next to ours, whose parents we called uncle and aunt following Bengali custom, performed this ritual. At dawn they had their plunge in the cold river and came back singing and shivering. We, the boys, quickly collected twigs, dry leaves, bamboo scrapings, even a log or two, and made a fire for them. After they had got a little warm the girls set to work and it went on till about ten o'clock. The girls chanted hymns to the sun and the moon which could be called a crude and rudimentary version of the canticles of St Francis. We could not go near or touch them because, being unbathed, we were unclean, but we did our best to make ourselves serviceable in every possible way.

This account of the process of the seasons at Kishorganj should now be closed. The campings and the rituals I have described were the rubrics of the year. Simultaneously, the ordinary text, though less colourful, was not unrolling itself less absorbingly. We were almost wild with excitement when the trees bought to supply the year's firewood arrived on the shoulders of men or on carts. The boles and the branches with leaves, buds, and even fruit were piled high on the wayside, on the riverside slope of the road, to dry. We climbed on them, heaved the whole green mass up and down, suddenly let go, and slid down to the ground. This lasted for about ten days, by which time the leaves withered and dropped off, and then the branches were cut up into logs.

After the firewood it was the turn of the year's supply of straw for our cows. Newly cut straw is lighter in colour, stiffer, and more hollow than dry straw. It is also sharp. After a bout of climbing and rolling on straw we had very fine invisible scratches all over the body, and these smarted when we entered water. That was why we were usually warned off the straw. But we did not rate too high the price which we had to pay for making free love to it at its most lovable age.

The oranges from the Khasi Hills, which are rather small in size, besides being smooth, thin-skinned, and very sweet, were our regular winter visitors. They were quite plentiful at Kishorganj, and the cold season was for us a season marked by the flavour, fragrance, and colour of oranges. Those were pre-vitamin days, when the eating of oranges was a pleasure and not a duty. The colour of the oranges was taken up by the gorgeous borders of African marigold (*Tagetes erecta*) or *Gainda*, as we called them, which was the most common and in my childhood the only cold-season annual we had. By chance I and two of my brothers had bright orange-coloured overcoats, and we stood in the sun in these overcoats every morning eating oranges. Perhaps I ought to explain here that from the bare skin of summer we passed to more adequate clothing in the winter.

As soon as the cold was passing off, our typical flowers began to come out. In addition to the marigold we cultivated another annual, the balsam, which, however, was a flower of the rainy season. In the meanwhile one glorious cycle of our prized blooms had come and gone. It was a remarkable thing that both the opening of the flowering season in spring and its final closing in the late autumn were marked by same two flowers, two of the most deliciously scented flowers we had. They were the Night-blooming Flower of Sadness (*Nyctanthes arbortristis*), called *Sewlee* in Bengali, and the *Champa* (*Michelia champaca*). Whiffs of their heavy scent came borne on every little breeze to us. Starting from the spring we had, in a steady stream, all the kinds of jasmine, also the so-called Cape Jasmine which was not a jasmine at all but our *Gandharaj* (*Gardenia florida*), the China Box or *Kamini* (*Murraya exotica*), the ravishing *Bakul* (*Mimusops elengi*) with its creamy green flowerets, and the exquisite Tuberose, *Rajanigandha* or *Gul-shabu* (*Polianthes tuberosa*). All these flowers, with the exception of the *Bakul* whose colour I have mentioned and the *Champa* which was pale golden yellow, were pure white, with scents which would be considered overpowering by many. The great floral attraction of the rainy season was the *Kadamva* (*Anthocephalus cadamva*), which one could regard as the link between our white scented flowers and coloured unscented flowers. It had only a very mild fragrance and its spherical flowers could be easily plucked bare of the innumerable white stamens to expose the orange core. The tall and large-leaved tree which bears this flower is famous in legend as that under which Krishna used to play his flute on the banks of the Jumna.

Among coloured flowers we had, of course, the highly perfumed Bussora rose, and the scentless hibiscus – the red, the light pink, and the pendulous; also the *Hibiscus mutabilis*, which we did not look upon as a hibiscus at all but called 'land lotus', the ixora, and the canna. Curiously enough, we never had oleanders. What passed as oleander or *Karavi* with us was a yellow, nectar-bearing, bell-shaped flower, to whose mildly poisonous fruit hysterical women bent on spiting their husbands by committing suicide sometimes had recourse. We, the children, loved all the flowers equally well. But our elders never thought much of any of the coloured flowers except the red hibiscus which was indispensable for worshipping the goddess Kali. Even the sweet-smelling Bussora rose was out of court because it was looked upon as an Islamic flower. China had got accepted at our hands, but neither Iran nor Araby.

It was an essential part of our education to be able to weave garlands of three kinds of flowers – the jasmine, the Night-blooming Flower of Sadness, and the Bakul. We sat still with needlefuls of thread pricking our way through the fine stalks of all these minute flowers. But when this task of infinite patience was over, we put the garlands round our necks for a few minutes and then tore them and threw them away on the ground to be trampled under foot. Our floors and inner court-yard in the summer were almost always strewn with the loose ends of garlands.

It was not by flowers alone that the seasons were marked for us at Kishorganj. There was another visitor both at the beginning and end of the cold weather, but mostly at the beginning, whom we did not like though we did not know him well. One day my father, who was the Vice-Chairman of the municipal-ity, would come home and say, 'There's cholera on the other bank.' We felt vaguely anxious and, going out on the road, stared long and thoughtfully at the other bank. What we gen-erally saw was very low strips of smoke and mist on the meadow across the stream. We came gradually to half-associ-ate cholera with those banks of smoke and mist. But there was another thing with which we wholly associated it, that being one of the regular sights of the cholera season. Every evening a municipal workman passed along the road swinging a censer-like pot in which sulphur was burning. Thus sulphur dioxide became firmly united in our sensations with cholera. We did not, however, know cholera at close quarters until our baby sister had it. Even then we were not allowed to approach the sickroom, although we were very curious to see what cholera was like. I saw a case with my own eyes only in 1913 and then I understood what cholera really was.

Kamala Markandaya

HUNGER

THAT YEAR THE rains failed. A week went by, two. We stared
at the cruel sky, calm, blue, indifferent to our need. We threw
ourselves on the earth and we prayed. I took a pumpkin and
a few grains of rice to my Goddess, and I wept at her feet. I
thought she looked at me with compassion and I went away
comforted, but no rain came.

'Perhaps tomorrow,' my husband said. 'It is not too late.'

We went out and scanned the heavens, clear and beautiful,
deadly beautiful, not one cloud to mar its serenity. Others did
so too, coming out, as we did, to gaze at the sky and murmur,
'Perhaps tomorrow.'

Tomorrows came and went and there was no rain. Nathan
no longer said perhaps; only a faint spark of hope, obstinately
refusing to die, brought him out each dawn to scour the
heavens for a sign.

Each day the level of the water dropped and the heads of
the paddy hung lower. The river had shrunk to a trickle, the
well was as dry as a bone. Before long the shoots of the paddy
were tipped with brown; even as we watched, the stain spread
like some terrible disease, choking out the green that meant
life to us.

Harvesting time, and nothing to reap. The paddy had
taken all our labour and lay now before us in faded, useless
heaps.

Sivaji came to collect his master's dues and his face fell

Extract from the novel *Nectar in a Sieve*.

when he saw how much was lost, for he was a good man and he felt for us.

'There is nothing this year,' Nathan said to him. 'Not even gleanings, for the grain was but little advanced.'

'You have had the land,' Sivaji said, 'for which you have contracted to pay: so much money, so much rice. These are just dues, I must have them. Would you have me return empty-handed?'

Nathan's shoulders sagged. He looked tired and dispirited. I came and stood beside him, Ira and the boys crouched near us, defensively.

'There is nothing,' Nathan repeated. 'Do you not see the crops are dead? There has been no rain and the river is dry.'

'Yet such was the contract, else the land would not have been rented to you.'

'What would you have me do? The last harvest was meagre; we have nothing saved.'

Sivaji looked away. 'I do not know. It is your concern. I must do as I am bid.'

'What then?'

'The land is to be given to another if you cannot make payment.'

'Go from the land after all these years? Where would we go? How would we live?'

'It is your concern. I have my orders and must obey them.'

Nathan stood there sweating and trembling.

'Give me time,' he said at last humbly, 'until the next crop. I will pay then, somehow.'

'Pay half now,' Sivaji said, 'and I will try and do as you wish.' He spoke quickly, as if to give himself no time to repent of his offer, and hurried away even before my husband had assented.

'No easy job for him,' I said. 'He is answerable, even as we are.'

'That is why he and his kind are employed,' Nathan said bitterly. 'To protect their overlords from such unpleasant tasks. Now the landlord can wring from us his moneys and care not for the misery he evokes, for indeed it would be difficult for any man to see another starve and his wife and children as well; or to enjoy the profits born of such travail.'

He went into the hut and I followed. A few mud pots and two brass vessels, the tin trunk I had brought with me as a bride, the two shirts my eldest sons had left behind, two ollocks of dhal and a handful of dried chillies left over from better times: these we put together to sell.

'Rather these should go,' said Nathan, 'than that the land should be taken from us; we can do without these, but if the land is gone our livelihood is gone, and we must thenceforth wander like jackals.' He stared awhile at what we had to sell, and made an effort to say something and tried again and at last he said, choking, 'The bullocks must go. Otherwise we shall not have enough.'

But when we had added them and reckoned and reckoned, there was still not enough. 'There are the saris left,' I said. 'Good ones and hardly worn, and these we must sell.'

I brought out the red sari that had served for both my wedding and my daughter's, and the sari and dhoti I had bought when Thambi worked at the tannery, made a parcel of them and set out.

'Ah, Rukmani,' said Biswas with false welcome. 'What brings you here? I have not seen you for a long time, nor had any of your succulent fruit. Would that be what you bear with you?'

'No indeed,' I answered shortly, his voice grating on me as always. 'For the earth is parched to dust and all that I grew is dead. The rains failed, as you know.'

'Yes, yes, yes,' he said, looking at me with his cunning eyes. 'These are hard times for us.'

Not for you, I thought. You thrive on others' misfortunes.

'We need money for the land,' I said. 'I have brought the two shirts my sons no longer need, being away, two saris I never wear and my husband's dhoti to sell to you. The saris are very finely worked, and worn but a few times.' I took them out and laid them before him.

He fingered the rich stuff, and measured the borders between outstretched thumb and little finger, and lifted up the silver threads to examine them the closer, and held up the shirts to the light for sign of wear.

'How much do you want for these?'

'It is for you to make the offer.'

'Tell me first how much you want and I will see what I can do.'

'Enough to pay the land dues.'

'How much is that?'

'It is my business.'

He was silent for a while, and I said to him exasperated, 'Tell me if you are not prepared to buy and I will go elsewhere.'

'Always in haste,' he rebuked me in that gentle, oily voice of his. 'Yet I think this time you will have to await my pleasure, Rukmani.'

'What do you mean?' I said, ruffled. 'There are many who would be pleased to buy such good material.'

'I think not,' he said. 'I think not. For, you see, the wives of other men have come to me, even as you have, and have gone away as you threaten, yet they have to come back to me because nobody else can afford to buy in these hard times.'

'As no doubt you can,' I said with contempt, and then an inspiration came to me and I went on: 'Unless you pay a fair price I shall take these saris elsewhere. There is the Muslim wife of a tannery official whom I know, and she will buy from me as she has done before.'

'Indeed,' he said, a little disconcerted. 'Well, Rukmani, since we have done business for a long time, and because you are a woman of spirit whom I have long admired, I will give you thirty rupees. Nobody could be fairer.'

'Fairer, by far,' I retorted. 'I will not take one pie under seventy-five rupees. Take it or not as you please.'

I put the clothes away, making a pretence of going to the door. I hoped he would call me back, for in truth I did not know where else to turn, but if not – well, thirty rupees was too far from our needs to be of use, and if I did not get what I asked I might as well keep the saris.

As I got to the door he called to me. 'Very well, Rukmani.

I will pay you what you ask, since it will help you.'

I waited. He disappeared into another room and came back in a few minutes with a sour face and a small leather pouch full of money. He pulled the drawstrings and took from it notes and silver, counting them twice over to make sure.

'A very rare price,' he said, handing me the money. 'Remember always the good turn I have done you.'

I tucked the money away, making no reply, and I went back with a lighter step than I had come out.

Nathan had returned too, having sold the pots and pans, the food and the bullocks. We pooled the money and counted it, and there was in all one hundred and twenty-five rupees, not even the half we had to pay.

'There is still the seed,' Nathan said. 'We must sell that.'

'What of the next crop?' I said. 'If we sell the seed we may as well give up the land too, for how shall we raise a new crop?'

'It is better to be without the seed than bereft of the land in which to plant it. Seed is cheap, it can be bought. I can earn a few rupees, or perhaps my sons . . .'

How? I cried to myself. How? Is not my son every day at the tannery, and no one will look at him because of his brothers! And you, my husband, what chance have you when so many young men are festering in idleness!

'It will mean only a few rupees,' I said. 'Let us not sacrifice the future to our immediate need.'

'What is the alternative?' he shouted. 'Do you think I am blind and do not see, or so stupid as to believe that crops are raised without seed? Do you take me for a fool that –'

He was not shouting at me but at the terrible choice forced upon us; this I knew, yet could not prevent my throat contracting, or force the tears back into their wells.

'Let us only try,' I said with the sobs coming fast. 'Let us keep our hope for a next harvest.'

'Very well, very well,' Nathan exclaimed. 'Let us try by all means. We may be kicked for our pains, but what of that! Anything to stop your wailing. Now go, do not cross me further.'

He is worried, I thought, smothering my sobs. He is distracted and does not mean to be harsh.

I went inside and lay down, with the money tied to my body, and at last dozed off into a troubled sleep.

In the morning Sivaji came, and my husband took the money and counted it out in front of him.

'One hundred and twenty-five rupees,' he said. 'Not half what we owe, but the best we can do without selling the seed for the next sowing.'

'It would raise only a few rupees,' I pleaded. 'Let us but keep it, and we will repay you twofold.'

'It is not for me,' Sivaji answered. 'You make payment to another. What shall I say to him that I bring so little? You made promise of half.'

'Give us a little grace,' Nathan said, dragging the words out. 'We will make full repayment and over after the next harvesting.'

So we stood and argued and begged, and in the end Sivaji agreed to wait. He took the money and turned to go, then he hesitated and said, a little wistfully: 'What I do I must, for I must think of my own . . . I do not wish to be hard. May you prosper.'

'May you prosper too,' I whispered, hardly able to speak, for his words had left me defenceless. 'May the Gods give you their blessing.' And so he departed.

The drought continued until we lost count of the time. Day after day the pitiless sun blazed down, scorching whatever still struggled to grow and baking the earth hard until at last it split and great irregular fissures gaped in the land. Plants died and the grasses rotted, cattle and sheep crept to the river that was no more and perished there for lack of water, lizards and squirrels lay prone and gasping in the blistering sunlight.

In the town a water reservoir had been built for the tannery workers and their families, but now others were allowed a limited quantity as well. So thither I journeyed every morning, and, when I said how many we were, perhaps half a mud pot would be doled out, sometimes a little more, depending upon who was in charge. Then some of the women in their greed began to claim to have more children than they had, and nonexistent relatives, and there were jealousies and spite and bitter argument. Until at last it was decreed that each person must come in his own right only, not for others, even children and old men, and this put an end to the cheating and quarrelling; but it was hard for many who had not their full strength.

Then, after the heat had endured for days and days, and our hopes had shrivelled with the paddy – too late to do any good – then we saw the storm clouds gathering, and before long the rain came lashing down, making up in fury for the long drought and giving the grateful land as much as it could suck and more. But in us there was nothing left – no joy, no call for joy. It had come too late.

As soon as the rains were over, and the cracks in the earth had healed, and the land was moist and ready, we took our seed to our Goddess and placed it at her feet to receive her blessing, and then we bore it away and made our sowing.

When a few weeks had gone by, the seed sprouted; tender shoots appeared, thrusting upwards with increasing strength, and soon we were able to transplant the seedlings one by one, and at first they stood out singly, slender, tremulous spires with spaces between: but grew and grew and soon were merged into one thick green field of rustling paddy. In that field, in the grain which had not yet begun to form, lay our future and our hope.

Hope, and fear. Twin forces that tugged at us first in one direction and then in another, and which was the stronger no one could say. Of the latter we never spoke, but it was always with us. Fear, constant companion of the peasant. Hunger, ever at hand to jog his elbow should he relax. Despair, ready to engulf him should he falter. Fear; fear of the dark future; fear of the sharpness of hunger; fear of the blackness of death.

Long before the paddy ripened we came to the end of our dried-fish stocks. There was no money left – every pie had gone to pay the land dues. Nothing left to sell. Nothing to be had from my efforts, for the vines and vegetables had withered in the long weeks of drought.

At last no option but to draw upon my secret hoard: a small stock of rice, ten ollocks in all, shielded from every temptation to sell or barter, kept even when the need to hold our land had squeezed us dry of everything else. Now I brought it out and measured it again, ten ollocks exactly. Then I divided it into several equal portions, each of the portions as little as would suffice for one day, and counted the portions, of which there were twenty-four, so that for nearly a month we would not starve. For a long time I hesitated, wondering whether we could do with less, thus making thirty divisions, but finally I decided against it, for Kuti was already ailing, and we needed to preserve our strength for the harvest.

For at least twenty-four days we shall eat, I thought. At the end of that time – well, we are in God's hands. He will not fail us. Sometimes I thought that, and at other times I was seized with trembling and was frightened, not knowing where to turn.

The nights were always the worst, and not for me alone. Peace then seemed to forsake our hut and I could hear my husband and children moving restlessly in their sleep and muttering, whether from hunger or fear I do not know. Once Nathan cried out loudly and sprang up in his sleep. I went to him, and he woke then and clung to me.

'Only a dream,' I said. 'Sleep, my dear one.'

'A nightmare,' he said sweating. 'I saw the paddy turned to straw, the grain lost . . . Oh God, all was lost.'

His voice was stark, bereft of the power of dissembling which full consciousness brings.

'Never fear,' I said with false courage lest panic should swoop down on us. 'All will be well.'

He composed himself for sleep again.

'You are a good wife,' he murmured. 'I would not have any other.'

I drifted at last into uneasy sleep, and dreamt many evil dreams, and in one I saw a shadowy figure with no face creeping into our hut and bearing away the ten ollocks of rice. I knew it was but the result of an over-burdened spirit, but the following night I had the same dream. As the days passed I found myself growing increasingly suspicious. Except for my family, I trusted no one. Only at night when there were no passers-by, did I feel completely safe. Then I would bring out the rice, and measure it, and run the grain through my fingers for sheer love of it, fondling it like a simpleton. When I had taken out the allotted portion for the next day I would bury the remainder: one half, tied in a white cloth, in a hole I dug some distance from our hut, the other half in our granary.

Several times I thought of going to Kenny, and twice I did go. He would have helped us, of that I am sure, but each time I was told he had gone away . . . the townsfolk had not seen him for many weeks. I would have gone again and again, but I had not my full strength; it was no longer easy to walk to the town and back. We might have borrowed from Biswas, but there was nothing left to pledge; in any event, we would not have been able even to pay the interest he demanded.

Seven days went by and seven precious portions of rice were eaten. On the eighth day Kunthi came as I was cooking the rice water.

I had not set eyes on her for a considerable time – not since the day I had seen her in her nakedness; and she had changed so much I scarcely recognised her. I gazed at her hardly believing. The skin of her face was stiff and shiny as if from over-stretching, elsewhere it showed folds and wrinkles. Under her faded sari her breasts hung loose; gone was the tense supple-ness that had been her pride and her power. Of her former beauty not a vestige remained. Well, I thought. All women come to it sooner or later: she has come off perhaps worse than most.

'Sit and rest awhile,' I said. 'What brings you hither?'

She made no answer, but walked to the pot on the fire and looked in.

'You eat well,' she said. 'Better than most.'

'Not well. We eat, that is all.'

'You still have your husband?'

'Why, yes,' I said staring at her, not quite taking her mean-ing. 'Why do you ask?'

She shrugged. 'I have lost mine. I wondered how you had fared.'

Poor thing, I thought. She has suffered. I looked on her pityingly.

'I do not want your pity,' she said savagely, 'nor does my husband. He is alive and well – he is living with another.'

I thought of her husband, slow, sturdy, dependable, rather like an ox, and I could not believe it of him; then I thought of Kunthi as I had once seen her, with painted mouth and scented thighs that had held so many men, and I wondered if after all these years he had not at last found out about her. Perhaps the truth has been forced upon him, I thought, looking at her with suspicion, and I gazed again upon that ravaged beauty.

'Stare your fill,' she said scornfully. 'You always lacked graces, Rukmani.'

I averted my eyes hastily. I hardly knew what to say.

'I have come,' she continued, 'not to be seen, or to see you, but for a meal. I have not eaten for a long time.'

I went to the pot and stirred it, scooped out a little, placed it in a bowl, handed it to her. She swallowed it quickly and put the bowl down.

'I must have some rice too. I cannot come every day . . . as it is I have waited a long time to make sure you were alone.'

'There is no rice to be given away,' I said. 'I must think of my husband and children. These are not times of plenty.'

'Nevertheless,' she replied. 'I will have some. The damage will never be repaired while I hunger. There is no life for me until I am whole again.'

She is mad, I thought. She believes what she says; does not realise there is no going back for her.

'Listen,' I said, 'there is none, or very little. Drink our rice water, come here daily, but do not ask for rice. I have a daughter and sons, even as you have, to consider. What I have belongs to us all. Can you not go to your sons?'

'My sons,' she said, looking at me speculatively, 'are not mine alone.' Seeing my bewilderment she added, 'They have wives. I would never approach them now.'

'What are sons for –' I began.

'Not to beg from,' she interrupted with a flicker of contempt. 'I can look after myself; but first the bloom must come back.'

I was mute: I had said all there was to say and now there was nothing more.

'Well,' she said, breaking the silence, and with an edge to her voice. 'How much longer have I to wait?'

She came close to me and put her face near mine. I saw the grey, drawn flesh and the hooded eyes, deep sunken in their sockets, and I made to turn away but she held me.

'I have not so much patience,' she said. 'I will have the rice now or your husband shall hear that his wife is not as virtuous as he believes – or she pretends.'

'He believes what is true,' I said with anger. 'I do not pretend.'

'Perhaps he has not seen what I have seen,' she said, and there was menace in her voice and threat in the words. 'Comings and goings in the twilight, and soft speech, and gifts of milk and honey such as men make to the women they have known.'

'Stop,' I howled at her, and put my hands to my ears. Thoughts kept hurtling through my head like frenzied squirrels in a new-forged cage. With sudden clarity I recalled my daughter's looks that far-off day when I had gone to Kenny; my son's words: 'Such men have power, especially over women'; remembered my own foolish silences. I closed my eyes and sank down. She came and sat beside me.

'Which is it to be? Which is it to be? . . .'

Her words were hammering at my brain, the horrible syllables were beating the air around me, the whole place was full of their sound.

I need you, I cried to myself, Nathan, my husband. I cannot take the risk, because there is a risk since she is clever and I am not. In your anger or your jealousy, or even because you are not yourself after these long strained months, you may believe what she says and what she means. Because I have deceived you and cannot deny all she proclaims, you may believe the more. I will kill her first, I thought, and the desire was strong.

I felt myself shaking. I raised my hands to my eyes and there was a quivering redness there. Then I heard a cry, whether of bird or child or my own tortured self I do not know, and the redness cleared. I felt the water oozing through my closed eyes, through my closed fingers. I took my hands away, and there was Kunthi waiting by my side with the patience of one who knows what power she wields, patient, like a vulture.

The ration of seven days to Kunthi, and eight already eaten. There is still enough for nine days, I thought, not with comfort but with desolation, and hatred came welling up again for her who had deprived me of the grain, and contempt for myself who had relinquished it.

I waited a long time that night before going out, for fear that Kunthi might be watching. There is nothing she would not do, I thought, lying there in the darkness. I must wait, and walk with care, and return unseen. I will match my wits against hers, I thought cunningly, lying and listening to uneasy slumber about me, and I will yet win; clever though she is, she shall not have all . . . I rose at last and went out softly, and looked about me, and went quickly to the hole I had dug, and clawed away the earth until I saw the bundle, white under the starlight. I squatted down, crooning silently, untied it, ran my fingers through the grain; and I knew then there was no more than a handful left – a day's supply, no more, not the nine days' supply I had looked to find.

My stomach lurched, blood came pounding to my head, I felt myself going dizzy. Who could have known, who had done this to me? I heard a voice moaning and it was mine and the sound was terrifying, for I had not meant to speak. I looked about me wildly, seeking to see even in that darkness. Nothing in sight, not a sound except my own loud heartbeats. I dug my nails into my palms, striving for calm, trying to think. Who could have done this? Kunthi? – but she only knew of the granary, not this other hiding place. My own family? No, I thought with despair, thrusting aside the small core of suspicion each time it formed. Surely not. Who else? Who?

A long time passed; when at last I rose, my limbs were stiff and prickling, and darkness had given way to the first grey beginnings of dawn.

Nathan was not in the hut when I went back: I saw him sitting beside the paddy fields as he often did when he could not sleep. The boys were still asleep, the two older ones side by side, Kuti squeezed close to Ira and she with her arm thrown across him. I shook her by the shoulder, and Kuti woke first and began to cry. I picked him up and took him outside and left him there, and when I went back the others were awake. I looked at the three faces and I thought bitterly. One of them has done this to me . . . Which one? Which one? I thought, questioning, looking at the three faces as if to read their thoughts; but there was nothing to see save alarm; they shrank a little from my vehemence.

'I must know,' I shouted. 'I must know who has done this thing.'

They looked at me as if I had lost my senses. Ira said timidly, 'We would not take what belonged to us all.'

'Tell me I am imagining the loss,' I stormed at her, 'or that I myself have eaten it.'

They stared at me in silence, amazed. Outside Kuti was bawling. Attracted by his cries, Nathan had come up, now he called to me.

'See to the child,' he said frowning. 'Can you not hear him? He will choke.'

'So much the better,' I said. 'It will be one mouth less to feed.'

'You are ill,' he said. 'You do not know what you are saying.' He picked up the child, soothing him in his arms, and then gave him to Ira.

'My heart is sick,' I said. 'I have been robbed, and by one of my own children, of rice, which above all things is most precious.'

'Is that what you have said to them?'

I nodded. I saw his face wither.

'I took it,' he said at last.

'You? My husband? I do not believe it!'

'It is true.'

Silence fell like a shroud. I listened to it locked in my own brooding bitterness. Then it was rent by a sound so raw, so painful, that my nerves began screaming in response. I looked up and it was Nathan. His face was working, from his throat came those dry hideous sobs.

'Not for myself,' he was muttering, trying to control his treacherous voice, 'for another. I took it for another. There was no other way. I hoped you would not notice. I had to do it.'

I went to him. I did not want to know any more why he had done it or for whom, it was no longer important; but he was still speaking: it was as if he could not stop.

'Kunthi took it all, I swear it. She forced me, I did not want you to know.'

Presently he was quiet.

'She has a strange power, this woman,' I said, half to myself.

'Not strange,' Nathan said. 'I am the father of her sons. She would have told you, and I was weak.'

Disbelief first; disillusionment; anger, reproach, pain. To find out, after so many years, in such a cruel way. Kali's words: 'She has fire in her body, men burn before and after.' My husband was of those men. He had known her not once but twice; he had gone back to give her a second son. And between, how many times, I thought, bleak of spirit, while her husband in his impotence and I in my innocence did nothing.

'It was a long time ago,' Nathan said. 'I was very young, and she a skilful woman.'

'The first time was before our marriage,' he said.

'One did not see the evil for the beauty,' he said.

At last I made an effort and roused myself.

'It is as you say a long time ago,' I said wearily. 'That she is evil and powerful I know myself. Let it rest.'

It became possible for me to speak as well. I told him of her earlier visit and the grain she had extorted from me also; and it seemed to me that a new peace came to us then, freed at last from the necessity for lies and concealment and deceit, with the fear of betrayal lifted from us, and with the power we ourselves had given her wrested finally from Kunthi.

Now that the last of the rice was gone it was in a sense a relief: no amount of scheming and paring would make it go any further: the last grain had been eaten.

Thereafter we fed on whatever we could find: the soft ripe fruit of the prickly pear; a sweet potato or two, blackened and half-rotten, thrown away by some more prosperous hand; sometimes a crab that Nathan managed to catch near the river. Early and late my sons roamed the countryside, returning with a few bamboo shoots, a stick of sugar cane left in some deserted field, or a piece of coconut picked from the gutter in the town. For these they must have ranged widely, for other farmers and their families, in like plight to ourselves, were also out searching for food; and for every edible plant or root there was a struggle – a desperate competition that made enemies of friends and put an end to humanity.

It was not enough. Sometimes from sheer rebellion we ate grass, although it always resulted in stomach cramps and violent retching. For hunger is a curious thing: at first it is with you all the time, waking and sleeping and in your dreams, and your belly cries out insistently, and there is a gnawing and a pain as if your very vitals were being devoured, and you must stop it at any cost, and you buy a moment's respite even while you know and fear the sequel. Then the pain is no longer sharp but dull, and this too is with you always, so that you think of food many times a day and each time a terrible sickness assails you, and because you know this you try to avoid the thought, but you cannot, it is with you. Then that too is gone, all pain, all desire, only a great emptiness is left, like the sky, like a well in drought, and it is now that the strength drains from your limbs, and you try to rise and find you cannot, or to swallow water and your throat is powerless, and both the swallow and the effort of retaining the liquid tax you to the uttermost.

'It will not be long before the harvest,' Nathan would murmur, and I would agree with him, stifling the query whether our strength would last till then, saying, 'Ah yes, not long now; only a little time before the grain is ripe.'

Mulk Raj Anand

THE LIAR

LABHU, THE OLD Shikari of my village, was a born liar.
Therefore he had won the reputation of being the best story-
teller in our parts. And though a sweeper of low caste, he was
honoured by all and sundry. He was tolerated even to the
extent of being given a seat at the foot of the banyan tree. And
my mother did not insist too harshly on the necessity of my
taking a bath to purify myself every time I had been seen listening to one of his uncanny tales with the other village boys.

Labhu was a thin, little man, with the glint of a lance and
the glide of an arrow. His wiry, weather-beaten frame must
have had immense reserves of energy, to judge by the way he
could chase stags up the steep crags of the hills behind our village and run abreast of the bay mare of Subedar Deep Singh
to whose household he was attached as a Shikari, except
when some English official, a rich white merchant, or a guest
of the Subedar, engaged him for a season. It was perhaps this
wonderful physical agility of his that had persuaded him to
adopt the profession of a Shikari. Labhu had also a sensitive,
dark face of which the lower lip trembled as it pronounced the
first accents of a poignant verse or the last words of a grue-
some hunting story. And it was the strange spell that his tragic
verses and weird stories cast on me that made me his devoted
follower through childhood. He taught me the way to track
all the wild animals; and he taught me how to concoct a cock-
and-bull story to tell my father if I had to make an excuse for
not being at home during the reign of the hot sun.

His teaching was, of course, by example, as I was rather a

critical pupil.

'Labhu,' I would say, 'I am sure it is impossible to track any prey when you are half up the side of a hillock.'

'*Achha*,' he would say, 'I will show you. Stand still and listen.' I did so and we both heard a pebble drop. Up he darted on the stony ridge in the direction whence the sound had come, jumping from crag to crag, securing a precarious foothold on a small stone here and a sure one on a boulder there, till he was tearing through a flock of sheep, towards a little gully where a ram had taken shelter in a cave, secure in the belief that it would escape its pursuer.

'All right,' I would say. 'You may have been able to track this ram, but I don't believe that yarn of yours about the devil ram you saw when you were hunting with the Subedar.'

'I swear by God Almighty,' he said, 'it is true. The Subedar will tell you that he saw this terrible apparition with me. It was a beast about the size of an elephant, with eyes as big as hens' eggs and a beard as long as that of Maulvi Shah Din, the priest of the mosque, not only henna-dyed and red, but blue-black; it had huge ears as big as an elephant's, which did not flap, however, but pricked up like the ears of the Subedar's horse; it had a nose like that of the wife of the missionary Sahib, and it had square jaws which showed teeth almost as big as the chunks of marble which lie outside the temple, as it laughed at the Subedar. It appeared unexpectedly near the peak of Devi Parbat. The Subedar and I had ascended about twelve thousand feet up the mountain in search of game, when suddenly, out of the spirit world that always waits about us in the living air, there was the clattering of stones and boulders, the whistling of sharp winds, the gurgling of thunder and a huge crack on the side of the mountain. Then an enormous figure seemed to rise. From a distance it seemed to both of us like a dark patch, and we thought it was an *oorial* and began to stalk towards it. What was our surprise, however, when, as soon as we saw it stand there, facing us with its glistening, white eyes as a hen's egg, it sneezed and ripped the mountainside with a kick of its forefeet and disappeared. The mountain shook and the Subedar trembled, while

I stood bravely where I was and laughed till I wept with joy at my good luck in having seen so marvellous a manifestation of the devil-god of the tribe of rams. I tell you, son, please God I shall show him to you one of these days.'

'Labhu, you don't mean to say so!' I said, half-incredulous, though I was fascinated by the chimaera.

'Of course I mean to say so, silly boy,' said Labhu. 'This is nothing compared to the other vision that was vouchsafed to me, praise be to God, when I was on the journey to Ladakh, hunting with Jolly John Sahib.' And he began to relate a fantastic story of a colossal snake, which was so improbable that even I did not believe it.

'Oh, you are a fool, Labhu,' I said. 'And you are a liar. Everybody says so. And I don't believe you at all. My mother says I am silly to believe your tales.'

'All right, then if you don't believe my stories why do you come here to listen to them?' he said, with wounded pride. 'Go, I shall never teach you anything more, and I shall certainly not let you accompany me to the hunts.'

'All right,' I said, chagrined and stubborn. 'I don't want to speak to you either.'

And I ran home bursting with indignation at having forced a quarrel upon Labhu, when really he only told me his stories for my amusement.

Labhu went away for a while on a hunting tour with the Subedar. He didn't come back to the village when this tour finished, because Subedar Deep Singh's eldest son, Kuldeep Singh, who was lieutenant in the army, took him for a trip across the Himalayas to Nepal.

During this time, though I regretted Labhu's absence, I lent my ear readily to the malicious misrepresentation of his character that the Subedar and his employers, and occasionally also my father, indulged in; because, though superior to Labhu by caste, they were not such good shots as he was.

'He can only wait by a forest pool or a safe footpath to shoot at some unfortunate beast, this Labhu!' said the Subedar. 'And often he shoots in the dark with that inefficient powdergun of his. He is no good except for tracking.'

'Yes,' said my father, 'he is a vain boaster and a liar. The only beast he dared to shoot at while he was with me was a hare, and even that he hit in the leg.'

I waited eagerly for Labhu's return to confirm from his very mouth these stories of his incompetence, because, though incredulous of this scandal, I had been driven to a frenzy of chagrin by his insulting dismissal of me. I thought I would ask him point-blank whether he was really as bad a hunter as the Subedar and my father made him out to be.

When Labhu came back, however, he limped about and seemed ill. It was very sad to see him broken and dispirited. And I forgot all the scandal I had heard about him in my bafflement at the sudden change that had come into his character, for he was now no longer the garrulous man who sat telling stories to old men and young boys, but a strangely reticent creature who lay in a stupor all day, moaning and murmuring to himself in a prolonged delirium, except that he occasionally hobbled out with a huge staff in his hand in the evenings.

I was afraid to go near him, because he always wore a forbidding, angry look. But the villagers didn't seem to think there was anything the matter with Labhu, as I heard them say, 'Now that we have no patience with him and his stories, he spends most of his time telling them to himself, the fool!'

I owed a loyalty to Labhu, for I had discovered a kinship in my make-up for all those extravagances for which the Shikari was so well known.

So I went up to him one day, as he lay on a broken string-bed near his mud hut, under the precarious shelter which a young pipal gave him.

'You have returned then, Master Labhu,' I said.

'Yes,' he said, 'I have been back some time, son. I looked for you, but you did not seem to be about. But you know, the man who is slain cannot walk even to his own house. This leg of mine pains me and I can't get about as I used to.'

'What happened to your leg, then?' I asked, realising that he had forgotten all about our past quarrels and was as kind and communicative to me as before. 'Did you fall down a cliff or something?'

'No,' he said in a tired voice. And he kept quiet for a long while.

'What happened then?' I persisted.

'You know, son,' Labhu began, at first pale and hesitant, then smiling and lifting his eyebrows in the familiar manner of the old days, 'I went away on a hunting tour in the pay of the Subedar's eldest son, Kuldeep Singh, and some of his friends. Well, we went to Nepal through the Kulu valley. They had no experience of hunting in this or in any other part of the world, and I led them across such trails as I knew and such as the local shikaris told me about. That boy, Kuldeep, I don't know what he does in the army, but he can't shoot at any range, and the Sahibs with him were clumsy, purblind white men. I would point to a beast with my stick, and, though they could see the hide before their eyes, they bungled with their guns or were too noisy on their feet, and away crashed the bull which we had been tracking. I would grunt, shrug my shoulders and did not mind, because they were like children. They had finished hundreds of cartridges and had not shot anything, and daily begged me to help them to secure some game.

'At first I told them that game doesn't taste sweet unless it is shot by oneself. But at length I took pity on them and thought that I would secure them a good mixed bag. I shot twelve tigers with my gun and fifteen panthers in the course of seven days, and many stags.

'On the eighth day we saw a monster which had the body of a wild bear, the head of a reindeer, the feet of a goat, the tail of a wild bull and a glistening, fibrous tissue all round it like the white silken veil which the Rani of Boondi wore when she came to visit Subedar Deep Singh's wife. Kuldeep Singh and the Sahibs were very frightened of this apparition and said it was the devil himself who had the shape of an earthly being and who would soon breathe a breath which would mix with the still air of the night and poison life.

'They were all for killing it outright, while I was sure that it was only a princess of the royal house of Nepal who had been transformed by some magician into this fantastic shape and size. And I wanted to catch it alive and bring it home to be my bride.'

Labhu went on to relate how beautiful she was and how he resolved to restore her to her normal self by reading magical incantations.

'I told her I loved her,' he continued, 'and she smiled shyly. But some fool, I think it was the Subedar's son, fired a volley of shots, which frightened her so that she ran, became one with the air and began to ascend the snowy peaks of Kailash Parbat.

'I was bent on rescuing my beloved, and I leaped from one mountain to another, calling after her to stop. But that idiot Kuldeep and the Sahibs kept on shooting and roused the magician who kept guard over her. And this evil sage threw a huge mountain of snow at me to kill me.

'I just blew a hot breath and the mountain of snow cracked into a million pieces and hung about the sky like glittering stars.

'Then the magician struck the earth with his feet and opened up a grave to bury me alive. I leapt right across the fissure and found myself on a peak in the land of the lama who never dies.

'By now, of course, the magician had hidden the beauty away in some cave. So, I gave up the chase, as there was the doom of death about his beauty, anyhow, and I made one leap across the Himalayas for home . . .'

'And as you landed this side of the mountains you sprained your foot,' I said.

Labhu lifted his eyebrows funnily in the manner of the old days and, laughing, said: 'Have I told you this story before, then?'

R. K. Narayan

FELLOW-FEELING

THE MADRAS–BANGALORE Express was due to start in a few minutes. Trolleys and barrows piled with trunks and beds rattled their way through the bustle. Fruit-sellers and *beedi*-and-betel-sellers cried themselves hoarse. Latecomers pushed, shouted and perspired. The engine added to the general noise with the low monotonous hum of its boiler; the first bell rang, the guard looked at his watch. Mr Rajam Iyer arrived on the platform at a terrific pace, with a small roll of bedding under one arm and an absurd yellow trunk under the other. He ran to the first third-class compartment that caught his eye, peered in and, since the door could not be opened on account of the congestion inside, flung himself in through the window.

Fifteen minutes later Madras flashed past the train in window-framed patches of sun-scorched roofs and fields. At the next halt, Mandhakam, most of the passengers got down. The compartment built to 'seat 8 passengers; 4 British Troops, or 6 Indian Troops' now carried only nine. Rajam Iyer found a seat and made himself comfortable opposite a sallow, meek passenger, who suddenly removed his coat, folded it and placed it under his head and lay down, shrinking himself to the area he had occupied while he was sitting. With his knees drawn up almost to his chin, he rolled himself into a ball. Rajam Iyer threw at him an indulgent, compassionate look. He then fumbled for his glasses and pulled out of his pocket a small book, which set forth in clear Tamil the significance of the obscure *Sandhi* rites that every Brahmin worth the name performs thrice daily.

He was startled out of this pleasant languor by a series of growls coming from a passenger who had got in at Katpadi. The newcomer, looking for a seat, had been irritated by the spectacle of the meek passenger asleep and had enforced the law of the third-class. He then encroached on most of the meek passenger's legitimate space and began to deliver home-truths which passed by easy stages from impudence to impertinence and finally to ribaldry.

Rajam Iyer peered over his spectacles. There was a dangerous look in his eyes. He tried to return to the book, but could not. The bully's speech was gathering momentum.

'What is all this?' Rajam Iyer asked suddenly, in a hard tone.

'What is what?' growled back the newcomer, turning sharply on Rajam Iyer.

'Moderate your style a bit,' Rajam Iyer said firmly.

'You moderate yours first,' replied the other.

A pause.

'My man,' Rajam Iyer began endearingly, 'this sort of thing will never do.'

The newcomer received this in silence. Rajam Iyer felt encouraged and drove home his moral: 'Just try and be more courteous, it is your duty.'

'You mind your business,' replied the newcomer.

Rajam Iyer shook his head disapprovingly and drawled out a 'No.' The newcomer stood looking out for some time and, as if expressing a brilliant truth that had just dawned on him, said, 'You are a Brahmin, I see. Learn, sir, that your days are over. Don't think you can bully us as you have been bullying us all these years.'

Rajam Iyer gave a short laugh and said, 'What has it to do with your beastly conduct to this gentleman?' The newcomer assumed a tone of mock humility and said, 'Shall I take the dust from your feet, O Holy Brahmin? O Brahmin, Brahmin.' He continued in a singsong fashion: 'Your days are over, my dear sir, learn that. I should like to see you trying a bit of bossing on us.'

'Whose master is who?' asked Rajam Iyer philosophically.

The newcomer went on with no obvious relevance: 'The cost of mutton has gone up out of all proportion. It is nearly double what it used to be.'

'Is it?' asked Rajam Iyer.

'Yes, and why?' continued the other. 'Because Brahmins have begun to eat meat and they pay high prices to get it secretly.' He then turned to the other passengers and added, 'And we non-Brahmins have to pay the same price, though we don't care for the secrecy.'

Rajam Iyer leaned back in his seat, reminding himself of a proverb which said that if you threw a stone into a gutter it would only spurt filth in your face.

'And,' said the newcomer, 'the price of meat used to be five annas per pound. I remember the days quite well. It is nearly twelve annas now. Why? Because the Brahmin is prepared to pay so much, if only he can have it in secret. I have with my own eyes seen Brahmins, pukkah Brahmins with sacred threads on their bodies, carrying fish under their arms, of course all wrapped up in a towel. Ask them what it is, and they will tell you that it is plantain. Plantain that has life, I suppose! I once tickled a fellow under the arm and out came the biggest fish in the market. Hey, Brahmin,' he said, turning to Rajam Iyer, 'what did you have for your meal this morning?' 'Who? I?' asked Rajam Iyer. 'Why do you want to know?' 'Look, sirs,' said the newcomer to the other passengers, 'why is he afraid to tell us what he ate this morning?' And turning to Rajam Iyer, 'Mayn't a man ask another what he had for his morning meal?'

'Oh, by all means. I had rice, ghee, curds, *brinjal* soup, fried beans.'

'Oh, is that all?' asked the newcomer, with an innocent look.

'Yes,' replied Rajam Iyer.

'Is that all?'

'Yes, how many times do you want me to repeat it?'

'No offence, no offence,' replied the newcomer.

'Do you mean to say I am lying?' asked Rajam Iyer.

'Yes,' replied the other, 'you have omitted from your list a few things. Didn't I see you this morning going home from the market with a banana, a water banana, wrapped up in a towel, under your arm? Possibly it was somebody very much like you. Possibly I mistook the person. My wife prepares excellent soup with fish. You won't be able to find the difference between *dhall* soup and fish soup. Send your wife, or the wife of the person that was exactly like you, to my wife to learn soup-making. Hundreds of Brahmins have smacked their lips over the *dhall* soup prepared in my house. I am a leper if there is a lie in anything I say.'

'You are,' replied Rajam Iyer, grinding his teeth. 'You are a rabid leper.'

'Whom do you call a leper!'

'You!'

'I? You call me a leper?'

'No. I call you a rabid leper.'

'You call me rabid?' the newcomer asked, striking his chest to emphasise 'me'.

'You are a filthy brute,' said Rajam Iyer. 'You must be handed over to the police.'

'Bah!' exclaimed the newcomer. 'As if I didn't know what these police were.'

'Yes, you must have had countless occasions to know the police. And you will see more of them yet in your miserable life, if you don't get beaten to death like the street mongrel you are,' said Rajam Iyer in great passion. 'With your foul mouth you are bound to come to that end.'

'What do you say?' shouted the newcomer menacingly. 'What do you say, you vile humbug?'

'Shut up,' Rajam Iyer cried.

'You shut up.'

'Do you know to whom you are talking?'

'What do I care who the son of a mongrel is?'

'I will thrash you with my slippers,' said Rajam Iyer.

'I will pulp you down with an old rotten sandal,' came the reply.

'I will kick you,' said Rajam Iyer.

'Will you?' howled the newcomer.

'Come on, let us see.'

Both rose to their feet simultaneously.

There they stood facing each other on the floor of the compartment. Rajam Iyer was seized by a sense of inferiority. The newcomer stood nine clean inches over him. He began to feel ridiculous, short and fat, wearing a loose dhoti and a green coat, while the newcomer towered above him in his grease-spotted khaki suit. Out of the corner of his eye he noted that the other passengers were waiting eagerly to see how the issue would be settled and were not in the least disposed to intervene.

'Why do you stand as if your mouth was stopped with mud?' asked the newcomer.

'Shut up,' Rajam Iyer snapped, trying not to be impressed by the size of the adversary.

'Your honour said that you would kick me,' said the newcomer, pretending to offer himself.

'Won't I kick you?' asked Rajam Iyer.

'Try.'

'No,' said Rajam Iyer, 'I will do something worse.'

'Do it,' said the other, throwing forward his chest and pushing up the sleeves of his coat.

Rajam Iyer removed his coat and rolled up his sleeves. He rubbed his hands and commanded suddenly, 'Stand still!' The newcomer was taken aback. He stood for a second baffled. Rajam Iyer gave him no time to think. With great force he swung his right arm and brought it near the other's cheek, but stopped it short without hitting him.

'Wait a minute, I think I had better give you a chance,' said Rajam Iyer.

'What chance?' asked the newcomer.

'It would be unfair if I did it without giving you a chance.'

'Did what?'

'You stand there and it will be over in a fraction of a second.'

'Fraction of a second? What will you do?'

'Oh, nothing very complicated,' replied Rajam Iyer, nonchalantly, 'nothing very complicated. I will slap your right cheek and at the same time tug your left ear, and your mouth, which is now under your nose, will suddenly find itself under your left ear, and, what is more, stay there. I assure you, you won't feel any pain.'

'What do you say?'

'And it will all be over before you say "Sri Rama".'

'I don't believe it,' said the newcomer.

'Well and good. Don't believe it,' said Rajam Iyer carelessly. 'I never do it except under extreme provocation.'

'Do you think I am an infant?'

'I implore you, my man, not to believe me. Have you heard of a thing called jujitsu? Well, this is a simple trick in jujitsu perhaps known to half a dozen persons in the whole of South India.'

'You said you would kick me,' said the newcomer.

'Well, isn't this worse?' asked Rajam Iyer. He drew a line on the newcomer's face between his left ear and mouth, muttering, 'I must admit you have a tolerably good face and round figure. But imagine yourself going about the streets with your mouth under your left ear . . .' He chuckled at the vision. 'I expect at Jalarpet station there will be a huge crowd outside our compartment to see you.' The newcomer stroked his chin thoughtfully. Rajam Iyer continued, 'I felt it my duty to explain the whole thing to you beforehand. I am not as hotheaded as you are. I have some consideration for your wife and children. It will take some time for the kids to recognise Papa when he returns home with his mouth under . . . How many children have you?'

'Four.'

'And then think of it,' said Rajam Iyer. 'You will have to take your food under your left ear, and you will need the assistance of your wife to drink water. She will have to pour it in.'

'I will go to a doctor,' said the newcomer.

'Do go,' replied Rajam Iyer, 'and I will give you a thousand rupees if you find a doctor. You may try even European doctors.'

The newcomer stood ruminating with knitted brow. 'Now prepare,' shouted Rajam Iyer, 'one blow on the right cheek. I will jerk your left ear, and your mouth . . .'

The newcomer suddenly ran to the window and leaned far out of it. Rajam decided to leave the compartment at Jalarpet.

But the moment the train stopped at Jalarpet station, the newcomer grabbed his bag and jumped out. He moved away at a furious pace and almost knocked down a coconut-seller and a person carrying a trayload of coloured toys. Rajam Iyer felt it would not be necessary for him to get out now. He leaned through the window and cried, 'Look here!' The newcomer turned.

'Shall I keep a seat for you?' asked Rajam Iyer.

'No, my ticket is for Jalarpet,' the newcomer answered and quickened his pace.

The train had left Jalarpet at least a mile behind. The meek passenger still sat shrunk in a corner of the seat. Rajam Iyer looked over his spectacles and said, 'Lie down if you like.'

The meek passenger proceeded to roll himself into a ball. Rajam Iyer added, 'Did you hear that bully say that his ticket was for Jalarpet?'

'Yes.'

'Well,' he lied, 'he is in the fourth compartment from here. I saw him get into it just as the train started.'

Though the meek passenger was too grateful to doubt this statement, one or two other passengers looked at Rajam Iyer sceptically.

Ved Mehta

ACTIVITIES AND OUTINGS

IT WAS EASTER. We all gathered on the veranda to greet Mrs Thomas, the school's superintendent. We boys stood in one line and the girls stood in another, in front of her and Mr Ras Mohun, and shouted, 'Good morning, Mrs Thomas!'

'Good morning, boys and girls,' she said, in funny-sounding Marathi.

Then she turned to Mr Ras Mohun, and they started talking together in fast English.

'You hear how respectfully Mr Ras Mohun talks to her?' Abdul whispered to me. 'That's because she's from the rich country of America and has a bigger ruler.'

'Thanks to the work of Mrs Thomas and her good husband, who couldn't be here today,' Mr Ras Mohun was saying to us, 'this school is a happy home. Mrs Thomas would like to hear you sing now.'

We boys had never sung together with the girls before, and there was a little confusion about whether they or we should start. But Deoji launched into 'When the Saints Go Marching In', and we all joined in.

Then Mrs Thomas gave a speech. 'Boys and girls, I want you all to grow up like Louis Braille,' she said, in her funny Marathi. 'He was a little boy, like the littlest of you here, who lived in a village far, far away, across the ocean, more than a hundred years ago. He had an accident when he was three years old and went blind. When he was ten, he went to a blind

Extract from the memoir *Vedi*.

school. There he learned to read with his fingers something called the line code. At the time, the blind could read the line code, but there was no way for them to write it. Then someone thought up a new code, which could be written. It was a twelve-dot-letter embossed code, and little Louis learned that, but its letters were too big for his fingers and those of his blind friends. So he decided he would think up a better code, and he spent many, many years working on it. He came up with one oblong cell of six embossed dots which could be easily recognised by the littlest fingers. It is because of Louis that you're able to read and write Braille and go to school. So every night when you go to sleep think of Louis, in Heaven with Jesus, thinking about you.'

'Let's give a good cheer for Mrs Thomas,' Mr Ras Mohun said. 'Hip, hip!'

'Hip, hip!' we shouted.

'Hi-i-ip, hip!'

'Hi-i-ip, hip!' we repeated.

'Hurrah!' we all shouted with Mr Ras Mohun.

Mrs Thomas thanked us and then came around with a basket and gave everyone a present. Paran got a hand mirror, Abdul got a small wooden cross, Deoji got a small wooden angel, Bhaskar got a rubber frog, and I got a metal car.

Mr Ras Mohun called on Deoji to thank Mrs Thomas on behalf of the school.

All of us boys pushed Deoji forward, and he said a few words in English and concluded, 'Mrs Thomas is our saint come marching in. Thank you.'

Whenever I asked Paran, from the boys' side of the classroom, 'What are you doing, Paran?' she would say, 'I'm looking into my mirror.'

'What do you see in a mirror?'

'My reflection.'

'What is that?'

'It's my double.'

'But how can it be your double? The mirror is thin and flat.'

'You have to be able to see to understand.'

I could not work out the puzzle of Paran and the mirror until some time after Abdul and I stumbled on to a heavy stone slab in the cellar. We moved it and discovered that under it was a big, sloping hole. We got down into the hole. I was frightened and wanted to run back, because the tunnel – for that was what it seemed to be – was knee-deep in water, and I could hear things splashing and swimming, scuttling and buzzing. The little noises were picked up and repeated all around me, until it seemed that the whole tunnel was full of ghosts, snakes, and wasps.

'I'm getting out of here!' I shouted.

'I'm getting out of here!' they shouted back.

Abdul and I almost fell over each other getting out of the tunnel.

We put the stone back over the hole and didn't go near it for a few days. But one day I told Deoji about the tunnel.

'That's an old, unused sewer,' he said. 'I don't know what things were swimming down there. But the sound you heard was an echo.'

'What is an echo?'

'It's when your voice bounces back from the walls and the ceiling.'

'Why doesn't it do that everywhere?'

'You have to be in a tight corner or the voice will escape.'

After that, I would often go down to the slab of stone, move it a chink, and shout, 'Hello, there!' As I listened to the echo, I felt that, like Paran, I was looking into a mirror.

One afternoon, Mr Ras Mohun took those of us boys who were totally blind behind the school building, past Abdul's boa-constrictor tree, to a little vacant area by the wall of the Tata Mill. Here he let us feel four waist-high metal wires and what he called the starting and finishing posts, between which the wires had been strung. The wires formed three long lanes, each a few feet wide. Each wire had a hoop about the size of a thick bangle hanging from it.

'This is a racing track,' he said. 'I have modelled it on a racing track for the blind which I saw at Perkins, in America. We will have races for you here every week.'

111

We were excited. At school, the most we could do was to run up and down the boys' stairs, and even that we were not supposed to do, because the Sighted Master didn't like the noise we made. When we went for our outings, we had to hold on to the partially sighted or half-sighted boys and walk slowly. But here, Mr Ras Mohun said, we could run, and by ourselves.

Mr Ras Mohun positioned Abdul Reuben, and me in separate lanes, at the starting posts, and showed us how to catch hold of the metal hoop by a string that hung from it, and then run with the wire as our guide.

'No, no, Reuben, don't hold on to the string with both hands,' Mr Ras Mohun said. 'Just catch hold of the string loosely with your right hand, like this.'

'I don't need the string, Uncle,' I said. 'I can run just holding on to the hoop.'

'You need the string for a certain amount of leeway,' he said. 'Let's have a trial race, and you'll see what I mean.'

I prayed to Jesus, Mary, and Joseph that I would win.

Mr Ras Mohun called out, 'Ready, steady, go!'

I had never run so fast. I imagined myself an arrow flying from one post to the other.

'Oh, my God, they're going to kill themselves!' I heard Mr Ras Mohun exclaim as I fell sidewise, almost wrapping myself around the finishing post, and hitting my mouth on it.

'Any of you badly hurt?' Mr Ras Mohun asked, running up to us.

All three of us had bleeding mouths and bleeding foreheads. There had been no way for us to know when we were coming to the end, so we had all fallen down and hurt ourselves on the finishing posts.

Mr Ras Mohun sent for tincture of iodine and bandages, and after he had attended to our injuries he said, almost to himself, 'Bless me, I can't remember how they prevented such mishaps at Perkins.' He paused, and then went on, to us, 'I know. I'll station the Sighted Master at the finishing posts with my bell. He can ring it during the races. From the sound of the ringing, you'll know how close you are to the end. As an added precaution, I'll have a nice, strong rope stretched across the lanes, at the height of the wires, just before the end, so that if you fall you won't hit the finishing posts.'

After that, every Saturday we had races at the racing track. Mr Ras Mohun would stand at the starting posts and get us off, and the Sighted Master would stand at the finishing posts, behind the newly stretched rope, and ring the bell. Abdul, Reuben, and I were the three fastest runners, and whenever the school had visitors – missionaries and benefactors, Bombay notables and Government officials – we three would be asked to put on a special racing exhibition, running different kinds of races we had learned. We would put on the Biscuit Race: Mr Ras Mohun would give us each a hard biscuit, and when he said 'Ready, steady, go!' we would eat the biscuit quickly, showing our mouths to him, and then run. We would put on the Leapfrog Race: we would leap frog-fashion along the racing track, hanging on to the string. We would put on the Dog Race, with two dogs, Bobby and Robby, which Mr Ras Mohun had just acquired for us to play with: Mr Ras Mohun would line up Bobby and Robby as best he could outside the lanes, and we would all race against one another. The Dog Race was not as satisfactory as the Biscuit Race or the Leapfrog Race, because Mr Ras Mohun never quite succeeded in starting Bobby and Robby at the right time and getting them to run exactly as he wanted them to.

As time went on, the boys from a sighted school nearby occasionally came and joined us at our Saturday races. They would run outside the lanes. I was so eager to compete with them on even terms that now and again I would slyly let go of the string and hurl the hoop forward, so that I could run along the track like them for a time.

One warm day, there was a series of explosions at the front gate. At first, I thought someone was setting off firecrackers, but then I realised that what I had heard was a motor car engine idling and repeatedly backfiring. We heard such engine sounds all the time – mixed in with the clip-clop of victoria horses, the clatter of handcarts, and the clink and ponk-ponk of bicycle bells and car klaxons – but they were always the sounds of passing traffic. No vehicle, it seemed, ever stopped in front of the school.

'Mr Ras Mohun wants us all at the front gate!' Bhaskar cried, running into the boys' dormitory. 'There's a lorry! We are really going to Juhu Beach!'

We had heard Mr Ras Mohun mention the visit to Juhu Beach as a 'red-letter day'. We had all talked about going to the seaside, without knowing exactly what it was. Abdul had once remarked, 'Mahim Sea Beach is not the seaside, and there is no stuffed sand or stuffed ocean for the blind to feel. They have to take us to Juhu Beach to show us what it is.'

'Why are we going in a lorry?' I asked now.

'Because there are no trams to Juhu Beach, you son of an owl,' Abdul said. 'It's really far.'

The lorry had no seats, so we all sat on the floor, the boys on one side and the girls on the other. I wanted to run around – perhaps try to sit with Paran – but Mr Ras Mohun was addressing us from the front of the lorry.

'Boys and girls, this is our first annual holiday at Juhu Beach,' he said. 'Juhu Beach is on the Arabian Sea, and we have a day's holiday there because of a special gift from Mrs Thomas and the American Marathi Mission. It will take us quite some time to reach Juhu Beach. I want you to stay in your places, because the ride to Juhu Beach is bumpy.'

To help us pass the time, Miss Mary led us in a new song. It really had only one line: 'John Brown's Whiskey Bottle Number One Hundred and One'. Each time we sang it, we would sing out one number less than the time before. The song sounded naughty and festive to us, and we felt we were really on an annual holiday.

At Juhu Beach, I heard a sound I'd never heard before – a gigantic roar alternating with the sound of a huge amount of water rushing out. The sound was very different from Mahim Sea Beach, which was quiet, like a canal in Lahore. (It was actually an inlet.) I wanted to run towards the sound and touch it – to feel what it was really like – but the Sighted Master herded us boys into the boys' shack. He gave us each a pair of bathing drawers and we got into them.

'Now you can do what you like,' the Sighted Master said. 'But don't go beyond the rope in the water.'

I hesitated for a moment, wondering if there were wired lanes and how, amid the roar and the rush, I would hear the Sighted Master ringing the bell on the other side of the rope, but the partially sighted boys started running towards the roar and the rush, calling back, 'Abdul! Reuben! Vedi! There is nothing in the way! You can run, too!'

I ran toward the roar and the rush. The air smelled of salt and coconut. There was hot, grainy, dry ground underfoot. It was so hot that I could scarcely bear to put my feet on it, so I had to run fast, and couldn't stop to examine it. Suddenly, I was in the water, being carried out. It closed over my head. I forgot everything. I felt I'd never been so happy. A jolt opened my mouth. I was rapidly swallowing water that tasted of tears – buckets of them. I was flung back, choking. Again the water closed over my head. The water retreated. I lay on the water, wondering if the sea could take me all the way to the Punjab. Then I came up against the rope, as thick as the one we used for the tug-of-war, and I heard the Sighted Master calling to me, 'That's far enough! Come back! You'll drown!'

We spent the day bathing in the water and running around on the new ground. I couldn't get over the way it shifted around, almost like the water. We could go into the water as often as we liked, and when we ran we just had to keep the sound of the ocean to our left and right, depending on which way we were facing. The school compound and the racing track suddenly shrank in my mind, like a woollen sock Mamaji had knitted for me which became so small after Heea's ayah washed it that I could scarcely get my hand in it.

At one point, we had a picnic – Mr Ras Mohun, the Sighted Master, Mrs Ras Mohun, Heea, the Matron, and all the boys and girls. We all sat down on bedsheets. For the first time, I was able to sit next to Deoji and eat with him. The food was not mutton and toast but thick, heavy potato-filled bread, with a chewy relish made of pickled mango skin.

It was Sunday, and all of us were excited because we had been brought in a fast, sootless electric train to the zoo. We walked in twos and threes along the cages and pens, holding one another or touching the outer railings with our hands. Mr Ras Mohun explained to us from the front about the animals we were going past while Mrs Ras Mohun pointed them out to Heea and the partially sighted boys and girls.

'Here is a lion,' Mr Ras Mohun said. 'He has a big mane.'

'Can I touch him, Uncle?' I asked, running up to him. I had learned the shape of the lion in the birds-and-animals class, but I had no idea how big a lion was. I wondered if the one behind the railing was ten times as big as the stuffed animal in our class, or twenty times, or a hundred times.

'Touch what? The lion?' he asked. 'If you touch him, he'll make lunch of your hands, and you'll never be able to read Braille again.'

I took a step, and I heard thunder underfoot. I jumped back. 'It's going to rain in the ground,' I said.

Mr Ras Mohun laughed. 'It's only the lion roaring,' he said. 'That's the way he talks.'

'I didn't know that the lion could make a sound,' I said. 'He sounds as big as our school.'

But Mr Ras Mohun had walked away, and Abdul said, 'You know what he's saying?'

'No. What?'

'He's saying, "I'm hungry, I want my food." You see, the lion is no different from me. Food is all I think about when I am in my cage at Dadar.'

Ahead, Mr Ras Mohun was walking along and saying, 'Here is a bear . . . You hear his growl? Notice how different it is from the roar of the lion . . . You hear that hooting? Well, that's an owl . . . Here are some monkeys.'

Mr Ras Mohun stopped, bought some groundnuts from a vender, and gave us a few to feed the monkeys. I put my hand with the nuts inside the railings. Suddenly, I felt a little pinch on my hand, and the nuts were gone.

'There, Vedi. He's eating the nuts now,' Mr Ras Mohun said. 'You can say now that at least you have touched a monkey.'

116

Mr and Mrs Ras Mohun walked Heea and me away from the other boys and girls, and took us up a very tall ladder – it had many more rungs than the climbing bars at the school – to the top of an elephant. Here there was a sofa with a cane seat and a cane back, and we sat on it, facing backward, as in a tonga.

'What's his name?' I asked the mahout, turning around.

'Dumbo, little Sahib,' he said. He clicked his tongue, as I had heard Lahore tongawallahs do, and the elephant set off. I expected the elephant to trot, like a tonga horse, but he rolled and pitched, throwing Mr and Mrs Ras Mohun, Heea, and me against one another on the sofa.

I felt I had never been so high up – so close to the sun, which was warm against my cheeks. I felt wonderfully dizzy.

I could hear the voices of Deoji, Abdul, Bhaskar, Tarak Nath, Dham, Miss Mary, and Paran far below. I was riding over the heads of the tallest of them.

'Uncle and Auntie, let's invite Deoji, Abdul, and Paran up,' I said.

'The ride on the elephant costs money,' Mrs Ras Mohun said. 'And they don't get that much pocket money. Only maharajas can ride elephants.'

I recalled that the boys' missionary mummies and daddies sometimes sent them a rupee or two for pocket money on the first day of the month. Even though the boys spent their pocket money only on snacks like mother's kisses at the Muhammadan Hotel, the money was gone before they knew it. Bhaskar would say when he received his money, 'This will last me for a month,' but within a few days the money would be gone, and he would already be looking forward to the first day of the month. Then every day he would ask Deoji 'How many days to the new month?' and sometimes on the same day 'Deoji, when did you say the new month is?'

I wished that Mamaji and Daddyji were there, so they could pay for everyone to ride on Dumbo. I decided that I would count every rung of the ladder on the way down, because then I could tell my friends below how tall the elephant really was.

*

'We are going to the grounds of the Bombay Studios!' Mr Ras Mohun shouted, standing near the driver of a lorry and addressing all of us, inside it. He had to shout because this lorry was, if anything, noisier than the one that had taken us to Juhu Beach. His thin voice cracked with the effort. 'You're going to be actors and actresses in a picture called *Andhera*! It will be shown in cinemas all over the country!' *Andhera* means 'darkness'.

I didn't know exactly what a picture was, but I was excited. I expected to meet Cousin Prakash at the cinema place.

The driver changed gears, and for a time I couldn't hear what Mr Ras Mohun was saying. But then the lorry slowed down, and I heard him say, 'Few people have heard of Dadar School. The public doesn't know about schools for the blind. The public doesn't know about the blind. But now Jesus, in his mercy, has given us the cinema to arouse the public's interest in both these matters.'

I didn't know what the public was, but I was all the more excited.

The lorry left us in some kind of park. There was no Cousin Prakash; instead, there were a lot of strangers, who surrounded us. They moved us this way and that way, making many of us change places several times.

'You are the smallest,' Mr Ras Mohun said, moving me to the front. 'Stand here.'

A stranger ran up and pressed down on my shoulders with rough hands. 'Down, boy,' he said, and I dropped my shoulders. He ran back to where he had been standing, and called out to me, 'Boy, look this way . . . No, no – in the direction of my voice . . . Now hold up your head . . . No, that's too high . . . That's right.'

A fly started buzzing around my ear. I tried furtively to flick it with my shoulder.

The stranger with the rough hands shouted, 'Stand by . . . Lights . . . Action.'

A yawn began to fill my mouth, and at the same time my left foot started to fall asleep. The sun was very hot, and lights hot as fire were turned on me. But I didn't move.

'Children of Darkness, come to me. Don't be frightened,' I heard a lady say kindly.

I started to step forward.

'Cut!'

'Mr Ras Mohun, tell him not to move – tell him he's on the set!' the stranger with the rough hands cried.

Mr Ras Mohun came up to me and put his ruler on my bare arm. It was the first time I had felt it, and, just as Abdul said it was heavy, round, and hard. 'You really mustn't move,' Mr Ras Mohun told me. 'You must stand still – at attention.'

'But there is a fly!' I cried.

'It won't hurt you. It will go away.'

It seemed that we had to do the exercise of standing at attention over and over.

I remember that finally Mr Ras Mohun called out, 'At ease! Boys and girls, you can play now and eat as much *bhel-puri* as you like. The studio's vender will give it to you free.'

There was something frightening about eating the secret hot, spicy snacks of the Muhammadan Hotel out in the open, under the eyes of Mr Ras Mohun. But we ran up to a vendor who was crying *'Bhel-puri! Bhel-puri!'* and crowded around him. He handed us *bhel-puri* in plantain leaves. We ate it with our fingers and licked them clean.

Abdul started chasing me. I ran into something, and I felt it to see what it was. It felt like a cart with a mysterious thing on it. I started to climb up on the cart to examine the thing.

The lady with the kind voice came rushing up to me. 'You don't want to play with that horrible camera,' she said. 'Let me show you a better game.'

I gave her my hand, and we walked along together. She was very different from Mr Ras Mohun; she let me walk any way I liked – turning my toes out, running from side to side, falling behind and catching up with her.

'What do you do?' I asked her.

'I am the Lady of Charity in the orphanage in the picture,' she said. 'You are all my Children of Darkness, and I take care of you.'

'Do you know Mrs Thomas?' I asked, jumping up and down.

'Who is Mrs Thomas?'

'She's our missionary lady. She came to our school at Easter and brought a present for everyone.'

She laughed. 'Well, I suppose I'm like her, but in the picture I live in the orphanage.'

'What is your new game?' I asked.

'Here it is,' she answered. She walked me up a ladder taller than the one on the elephant. Then she sat me down at the top and pushed me. I laughed and shrieked with delight, for I was on a slide and it seemed endless. Every time I thought I had come to the bottom of the slide, it turned out to be only a landing and there was another slope. The school slide had one slope, but this slide had many slopes.

'Again!' I cried when I reached the bottom. I was so light-headed I could scarcely stand up.

'That's enough for today,' she said. 'You can go on the slide again tomorrow.'

Every day for the next month or two, the lorry came for us and took us to the cinema place. Every day, we had to stand still under the hot sun near the fire of lights. Every day, there was a lot of *bhel-puri* to eat and many rides down the slide. But, for some reason, except for these few memories of routine – and, of course, the remarkable first day – I remember little about *Darkness*. (According to the National Film Archive of India, the film eventually made was quite different: 'The story tells the heart-rending saga of Jyoti – a girl – who is caught in a dilemma between her lover who blames her for being ungrateful and cause for his blindness and a father, who blames her for deserting her blind father and blind sister. She serves them both in disguise as a nurse and eventually her lover on regaining his sight realises the folly committed by him in judging Jyoti.')

Anita Desai

GAMES AT TWILIGHT

IT WAS STILL too hot to play outdoors. They had had their tea, they had been washed and had their hair brushed, and after the long day of confinement in the house that was not cool but at least a protection from the sun, the children strained to get out. Their faces were red and bloated with the effort, but their mother would not open the door, everything was still curtained and shuttered in a way that stifled the children, made them feel that their lungs were stuffed with cotton wool and their noses with dust and if they didn't burst out into the light and see the sun and feel the air, they would choke.

'Please, Ma, please,' they begged. 'We'll play in the veranda and porch – we won't go a step out of the porch.'

'You will, I know you will, and then –'

'No – we won't, we won't,' they wailed so horrendously that she actually let down the bolt of the front door so that they burst out like seeds from a crackling, over-ripe pod into the veranda, with such wild, maniacal yells that she retreated to her bath and the shower of talcum powder and the fresh sari that were to help her face the summer evening.

They faced the afternoon. It was too hot. Too bright. The white walls of the veranda glared stridently in the sun. The bougainvillea hung about it, purple and magenta, in livid balloons. The garden outside was like a tray made of beaten brass, flattened out on the red gravel and the stony soil in all shades of metal – aluminium, tin, copper and brass. No life

121

stirred at this arid time of day – the birds still drooped, like dead fruit, in the paper tents of the trees; some squirrels lay limp on the wet earth under the garden tap. The outdoor dog lay stretched as if dead on the veranda mat, his paws and ears and tail all reaching out like dying travellers in search of water. He rolled his eyes at the children – two white marbles rolling in the purple sockets, begging for sympathy – and attempted to lift his tail in a wag but could not. It only twitched and lay still.

Then, perhaps roused by the shrieks of the children, a band of parrots suddenly fell out of the eucalyptus tree, tumbled frantically in the still, sizzling air, then sorted themselves out into battle formation and streaked away across the white sky.

The children, too, felt released. They too began tumbling, shoving, pushing against each other, frantic to start. Start what? Start their business. The business of the children's day which is – play.

'Let's play hide-and-seek.'

'Who'll be It?'

'You be It.'

'Why should I? You be –'

'You're the eldest –'

'That doesn't mean –'

The shoves became harder. Some kicked out. The motherly Mira intervened. She pulled the boys roughly apart. There was a tearing sound of cloth but it was lost in the heavy panting and angry grumbling and no one paid attention to the small sleeve hanging loosely off a shoulder.

'Make a circle, make a circle!' she shouted, firmly pulling and pushing till a kind of vague circle was formed. 'Now clap!' she roared and, clapping, they all chanted in melancholy unison: 'Dip, dip, dip – my blue ship –' and every now and then one or the other saw he was safe by the way his hands fell at the crucial moment – palm on palm, or back of hand on palm – and dropped out of the circle with a yell and a jump of relief and jubilation.

Raghu was It. He started to protest, to cry 'You cheated – Mira cheated – Anu cheated –' but it was too late, the others had all already streaked away. There was no one to hear when he called out, 'Only in the veranda – the porch – Ma said – Ma *said* to stay in the porch!' No one had stopped to listen, all he saw were their brown legs flashing through the dusty shrubs, scrambling up brick walls, leaping over compost heaps and hedges, and then the porch stood empty in the purple shade of the bougainvillea and the garden was as empty as before; even the limp squirrels had whisked away, leaving everything gleaming, brassy and bare.

Only small Manu suddenly reappeared, as if he had dropped out of an invisible cloud or from a bird's claws, and stood for a moment in the centre of the yellow lawn, chewing his finger and near to tears as he heard Raghu shouting, with his head pressed against the veranda wall, 'Eighty-three, eighty-five, eighty-nine, ninety . . .' and then made off in a panic, half of him wanting to fly north, the other half counselling south. Raghu turned just in time to see the flash of his white shorts and the uncertain skittering of his red sandals, and charged after him with such a blood-curdling yell that Manu stumbled over the hosepipe, fell into its rubber coils and lay there weeping, 'I won't be It – you have to find them all – all – All!'

'I know I have to, idiot,' Raghu said, superciliously kicking him with his toe. 'You're dead,' he said with satisfaction, licking the beads of perspiration off his upper lip, and then stalked off in search of worthier prey, whistling spiritedly so that the hiders should hear and tremble.

Ravi heard the whistling and picked his nose in panic, trying to find comfort by burrowing the finger deep-deep into that soft tunnel. He felt himself too exposed, sitting on an upturned flower pot behind the garage. Where could he burrow? He could run around the garage if he heard Raghu come – around and around and around – but he hadn't much faith in his short legs when matched against Raghu's long, hefty, hairy footballer legs. Ravi had a frightening glimpse of them as Raghu combed the hedge of crotons and hibiscus, trampling delicate ferns underfoot as he did so. Ravi looked about him desperately, swallowing a small ball of snot in his fear.

The garage was locked with a great heavy lock to which the driver had the key in his room, hanging from a nail on the wall under his work-shirt. Ravi had peeped in and seen him still sprawling on his string-cot in his vest and striped under-pants, the hair on his chest and the hair in his nose shaking with the vibrations of his phlegm-obstructed snores. Ravi had wished he were tall enough, big enough to reach the key on the nail, but it was impossible, beyond his reach for years to come. He had sidled away and sat dejectedly on the flower pot. That at least was cut to his own size.

But next to the garage was another shed with a big green door. Also locked. No one even knew who had the key to the lock. That shed wasn't opened more than once a year when Ma turned out all the old broken bits of furniture and rolls of matting and leaking buckets, and the white ant hills were broken and swept away and Flit sprayed into the spider webs and rat holes so that the whole operation was like the looting of a poor, ruined and conquered city. The green leaves of the door sagged. They were nearly off their rusty hinges. The hinges were large and made a small gap between the door and the walls – only just large enough for rats, dogs and, possibly, Ravi to slip through.

Ravi had never cared to enter such a dark and depressing mortuary of defunct household goods seething with such unspeakable and alarming animal life but, as Raghu's whistling grew angrier and sharper and his crashing and storming in the hedge wilder, Ravi suddenly slipped off the flower pot and through the crack and was gone. He chuckled aloud with astonishment at his own temerity so that Raghu came out of the hedge, stood silent with his hands on his hips, listening, and finally shouted 'I heard you! I'm coming! *Got* you –' and came charging round the garage only to find the upturned flower pot, the yellow dust, the crawling of white ants in a mud hill against the closed shed door – nothing. Snarling, he bent to pick up a stick and went off, whacking it against the garage and shed walls as if to beat out his prey.

*

Ravi shook, then shivered with delight, with self-congratulation. Also with fear. It was dark, spooky in the shed. It had a muffled smell, as of graves. Ravi had once got locked into the linen cupboard and sat there weeping for half an hour before he was rescued. But at least that had been a familiar place, and even smelt pleasantly of starch, laundry and, reassuringly, of his mother. But the shed smelt of rats, ant hills, dust and spider webs. Also of less definable, less recognisable horrors. And it was dark. Except for the white-hot cracks along the door, there was no light. The roof was very low. Although Ravi was small, he felt as if he could reach up and touch it with his finger tips. But he didn't stretch. He hunched himself into a ball so as not to bump into anything, touch or feel anything. What might there not be to touch him and feel him as he stood there, trying to see in the dark? Something cold, or slimy – like a snake. Snakes! He leapt up as Raghu whacked the wall with his stick – then, quickly realising what it was, felt almost relieved to hear Raghu, hear his stick. It made him feel protected.

But Raghu soon moved away. There wasn't a sound once his footsteps had gone around the garage and disappeared. Ravi stood frozen inside the shed. Then he shivered all over. Something had tickled the back of his neck. It took him a while to pick up the courage to lift his hand and explore. It was an insect – perhaps a spider – exploring *him*. He squashed it and wondered how many more creatures were watching him, waiting to reach out and touch him, the stranger.

There was nothing now. After standing in that position – his hand still on his neck, feeling the wet splodge of the squashed spider gradually dry – for minutes, hours, his legs began to tremble with the effort, the inaction. By now he could see enough in the dark to make out the large solid shapes of old wardrobes, broken buckets and bedsteads piled on top of each other around him. He recognised an old bathtub – patches of enamel glimmered at him and at last he lowered himself on to its edge.

He contemplated slipping out of the shed and into the fray. He wondered if it would not be better to be captured by

Raghu and be returned to the milling crowd as long as he could be in the sun, the light, the free spaces of the garden and the familiarity of his brothers, sisters and cousins. It would be evening soon. Their games would become legitimate. The parents would sit out on the lawn on cane basket chairs and watch them as they tore around the garden or gathered in knots to share a loot of mulberries or black, teeth-splitting *jamun* from the garden trees. The gardener would fix the hosepipe to the water tap and water would fall lavishly through the air to the ground, soaking the dry yellow grass and the red gravel and arousing the sweet, intoxicating scent of water on dry earth – that loveliest scent in the world. Ravi sniffed for a whiff of it. He half-rose from the bathtub, then heard the despairing scream of one of the girls as Raghu bore down upon her. There was the sound of a crash, and of rolling about in the bushes, the shrubs, then screams and accusing sobs of, 'I touched the den –' 'You did not –' 'I did –' 'You liar, you did *not*' and then a fading away and silence again.

Ravi sat back on the harsh edge of the tub, deciding to hold out a bit longer. What fun if they were all found and caught – he alone left unconquered! He had never known that sensation. Nothing more wonderful had ever happened to him than being taken out by an uncle and bought a whole slab of chocolate all to himself, or being flung into the soda-man's pony cart and driven up to the gate by the friendly driver with the red beard and pointed ears. To defeat Raghu – that hirsute, hoarse-voiced football champion – and to be the winner in a circle of older, bigger, luckier children – that would be thrilling beyond imagination. He hugged his knees together and smiled to himself almost shyly at the thought of so much victory, such laurels.

There he sat smiling, knocking his heels against the bathtub, now and then getting up and going to the door to put his ear to the broad crack and listening for sounds of the game, the pursuer and the pursued, and then returning to his seat with the dogged determination of the true winner, a breaker of records, a champion.

It grew darker in the shed as the light at the door grew softer, fuzzier, turned to a kind of crumbling yellow pollen that turned to yellow fur, blue fur, grey fur. Evening. Twilight. The sound of water gushing, falling. The scent of earth receiving water, slaking its thirst in great gulps and releasing that green scent of freshness, coolness. Through the crack Ravi saw the long purple shadows of the shed and the garage lying still across the yard. Beyond that, the white walls of the house. The bougainvillea had lost its lividity, hung in dark bundles that quaked and twittered and seethed with masses of homing sparrows. The lawn was shut off from his view. Could he hear the children's voices? It seemed to him that he could. It seemed to him that he could hear them chanting, singing, laughing. But what about the game? What had happened? Could it be over? How could it when he was still not found?

It then occurred to him that he could have slipped out long ago, dashed across the yard to the veranda and touched the 'den'. It was necessary to do that to win. He had forgotten. He had only remembered the part of hiding and trying to elude the seeker. He had done that so successfully, his success had occupied him so wholly that he had quite forgotten that success had to be clinched by that final dash to victory and the ringing cry of 'Den!'

With a whimper he burst through the crack, fell on his knees, got up and stumbled on stiff, benumbed legs across the shadowy yard, crying heartily by the time he reached the veranda so that when he flung himself at the white pillar and bawled, 'Den! Den! Den!' his voice broke with rage and pity at the disgrace of it all and he felt himself flooded with tears and misery.

Out on the lawn, the children stopped chanting. They all turned to stare at him in amazement. Their faces were pale and triangular in the dusk. The trees and bushes around them stood inky and sepulchral, spilling long shadows across them. They stared, wondering at his reappearance, his passion, his wild animal howling. Their mother rose from her basket chair and came towards him, worried, annoyed, saying, 'Stop it, stop it, Ravi. Don't be a baby. Have you hurt yourself?' Seeing him attended to, the children went back to clasping their hands and chanting 'The grass is green, the rose is red . . .'

But Ravi would not let them. He tore himself out of his mother's grasp and pounded across the lawn into their midst, charging at them with his head lowered so that they scattered in surprise. 'I won, I won, I won,' he bawled, shaking his head so that the big tears flew. 'Raghu didn't find me. I won, I won –'

It took them a minute to grasp what he was saying, even who he was. They had quite forgotten him. Raghu had found all the others long ago. There had been a fight about who was to be It next. It had been so fierce that their mother had emerged from her bath and made them change to another game. Then they had played another and another. Broken mulberries from the tree and eaten them. Helped the driver wash the car when their father returned from work. Helped the gardener water the beds till he roared at them and swore he would complain to their parents. The parents had come out, taken up their positions on the cane chairs. They had begun to play again, sing and chant. All this time no one had remembered Ravi. Having disappeared from the scene, he had disappeared from their minds. Clean.

'Don't be a fool,' Raghu said roughly, pushing him aside, and even Mira said, 'Stop howling, Ravi. If you want to play, you can stand at the end of the line,' and she put him there very firmly.

The game proceeded. Two pairs of arms reached up and met in an arc. The children trooped under it again and again in a lugubrious circle, ducking their heads and intoning

> The grass is green,
> The rose is red;
> Remember me
> When I am dead, dead, dead, dead . . .

And the arc of thin arms trembled in the twilight, and the heads were bowed so sadly, and their feet tramped to that melancholy refrain so mournfully, so helplessly, that Ravi could not bear it. He would not follow them, he would not be included in this funereal game. He had wanted victory and triumph – not a funeral. But he had been forgotten, left out and he would not join them now. The ignominy of being forgotten – how could he face it? He felt his heart go heavy and ache inside him unbearably. He lay down full length on the damp grass, crushing his face into it, no longer crying, silenced by a terrible sense of his insignificance.

Ruth Prawer Jhabvala

IN THE MOUNTAINS

WHEN ONE LIVES alone for most of the time and meets almost nobody, then care for one's outward appearance tends to drop away. That was what happened to Pritam. As the years went by and she continued living by herself, her appearance became rougher and shabbier, and though she was still in her thirties, she completely forgot to care for herself or think about herself as a physical person.

Her mother was just the opposite. She was plump and pampered, loved pastries and silk saris, and always smelled of lavender. Pritam smelled of – what was it? Her mother, enfolded in Pritam's embrace after a separation of many months, found herself sniffing in an attempt to identify the odour emanating from her. Perhaps it was from Pritam's clothes, which she probably did not change as frequently as was desirable. Tears came to the mother's eyes. They were partly for what her daughter had become and partly for the happiness of being with her again.

Pritam thumped her on the back. Her mother always cried at their meetings and at their partings. Pritam usually could not help being touched by these tears, even though she was aware of the mixed causes that evoked them. Now, to hide her own feelings, she became gruffer and more manly, and even gave the old lady a push toward a chair. 'Go on, sit down,' she said. 'I suppose you are dying for your cup of tea.' She had it all ready, and the mother took it gratefully, for she loved and needed tea, and the journey up from the plains had greatly tired her.

But she could not drink with enjoyment. Pritam's tea was always too strong for her – a black country brew such as peasants drink, and the milk was also that of peasants, too newly rich and warm from the buffalo. And they were in this rough and barely furnished room in the rough stone house perched on the mountainside. And there was Pritam herself. The mother had to concentrate all her energies on struggling against more tears.

'I suppose you don't like the tea,' Pritam said challengingly. She watched severely while the mother proved herself by drinking it up to the last drop, and Pritam refilled the cup. She asked, 'How is everybody? Same as usual? Eating, making money?'

'No, no,' said the mother, not so much denying the fact that this was what the family was doing as protesting against Pritam's saying so.

'Aren't they going up to Simla this year?'

'On Thursday,' the mother said, and shifted uncomfortably.

'And stopping here?'

'Yes. For lunch.'

The mother kept her eyes lowered. She said nothing more, though there was more to say. It would have to wait till a better hour. Let Pritam first get over the prospect of entertaining members of her family for a few hours on Thursday. It was nothing new or unexpected, for some of them stopped by every year on their way farther up the mountains. However much they may have desired to do so, they couldn't just drive past; it wouldn't be decent. But the prospect of meeting held no pleasure for anyone. Quite often there was a quarrel, and then Pritam cursed them as they drove away, and they sighed at the necessity of keeping up family relationships, instead of having their lunch comfortably in the hotel a few miles farther on.

Pritam said, 'I suppose you will be going with them,' and went on at once, 'Naturally, why should you stay? What is there for you here?'

'I want to stay.'

'No, you love to be in Simla. It's so nice and jolly, and meeting everyone walking on the Mall, and tea in Davico's. Nothing like that here. You even hate my tea.'

'I want to stay with you.'

'But I don't want you!' Pritam was laughing, not angry. 'You will be in my way, and then how will I carry on all my big love affairs?'

'What, what?'

Pritam clapped her hands in delight. 'Oh no. I'm telling you nothing, because then you will want to stay and you will scare everyone away.' She gave her mother a sly look and added, 'You will scare poor Doctor Sahib away.'

'Oh, Doctor Sahib,' said the old lady, relieved to find it had all been a joke. But she continued with disapproval, 'Does he still come here?'

'Well, what do you think?' Pritam stopped laughing now and became offended. 'If he doesn't come, then who will come? Except some goats and monkeys, perhaps. I know he is not good enough for you. You don't like him to come here. You would prefer me to know only goats and monkeys. And the family, of course.'

'When did I say I don't like him?' the mother said.

'People don't have to say. And other people are quite capable of feeling without anyone saying. Here.' Pritam snatched up her mother's cup and filled it, with rather a vengeful air, for the third time.

Actually, it wasn't true that the mother disliked Doctor Sahib. He came to visit the next morning, and as soon as she saw him she had her usual sentiment about him – not dislike but disapproval. He certainly did not look like a person fit to be on terms of social intercourse with any member of her family. He was a tiny man, shabby and even dirty. He wore a kind of suit, but it was in a terrible condition and so were his shoes. One eye of his spectacles, for some reason, was blacked out with a piece of cardboard.

'Ah!' he exclaimed when he saw her. 'Mother has come!' And he was so genuinely happy that her disapproval could not stand up to him – at least, not entirely.

'Mother brings us tidings and good cheer from the great world outside,' Doctor Sahib went on. 'What are we but two mountain hermits? Or I could even say two mountain bears.'

He sat at a respectful distance away from the mother, who was ensconced in a basket chair. She had come to sit in the garden. There was a magnificent view from here of the plains below and the mountains above; however, she had not come out to enjoy the scenery but to get the benefit of the morning sun. Although it was the height of summer, she always felt freezing cold inside the house, which seemed like a stone tomb.

'Has Madam told you about our winter?' Doctor Sahib said. 'Oh, what these two bears have gone through! Ask her.'

'His roof fell in,' Pritam said.

'One night I was sleeping in my bed. Suddenly – what shall I tell you – crash, bang! Boom and bang! To me it seemed that all the mountains were falling and, let alone the mountains, heaven itself was coming down into my poor house. I said, "Doctor Sahib, your hour has come."'

'I told him, I told him all summer, "The first snowfall and your roof will fall in." And when it happened all he could do was stand there and wring his hands. What an idiot!'

'If it hadn't been for Madam, God knows what would have become of me. But she took me in and all winter she allowed me to have my corner by her own fireside.'

The mother looked at them with startled eyes.

'Oh yes, all winter,' Pritam said, mocking her. 'And all alone, just the two of us. Why did you have to tell her?' she reproached Doctor Sahib. 'Now she is shocked. Just look at her face. She is thinking we are two guilty lovers.'

The mother flushed, and so did Doctor Sahib. An expression of bashfulness came into his face, mixed with regret, with melancholy. He was silent for some time, his head lowered. Then he said to the mother, 'Look, can you see it?' He pointed at his house, which nestled farther down the mountainside, some way below Pritam's. It was a tiny house, not much more than a hut. 'All hale and hearty again. Madam had the roof fixed, and now I am snug and safe once more in my own little kingdom.'

Pritam said, 'One day the whole place is going to come down, not just the roof, and then what will you do?'

He spread his arms in acceptance and resignation. He had no choice as to place of residence. His family had brought him here and installed him in the house; they gave him a tiny allowance but only on condition that he wouldn't return to Delhi. As was evident from his fluent English, Doctor Sahib was an educated man, though it was not quite clear whether he really had qualified as a doctor. If he had, he may have done something disreputable and been struck off the register. Some such air hung about him. He was a great embarrassment to his family. Unable to make a living, he had gone around scrounging from family friends, and at one point had sat on the pavement in New Delhi's most fashionable shopping district and attempted to sell cigarettes and matches.

Later, when he had gone, Pritam said, 'Don't you think I've got a dashing lover?'

'I know it's not true,' the mother said, defending herself. 'But other people, what will they think – alone with him in the house all winter? You know how people are.'

'What people?'

It was true. There weren't any. To the mother, this was a cause for regret. She looked at the mountains stretching away into the distance – a scene of desolation. But Pritam's eyes were half-shut with satisfaction as she gazed across the empty spaces and saw birds cleaving through the mist, afloat in the pure mountain sky.

'I was waiting for you all winter,' the mother said. 'I had your room ready, and every day we went in there to dust and change the flowers.' She broke out, 'Why didn't you come? Why stay in this place when you can be at home and lead a proper life like everybody else?'

Pritam laughed. 'Oh but I'm not like everybody else! That's the last thing!'

The mother was silent. She could not deny that Pritam was different. When she was a girl, they had worried about her and yet they had also been proud of her. She had been a big, handsome girl with independent views. People admired her and thought it a fine thing that a girl could be so emancipated in India and lead a free life, just as in other places.

Now the mother decided to break the news. She said, 'He is coming with them on Thursday.'

'Who is coming with them?'

'Sarla's husband.' She did not look at Pritam after saying this.

After a moment's silence Pritam cried, 'So let him come! They can all come – everyone welcome. My goodness, what's so special about him that you should make such a face? What's so special about any of them? They may come, they may eat, they may go away again, and good-bye. Why should I care for anyone? I don't care. And also you! You also may go – right now, this minute, if you like – and I will stand here and wave to you and laugh!'

In an attempt to stop her, the mother asked, 'What will you cook for them on Thursday?'

That did bring her up short. For a moment she gazed at her mother wildly, as if she were mad herself or thought her mother mad. Then she said, 'My God, do you ever think of anything except food?'

'I eat too much,' the old lady gladly admitted. 'Dr Puri says I must reduce.'

Pritam didn't sleep well that night. She felt hot, and tossed about heavily, and finally got up and turned on the light and wandered around the house in her nightclothes. Then she unlatched the door and let herself out. The night air was crisp, and it refreshed her at once. She loved being out in all this immense silence. Moonlight lay on top of the mountains, so that even those that were green looked as if they were covered in snow.

There was only one light – a very human little speck – in all that darkness. It came from Doctor Sahib's house, some way below hers. She wondered if he had fallen asleep with the light on. It happened sometimes that he dozed off where he was sitting and when he woke up again it was morning. But other times he really did stay awake all night, too excited by his

135

reading and thinking to be able to sleep. Pritam decided to go down and investigate. The path was very steep, but she picked her way down, as sure and steady as a mountain goat. She peered in at his window. He was awake, sitting at his table with his head supported on his hand, and reading by the light of a kerosene lamp. His house had once had electricity, but after the disaster last winter it could not be got to work again. Pritam was quite glad about that, for the wiring had always been uncertain, and he had been in constant danger of being electrocuted.

She rapped on the glass to rouse him, then went around to let herself in by the door. At the sound of her knock, he had jumped to his feet; he was startled, and no less so when he discovered who his visitor was. He stared at her through his one glass lens, and his lower lip trembled in agitation.

She was irritated. 'If you're so frightened, why don't you lock your door? You should lock it. Any kind of person can come in and do anything he wants.' It struck her how much like a murder victim he looked. He was so small and weak – one blow on the head would do it. Some morning she would come down and find him lying huddled on the floor.

But there he was, alive, and, now that he had got over the shock, laughing and flustered and happy to see her. He fussed around and invited her to sit on his only chair, dusting the seat with his hand and drawing it out for her in so courtly a manner that she became instinctively graceful as she settled herself on it and pulled her nightdress over her knees.

'Look at me, in my nightie,' she said, laughing. 'I suppose you're shocked. If Mother knew. If she could see me! But of course she is fast asleep and snoring in her bed. Why are you awake? Reading one of your stupid books – what stuff you cram into your head day and night. Anyone would go crazy.'

Doctor Sahib was very fond of reading. He read mostly historical romances and was influenced and even inspired by them. He believed very strongly in past births, and these books helped him to learn about the historical eras through which he might have passed.

'A fascinating story,' he said. 'There is a married lady – a queen, as a matter of fact – who falls hopelessly in love with a monk.'

'Goodness! Hopelessly?'

'You see, these monks – naturally – they were under a vow of chastity and that means – well – you know . . .'

'Of course I know.'

'So there was great anguish on both sides. Because he also felt burning love for the lady and endured horrible penances in order to subdue himself. Would you like me to read to you? There are some sublime passages.'

'What is the use? These are not things to read in books but to experience in life. Have you ever been hopelessly in love?'

He turned away his face, so that now only his cardboard lens was looking at her. However, it seemed not blank but full of expression.

She said, 'There are people in the world whose feelings are much stronger than other people's. Of course they must suffer. If you are not satisfied only with eating and drinking but want something else . . . You should see my family. They care for nothing – only physical things, only enjoyment.'

'Mine exactly the same.'

'There is one cousin, Sarla – I have nothing against her, she is not a bad person. But I tell you it would be just as well to be born an animal. Perhaps I shouldn't talk like this, but it's true.'

'It is true. And in previous births these people really were animals.'

'Do you think so?'

'Or some very low form of human being. But the queens and the really great people, they become – well, they become like you. Please don't laugh! I have told you before what you were in your last birth.'

She went on laughing. 'You've told me so many things,' she said.

'All true. Because you have passed through many incarnations. And in each one you were a very outstanding personality, a highly developed soul, but each time you also had a difficult life, marked by sorrow and suffering.'

137

Pritam had stopped laughing. She gazed sadly at the blank wall over his head.

'It is the fate of all highly developed souls,' he said. 'It is the price to be paid.'

'I know.' She fetched a sigh from her innermost being.

'I think a lot about this problem. Just tonight, before you came, I sat here reading my book. I'm not ashamed to admit that tears came streaming from my eyes, so that I couldn't go on reading, on account of not being able to see the print. Then I looked up and I asked, "Oh, Lord, why must these good and noble souls endure such torment, while others, less good and noble, can enjoy themselves freely?"'

'Yes, why?' Pritam asked.

'I shall tell you. I shall explain.' He was excited, inspired now. He looked at her fully, and even his cardboard lens seemed radiant. 'Now, as I was reading about this monk – a saint, by the way – and how he struggled and battled against nature, then I could not but think of my own self. Yes, I too, though not a saint, struggle and battle here alone in my small hut. I cry out in anguish, and the suffering endured is terrible but also – oh, Madam – glorious! A privilege.'

Pritam looked at a crack that ran right across the wall and seemed to be splitting it apart. One more heavy snowfall, she thought, and the whole hut would come down. Meanwhile he sat here and talked nonsense and she listened to him. She got up abruptly.

He cried, 'I have talked too much! You are bored!'

'Look at the time,' she said. The window was milk-white with dawn. She turned down the kerosene lamp and opened the door. Trees and mountains were floating in a pale mist, attempting to surface like swimmers through water. 'Oh my God,' she said, 'it's time to get up. And I'm going to have such a day today, with all of them coming.'

'They are coming today?'

'Yes, and you needn't bother to visit. They are not your type at all. Not one bit.'

He laughed. 'All right.'

'Not mine, either,' she said, beginning the upward climb

138

back to her house.

Pritam loved to cook and was very good at it. Her kitchen was a primitive little outbuilding in which she bustled about. Her hair fell into her face and stuck to her forehead; several times she tried to push it back with her elbow but only succeeded in leaving a black soot mark. When her mother pointed this out to her, she laughed and smeared at it and made it worse.

Her good humour carried her successfully over the arrival of the relatives. They came in three carloads, and suddenly the house was full of fashionably dressed people with loud voices. Pritam came dashing out of the kitchen just as she was and embraced everyone indiscriminately, including Sarla and her husband, Bobby. In the bustle of arrival and the excitement of many people, the meeting went off easily. The mother was relieved. Pritam and Bobby hadn't met for eight years – in fact, not since Bobby had been married to Sarla.

Soon Pritam was serving a vast, superbly cooked meal. She went around piling their plates, urging them to take, take more, glad at seeing them enjoy her food. She still hadn't changed her clothes, and the smear of soot was still on her face. The mother – whose main fear had been that Pritam would be surly and difficult – was not relieved but upset by Pritam's good mood. She thought to herself, why should she be like that with them – what have they ever done for her that she should show them such affection and be like a servant to them? She even looked like their servant. The old lady's temper mounted, and when she saw Pritam piling rice on to Bobby's plate – when she saw her serving *him* like a servant, and the way he turned around to compliment her about the food, making Pritam proud and shy and pleased – then the mother could not bear any more. She went into the bedroom and lay down on the bed. She felt ill; her blood pressure had risen and all her pulses throbbed. She shut her eyes and tried to shut out the merry, sociable sounds coming from the next room.

After a while Pritam came in and said, 'Why aren't you eating?'

The old lady didn't answer.

'What's the matter?'

'Go. Go away. Go to your guests.'

'Oh my God, she is sulking!' Pritam said, and laughed out loud – not to annoy her mother but to rally her, the way she would a child. But the mother continued to lie there with her eyes shut.

Pritam said, 'Should I get you some food?'

'I don't want it,' the mother said. But suddenly she opened her eyes and sat up. She said, 'You should give food to him. He also should be invited. Or perhaps you think he is not good enough for your guests?'

'Who?'

'Who. You know very well. You should know. You were with him the whole night.'

Pritam gave a quick glance over her shoulder at the open door, then advanced toward her mother. 'So you have been spying on me,' she said. The mother shrank back. 'You pretended to be asleep, and all the time you were spying on me.'

'Not like that, Daughter –'

'And now you are having filthy thoughts about me.'

'Not like that!'

'Yes, like that!'

Both were shouting. The conversation in the next room had died down. The mother whispered, 'Shut the door,' and Pritam did so.

Then the mother said in a gentle, loving voice, 'I'm glad he is here with you. He is a good friend to you.' She looked into Pritam's face, but it did not lighten, and she went on, 'That is why I said he should be invited. When other friends come, we should not neglect our old friends who have stood by us in our hour of need.'

Pritam snorted scornfully.

'And he would have enjoyed the food so much,' the mother said. 'I think he doesn't often eat well.'

Pritam laughed. 'You should see what he eats!' she said. 'But he is lucky to get even that. At least his family send him money now. Before he came here, do you want to hear what he did? He has told me himself. He used to go to the kitchens of the restaurants and beg for food. And they gave him scraps and he ate them – he has told me himself. He ate leftover scraps from other people's plates like a sweeper or a dog. And you want such a person to be my friend.'

She turned away from her mother's startled, suffering face. She ran out of the room and out through the next room, past all the guests. She climbed up a path that ran from the back of her house to a little cleared plateau. She lay down in the grass, which was alive with insects; she was level with the tops of trees and with the birds that pecked and called from inside them. She often came here. She looked down at the view but didn't see it, it was so familiar to her. The only unusual sight was the three cars parked outside her house. A chauffeur was wiping a windshield. Then someone came out of the house and, reaching inside a car door, emerged with a bottle. It was Bobby.

Pritam watched him, and when he was about to go back into the house, she aimed a pebble that fell at his feet. He looked up. He smiled. 'Hi, there!' he called.

She beckoned him to climb up to her. He hesitated for a moment, looking at the bottle and towards the house, but then gave the toss of his head that she knew well, and began to pick his way along the path. She put her hand over her mouth to cover a laugh as she watched him crawl up towards her on all fours. When finally he arrived, he was out of breath and dishevelled, and there was a little blood on his hand where he had grazed it. He flung himself on the grass beside her and gave a great 'Whoof!' of relief.

She hadn't seen him for eight years, and her whole life had changed in the meantime, but it didn't seem to her that he had changed all that much. Perhaps he was a little heavier, but it suited him, made him look more manly than ever. He was lying face down on the grass, and she watched his shoulder blades twitch inside his finely striped shirt as he breathed in exhaustion.

'You are in very poor condition,' she said.

'Isn't it terrible?'

'Don't you play tennis any more?'

'Mostly golf now.'

He sat up and put the bottle to his mouth and tilted back his head. She watched his throat moving as the liquid glided down. He finished with a sound of satisfaction and passed the bottle to her, and without wiping it she put her lips where his had been and drank. The whisky leaped up in her like fire. They had often sat like this together, passing a bottle of Scotch between them.

He seemed to be perfectly content to be there with her. He sat with his knees drawn up and let his eyes linger appreciatively over the view. It was the way she had often seen him look at attractive girls. 'Nice,' he said, as he had said on those occasions. She laughed, and then she too looked and tried to imagine how he was seeing it.

'A nice place,' he said. 'I like it. I wish I could live here.'

'You!' She laughed again.

He made a serious face. 'I love peace and solitude. You don't know me. I've changed a lot.' He turned right around towards her, still very solemn, and for the first time she felt him gazing full into her face. She put up her hand and said quickly, 'I've been cooking all day.'

He looked away, as if wanting to spare her, and this delicacy hurt her more than anything. She said heavily, 'I've changed.'

'Oh no!' he said in haste. 'You are just the same. As soon as I saw you, I thought: Look at Priti, she is just the same.' And again he turned towards her to allow her to see his eyes, stretching them wide open for her benefit. It was a habit of his she knew well; he would always challenge the person to whom he was lying to read anything but complete honesty in his eyes.

She said, 'You had better go. Everyone will wonder where you are.'

'Let them.' And when she shook her head, he said, in his wheedling voice, 'Let me stay with you. It has been such a long time. Shall I tell you something? I was so excited yesterday thinking: Tomorrow I shall see her again. I couldn't sleep all night. No, really – it's true.'

Of course she knew it wasn't. He slept like a bear; nothing could disturb that. The thought amused her, and her mouth corners twitched. Encouraged, he moved in closer. 'I think about you very often,' he said. 'I remember so many things – you have no idea. All the discussions we had about our terrible social system. It was great.'

Once they had had a very fine talk about free love. They had gone to a place they knew about, by a lake. At first they were quite frivolous, sitting on a ledge overlooking the lake, but as they got deeper into their conversation about free love (they both, it turned out, believed in it) they became more and more serious and, after that, very quiet, until in the end they had nothing more to say. Then they only sat there, and though it was very still and the water had nothing but tiny ripples on it, like wrinkles in silk, they felt as if they were in a storm. But of course it was their hearts beating and their blood rushing. It was the most marvellous experience they had ever had in their whole lives. After that, they often returned there or went to other similar places that they found, and as soon as they were alone together that same storm broke out.

Now Bobby heaved a sigh. To make himself feel better, he took another drink from his bottle and then passed it to her. 'It's funny,' he said. 'I have this fantastic social life. I meet such a lot of people, but there isn't one person I can talk with the way I talk with you. I mean, about serious subjects.'

'And with Sarla?'

'Sarla is all right, but she isn't really interested in serious subjects. I don't think she ever thinks about them. But I do.'

To prove it, he again assumed a very solemn expression and turned his face toward her, so that she could study it. How little he had changed!

'Give me another drink,' she said, needing it.

He passed her the bottle. 'People think I'm an extrovert type, and of course I do have to lead a very extrovert sort of life,' he said. 'And there is the business too – ever since Daddy had his stroke, I have to spend a lot of time in the office. But very often, you know what I like to do? Just lie on my bed and listen to nice tunes on my cassette. And then I have a lot of thoughts.'

'What about?'

'Oh, all sorts of things. You would be surprised.'

She was filled with sensations she had thought she would never have again. No doubt they were partly due to the whisky; she hadn't drunk in a long time. She thought he must be feeling the way she did; in the past they had always felt the same. She put out her hand to touch him – first his cheek, which was rough and manly, and then his neck, which was soft and smooth. He had been talking, but when she touched him he fell silent. She left her hand lying on his neck, loving to touch it. He remained silent, and there was something strange. For a moment, she didn't remove her hand – she was embarrassed to do so – and when at last she did, she noticed that he looked at it. She looked at it too. The skin was rough and not too clean, and neither were her nails, and one of them was broken. She hid her hands behind her back.

Now he was talking again, and talking quite fast. 'Honestly, Priti, I think you're really lucky to be living here,' he said. 'No one to bother you, no worries, and all this fantastic scenery.' He turned his head again to admire it and made his eyes sparkle with appreciation. He also took a deep breath.

'And such marvellous air,' he said. 'No wonder you keep fit and healthy. Who lives there?' He pointed at Doctor Sahib's house below.

Pritam answered eagerly. 'Oh, I'm very lucky – he is such an interesting personality. If only you could meet him.'

'What a pity,' Bobby said politely. Down below, there was a lot of activity around the three cars. Things were being rolled up and stowed away in preparation for departure.

'Yes, you don't meet such people every day. He is a doctor, not only of medicine but all sorts of other things too. He does a lot of research and thinking, and that is why he lives up here. Because it is so quiet.'

Now people could be seen coming out of Pritam's house.

They turned this way and that, looking up and calling Pritam's name.

'They are looking for you,' Bobby said. He replaced the cap of his whisky bottle and got up and waited for her to get up too. But she took her time.

'You see, for serious thinking you have to have absolute peace and quiet,' she said. 'I mean, if you are a real thinker, a sort of philosopher type.'

She got up. She stood and looked down at the people searching and calling for her. 'Whenever I wake up at night, I can see his light on. He is always with some book, studying, studying.'

'Fantastic,' Bobby said, though his attention was distracted by the people below.

'He knows all about past lives. He can tell you exactly what you were in all your previous births.'

'Really?' Bobby said, turning towards her again.

'He has told me all about my incarnations.'

'Really? Would he know about me too?'

'Perhaps. If you were an interesting personality. Yes all right, coming!' she called down at last.

She began the steep climb down, but it was so easy for her that she could look back at him over her shoulder and continue talking. 'He is only interested in studying highly developed souls, so unless you were someone really quite special in a previous birth he wouldn't be able to tell you anything.'

'What were you?' Bobby said. He had begun to follow her. Although the conversation was interesting to him, he could not concentrate on it, because he had to keep looking down at the path and place his feet with caution.

'I don't think I can tell you,' she said, walking on ahead. 'It is something you are supposed to know only in your innermost self.'

'What?' he said, but just then he slipped, and it was all he could do to save himself from falling.

'In your innermost self!' she repeated in a louder voice, though without looking back. Nimbly, she ran down the remainder of the path and was soon among the people who had been calling her.

They were relieved to see her. It seemed the old lady was being very troublesome. She refused to have her bag packed, refused to get into the car and be driven up to Simla. She said she wanted to stay with Pritam.

'So let her,' Pritam said.

Her relatives exchanged exasperated glances. Some of the ladies were so tired of the whole thing that they had given up and sat on the steps of the veranda, fanning themselves. Others, more patient, explained to Pritam that it was all very well for her to say let her stay, but how was she going to look after her? The old lady needed so many things – a masseuse in the morning, a cup of Horlicks at eleven and another at three, and one never knew when the doctor would have to be called for her blood pressure. None of these facilities was available in Pritam's house, and they knew exactly what would happen – after a day, or at the most two, Pritam would send them an SOS, and they would have to come back all the way from Simla to fetch her away.

Pritam went into the bedroom, shutting the door behind her. The mother was lying on her bed, with her face to the wall. She didn't move or turn around or give any sign of life until Pritam said, 'It's me.' Then her mother said, 'I'm not going with them.'

Pritam said, 'You will have to have a cold bath every day, because I'm not going to keep lighting the boiler for you. Do you know who has to chop the wood? Me, Pritam.'

'I don't need hot water. If you don't need it, I don't.'

'And there is no Horlicks.'

'Tcha!' said her mother. She was still lying on the bed, though she had turned around now and was facing Pritam. She did not look very well. Her face seemed puffed and flushed.

'And your blood pressure?' Pritam asked.

'It is quite all right.'

'Yes, and what if it isn't? There is no Dr Puri here, or anyone like that.'

The mother shut her eyes, as if it were a great effort. After a time, she found the strength to say, 'There is a doctor.'

'God help us!' Pritam said, and laughed out loud.

'He *is* a doctor.' The mother compressed her little mouth stubbornly over her dentures. Pritam did not contradict her, though she was still laughing to herself. They were silent together but not in disagreement. Pritam opened the door to leave.

'Did you keep any food for him?' the mother said.

'There is enough to last him a week.'

She went out and told the others that her mother was staying. She wouldn't listen to any arguments, and after a while they gave up. All they wanted was to get away as quickly as possible. They piled into their cars and waved at her from the windows. She waved back. When she was out of sight, they sank back against the upholstery with sighs of relief. They felt it had gone off quite well this time. At least there had been no quarrel. They discussed her for a while and felt that she was improving; perhaps she was quietening down with middle age.

Pritam waited for the cars to reach the bend below and then – quite without malice but with excellent aim – she threw three stones. Each one squarely hit the roof of a different car as they passed, one after the other. She could hear the sound faintly from up here. She thought how amazed they would be inside their cars, wondering what had hit them, and how they would crane out of the windows but not be able to see anything. They would decide that it was just some stones crumbling off the hillside – perhaps the beginning of a landslide; you never could tell in the mountains.

She picked up another stone and flung it all the way down at Doctor Sahib's corrugated tin roof. It landed with a terrific clatter, and he came running out. He looked straight up to where she was standing, and his one lens glittered at her in the sun.

She put her hands to her mouth and called, 'Food!' He gave a sign of joyful assent and straightaway, as nimble as herself, began the familiar climb up.

147

Satyajit Ray

BIG BILL

BY TULSI BABU'S desk in his office on the ninth floor of a
building in Old Court House Street there is a window which
opens onto a vast expanse of the western sky. Tulsi Babu's
neighbour Jaganmoy Dutt had just gone to spit betel juice out
of the window one morning in the rainy season when he
noticed a double rainbow in the sky. He uttered an exclamation of surprise and turned to Tulsi Babu. 'Come here, sir.
You won't see the like of it every day.'

Tulsi Babu left his desk, went to his window, and looked
out.

'What are you referring to?' he asked.

'Why, the double rainbow!' said Jaganmoy Dutt. 'Are you
colour-blind?'

Tulsi Babu went back to his desk. 'I can't see what is so
special about a double rainbow. Even if there were twenty
rainbows in the sky, there would be nothing surprising about
that. Why, one can just as well go and stare at the double-
spired church in Lower Circular Road!'

Not everyone is endowed with the same sense of wonder,
but there is good reason to doubt whether Tulsi Babu possesses any at all. There is only one thing that never ceases to
surprise him, and that is the excellence of the mutton *kebab*
at Mansur's. The only person who is aware of this is Tulsi
Babu's friend and colleague, Prodyot Chanda.

Being of such a sceptical temperament, Tulsi Babu was not
particularly surprised to find an unusually large egg while
looking for medicinal plants in the forests of Dandakaranya.

148

Tulsi Babu had been dabbling in herbal medicine for the last fifteen years; his father was a well-known herbalist. Tulsi Babu's main source of income is as an upper division clerk in Arbuthnot & Co but he has not been able to discard the family profession altogether. Of late he has been devoting a little more time to it because two fairly distinguished citizens of Calcutta have benefited from his prescriptions, thus giving a boost to his reputation as a part-time herbalist.

It was herbs again which had brought him to Dandakaranya. He had heard that thirty miles to the north of Jagdalpur there lived a holy man in a mountain cave who had access to some medicinal plants including one for high blood pressure which was even more efficacious than *rawolfa serpentina*. Tulsi Babu suffered from hypertension; *serpentina* hadn't worked too well in his case, and he had no faith in homeopathy or allopathy.

Tulsi Babu had taken his friend Prodyot Babu with him on this trip to Jagdalpur. Tulsi Babu's inability to feel surprise had often bothered Prodyot Babu. One day he was forced to comment, 'All one needs to feel a sense of wonder is a little imagination. You are so devoid of it that even if a full-fledged ghost were to appear before you, you wouldn't be surprised.' Tulsi Babu had replied calmly, 'To feign surprise when one doesn't actually feel it, is an affectation. I do not approve of it.'

But this didn't get in the way of their friendship.

The two checked into a hotel in Jagdalpur during the autumn vacation. On the way, in the Madras Mail, two foreign youngsters had got into their compartment. They turned out to be Swedes. One of them was so tall that his head nearly touched the ceiling. Prodyot Babu had asked him how tall he was and the young man had replied, 'Two metres and seven centimetres.' Which is nearly seven feet. Prodyot Babu couldn't take his eyes away from this young giant during the rest of the journey; and yet Tulsi Babu was not surprised. He said such extraordinary height was simply the result of the diet of the Swedish people, and therefore nothing to be surprised at.

They reached the cave of the holy man Dhumai Baba after walking through the forest for a mile or so then climbing up about five hundred feet. The cave was a large one, but since no sun ever reached it, they only had to take ten steps to be engulfed in darkness, thickened by the ever present smoke from the Baba's brazier. Prodyot Babu was absorbed in watching, by the light of his torch, the profusion of stalactites and stalagmites while Tulsi Babu inquired after his herbal medicine. The tree that Dhumai Baba referred to was known as *chakraparna*, which is the Sanskrit for 'round leaves'. Tulsi Babu had never heard of it, nor was it mentioned in any of the half-dozen books he had read on herbal medicine. It was not a tree, but a shrub. It was found only in one part of the forest of Dandakaranya, and nowhere else. Baba gave adequate directions which Tulsi Babu noted down carefully.

Coming out of the cave, Tulsi Babu lost no time in setting off in quest of the herb. Prodyot Babu was happy to keep his friend company; he had hunted big game at one time – conservation had put an end to that, but the lure of the jungle persisted.

The holy man's directions proved accurate. Half an hour's walk brought them to a ravine which they crossed and in three minutes they found the shrub seven steps to the south of a *neem* tree scorched by lightning – a waist-high shrub with round green leaves, each with a pink dot in the centre.

'What kind of a place is this?' asked Prodyot Babu, looking around.

'Why, what's wrong with it?'

'But for the *neem*, there isn't a single tree here that I know. And see how damp it is. Quite unlike the places we've passed through.'

It *was* moist underfoot, but Tulsi Babu saw nothing strange in that. Why, in Calcutta itself, the temperature varied between one neighbourhood and another. Tollygunge in the south was much cooler than Shambazar in the north. What was so strange about one part of a forest being different from another? It was nothing but a quirk of nature.

Tulsi Babu had just put the bag down on the ground and

stooped towards the shrub when a sharp query from Prodyot Babu interrupted him.

'What on earth is that?'

Tulsi Babu had seen the thing too, but was not bothered by it. 'Must be some sort of egg,' he said.

Prodyot Babu had thought it was a piece of egg-shaped rock, but on getting closer he realised that it was a genuine egg, yellow, with brown stripes flecked with blue. What could such a large egg belong to? A python?

Meanwhile, Tulsi Babu had already plucked some leafy branches off the shrub and put them in his bag. He wanted to take some more but something happened then which made him stop.

The egg chose this very moment to hatch. Prodyot Babu had jumped back at the sound of the cracking shell, but now he took courage to take a few steps towards it.

The head was already out of the shell. Not a snake, nor a croc or a turtle, but a bird.

Soon the whole creature was out. It stood on spindly legs and looked around. It was quite large; about the size of a hen. Prodyot Babu was very fond of birds and kept a mynah and a bulbul as pets; but he had never seen a chick as large as this, with such a large beak and long legs. Its purple plumes were unique, as was its alert behaviour so soon after birth.

Tulsi Babu, however, was not in the least interested in the chick. He had been intent on stuffing his bag with as much of the herb as would go into it.

Prodyot Babu looked around and commented, 'Very surprising; there seems to be no sign of its parents, at least not in the vicinity.'

'I think that's enough surprise for a day,' said Tulsi Babu, hoisting his bag on his shoulder. 'It's almost four. We must be out of the forest before it gets dark.'

Somewhat against his wish, Prodyot Babu turned away from the chick and started walking with Tulsi Babu. It would take at least half an hour to reach the waiting taxi.

A patter of feet made Prodyot Babu stop and turn round.

The chick was following them.

151

'I say –' called out Prodyot Babu.

Tulsi Babu now stopped and turned. The chick was looking straight at him.

Then it padded across and stopped in front of Tulsi Babu where it opened its unusually large beak and gripped the edge of Tulsi Babu's dhoti.

Prodyot Babu was so surprised that he didn't know what to say, until he saw Tulsi Babu pick up the chick and shove it into his bag. 'What d'you think you're doing?' he cried in consternation. 'You put that nameless chick in your bag?'

'I've always wanted to keep a pet,' said Tulsi Babu, resuming his walk. 'Even mongrels are kept as pets. What's wrong with a nameless chick?'

Prodyot Babu saw the chick sticking its neck out of the swinging bag and glancing around with wide-open eyes.

Tulsi Babu lived in a flat on the second floor of a building in Masjidbari Street. Besides Tulsi Babu, who was a bachelor, there was his servant Natobar and his cook Joykesto. There was another flat on the same floor, and this was occupied by Tarit Sanyal, the proprietor of the Nabarun Press. Mr Sanyal was a short-tempered man made even more so by repeated power failures in the city which seriously affected the working of his press.

Two months had passed since Tulsi Babu's return from Dandakaranya. He had put the chick in a cage which he had specially ordered immediately upon his return. The cage was kept in a corner of the inner veranda. He had found a Sanskrit name for the chick: *Brihat-Chanchu*, or Big Bill; soon the Big was dropped and now it was just Bill.

The very first day he had acquired the chick in Jagdalpur, Tulsi Babu had tried to feed it grain. The chick had refused. Tulsi Babu had guessed, and rightly, that it was probably a meat eater; ever since he has been feeding it insects. Of late the bird's appetite seems to have grown, and Tulsi Babu has been obliged to feed it meat; Natobar buys meat from the market regularly, which may explain the bird's rapid growth in size.

Tulsi Babu had been far-sighted enough to buy a cage

which was several sizes too large for the bird. His instinct had told him that the bird belonged to a large species. The roof of the cage was two and a half feet from the ground, but only yesterday Tulsi Babu had noticed that when Bill stood straight its head nearly touched the roof; even though the bird was only two months old, it would soon need a larger cage.

Nothing has so far been said about the cry of the bird, which made Mr Sanyal choke on his tea one morning while he stood on the veranda. Normally the two neighbours hardly spoke to each other; today, after he had got over his fit of coughing, Mr Sanyal demanded to know what kind of an animal Tulsi Babu kept in his cage that yelled like that. It was true that the cry was more beast-like than bird-like.

Tulsi Babu was getting dressed to go to work. He appeared at the bedroom door and said, 'Not an animal, but a bird. And whatever its cry, it certainly doesn't keep one awake at night the way your cat does.'

Tulsi Babu's retort put an end to the argument, but Mr Sanyal kept grumbling. It was a good thing the cage couldn't be seen from his flat; a sight of the bird might have given rise to even more serious consequences.

Although its looks didn't bother Tulsi Babu, they certainly worried Prodyot Babu. The two met rarely outside office hours, except once a week for a meal of *kebab* and *paratha* at Mansur's. Prodyot Babu had a large family and many responsibilities. But since the visit to Dandakaranya, Tulsi Babu's pet was often on his mind. As a result he had started to drop in at Tulsi Babu's from time to time in the evenings. The bird's astonishing rate of growth and the change in its appearance were a constant source of surprise to Prodyot Babu. He was at a loss to see why Tulsi Babu should show no concern about it. Prodyot Babu had never imagined that the look in a bird's eye could be so malevolent. The black pupils in the amber irises would fix Prodyot Babu with such an unwavering look that he would feel most uneasy. The bird's beak naturally grew as well as its body; shiny black in colour, it resembled an eagle's beak but was much larger in relation to the rest of the body. It was clear, from its rudimentary wings and its long sturdy legs and sharp talons, that the bird couldn't fly. Prodyot Babu had described the bird to many acquaintances, but no one had been able to identify it.

One Sunday Prodyot Babu came to Tulsi Babu with a camera borrowed from a nephew. There wasn't enough light in the cage, so he had come armed with a flash gun. Photography had been a hobby with him once, and he was able to summon up enough courage to point the camera at the bird in the cage and press the shutter. The scream of protest from the bird as the flash went off sent Prodyot Babu reeling back a full yard, and it struck him that the bird's cry should be recorded; showing the photograph and playing back the cry might help in the identification of the species. Something rankled in Prodyot Babu's mind; he hadn't yet mentioned it to Tulsi Babu but somewhere in a book or a magazine he had seen a picture of a bird which greatly resembled this pet of Tulsi Babu's. If he came across the picture again, he would compare it with the photograph.

When the two friends were having tea, Tulsi Babu came out with a new piece of information. Ever since Bill had arrived, crows and sparrows had stopped coming to the flat. This was a blessing because the sparrows would build nests in the most unlikely places, while the crows would make off with food from the kitchen. All that had stopped.

'Is that so?' asked Prodyot Babu, surprised as usual.

'Well, you've been here all this time; have you seen any other birds?'

Prodyot Babu realised that he hadn't. 'But what about your two servants? Have they got used to Bill?'

'The cook never goes near the cage, but Natobar feeds it meat with pincers. Even if he does have any objection, he hasn't come out with it. And when the bird turns nasty, one sight of me calms it down. By the way, what was the idea behind taking the photograph?'

Prodyot Babu didn't mention the real reason. He said, 'When it's no more, it'll remind you of it.'

Prodyot Babu had the photograph developed and printed the

following day. He also had two enlargements made. One he gave to Tulsi Babu and the other he took to the ornithologist Ranajoy Shome. Only the other day an article by Mr Shome on the birds of Sikkim had appeared in the weekly magazine *Desh*.

But Mr Shome failed to identify the bird from the photograph. He asked where the bird could be seen, and Prodyot Babu answered with a bare-faced lie. 'A friend of mine has sent this photograph from Osaka. He wanted me to identify the bird for him.'

Tulsi Babu noted the date in his diary: February the fourteenth, 1980. Big Bill, who had been transferred from a three-and-a-half-foot cage to a four-and-a-half-foot one only last month, had been guilty of a misdeed last night.

Tulsi Babu had been awakened by a suspicious sound in the middle of the night. A series of hard, metallic twangs. But the sound had soon stopped and had been followed by total silence.

Still, the suspicion that something was up lingered in Tulsi Babu's mind. He came out of the mosquito net. Moonlight fell on the floor through the grilled window. Tulsi Babu put on his slippers, took the electric torch from the table, and came out on to the veranda.

In the beam of the torch he saw that the meshing on the cage had been ripped apart and a hole large enough for the bird to escape from had been made. The cage was now empty.

Tulsi Babu's torch revealed nothing on this side of the veranda. At the opposite end, the veranda turned right towards Mr Sanyal's flat.

Tulsi Babu reached the corner in a flash and swung his torch to the right.

It was just as he feared.

Mr Sanyal's cat was now a helpless captive in Bill's beak. The shiny spots on the floor were obviously drops of blood. But the cat was still alive and thrashing its legs about.

Tulsi Babu now cried out 'Bill' and the bird promptly dropped the cat from its beak.

Then it advanced with long strides, turned the corner, and

went quietly back to its cage.

Even in this moment of crisis, Tulsi Babu couldn't help heaving a sigh of relief.

A padlock hung on the door of Mr Sanyal's room; Mr Sanyal had left three days ago for a holiday, after the busy months of December and January when school books were printed in his press.

The best thing to do with the cat would be to toss it out of the window on to the street. Stray cats and dogs were run over every day on the streets of Calcutta; this would be just one more of them.

The rest of the night Tulsi Babu couldn't sleep.

The next day Tulsi Babu had to absent himself from work for an hour or so while he went to the railway booking office; he happened to know one of the booking clerks which made his task easier. Prodyot Babu had asked after the bird and Tulsi Babu had replied he was fine. Then he had added after a brief reflection – 'I'm thinking of framing the photo you took of it.'

On the twenty-fourth of February, Tulsi Babu arrived in Jagdalpur for the second time. A packing case with Bill in it arrived in the luggage van in the same train. The case was provided with a hole for ventilation.

From Jagdalpur, Tulsi Babu set off in a luggage caravan with two coolies and the case, for the precise spot in the forest where he had found the bird.

At a certain milepost on the main road, Tulsi Babu got off the vehicle and, with the coolies carrying the packing case, set off for the scorched *neem* tree. It took nearly an hour to reach the spot. The coolies put the case down. They had already been generously tipped and told that they would have to open the packing case. This was done, and Tulsi Babu was relieved to see that Bill was in fine fettle. The coolies, of course, bolted screaming at the sight of the bird, but that didn't worry Tulsi Babu. His purpose had been served. Bill was looking at him with a fixed stare. Its head already touched the four and a half foot high roof of the cage.

'Good-bye, Bill.'

The sooner the parting took place the better.

Tulsi Babu started his journey back to the Tempo.

Tulsi Babu hadn't told anybody in the office about his trip, not even Prodyot Babu, who naturally asked where he had been when he appeared at his desk on Monday. Tulsi Babu replied briefly that he had been to a niece's wedding in Naihati.

About a fortnight later, on a visit to Tulsi Babu's place, Prodyot Babu was surprised to see the cage empty. He asked about the bird. 'It's gone,' said Tulsi Babu.

Prodyot Babu naturally assumed that the bird was dead. He felt a twinge of remorse. He hadn't meant it seriously when he had said that the photo would remind Tulsi Babu of his pet when it was no more; he had no idea the bird would die so soon. The photograph he had taken had been framed and was hanging on the wall of the bedroom. Tulsi Babu seemed out of sorts; altogether the atmosphere was gloomy. To relieve the gloom, Prodyot Babu made a suggestion. 'We haven't been to Mansur's in long while. What about going tonight for a meal of *kebab* and *paratha*?'

'I'm afraid I have quite lost my taste for them.'

Prodyot Babu couldn't believe his ears. 'Lost your taste for *kebabs*? What's the matter? Aren't you well? Have you tried the herb the holy man prescribed?'

Tulsi Babu said that his blood pressure had come down to normal since he tried the juice of the *chakra-parna*. What he didn't bother to mention was that he had forgotten all about herbal medicines as long as Bill had been with him, and that he had gone back to them only a week ago.

'By the way,' remarked Prodyot Babu, 'the mention of the herb reminds me – did you read in the papers today about the forest of Dandakaranya?'

'What did the papers say?'

Tulsi Babu bought a daily newspaper all right, but rarely got beyond the first page. The paper was near at hand. Prodyot Babu pointed out the news to him. The headline said 'The Terror of Dandakaranya'.

The news described a sudden and unexpected threat to the

domestic animals and poultry in the villages around the forests of Dandakaranya. Some unknown species of animal had started to devour them. No tigers are known to exist in that area, and proof has been found that something other than a feline species had been causing the havoc. Tigers usually drag their prey to their lairs; this particular beast doesn't. The shikaris engaged by the Madhya Pradesh Government had searched for a week but failed to locate any beasts capable of such carnage. As a result, panic has spread amongst the villagers. One particular villager claims that he had seen a two-legged creature running away from his cowshed. He had gone to investigate, and found his buffalo lying dead with a sizeable portion of his lower abdomen eaten away.

Tulsi Babu read the news, folded the paper, and put it back on the table.

'Don't tell me you don't find anything exceptional in the story?' said Prodyot Babu.

Tulsi Babu shook his head. In other words, he didn't.

Three days later a strange thing happened to Prodyot Babu.

At breakfast, his wife opened a tin of Digestive biscuits and served them to her husband with his tea.

The next moment Prodyot Babu had left the dining-table and rushed out of the house.

By the time he reached his friend Animesh's flat in Ekdalia Road, he was trembling with excitement.

He snatched the newspaper away from his friend's hands, threw it aside and said panting: 'Where d'you keep your copies of *Readers' Digest*? Quick – it's most important!'

Animesh shared with millions of others a taste for *Readers' Digest*. He was greatly surprised by his friend's behaviour but scarcely had the opportunity to show it. He went to a book-case and dragged out some dozen issues of the magazine from the bottom shelf.

'Which number are you looking for?'

Prodyot Babu took the whole bunch, flipped through the pages issue after issue, and finally found what he was looking for.

'Yes – this is the bird. No doubt about it.'

His fingers rested on a picture of a conjectural model of a bird kept in the Chicago Museum of Natural History. It showed an attendant cleaning the model with a brush.

'*Andalgalornis*,' said Prodyot Babu, reading out the name. The name meant terror-bird. A huge prehistoric species, carnivorous, faster than a horse, and extremely ferocious.

The doubt which had crept into Prodyot Babu's mind was proved right when in the office next morning Tulsi Babu came to him and said that he had to go to Dandakaranya once again, and that he would be delighted if Prodyot Babu would join him and bring his gun with him. There was too little time to obtain sleeping accommodation in the train, but that couldn't be helped as the matter was very urgent.

Prodyot Babu agreed at once.

In the excitement of the pursuit, the two friends didn't mind the discomfort of the journey. Prodyot Babu said nothing about the bird in the *Readers' Digest*. He could do so later; there was plenty of time for that. Tulsi Babu had in the meantime told everything to Prodyot Babu. He had also mentioned that he didn't really believe the gun would be needed; he had suggested taking it only as a precaution. Prodyot Babu, on the other hand, couldn't share his friend's optimism. He believed the gun was essential, and he was fully prepared for any eventuality. Today's paper had mentioned that the Madhya Pradesh Government had announced a reward of 5,000 rupees to anyone who succeeded in killing or capturing the creature, which had been declared a man-eater ever since a woodcutter's son had fallen victim to it.

In Jagdalpur, permission to shoot the creature was obtained from the conservator of forests, Mr Tirumalai. But he warned that Tulsi Babu and Prodyot Babu would have to go on their own as nobody could be persuaded to go into the forest any more.

Prodyot Babu asked if any information had been received from the shikaris who had preceded them. Tirumalai turned grave. 'So far four shikaris have attempted to kill the beast. Three of them had no success. The fourth never returned.'

'Never returned?'

'No. Ever since then shikaris have been refusing to go. So you had better think twice before undertaking the trip.'

Prodyot Babu was shaken, but his friend's nonchalance brought back his courage. 'I think we will go,' he said.

This time they had to walk a little further because the taxi refused to take the dirt road which went part of the way into the forest. Tulsi Babu was confident that the job would be over in two hours, and the taxi agreed to wait that long upon being given a tip of fifty rupees. The two friends set off on their quest.

It being springtime now, the forest wore a different look from the previous trips. Nature was following its course, and yet there was an unnatural silence. There were no bird calls; not even the cries of cuckoos.

As usual, Tulsi Babu was carrying his shoulder bag. Prodyot Babu knew there was a packet in it, but he didn't know what it contained. Prodyot Babu himself was carrying his rifle and bullets.

As the undergrowth was thinner they could see farther into the forest. That is why the two friends were able to see from a distance the body of a man lying spread-eagled on the ground behind a jackfruit tree. Tulsi Babu hadn't noticed it, and stopped only when Prodyot Babu pointed it out to him. Prodyot Babu took a firm grip on the gun and walked towards the body. Tulsi Babu seemed only vaguely interested in the matter.

Prodyot Babu went halfway, and then turned back.

'You look as if you've seen a ghost,' said Tulsi Babu when his friend rejoined him. 'Isn't that the missing shikari?'

'It must be,' said Prodyot Babu hoarsely. 'But it won't be easy to identify the corpse. The head's missing.'

The rest of the way they didn't speak at all.

It took one hour to reach the *neem* tree, which meant they must have walked at least three miles. Prodyot Babu noticed that the medicinal shrub had grown fresh leaves and was back to its old shape.

'Bill! Billie!'

There was something faintly comic about the call, and Prodyot Babu couldn't help smiling. But the next moment he realised that for Tulsi Babu the call was quite natural. That he had succeeded in taming the monster bird, Prodyot Babu had seen with his own eyes.

Tulsi Babu's call resounded in the forest.

'Bill! Bill! Billie!'

Now Prodyot Babu saw something stirring in the depths of the forest. It was coming towards them, and at such a speed that it seemed to grow bigger and bigger every second.

It was the monster bird.

The gun in Prodyot Babu's hand suddenly felt very heavy. He wondered if he would be able to use it at all.

The bird slowed down and approached them stealthily through the vegetation.

Andalgalornis. Prodyot Babu would never forget the name. A bird as tall as a man. Ostriches were tall too; but that was largely because of their neck. This bird's back itself was as high as an average man. In other words, the bird had grown a foot and a half in just about a month. The colour of its plumes had changed too. There were blotches of black on the purple. And the malevolent look in its amber eyes which Prodyot Babu found he could confront when the bird was in captivity, was now for him unbearably terrifying. The look was directed at its ex-master.

There was no knowing what the bird would do. Thinking its stillness to be a prelude to an attack, Prodyot Babu had made an attempt to raise the gun with his shaking hands. But the moment he did so, the bird turned its gaze at him, its feathers puffing out to give it an even more terrifying appearance.

'Lower the gun,' hissed Tulsi Babu in a tone of admonition.

Prodyot Babu obeyed. Now the bird lowered its feathers too and transferred its gaze to its master.

'I don't know if you are still hungry,' said Tulsi Babu, 'but I hope you will eat this because I am giving it to you.'

Tulsi Babu had already brought out the packet from the bag. He now unwrapped it and tossed the contents towards the bird. It was a large chunk of meat.

'You've been the cause of my shame. I hope you will behave yourself from now on.'

Prodyot Babu saw that the bird picked up the chunk with its huge beak, and proceeded to masticate it.

'This time it really is good-bye.'

Tulsi Babu turned. Prodyot Babu was afraid to turn his back on the bird, and for a while walked backwards with his eyes on the bird. When he found that the bird was making no attempt to follow him or attack him, he too turned round and joined his friend.

A week later the news came out in the papers of the end of the terror in Dandakaranya. Prodyot Babu had not mentioned anything to Tulsi Babu about *Andalgalornis*, and the fact that the bird had been extinct for three million years. But the news in the papers today obliged him to come to his friend. 'I'm at a loss to know how it happened,' he said. 'Perhaps you may throw some light on it.'

'There's no mystery at all,' said Tulsi Babu. 'I only mixed some of my medicine with the meat I gave him.'

'Medicine?'

'An extract of *chakra-parna*. It turns one into a vegetarian. Just as it has done me.'

Salman Rushdie

THE PERFORATED SHEET

I WAS BORN IN the city of Bombay . . . once upon a time. No, that won't do, there's no getting away from the date: I was born in Doctor Narlikar's Nursing Home on August 15th, 1947. And the time? The time matters, too. Well then: at night. No, it's important to be more . . . On the stroke of midnight, as a matter of fact. Clock-hands joined palms in respectful greeting as I came. Oh, spell it out, spell it out: at the precise instant of India's arrival at independence, I tumbled forth into the world. There were gasps. And, outside the window, fireworks and crowds. A few seconds later, my father broke his big toe; but his accident was a mere trifle when set beside what had befallen me in that benighted moment, because thanks to the occult tyrannies of those blandly saluting clocks I had been mysteriously handcuffed to history, my destinies indissolubly chained to those of my country. For the next three decades, there was to be no escape. Soothsayers had prophesied me, newspapers celebrated my arrival, politicos ratified my authenticity. I was left entirely without a say in the matter. I, Saleem Sinai, later variously called Snotnose, Stainface, Baldy, Sniffer, Buddha and even Piece-of-the-Moon, had become heavily embroiled in Fate – at the best of times a dangerous sort of involvement. And I couldn't even wipe my own nose at the time.

Now, however, time (having no further use for me) is running out. I will soon be thirty-one years old. Perhaps. If my

Extracts from the novel *Midnight's Children*.

crumbling, over-used body permits. But I have no hope of saving my life, nor can I count on having even a thousand nights and a night. I must work fast, faster than Scheherazade, if I am to end up meaning – yes, meaning – something. I admit it: above all things, I fear absurdity.

And there are so many stories to tell, too many, such an excess of intertwined lives events miracles places rumours, so dense a commingling of the improbable and the mundane! I have been a swallower of lives; and to know me, just the one of me, you'll have to swallow the lot as well. Consumed multitudes are jostling and shoving inside me; and guided only by the memory of a large white bedsheet with a roughly circular hole some seven inches in diameter cut into the centre, clutching at the dream of that holey, mutilated square of linen, which is my talisman, my open-sesame, I must commence the business of remaking my life from the point at which it really began, some thirty-two years before anything as obvious, as *present*, as my clock-ridden crime-stained birth.

(The sheet, incidentally, is stained too, with three drops of old, faded redness. As the Quran tells us: *Recite, in the name of the Lord thy Creator, who created Man from clots of blood.*)

One Kashmiri morning in the early spring of 1915, my grandfather Aadam Aziz hit his nose against a frost-hardened tussock of earth while attempting to pray. Three drops of blood plopped out of his left nostril, hardened instantly in the brittle air and lay before his eyes on the prayer-mat, transformed into rubies. Lurching back until he knelt with his head once more upright, he found that the tears which had sprung to his eyes had solidified, too; and at that moment, as he brushed diamonds contemptuously from his lashes, he resolved never again to kiss earth for any god or man. This decision, however, made a hole in him, a vacancy in a vital inner chamber, leaving him vulnerable to women and history. Unaware of this at first, despite his recently completed medical training, he stood up, rolled the prayer-mat into a thick cheroot, and holding it under his right arm surveyed the valley through clear, diamond-free eyes.

The world was new again. After a winter's gestation in its eggshell of ice, the valley had beaked its way out into the open, moist and yellow. The new grass bided its time underground; the mountains were retreating to their hill-stations for the warm season. (In the winter, when the valley shrank under the ice, the mountains closed in and snarled like angry jaws around the city on the lake.)

In those days the radio mast had not been built and the temple of Sankara Acharya, a little black blister on a khaki hill, still dominated the streets and lake of Srinagar. In those days there was no army camp at the lakeside, no endless snakes of camouflaged trucks and jeeps clogged the narrow mountain roads, no soldiers hid behind the crests of the mountains past Baramulla and Gulmarg. In those days travellers were not shot as spies if they took photographs of bridges, and apart from the Englishmen's houseboats on the lake, the valley had hardly changed since the Mughal Empire, for all its springtime renewals; but my grandfather's eyes – which were, like the rest of him, twenty-five years old – saw things differently . . . and his nose had started to itch.

To reveal the secret of my grandfather's altered vision: he had spent five years, five springs, away from home. (The tussock of earth, crucial though its presence was as it crouched under a chance wrinkle of the prayer-mat, was at bottom no more than a catalyst.) Now, returning, he saw through travelled eyes. Instead of the beauty of the tiny valley circled by giant teeth, he noticed the narrowness, the proximity of the horizon; and felt sad, to be at home and feel so utterly enclosed. He also felt – inexplicably – as though the old place resented his educated, stethoscoped return. Beneath the winter ice, it had been coldly neutral, but now there was no doubt; the years in Germany had returned him to a hostile environment. Many years later, when the hole inside him had been clogged up with hate, and he came to sacrifice himself at the shrine of the black stone god in the temple on the hill, he would try and recall his childhood springs in Paradise, the way it was before travel and tussocks and army tanks messed everything up.

On the morning when the valley, gloved in a prayer-mat,

punched him on the nose, he had been trying, absurdly, to pretend that nothing had changed. So he had risen in the bitter cold of four-fifteen, washed himself in the prescribed fashion, dressed and put on his father's astrakhan cap; after which he had carried the rolled cheroot of the prayer-mat into the small lakeside garden in front of their old dark house and unrolled it over the waiting tussock. The ground felt deceptively soft under his feet and made him simultaneously uncertain and unwary. 'In the Name of God, the Compassionate, the Merciful . . .' – the exordium, spoken with hands joined before him like a book, comforted a part of him, made another, larger part feel uneasy – '. . . Praise be to Allah, Lord of the Creation . . .' – but now Heidelberg invaded his head; here was Ingrid, briefly his Ingrid, her face scorning him for this Mecca-turned parroting; here, their friends Oskar and Ilse Lubin the anarchists, mocking his prayer with their anti-ideologies – '. . . The Compassionate, the Merciful, King of the Last Judgment! . . .' – Heidelberg, in which, along with medicine and politics, he learned that India – like radium – had been 'discovered' by the Europeans; even Oskar was filled with admiration for Vasco da Gama, and this was what finally separated Aadam Aziz from his friends, this belief of theirs that he was somehow the invention of their ancestors – '. . . You alone we worship, and to You alone we pray for help . . .' – so here he was, despite their presence in his head, attempting to re-unite himself with an earlier self which ignored their influence but knew everything it ought to have known, about submission for example, about what he was doing now, as his hands, guided by old memories, fluttered upwards, thumbs pressed to ears, fingers spread, as he sank to his knees – '. . . Guide us to the straight path, The path of those whom You have favoured . . .' But it was no good, he was caught in a strange middle ground, trapped between belief and disbelief, and this was only a charade after all – '. . . Not of those who have incurred Your wrath, Nor of those who have gone astray.' My grandfather bent his forehead towards the earth. Forward he bent, and the earth, prayer-mat-covered, curved up towards him. And now it was the tussock's time. At one and the same time a rebuke from Ilse-Oskar-Ingrid-Heidelberg as well as valley-and-God, it smote him upon the point of the nose. Three drops fell. There were rubies and diamonds. And my grandfather, lurching upright, made a resolve. Stood. Rolled cheroot. Stared across the lake. And was knocked forever into that middle place, unable to worship a God in whose existence he could not wholly disbelieve. Permanent alteration: a hole.

The lake was no longer frozen over. The thaw had come rapidly, as usual; many of the small boats, the shikaras, had been caught napping, which was also normal. But while these sluggards slept on, on dry land, snoring peacefully beside their owners, the oldest boat was up at the crack as old folk often are, and was therefore the first craft to move across the unfrozen lake. Tai's shikara . . . this, too, was customary.

Watch how the old boatman, Tai, makes good time through the misty water, standing stooped over at the back of his craft! How his oar, a wooden heart on a yellow stick, drives jerkily through the weeds! In these parts he's considered very odd because he rows standing up . . . among other reasons. Tai, bringing an urgent summons to Doctor Aziz, is about to set history in motion . . . while Aadam, looking down into the water, recalls what Tai taught him years ago: 'The ice is always waiting, Aadam baba, just under the water's skin.' Aadam's eyes are a clear blue, the astonishing blue of mountain sky, which has a habit of dripping into the pupils of Kashmiri men; they have not forgotten how to look. They see – there! like the skeleton of a ghost, just beneath the surface of Lake Dal! – the delicate tracery, the intricate crisscross of colourless lines, the cold waiting veins of the future. His German years, which have blurred so much else, haven't deprived him of the gift of seeing. Tai's gift. He looks up, sees the approaching V of Tai's boat, waves a greeting. Tai's arm rises – but this is a command. 'Wait!' My grandfather waits; and during this hiatus, as he experiences the last peace of his life, a muddy, ominous sort of peace, I had better get round to describing him.

Keeping out of my voice the natural envy of the ugly man for the strikingly impressive, I record that Doctor Aziz was a tall man. Pressed flat against a wall of his family home, he measured twenty-five bricks (a brick for each year of his life), or just over six foot two. A strong man also. His beard was thick and red – and annoyed his mother, who said only Hajis, men who had made the pilgrimage to Mecca, should grow red beards. His hair, however, was rather darker. His sky-eyes you know about. Ingrid had said, 'They went mad with the colours when they made your face.' But the central feature of my grandfather's anatomy was neither colour nor height, neither strength of arm nor straightness of back. There it was, reflected in the water, undulating like a mad plantain in the centre of his face . . . Aadam Aziz, waiting for Tai, watches his rippling nose. It would have dominated less dramatic faces than his easily; even on him, it is what one sees first and remembers longest. 'A cyranose,' Ilse Lubin said, and Oskar added, 'A proboscissimus.' Ingrid announced, 'You could cross a river on that nose.' (Its bridge was wide.)

My grandfather's nose: nostrils flaring, curvaceous as dancers. Between them swells the nose's triumphal arch, first up and out, then down and under, sweeping in to his upper lip with a superb and at present red-tipped flick. An easy nose to hit a tussock with. I wish to place on record my gratitude to this mighty organ – if not for it, who would ever have believed me to be truly my mother's son, my grandfather's grandson? – this colossal apparatus which was to be my birthright, too. Doctor Aziz's nose – comparable only to the trunk of the elephant-headed god Ganesh – established incontrovertibly his right to be a patriarch. It was Tai who taught him that, too. When young Aadam was barely past puberty the dilapidated boatman said, 'That's a nose to start a family on, my princeling. There'd be no mistaking whose brood they were. Mughal Emperors would have given their right hands for noses like that one. There are dynasties waiting inside it,' – and here Tai lapsed into coarseness – 'like snot.'

Nobody could remember when Tai had been young. He

had been plying this same boat, standing in the same hunched position, across the Dal and Nageen Lakes . . . forever. As far as anyone knew. He lived somewhere in the insanitary bowels of the old wooden-house quarter and his wife grew lotus roots and other curious vegetables on one of the many 'floating gardens' lilting on the surface of the spring and summer water. Tai himself cheerily admitted he had no idea of his age. Neither did his wife – he was, she said, already leathery when they married. His face was a sculpture of wind on water: ripples made of hide. He had two golden teeth and no others. In the town, he had few friends. Few boatmen or traders invited him to share a hookah when he floated past the shikara moorings or one of the lakes' many ramshackle, waterside provision-stores and tea-shops.

The general opinion of Tai had been voiced long ago by Aadam Aziz's father the gemstone merchant: 'His brain fell out with his teeth.' It was an impression the boatmen fostered by his chatter, which was fantastic, grandiloquent and ceaseless, and as often as not addressed only to himself. Sound carries over water, and the lake people giggled at his monologues; but with undertones of awe, and even fear. Awe, because the old halfwit knew the lakes and hills better than any of his detractors; fear, because of his claim to an antiquity so immense it defied numbering, and moreover hung so lightly round his chicken's neck that it hadn't prevented him from winning a highly desirable wife and fathering four sons upon her . . . and a few more, the story went, on other lakeside wives. The young bucks at the shikara moorings were convinced he had a pile of money hidden away somewhere – a hoard, perhaps, of priceless golden teeth, rattling in a sack like walnuts. And, as a child, Aadam Aziz had loved him.

He made his living as a simple ferryman, despite all the rumours of wealth, taking hay and goats and vegetables and wood across the lakes for cash; people, too. When he was running his taxi-service he erected a pavilion in the centre of the shikara, a gay affair of flowered-patterned curtains and canopy, with cushions to match; and deodorised his boat with

incense. The sight of Tai's shikara approaching, curtains flying, had always been for Doctor Aziz one of the defining
images of the coming of spring. Soon the English sahibs
would arrive and Tai would ferry them to the Shalimar
Gardens and the King's Spring, chattering and pointy and
stooped, a quirky, enduring familiar spirit of the valley. A
watery Caliban, rather too fond of cheap Kashmiri brandy.

The Boy Aadam, my grandfather-to-be, fell in love with the
boatman Tai precisely because of the endless verbiage which
made others think him cracked. It was magical talk, words
pouring from him like fools' money, past his two gold teeth,
laced with hiccups and brandy, soaring up to the most remote
Himalayas of the past, then swooping shrewdly on some present detail. Aadam's nose for instance, to vivisect its meaning
like a mouse. This friendship had plunged Aadam into hot
water with great regularity. (Boiling water. Literally. While
his mother said, 'We'll kill that boatman's bugs if it kills
you.') But still the old soliloquist would dawdle in his boat at
the garden's lakeside toes and Aziz would sit at his feet until
voices summoned him indoors to be lectured on Tai's filthi-
ness and warned about the pillaging armies of germs his
mother envisaged leaping from that hospitably ancient body
on to her son's starched white loose-pajamas. But always
Aadam returned to the water's edge to scan the mists for the
ragged reprobate's hunched-up frame steering its magical
boat through the enchanted waters of the morning.

'But how old are you really, Taiji?' (Doctor Aziz, adult, red-
bearded, slanting towards the future, remembers the day he
asked the unaskable question.) For an instant, silence, noisier
than a waterfall. The monologue, interrupted. Slap of oar in
water. He was riding in the shikara with Tai, squatting
amongst goats, on a pile of straw, in full knowledge of the
stick and bathtub waiting for him at home. He had come for
stories – and with one question had silenced the storyteller.

'No, tell, Taiji, how old, *truly*?' And now a brandy bottle,
materialising from nowhere: cheap liquor from the folds of
the great warm chugha-coat. Then a shudder, a belch, a glare.
Glint of gold. And – at last! – speech. 'How old? You ask how

old, you little wet-head, you nosey . . .' Tai pointed at the mountains. 'So old, nakkoo!' Aadam, the nakkoo, the nosey one, followed his pointing finger. 'I have watched the mountains being born; I have seen Emperors die. Listen. Listen, nakkoo . . .' – the brandy bottle again, followed by brandy-voice, and words more intoxicating than booze – '. . . I saw that Isa, that Christ, when he came to Kashmir. Smile, smile, it is your history I am keeping in my head. Once it was set down in old lost books. Once I knew where there was a grave with pierced feet carved on the tombstone, which bled once a year. Even my memory is going now; but I know, although I can't read.' Illiteracy, dismissed with a flourish; literature crumbled beneath the rage of his sweeping hand. Which sweeps again to chugha-pocket, to brandy bottle, to lips chapped with cold. Tai always had woman's lips. 'Nakkoo, listen, listen. I have seen plenty. Yara, you should've seen that Isa when he came, beard down to his balls, bald as an egg on his head. He was old and fagged-out but he knew his manners. "You first, Taiji," he'd say, and "Please to sit"; always a respectful tongue, he never called me crackpot, never called me *tu* either. Always *aap*. Polite, see? And what an appetite! Such a hunger, I would catch my ears in fright. Saint or devil, I swear he could eat a whole kid in one go. And so what? I told him, eat, fill your hole, a man comes to Kashmir to enjoy life, or to end it, or both. His work was finished. He just came up here to live it up a little.' Mesmerised by this brandied portrait of a bald, gluttonous Christ, Aziz listened, later repeating every word to the consternation of his parents, who dealt in stones and had no time for 'gas'.

'Oh, you don't believe?' – licking his sore lips with a grin, knowing it to be the reverse of the truth; 'Your attention is wandering?' – again, he knew how furiously Aziz was hanging on his words. 'Maybe the straw is pricking your behind, hey? Oh, I'm so sorry, babaji, not to provide for you silk cushions with gold brocade-work – cushions such as the Emperor Jehangir sat upon! You think the Emperor Jehangir as a gardener only, no doubt,' Tai accused my grandfather, 'because he built Shalimar. Stupid! What do you know? His name meant Encompasser of the Earth. Is that a gardener's name? God knows what they teach you boys these days. Whereas I' . . . puffing up a little here . . . 'I knew his precise weight, to the tola! Ask me how many maunds, how many seers! When he was happy he got heavier and in Kashmir he was heaviest of all. I used to carry his litter . . . no, no, look, you don't believe again, that big cucumber in your face is waggling like the little one in your pajamas! So, come on, come on, ask me questions! Give examination! Ask how many times the leather thongs wound round the handles of the litter – the answer is thirty-one. Ask me what was the Emperor's dying word – I tell you it was "Kashmir". He had bad breath and a good heart. Who do you think I am? Some common ignorant lying pie-dog? Go, get out of the boat now, your nose makes it too heavy to row; also your father is waiting to beat my gas out of you, and your mother to boil off your skin.'

Despite beating and boiling, Aadam Aziz floated with Tai in his shikara, again and again, amid goats hay flowers furniture lotus-roots, though never with the English sahibs, and heard again and again the miraculous answers to that single terrifying question: 'But Taiji, how old are you, *honestly*?'

From Tai, Aadam learned the secrets of the lake – where you could swim without being pulled down by weeds; the eleven varieties of water-snake; where the frogs spawned; how to cook a lotus-root; and where the three English women had drowned a few years back. 'There is a tribe of feringhee women who come to this water to drown,' Tai said. 'Sometimes they know it, sometimes they don't, but I know the minute I smell them. They hide under the water from God knows what or who – but they can't hide from me, baba!' Tai's laugh, emerging to infect Aadam – a huge, booming laugh that seemed macabre when it crashed out of that old, withered body, but which was so natural in my giant grandfather that nobody knew, in later times, that it wasn't really his. And, also from Tai, my grandfather heard about noses.

Tai tapped his left nostril. 'You know what this is, nakkoo? It's the place where the outside world meets the world inside you. If they don't get on, you feel it here. Then you rub your nose with embarrassment to make the itch go away. A nose like that, little idiot, is a great gift. I say: trust it. When it warns you, look out or you'll be finished. Follow your nose and you'll go far.' He cleared his throat; his eyes rolled away into the mountains of the past. Aziz settled back on the straw. 'I knew one officer once – in the army of that Iskandar the Great. Never mind his name. He had a vegetable just like yours hanging between his eyes. When the army halted near Gandhara, he fell in love with some local floozy. At once his nose itched like crazy. He scratched it, but that was useless. He inhaled vapours from crushed boiled eucalyptus leaves. Still no good, baba! The itching sent him wild; but the damn fool dug in his heels and stayed with his little witch when the army went home. He became – what? – a stupid thing, neither this nor that, a half-and-halfer with a nagging wife and an itch in the nose, and in the end he pushed his sword into his stomach. What do you think of that?'

Doctor Aziz in 1915, whom rubies and diamonds have turned into a half-and-halfer, remembers this story as Tai enters hailing distance. His nose is itching still. He scratches, shrugs, tosses his head; and then Tai shouts.

'Ohé! Doctor Sahib! Ghani the landowner's daughter is sick.'

. . . The young Doctor has entered the throes of a most unhippocratic excitement at the boatman's cry, and shouts, 'I'm coming just now! Just let me bring my things!' The shikara's prow touches the garden's hem. Aadam is rushing indoors, prayer-mat rolled like a cheroot under one arm, blue eyes blinking in the sudden interior gloom; he has placed the cheroot on a high shelf on top of stacked copies of *Vorwärts* and Lenin's *What Is To Be Done?* and other pamphlets, dusty echoes of his half-faded German life; he is pulling out, from under his bed, a second-hand leather case which his mother called his 'doctori-attaché', and as he swings it and himself upwards and runs from the room, the word HEIDELBERG is briefly visible, burned into the leather on the bottom of the bag. A landowner's daughter is good news indeed to a doctor with a career to make, even if she is ill. No: *because* she is ill.

. . . Slap of oar in water. Plop of spittle in lake. Tai clears his throat and mutters angrily, 'A fine business. A wet-head nakkoo child goes away before he's learned one damn thing and he comes back a big doctor sahib with a big bag full of foreign machines, and he's still as silly as an owl. I swear: a too bad business.'

. . . 'Big shot,' Tai is spitting into the lake, 'big bag, big shot. Pah! We haven't got enough bags at home that you must bring back that thing made of a pig's skin that makes one unclean just by looking at it? And inside, God knows what all.' Doctor Aziz, seated amongst flowery curtains and the smell of incense, has his thoughts wrenched away from the patient waiting across the lake. Tai's bitter monologue breaks into his consciousness, creating a sense of dull shock, a smell like a casualty ward overpowering the incense . . . the old man is clearly furious about something, possessed by an incomprehensible rage that appears to be directed at his erstwhile acolyte, or, more precisely and oddly, at his bag. Doctor Aziz attempts to make small talk . . . 'Your wife is well? Do they still talk about your bag of golden teeth?' . . . tries to remake an old friendship; but Tai is in full flight now, a stream of invective pouring out of him. The Heidelberg bag quakes under the torrent of abuse. 'Sistersleeping pigskin bag from Abroad full of foreigners' tricks. Big-shot bag. Now if a man breaks an arm that bag will not let the bone-setter bind it in leaves. Now a man must let his wife lie beside that bag and watch knives come and cut her open. A fine business, what these foreigners put in our young men's heads. I swear: it is a too-bad thing. That bag should fry in Hell with the testicles of the ungodly.'

. . . 'Do you still pickle water-snakes in brandy to give you virility, Taiji? Do you still like to eat lotus-root without any spices?' Hesitant questions, brushed aside by the torrent of Tai's fury. Doctor Aziz begins to diagnose. To the ferryman, the bag represents Abroad; it is the alien thing, the invader, progress. And yes, it has indeed taken possession of the young Doctor's mind; and yes, it contains knives, and cures for cholera and malaria and smallpox; and yes, it sits between doctor and boatman, and has made them antagonists. Doctor Aziz begins to fight, against sadness, and against Tai's anger, which is beginning to infect him, to become his own, which erupts only rarely, but comes, when it does come, unheralded in a roar from his deepest places, laying waste everything in sight; and then vanishes, leaving him wondering why everyone is so upset . . . They are approaching Ghani's house. A bearer awaits the shikara, standing with clasped hands on a little wooden jetty. Aziz fixes his mind on the job in hand.

The bearer holds the shikara steady as Aadam Aziz climbs out, bag in hand. And now, at last, Tai speaks directly to my grandfather. Scorn in his face, Tai asks, 'Tell me this, Doctor Sahib: have you got in that bag made of dead pigs one of those machines that foreign doctors use to smell with?' Aadam shakes his head, not understanding. Tai's voice gathers new layers of disgust. 'You know, sir, a thing like an elephant's trunk.' Aziz, seeing what he means, replies: 'A stethoscope? Naturally.' Tai pushes the shikara off from the jetty. Spits. Begins to row away. 'I knew it,' he says. 'You will use such a machine now, instead of your own big nose.'

My grandfather does not trouble to explain that a stethoscope is more like a pair of ears than a nose. He is stifling his own irritation, the resentful anger of a cast-off child; and besides, there is a patient waiting.

The house was opulent but badly lit. Ghani was a widower and the servants clearly took advantage. There were cobwebs in corners and layers of dust on ledges. They walked down a long corridor; one of the doors was ajar and through it Aziz saw a room in a state of violent disorder. This glimpse, connected with a glint of light in Ghani's dark glasses, suddenly informed Aziz that the landowner was blind. This aggravated his sense of unease . . . They halted outside a thick teak door. Ghani said, 'Wait here two moments,' and went into the room behind the door.

In later years, Doctor Aadam Aziz swore that during those two moments of solitude in the gloomy spidery corridors of the landowner's mansion he was gripped by an almost uncontrollable desire to turn and run away as fast as his legs would carry him. Unnerved by the enigma of the blind art-lover, his insides filled with tiny scrabbling insects as a result of the insidious venom of Tai's mutterings, his nostrils itching to the point of convincing him that he had somehow contracted venereal disease, he felt his feet begin slowly, as though encased in boots of lead, to turn; felt blood pounding in his temples; and was seized by so powerful a sensation of standing upon a point of no return that he very nearly wet his German woollen trousers. He began, without knowing it, to blush furiously; and at this point a woman with the biceps of a wrestler appeared, beckoning him to follow her into the room. The state of her sari told him that she was a servant; but she was not servile. 'You look green as a fish,' she said. 'You young doctors. You come into a strange house and your liver turns to jelly. Come, Doctor Sahib, they are waiting for you.' Clutching his bag a fraction too tightly, he followed her through the dark teak door.

. . . Into a spacious bedchamber that was as ill-lit as the rest of the house; although here there were shafts of dusty sunlight seeping in through a fanlight high on one wall. These fusty rays illuminated a scene as remarkable as anything the Doctor had ever witnessed: a tableau of such surpassing strangeness that his feet began to twitch towards the door once again. Two more women, also built like professional wrestlers, stood stiffly in the light, each holding one corner of an enormous white bedsheet, their arms raised high above their heads so that the sheet hung between them like a curtain. Mr Ghani welled up out of the murk surrounding the sunlit sheet and permitted the nonplussed Aadam to stare stupidly at the peculiar tableau for perhaps half a minute, at the end of which, and before a word had been spoken, the Doctor made a discovery:

In the very centre of the sheet, a hole had been cut, a crude circle about seven inches in diameter.

'Close the door, ayah,' Ghani instructed the first of the lady wrestlers, and then, turning to Aziz, became confidential. 'This town contains many good-for-nothings who have on

occasion tried to climb into my daughter's room. She needs,'
he nodded at the three musclebound women, 'protectors.'

Aziz was still looking at the perforated sheet. Ghani said,
'All right, come on, you will examine my Naseem right now.
Pronto.'

My grandfather peered around the room. 'But where is she,
Ghani Sahib?' he blurted out finally. The lady wrestlers
adopted supercilious expressions and, it seemed to him, tightened their musculatures, just in case he intended to try something fancy.

'Ah, I see your confusion,' Ghani said, his poisonous smile
broadening, 'You Europe-returned chappies forget certain
things. Doctor Sahib, my daughter is a decent girl, it goes
without saying. She does not flaunt her body under the noses
of strange men. You will understand that you cannot be permitted to see her, no, not in any circumstances; accordingly I
have required her to be positioned behind that sheet. She
stands there, like a good girl.'

A frantic note had crept into Doctor Aziz's voice. 'Ghani
Sahib, tell me how I am to examine her without looking at
her?' Ghani smiled on.

'You will kindly specify which portion of my daughter it is
necessary to inspect. I will then issue her with my instructions
to place the required segment against that hole which you see
there. And so, in this fashion the thing may be achieved.'

'But what, in any event, does the lady complain of?' – my
grandfather, despairingly. To which Mr Ghani, his eyes rising
upwards in their sockets, his smile twisting into a grimace of
grief, replied: 'The poor child! She has a terrible, a too dreadful stomach-ache.'

'In that case,' Doctor Aziz said with some restraint, 'will
she show me her stomach, please.'

My grandfather's premonitions in the corridor were not without foundation. In the succeeding months and years, he fell
under what I can only describe as the sorcerer's spell of that

enormous – and as yet unstained – perforated cloth.

In those years, you see, the landowner's daughter Naseem Ghani contracted a quite extraordinary number of minor ill-nesses, and each time a shikara-wallah was dispatched to summon the tall young Doctor sahib with the big nose who was making such a reputation for himself in the valley. Aadam Aziz's visits to the bedroom with the shaft of sunlight and the three lady wrestlers became weekly events; and on each occasion he was vouchsafed a glimpse, through the muti-lated sheet, of a different seven-inch circle of the young woman's body. Her initial stomach-ache was succeeded by a very slightly twisted right ankle, an ingrowing toenail on the big toe of the left foot, a tiny cut on the lower left calf. 'Tetanus is a killer, Doctor Sahib,' the landowner said, 'My Naseem must not die for a scratch.' There was the matter of her stiff right knee, which the Doctor was obliged to manipu-late through the hole in the sheet . . . and after a time the ill-nesses leapt upwards, avoiding certain unmentionable zones, and began to proliferate around her upper half. She suffered from something mysterious which her father called Finger Rot, which made the skin flake off her hands; from weakness of the wrist-bones, for which Aadam prescribed calcium tablets; and from attacks of constipation, for which he gave her a course of laxatives, since there was no question of being permitted to administer an enema. She had fevers and she also had subnormal temperatures. At these times his thermometer would be placed under her armpit and he would hum and haw about the relative inefficiency of the method. In the opposite armpit she once developed a slight case of tineachlo-ris and he dusted her with yellow powder; after this treatment – which required him to rub the powder in, gently but firmly, although the soft secret body began to shake and quiver and he heard helpless laughter coming through the sheet, because Naseem Ghani was very ticklish – the itching went away, but Naseem soon found a new set of complaints. She waxed anaemic in the summer and bronchial in the winter. ('Her tubes are most delicate,' Ghani explained, 'like little flutes.') Far away the Great War moved from crisis to crisis, while in the cobwebbed house Doctor Aziz was also engaged in a total war against his sectioned patient's inexhaustible complaints. And, in all those war years, Naseem never repeated an illness. 'Which only shows,' Ghani told him, 'that you are a good doctor. When you cure, she is cured for good. But alas!' – he struck his forehead – 'She pines for her late mother, poor baby, and her body suffers. She is a too loving child.'

So gradually Doctor Aziz came to have a picture of Naseem in his mind, a badly-fitting collage of her severally-inspected parts. This phantasm of a partitioned woman began to haunt him, and not only in his dreams. Glued together by his imagination, she accompanied him on all his rounds, she moved into the front room of his mind, so that waking and sleeping he could feel in his fingertips the softness of her ticklish skin or the perfect tiny wrists or the beauty of the ankles; he could smell her scent of lavender and chambeli; he could hear her voice and her helpless laughter of a little girl; but she was headless, because he had never seen her face.

By 1918, Aadam Aziz had come to live for his regular trips across the lake. And now his eagerness became even more intense, because it became clear that, after three years, the landowner and his daughter had become willing to lower certain barriers. Now, for the first time, Ghani said, 'A lump in the right chest. Is it worrying, Doctor? Look. Look well.' And there, framed in the hole, was a perfectly-formed and lyrically lovely . . . 'I must touch it,' Aziz said, fighting with his voice. Ghani slapped him on the back. 'Touch, touch!' he cried. 'The hands of the healer! The curing touch, eh, Doctor?' And Aziz reached out a hand . . . 'Forgive me for asking; but is it the lady's time of the month?' . . . Little secret smiles appearing on the faces of the lady wrestlers. Ghani, nodding affably: 'Yes. Don't be so embarrassed, old chap. We are family and doctor now.' And Aziz, 'Then don't worry. The lumps will go when the time ends.' . . . And the next time, 'A pulled muscle in the back of her thigh, Doctor Sahib. Such pain!' And there, in the sheet, weakening the eyes of Aadam Aziz, hung a superbly rounded and impossible buttock . . . And now Aziz: 'Is it permitted that . . .' Whereupon a word from Ghani; an obedient reply from behind the sheet; a drawstring pulled; and pajamas fall from the celestial rump, which swells wondrously through the hole. Aadam Aziz forces himself into a medical frame of mind . . . reaches out . . . feels. And swears to himself, in amazement, that he sees the bottom reddening in a shy, but compliant blush.

That evening, Aadam contemplated the blush. Did the magic of the sheet work on both sides of the hole? Excitedly, he envisaged his headless Naseem tingling beneath the scrutiny of his eyes, his thermometer, his stethoscope, his fingers, and trying to build a picture in her mind of *him*. She was at a disadvantage, of course, having seen nothing but his hands . . . Aadam began to hope with an illicit desperation for Naseem Ghani to develop a migraine or graze her unseen chin, so they could look each other in the face. He knew how unprofessional his feelings were; but did nothing to stifle them. There was not much he could do. They had acquired a life of their own. In short: my grandfather had fallen in love, and had come to think of the perforated sheet as something sacred and magical, because through it he had seen the things which had filled up the hole inside him which had been created when he had been hit on the nose by a tussock and insulted by the boatman Tai.

On the day the World War ended, Naseem developed the longed-for headache. Such historical coincidences have littered, and perhaps befouled, my family's existence in the world.

He hardly dared to look at what was framed in the hole in the sheet. Maybe she was hideous; perhaps that explained all this performance . . . he looked. And saw a soft face that was not at all ugly, a cushioned setting for her glittering, gemstone eyes, which were brown with flecks of gold: tiger's-eyes. Doctor Aziz's fall was complete. And Naseem burst out, 'But Doctor, my God, what a *nose*!' Ghani, angrily, 'Daughter, mind your . . .' But patient and doctor were laughing together, and Aziz was saying, 'Yes, yes, it is a remarkable specimen. They tell me there are dynasties waiting in it . . .' And he bit his tongue because he had been about to add, '. . . like snot.'

And Ghani, who had stood blindly beside the sheet for three long years, smiling and smiling and smiling, began once again to smile his secret smile, which was mirrored in the lips of the wrestlers.

Padma Perera

DR SALAAM

DR 'SALAAM' WAS what he eventually came to be called by his patients, because they couldn't twist their tongues around his real name, which was Schlamm. 'Salaam,' they would greet him, 'salaam, Dr Salaam,' and he would salaam back with equal gravity.

We saw him first when he moved into the Hibinett house, next door. It was called the Hibinett house because a wealthy Swedish match manufacturer of that name had once lived there and startled the entire neighbourhood by singing operatic arias at the top of his voice in the middle of the night. But nobody complained, because, after all, the man had a right to sing in his own house, and since he was far from his country and did not have any family in evidence, it was concluded that he must be lonely and in need of recreation. Foreigners had strange ideas; this was probably one of them.

The Hibinett house was the newest building in the Nungambakam locality of Madras, where we lived, and where most of the other houses were about a hundred years old. The oldest servants in the servants' quarters said that our particular neighbourhood had been inhabited at the turn of the century by Japanese merchants, some of whom had continued to live there until just a few years before the Second World War. These men kept cats, and in the half-dark of an early southern twilight you could still see silent feline shapes skulking along the garden walls or rummaging through the garbage. It wasn't until Dr Schlamm arrived with his enormous marmalade, Toni, that the Japanese cats were routed once and for all; Toni emerged from his battles with a ragged tail and generally moth-eaten fur, but the earlier cats left and Dr Schlamm and his Toni considered themselves well established in their own domain. Every evening, we heard the Doctor, who was both absent-minded and near-sighted, walk up and down the gravelled drive, calling for his cat.

The driveways of the Nungambakam houses were all shadowed and cool; their gardens stirred with green depths. The garden walls were mellowed to the beautiful dignity of sunwarmed stone, and the tamarind trees that lined the drives had a way of placing a person in his perspective, giving him an inevitable location, with textures of his past and present woven into the shadows they threw around him. Under those trees you could see, for instance, that Dr Schlamm was an Austrian Jewish refugee, about thirty-five, a lonely man; that he had come to India some years ago and taken it to heart – the whole unwieldy, contradictory mass of it – and been embraced as cordially in return. But the sense of being alien had remained, and he was assuaging his loneliness for the first time now, as he told us, by smiling at his neighbours.

Actually, Dr Schlamm had met my father long before he smiled at any of us. In fact, his decision to move into the Hibinett house had stemmed from this meeting, which had occurred soon after his arrival in India during the early years of the war. Characteristically, my father had spoken little of this, so it wasn't until very much later that I heard the incident described by Dr Schlamm himself. My sister and I were sitting together on the front steps of our house on a spring evening, when he came and ensconced himself comfortably between the two of us, announcing that he liked the idea of sitting between sisters, and going on from there to talk of his friendship with our father and the events that had led to his moving in next door.

Ten years ago, he said, he had started his practice in Madras by establishing the Schlamm Clinic on Mount Road, where he lived in a poky little room above the office and ate at an Irani restaurant across the street. The practice fared better than he expected, and when the New Year came around, he took two weeks off to go down to a seaside village he had heard about, four hundred miles south and facing the strait between India and Ceylon. My father, in Government service, happened at that time to be magistrate for the district in which the village lay.

It was a smaller village than any Dr Schlamm had yet seen. There was a cluster of mud huts along the coast (fishermen), near the fields (farmers), and beside the new road (labourers); and one solitary brick house with a bright-red tiled roof. The brick house, staffed by a cook and a caretaker, was called a Travellers' Bungalow, and had been built by the Government to accommodate officers touring on duty in the more remote districts. It consisted of two sets of rooms with a veranda all around, where the roof sloped steeply down to meet a row of supporting wooden pillars. Here Dr Schlamm sat in an easy chair, smoking and watching the sea and thinking his thoughts. In the mornings, he swam; in the afternoons he went for a walk along the fields or by the sea, followed by an inevitable column of ragged children with their fingers in their mouths, staring at him because he was probably the first white man they had ever seen – apart from a British official who had once visited the village six years ago, when they were too young to remember anyway.

But it was understood that Dr Schlamm was not an official; neither was he British. He spoke German, and this was during the war, so, though they smiled shyly at him, they kept their distance. Then one day the sleepy old caretaker suddenly came to life and began to sweep the veranda; the cook rushed around with preparations for an elaborate meal – until a dusty jeep came bumping along the village road and a red-coated peon from the magistrate's office hopped out and told them to keep everything as simple as possible because the magistrate-*dorai* disliked fuss.

The magistrate-*dorai* arrived late at night, and turned out to have an unobtrusive chuckle at the back of his voice. When he invited Dr Schlamm to dinner, the Doctor told us he found a man who bore his authority without pretensions, wearing it rather like a dispensable suit – a man who had travelled much and read much and knew his country with the precision and detachment of an ideal Man of Duty lauded by the Bhagavid-Gita. 'It was there in your father that I saw for the first time all the qualities embodied in one man,' he said. 'The combination of a personal and impersonal integrity, the emphasis on a deed for its own sake, the irrelevance of any reward – all of it lightened by a sense of humour. It was fascinating.'

Next day, Father was away on a tour of inspection, and during the drowsy part of the afternoon the hum of an aeroplane first began. Dr Schlamm was reading, and only registered the fact at the back of his mind. It was a common enough sound in Madras; it did not strike him that this was a remote village, that the sound might be alien here. It died away in the distance and then came back again, faded and reappeared, getting louder and louder – apparently the plane was circling the bungalow. He put down his book and went out to investigate. He was still standing on the veranda, leaning against a wooden pillar and blinking up at the afternoon sky, when he became aware of something else. A crowd was collecting at the gate of the Travellers' Bungalow – a crew of dusty roadworkers and angry-looking farmers. The women and children had been shooed off to one side, where they stood clustered and apprehensive in the scraggly shade of a thorn tree. All of them were talking at the same time, looking from Dr Schlamm to the aeroplane and then from the plane back to Dr Schlamm again. Meanwhile, the plane itself continued to circle, drowning the chatter of voices each time it came overhead. Dr Schlamm sensed something more than excitement now. The men were gesticulating, pointing to him and drawing closer together. Suddenly uneasy, he called to the caretaker, who was staring up at the sky, open-mouthed and speechless. Asked for an explanation, the man only shook his head. Either his English was not equal to the occasion or, more likely, he was unwilling to speak; and Dr Schlamm, at this stage of his stay in India, knew no Tamil. Then there was a sudden concerted movement in the crowd.

'What is it?' the Doctor demanded. 'For God's sake, man, what is it?'

The note of urgency in his voice penetrated at last to the caretaker. He grinned nervously, and jerked his thumb at the plane. 'You bring?' he suggested, and grinned again.

'*No!*' Dr Schlamm said. 'I don't know anything about it. Tell them so! Look.' He turned to the angry, frightened faces at the gate and shook his head, pointing up at the plane and making vehemently negative gestures.

Their expressions did not change. They had stopped talking now; the silence had grown ugly. Just then the plane swept down again, lower than it had before, and started to drop leaflets.

He stared in a kind of petrified amazement. The papers floated down, swaying and eddying in the sea breeze and then being carried off to the sands beyond the gate. One of the children ran to pick them up and was arrested by a hoarse shout from his mother – as if in terror of unknown dangers from the sky. With that shout, something broke loose in the crowd. They pushed the gate open and started towards Dr Schlamm with a furious, low-throated roar. 'I thought I was finished,' he said. 'They were going to kill me.' At that moment, like a rattling *deus ex machina*, the jeep came bumping down the road. Before the red-coated peon could hop off, Father was out of the jeep and in among the men. Dr Schlamm had a confused impression of voices and hands, as the crowd was made to halt in its tracks.

'Don't thank me,' Father said afterwards, smiling rather dryly. 'It was only the voice of authority they listened to.' He poured the Doctor a stiff drink and explained that the plane had apparently been on a reconnoitring flight, dropping leaflets to assure the people (in English, which not one of them could read) of the harmlessness of its purpose and the need for secrecy.

'But why *me*?' Dr Schlamm demanded, bewildered.

'The villagers knew you'd come from Germany. There were rumours of a raid. So they put two and two together and made five and a half . . .'

And there, in the red-tiled house by the sea, Father and Dr Schlamm had laughed together and become friends.

'Which was why I chose to come and live here when I heard a couple of years later that this house was vacant,' the Doctor concluded, squirming a little as he sat between us on the steps, and gesturing at the Hibinett house in hurried dismissal, as if he already regretted his confidence and would retrieve it if he could.

But in any case we could not have guessed all this in the beginning, when the Doctor first arrived next door. My father had long since handed over his post to his successor in that southern district; his offices were now in the Madras Secretariat buildings behind the massive walls of Fort St George. He and my mother happened to be away when Dr Schlamm moved in, so we first heard of him when our gardener announced that the man next door seemed rather unusual for a foreigner – quite apart from his habit of calling for his cat up and down the drive. For one thing, he did not have a car; he rode a bicycle. For another, instead of an elaborate staff to run his house, he had a single rascally man-servant called Joe, who served a cook, office boy, and general factotum. Joe came from a family of second-generation Christian converts, all of whom had died except his mother, a pious and self-effacing woman, who helped her son clean the house, prayed for his soul, and lived in the low-roofed rooms behind the courtyard.

All day, the Hibinett house lay closed and silent. It was built of a particularly dingy shade of bricks; the roof hung low, its eaves beetling like eyebrows over the upstairs windows. The quiet clung everywhere – to the house and the garden and the gravelled drive – until evening, when Dr Schlamm and Joe returned from the clinic. Then Joe set up a terrific banging clatter of pans in the kitchen (as if his mother hadn't done most of the cooking already), and Dr Schlamm went into his study and started to play his records.

He had a magnificent collection, which not only began my personal introduction to Western music but also initiated the neighbourhood's acquaintance with the Doctor himself. Again nobody objected to the volume at which the music was played. My older sister, dreamy and exquisite, and with memories of a European childhood, loved the symphonies that spilled out of his windows and through the trees. But to me these were unknown sounds, and every evening after tea I stood by the hedge between our houses and tried to make sense out of them. One day, I was in my usual place, sucking a surreptitious tamarind (eating too many made you sick), listening to every note and wondering where the next one would fall – too high or too low or not at all – when the hedge parted and a spectacled head thrust itself cautiously through.

'Do you like the music?' Dr Schlamm asked.

Laws of courtesy demanded a positive answer, and laws of truth a negative one; solving the problem, I offered him half my tamarind to suck. He accepted it with a murmured thanks, and clambered through the hedge into our garden and into our lives.

Our household consisted at this time of my parents, whom the Doctor already knew; my older sister, whom he promptly started to fall in love with; me, whose cultural education he took in hand as a matter of course; and a great-aunt, who was alternately charmed and irritated by him but maintained a stony distance (she was fiercely nationalistic and detested Europeans on principle, as part of her fight for freedom). Then there was also Govinda. He was ostensibly a cook but actually more of an old friend, who had come from Malabar to work for my parents long before we were born, bossed us left and right, and had a phobia about cats. He'd disposed of the earlier ones with a summary brandish of his bread knife when they approached too close to the kitchen, but Toni was a different matter. Accepting Dr Schlamm meant making truce with Toni, so Govinda glowered forbiddingly at the Doctor through the kitchen window, while the Doctor, all oblivious, progressed from neighbour to friend to something much rarer.

It was as if our home reshaped itself subtly around his presence, in a shifting of balance so delicate that neither he nor we were aware of any change. The hedge parted, footsteps sounded across the lawn, and there he was – never a 'visitor', never interrupting the rhythm of the household. His sudden snort of laughter over whatever he was reading became as much a part of the evening as the whir of the ceiling fan in my father's office room, the rustle of papers on his desk, the soft jingle of household keys as my mother moved in and out of the rooms, the tuneless, thumping harvest songs from the radio programme in Kannada, which was our great-aunt's favourite language, and the crunch of wheels on the gravel as the newsboy delivered the evening paper. When I ran out to read the day's cartoon strip, Dr Schlamm raced me to the doormat and peered over my shoulder. Later, he and my sister did the London *Times* crossword together. And still later, long after we were in bed and the old house had settled down for the night with its customary creaks and groans, he sat out on the lawn with my parents, their voices blending companionably under the stars. There were some nights when they did not talk at all; the only sound then was of the wind lifting the branches of the neem trees – gently, as a woman will lift her hair with her hand to cool the nape of her neck. Often the silence lasted half the night, or so it seemed to us. For my mother – with her intuition so fine-grained, so unerring, that only the faintest Japanese brushstroke could begin to define it – always seemed to know when he wanted conversation and when merely the comfort of a human presence.

Others in the neighbourhood were understandably more obtuse. All the same, after that first day when he clambered through the hedge, it was as if Dr Schlamm had moved into the Hibinett house not only physically but with a much deeper tenancy, implying access to our collective loyalty and concern. Our great-aunt, for instance, for all her disapproval, sent up a prayer for the Doctor's safety every time he set out on his bicycle, because she was sure he would end in a ditch. Dr Schlamm's bicycle was an old rattletrap; the brakes never worked; he rode with three fingers of his left hand casually guiding the handlebar, his right hand on his hip and his gaze directed upwards to sky or tree-top or telegraph pole, while the bicycle teetered from one side of the road to the other, depending on whether or not he remembered to keep left.

'That man will forget his patients' names next,' our great-aunt scolded.

The trouble was, he did forget them. And Joe was no help, because Joe had a genius for offering his own tactless interpretation of foreign names. 'Oliphants' became Elephants; 'Henri Couchon' turned into Air Cushion; and once a Mrs Willoughby, friend of a friend from a Commonwealth High Commission, departed highly affronted after he had called her Bumblebee, which was unfortunate, because she happened to be a large and buzzing sort of woman. This, though, was not the least of Joe's weaknesses. Every Saturday night, he got roaring drunk and staggered down the road singing lewd songs. Dr Schlamm was never unduly upset, but the auctioneers who had taken the building across the road from his saw to it, in a burst of neighbourliness, that Joe was taken safely home each week. Fortunately, Joe yielded to his mother's importunities not to drink on Sundays and spent an abstemious Sabbath nursing his hangover. The auctioneers, however, attributed this to the Doctor's good influence and sent him invitations to all their auctions. So one Sunday in every month, Dr Schlamm got the catalogue at their door and wandered dutifully past gate-leg tables and standard lamps and mahogany dressers and out again.

If Joe introduced the Doctor to the auctioneers, Toni was responsible for getting him acquainted with the house on our left. Toni, for all his prowess in battle, was neurotic about thunderstorms. They drove him under the Doctor's bed, where he crouched, baleful and cowering; and when he did finally emerge, it was to do unpredictable things. Once, he ventured right into our kitchen. We saw a streak of orange, which was Toni, followed by a streak of silver, which was Govinda's dhoti, shoot through the garden and out of the gate. Govinda apologised later, grudgingly, for it had cost him his dignity. But the Doctor proved equally magnanimous. He quite understood Govinda's feelings about cats, he said; why, the cat itself had feelings about thunderstorms, so what could one do? At any rate, one couldn't do anything for the next few days, because Toni disappeared. We looked for him everywhere, but nobody saw so much as a flick of his tail. Then he was discovered hiding in one of the disused lofts in the house to our left.

This belonged to a minor rajah of sorts; he was an obliging little man, tiny and amiable and bald as an egg, and the house to our left was what was discreetly known as his 'establishment'. There was a woman there, buxomly established and with long black hair that she dried in the sunlight up on the roof after her bath. Most of the year, the rajah was away, and the whole place – a huge, humped structure with many rooms – was left to the lady and numerous male servants who spent their time yelling raucously up and down the stairs. One of them found the cat in the loft, but none of them could get near the animal, because of all the hissing and spitting it aimed at them, so finally the lady sent a message asking Dr Schlamm to come and fetch Toni himself.

I watched him over the garden wall, absurdly anxious; that house, for all its noise, had a way of swallowing people up. Dr Schlamm himself seemed embarrassed. He shuffled his shoulders beneath his shirt, scrubbed his feet assiduously on the doormat, and went in. After a while, there was a murmur of voices and a sudden yowl from indignant Toni followed by another murmur. Eventually, the Doctor appeared, a streak of cobweb trailing his cheek, scratches along his hand, bearing Toni in his arms. 'Nice woman, that,' he said to us over his shoulder. 'I told her I'd attend on her if she needed any medical help. You don't suppose the rajah will mind, do you?'

The rajah did not seem to mind. He came and went; the lady stayed on the roof drying her hair. Meanwhile, the Doctor's ideal continued to be my sister – an ideal cherished with a combination of personal need and Petrarchan distance, almost as if her very remoteness was a necessary source of his sustenance: as long as she remained inaccessible, he could remain constant. He probably could have proposed to her at any time, but he never did. The nearest he came to declaring his devotion was murmuring wistfully that this was the kind of girl he'd like to marry; the nearest he came to showing his feelings was by being acutely embarrassed if he happened to be unshaven when she came into the room. How this admiration affected her, I could not tell. She continued exquisite and elusive, away at college or upstairs in her room most of the time, writing poetry or playing on her sitar. My parents, with their usual tolerance, accepted the situation; my mother, with her usual insight, remarked one evening that Dr Schlamm was an anachronism in time and space – no matter where he lived or when he would be out of his context, out of his time. She might have added that when his century caught up with him the disaster would begin, but that we did not know yet.

Or perhaps we did – for with the coming of Medora Hane the neighbourhood arrayed itself on the side of his survival and the fight was on. He told me of the lady one afternoon when I had dragged him off to the Asia Library because I thought I'd discovered a first edition of Burke's *Reflections on the French Revolution* in one of its back rooms. The back room had no door; you jumped over a high window and into another world, filtered with sunlight and dust motes. We sat on the window-sill, swinging our legs, our whispers in that place becoming dry as old paper, scrapy as the neem leaves brushing the sandstone ceiling. For when the Doctor discovered it *was* a first edition, he unbent enough to tell me about Medora Hane.

'She works at the US Consulate,' he said. 'One of the staff, in fact. The most beautiful girl I have ever met.'

If that had been all, we might have given our blessing; but she made him sleepless and hollow-eyed, irascible and tormented; what was worse, he lost his appetite and would not eat. There wasn't a moment's joy in the man; he looked almost famine-stricken – and in a country keenly conscious of hunger this would never do. Joe's mother made the first move. She came over, as most of the neighbourhood did in moments of stress, to ask my mother's help. But for once my mother had nothing to suggest. 'There are other needs than the need for rice,' was all she said. So Joe's mother went over to the rajah's establishment, and two days later the lady of the house was ill and needed attention. Dr Schlamm attended her as promised, and before he had time to wonder a little about the symptoms, our gardener's entire family – himself, his wife, his children – had one thing or another wrong with them. They straggled up to his veranda complaining of varied and original illnesses, and Dr Schlamm was too kind to call their bluff. If he did, there was still our chauffeur to be accounted for, and the auctioneer's second cousin, and the Punjabi refugees who were staying with them, and the caretaker from the house behind ours, and lots of runny-nosed two-year-olds, dragged in, protesting, by their mothers, who worked in the houses along the street. Soon there were more patients than he could keep track of. 'Salaam,' they greeted him solemnly every evening. 'Salaam, Dr Salaam.' A makeshift clinic evolved on his veranda; it was always crammed.

All this combined effort paid off. Besides, the glamorous Miss Hane (we saw her once at a concert, and she was every bit as blonde and capricious as expected) had agreed to be escorted to the Saturday-afternoon races at Guindy. Dr Schlamm waited and waited at the appointed hour, but, whether from overpopularity or oversight, she never appeared. After that, the scales fell slowly and obligingly from his eyes, and he went back to eating and sleeping and adoring my sister as usual.

The patients, however, continued to patronise his veranda. Now when we took him to plays, he understood what was being said; when we took him to concerts, he waggled his head in appreciation as enthusiastically as anyone in the audience; he was asked to weddings and was wept on at funerals ('If *you* had treated him, Dr Schlamm, he might have lived') – until it seemed as if nothing could dislodge this man from the place they had carved for him and buttressed with their need.

The Medora Hane affair was, however, only part of a nameless battle – easier because it involved a recognisable adversary and a tangible end. There had been other crises right from the beginning. Now they recurred. Nothing altered on the surface; he was busy as usual, going from the clinic on Mount Road to the clinic on his veranda. But in the evenings no music spilled out of his windows, no footsteps came across the lawn – they only sounded in his study; ceaselessly up and down. Any relationship with Dr Schlamm was always full of lights and darks, and in times like these it was as if the dark had laid siege to his house. In our house there were stern injunctions not to intrude on the Doctor's privacy when he wanted to be alone. Once, when things had been at their worst in the early days of his arrival, I had begged, 'Can't we *do* something to help him?' and was told quite simply that the first thing to know about helping was when not to try. Eventually, as if of its own accord, a camping trip would materialise, or perhaps a fortnight in one of the huge game sanctuaries in the Western Ghats, and before we knew what had happened the dark was as if it had never been – until the next time it descended on him. But this time, after a week's pacing and before Joe's mother could approach us, Dr Schlamm himself did. He walked through the hedge (which had acquired a noticeable gap by now) and asked my mother what kind of religious instruction she gave to her children.

'Religious instruction?' my mother said, nonplussed. 'I never thought of it as that. I couldn't really tell you. Why don't you watch and see for yourself?'

So Dr Schlamm watched and learned – in three easy lessons, he told me afterwards.

The first occurred soon after, when I joined a convent school run by French nuns. Within a few days of my admission, there was a problem to be brought to my mother: would I have to say Hail Marys with the rest of the girls? As the Doctor listened, she told me matter-of-factly that prayer was prayer whether I hailed Mary or anyone else – so I went and said my prayers, loud and devout and righteous as the next pupil. When the monsoons came and thunder lilies bloomed in sprays of audacious white all over our garden, I took some to decorate the chapel, saw their whiteness transformed from the dauntless to the sacerdotal; and came home stammering at the shadowed beauty of the shrine and the candlelight and the stained-glass windows.

Our great-aunt, hearing me, commented acidly, 'Take care they don't convert you,' at which I began at once to have nightmares of kind, dimpled Sister Véronique standing over me brandishing a bread knife, for all the world like Govinda with the cats. Dr Schlamm was with us in time for his second lesson when I mentioned this to my mother. She said nothing; she only laughed, but with such a curiously undisturbed quality to her laughter that things tilted back into focus, as much for the Doctor as for myself, apparently, because after that he argued less about Miss Logge.

Miss Logge was an English missionary lady of uncertain age who waylaid us on buses and even in our own home, to preach fire and brimstone at us. Much to Dr Schlamm's annoyance, we heard her out every time, no matter how long she talked. 'Why do you *suffer* her so?' he would demand, infuriated.

'It's merely a question of courtesy,' my mother replied. 'The courtesy of allowing her to uphold the faith she believes in.'

'And what if she hasn't the courtesy to let you uphold yours?'

My mother dismissed the matter with a wave of her hand. 'That is her concern, not ours.'

One day, Miss Logge cornered us at his clinic, where we had gone to leave some urgent letters on the Doctor's desk. She kept us there, preaching, while I tried not to fidget and Dr Schlamm waited in growing exasperation. After half an hour's eloquence, the lady caught my mother by the shoulders and thrust her face close to demand, in a passionate finale, 'Don't you want your soul to be *saved*?'

My mother stepped adroitly aside. 'Some other time, thank you,' she said, polite as ever, and we escaped.

That did it, Dr Schlamm said afterward. He seemed hugely delighted by the whole episode, but not more delighted than our great-aunt.

Great-aunt, after the founding of the impromptu clinic on his veranda, had started to thaw in her attitude toward him. She began by conceding that he was a good man, and went on to evince an extraordinary interest in his background, as if, his character now having been established, she recognised his validity to claim a past. Her final reservations fell away when she discovered he was Jewish ('Ah, then he is like one of us; he's from an old people'), and the surrender was complete once he admitted his weakness for the *halva* she made.

After this, nothing was too good for Dr Schlamm; no amount of information about him ever really satisfied her. She asked my parents all kinds of questions and set out their answers before her, laying one against the other, as if playing a sort of mental solitaire where every move was speculated aloud. It was her only suggestion of senility, for most of the day she ruled her old age with indomitable vigour. Then at night she would sit on the upstairs veranda, where my sister and I slept in summer, fanning herself with a palm-leaf fan, murmuring her conjectures half to herself and half to us. Sometimes we answered her, sometimes we didn't. It made no difference; she went on murmuring. Once it had been about Independence, then the Partition of the country after Independence, then some local politics; now it was Dr Schlamm.

This musing every night brought to light many things about the Doctor, especially those unspoken terrors behind his darkness. We knew the vague details, of course: the uncle whom he hated but who always knew which way the wind was blowing; the night when this uncle called Dr Schlamm and told him dryly that he might as well get out of the country while he could; Dr Schlamm's own mystique about India and the early years here, binding though alien. One evening, lying on my stomach in the middle of his study and listening to his records, I asked him about his childhood. He started to tell me of Innsbruck, where he was born; Munich, where his family had moved when he was still a child, the street where they lived and the number of the house. Then there was a sudden silence.

'Go on,' I said. 'What was Munich like?'

Dr Schlamm was staring out the window. The record scraped to an end; the rug smelled faintly of cat and floor polish. (Years later, when I walked down a bombed, partly rebuilt street in Munich, trying to locate No 21, that same smell of cat and floor polish was to come back, tenuous and insistent.) Finally, the Doctor shrugged, and turned away from the window. 'Munich? Munich is ten miles from Dachau. Now go on home.'

He did not need to tell me. There was a note in his voice I had never heard before, and, hearing it, I was already stumbling toward the door. Two days later, when he called me through the hedge to give me a dog-eared copy of Gogol's *Dead Souls*, and three days later, when he upbraided me for yawning so prodigiously over it, that note wasn't there. I don't remember its ever recurring. But it echoed in his footsteps the next time he paced, and my great-aunt recognised it, too. She jerked her head towards the Hibinett house and said, 'Now I know what your mother meant.'

'About what?'

'About him. It was in the last days of the war. When he first moved in. I said to your mother, "What ails the man?" and she said quite angrily, 'If your people are driven and dying and you are safe and alive, isn't that reason enough?"'

It was reason enough for something else, too, which had never been mentioned at home. I was looking up four-year-old issues of the local newspaper in the Asia Library, for some essay to be written for school, when I came across a small item tucked away on the third page. It was brief. Karl Jacob Schlamm, the Austrian physician, of 1238 Mount Road, had been admitted to the General Hospital after he had taken an overdose of sleeping pills. His condition was reported satisfactory.

I stared at it, uncomprehending, and when Dr Schlamm came to dinner that night, I stared at him as well. It was hard to merge the man in the newspaper column with the man sitting across from me at table. Our great-aunt's endless curiosities and conclusions, the Doctor's own darkness, and now this, gathered together, emerging from the background into a cumulative effect of horror and tragedy that made his image somehow indistinct.

I was squinting at him, trying to focus, when his voice broke through. 'Why are you staring at me, young woman?'

Taken aback, I said nothing. So he repeated the question,

and I was overcome with inexplicable guilt and yelled, 'I'm *not* staring!' at the top of my voice.

'Sh-h-h,' he said. 'Ladies don't shout.'

At that, I thought he had begun to be recognisable again. This was the Dr Schlamm who inspected my nails and improved my mind and dabbed mercurochrome on scratched knees, while holding forth sternly on the unseemliness of young ladies climbing trees.

It was the same man, but something had changed. Studying him more covertly across the table, I saw the change: not in him but in the burden of my new knowledge of him. There was now a dim, incipient realisation that if Dr Schlamm brought out the hoyden in me, he brought out the serenity in my mother. When he was among us, he gave us back ourselves, mirrored but somehow accented, refracted, so that my father was stronger than ever, my sister more unlimnable, our great-aunt more opinionated. It was the opposite face of the same thing that held us back, however close we felt toward him, from referring to him as a part of the family. We might love him or grieve with him or feel the palpable weight of his guilt on our shoulders, but Dr Schlamm carried an uncompromising loneliness with him that demanded a reticence between us. He seemed to imply all the time that no matter how valid our own sorrows, our own understanding, our lives had been rooted in our land for centuries and we could not really begin to know.

Sometimes this emerged directly, as in arguments with our great-aunt over the refugee problem in north India, when he accused her of not even knowing the meaning of the word 'dispossessed'. Sometimes it was more oblique, as when I caught him by the hedge the following morning, staring up at our house. Asked what he was looking for, he tweaked my braids and scowled and said, 'It wasn't only your father who saved my life, damn it.' He sounded more angry than anything else, but I accepted that, as I accepted most of his remarks, with a margin left for future cogitation. Having Dr Schlamm next door had become part of the bewildering business of growing up, of learning to fill in blanks that one hadn't even known existed. This statement now could probably be construed – or misconstrued; it didn't matter which – either the next day or the next month or the next year. Where Dr Schlamm was concerned, nothing was ever really finished; there would always be threads and echoes, ravelled or reappearing, to be tied up in retrospect or matched to a subsequent discovery. So that when he went on to say he was going away to Edinburgh for a couple of years, I did not believe him at first.

'You're what?'

'Leaving. Edinburgh. You know, in Scotland?'

'Of course I know, in Scotland. But why?'

It turned out to be a matter of a specialised medical degree – one he had already. The Indian Government at that point of political turnover did not recognise the degree from Munich, so it had to be Edinburgh. I turned and stared at the Hibinett house, suddenly bleak and bereft, knowing for the first time what it was to miss someone who was standing next to you, so close you could hear him breathe; then wishing there was a tamarind to offer him, to divert his attention; then asking him gruffly if my parents knew.

'Yes, they know, but I wanted to tell you myself. I'll be back. It's only two years.'

'That's a long time.'

'When you haven't begun to tread your teens, yes. When you're riding your thirties, no. I'll be back before you know it. You'll see. Just two years.'

It might have been two hundred for all the farewell gestures from the neighbourhood. Dr Schlamm's portly Muslim landlord arrived on his doorstep with the noble suggestion that the next tenants be confined to a two-year lease, so that the Hibinett house could wait for the Doctor when he returned. Joe got more drunk than ever. His mother wept copiously on hearing of the Doctor's departure and refused to leave the two rooms behind the courtyard, preferring, she said, to wait for him as the house did. Our great-aunt, of course, filled two biscuit tins full of *halva*. The rajah and his lady offered to look after Toni. The auctioneers presented him with a massive mahogany whatnot, so heavy it had to be left behind. And finally a deputation of patients arrived at the railway station with garlands of jasmine and marigolds, to give him a royal sendoff.

He was travelling to Bombay to catch a P & O liner, but kept reiterating, as if it were some obscure kind of promise, that the Madras seafront was the most beautiful he had ever seen, and that he would never forget the day he first sailed into the harbour. His fellow-travellers surged around us, bristling with tightly strapped holdalls and tiffin carriers gleaming brassily beneath the station light. Porters trundled wheelbarrows right into our ankles; vendors thrust laden wooden trays under our noses, screaming panegyrics to soft drinks and cigarettes, betel leaves and magazines. Dodging each as he came by, we stood and gazed up at the Doctor's spectacled face, framed embarrassedly over his garlands in the dusty square outline of the train window.

'Write to me,' he kept saying at intervals, and then reached out to tweak my braids in the familiar gesture. 'And you, remember to say goodbye to your sister from me. And for God's sake, *finish Dead Souls*.'

My sister was away at college. Before I could begin to nod, the clamour of the station was wiped out by a single shriek from the engine whistle, and Dr Schlamm's carriage started to lurch forward. We watched the train until it had dwindled to a receding dot and then went home in silence.

The silence lasted underneath for a year and a half in an unspoken anxiety about the Doctor, while we remembered the rickety bicycle or laughed over the rascally Joe. Old acquaintances of ours moved into the Hibinett house, but I always thought of them as intruders; they 'visited' us, walking sedately through the front gate and down our drive. The sounds that issued from the Hibinett house were equally commonplace. There were no noises to startle the night, no symphonies, no cries for straying cats or countries left behind.

At the end of the first year, my sister was married. Dr Schlamm did not react to that as I imagined he would. He

seemed rather vague – sent her a charming letter and spoke of
cutting cords. I graduated from skirts to saris with all the
attendant implications of trying to move gracefully in new
awareness as one tried to move gracefully in grown-up
clothes. Meanwhile, letters from the Doctor continued to
trickle in, written on long, narrow strips of paper rather like
the discarded edges of new sets of postage stamps, on which
his crabbed handwriting descended in jagged steps to tell us of
his English landlady and what I'd considered to be the out-
moded cliché of a rooming house smelling of boiled beef and
cabbage. Sometimes a more disturbing phrase jangled: 'Living
there, next door to you, was all right. Here in Europe the horror comes too close.' Then the inconsequentialities closed
smoothly in again. In return, we sent him joint family missives
– long, chatty, and disconnected. When my turn came, I wrote
primly of things seen and done; the important things had to
wait and be spoken in person. Look, I told him, my nails are
manicured and I finished *Dead Souls*, but I climb all the trees
I want.

Then on a summer evening just two months short of the
second year, the slap of the newspaper sounded, falling
against the doormat, and the newsboy crunched his way out
of the gate as usual. I dashed out to the front steps from sheer
habit, shuffling cursorily past the political items to get to the
cartoon. That was when his name sprang out from a blur of
print. It was a brief paragraph again, and on the third page
again: a report of the death in Edinburgh of Dr Karl Jacob
Schlamm, of 1238 Mount Road. Later, we heard the facts –
that he had gone to the music festival, that he had listened to
a Wagner concert, that he had come home and put a bullet
through his head. The world braked to a stop; I could neither
move nor breathe, standing on the doormat trembling and
trying to call out. When they took the paper from my hand,
part of the business of growing up was over and nothing
could be the same again, either for me or for the rest of the
neighbourhood.

The auctioneers were closed on the following Sunday, 'In
memory of Dr Karl Jacob Schlamm'. As if in an appropriate

coda to the question he had asked my mother about religion, our great-aunt observed the Hindu ritual of his death anniversary, cooking his favourite food and giving it away in charity; Joe's mother offered her prayers in church; the landlord offered his at the mosque. The runny-nosed two-year-olds who had come to the clinic on the veranda cried, whether from grief or hunger. And nobody ever used the hedge. That gap was soon overgrown, and scratched across with tentative new twigs: a bedraggled testament to the coming and the going between us.

Upamanyu Chatterjee

THE ASSASSINATION OF INDIRA GANDHI

BUNNY THREW HIS glass meditatively at the wall. It tinkled into large ugly pieces. One fell on Randeep's head. 'We'd better look out,' he said, 'Cut Surd's getting violent.'

Bunny took off his goggles. His eyes were very red. 'Give me a glass.' Shashi did. Bunny finished it and threw it slowly up at the ceiling fan. Ramnath caught it. 'Stop it Cut Surd.'

'Stop calling me Cut Surd.'

Mirza fixed Bunny another drink. 'These bloody Hindus yaar Surd.' Everyone laughed drunkenly.

'I'm feeling sick.' Bunny put on his goggles. 'Not pukey, just sick.'

'Throw up in the bathroom. Not here.' said Ramnath.

'Why didn't we get women. I'm sick of just men. I want some sex.'

Shashi said, 'Rum before sundown, that's the problem. I kept saying let's get beer.'

Bunny got up slowly from the floor. He tucked in his T-shirt. He kicked Ramnath. 'I'm going out. I'm getting myself a ticket home.' He felt his pockets. 'Where are the keys? I'll leave the bike with you. Don't kill it.'

Outside, a very loud motorcycle went by. Bunny drew back the curtain and opened the window. The late-afternoon late-October light bounded in, along with the noises of horns and accelerating cars. He spoke to the traffic. 'I'm sick to my balls of Delhi. A dog of a city. It's almost like Chandigarh.' Bunny looked around the room and looked out again. 'Sick.' His knees and right ankle ached faintly.

'No, Surd, this is just a bad trip. Get some ganja and some sleep, you'll be fine.'

'No, I'm just sick. Dog city.' He liked the phrase. He scratched his beard. 'Next June I'll be apprenticed in Chandigarh, horny and alone.' Drink made Bunny articulate. 'The hep Surds call Chandigarh Chandy. Just red brick and empty spaces.' He moved around the room, leaned against the bathroom door and watched Shashi urinate. 'Your piss is yellow like mustard oil. Maybe you have jaundice.' At the table he slowly poured himself a large rum. 'These days I ejaculate too quickly. It's like school, those jerk-off competitions.'

'Fix me one, Surd, thanks.'

Bunny took off his goggles and sat them carefully on the knob of the cupboard door. 'Randeep, just fix my attendance with Kapila. I'll be back maybe in a month or something. Bye everybody.' He put on his goggles and left.

An orange October sun, but Bunny was only faintly conscious of it. He was drunk, but not uncontrollably. He was depressed too, but he did not know it. Bunny was twenty-three, and inarticulate and silent when sober. He put on his crash helmet and left the straps loose. He rode off at a frightening speed.

He stopped on the peak of a flyover to watch, in the mild light, the traffic and the teenagers around the ice-cream man. He said to himself, if there's a queue at the ticket counter, even a line of three bastards, I'm not going home. He rode away. But there was only one. So he bought a seat on the night bus to Mussoorie. From the bus station, he went for a haircut.

At traffic lights, at other places where he had to slow down or stop, Bunny felt quite ill. He attributed his weakness to his ennui, the drink, the inadequate sleep, Delhi's fickle October weather, his vague distaste for the way he lived his life. But self-examination was not his practice. He lived unthinkingly and encouraged in himself random impulses.

At the saloon, while waiting, he flipped blindly through a film magazine. At saloons, he always remembered his first haircut, in Darjeeling, about eight years ago, the barber's smiles and enthusiasm. He had written to his parents about it.

He never wrote letters, for he found expression tiresome, but his parents had had to be forewarned before his return home. They had disapproved vastly. Even now his father, when really angry, called him a bastard Sikh.

Abruptly he felt queasy. He skipped the haircut and rode back to the hostel with a headache. He woke up Yudhvir, a friend. 'This is no time to sleep.'

'What time is it?' Red drugged eyes and porcupine hair, but Yudhvir never got angry.

'Sixish. I've got myself a ticket on the night bus home. You take care of the bike.'

'Okay.'

'And fix Kapila about attendance. I'm going to sleep too. I'll wake you up later to drop me to the bus.'

Bunny liked night bus journeys. The seats were quite comfortable, and he could sleep anywhere. The jolts even lulled him, but during the journey, when he woke up, his knees were stiff and aching.

He wasn't particularly fond of his parents. They bored him. Home was not an exciting place, but he could unwind there, sleep in the sun and eat really well. His mother opened the door. She was not surprised to see him. He always came home unexpectedly. She said, 'You look awful. Are you ill?'

'I just feel exhausted. Must be the journey.'

He went to his room with his bag. His father grunted as he passed his parents' room. Bunny mumbled a reply. His mother came in with two blankets. It was six in the morning. Bunny slept uneasily till nine, and got out of bed after ten.

His father was in the garden, in a white cane chair. 'What, Law Faculty again on strike?'

'Yes.' An easy lie, for at any time, Bunny would have found it difficult to tell his father he had just *felt* like coming home. He sat down. The small lawn was an odd triangle in shape, the wooden fence a bright white. Beyond the fence, the hill tumbled down to the narrow road, the tea stalls, the shacks selling wooden Taj Mahals and walking-sticks, the Tibetans in bright quilted jackets. Then the hill lurched further down the main road. Behind it lay the vast valley, surrounded by curve after curve of denuded hill. On a clear day, one could see in the valley the dots and dashes of the houses of Dehradun. Above this was an immense pale sky. At ten in the morning it still waited for the sun.

Bunny's mother emerged, in a salwar-kameez and a grey sweater. 'Come, breakfast is ready.'

Bunny didn't want to move or eat. 'Later.'

'What, shall I bring your food here?'

'No, I don't want to eat just now.'

His mother came up. Bunny looked at her defensively and noticed again his own face in hers. 'Are you feeling all right?' She put her hand on his shoulder. He cringed a little.

'You look horrible,' Mr Kairon said, staring steadily at Bunny over his reading glasses. *A History of the Sikhs* dropped onto the table. With a pencil he pushed stray hair into his turban. 'You've lost weight and colour. You don't *look* healthy.'

'Shall we call a doctor?'

'No. I think I'll be okay in a day or two.'

'But do you *feel* ill?' His mother half-bent down and examined Bunny's face.

Then Bunny's resistance collapsed. 'Yes. Maybe we should call Malviya.' He felt a little better. Just the admission of illness eased him, allowed him deeper breaths.

His mother left. His father said, 'What's wrong? Any symptoms?'

'Weakness. No appetite. That's all.' He forgot the faint pain in his knees, and now occasionally, his back.

Mr Kairon pushed his lips up and out till the upper lip touched his nose and breathed heavily into his moustache. He was a cliché of a man, once a brigadier, tall, with an inflexible back, now horribly active after retirement. He used his leisure for his garden and for long walks on the hill roads, and for educative books. He wasn't scholarly or even contemplative, but with the years he had been increasingly assailed by a conviction of his ignorance. One mild heart attack had even made him religious, and now his daily ritual included the Granth Saheb.

Bunny went in and returned with a camp cot. Dragging it tired him incredibly. He lay down. The weakness encouraged only unpleasant thoughts, it only allowed for images of depression, of Chandigarh and some lawyer's chambers, of law tomes and loneliness, of professional inadequacy and dislocation in a dead town.

'Fever?'

'No.'

'Stomach all right?'

'Oh yes.'

Then the sun broke through and warmed them. Somewhere in the house, Bunny could hear his mother giving the maid-servant hell. His mother had a pleasant rich voice. To avoid his father's questions, Bunny pretended to doze.

Mr Kairon was proud of his son's good looks, but Bunny had often disappointed him. For one, he had not joined the army. And though Mr Kairon admitted that short hair suited Bunny, he had been outraged that Bunny had not asked him *before* the haircut. Now he watched him sleeping in the sun and said, 'I hope your illness is not serious.'

They heard the gate and Dr Malviya appeared, clean, pink and busy. Bunny disliked doctors because they made him insecure. Standing over Bunny, Dr Malviya announced immediately, 'This is jaundice, Kaironji. What, Bunny boy, you've been drinking a lot?' He checked his eyes, spleen and liver, questioned him about his whisky and his urine, ordered blood tests, a special diet and lots of rest and left.

Jaundice. Bunny wondered if it could have been worse and almost immediately told himself yes. The blue of the sky was gathering richer tones. Light cottonwool clouds just above him, long flat strips of grey on the horizon, tiny white waves of cloud, ribbed like desert sand, on the left, and the warm sun. When his father wasn't going on and on about his dissipation and abysmal lack of care, Bunny could hear different birds, on the lawn, and in the distant trees. He knew nothing about them, but they sounded nice.

Out on the lawn time passed easily. Bunny ate a little and drank some juice. Mr Kairon, perhaps regretting his earlier sharpness, asked him if he felt better. Bunny said yes. The telephone rang. Mrs Kairon picked it up, then shrieked through the large white windows, 'from New York!'

'Rajwant,' muttered Mr Kairon. He rushed inside and pushed his hand out peremptorily for the phone. 'Here.'

Bunny turned on his side and observed them. He didn't think his sister worth the effort of leaving the camp cot. Older by nine years his sister, like the rest of the family, was distant. He saw his father's back jerk with surprise and heard a loud incredulous 'What!' Bunny turned back to the sky. His mother hurried out a few moments later and blurted out, 'Indira Gandhi has been shot dead. By two of her guards, both Sikhs. In her house in Delhi.' Mrs Kairon looked around uncertainly.

The news was unnerving. 'What else did Rajju say?'

'She wanted details from us, imagine. We didn't know anything, she said it's all over American news, even BBC and Radio Australia. She was taken to hospital but she died quickly. It happened in the morning at about nine-thirty.' Mrs Kairon gulped and sat down.

Just my luck, thought Bunny, to leave the dog city just when something exciting happened. His father returned to his chair, eyes agleam, intently twirling the knobs of a transistor.

'Will Rajju telephone again?' asked Mrs Kairon.

'Yes. As soon as she hears more news.'

All the radio stations played the same mournful song. 'She can't be dead. If she was dead, there'd be no voices and no drums and dholaks.'

'But something *has* happened, all the stations are playing the same music.'

'But this is terrible,' said Mr Kairon, looking out over the valley.

No one spoke, Bunny turned over, now warming his right arm and shoulder. Mr Kairon said, 'In New York the Sikhs are out on the roads, celebrating and distributing mithai. Rajju didn't say so, but even Manjeet seems to be celebrating.' Manjeet was the son-in-law. On the faces of Mr and Mrs Kairon could be discerned a daze, an initial shock, and an inchoate ethnic guilt.

Bunny watched the green and dull-brown ground, a few weeds among the grass. The news thrilled him, momentarily distracted him from himself. Against the white fence and footrule-strips of sky, Bunny visualised the blood dyeing the sari and the collapsing, crumpling female form. Maybe she had even said something to her assassins or to someone near by. Mr Kairon got up, said, 'I'm telephoning Duggal,' and went inside. The songs from the transistor continued.

Mr Kairon returned, more composed. 'Duggal says AIR is still saying she was shot, but BBC announced her death long ago. The killers are Sikhs, no doubt about that.'

Mrs Kairon said, 'For shame.'

Lunch was dreary and silent. Duggal arrived soon after. Bunny did not move to acknowledge him. 'Hallo Balwinder,' Duggal said, 'when did you come?' Bunny disliked Duggal because he called him Balwinder and because Duggal disliked Bunny for his good looks, his haircut, his jeans and T-shirts. Duggal was uninterested in Bunny's illness. He sipped his tea noisily and said, 'This is going to cause many problems.'

'A shameful death. This is no way for a person of her stature to go,' said Mrs Kairon.

'But it's no surprise. She had it coming to her.'

Bunny eyed Duggal with amusement and contempt. What a stupid perspective, he thought. In the black and white of Duggal's mind, pain and annihilation, even jaundice probably, were merely retributive. As one sows, so one reaps, even when the harvest was a spray of unexpected bullets, or a debilitating illness. Bunny thought of his own past but could hunt out no redeeming image to refute Duggal's argument. Oh well. His parents and Duggal continued to talk. Bunny dozed off to a constraint in the air and to polite, firm disagreement.

In the late afternoon Mr Kairon and Duggal walked out to get Bunny's blood reports. They sensed, or imagined they sensed, a difference in the narrow lanes of Mussoorie. To them, the honeymooners looked sombre, there were lesser aimless throngs of tourists, an unusually large number of shops was shut, there were fewer lights. The blood reports confirmed acute jaundice. After seeing Duggal off to his dental clinic, Mr Kairon stopped for bread and soap. The grocer said, very gravely, 'Kairon Saab, your people ought not to have done this,' and overcharged him just a little. Mr Kairon could think of nothing in reply.

When Bunny woke up, the pain in his knees and ankles had increased. Must be the weakness, he thought. He found it a little difficult to move back into the house. With each step even the soles of his feet hurt. Bunny was suddenly not sure that he could rely on his body for even the simplest acts. 'Tomorrow morning I'll ring up Pammi,' announced his father over tea. 'Find out what's happening in Delhi.' In the lanes Mr Kairon had sensed a tension, an antagonism. So father and son had lost their different confidences together. At six, TV finally said that Indira Gandhi was dead. Mr Kairon was outraged at the delay in the announcement. 'We first heard the news,' he snorted, 'through a call from New York, what rubbish.' Bunny walked carefully to the telephone, not wanting to exhibit his pain. 'Hallo, may I speak to Dr Malviya? . . . Hallo this is Bunny here . . . Now my knees and ankles are paining quite a lot . . . I don't know, for about a week I think.' Dr Malviya asked Bunny not to worry, and not to take any painkiller. He attributed the pain to Bunny's exhaustion and weakness. 'You must've slept in some odd position during the day. And perhaps you're not used to the Mussoorie chill, having come up from Delhi.' 'Where things are hotting up,' said Bunny. Dr Malviya's laugh was forced and embarrassed.

'What's this pain?' asked Mr Kairon suspiciously, turning away for a moment from the TV.

'Oh nothing.'

His mother watched Bunny walk slowly to his room. She wished that he would communicate more. She had placed a heater in his room. Through the window the fading sun depressed him. The room was small, with a single bed. The bedspread was a present from Rajwant on her last visit. On it, on a yellow background, there romped one large red dragon. Bunny looked out at the sun and said to himself, No, I'm not weak. He closed the door and got down slowly onto the floor to exercise. At his third push-up the floor rushed up and hit him. He lost consciousness for a moment or two. When he came to, the cold cement against his left cheek was quite comfortable. An ant hurried by two inches from his right eye. He got into bed slowly, pulled the quilt right up and waited for the warmth. He felt defeated, empty, and now the twilight seemed soothing, like a dying glow. Moments passed and he breathed deeply. He tried momentarily to divert himself with a thought for Indira Gandhi but, like the rest of the world, she was remote and cold. They had in common only a numbness. Under the quilt Bunny felt his knees and tried to rotate his ankles. That pain was his only distraction from nothingness. Outside he could hear his parents, the TV and the foreign stations on the radio. All three were going on and on about Indira Gandhi.

After some time his mother pushed the door open. 'Sleeping?'

'No.'

'What did Malviya say about the pain?'

Bunny answered, but wondered why his mother wanted to know. One's own pain was one's own, secret and unshareable, even incommunicable. Someone else's pain must be tedium, the cause of boredom and irritation. The ill were always alone, hugging their illness.

'You'd better have a hot-water bottle.'

'Okay.'

Bunny's father locked up early, at about seven. He then checked his Service revolver. From the lawn, the hills and the valley were a black menacing mass, shrouded by mist and topped by a clouded night sky. The quiet of Mussoorie normally gladdened him, but now it made him irascible and uneasy. No intermittent laughter from the tea-stalls below them, no wink of light from a neighbouring hill. Just the evening chill, the opaque mist, behind it the dark, and an underwater silence. Mr Kairon felt nervy, irrationally remembering the riots of Partition and the wars of '65 and '71. Indoors, the tension was alleviated only by the depression at Bunny's illness. Dinner was short. Bunny nibbled something in bed. His mother asked him to leave his door open and to call whenever necessary.

That night Bunny entered a private, nightmare world. His ankles and knees turned red and doubled in size. His skin burned with fever. Very very slowly he struggled to sit up in bed. He touched his left knee and the pain stunned him. He just looked at his legs and could not believe the horror. Then Bunny heard the telephone ring and ring, loud and frightening. At last his father picked it up. 'Oh Pammi, hello . . . what, I hope . . . oh no . . . God . . . no . . .' From his father, Bunny heard only exclamations. Mrs Kairon joined him. 'What, what's happened?'

Bunny carefully put his two pillows beneath his knees. He couldn't scream because he was not used to expressing pain or to pleading for help. His fear and helplessness drew tears out of his eyes. His face crumpled. But he cried without sound. Jerking his head from side to side, his fists squeezing the pliant quilt, he decided to fight his battles silently and alone.

'Riots in Delhi.' Mr Kairon walked around helplessly. 'Sikhs pulled out of buses and killed. Some've been burnt. Bonfires of turbans. Houses attacked and looted. Hundreds dead already.' Mr Kairon's slippers made the only sound. 'And Pammi?' asked Mrs Kairon.

'No problem in his area yet.'

Mrs Kairon's eyes followed Mr Kairon. 'And Punjab?'

'No news. There's a news ban there.'

To Bunny in his delirious state, it seemed that the world's chaos merely mirrored his own. He again tried to move. The pain rushed up to his hip and back. He sat motionless for what seemed ages. Bunny eventually began to realise for the first time, what he was later to get used to, that pain cannot be acute forever. After a time it turns monotonous, even becomes boring. So, sitting up in bed, he dozed a little, till some inadvertent movement wrenched him out of sleep. Awake, he would suffer, grow bored, and doze till the next wrench. Then finally, through the window behind him, he heard the chirrup of the birds and sensed the new dawn.

Thus Bunny provided his parents with something other than

Indira Gandhi to think about. Dr Malviya checked Bunny's heart and said, avoiding Mr Kairon's eyes, that apart from jaundice, Bunny probably also had rheumatic arthritis. Dr Malviya called for more blood tests and even an ECG. Rheumatic arthritis stunned and later scared and disgusted Mr Kairon. It was *not* an illness for a young, strong, good-looking Sikh. When the sun came up he dragged his son out onto the lawn.

In the sunny cottage that he had bought for a song, Mr Kairon now felt helpless and isolated. He was cut off, lost in an idyllic location, while epochal events were taking place elsewhere. He looked at Bunny, lying there with arms folded and eyes closed, with bewilderment.

Out under the sun, Bunny was less scared. He sensed the security of the house, aloof and removed. He was living with people who meant well, who would never do him harm. Home. Though home didn't mean that for everybody, I mean, he chuckled to himself, seeing the orange of the sun under his eyelids, look at Indira Gandhi.

Mrs Kairon brought out the portable black and white TV, another present from Rajwant. They watched Mrs Gandhi lying in state. Initially they all felt solemn. Bunny said, 'She still looks dignified.' Later he looked down at his torso and then up at her aquiline nose in that grey face surrounded by flowers, and thought, Just an old woman. Mrs Kairon murmured obscene expressions of sorrow every time Mrs Gandhi was shown. But Bunny soon wearied of this and returned to the infinite variety of the sky. Malviya's pills were good. If he lay still he could even forget the pain for a while. The weeping women on TV distracted and disgusted him. He watched them beat their breasts and wail on shoulders. But surely tears were more valuable than that, thought Bunny, remembering only his own. The TV continued to spew out words of grief and immediately to deprive them of meaning.

Duggal came again that afternoon and was quite happy to hear of Bunny's new illness. He and Bunny's parents talked interminably, about the assassins, the riots, Punjab, the Anandpur Saheb Resolution, Khalistan, Trilokpuri. 'A communal carnage,' said Mr Kairon, picking up the jargon of the newspapers from Delhi that had just come in. 'The riots are also against the financial dominance of the Sikhs in Delhi.' 'They'll announce the elections soon and this killing will win it.' 'Some young Sikhs are cutting their hair, turning out like Bunny.'

Bunny loved the discussion as background and the stray sentences that registered with him. He idly wondered what Khalistan would be like. He was a little surprised at the fervour of the elders. To him religion was alien. But he liked his state, without roots or history. With his ugly past and ugly future, nothing could claim him.

Dr Malviya came again. 'The fever will return. The swelling will subside in three weeks or so. Later you will need a physiotherapist.' Over the next few days he visited regularly. 'We must be careful, Bunny. We must not allow the pain to move into your wrists and fingers, or up your backbone. No exertion, complete rest.' 'You'll have to forget alcohol for ever, or almost for ever. The jaundice will pass, but the arthritis is going to stay.' Sometimes Dr Malviya turned quite philosophical. 'You will have to learn to live with pain, with limitations. Learning to live, that can be quite rewarding, Bunny.' 'Don't think of it too much, and don't talk about it with others. They'll all have stupid theories. Don't you have hobbies, or something like that to occupy you?' Bunny said no. He never read, he had no ear for music, he collected nothing. He wasn't even used to thought.

As Dr Malviya had prophesied, the fever returned, fitfully. Then when his mother asked every hour if he felt better, he couldn't even snap at her because he felt so dulled. Sometimes he would press his hand to his heart, hard, and say, you are strong. Sometimes he would giggle when he recalled that earlier, in Delhi, he had thought that he had problems, and now. Sometimes he would glaze his eyes and not recognise his mother when she bent over him because he found her concern irritating. Sometimes he played a game of exaggerating the pain, for the pain was boring and needed to be embellished.

On the second and third of November 1984, Indira Gandhi lay in state and Delhi, as the newspapers said, was in flames.

On the fourth she was cremated. On the eleventh her ashes were flung all over Gangotri, a cold dead place. The nineteenth was her birthday. Thus the days passed for Bunny, and every day he saw the same images of her on TV.

Surprisingly Randeep wrote him a letter. 'My dear Bunny, where do I begin? I can't believe that I really saw what I am about to describe to you . . .' I can't read this rubbish, said Bunny to himself, and crumpled up and threw away the letter. Hours of introspection had made him love and long only for his own self. His mother sensed this as she watched him spend his hours examining the sky. 'I wish there were more people of your age here, Bunny.' Randeep's letter had broken Bunny's cocoon and the world had rushed in. He thought of his friends and his Delhi life with distaste. He couldn't return there. Bunny hated his past, it had given him his illness, and he distrusted his future, it would bring no respite.

Bunny bathed after the first few days, using an aluminium chair. The skin on his feet was thin and wrinkled. His toes looked like pieces of ginger. He thought, I had once been innocent, when I had assumed I could sprint a hundred yards with ease.

Then Mr Kairon asked once, on a bright morning, again over tea on the lawn, 'Bunny, will you grow your hair? And wear a turban? For my sake?' Mr Kairon did not know what role to assume, that of a liberal Sikh, a nationalist Sikh, or what Duggal called a true Sikh. 'And for Chandigarh, when you're a lawyer.' Bunny said yes immediately. He would have said yes to any request, it was not important. There were still months before Chandigarh, and the disease and the assassination had made it clear that the world was a wonderfully unstable place, where anything could happen. The two events ratified Bunny's inaction. One had to wait for the mad event, that was all. Where were the certainties? In the sky and sun? To the questions, there were no solutions; there was only a life, and only one life. Ambition was an absurdity; so-much-to-do-and-so-little-time-to-do-it-in, how pointless an outlook, here, look at Indira Gandhi, Bunny used to think, and often smile at the recollection.

Rohinton Mistry

THE COLLECTORS

I

WHEN DR BURJOR MODY was transferred from Mysore to assume the principalship of the Bombay Veterinary College, he moved into Firozsha Baag with his wife and son Pesi. They occupied the vacant flat on the third floor of C Block, next to the Bulsara family.

Dr Mody did not know it then, but he would be seeing a lot of Jehangir, the Bulsara boy; the boy who sat silent and brooding, every evening, watching the others at play, and called *chaarikhao* by them – quite unfairly, since he never tattled or told tales – (Dr Mody would call him, affectionately, the observer of C Block). And Dr Mody did not know this, either, at the time of moving, that Jehangir Bulsara's visits at ten a.m. every Sunday would become a source of profound joy for himself. Or that just when he would think he had found someone to share his hobby with, someone to mitigate the perpetual disappointment about his son Pesi, he would lose his precious Spanish dancing-lady stamp and renounce Jehangir's friendship, both in quick succession. And then two years later, he himself would – but *that* is never knowable.

Soon after moving in, Dr Burjor Mody became the pride of the Parsis in C Block. C Block, like the rest of Firozsha Baag, had a surfeit of low-paid bank clerks and bookkeepers, and the arrival of Dr Mody permitted them to feel a little better about themselves. More importantly, in A Block lived a prominent priest, and B Block boasted a chartered accountant. Now C Block had a voice in Baag matters as important as the others did.

While C Block went about its routine business, confirming and authenticating the sturdiness of the object of their pride, the doctor's big-boned son Pesi established himself as leader of the rowdier elements among the Baag's ten-to-sixteen population. For Pesi, too, it was routine business; he was following a course he had mapped out for himself ever since the family began moving from city to city on the whims and megrims of his father's employer, the Government.

To account for Pesi's success was the fact of his brutish strength. But he was also the practitioner of a number of minor talents which appealed to the crowd where he would be leader. The one no doubt complemented the other, the talents serving to dissemble the brutish qualifier of strength, and the brutish strength encouraging the crowd to perceive the appeal of his talents.

Hawking, for instance, was one of them. Pesi could summon up prodigious quantities of phlegm at will, accompanied by sounds such as the boys had seldom heard except in accomplished adults: deep, throaty, rasping, resonating rolls which culminated in a pthoo, with the impressive trophy landing in the dust at their feet, its size leaving them all slightly envious. Pesi could also break wind that sounded like questions, exclamations, fragments of the chromatic scale, and clarion calls, while the others sniffed and discussed the merits of pungency versus tonality. This ability earned him the appellation of Pesi *paadmaroo*, and he wore the sobriquet with pride.

Perhaps his single most important talent was his ability to improvise. The peculiarities of a locale were the raw material for his inventions. In Firozsha Baag, behind the three buildings, or blocks, as they were called, were spacious yards shared by all three blocks. These yards planted in Pesi's fecund mind the seed from which grew a new game: stoning-the-cats.

Till the arrival of the Mody family the yards were home for stray and happy felines, well fed on scraps and leftovers disgorged regularly as clockwork, after mealtimes, by the three blocks. The ground floors were the only ones who refrained.

217

They voiced their protests in a periodic cycle of reasoning, pleading, and screaming of obscenities, because the garbage collected outside their windows where the cats took up permanent residency, miaowing, feasting and caterwauling day and night. If the cascade of food was more than the cats could devour, the remainder fell to the fortune of the rats. Finally, flies and insects buzzed and hovered over the dregs, little pools of pulses and curries fermenting and frothing, till the *kuchrawalli* came next morning and swept it all away.

The backyards of Firozsha Baag constituted its squalid underbelly. And this would be the scenario for stoning-the-cats, Pesi decided. But there was one hitch: the backyards were off limits to the boys. The only way in was through the *kuchrawalli*'s little shack standing beyond A Block, where her huge ferocious dog, tied to the gate, kept the boys at bay. So Pesi decreed that the boys gather at the rear windows of their homes, preferably at a time of day when the adults were scarce, with the fathers away at work and the mothers not yet finished with their afternoon naps. Each boy brought a pile of small stones and took turns, chucking three stones each. The game could just as easily have been stoning-the-rats; but stoned rats quietly walked away to safety, whereas the yowls of cats provided primal satisfaction and verified direct hits: no yowl, no point.

The game added to Pesi's popularity – he called it a howling success. But the parents (except the ground floor) complained to Dr Mody about his son instigating the children to torment poor dumb and helpless creatures. For a veterinarian's son to harass animals was shameful, they said.

As might be supposed, Pesi was the despair of his parents. Over the years Dr Mody had become inured to the initial embarrassment in each new place they moved to. The routine was familiar: first, a spate of complaints from indignant parents claiming their sons *bugree nay dhoor thai gaya* – were corrupted to become useless as dust; next, the protestations giving way to sympathy when the neighbours saw that Pesi was the worm in the Modys' mango.

And so it was in Firozsha Baag. After the furor about stoning-the-cats had died down, the people of the Baag liked Dr Mody more than ever. He earned their respect for the initiative he took in Baag matters, dealing with the management for things like broken lifts, leaking water tanks, crumbling plaster, and faulty wiring. It was at his urging that the massive iron gate, set in the stone wall which ran all around the buildings, compound and backyards, was repaired, and a watchman installed to stop beggars and riff-raff. (And although Dr Mody would be dead by the time of the *Shiv Sena* riots, the tenants would remember him for the gate which would keep out the rampaging mobs.) When the Bombay Municipality tried to appropriate a section of Baag property for its road-widening scheme, Dr Mody was in the forefront of the battle, winning a compromise whereby the Baag only lost half the proposed area. But the Baag's esteem did nothing to lighten the despair for Pesi that hung around the doctor.

At the birth of his son, Dr Mody had deliberated long and hard about the naming. Peshotan, in the Persian epic, *Shah-Nameh*, was the brother of the great Asfandyar, and a noble general, lover of art and learning, and man of wise counsel. Dr Mody had decided his son would play the violin, acquire the best from the cultures of East and West, thrill to the words of Tagore and Shakespeare, appreciate Mozart and Indian ragas; and one day, at the proper moment, he would introduce him to his dearest activity, stamp-collecting.

But the years passed in their own way. Fate denied fruition to all of Dr Mody's plans; and when he talked about stamps, Pesi laughed and mocked his beloved hobby. This was the point at which, hurt and confused, he surrendered his son to whatever destiny was in store. A perpetual grief entered to occupy the void left behind after the aspirations for his son were evicted.

The weight of grief was heaviest around Dr Mody when he returned from work in the evenings. As the car turned into the compound he usually saw Pesi before Pesi saw him, in scenes which made him despair, scenes in which his son was abusing someone, fighting, or making lewd gestures.

But Dr Mody was careful not to make a public spectacle of

his despair. While the car made its way sluggishly over the uneven flagstones of the compound, the boys would stand back and wave him through. With his droll comments and jovial countenance he was welcome to disrupt their play, unlike two other car-owners of Firozsha Baag: the priest in A Block and the chartered accountant in B who habitually berated, from inside their vehicles, the sons of bank clerks and bookkeepers for blocking the driveway with their games. Their well-worn curses had become so predictable and ineffective that sometimes the boys chanted gleefully, in unison with their nemeses: 'Worse than *saala* animals!' or '*junglee* dogs – cats have more sense!' or 'you *sataans* ever have any lesson-*paani* to do or not!'

There was one boy who always stayed apart from his peers – the Bulsara boy, from the family next door to the Modys. Jehangir sat on the stone steps every evening while the gentle land breezes, drying and cooling the sweaty skins of the boys at play, blew out to sea. He sat alone through the long dusk, a source of discomfiture to the others. They resented his melancholy, watching presence.

Dr Mody noticed Jehangir, too, on the stone steps of C Block, the delicate boy with the build much too slight for his age. Next to a hulk like Pesi he was diminutive, but things other than size underlined his frail looks: he had slender hands, and forearms with fine downy hair. And while facial fuzz was incipient in most boys of his age (and Pesi was positively hirsute), Jehangir's chin and upper lip were smooth as a young woman's. But it pleased Dr Mody to see him evening after evening. The quiet contemplation of the boy on the steps and the noise and activity of the others at play came together in the kind of balance that Dr Mody was always looking for and was quick to appreciate.

Jehangir, in his turn, observed the burly Dr Mody closely as he walked past him each evening. When he approached the steps after parking his car, Jehangir would say '*Sahibji*' in greeting, and smile wanly. He saw that despite Dr Mody's constant jocularity there was something painfully empty about his eyes. He noticed the peculiar way he scratched the greyish-red patches of psoriasis on his elbows, both elbows simultaneously, by folding his arms across his chest. Sometimes Jehangir would arise from the stone steps and the two would go up together to the third floor. Dr Mody asked him once, 'You don't like playing with the other boys? You just sit and watch them?' The boy shook his head and blushed, and Dr Mody did not bring up the matter after that.

Gradually, a friendship of sorts grew between the two. Jehangir touched a chord inside the doctor which had lain silent for much too long. Now affection for the boy developed and started to linger around the region hitherto occupied by grief bearing Pesi's name.

II

One evening, while Jehangir sat on the stone steps waiting for Dr Mody's car to arrive, Pesi was organising a game of *naargolio*. He divided the boys into two teams, then discovered he was one short. He beckoned to Jehangir, who said he did not want to play. Scowling, Pesi handed the ball to one of the others and walked over to him. He grabbed his collar with both hands, jerking him to his feet. '*Arré choosya!*' he yelled, 'want a pasting?' and began dragging him by the collar to where the boys had piled up the seven flat stones for *naargolio*.

At that instant, Dr Mody's car turned into the compound, and he spied his son in one of those scenes which could provoke despair. But today the despair was swept aside by rage when he saw that Pesi's victim was the gentle and quiet Jehangir Bulsara. He left the car in the middle of the compound with the motor running. Anger glinted in his eyes. He kicked over the pile of seven flat stones as he walked blindly towards Pesi who, having seen his father, had released Jehangir. He had been caught by his father often enough to know that it was best to stand and wait. Jehangir, meanwhile, tried to keep back the tears.

Dr Mody stopped before his son and slapped him hard, once on each cheek, with the front and back of his right hand.

He waited, as if debating whether that was enough, then put his arm around Jehangir and led him to the car.

He drove to his parking spot. By now, Jehangir had control of his tears, and they walked to the steps of C Block. The lift was out of order. They climbed the stairs to the third floor and knocked. He waited with Jehangir.

Jehangir's mother came to the door. '*Sahibji*, Dr Mody,' she said, a short, middle-aged woman, very prim, whose hair was always in a bun. Never without a *mathoobanoo*, she could do wonderful things with that square of fine white cloth which was tied and knotted to sit like a cap on her head, snugly packeting the bun. In the evenings, after the household chores were done, she removed the *mathoobanoo* and wore it in a more conventional manner, like a scarf.

'*Sahibji*,' she said, then noticed her son's tear-stained face. '*Arré*, Jehangoo, what happened, who made you cry?' Her hand flew automatically to the *mathoobanoo*, tugging and adjusting it as she did whenever she was concerned or agitated.

To save the boy embarrassment, Dr Mody intervened: 'Go, wash your face while I talk to your mother.' Jehangir went inside, and Dr Mody told her briefly about what had happened. 'Why does he not play with the other boys?' he asked finally.

'Dr Mody, what to say. The boy never wants even to go out. *Khoedai salaamat raakhé*, wants to sit at home all the time and read story books. Even this little time in the evening he goes because I force him and tell him he will not grow tall without fresh air. Every week he brings new-new story books from school. First, school library would allow only one book per week. But he went to Father Gonzalves who is in charge of the library and got special permission for two books. God knows why he gave it.'

'But reading is good, Mrs Bulsara.'

'I know, I know, but a mania like this, all the time?'

'Some boys are outdoors types, some are indoor types. You shouldn't worry about Jehangir, he is a very good boy. Look at my Pesi, now there is a case for worry,' he said, meaning to reassure her.

'No, no. You mustn't say that. Be patient, *Khoedai* is great,' said Mrs Bulsara, consoling him instead. Jehangir returned, his eyes slightly red but dry. While washing his face he had wet a lock of his hair which hung down over his forehead.

'Ah, here comes my indoor champion,' smiled Dr Mody, and patted Jehangir's shoulder, brushing back the lock of hair. Jehangir did not understand, but grinned anyway; the doctor's joviality was infectious. Dr Mody turned again to his mother. 'Send him to my house on Sunday at ten o'clock. We will have a little talk.'

After Dr Mody left, Jehangir's mother told him how lucky he was that someone as important and learned as Burjor Uncle was taking an interest in him. Privately, she hoped he would encourage the boy towards a more all-rounded approach to life and to the things other boys did. And when Sunday came she sent Jehangir off to Dr Mody's promptly at ten.

Dr Mody was taking his bath, and Mrs Mody opened the door. She was a dour-faced woman, spare and lean – the opposite of her husband in appearance and disposition, yet retaining some quality from long ago which suggested that it had not always been so. Jehangir had never crossed her path save when she was exchanging civilities with his mother, while making purchases out by the stairs from the vegetable-walla or fruitwalla.

Not expecting Jehangir's visit, Mrs Mody stood blocking the doorway and said: 'Yes?' Meaning, what nuisance now?

'Burjor Uncle asked me to come at ten o'clock.'

'Asked you to come at ten o'clock? What for?'

'He just said to come at ten o'clock.'

Grudgingly, Mrs Mody stepped aside. 'Come in then. Sit down there.' And she indicated the specific chair she wanted him to occupy, muttering something about a *baap* who had time for strangers' children but not for his own son.

Jehangir sat in what must have been the most uncomfortable chair in the room. This was his first time inside the Modys' flat, and he looked around with curiosity. But his gaze was quickly restricted to the area of floor directly in front of him when he realised that he was the object of Mrs Mody's watchfulness.

Minutes ticked by under her vigilant eye. Jehangir was grateful when Dr Mody emerged from the bedroom. Being Sunday, he had eschewed his usual khaki half-pants for loose and comfortable white pyjamas. His *sudra* hung out over it, and he strode vigorously, feet encased in a huge pair of *sapaat*. He smiled at Jehangir, who happily noted the crow's-feet appearing at the corners of his eyes. He was ushered into Dr Mody's room, and man and boy both seemed glad to escape the surveillance of the woman.

The chairs were more comfortable in Dr Mody's room. They sat at his desk and Dr Mody opened a drawer to take out a large book.

'This was the first stamp album I ever had,' said Dr Mody. 'It was given to me by my Nusserwanji Uncle when I was your age. All the pages were empty.' He began turning them. They were covered with stamps, each a feast of colour and design. He talked as he turned the pages, and Jehangir watched and listened, glancing at the stamps flying past, at Dr Mody's face, then at the stamps again.

Dr Mody spoke not in his usual booming, jovial tones but softly, in a low voice charged with inspiration. The stamps whizzed by, and his speech was gently underscored by the rustle of the heavily laden pages that seemed to turn of their own volition in the quiet room. (Jehangir would remember this peculiar rustle when one day, older, he'd stand alone in this very room, silenced now for ever, and turn the pages of Nusserwanji Uncle's album.) Jehangir watched and listened. It was as though a mask had descended over Dr Mody, a far-away look upon his face, and a shining in the eyes which heretofore Jehangir had only seen sad with despair or glinting with anger or just plain and empty, belying his constant drollery. Jehangir watched, and listened to the euphonious voice hinting at wondrous things and promises and dreams.

The album on the desk, able to produce such changes in Dr Mody, now worked its magic through him upon the boy.

Jehangir, watching and listening, fascinated, tried to read the names of the countries at the top of the pages as they sped by: Antigua . . . Australia . . . Belgium . . . Bhutan . . . Bulgaria . . . and on through to Malta and Mauritius . . . Romania and Russia . . . Togo and Tonga . . . and a final blur through which he caught Yugoslavia and Zanzibar.

'Can I see it again?' he asked, and Dr Mody handed the album to him.

'So what do you think? Do you want to be a collector?'

Jehangir nodded eagerly and Dr Mody laughed. 'When Nusserwanji Uncle showed me his collection I felt just like that. I'll tell your mother what to buy for you to get you started. Bring it here next Sunday, same time.'

And next Sunday Jehangir was ready at nine. But he waited by his door with a Stamp Album For Beginners and a packet of 100 Assorted Stamps – All Countries. Going too early would mean sitting under the baleful eyes of Mrs Mody.

Ten o'clock struck and the clock's tenth bong was echoed by the Modys' door chimes. Mrs Mody was expecting him this time and did not block the doorway. Wordlessly, she beckoned him in. Burjor Uncle was ready, too, and came out almost immediately to rescue him from her arena.

'Let's see what you've got there,' he said when they were in his room. They removed the cellophane wrapper, and while they worked Dr Mody enjoyed himself as much as the boy. His deepest wish appeared to be coming true: he had at last found someone to share his hobby with. He could not have hoped for a finer neophyte than Jehangir. His young recruit was so quick to learn how to identify and sort stamps by countries, learn the different currencies, spot watermarks. Already he was skilfully folding and moistening the little hinges and mounting the stamps as neatly as the teacher.

When it was almost time to leave, Jehangir asked if he could examine again Nusserwanji Uncle's album, the one he had seen last Sunday. But Burjor Uncle led him instead to a cupboard in the corner of the room. 'Since you enjoy looking at my stamps, let me show you what I have here.' He unlocked its doors.

Each of the cupboard's four shelves was piled with biscuit tins and sweet tins: round, oval, rectangular, square. It puzzled Jehangir: all this bore the unmistakable stamp of the worthless hoardings of senility, and did not seem at all like Burjor Uncle. But Burjor Uncle reached out for a box at random and showed him inside. It was chock-full of stamps! Jehangir's mouth fell open. Then he gaped at the shelves, and Burjor Uncle laughed. 'Yes, all these tins are full of stamps. And that big cardboard box at the bottom contains six new albums, all empty.'

Jehangir quickly tried to assign a number in his mind to the stamps in the containers of Maghanlal Biscuitwalla and Lokmanji Mithaiwalla, to all of the stamps in the round tins and the oval tins, the square ones and the oblong ones. He failed.

Once again Dr Mody laughed at the boy's wonderment. 'A lot of stamps. And they took me a lot of years to collect. Of course, I am lucky I have many contacts in foreign countries. Because of my job, I meet the experts from abroad who are invited by the Indian Government. When I tell them about my hobby they send me stamps from their countries. But no time to sort them, so I pack them in boxes. One day, after I retire, I will spend all my time with my stamps.' He paused, and shut the cupboard doors. 'So what you have to do now is start making lots of friends, tell them about your hobby. If they also collect, you can exchange duplicates with them. If they don't, you can still ask them for all the envelopes they may be throwing away with stamps on them. You do something for them, they will do something for you. Your collection will grow depending on how smart you are.'

He hesitated, and opened the cupboard again. Then he changed his mind and shut it – it wasn't yet time for the Spanish dancing-lady stamp.

III

On the pavement outside St Xavier's Boys School, not far from the ornate iron gates, stood two variety stalls. They were the stalls of *Patla Babu* and *Jhaaria Babu*. Their real names were never known. Nor was known the exact source of the schoolboy inspiration that named them thus, many years ago, after their respective thinness and fatness.

Before the schoolboys arrived in the morning, the two would unpack their cases and set up the displays, beating the beggars to the choice positions. Occasionally, there were disputes if someone's space was violated. The beggars did not harbour great hopes for alms from schoolboys but they stood there, none the less, like mute lessons in realism and the harshness of life. Their patience was rewarded when they raided the dustbins after breaks and lunches.

At the end of the school day the pavement community packed up. The beggars shuffled off into the approaching dark, *Patla Babu* went home with his cases, and *Jhaaria Babu* slept near the school gate under a large tree to whose trunk he chained his boxes during the night.

The two sold a variety of nondescript objects and comestibles, uninteresting to any save the eyes and stomachs of schoolboys: *supari*, A-1 chewing gum (which, in a most ungumlike manner, would, after a while, dissolve in one's mouth), *jeeragoli*, marbles, tops, *aampapud* during the mango season, pens, Camel Ink, pencils, rulers, and stamps in little cellophane packets.

Patla Babu and *Jhaaria Babu* lost some of their goods regularly due to theft. This was inevitable when doing business outside a large school like St Xavier's, with a population as varied as its was. The loss was an operating expense stoically accepted, like the success or failure of the monsoons, and they never complained to the school authorities or held it against the boys. Besides, business was good despite the losses: insignificant items like a packet of *jeeragoli* worth ten paise, or a marble of the kind that sold for three or five paise. More often than not, the stealing went on for the excitement of it, out of bravado or on a dare. It was called 'flicking' and was done without any malice towards *Patla* and *Jhaaria*.

Foremost among the flickers was a boy in Jehangir's class called Eric D'Souza. A tall, lanky fellow who had been suspended a couple of times, he had had to repeat the year on two occasions, and held out the promise of more repetitions. Eric also had the reputation of doing things inside his half-pants under cover of his desk. In a class of fifty boys it was easy to go unobserved by the teacher, and only his immediate neighbours could see the ecstasy on his face and the vigorous back and forth movement of his hand. When he grinned at them they looked away, pretending not to have noticed anything.

Jehangir sat far from Eric and knew of his habits only by hearsay. He was oblivious to Eric's eye which had been on him for quite a while. In fact, Eric found Jehangir's delicate hands and fingers, his smooth legs and thighs very desirable. In class he gazed for hours, longingly, at the girlish face, curly hair, long eyelashes.

Jehangir and Eric finally got acquainted one day when the class filed out for games period. Eric had been made to kneel down by the door for coming late and disturbing the class, and Jehangir found himself next to him as he stood in line. From his kneeling position Eric observed the smooth thighs emerging from the half-pants (half-pants was the school uniform requirement), winked at him and, unhindered by his underwear, inserted a pencil up the pant leg. He tickled Jehangir's genitals seductively with the eraser end, expertly, then withdrew it. Jehangir feigned a giggle, too shocked to say anything. The line started to move for the playground.

Shortly after this incident, Eric approached Jehangir during breaktime. He had heard that Jehangir was desperate to acquire stamps.

'*Arré* man, I can get you stamps, whatever kind you want,' he said.

Jehangir stopped. He had been slightly confused ever since the pass with the pencil; Eric frightened him a little with his curious habits and forbidden knowledge. But it had not been easy to accumulate stamps. Sundays with Burjor Uncle continued to be as fascinating as the first. He wished he had new stamps to show – the stasis of his collection might be interpreted as lack of interest. He asked Eric: 'Ya? You want to exchange?'

'No *yaar*, I don't collect. But I'll get them for you. As a favour, man.'

'Ya? What kind do you have?'

'I don't have, man. Come on with me to *Patla* and *Jhaaria*, just show me which ones you want. I'll flick them for you.'

Jehangir hesitated. Eric put his arm around him: 'C'mon man, what you scared for, I'll flick. You just show me and go away.' Jehangir pictured the stamps on display in cellophane wrappers: how well they would add to his collection. He imagined album pages bare no more but covered with exquisite stamps, each one mounted carefully and correctly, with a hinge, as Burjor Uncle had showed him to.

They went outside, Eric's arm still around him. Crowds of schoolboys were gathered around the two stalls. A multitude of groping, exploring hands handled the merchandise and browsed absorbedly, a multitude that was a prerequisite for flicking to begin. Jehangir showed Eric the individually wrapped stamps he wanted and moved away. In a few minutes Eric joined him triumphantly.

'Got them?'

'Ya ya. But come inside. He could be watching, man.'

Jehangir was thrilled. Eric asked, 'You want more or what?'

'Sure,' said Jehangir.

'But not today. On Friday. If you do me a favour in visual period on Thursday.'

Jehangir's pulse speeded slightly – visual period, with its darkened hall and projector, and the intimacy created by the teacher's policing abilities temporarily suspended. He remembered Eric's pencil. The cellophane-wrapped stamp packets rustled and crackled in his hand. And there was the promise of more. There had been nothing unpleasant about the pencil. In fact it had felt quite, well, exciting. He agreed to Eric's proposal.

On Thursday, the class lined up to go to the Visual Hall. Eric stood behind Jehangir to ensure their seats would be together.

When the room was dark he put his hand on Jehangir's thigh and began caressing it. He took Jehangir's hand and placed it on his crotch. It lay there inert. Impatient, he whispered, 'Do it, man, c'mon!' But Jehangir's lack-lustre stroking was highly unsatisfactory. Eric arrested the hand, reached inside his pants and said, 'Okay, hold it tight and rub it like this.' He encircled Jehangir's hand with his to show him how. When Jehangir had attained the right pressure and speed he released his own hand to lean back and sigh contentedly. Shortly, Jehangir felt a warm stickiness fill his palm and fingers, and the hardness he held in his hand grew flaccid.

Eric shook off the hand. Jehangir wiped his palm with his hanky. Eric borrowed the hanky to wipe himself. 'Want me to do it for you?' he asked. But Jehangir declined. He was thinking of his hanky. The odour was interesting, not unpleasant at all, but he would have to find some way of cleaning it before his mother found it.

The following day, Eric presented him with more stamps. Next Thursday's assignation was also fixed.

And on Sunday Jehangir went to see Dr Mody at ten o'clock. The wife let him in, muttering something under her breath about being bothered by inconsiderate people on the one day that the family could be together.

Dr Mody's delight at the new stamps fulfilled Jehangir's every expectation: 'Wonderful, wonderful! Where did you get them all? No, no, forget it, don't tell me. You will think I'm trying to learn your tricks. I already have enough stamps to keep me busy in my retirement. Ha! ha!'

After the new stamps had been examined and sorted Dr Mody said, 'Today, as a reward for your enterprise, I'm going to show you a stamp you've never seen before.' From the cupboard of biscuit and sweet tins he took a small satin-covered box of the type in which rings or bracelets are kept. He opened it and, without removing the stamp from inside, placed it on the desk.

The stamp said España Correos at the bottom and its denomination was noted in the top left corner: 3 PTAS. The face of the stamp featured a flamenco dancer in the most exquisite detail and colour. But it was something in the woman's countenance, a look, an ineffable sparkle he saw in her eyes, which so captivated Jehangir.

Wordlessly, he studied the stamp. Dr Mody waited restlessly as the seconds ticked by. He kept fidgeting till the little satin-covered box was shut and back in his hands, then said, 'So you like the Spanish dancing-lady. Everyone who sees it likes it. Even my wife who is not interested in stamp-collecting thought it was beautiful. When I retire I can spend more time with the Spanish dancing-lady. And all my other stamps.' He relaxed once the stamp was locked again in the cupboard.

Jehangir left, carrying that vision of the Spanish dancer in his head. He tried to imagine the stamp inhabiting the pages of his album, to greet him every time he opened it, with the wonderful sparkle in her eyes. He shut the door behind him and immediately, as though to obliterate his covetous fantasy, loud voices rose inside the flat.

He heard Mrs Mody's, shrill in argument, and the doctor's, beseeching her not to yell lest the neighbours would hear. Pesi's name was mentioned several times in the quarrel that ensued, and accusations of neglect, and something about the terrible affliction on a son of an unloving father. The voices followed Jehangir as he hurried past the inquiring eyes of his mother, till he reached the bedroom at the other end of the flat and shut the door.

When the school week started, Jehangir found himself looking forward to Thursday. His pulse was racing with excitement when visual period came. To save his hanky this time he kept some paper at hand.

Eric did not have to provide much guidance. Jehangir discovered he could control Eric's reactions with variations in speed, pressure, and grip. When it was over and Eric offered to do it to him, he did not refuse.

The weeks sped by and Jehangir's collection continued to grow, visual period by visual period. Eric's and his masturbatory partnership was whispered about in class, earning the pair the title of *moothya-maroo*. He accompanied Eric on the flicking forays, helping to swell the milling crowd and add to the browsing hands. Then he grew bolder, studied Eric's methods, and flicked a few stamps himself.

But this smooth course of stamp-collecting was about to end. *Patla Babu* and *Jhaaria Babu* broke their long tradition of silence and complained to the school. Unlike marbles and *supari*, it was not a question of a few paise a day. When Eric and Jehangir struck, their haul could be totalled in rupees reaching double digits; the loss was serious enough to make the *Babus* worry about their survival.

The school assigned the case to the head prefect to investigate. He was an ambitious boy, always snooping around, and was also a member of the school debating team and the Road Safety Patrol. Shortly after the complaint was made he marched into Jehangir's class one afternoon just after lunch break, before the teacher returned, and made what sounded very much like one of his debating speeches: 'Two boys in this class have been stealing stamps from *Patla Babu* and *Jhaaria Babu* for the past several weeks. You may ask: who are those boys? No need for names. They know who they are and I know who they are, and I am asking them to return the stamps to me tomorrow. There will be no punishment if this is done. The *Babus* just want their stamps back. But if the missing stamps are not returned, the names will be reported to the principal and to the police. It is up to the two boys.'

Jehangir tried hard to appear normal. He was racked with trepidation, and looked to the unperturbed Eric for guidance. But Eric ignored him. The head prefect left amidst mock applause from the class.

After school, Eric turned surly. Gone was the tender, cajoling manner he reserved for Jehangir, and he said nastily: 'You better bring back all those fucking stamps tomorrow.' Jehangir, of course, agreed. There was no trouble with the prefect or the school after the stamps were returned.

But Jehangir's collection shrunk pitiably overnight. He slept badly the entire week, worried about explaining to Burjor Uncle the sudden disappearance of the bulk of his collection. His mother assumed the dark rings around his eyes were due to too much reading and not enough fresh air. The thought of stamps or of *Patla Babu* or *Jhaaria Babu* brought an emptiness to his stomach and a bitter taste to his mouth. A general sense of ill-being took possession of him.

He went to see Burjor Uncle on Sunday, leaving behind his stamp album. Mrs Mody opened the door and turned away silently. She appeared to be in a black rage, which exacerbated Jehangir's own feelings of guilt and shame.

He explained to Burjor Uncle that he had not bothered to bring his album because he had acquired no new stamps since last Sunday, and also, he was not well and would not stay for long.

Dr Mody was concerned about the boy, so nervous and uneasy; he put it down to his feeling unwell. They looked at some stamps Dr Mody had received last week from his colleagues abroad. Then Jehangir said he'd better leave.

'But you *must* see the Spanish dancing-lady before you go. Maybe she will help you feel better. Ha! ha!' and Dr Mody rose to go to the cupboard for the stamp. Its viewing at the end of each Sunday's session had acquired the significance of an esoteric ritual.

From the next room Mrs Mody screeched: 'Burjorji! Come here at once!' He made a wry face at Jehangir and hurried out.

In the next room, all the vehemence of Mrs Mody's black rage of that morning poured out upon Dr Mody: 'It has reached the limit now! No time for your own son and Sunday after Sunday sitting with some stranger! What does he have that your own son does not? Are you a *baap* or what? No wonder Pesi has become this way! How can I blame the boy when his own *baap* takes no interest . . .'

'Shh! The boy is in the next room! What do you want, that all the neighbours hear your screaming?'

'I don't care! Let them hear! You think they don't know already? You think you are . . .'

Mrs Bulsara next door listened intently. Suddenly, she realised that Jehangir was in there. Listening from one's own house was one thing – hearing a quarrel from inside the quarrellers' house was another. It made feigning ignorance very difficult.

She rang the Modys' doorbell and waited, adjusting her *mathoobanoo*. Dr Mody came to the door.

'Burjorji, forgive me for disturbing your stamping and collecting work with Jehangir. But I must take him away. Guests have arrived unexpectedly. Jehangir must go to the Irani, we need cold drinks.'

'That's okay, he can come next Sunday.' Then added, 'He *must* come next Sunday,' and noted with satisfaction the frustrated turning away of Mrs Mody who waited out of sight of the doorway. 'Jehangir! Your mother is calling.'

Jehangir was relieved at being rescued from the turbulent waters of the Mody household. They left without further conversation, his mother tugging in embarrassment at the knots of her *mathoobanoo*.

As a result of this unfortunate outburst, a period of awkwardness between the two women was unavoidable. Mrs Mody, though far from garrulous, had never let her domestic sorrows and disappointments interfere with the civilities of neighbourly relations, which she respected and observed at all times. Now for the first time since the arrival of the Modys in Firozsha Baag these civilities experienced a hiatus.

When the *muchhiwalla* arrived next morning, instead of striking a joint deal with him as they usually did, Mrs Mody waited till Mrs Bulsara had finished. She stationed an eye at her peephole as he emphasised the freshness of his catch. 'Look *bai*, it is *saféd paani*,' he said, holding out the pomfret and squeezing it near the gills till white fluid oozed out. After Mrs Bulsara had paid and gone, Mrs Mody emerged, while the former took her turn at the peephole. And so it went for a few days till the awkwardness had run its course and things returned to normal.

But not so for Jehangir; on Sunday, he once again had to leave behind his sadly depleted album. To add to his uneasiness, Mrs Mody invited him in with a greeting of 'Come *bawa* come,' and there was something malignant about her smile.

Dr Mody sat at his desk, shoulders sagging, his hands dangling over the arms of the chair. The desk was bare – not a single stamp anywhere in sight, and the cupboard in the corner locked. The absence of his habitual, comfortable clutter made the room cold and cheerless. He was in low spirits; instead of the crow's-feet at the corners of his eyes were lines of distress and dejection.

'No album again?'

'No. Haven't got any new stamps yet,' Jehangir smiled nervously.

Dr Mody scratched the psoriasis on his elbows. He watched Jehangir carefully as he spoke. 'Something very bad has happened to the Spanish dancing-lady stamp. Look,' and he displayed the satin-covered box minus its treasure. 'It is missing.' Half-fearfully, he looked at Jehangir, afraid he would see what he did not want to. But it was inevitable. His last sentence evoked the head prefect's thundering debating-style speech of a few days ago, and the ugliness of the entire episode revisited Jehangir's features – a final ignominious postscript to Dr Mody's loss and disillusion.

Dr Mody shut the box. The boy's reaction, his silence, the absence of his album, confirmed his worst suspicions. More humiliatingly, it seemed his wife was right. With great sadness he rose from his chair. 'I have to leave now, something urgent at the College.' They parted without a word about next Sunday.

Jehangir never went back. He thought for a few days about the missing stamp and wondered what could have happened to it. Burjor Uncle was too careful to have misplaced it; besides, he never removed it from its special box. And the box was still there. But he did not resent him for concluding he had stolen it. His guilt about *Patla Babu* and *Jhaaria Babu*, about Eric and the stamps was so intense, and the punishment deriving from it so inconsequential, almost non-existent, that he did not mind this undeserved blame. In fact, it served to equilibrate his scales of justice.

His mother questioned him the first few Sundays he stayed home. Feeble excuses about homework, and Burjor Uncle not having new stamps, and it being boring to look at the same stuff every Sunday did not satisfy her. She finally attributed his abnegation of stamps to sensitivity and a regard for the unfortunate state of the Modys' domestic affairs. It pleased her that her son was capable of such concern. She did not press him after that.

IV

Pesi was no longer to be seen in Firozsha Baag. His absence brought relief to most of the parents at first, and then curiosity. Gradually, it became known that he had been sent away to a boarding-school in Poona.

The boys of the Baag continued to play their games in the compound. For better or worse, the spark was lacking that lent unpredictability to those languid coastal evenings of Bombay; evenings which could so easily trap the unwary, adult or child, within a circle of lassitude and depression in which time hung heavy and suffocating.

Jehangir no longer sat on the stone steps of C Block in the evenings. He found it difficult to confront Dr Mody day after day. Besides the boys he used to watch at play suspected some kind of connection between Pesi's being sent away to boarding-school, Jehangir's former friendship with Dr Mody, and the emerging of Dr Mody's constant sorrow and despair (which he had tried so hard to keep private all along, and had succeeded, but was now visible for all to see). And the boys resented Jehangir for whatever his part was in it – they bore him open antagonism.

Dr Mody was no more the jovial figure the boys had grown to love. When his car turned into the compound in the evenings, he still waved, but no crow's-feet appeared at his eyes, no smile, no jokes.

Two years passed since the Mody family's arrival in Firozsha Baag.

In school, Jehangir was as isolated as in the Baag. Most of his effeminateness had, of late, transformed into vigorous signs of impending manhood. Eric D'Souza had been expelled for attempting to sodomise a junior boy. Jehangir had not been involved in this affair, but most of his classmates related it to the furtive activities of their callow days and the stamp-flicking. *Patla Babu* and *Jhaaria Babu* had disappeared from the pavement outside St Xavier's. The Bombay police, in a misinterpretation of the nation's mandate: *garibi hatao* – eradicate poverty, conducted periodic round-ups of pavement dwellers, sweeping into their vans beggars and street-vendors, cripples and alcoholics, the homeless and the hungry, and dumped them somewhere outside the city limits; when the human detritus made its way back into the city, another clean-up was scheduled. *Patla* and *Jhaaria* were snared in one of these raids, and never found their way back. Eye-witnesses said their stalls were smashed up and *Patla Babu* received a *lathi* across his forehead for trying to salvage some of his inventory. They were not seen again.

Two years passed since Jehangir's visits to Dr Mody had ceased.

It was getting close to the time for another transfer for Dr Mody. When the inevitable orders were received, he went to Ahmedabad to make arrangements. Mrs Mody was to join her husband after a few days. Pesi was still in boarding-school, and would stay there.

So when news arrived from Ahmedabad of Dr Mody's death of heart failure, Mrs Mody was alone in the flat. She went next door with the telegram and broke down.

The Bulsaras helped with all the arrangements. The body was brought to Bombay by car for a proper Parsi funeral. Pesi came from Poona for the funeral, then went back to boarding-school.

The events were talked about for days afterwards, the stories spreading first in C Block, then through A and B. Commiseration for Mrs Mody was general. The ordeal of the body during the two-day car journey from Ahmedabad was particularly horrifying, and was discussed endlessly. Embalming was not allowed according to Parsi rituals, and the body in the trunk, although packed with ice, had started to smell horribly in the heat of the Deccan Plateau which the car had had to traverse. Some hinted that this torment suffered by Dr Mody's earthly remains was the Almighty's punishment for neglecting his duties as a father and making Mrs Mody so unhappy. Poor Dr Mody, they said, who never went a day without a bath and talcum powder in life, to undergo this in death. Someone even had, on good authority, a count of the number of eau de cologne bottles used by Mrs Mody and the three occupants of the car over the course of the journey – it was the only way they could draw breath, through cologne-watered handkerchiefs. And it was also said that ever after, these four could never tolerate eau de cologne – opening a bottle was like opening the car trunk with Dr Mody's decomposing corpse.

A year after the funeral, Mrs Mody was still living in Firozsha Baag. Time and grief had softened her looks, and she was no longer the harsh and dour-faced woman Jehangir had seen during his first Sunday visit. She had decided to make the flat her permanent home now, and the trustees of the Baag granted her request 'in view of the unfortunate circumstances'.

There were some protests about this, particularly from those whose sons or daughters had been postponing marriages and families till flats became available. But the majority, out of respect for Dr Mody's memory, agreed with the trustees' decision. Pesi continued to attend boarding-school.

One day, shortly after her application had been approved by the trustees, Mrs Mody visited Mrs Bulsara. They sat and talked of old times, when they had first moved in, and about how pleased Dr Mody had been to live in a Parsi colony like Firozsha Baag after years of travelling, and then the disagreements she had had with her husband over Pesi and Pesi's future; tears came to her eyes, and also to Mrs Bulsara's, who tugged at a corner of her *mathoobanoo* to reach it to her eyes and dry them. Mrs Mody confessed how she had hated Jehangir's Sunday visits although he was such a fine boy, because she was worried about the way poor Burjorji was neglecting Pesi: 'But he could not help it. That was the way he was. Sometimes he would wish *Khoedai* had given him a daughter instead of a son. Pesi disappointed him in everything, in all his plans, and . . .' and here she burst into uncontrollable sobs.

Finally, after her tears subsided she asked, 'Is Jehangir home?' He wasn't. 'Would you ask him to come and see me this Sunday? At ten? Tell him I won't keep him long.'

Jehangir was a bit apprehensive when his mother gave him the message. He couldn't imagine why Mrs Mody would want to see him.

On Sunday, as he prepared to go next door, he was reminded of the Sundays with Dr Mody, the kindly man who had befriended him, opened up a new world for him, and then repudiated him for something he had not done. He remembered the way he would scratch the greyish-red patches of psoriasis on his elbows. He could still picture the sorrow on his face as, with the utmost reluctance, he had made his decision to end the friendship. Jehangir had not blamed Dr Mody then, and he still did not; he knew how overwhelmingly the evidence had been against him, and how much that stamp had meant to Dr Mody.

Mrs Mody led him in by his arm: 'Will you drink something?'

'No, thank you.'

'Not feeling shy, are you? You always were shy.' She asked him about his studies and what subjects he was taking in high school. She told him a little about Pesi, who was still in boarding-school and had twice repeated the same standard. She sighed. 'I asked you to come today because there is something I wanted to give you. Something of Burjor Uncle's. I thought about it for many days. Pesi is not interested, and I don't know anything about it. Will you take his collection?'

'The album in his drawer?' asked Jehangir, a little surprised.

'Everything. The album, all the boxes, everything in the cupboard. I know you will use it well. Burjor would have done the same.'

Jehangir was speechless. He had stopped collecting stamps, and they no longer held the fascination they once did. None the less, he was familiar with the size of the collection, and the sheer magnitude of what he was now being offered had its effect. He remembered the awe with which he had looked inside the cupboard the first time its doors had been opened before him. So many sweet tins, cardboard boxes, biscuit tins . . .

'You will take it? As a favour to me, yes?' she asked a second time, and Jehangir nodded. 'You have some time today? Whenever you like, just take it.' He said he would ask his mother and come back.

There was a huge, old iron trunk which lay under Jehangir's bed. It was dented in several places and the lid would not shut properly. Undisturbed for years, it had rusted peacefully beneath the bed. His mother agreed that the rags it held could be thrown away and the stamps temporarily stored in it till Jehangir organised them into albums. He emptied the trunk, wiped it out, lined it with brown paper and went next door to bring back the stamps.

Several trips later, Dr Mody's cupboard stood empty. Jehangir looked around the room in which he had once spent so many happy hours. The desk was in exactly the same position, and the two chairs. He turned to go, almost forgetting, and went back to the desk. Yes, there it was in the drawer, Dr Mody's first album, given him by his Nusserwanji Uncle.

He started to turn the heavily laden pages. They rustled in a peculiar way – what was it about that sound? Then he remembered: that first Sunday, and he could almost hear Dr Mody again, the soft inspired tones speaking of promises and dreams, quite different from his usual booming, jovial voice, and that faraway look in his eyes which had once glinted with rage when Pesi had tried to bully him . . .

Mrs Mody came into the room. He shut the album, startled: 'This is the last lot.' He stopped to thank her but she interrupted: 'No, no. What is the thank-you for? You are doing a favour to me by taking it, you are helping me to do what Burjor would like.' She took his arm. 'I wanted to tell you. From the collection one stamp is missing. With the picture of the dancing-lady.'

'I know!' said Jehangir. 'That's the one Burjor Uncle lost and thought that I . . .'

Mrs Mody squeezed his arm which she was still holding

and he fell silent. She spoke softly, but without guilt: 'He did not lose it. I destroyed it.' Then her eyes went moist as she watched the disbelief on his face. She wanted to say more, to explain, but could not, and clung to his arm. Finally, her voice quavering pitiably, she managed to say, 'Forgive an old lady,' and patted his cheek. Jehangir left in silence, suddenly feeling very ashamed.

Over the next few days, he tried to impose some order on that greatly chaotic mass of stamps. He was hoping that sooner or later his interest in philately would be rekindled. But that did not happen; the task remained futile and dry and boring. The meaningless squares of paper refused to come to life as they used to for Dr Mody in his room every Sunday at ten o'clock. Jehangir shut the trunk and pushed it back under his bed where it had lain untroubled for so many years.

From time to time his mother reminded him about the stamps: 'Do something Jehangoo, do something with them.' He said he would when he felt like it and had the time; he wasn't interested for now.

Then, after several months, he pulled out the trunk again from under his bed. Mrs Bulsara watched eagerly from a distance, not daring to interrupt with any kind of advice or encouragement: her Jehangoo was at that difficult age, she knew, when boys automatically did the exact reverse of what their parents said.

But the night before, Jehangir's sleep had been disturbed by a faint and peculiar rustling sound seeming to come from inside the trunk. His reasons for dragging it out into daylight soon became apparent to Mrs Bulsara.

The lid was thrown back to reveal clusters of cockroaches. They tried to scuttle to safety, and he killed a few with his slipper. His mother ran up now, adding a few blows of her own *chappal*, as the creatures began quickly to disperse. Some ran under the bed into hard-to-reach corners; others sought out the trunk's deeper recesses.

A cursory examination showed that besides cockroaches, the trunk was also infested with white ants. All the albums had been ravaged. Most of the stamps which had not been destroyed outright were damaged in one way or another. They bore haphazard perforations and brown stains of the type associated with insects and household pests.

Jehangir picked up an album at random and opened it. Almost immediately, the pages started to fall to pieces in his hands. He remembered what Dr Mody used to say: 'This is my retirement hobby. I will spend my retirement with my stamps.' He allowed the tattered remains of Burjor Uncle's beloved pastime to drop back slowly into the trunk.

He crouched beside the dented, rusted metal, curious that he felt no loss or pain. Why, he wondered. If anything, there was a slight sense of relief. He let his hands stray through the contents, through worthless paper scraps, through shreds of the work of so many Sunday mornings, stopping now and then to regard with detachment the bizarre patterns created by the mandibles of the insects who had feasted night after night under his bed, while he slept.

With an almost imperceptible shrug, he arose and closed the lid. It was doubtful if anything of value remained in the trunk.

Bapsi Sidhwa

RANNA'S STORY

LATE THAT AFTERNOON the clamour of the monsoon downpour suddenly ceased. Chidda raised her hands from the dough she was kneading and, squatting before the brass tray, turned to her mother-in-law. Sitting by his grandmother Ranna sensed their tension as the old woman stopped chaffing the wheat. She slowly pushed back her age-brittle hair and, holding her knobbly fingers immobile, grew absolutely still.

Chidda stood in their narrow doorway, her eyes nervously scouring the courtyard. Ranna clung to her shalwar, peering out. His cousins, almost naked in their soaking rags, were shouting and splashing in the slush in their courtyard. 'Shut up. Oye!' Chidda shouted in a voice that rushed so violently from her strong chest that the children quietened at once and leaned and slid uneasily against the warm black hides of the buffaloes tethered to the rough stumps. The clouds had broken and the sun shot beams that lit up the freshly bathed courtyard.

The other members of the household, Ranna's older brothers, his uncles, aunts and cousins were quietly filing into the courtyard. When she saw Khatija and Parveen, Chidda strode to her daughters and pressed them fiercely to her body. The village was so quiet it could be the middle of the night: and from the distance, buffeting the heavy, moisture-laden air, came the wails and the hoarse voices of men shouting.

Already their neighbours' turbans skimmed the tall mud

Extract from the novel *Ice-Candy-Man*.

243

ramparts of their courtyard, their bare feet squelching on the path the rain had turned into a muddy channel.

I can imagine the old mullah, combing his faded beard with trembling fingers as he watches the villagers converge on the mosque with its uneven green dome. It is perched on an incline; and seen from there the fields, flooded with rain, are the same muddy colour as the huts. The mullah drags his cot forward as the villagers, touching their foreheads and greeting him sombrely, fill the prayer ground. The *chaudhry* joins the mullah on his charpoy. The villagers sit on their haunches in uneven rows lifting their confused and frightened faces. There is a murmur of voices. Conjectures. First the name of one village and then of another. The Sikhs have attacked Kot-Rahim. No, it sounds closer . . . It must be Makipura.

The *chaudhry* raises his heavy voice slightly: 'Dost Mohammad and his party will be here soon . . . We'll know soon enough what's going on.'

At his reassuring presence the murmuring subsides and the villagers nervously settle down to wait. Some women draw their veils across their faces and, shading their bosoms, impatiently shove their nipples into the mouths of whimpering babies. Grandmothers, mothers and aunts rock restive children on their laps and thump their foreheads to put them to sleep. The children, conditioned to the numbing jolts, grow groggy and their eyes become unfocused. They fall asleep almost at once.

Half an hour later the scouting party, drenched and muddy, the lower halves of their faces wrapped in the ends of their turbans, pick their way through the squatting villagers to the *chaudhry*.

Removing his wet puggaree and wiping his head with a cloth the mullah hands him, Dost Mohammad turns on his haunches to face the villagers. His skin is grey, as if the rain has bleached the colour. Casting a shade across his eyes with a hand that trembles slightly, speaking in a matter-of-fact voice that disguises his ache and fear, he tells the villagers that the Sikhs have attacked at least five villages around Dehra

Misri, to their east. Their numbers have swollen enormously. They are like swarms of locusts, moving in marauding bands of thirty and forty thousand. They are killing all Muslims. Setting fires, looting, parading the Muslim women naked through the streets – raping and mutilating them in the centre of villages and in mosques. The Bias, flooded by melting snow, and the monsoon, is carrying hundreds of corpses. There is an intolerable stench where the bodies, caught in the bends, have piled up.

'What are the police doing?' a man shouts. He is Dost Mohammad's cousin. One way or another the villagers are related.

'The Muslims in the force have been disarmed at the orders of a Hindu Sub-Inspector; the dog's penis!' says Dost Mohammad, speaking in the same flat monotone. 'The Sikh and Hindu police have joined the mobs.'

The villagers appear visibly to shrink – as if the loss of hope is a physical thing. A woman with a child on her lap slaps her forehead and begins to wail: *'Hai! Hai!'* The other women join her: *'Hai! Hai!'* Older women, beating their breasts like hollow drums, cry, 'Never mind us . . . save the young girls! The children! *Hai! Hai!'*

Ranna's two-toothed old grandmother, her frail voice quavering bitterly, shrieks: 'We should have gone to Pakistan!'

It was hard to believe that the decision to stay was taken only a month ago. Embedded in the heart of the Punjab, they had felt secure, inviolate. And to uproot themselves from the soil of their ancestors had seemed to them akin to tearing themselves, like ancient trees, from the earth.

And the messages filtering from the outside had been reassuring. Gandhi, Nehru, Jinnah, Tara Singh were telling the peasants to remain where they were. The minorities would be a sacred trust . . . The communal trouble was being caused by a few mischief-makers and would soon subside – and then there were their brothers, the Sikhs of Dera Tek Singh, who would protect them.

But how many Muslims can the Sikh villagers befriend? The mobs, determined to drive the Muslims out, are prepared for the carnage. Their ranks swollen by thousands of refugees recounting fresh tales of horror they roll towards Pir Pindo like the heedless swells of an ocean.

The *chaudhry* raises his voice: 'How many guns do we have now?'

The women quieten.

'Seven or eight,' a man replies from the front.

There is a disappointed silence. They had expected to procure more guns but every village is holding on to its meagre stock of weapons.

'We have our axes, knives, scythes and staves!' a man calls from the back. 'Let those bastards come. We're ready!'

'Yes . . . we're as ready as we'll ever be,' the *chaudhry* says, stroking his thick moustache. 'You all know what to do . . .'

They have been over the plan often enough recently. The women and the girls will gather at the *chaudhry*'s. Rather than face the brutality of the mob they will pour kerosene around the house and burn themselves. The canisters of kerosene are already stored in the barn at the rear of the *chaudhry*'s sprawling mud house. The young men will engage the Sikhs at the mosque, and at other strategic locations, for as long as they can and give the women a chance to start the fire.

A few men from each family were to shepherd the younger boys and lock themselves into secluded back rooms, hoping to escape detection. They were peaceable peasants, not skilled in such matters, and their plans were sketchy and optimistic. Comforted by each other's presence, reluctant to disperse, the villagers remained in the prayer yard as dusk gathered about them. The distant wailing and shouting had ceased. Later that night it rained again, and comforted by its seasonal splatter the tired villagers curled up on their mats and slept.

The attack came at dawn. The watch from the mosque's single minaret hurtled down the winding steps to spread the alarm. The panicked women ran to and fro screaming and snatching up their babies, and the men barely had time to get to their posts. In fifteen minutes the village was swamped by the Sikhs – tall men with streaming hair and thick biceps and thighs, waving full-sized swords and sten-guns, roaring, 'Bolay so Nihal! Sat Siri Akal!'

They mowed down the villagers in the mosque with the sten-guns. Shouting 'Allah-o-Akbar!' the peasants died of sword and spear wounds in the slushy lanes and courtyards, the screams of women from the *chaudhry*'s house ringing in their ears, wondering why the house was not burning.

Ranna, abandoned by his mother and sisters halfway to the *chaudhry*'s house, ran howling into the courtyard. Chidda had spanked his head and pushed him away, shrieking, 'Go to your father! Stay with the men!'

Ranna ran through their house to the room the boys had been instructed to gather in. Some of his cousins and uncles were already there. More men stumbled into the dark windowless room – then his two older brothers. There must be at least thirty of them in the small room. It was stifling. He heard his father's voice and fought his way towards him. Dost Mohammad shouted harshly: 'Shut up! They'll kill you if you make a noise.'

The yelling in the room subsided. Dost Mohammad picked up his son, and Ranna saw his uncle slip out into the grey light and shut the door, plunging the room into darkness. Someone bolted the door from inside, and they heard the heavy thud of cotton bales stacked against the door to disguise the entrance. With luck they would remain undetected and safe.

The shouting and screaming from outside appeared to come in waves: receding and approaching. From all directions. Sometimes Ranna could make out the words and even whole sentences. He heard a woman cry, 'Do anything you want with me, but don't torment me . . . For God's sake, don't torture me!' And then an intolerable screaming. 'Oh God!' a man whispered on a sobbing intake of breath. 'Oh God, she is the mullah's daughter!' The men covered their ears – and the boys' ears – sobbing unaffectedly like little children.

A teenager, his cracked voice resounding like the honk of geese, started wailing: 'I don't want to die . . . I don't want to die!' Catching his fear, Ranna and the other children set to whimpering: 'I don't want to die . . . Abba, I don't want to die!'

'Hush,' said Dost Mohammad gruffly. 'Stop whining like girls!' Then, with words that must have bubbled up from a deep source of strength and compassion, with infinite gentleness, he said, 'What's there to be afraid of? Are you afraid to die? It won't hurt any more than the sting of a bee.' His voice, unseasonably light-hearted, carried a tenderness that soothed and calmed them. Ranna fell asleep in his father's arms.

Someone was banging on the door, shouting: 'Open up! Open up!'

Ranna awoke with a start. Why was he on the floor? Why were there so many people about in the dark? He felt the stir of men getting to their feet. The air in the room was oppressive: hot and humid and stinking of sweat. Suddenly Ranna remembered where he was and the darkness became charged with terror.

'We know you're in there. Come on, open up!' The noise of the banging was deafening in the pitch-black room, drowning the other children's alarmed cries. 'Allah! Allah! Allah!' an old man moaned non-stop.

'Who's there?' Dost Mohammad called; and putting Ranna down, stumbling over the small bodies, made his way to the door. Ranna, terrified, groping blindly in the dark, tried to follow.

'We're Sikhs!'

There was a pause in which Ranna's throat dried up. The old man stopped saying 'Allah'. And in the deathly stillness, his voice echoing from his proximity to the door, Dost Mohammad said, 'Kill us . . . Kill us all . . . but spare the children.'

'Open at once!'

'I beg you in the name of all you hold sacred, don't kill the little ones,' Ranna heard his father plead. 'Make them Sikhs . . . Let them live . . . they are so little . . .'

Suddenly the noon light smote their eyes. Dost Mohammad stepped out and walked three paces. There was a sunlit sweep of curved steel. His head was shorn clear off his neck. Turning once in the air, eyes wide open, it tumbled in the dust. His hands jerked up slashing the air above the bleeding stump of his neck.

Ranna saw his uncles beheaded. His older brothers, his cousins. The Sikhs were among them like hairy vengeful demons, wielding bloodied swords, dragging them out as a sprinkling of Hindus, darting about at the fringes, their faces vaguely familiar, pointed out and identified the Mussulmans by name. He felt a blow cleave the back of his head and the warm flow of blood. Ranna fell just inside the door on a tangled pile of unrecognisable bodies. Someone fell on him, drenching him in blood.

Every time his eyes open the world appears to them to be floating in blood. From the direction of the mosque come the intolerable shrieks and wails of women. It seems to him that a woman is sobbing just outside their courtyard: great anguished sobs – and at intervals she screams: 'You'll kill me! *Hai Allah* . . . Y'all will kill me!'

Ranna wants to tell her, 'Don't be afraid to die . . . It will hurt less than the sting of a bee.' But he is hurting so much . . . Why isn't he dead? Where are the bees? Once he thought he saw his eleven-year-old sister, Khatija, run stark naked into their courtyard: her long hair dishevelled, her boyish body bruised, her lips cut and swollen and a bloody scab where her front teeth were missing.

Later in the evening he awoke to silence. At once he became fully conscious. He wiggled backwards over the bodies and slipping free of the weight on top of him felt himself sink knee-deep into a viscous fluid. The bodies blocking the entrance had turned the room into a pool of blood.

Keeping to the shadows cast by the mud walls, stepping over the mangled bodies of people he knew, Ranna made his way to the *chaudhry*'s house. It was dark inside. There was a nauseating stench of kerosene mixed with the smell of spilt curry. He let his eyes get accustomed to the dimness. Carefully he explored the rooms cluttered with smashed clay pots, broken charpoys, spilled grain and chapatis. He had not realised how hungry he was until he saw the pile of stale bread. He crammed the chapatis into his mouth.

His heart gave a lurch. A woman was sleeping on a char-poy. He reached for her and his hand grasped her clammy, inert flesh. He realised with a shock she was dead. He walked round the cot to examine her face. It was the *chaudhry*'s older wife. He discovered three more bodies. In the dim light he turned them over and peered into their faces searching for his mother.

When he emerged from the house it was getting dark. Moving warily, avoiding contact with the bodies he kept stumbling upon, he went to the mosque.

For the first time he heard voices. The whispers of women comforting each other – of women softly weeping. His heart pounding in his chest he crept to one side of the arching mosque entrance. He heard a man groan, then a series of animal-like grunts.

He froze near the body of the mullah. How soon he had become accustomed to thinking of people he had known all his life as bodies. He felt on such easy terms with death. The old mullah's face was serene in death, his beard pale against the brick plinth. The figures in the covered portion at the rear of the mosque were a dark blur. He was sure he had heard Chidda's voice. He began inching forward, prepared to dash across the yard to where the women were, when a man yawned and sighed, '*Wah Guru!*'

'*Wah Guru! Wah Guru!*' responded three or four male voices, sounding drowsy and replete. Ranna realised that the men in the mosque were Sikhs. A wave of rage and loathing swept his small body. He knew it was wrong of the Sikhs to be in the mosque with the village women. He could not explain why: except that he still slept in his parents' room.

'Stop whimpering, you bitch, or I'll bugger you again!' a man said irritably.

Other men laughed. There was much movement. Stifled exclamations and moans. A woman screamed, and swore in Punjabi. There was a loud cracking noise and the rattle of breath from the lungs. Then a moment of horrible stillness.

Ranna fled into the moonless night. Skidding on the slick wet clay, stumbling into the irrigation ditches demarcating the fields, he ran in the direction of his Uncle Iqbal and his Noni *chachi*'s village. He didn't stop until deep inside a thicket of sugar-cane he stumbled on a slightly elevated slab of drier ground. The clay felt soft and caressing against his exhausted body. It was a safe place to rest. The moment Ranna felt secure his head hurt and he fainted.

Ranna lay unconscious in the cane field all morning. Intermittent showers washed much of the blood and dust off his limbs. Around noon two men walked into the cane field, and at the first rustle of the dried leaves Ranna became fully conscious.

Sliding on his butt to the lower ground, crouching amidst the pricking tangle of stalks and dried leaves, Ranna followed the passage of the men with his ears. They trampled through the field, selecting and cutting the sugarcane with their *kirpans*, talking in Punjabi. Ranna picked up an expression that warned him that they were Sikhs. Half-buried in the slush he scarcely breathed as one of the men came so close to him that he saw the blue check on his lungi and the flash of a white singlet. There was a crackling rustle as the man squatted to defecate.

Half an hour later when the men left, Ranna moved cautiously towards the edge of the field. A cluster of about sixty Sikhs in lungis and singlets, their carelessly knotted hair snaking down their backs, stood talking in a fallow field to his right. At some distance, in another field of young green shoots, Sikhs and Hindus were gathered in a much larger bunch. Ranna sensed their presence behind him in the fields he couldn't see. There must be thousands of them, he thought. Shifting to a safe spot he searched the distance for the green dome of his village mosque. He had travelled too far to spot it. But he knew where his village lay and guessed from the coiling smoke that his village was on fire.

Much later, when it was time for the evening meal, the fields cleared. He could not make out a single human form for miles. As he ran again towards his aunt's village, the red sun, as if engorged with blood, sank into the horizon.

All night he moved, scuttling along the mounds of earth protecting the waterways, running in shallow channels, burrowing like a small animal through the standing crop. When he stopped to catch his breath, he saw the glow from burning villages measuring the night distances out for him.

Ranna arrived at his aunt's village just after dawn. He watched it from afar, confused by the activity taking place around five or six huge lorries parked in the rutted lanes. Soldiers, holding guns with bayonets sticking out of them, were directing the villagers. The villagers were shouting and running to and fro, carrying on their heads charpoys heaped with their belongings. Some were herding their calves and goats towards the trucks. Others were dumping their household effects in the middle of the lanes in their scramble to climb into the lorries.

There were no Sikhs about. The village was not under attack. Perhaps the army trucks were there to evacuate the villagers and take them to Pakistan.

Ranna hurtled down the lanes, weaving through the burdened and distraught villagers and straying cattle, into his aunt's hut. He saw her right away, heaping her pots and pans on a cot. A fat roll of winter bedding tied with a string lay to one side. He screamed: 'Noni *chachi*! It's me!'

'*For a minute I thought: Who is this filthy little beggar?*' Noni *chachi* says, when she relates her part in the story. '*I said: Ranna? Ranna? Is that you? What're you doing here!*'

The moment he caught the light of recognition and concern in her eyes, the pain in his head exploded and he crumpled at her feet unconscious.

'*It is funny,*' Ranna says. '*As long as I had to look out for myself, I was all right. As soon as I felt safe, I fainted.*'

Her hands trembling, his *chachi* washed the wound on his head with a wet rag. Clots of congealed blood came away and floated in the pan in which she rinsed the cloth. '*I did not dare remove the thick scabs that had formed over the wound,*' she says. '*I thought I'd see his brain!*' The slashing blade had scalped him from the rise in the back of his head to the top, exposing a wound the size of a large bald patch on a man. She wondered he had lived; found his way to their village. She was sure he would die in a few moments. Ranna's *chacha*, Iqbal, and other members of the house gathered about him. An old woman, the village *dai*, checked his pulse and his breath and, covering him with a white cloth, said: 'Let him die in peace!'

A terrifying roar, like the warning of an alarm, throbs in his ears. He sits up on the charpoy, taking in the disorder in the hastily abandoned room. The other cot, heaped with his aunt's belongings, lies where it was. He can see the bedding roll abandoned in the courtyard. Clay dishes, mugs, chipped crockery, and hand-fans lie on the floor with scattered bits of clothing. Where are his aunt and uncle? Why is he alone? And in the fearsome noise drawing nearer, he recognises the rhythm of the Sikh and Hindu chants.

Ranna leapt from the cot and ran through the lanes of the deserted village. Except for the animals lowing and bleating and wandering ownerless on the slushy paths there was no one about. Why hadn't they taken him with them?

His heart thumping, Ranna climbed to the top of the mosque minaret. He saw the mob of Sikhs and Hindus in the fields scuttling forward from the horizon like giant ants. Roaring, waving swords, partly obscured by the veil of dust raised by their trampling feet, they approached the village.

Ranna flew down the steep steps. He ran in and out of the empty houses looking for a place to hide. The mob sounded close. He could hear the thud of their feet, make out the words of their chants. Ranna slipped through the door into a barn. It was almost entirely filled with straw. He dived into it.

He heard the Sikhs' triumphant war cries as they swarmed into the village. He heard the savage banging and kicking open of doors: and the quick confused exchange of shouts as the men realised that the village was empty. They searched all the houses, moving systematically, looting whatever they could lay their hands on.

Ranna held his breath as the door to the barn opened.

'Oye! D'you think the Musslas are hiding here?' a coarse voice asked.

'We'll find out,' another voice said.

Ranna crouched in the hay. The men were climbing all over the straw, slashing it with long sweeps of their swords and piercing it with their spears.

Ranna almost cried out when he felt the first sharp prick. He felt steel tear into his flesh. As if recalling a dream, he heard an old woman say: He's lost too much blood. Let him die in peace.

Ranna did not lose consciousness again until the last man left the barn.

And while the old city in Lahore, crammed behind its dilapidated Mogul gates, burned, thirty miles away Amritsar also burned. No one noticed Ranna as he wandered in the burning city. No one cared. There were too many ugly and abandoned children like him scavenging in the looted houses and the rubble of burnt-out buildings.

His rags clinging to his wounds, straw sticking in his scalped skull, Ranna wandered through the lanes stealing chapatis and grain from houses strewn with dead bodies, rifling the corpses for anything he could use. He ate anything. Raw potatoes, uncooked grains, wheat-flour, rotting peels and vegetables.

No one minded the semi-naked spectre as he looked in doors with his knowing, wide-set peasant eyes as men copulated with wailing children – old and young women. He saw a naked woman, her light Kashmiri skin bruised with purple splotches and cuts, hanging head down from a ceiling fan. And looked on with a child's boundless acceptance and curiosity as jeering men set her long hair on fire. He saw babies, snatched from their mothers, smashed against walls and their howling mothers brutally raped and killed.

Carefully steering away from the murderous Sikh mobs he arrived at the station on the outskirts of the city. It was cordoned off by barbed wire, and beyond the wire he recognised a huddle of Muslim refugees surrounded by Sikh and Hindu police. He stood before the barbed wire screaming, *'Amma! Amma!* Noni *chachi!* Noni *chachi!'*

A Sikh sepoy, his hair tied neatly in a khaki turban, ambled up to the other side of the wire. 'Oye! What're you making such a racket for? Scram!' he said, raising his hand in a threatening gesture.

Ranna stayed his ground. He could not bear to look at the Sikh. His stomach muscles felt like choked drains. But he stayed his ground: *'I was trembling from head to toe,'* he says.

'O, *me-kiya!* I say!' the sepoy shouted to his cronies standing by an opening in the wire. 'This little mother-fucker thinks his mother and aunt are in that group of Musslas.'

'Send him here,' someone shouted.

Ranna ran up to the men.

'Don't you know? Your mother married me yesterday,' said a fat-faced, fat-bellied Hindu, his hairy legs bulging beneath the shorts of his uniform. 'And your *chachi* married Makhan Singh,' he said, indicating a tall young sepoy with a shake of his head.

'Let the poor bastard be,' Makhan Singh said. 'Go on: run along.' Taking Ranna by his shoulder he gave him a shove.

The refugees in front watched the small figure hurtle towards them across the gravelly clearing. A middle-aged women without a veil, her hair dishevelled, moved forward holding out her arms.

The moment Ranna was close enough to see the compassion in her stranger's eyes, he fainted.

With the other Muslim refugees from Amritsar, Ranna was herded into a refugee camp at Badami Baug. He stayed in the camp, which is quite close to our Fire Temple, for two months, queuing for the doled-out chapatis, befriended by improvident refugees, until chance – if the random queries of five million refugees seeking their kin in the chaos of mammoth camps all over West Punjab can be called anything but chance – reunited him with his Noni *chachi* and Iqbal *chacha*.

I. Allan Sealy

THE TROTTER-NAMA

BEING THE CHRONICLE OF THE TROTTERS AS SET OUT BY EUGENE SEVENTH TROTTER

ON THE TWENTY-FIRST of June, 1799, from ten minutes past ten in the morning until the stroke of noon, a man not much above four feet tall, portly, handsome, eighty, alive and well, floated in the sky above Sans Souci, looking down in unspeakable wonder upon the dwarfed features of his château and the lands about it.

> *How came he there, Narrator? Once more, how came he there?*
> *Bring me first the cup.*
> *Will you start with a dessert wine, Narrator?*
> *My own Cup-Bearer! Better still a liqueur.*
> *Here is a potent little Mexican blend, wheedled from ripe cherries and the cocoa bean.*
> *Oh heavenly! Now answer me. Which is the most perfect of days?*
> *The twenty-first of June, it being the longest of days, when the ice is dearest.*
> *Well said. Now listen. I have heard from the cranny bird, sometimes called the writer bird, that it happened in this way.*

Justine Aloysius Trotter rose late that morning. He passed the night's water, its dark soil, purified his hands and rinsed his

Extract from the novel *The Trotter-Nama*.

mouth, stood under his watering-can on a pallet of mango wood, towelled his bulk, put on fresh clothes, and composed himself for breakfast. Before him there appeared his customary eight chapatis spread with ghi, a pigeon curry, and a cliff of white rice topped with three pats of unsalted butter. He ate. Satisfied, he turned to his toast, which he dipped in a bowl of tea neither seasoned with cloves nor sweetened with honey. Sated, he called down for his shoes. There being no guests at this morning's breakfast, he did not need to excuse himself, for he was not at table in the Rain Room. His breakfast tray had been brought to his rooms in the West Tower where he sat on a patterned rug to eat. In its place now appeared his walking shoes, a pair of closed-in black Jodhpuris filigreed with gold. They were sadly worn, but the master of all Sans Souci slipped them onto his illustrious feet and made his way downstairs to the Audience Hall. Flapping aside the servants gathered there, he crossed the inlaid floor and descended the flight of steps into the Indigo Court on the north-east side of Sungum, sometimes called the Watersmeet. Stooping, he threaded the eye of a massive iron gate though he could have gone around, there being no fence on either side. He walked unaccompanied but not unseen between the Glacerie and the Hava Manzil, past the kitchens, past the music pavilion, between a row of mulberry trees and the indigo baths, and up the slope of the saltpetre hill. At the top, which was not far from the bottom, he came upon a wicker basket lined with blue-and-green silk cushions. The Great Trotter stepped into this basket.

The basket was capacious. It might have held forty chickens or twelve dogs or mangoes without number. Instead there were, besides a rug and the cushions: a spy-glass, an astrolabe, an horologe, an horoscope, a barometer, a gypsonometer, one hundred and forty meteorological instruments, four sheets of writing paper of the Great Trotter's own manufacture and bearing his watermark, an ink-horn, three pens, two curried doves, and a partridge in a covered dish. There was also a skin of iced water.

Into this basket the Great Trotter stepped. The watching

crowd of Sagarpaysans tensed, held at bay by a cordon strung fifty feet all round from the basket. They had collectively abstained from work, knowing that today it would not matter, and turned out for the floating. Since five o'clock that morning, the stream of servants that ordinarily flowed from the hutments near the mines to Sans Souci had turned the other way, running uphill like the water in the Great Trotter's fountains. They fell silent as the bamboo ladder by which the master entered the basket, leaning on Yakub Khan as he climbed, was taken away. This was a sign for the ropers on the three platforms to begin their work, two teams pulling and one paying out. When the huge yellow bladder of close-silk stuff was swung into place above the basket, it at once bloated out. Its mouth, stiffened with whalebone, gaped over a fire-bucket intensely hot from its freight of living coals. The bucket, lined with clay, hung from a tripod whose base was the gondola in which the old man stood. At the top of the tripod was a hoop whose diameter matched the balloon-mouth. To the hoop were secured both balloon and fire-bucket, the bucket suspended by chains five feet above the Great Trotter's head.

One week earlier, the First Trotter had all but left the earth when the balloon collapsed onto the fire-bucket and was singed. In a flash of inspiration the old man had made good the damage with a large patch upon which he caused to be embroidered his crest. All that week Zuhur Ali, bespoke tailor, laboured with silk skeins, blue, green, and orange, on his ear. Today the balloon rode proudly above the flame, tethered by its net to the hoop. On one side it wore, in place of last week's scar, a sun of orange above a castle of yellow, a ship of blue upon a sea of green, the whilom Frenchman's fleurs-de-lis coupled with the fishes of Tirnab, and a scroll to complete the device with the motto: TERTIUM QUID. On the other side it wore in black letters the name: SALAMANDRE.

If a cry went up from the Sagarpaysans, the Great Trotter did not hear it. *For why?* Because he was jolted off the earth with a suddenness he had not anticipated. *For why?* Because no allowance had been made for a mooring rope. *What a marvel is this man!* Thereafter the Great Trotter floated in peace. The balloon rose rapidly above the toddy-palm trees and he watched them shrink into bent pins pricked into the tawny pin-cushion of the saltpetre hill. Above, the sky was cloudless. Its indigo grew deeper as the horizon dropped away. Nor were there any gusts to buffet the *Salamandre*, though the month of June is plagued with fiery winds called loo. *Thanks be to God. But He has further given us Intelligence, which when applied brings Knowledge, which when ordered is Science.*

It was not for nothing that the First Trotter had chosen the month of June. He knew of a cool circuit of air which flowed during this month in an echelon apart, far above the fume and fret of loo. Once latched onto this current, he reasoned, a balloon should describe a calm and constant orbit about Sans Souci until its fires cooled. He had demonstrated the surmise to his own satisfaction with a smaller, unmanned craft in the June of 1798.

At the height of two thousand feet the First Trotter did a strange thing. Standing among his one hundred and forty meteorological instruments, he brought the tip of his finger to his mouth. As if he were about to turn a page of his Bible or his writing paper, he moistened the fingertip with a furtive tongue. But he had not brought the great black Book and he had written nothing in the past quarter of an hour. Instead he held the finger up this way and that until it caught a cool breath from that same upper current. There it was! At once he began to operate a rope which connected, by a system of pulleys, with a broad vane suspended below the gondola in which he stood. Once set, the vane would deflect the current of air at a constant rate and the *Salamandre* lock onto the inner track of the current's course. The balloon began to list, and in a few moments was drawn into its chosen course. Now the Great Trotter glided in the company of those kites whose effortless flight he had often marvelled at when, some hot afternoon, the promise of rain set them wheeling about the sky.

His course fixed, Justin Aloysius Trotter had nothing to do

but gaze down upon the earth he had so lately trod. It passed beneath him like a dream. *And is it not?* First his eye was drawn to the four towers of Sungum with their joint crown, then with a wrench of especial possessiveness to his own West Tower. From there it shifted a finger's width to the domeless South Tower. On the earth it was his practice to look the other way when passing this tower. Now, at so great a distance, it did not seem to matter if his eye strayed. And having once looked, it seemed he could look at nothing else. Was she at her window? But why should she be? How should she know? He had told her nothing. Nor did he ever now: they did not speak or even meet. He ate in his tower; she had the dining table to herself. He imagined her there, sipping the endless glasses of water that were her sustenance, the table companion he had longed for in the old days, the only one of his wives he had ever talked to, until he made the mistake of sharing her bed. The one in the East Tower, now, was fierce in love and prayer but spoke little and took her meals in seclusion. He never saw her now, not even on moonless nights. The one in the North Tower did nothing but weep. Only the German's daughter was interesting and, latterly, interested. Why then had *he* lost interest? Why had he not left it at table-talk?

But – wait! Was that a speck of white framed in the upper-most window of her tower?

He sprang at his spy-glass and, fumbling, put it to his eye. What was this? All Sungum reduced to a grain of sand! The South Tower to the tip of a needle! Did his angel dance there? He saw he was looking down the wrong end of the telescope. Impatiently he spun it about, but as he did so it slipped from his grasp and fell, the kites swooping after it, until it parted the ripples of the Tank far below and was swallowed up.

For fully one circuit the Great Trotter was sunk in the pro-foundest gloom. He sat among the cushions heedless of all that passed below, feeding only on his sorrow and rage. As this mood began to abate, he cast an eye about the gondola over each of the objects with which it had been furnished. It alighted upon the luncheon dish which kept company with the gypsonometer. He lifted the lid of the dish. Abstractedly he tore off the leg of the tandoori partridge and ate. He tossed the bone over the side of the gondola, where a kite caught it up. His disposition much improved, he fondled the gypsonometer. He traced with a thumbnail the calibrations of its brass arc. At the forty-fifth degree he stopped: he must waste no more time. There were measurements to take, a piece of writing to begin, and here he sat idling! He got up, clutching the rim of the basket to steady himself. It was then that the beauty of the earth spread out below struck him. The gypsonometer slid from his grasp. It followed the telescope over the edge of the gondola and fell into the desert south of the Tank. He let it go.

Looking east, Justin saw littered the fallen new moons of a dozen ox-bow lakes – his lakes! – stretching out towards the horizon. There, to one side, ran the crystal waters of the Kirani river, a tiny winding stream. Further out, well beyond the lakes, sprawled Nakhlau's river, the Moti Ganga, broad, silted, indulgent. Far away on the horizon glinted the mother of rivers, the Ganges, into which the Moti Ganga emptied. Together the three rivers gave the kingdom of Tirnab its name. On the far side of the Kirani river squatted little villages where the land showed brown on ochre. His villages! From them white dust tracks led to open fields, purple with sugarcane, green with chick-peas, yellow with mustard. His fields! All ripening together in June, but he did not think it strange. A dozen mango topes stood out of this mosaic, embossed in a darker green. His mangoes! Here and there a gulmohar tree shone red. His trees! His forest, his quarry, his desert, his stream! His plateau – the saltpetre hill where it all started. His indigo baths – spread out like a bracelet at the edge of the plateau – the product of his science! His gardens – here formal and pleasing, there rambling and sweet – the product of his art! His fountains, his parklands, his groves, his canal, his Tank, his château! His Sungum! His Sans Souci!

The Great Trotter's breast swelled with satisfaction. All this was his. He spread his arms. He turned around. All, all, his. All good and fat. Would that Mama were alive – and poor Papa! And what should his former mates think could they but see him now from the France to which all had safely returned?

A thought struck him. *Could* they see him at this moment? Might he see them?

He looked west. France was there, a film of green on the horizon. Fighting some fruitless war, no doubt. Losing the New World. Concluding some base treaty. He lowered his eyes. When he left America it seemed certain that France would inherit Spain's empire. Britain had won. When he arrived in India it seemed certain that France would succeed the Mughals. Britain had won. Well, let it go. What had he to do with either France or Britain? This was his home – all this. Here he would die – an event that could not be far off, for he was old – here he would be buried.

The *Salamandre*, travelling south by east from the plateau, was passing over the jujube groves that fringed the desert. From here the Great Trotter could look down and see the towers of Sungum reflected on the face of the Tank. He recalled the accidental beginning of this lake, the result of the artificial hill on which Sungum stood. It had occurred to him that there was no reason why the widening hollow should not take a definite shape. Accordingly the Tank was designed. It was to take the shape of a fleur-de-lis stretching outwards from the Grand Steps, its elongate head pointing between south and east. It was served by a gate, the Water Gate, which lent its name to the court at the top of the Steps, the Water Court. As work proceeded on the buildings, the cutting of the lake was neglected. Divided between Tank and Sungum, the Great Trotter came to sacrifice the cause of the one at the altar of the other. So where the gate and head were done with care, the lyrate scrolls on either side were indifferent things. Twenty monsoons had reduced them to a sorry pair of fins. Looking down now, the Great Trotter was astonished to find swimming far beneath, not his firangi fleur-de-lis but the fish on the seal of Tirnab.

Swayed by this consideration, Justin Trotter turned his gaze upon the Nawab's capital. As if sensible of his intent, the balloon, which had been travelling south by east, bucked and broke loose from its circuit. It struck out westward, bisecting the circle it had so far calmly described. No matter which way Justin worked his pulleys, no matter how many instruments he jettisoned, the balloon held its new course. The Great Trotter soon found himself directly above Sungum and travelling northwest. He stared down into the funnel that was the South Tower. Her tower. He watched the château recede as the craft swept on. At the opposite side of the circle the *Salamandre* returned to its course with a second twist and flourish that brought him Nakhlau. What a glittering of domes and minarets was there!

Lines in praise of Nakhlau (from Qaiyum)

Well it is known to all the people of the earth that the city of Nakhlau (which the vulgar and rough-tongued call Lakhnau, or One Hundred Thousand Boats) stands without equal for the beauty of its gateways, the majesty of its walls, the grace of its towers, the sheen of its domes, the lustre of its meanest dwellings washed with lime and shimmering under an indigo sky. Who has not heard of Chowk, with its heaven-embracing markets loaded with silks and incense, sugar and mangoes, its colonnades festooned with peacocks, its fragrant stairs washed hourly with crimson juices? Here, veiled, pass heart-expanding women with chaplets of flowers and comely boys with languid gait. Here are bejewelled elephants and haughty eunuchs, there frolic charioteers and vegetable lambs. Here are pannikins of crushed pearls, trays heavy with sweetmeats, the mouth-rejoicing gulab jamun, the tongue-delighting jalebi, the tooth-vibrating kulfi, the universe-arresting Sandila laddu; there are love philtres, a thousand roses distilled in a vial; here again are gossamer bodices, chikan-worked, of which a courtesan may put on twelve and still not be modestly clad. You who have feasted on the coconuts of Cashmere, who have lolled upon the nag-phan of Ceylon, who have slumbered beneath the kamchors of Thibet, and found no peace, stop in these scented gardens. Pause by some twilit lake whose ripples finely slice the clove-of-lahsan moon, whose shores are fringed with rubber trees and broad-leaved grasses where some dark lady clothed with the night plays on her flute a solemn air and one rapt bird stands unmolested by a company of pythons. And when, borne on cool breezes, the laughter of the citizenry wafts to you down some perfumed canal, voices so mellifluous that the traveller Kuo Chin-wu once asked where were these heart-easing bells that he might buy one, board you your sandalwood barge and hope to leave. Alas! There is no leaving. Have not visitors from Constantinople and St Petersburg, Toledo and Tashkent, Peiping and Aleppo, Bokhara, Kon, and Mandalay, stood speechless on the top of Lakshman Tila? And do they not then burst into tears and coming down disband their retinues, paying off their ass-herds and muleteers, their cooks and compote factors, their masalchis, sutlers, food-tasters, scullions, guides, guards, unguent-mixers, herbelots, mustard-oil-pressers and masseurs, because after this there can be no more travel?

(CHRONICLE RESUMED)

At the edge of all this magnificence Justin Aloysius Trotter had set his fleur-de-lis seal. And now it was turned fish. He squinted at the city. Its domes winked back at him: the Nawab's domes. Its whitewashed towers shimmered in the sun: the Nawab's towers. From the city wall a road ran east towards Sans Souci, but it was not Justin's road. It did not become the Trotter Road until it reached the Ganda Nala, a sewage canal which divided Nakhlau from Sans Souci – and then not until half-way across the bridge which spanned the canal.

Meditating on this injustice, the Great Trotter was visited by an old passion. Often it had seized him when he stood of an evening at his favourite window in the West Tower, an urge deep and hot for enlarging his domain, by main force if need be. Had he not been the Nawab's Commander-in-Chief? And who else in Tirnab could match his cannon? Who better for military survey, for teaching ballistics, training up troops? This passion he had confessed to no one, man or woman, and as he grew older he locked it away in his breast, examining it but rarely. Lately when he took it out he found it shrivelled into a contentment that he might do much if he wished. But now – here – in the air above Nakhlau what swept over him was the original lust, that suzerain impulse which once shook to his vitals a younger man. Take this city, then all Tirnab, and who was to say what else might follow? Instal the Nawab in some petty principality. Drive the British down the Ganges into Fort William, thence into the Bay of Bengal. Invite General Petitjohn up from his Deccan pasture. Recall Dupleix – was he alive? Wipe clean his disgrace. Appoint these men his deputies. Recruit, train, rearm, fortify, advance, annex, consolidate. Drive deep into the south. Pacify the north-west. Send an embassy to the Czar with Easter eggs. Dispatch an emissary to China complaining of her maps.

Borne from height to height, the Great Trotter leaned over the edge of the gondola now sailing far above the Ganda Nala, which marked the westward limit of his demesne. Lips chumbling, he made to encircle with his arms what he could no longer hope to win with a confection of strategy and gunpowder. In a younger man the gesture might have passed for a rush of hot blood, had any been by to observe it. In an octogenarian – a man already half angel – the cacoethes was strangely moving. The effect did not escape Justin himself. A man once given to irony, he pictured all that happened next before it came to pass, the whole of his future flashing before his eyes as the past is more commonly said to do when death comes suddenly.

(INTERPOLATION)

An Apology

Peccavi! The chronicler has sinned and you have every right to complain. Half a dozen pages of this *nama* and still no frontispiece! Mea culpa, mea culpa, me a Mexican cowboy. The bed of nails tonight. Not one illustration from the master painter of the age – certainly for the late yellow period of the

Kirani School – giant among miniaturists, darling of auctioneers, envy of collectors, copyist par excellence, his work
highly prized but modestly priced, hung in the great museums
of the world, everywhere sought, nowhere sufficient. Let me
then make good the omission.

Frontispiece

A ruled border of alternating fish and fleurs-de-lis in blue and
green on a pink ground. The border dusted with silver.

In the upper centre, a balloon in shape like a papaya, in
colour like a ripe papaya. Its crest as given above, in orange,
blue, and green; the name SALAMANDRE also visible on the
other side but upside down along the upper edge. Dependent
from the balloon a gondola, tilted. In it, or perhaps just outside, a figure in white, a halo about its head. The head, exact
centre, shown in three-quarter face. All other heads in the picture appear in profile.

The figure. The Great Trotter wears on his head a wig. It
is the only item of Western dress he has retained and it
assorts well with his white kurta, being powdered daily by
Fonseca. The kurta is embroidered in white after the
Nakhlau chikan style. Lesser painters cannot achieve this
effect, white on white. The face is that of an old man, but a
stout old man and therefore devoid of unsightly hollows. Its
curves are honest, the cheeks rounded and nowise haggard.
Such wrinkles as might have distressed a thinner man have
been smoothed away from beneath by a warm and generous
unction. The forehead is regular, receding perhaps, sweating
certainly, the nose prominent and slightly upturned at the
tip, its nostrils inclined to flare. The eyes are round,
famished, but not unduly large, and – wonder of wonders! –
the left more blue than brown, the right more brown than
blue. The hands, one upraised, are podgy, with short blunt
graceful fingers such as a painter or singer might covet. One
of the fingers might be brought to the tip of the tongue. The
skin is that of a Gaul, with some slight Nilotic tint, after
forty summers at the twenty-fourth parallel. The discerning

viewer will find the chin touched with a tarbrush of pig's bristle. One moment.

(INTERPOLATION)

Concerning an alleged painter, one Zoffanij

Two other portraits of the Great Trotter exist, oils both, by that relative wisp of a man, Zoffanij. What his contemporaries saw in him I don't know, but it's said they queued for hours outside his studio, ladies of quality too. Well, I too have had my sitters – but let us look objectively at the portraits.

The first shows a frail Justin lost in a vast concourse of men gathered for a cock-fight. There are some firangis in the foreground, but the great mass are Indians, courtiers and hangers-on to the Nawab whose own august presence fills the centre of the canvas. Bets are being laid, a circle drawn, and the air is thick with dust and cries. The supposed Justin is seated on a European chair, one bony leg crossed over the other, and a prissy look on his gaunt face. It's not clear whether he's examining a cock held out to him by a lean pencil-bearded half-Turkish steward-and-cocksman or just gazing feebly into the air, reckoning up his millions. In the right foreground sits a virile fellow in a mince-pie hat and curl-toed shoes, the picture of plump good health and doubtless modelled on the real Justin until the painter in a fit of malice or faint-heartedness put the Great Trotter further back. Zoffanij himself is off to one side, staring dully at the viewer, with one hand waving at his own imagined scene. Romantic fiction! Conjured up by an envious man who saw the Great Trotter once and then at a distance. And doesn't distance diminish? Here is a painting very likely done from memory in London on the celebrity's return from his Grand Oriental Tour. And doesn't memory thin?

The other, even less reliable painting is entitled 'The Great Trotter and His Friends'. It shows three friends – among whom Zoff not only numbers himself, but, in a forgivable lapse, places himself squarely in the centre – and of course the great man. The putative Justin is squinting at a worthless miniature by Tulsi the Younger or one of those insipid Mughals and turning his back on some exquisite bananas. Zoffanij – let us give the man his due – could do a banana. Though judging from his one self-portrait, in the Uffizi gallery in Florence, he might have profitably eaten a couple after. As it is he remains, if not gaunt, visibly wanting. In the Uffizi self-portrait he hopes to distract the viewer from his unfortunate face by posing as a kind of clownish Hamlet. His only endearing feature is a gap between his two front teeth – unless some later visitor inked it in while passing through. He leans on one elbow, holding up a skull which can't help but make his own look lively. ARS LONGA, VITA BREVIS on the spines of nearby books. You can see him there leaning in front of a mirror with his skull, then making a dash for the brushes, then back to the skull, then back to the canvas and so on until the travesty is complete. Ars longa? Zoffanij's! God forbid. The only thing long about this bounder, fingers apart, are his teeth. Vita not brevis enough by half, or the world might have been spared this piece of middle-aged dementia.

But to return in calmness to his so-called Justins. There is a conceivable excuse for these fleshless representations. The paintings, if genuine, may date from the summer of 1789 when the Great Trotter was recovering from a grievous illness and much reduced thanks to an ill-considered vow. But if so, he filled out again shortly after, perhaps not to the old Justin, but enough to make him recognisable, respectable, lovable. And portraiture, let me remind the admirers of Zoffanij and all his works, is a plunder of the general character, not a petty pilfering of some specific and transient frailty.

Jealousy, you say? Very well. Let someone else speak. I draw your attention to an Italian engraving which, though not exactly of the Great Trotter, closely resembles him. It is of the famous eighteenth-century castrato, Carlo Broschi Farinelli, in his classic role, *The Great Mogul*. Look it up some time.

But, the frontispiece.

Frontispiece continued

Above the balloon the sky is first blue, then indigo. There are no clouds, but one is being born in the upper or indigo sky.

Beneath the balloon stretches an ochre plain cleft by a canal, the Ganda Nala. The canal flows into a broad river, the Moti Ganga. A small winding stream, the Kirani or Cranny river, which arises in the saltpetre hill, also empties into the Moti Ganga. On the near side of the canal is spread Sans Souci, its buildings of mixed stucco and sandstone. Its crown and glory, Sungum, sits with its towers upon a man-made elevation. The result of this mound is a hollow that has formed a lake or Tank in which Sungum is reflected. To the right of Sungum, two fingers' width above, is a low square table-land, the saltpetre hill. On it are raised three bamboo platforms around a launching pad. Beyond are a jungle, a small stream, villages, several ox-bow lakes, and a broad river. On the far side of the canal is the city of Nakhlau.

Birds and animals fill the parklands and jungle. The peacock is one. The pigeon is another. The black partridge is another. The dog is another. He is a crafty beast. The tiger is another. The camel and elephant are others. The horse is another.

Trees are many: the jamun (*Eugenia jambolana*), the mango, the guava, the jakfruit, the imli or tamarind, the English tamarind, the nim, the pipal, the silk-cotton, the gulmohar or flame, the laburnum, the oracle, the papaya, the banana, the Chinese orange.

Flowers are some: the canna in rows, the rose in beds, the lotus in ponds, the daffodil, the bougainvillea, the Persian rose, phlox, and on the banks of the Kirani stream, the rat-kirani or queen of the night.

Men also abound, and women. On the table-land is a crowd of persons in ragged dress. These are the Sagarpaysans or camp-followers or simply ocean-of-peasants. They gaze in rural idiocy at the sky, some pointing. Among them, in richer dress, may be told a baker-and-Chief Steward, a head-poulterer, and a folk-doctor-and-dentist. Apart from the crowd, a dhobi-and-dyer is at work by a pool, beating a white gown on a rock by his hut. Beside him is an indigo vat, full. At a lower window in Sungum, an aged man sits bent in half at his desk. At another, lounges a man once fat but still handsome, a book of verse in his hand, a cup of wine resting on his belly. At another window, a middle-aged man, pock-marked, looks in a mirror. A crack in an East Tower window shows two women, one pink and one purple (the pink in truth a girl), singing. At an upper window in the South Tower is a woman in white gazing also at the sky. She is the colour of ice. In her hand is a quill, a drop of ink fresh upon the tip.

This was the frontispiece.

Entry in Jarman Began's diary for June 21, 1799

I awoke at five o'clock this morning, the sky being neither dark nor light. It is my favourite hour at this time of year – small respite from the sun's wrath, which is already mounting at breakfast – but today is of especial note – and not for that it is to be the longest and hottest day of the year – for today Trot is to go up in his *Salamandre*. He has not said a word, of course, but the servants are all abuzz with *zulmundur, zulmundur*. I must watch at the window when the time comes. Shall I be able to see him? Had I only his spy-glass – but he would not leave that behind. I wonder how Yaqoob Khaun has provisioned the craft, for Trot is sure to be hungry. Heaven knows how long he will be up there. He must eat – he has been looking so [*illegible*] of late. And his parasol – if Fonseca has not had the good sense to fetch it there I shall scold him most severely. It will be hot at ten and can only become hotter as he is borne nearer the sun. He will be able to see France from up there – and America too, Fonseca says. That will mean Germany, which is on this side, will show more clearly still. Could I get but one glimpse of the fatherland! Would that I were going up instead! I flatter myself I should not be in the least frightened though I were tossed most handsomely by the loo. It would be infinitely more diverting than cutting paper, which Fonseca has of late been distracting me with and which he says is the best ton in Calcutta. Yesterday he made a great many Japanese lanterns and hats and Canton doilies, I asked him to fashion me a balloon, but he answered – 'Madam, a balloon with holes is like

Lord Swan with Mister Chicken's feet!' I thought this a most elegant jest and asked him whether it was original. He simply smiled in his enigmatic way and inclined his head sagely.

Today it is still Thursday's white, with a yellow kerchief, because that scoundrel Dhunee Dass is late with the wash. 'Memsahib,' he declares, 'in this season I must go *very* far to find good water.' As if he dipt my cloathes in Himalayan streams! His wash dazzles only because he pilfers indigo dust from the factory.

Will Trot see me, I wonder? If I stand at the window and wave, he is sure to look. I am smaller than America but not so far away. What would Fonseca say to that! I shall try it on him. But for his company, which I confess most agreeable, I should be much vext with solitariness, for the women here are such vapid creatures. And since I write for myself I might confess a little more – for am I not at liberty to digress as I chuse? He is a handsome enough creature with his beetling forehead and lively eyes, though I did not think him so when first I saw him in Trot's tower. Then I noticed only the pock marks and the irresolute chin. I forgive him his finical hairdresser's manner, for there is nothing effeminate in his speech. He has the gait of, I should think, a peacock – but he would be much teased if I told him so, being not a little vain and therefore anxious to conceal his vanity. His hair is not in the least grey though he cannot be less than forty, and his teeth are not in the least yellow though he is inordinately fond of tobacco – not that he would smoak or chew it in my presence. He cannot play chess, but he is full of extravagant tales, told so rapidly one might lose one's way with a smaller talent. He is clever, for a man, though in a different way from Trot or Moonsheejee. They say Father was a wit, but then a travelling seller of inks must be quick if he is to profit in a foreign land. What brought him here? He never spoke of his travels except curtly, and of Germany not at all. Had he already a wife there? Have I sisters and brothers walking cobbled streets and sleeping under pointed roofs? Fonseca declares that Europe is paved from end to end so that carriages may cross it in a week, but he has never been there or seen the Portugal he prates of. He would see it, in purple, if he went up with Trot – this side of Florida with some little blue in between. He has seen only Bombay, and now his heart is set on Calcutta. He would fain go there this day were there not a surfeit of hairdressers that side. I fear he will never get there, for all that he cuts and dresses to perfection. If he should go, there would be none to entertain me when I am tired of pure mathematics – which I confess is often of late. To think that I ignored him these many years! Doubtless his travel tales of Thugs and Mahrattas and Ranas could be spun out endlessly. 'Madam,' he will cry – though he well knows my birth – seizing a lock from my shoulder, 'a hair-breadth 'scape, madam!' Lately he has taken to coming here on the smallest pretext. Rekha has begun to make eyes when she announces him, and she has a loose tongue, that one. I have seen her behave most familiar with Yaqoob Khaun. Why do I mistrust this baker-man? Could it be a clew that he appears to cultivate the saucy girl for some design she cannot know? Desire her person he surely cannot – it is alien to his temper – handling her as if she were a key.

I must resolve to be more faithful to the pages of this journal. Moonsheejee must be my model – the good man unbends from his desk only to send me the volumes I ask for, and always one more which he deems necessary to my education. 'Too much numbering will congeal the fluids of your brain,' says he. Last week it was Kautilya's *Discourses*, Aboolphargius's *Dynasties*, and the *Tota-Nama* of Kapildev. Yesterday it was Ibn-i-qasim's *Mirror of State* and *Cup of State*, Englished some forty years ago by Colonel Townshend and bound up in one volume. There are some few things in it of interest, but little that I could not have counselled myself. In the afternoon he sent up for my inspection (I think he must allow me sense) through Fonseca – who professes not to understand the man, or to be out of sympathy with 'all your statecraft' says he – the first fruits of his own labours in translating from the Turki a fragment of the *Babar-Nama* beginning with the three hundred-and-eighty-third folio. There are another seventy-two, widely supposed lost, which he has dredged up from Trot's chambers of unsorted books and manuscripts. He bravely proposes to classify every last item gathered there, and swears he would translate all such as wanted translation – were he not besieged with requests for formal odes and qasidas from all the grandees of Nakhlau. God grant the old librarian a long and quiet life! His deputy, Qaiyum, is a [*illegible*] wastrel.

But here it is already eleven – Trotter will have gone up – and I had meant to watch at the window –

(CHRONICLE RESUMED)

The gondola rocked sharply upon Justin's tilt at the city that would never be his. As if abetting him in his desperate enterprise, the *Salamandre* tipped him into the air in the direction of Nakhlau. With a crash the horologe, the astrolabe, the meteorological instruments, and the luncheon dish slid into a corner of the basket. The horologe began to strike the hour of noon but got no further than one silvery chime when its mechanism froze, the hands stopping at twelve.

Without a word the Great Trotter fell. The crash and chime alerted him to a state which had earlier escaped his notice: he was wrapped about in a sheet of silence. The invisible current of air played on his cheek but made no sound. He looked up but the heavens gave him no answer; the sun's gong hung mute. And in the silence long chains of mathematical problems cannoned through his brain, effortlessly resolved. Numerical figures of every description – the dimensions of Sans Souci, the distance to the pole, the weight of the earth, an imbalance in the ice account, the specific gravity of lead, the survey tables of Tirnab, an unpaid dhobi's bill – all rippled into crystal tropes and streamed silently before his eyes. This was curious, because on earth he had been unable to proceed beyond long division, a source of much amusement to his prodigy of a Burgher mistress. He was marvelling at the transformation when his eye was held by a still greater wonder: the sky was empty of the stars which he and he alone saw by day below.

Justin stared. Until yesterday, his nights were starless while the day-sky tormented him with a dazzling display of heavenly bodies. Now the clock was turned back and all was blue again. What did it mean? The sky's colours changed subtly, but where the blue ran into the indigo, or where the indigo received the blue, he could not say. Nor could he point to where the colour was purest. To an indigo manufacturer the realisation was a blow. At the zenith, where the colour seemed true, seamless, and virginal, where purity was most insistent, there it was that Justin longed with a fierce longing to install the absolute. But he could not. For was there not a purer spot just beside it? Falling, he searched for the elusive point, but now the sun which had reached the zenith stood in the way. It was noon.

In that elastic moment Justin examined his perplexity.

The Great Trotter considers the heavens

There it goes. The space of my finest hesitation filled with blinding light. Complete uncertainty, complete knowledge! A sky with stars, a sky devoid of stars: one or the other, all or nothing? But tell me, Trotter, have you not seen those stars that one sees only by indirection, only by looking beside them? And by the same token, might there not be infinitudes of blankness one can know only by looking at stars? Blanknesses not to be confused with those wider spaces of vulgar blue that distinguish star from star, and exist only to serve the stars, so that each might enjoy quality and particularity. These other spaces the stars in turn serve, being harbingers of a void mightily small, a space neither in them nor behind them but other than them, a scruple which their faint light invokes by shedding darkness. Here is knowledge of a kind, for though it does not announce itself, whether as common darkness or as specific light, yet it has considerable being. The blue is too fickle, and as for the sun, it drowns the shy signal in an unending torrent of light.

*

274

(CHRONICLE RESUMED)

Justin remembered the first trial of his indigo. After an hour's simmering in the vat his bolt of cloth had come out white – if anything, more dazzlingly white than when it had first gone in. He cursed the indigo, ladling some of the dye into a bowl for inspection. The liquor was true blue. Then what was the matter? He examined the cloth once more: it was ordinary cotton, unwaxed. He was on the point of flinging it back in when before his very eyes the cloth began, very faintly, to darken. He took it out into the sunlight and watched it go from pale blue through an infinite number of stages to a dark and fast indigo. The secret, it seemed, was neither in the dye nor in the cloth but in a third place. It was in the air.

Above him, Justin's *Salamandre* righted itself, and the lid of the luncheon dish slid back with a clink. The sun struck him full in the face and he turned over as he fell, looking downwards now at an earth that flew towards him at a terrifying speed. Yet his senses were more alert than at any time since he entered the world.

The Great Trotter considers the earth

It seems I am to exchange one vat for the other: out of the blue into the brown. So be it. I make no complaint.

That, directly below me, is the Ganda Nala, there is the city, there is the river —— but hold – hold – *hold!* The canal is flowing *backwards*, running from the river to the city! Or why would the trunk of a toddy palm drift that way under the Ice Bridge instead of this? Or the scum run against the stream? Wait – the parklands are turning green – in June! – when they should be the colour of bread. On the hottest day of the year! Where are the dust storms down below? Why are sands by the river turning black when there are no clouds? Why is there a swamp where my indigo fields should be? Who has torn up the baths? Where are the mango topes? The river has changed its course. The sugar-cane is early, the wheat is late – no, there's wheat in the sugar-cane fields, but now again sugar-cane! It goes from yellow to green to purple and back again in the twinkling of an eye – merciful heavens, what is happening down there? The grass flickers orange, the trees are blue, the colours shift and ripple as if some lunatic wind were scattering the pages of an illustrated book. Can it be true after all, as Timur Beg wrote, that in Hindoostan everything is backwards, the elephants' trunks being their tails carried in front? Look! The smoke from my brickworks is being sucked back into the chimney, and it's the same with those wisps curling back down over the city. That blue cloud is sinking, yes, back onto the many dung fires of the Sagarpaysans, and there above the forest a milky green strand returns to some charcoal-burner's stump fire – in *my* forest! But where are the trees? My tamarinds are gone, my avenues retreating into saplings and seed pods. My gardens lie all unravelled, the shrubs pulled under by the fuse, the flowers closing up and turning into buds. The wrong birds are singing – where is the cranny bird? – now they are not singing at all; now they fly backwards to their nests, climb into their eggs, tender beaks remaking their shells, sealing themselves in; buildings are coming down everywhere, my Sungum is undone, where is the Glacerie, why is the West Tower half-finished, who has put the scaffolding back on, but what do the workers think they're doing, the stonemasons' bullock-carts are hauling slabs to the quarry, the bricklayer returns mortar to his hod, removes a brick, takes his hod to the trough, where bhistis extract the water, mazdoors separate the sand from the lime, unslake the lime, the tiler comes down the ladder with tiles on his head, the sawyer dislodges his saw, the sawdust rising to heal the cut, the painters are stripping the walls, the carpenters taking out windows, the glaziers restacking their panes, the grinders and finishers breaking up the floor, the sealers exposing the foundations, women carry away baskets of earth on their heads to the Tank, its waters have dried up, the hollow filled in, the hill eroded; holes, then blank spaces appear where the other buildings stood, then other, prior structures take their place, mud huts, twelve villages, then these too give way to fields, the fields to a fort, the fort to mean dwellings, these to a river, a jungle, a jheel covered with ducks, a swamp full of crocodiles.

There – now the colours begin to run the other way. My vat is muddied. I must scold that Munnoo – what am I saying! I'm a dead man. Where is my son who went from brown to blue? There, in France? There, in the Deccan? Might he see me now? Would he turn away? Well, let it come – his father is beyond help. I will suffer nothing, simply a change of identity – and what of that? Did I not ask for my stone to read:

JUSTIN ALOYSIUS TROTTER
WHO
LIVED AND DIED

The Great Trotter considers what is in between

For that matter, if at every stage in my descent I am at rest, can I be truly said to fall at all? Is there nothing in between? Is the third thing nothing?

> Excuse me, Narrator. But could we have a little less specu-
> lation and a little more story?
> Impertinent Cup-Bearer! Could I have a little more
> patience? And a little more of that Mexican blend. In a
> little while you shall have more story than you could
> wish for.
> I take it on faith, Narrator.
> Believe me, I have a mystery brewing for you, told me by
> the Did-you-do-it. But first some praise of sugar and then
> a very foul smell.

(CHRONICLE RESUMED)

Justin Aloysius Trotter drew at a constant speed towards the earth. There fell with him, on either side, his wig and his masak of ice-water, the one a little higher than the other. Below, to one side, he saw his lands swiftly accumulate details not visible from the Salamandre. To the other side of the canal, and still through the pincer of his clasped arms, he observed a like multiplication of Nakhlau minutiae. A parkland with tombs/a city with tombs. His/the Nawab's. Blades of grass now returned to brown/blades of grass now returned to brown. His/the Nawab's. The earth on both sides was scorched.

Hot, Justin felt his throat rowelled by thirst. His white kurta billowed out and flapped at his shoulders, but it gave him no comfort. He reached for his masak but it danced away at his touch, and the ice cubes gave a liquid chuckle. Exposed to the sun, his scalp prickled. He stretched out a hand for his peruke. Easier to snatch a dandelion boll: a cloud of talcum came away on his hand.

And now it was not only thirst that distressed him. Justin was hungry. Might the *Salamandre* have sent down the tandoori partridge? He looked about him: it had not. The bird was wasted, his lunch floating away. But it was not a tandoori partridge he craved, nor was it the curried doves. It was nothing savoury; rather, a taste he had almost forgotten thanks to a hasty vow. It flashed through his mind that today was his birthday, and this recollection only made the absence the more poignant. He felt a quivering of taste buds at the utmost tip of the tongue, an ungovernable tickling at the root, neither salt nor sour nor bitter. It held promise of a sensation intensely pleasurable – sinfully, maddeningly, cripplingly, suffocatingly pleasurable; it was a siren song calling one to an endless debauch, inviting surrender to pleasures unspeakable, to a long sweet slavery, to sweetness without end.

Sugar was Justin's present and most abject craving. Had only Yakub Khan sent up, instead of those spiced birds, a baker's dozen of his sweet roggen loaves – a poulterer's dozen – a single loaf – a slice – a crumb! Partridges – pah! Did not the king of partridges himself trumpet his surrender?

The black partridge (Francolinus francolinus) *praises sugar*

Shir daram shakrak. With this sound the durraj (black partridge) of Hindoostan greets the dawn. He is the size of a dog's head, and his plumage is of many colours, the body between black and green, the neck green without black, the gorget purple, the head rufous, the bill yellow, the wing brown above and black beneath and speckled black on white at the tip. He is a handsome bird, as road-travellers (poets) know. Hear him in the sugar-cane fields, his head turned towards the east. He has run careless of snakes (ill-natured poets, senior librarians) among the purple stalks. He pauses on the bund, looks this way and that. See him lift his head. See his purple throat swell. See his beak open. Sing, bird, sing. Hear now: *Shir daram shakrak!* The first syllable is quick: *shir*. The rest is measured but not slow. *Daram* is voiced with care but not conviction; to tell the truth, it is thin (ugly, spoken without elocution). But there is more: see the proud bird's eye glaze, feel the pulse quicken in his jugular. Hear him redeem himself. *Shakrak* – sugar! It comes quickly at the end, climbing to a peak. *Shir daram shakrak* – 'I have a little milk and sugar.' Who has told me this? The emperor Babar records it in his *nama*. The good Englishwoman, Annette Susannah Beveridge (sharbat, sorbet) has put it in English. The Frenchman de Courteille renders it: '*J'ai du lait, un peu de sucre*,' but on what authority? Why 'a little sugar' and not 'a little milk'? Effrontery, the bitter (the Gaul); Hazard, the salt; Envy, the sour; or Indifference, the bland. Cowardly de Courteille, no friend of India, enemy of Nakhlau whose sugar once travelled as far as Cathay. Sugar gives courage: let us follow the greater heart. Padshah Babar the Brave writes more: 'The partridge of Arabia and those parts is understood to cry, *Bi'l shakar tadawm al ni'am* (with sugar pleasure endures)!' Wants there greater proof?

(CHRONICLE RESUMED)

Justin fell. As he fell, he felt a surge of regret. On his mind's tongue he knew again the kiss of sweet roggen. He recalled breakfasts past when the baker-and-(then still) steward reserved for himself the honour of waiting. The future baker-and-Chief Steward would glide into the barsati or Rain Room on the roof of the Glacerie, where breakfast was customarily taken, one hand held high above his head in the French waiting fashion. In place of a tray there floated, just above the baker's hand, a basket of varnished reeds lined with a green napkin. In it nestled a covey of soft brown loaves. These he would offer first his master, then the favoured Jarman Begam, then any others who happened to be at table (which was rare). Taking one, Justin would preserve a short silence. Then he would lean over his plate and inhale deeply. Lastly, he would break off a piece, dip it in his tea (which he took with a lump of yak's butter), and sticking out his tongue a short way he would ferry the morsel into his impatient mouth. The ritual was respected even by the literal Jarman Begam from whose recipe the loaves had first been baked. The Great Trotter had himself undone it, forswearing sweetness in a fit of abstract piety (*Headstrong Trotter, Senseless Vow*). Every morning thenceforward the First Trotter had his breakfast brought to his chambers in the West Tower. No longer did the first sunlight flood the barsati; undrawn, the Rain Room curtains grew brittle. The breakfast table stood cold and joyless, its mitred napkins gathering dust. The ovens baked common bread, the baker-and-major-domo glowered and spat into the ashes and gave the making of Justin's chapatis to a cook, the same who specialised in pigeon curries.

Today, as he fell, after an eternity of unleavened, unsweetened bread, Justin longed for a crumb from his own table. An infusion of tea-red sunlight, the face of his transparent mistress, a loaf of her sweet roggen, all newly risen – ah! here was bliss sufficient. He leaned forward in the silence and inhaled deeply, expectantly.

What was this? A stink, foul and sewagey, was coiling in his nostrils, an odour to which every pestilential thing in India seemed to have contributed its part.

What the Ganda Nala offers

The brimmings of cesspits, the green rot of markets, the scum of sewers, the swill of gutters, the refuse of gullies, the stench of offal, the vapour of privies, the crust of drains, the sweat of bird-catchers, the lime of seducers, the lint of navels, the foulings of footpaths, the footbaths of postmen, the leakings of oilmen, the oilings of lechers, the slime of ruttings, the scale-cakes of fish-stands, the mire of fowl-houses, the squirtings of cats, the grime of urchins, the dribblings of ancients, the pap of infants, the navel-cords of outcastes, the flickings of brahmins, the swabs of morticians, the sweepings of barbershops, the flushings of abattoirs, the slops of stews, the slab of neat-sheds, the parings of pariahs, the dressings of doctors, the wipings of cooks, the findings of ear-cleaners, the leavings of surgeons, the muck of mullahs, the waterbrash of lalas, the scrapings of tanners, the mange of muskrats, the pressings of beauticians, the rootings of scavengers, the semen of eunuchs, the shavings of padres, the spittle of mendicants, the turds of soldiers, the pickings of schoolboys, the scabs of traitors, the piss of bullies, the blisters of tabla-masters, the phlegm of palki-bearers, the ordure of chamberpots, the dung –

– Narrator –

of bats, the rummage of middens, the sludge of sluices, the dunnage of pyres, the rankling of boils, the rakings of gutters, the guttings of butchers, the gougings of taxidermists, the disjecta of ragmen, the rags of acrobats, the bones of hunters, the hair of criminals, the ears of informers, the eyes of spies, the stools of sentries, the droppings of politicians, the lather of courtesans, the glow of wrestlers, the emptying of yogis, the heavings of gluttons, the hawkings of vendors, the retchings of beggars, the warts of harlots, the chancres of students, the rattle of consumptives, the matter of sores, the armpit hair of cowards, the oozings of sweat-shops, the cuckings of cloaca, the cotton of monthly-pads, the voidings –

– Narrator –

of cretins, the discharge of pimps, the lavings of lepers, the spewings of drunkards, the effluvia of pickleworks, the ebullitions of smelters, the slag of armourers, the acid of carters, the moultings of reptiles, the crackling of corpses –

– Narrator, do you hear me? Your eyes are rolling! –

the bedding of incontinents, the bile of oil painters, the gall of historians, the swaddling of infants, the stillbirths of virgins, the scribbling of weavers, the weaving of scribblers, the betel-juice of bicyclists, the chewing-gum of motorcyclists –

> *Enough, Narrator.*
> *What is it, Cup-Bearer? Where am I?*
> *It's past, Narrator, there now, there now. Here is a little rice wine from Japan. It will calm you.*
> *O my sweet Ganymede! For a moment I thought I was – no it is too horrible . . .*
> *Then leave it. Let us go on.*

(CHRONICLE RESUMED)

The smell of these things, channelled by the Ganda Nala, rose to meet the Great Trotter. Other things too, but who will record them? *Life is short.*

Justin well knew it as he drew to his life's close. Falling, he looked southwards. At a stone's throw was the Ice Bridge, with whose central arch he had now almost drawn level (for he had been falling some time). The bridge was bare: men do not go abroad at noonday in June unless on an urgent mission. The Trotter Road was untrafficked as far as Sans Souci, the Nawab's road unpeopled as far as Nakhlau. Then what was this new sound, sharp and repetitive, pecking its way through the heat like a woodpecker? It was no living thing; rather it seemed the report of some engine to come, a chatter of pistons pumping furiously. And shortly a machine did appear from the direction of Sans Souci. It had two wheels and a lamp in front, and astride the belly was a man in uniform who stood racing his motor, once, twice, three times. Then, chewing calmly, he threw the machine into motion and hurtled towards the Ice Bridge. Halfway across he disappeared and angel voices sounded, rising to fever pitch and ending abruptly. In the stillness there appeared from the direction of Nakhlau another man. His kurta-pyjama was dazzling in the midday sun, almost blue with whiteness. His lank hair was freshly oiled and might have hung to his shoulders if it hadn't streamed out behind him, for he rode a machine not unlike the other. It had two wheels and a lamp, but no engine. The man glided along silently, his feet pedalling in circles. As he crossed the bridge he spat a merry curlicue of betel-juice into the Ganda Nala. The spittle turned the water a brief red, then it was gone. Then the man himself vanished.

Justin was amazed at these apparitions. So many wonders in one day! Might it all be some exotic romance, a tall tale trotted out? He shook his head.

It felt strangely light, and he remembered his peruke just in time to see it fall with a chalky plash into the canal, tail first. It floated a little way, then was sucked under. Faithful creature! Ten winters, summers too, it had covered his pate, fitting snugly, hatching notions, conjuring youth. Well, let it go. Youth had fled; the stars played tricks; summer and winter were unpinned. Did anything else of substance remain? The masak: his leathern flask of ice-water had fallen behind in the race, being heavier. For an instant it hung above the turbid waters, its skin purple like one of those dark plums remembered from his boyhood. It wore a fragile bloom of moisture, and for a moment Justin saw behind it a shade of green not to be found in his adopted land. The masak met the water with a smack, the ice-cubes gave a last mocking chuckle and went down. What could they mean? A jostle of cubes . . . three syllables of ice. Man . . . da . . . The *Mandalay*! His ship had not come in: his Quebec ice was late. Never again would he taste of those distant ponds where once, in the fire of youth, he had gone skating in May. The pity of it! Now when his thirst was greatest, now when his senses were so keenly awake. That he should feel most alive when life was no longer his to command!

A note on the crocodile of Hindoostan

The crocodile is a freshwater reptile, amphibious and wily. He is the length of one dog when small, two when grown. He feeds on fish and birds but has been hearsaid to prey on humans, prizing especially the pancreas or sweetbread. A washerman was taken from the Moti Ganga near the Bridge of Boats, a young girl lower down in the same stream. Crocodiles wait in muddy waters, floating like toddy palm logs. A story attaches to this beast. Once Crocodile said: 'Monkey, the jamuns (*Eugenia jambolana*) in yonder tree are purple and sweet.' Monkey replied: 'But who will ferry me across the river?' Crocodile said: 'I will.' So Monkey got on Crocodile's back. Halfway across the river he grinned and said, 'Now I will eat you. Already I can taste your pancreas. It is purple and sweet.' Monkey was greatly alarmed, but said, 'O Crocodile! You are my best friend. I would happily give you my pancreas, but my liver is still better. Only, I have left it in that fig tree on the bank whence we came. Take me back and I will exchange it with you for one of those sweet jamuns.' 'Very well,' said Crocodile, and he carried Monkey back to his bank. To this day Monkey has not tasted the jamuns of that tree, but he has his pancreas. This shows the wile of the Crocodile. Another proof is that he will sometimes snap at the bird which cleans his teeth. The Monkey story is told by the mendacious Indians. Another concerns the Elephant. For that you must go to the deceitful British. But who will trust either? Trust me; I will tell a better tale than both. The wonder is I do not know it yet myself. A further remark about this beast. When about to die, or when his mate is killed, he is said to shed a single tear in the shape of an egg. Within, you will find a tiny creature made in the image of the parent. Thus is the crocodile species propagated. He is best killed from under, for from above you will not. His flesh makes poor eating, being flat, cold, and lengthwise.

A word about ocean currents

The ocean does not stand still. After wetness, motion is its chief attribute. It is just always coming and going. Boats upon its surface and living creatures below may each avail of this shifting, going when it goes, coming when it comes. What is the first cause of this motion? Whose hand rocks this cradle? The hand of God. But directly? No, not directly. Indirectly. God has made the sun and the moon, his instruments and his glory, the one to chafe the earth (and its waters) and the other to chill the earth (and its waters). The warm attracts, the cold repels, and currents follow. Winds help them and rivers hinder. The warm are red, the cold blue: every schoolboy knows this. Currents have names from their discoverers, their navigators, their neighbouring land masses, their fish, but not their reptiles. Such as: the von Humboldt, the Quiros, the Labrador, the Eel; but never the Crocodile.

(CHRONICLE RESUMED)

Justin saw his end had come. He raised his eyes towards Nakhlau, meaning to look his last, but an embankment of earth stood in the way. Sorrowfully he turned and looked towards Sans Souci, but there too a curtain was built up; the Ganda Nala's banks are steep in June, the waters having run low. The First Trotter closed his eyes. He wished to sleep the long, still sleep of the tomb. Left bank or right, it did not matter where he fell. Let it be in Nakhlau or in Sans Souci, so long as his grave was dug deep, his sleep unbroken. Here Yakub Khan would find him – no one crossed the Ice Bridge as often as he – and follow his orders. Where he fell he was to be buried. *Vanity of vanities!*

What remains?

Neither bank is to be the Great Trotter's resting place. All solid things have deserted him: his *Salamandre*, his wig, his ice, his *Mandalay*. What remains?

The lust that engorged his heart, spurring him to rashness, has run its course. His pincer is undone: the hands unclasped come apart, obeying no centre, the feet drift together unbeknownst. The Ganda Nala's surface is broken by the slippers of Sans Souci, whose pointed toes slip noiselessly into the stream. Without a splash, without so much as a ripple, Justin Aloysius Trotter passes from air to water. One last vision is his: reflected on the glittering surface of the canal he sees, opening his eyes, a tawny sky spread with stars. I am still alive, he declares as life is taken from him. When the head has slipped below, there remains an arm upraised, and after the arm a finger, the same whose tip not two hours ago the tongue moistened. Escorted by a toddy palm log, the newest cess to the Ganda Nala is swept downstream to the Moti Ganga and thence into the mother of rivers. In a muddy stretch patrolled by crocodiles the body is unpicked. God's will be done. One part alone continues downriver, whole and unhurt, and at last out into the sea. It is jelly-like, purple and sweet. It is the pancreas. Coaxed by the action of a warm current, it inches with a flopping rise and fall along the ocean floor, staining with its dye the Bay of Bengal

(CHRONICLE RESUMED)

No one but Justin himself witnessed the fall. The Sagar-paysans who had raced along below the balloon, chasing a shadow that slid down the glacis of the saltpetre hill, sailed around the indigo baths, and skirting the Tank on the east side, shot across the desert, tired once the front runners got as far as the jujube groves and fell back. Hooting, they watched the *Salamandre* sweep westwards along the edge of Dilkhusha or the Heart's Ease (tracing a path which the railway would follow when it came to be laid by their children's children) and curve back towards Nakhlau.

After three further revolutions about the hub of Sans Souci, the *Salamandre* descended upon the plateau, its fires at last cooled. It came to rest within the triangle formed by the bamboo platforms at a point equal in distance from each. Its vane folded gently under the gondola, and the gondola met the earth without the jolt with which it had left. For a moment the vessel balanced there, trembling like a creature possessed of supernal intelligence. The Sagarpaysans, gathered once more at the cordon, sensed this presence and respected it with silence. Then the balloon, which in that space had preserved the dignity of its crest, gave a sigh and sank with a silken murmur. Released from awe the Sagarpaysans surged forward, breaking the cordon, and ran to the gondola meaning to carry off the Great Trotter in a triumphal palki.

There was another space of dusty silence when the crowd, which had had eyes only for the balloon, discovered the gondola was empty. Then Yakub Khan, baker-and-chandler and balloon master, who had the keeping of the ladder, vaulted into the basket and began to toss the parti-coloured cushions about as if he expected to find his master hidden in some cranny. Upon this sign – the baker-and-victualler might have been tossing sweets among them – the crowd began to heave and babble.

Yakub stood up and looked wildly around, sensible in spite of his surprise of the danger in which he stood. Sunya the egg-brahmin, he saw, was looking not at the *Zalmandar* but at him, and his eyes were heavy with mischief. He must act at once and with all the authority he had so sedulously shaped over the years, kneading into the lump of his advancement minute yet ever increasing measures of a yeast fermented in the still of his patient breast.

– Wah! Metaphor, Narrator! –

He found his voice. 'Some of you run Tankside! See if he has fallen there. Sunya, you lead them! Scatter them about on every side. Send one as far as the ber grove. You, Salim, go to the zenana. Ask if any saw him fall. No – wait! Yes, go. But do not speak of it before Jarman Begam, hear me? Ask the other two. Gunga, you search the marsh down to the river. Rekha and you children go home quickly. The women also will please return to the village and shut themselves in. I say so. Zuhur, you run to the Gunpowder Gate and stand duty. Wazir, you go and get any stragglers and comb the parklands. And, hé Wazira, send one to the house-servants to look on the rooftops and between the buildings. Rouse that slugabed Qaiyum, but leave the old librarian. Ré Munnoo and Nankoo, silly fools, you two scan the heavens. Go to the top of the Crown, one, and the other to the roof of the Rib above the Balloon Room. Hakimji, it is best if you wait with me.'

The men began to move off, but Yakub called after them.

'And, ohé, listen well. *No two must search together*, and no one is to wait for another. Split up when you reach your beat. If anyone finds the Master he must report at once to the Audience Hall, where Hakimji will be waiting. Do not on any account touch the body. Cover it decently if you can, but do not move it. Go.'

When the crowd had dispersed, Yakub turned to Hakim Ahmed.

'Brother,' he said, 'this is surely the most fateful hour of our lives. We must act boldly but calmly as befits worthy men. That is why I have asked you to remain. You are a responsible man, unlike that Sunya. Here is what I want you to do. It's very simple. If someone has found the body, you must detain him. You are a hakim; you know about herbs and suchlike. He will have come running in the heat. Give him a cool green draught. Lock him up somewhere, somehow. Then go at once to Tartar Sahib's tower – making sure that barber doesn't see you – and hang out the flag – the blue-and-green standard – at the uppermost window. It is kept in the chest in the vestibule of his chambers. Here is the key to the chambers, here is the key to the chest. That will be a sign to me and I will come without delay. As you know, I cannot leave the *Zalmandar*.'

Hakim Ahmed nodded his head slowly. He was a somnolent giant with a slack, bearded jaw, the beard dyed red with henna. His puffy eyes were solemn and generally upturned, giving him an air contemplative and idiotic. He liked to mull things over as he ground his roots and herbs, scanning the roof of his brain for stray wisps of intimation that might happen to drift by. He disliked haste, but he liked a scheme, and the prospect of one made him submit to the present urgency. It made a folk doctor, a man given to prescriptions and pronouncements, himself wholly biddable. The hakim had always suspected that some day Yakub, many years his junior, would give him an order. Unable to decide how he would respond, he had postponed the decision. Now it was taken from him, and he hurried away wordlessly, tucking the keys into his cummerbund. As he went he comforted himself with the thought that his patients, who knew less about certain things than he, took his twists of mauve powder and pellets of ear-wax without question.

When the hakim had gone, Yakub Khan wiped his face on his pocket handkerchief and scoffed into the damp cloth.

'Simple physician!'

He looked about the gondola in which he stood and kicked aside a cushion. 'And you, precious metaphysician. Where have you fallen?'

He was a tall slender loosely knit man, with a camel's neck and sound teeth. Coming at the top, his head might have been an afterthought, a dot on an inverted question mark whose drift was a constant torment. The face was lit by a pair of hazel eyes burning fitfully two inches above a wick-moustache that Yakub trimmed twice a day. He noticed the covered dish. He bent down, removed the lid, and with a turn of his wrist scooped up the one-winged bird and crammed it into his mouth. Then, with a curried dove in each fist, he jumped over the side of the gondola and began to lope softly towards Nakhlau.

When Jarman Begam broke off her journal entry and ran to the window she saw no sign of a balloon in the sky. She reproached herself for having sat dreaming with a pen while such a memorable journey was in progress. She had meant to catch the first possible glimpse of the *Salamandre*; instead she had been fussing with words while the world, or a significant fragment of it, went by. 'A window is worth a thousand books,' Fonseca had said the other day, opening one. She remembered his illustrated lecture on the subject, and with a guilty twist of the head dismissed him.

It was past eleven, and the sky remained blue and empty.

She craned out of the window: there was no one to be seen either on the ochre earth or in the sky above it. Then, as if issuing out of a window in the East Tower, the yellow bulb of the *Salamandre* hove into view and sailed silently, with scarcely a tremor, around the Tank. On the glassy black waters its image, inverted and unbroken, glided like a ghost. Elise screwed up her eyes and scanned the gondola for any sign of movement which would show her husband busy with his instruments or signalling France. But there was no silhouette, idle or busy. Shall I wave, shall I shout, she wondered, stepping from one window to the next in her tower as the balloon travelled west by south. Perhaps he is asleep or resting, she said. No – he has lost something and is sulking. The *Salamandre* disappeared from view behind the West Tower.

There was nothing to do now but wait at the first window while the balloon completed its circle. Elise stood at the window-sill careless of the sun. Once she glanced over her shoulder at the octagonal turret room. It looked unnaturally bright. Ordinarily at this hour all the windows would have been doubly secured against the sun, the green louvre shutters on the outside and the pane windows within bolted and latched. The heavy curtains of twilled cotton would snuff out any stray beam of light or dust and the room would be steeped in a cool subaqueous gloom lit only by a tube of mirrors opening onto the escritoire. On the hottest days Elise withdrew to an inner chamber or descended to lower and lower refuges in her tower. Today she was in the uppermost room, with all its windows thrown open. Each was a harsh rectangle of blue, and at the first of them Justin Trotter's consort stood, a little before noon, awaiting the return of the *Salamandre*.

In the silence a crow rasped from the banyan tree below. Now and then there blew a ripe gust from the elephant stables. A fine rain of sand fretted away at the rock and stucco pile of Sungum.

At last the balloon drifted past the edge of the East Tower and began once more its double track around the Tank. This time Elise fancied she saw a figure lean over the rim of the basket, looking out towards the ox-bow lakes. The figure spread its arms and turned around. Elise bent her head back and shaded her eyes with a hand that might have been made of glass. The glare was fierce all the same, and she found it easier to follow the inverted figure of the *Salamandre* reflected on the blue-black sheet of water. She had fastened her eyes on this image, when it appeared to halt in its track and return the way it came. The brief illusion, she saw, was created by the balloon's becoming larger: the craft had in fact stopped, but it was not returning the way it came – it was coming her way!

Elise began to wave first her handkerchief, then both hands at the approaching balloon. She saw the Great Trotter tug furiously at a set of ropes like a rebellious puppet. Next, a row of missiles began to punctuate the surface of the Tank, the sound of each splash – *bhut-oosh* – carrying dimly to her as the newest ring of ripples criss-crossed the last. *Bhut-oosh! Bhut-oosh!* When the *Salamandre* was past the Tank and above the Water Gate, she began to call: 'Just-in! Ju-stin!' But her voice was hoarse at the best of times, and she was used to calling him by another name. The tiny figure, enmeshed in ropes, did not respond. The gondola swept overhead, surely grazing the Crown, and the *Salamandre* disappeared from view.

Elise did not see the Great Trotter look down into her tower, nor could she follow his flight around to the West Tower, window by window, as before. He simply shot over the Crown and was gone. The next time the balloon appeared, the gondola was empty, and so too the time after, and the time after that. Then it did not appear at all. Forty minutes later Rekha ran into the room, burst into tears, and ran downstairs again without uttering a word.

Shashi Tharoor

A Raj Quartet

THE NEWS OF the annexation of Hastinapur by the British Raj was announced by the brusque communiqué one morning. There was none of the subtle build-up one might have expected, Ganapathi; no carefully planted stories in the press about official concern at the goings-on in the palace, no simulated editorial outrage about the degree of political misbehaviour being tolerated from a sitting Regent, not even the wide bureaucratic circulation of proposals, notes and minutes that Vidur, now a junior functionary in the States Department, might have seen and tried to do something about. No, Ganapathi, none of the niceties this time, none of the fabled British gentlemanliness and let-me-take-your-glasses-off-your-face-before-I-punch-you-in-the-nose; no sir, John Bull had seen red and was snorting at the charge. One day Hastinapur was just another princely state, with its flag and its crest and its eleven-gun salute; the next morning it was part of the British Presidency of Marabar, with its cannon spiked, its token frontier-post dismantled and the Union Jack flying outside Gandhari's bedroom window.

Sir Richard, former Resident of Hastinapur, now Special Representative of the Viceroy in charge of Integration, and a hot favourite to succeed the retiring Governor of Marabar himself, breakfasted well that morning on eggs and kedgeree, and his belly rumbled in satisfaction. He had just wiped his mouth with a damask napkin when an agitated Heaslop burst in.

Extract from *The Great Indian Novel*.

'Come in, Heaslop, come in,' said Sir Richard expansively if unnecessarily, for the equerry was already within sneezing distance of the pepper-pot. 'Tea?'

'No, thank you, sir. I'm sorry to barge in like this, sir, but I'm afraid the situation is beginning to look very ugly. Your intervention may be required.'

'What on earth are you on about, man? Sit down, sit down and tell me all about it.' Sir Richard reached for the teapot, a frown creasing his pink forehead. 'Are you sure you won't have some tea?'

'Absolutely sure, sir. The people of Hastinapur haven't reacted very well to the news of the annexation, sir. Ever since this morning's radio broadcast they have been pouring out on the streets, sir, milling about, listening to street-corner speakers denouncing the imperialist yoke. The shops are all closed, children aren't going to school nor their parents to work, and the atmosphere in the city centre and the *maidan* is, to say the least, disturbing.'

Sir Richard sipped elegantly, but two of his chins were quivering. 'Any violence?'

'A little. Some window-panes of English businesses smashed, stones thrown, that sort of thing. Not many targets hereabouts to aim at, of course, in a princely state. It's not as if this were British India, with assorted symbols of the Raj to set fire to. A crowd did try to march towards the residency, but the police stopped them at the bottom of the road.' Heaslop hesitated. 'My own car took a couple of knocks, sir, as I tried to get through. Stone smashed the windscreen.'

'Good Lord, man! Are you hurt?'

'Not a scratch, sir.' Heaslop seemed not to know whether to look relieved or disappointed. 'But the driver's cut up rather badly. He says he's all right, but I think we need to get him to the hospital.'

'Well, go ahead, Heaslop. What are you waiting for?'

'There's one more thing, sir. Word is going round that Ganga Datta will address a mass rally on the annexation this afternoon, sir. At the Bibigarh Gardens. People are flocking to the spot from all over the state, sir, hours before the Regent, that is, the ex-Regent, is supposed to arrive.'

'Ganga Datta? At the Bibigarh Gardens? Are you sure?'

'As sure as we can be of anything in these circumstances, sir.'

Sir Richard harrumphed. 'We've got to stop them, Heaslop.'

'Yes, sir, I thought you might want to consider that, sir, that's why I'm here. I'm afraid we might not be able to block off the roads to the gardens, though. The police are quite ineffectual, and I wouldn't be too sure of their loyalties either, in the circumstances.'

'What would you advise, Heaslop?'

'Well, sir, I wonder if we don't stand to lose more by trying to stop a rally we can't effectively prevent from taking place.'

'Yes?'

'So my idea would be a sort of strategic retreat, sir. Let them go ahead with their rally, let off steam.'

'You mean, do nothing?'

'In a manner of speaking, yes, sir. But then passions would subside. Once they've had their chance to listen to a few speeches and shout a few slogans, they'll go back to their normal lives soon enough.'

'Stuff and nonsense, Heaslop. Once they've listened to a few speeches from the likes of Ganga Datta and his treacherous ilk, there's no telling what they might do. Burn down the residency, like as not. No, this rally of theirs has to be stopped. But you're right about the police. They won't be able to do it.'

'That's what I thought, sir,' Heaslop said unhappily. 'Not much we can do, then.'

'Oh yes, there is,' Sir Richard retorted decisively. 'There's only one thing for it, Heaslop. Get me Colonel Rudyard at the cantonment. This situation calls for the army.'

The Bibigarh Gardens were no great masterpiece of landscaping, Ganapathi, but they were the only thing in Hastinapur that could pass for a public park. The plural came from the fact that Bibigarh was not so much one garden as a succession of them separated by high walls and hedges into little plots of varying sizes. The enclosures permitted the municipal author- ities the mild conceit of creating different effects in each gar- den, a little rectangular pool surrounded by a paved walkway in one, fountains and rose-beds in another, a small open park for children in a third. There was even a ladies' park in which women in and out of purdah could ride or take the air, free from the prying eyes of male intruders; here the hedge was particularly high and thick. The gardens were connected to each other and to the main road only by narrow gates, which normally were quite wide enough for the decorous entrances and exits of pram-pushing ayahs and strolling wooers. On this day, however, they were to prove hopelessly inadequate.

One of the gardens, a moderately large open space entirely surrounded by a high brick wall, was used – when it was not taken over by the local teenagers for impromptu games of cricket – as a sort of traditional open-air theatre-cum- Speaker's Corner. It was the customary venue (since the *maidan* was too big) for the few public meetings anyone in Hastinapur bothered to hold. These were usually *mushairas* featuring local poetic talent or folk-theatre on a rudimentary stage, neither of which ever attracted more than a few hun- dred people. It was the mere fact of having staged such func- tions that gave the Bibigarh Gardens their credentials for this more momentous occasion.

When news spread of a possible address by Gangaji on the day of the State's annexation, Bibigarh seemed the logical place to drift towards. Soon the garden was full, Ganapathi; not of a few hundred, not of a thousand, but of ten thousand people, men, women, even some children, squeezed uncom- plainingly against each other, waiting with the patience instilled in them over timeless centuries.

When Colonel Rudyard of the Fifth Baluch arrived at the spot with a detachment, it did not take him long to assess the scene. He saw the crowd of fathers, mothers, brothers, sisters, sons, daughters, standing, sitting, talking, expectant but not restless, as a milling mob. He also saw very clearly – more clearly than God allows the rest of us to see – what he had to do. He ordered his men to take up positions on the high ground all round the enclosure, just behind the brick walls.

It is possible that his instructions had been less than precise. Perhaps he was under the assumption that the people of Hastinapur had already been ordered not to assemble for any purpose and that these were, therefore, defiant trouble-makers. Perhaps all he had was a barked command from Sir Richard, telling him to put an end to an unlawful assembly, and his own military mind devised the best means of implementing the instruction. Or perhaps he just acted in the way dictated by the simple logic of colonialism, under which the rules of humanity applied only to the rulers, for the rulers were people and the people were objects. Objects to be controlled, disciplined, kept in their place and taught lessons like so many animals: yes, the civilising mission upon which Rudyard and his tribe were embarked made savages of all of us, and all of them.

Whatever it may be, Ganapathi – and who are we, all these decades later, to speculate on what went on inside the mind of a man we never knew and will never understand – Colonel Rudyard asked his men to level their rifles at the crowd barely 150 yards away and fire.

There was no warning, no megaphone reminder of the illegality of their congregation, no instruction to leave peacefully: nothing. Rudyard did not even command his men to fire into the air, or at the feet of their targets. They fired, at his orders, into the chests and the faces and the wombs of the unarmed, unsuspecting crowd.

Historians have dubbed this event the Hastinapur Massacre. How labels lie. A massacre connotes the heat and fire of slaughter, the butchery by bloodthirsty fighters of an outgunned opposition. There was nothing of this at the Bibigarh Gardens that day. Rudyard's soldiers were lined up calmly, almost routinely; they were neither disoriented nor threatened by the crowd; it was just another day's work, but one unlike any other. They loaded and fired their rifles coldly, clinically, without haste or passion or sweat or anger, resting their weapons against the tops of the brick walls so thoughtfully built in Shantanu's enlightened reign and emptying their magazines into the human beings before them with trained precision. I have often wondered whether they heard the screams of the crowd, Ganapathi, whether they noticed the blood, and the anguished wails of the women, and the stampeding of the trampling feet as panic-stricken villagers sought to get away from the sudden hail of death raining remorselessly down upon them. Did they hear the cries of the babies being crushed underfoot as dying men beat their mangled limbs against each other to get through those tragically narrow gateways? I cannot believe they did, Ganapathi, I prefer not to believe it, and so I think of the Bibigarh Gardens Massacre as a frozen tableau from a silent film, black and white and mute, an Indian *Guernica*.

The soldiers fired just 1,600 bullets that day, Ganapathi. It was so mechanical, so precise; they used up only the rounds they were allocated, nothing was thrown away, no additional supplies sent for. Just 1,600 bullets into the unarmed throng, and when they had finished, oh, perhaps ten minutes later, 379 people lay dead, Ganapathi, and 1,137 lay injured, many grotesquely maimed. When Rudyard was given the figures later he expressed satisfaction with his men. 'Only 84 bullets wasted,' he said. 'Not bad.'

Even those figures were, of course, British ones; in the eyes of many of us the real toll could never be known, for in the telling many more bled their lives into the ground than the British and the press and the official Commission of Inquiry ever acknowledged. Who knows, Ganapathi, perhaps each of Rudyard's bullets sent more than one soul to another world, just as they did the Raj's claims to justice and decency.

Gangaji came later, at the appointed hour of his address, and when he saw what had happened he doubled over in pain and was sick into an ornamental fountain. He stumbled among the bodies, hearing the cries of the injured and the moans of the dying, and he kept croaking to himself in Sanskrit. I was there, Ganapathi, and I caught the words, *'Vinasha kale, viparita buddhi'* – our equivalent of the Greek proverb: 'Whom the gods wish to destroy, they first make mad.'

It was Gangaji's strength to see meaning in the most mindless and perverse of human actions, and this time he was both wrong and right. He was wrong because the Massacre was no act of insane frenzy but a conscious, deliberate imposition of colonial will; yet he was right, because it was sheer folly on the part of the British to have allowed it to happen. It was not, Ganapathi, don't get me wrong, it was not as if the British were going around every day of the week shooting Indians in enclosed gardens. Nor was Rudyard particularly evil in himself; his was merely the evil of the unimaginative, the cruelty of the literal-minded, the brutality of the direct. And because he was not evil in himself he came to symbolise the evil of the system on whose behalf, and in whose defence, he was acting. It was not Rudyard who had to be condemned, not even his actions, but the system that permitted his actions to occur. In allowing Indians to realise this lay the true madness of the Hastinapur Massacre. It became a symbol of the worst of what colonialism could come to mean. And by letting it happen, the British crossed that point of no return that exists only in the minds of men, that point which, in any unequal relationship, a master and a subject learn equally to respect.

At the time this was perhaps not so evident. The incident left the population in a state of shock; if you think it provoked a further violent reaction, you would be wrong, Ganapathi, for no father of a family willingly puts himself in the firing-line if he knows what bullets can do to him. After Bibigarh everyone knew, and the people subsided into subordination.

Gangaji told me later that the Massacre confirmed for him the wisdom of the principles of non-violence he had preached and made us practise at Motihari. 'There is no point,' he said candidly, 'in choosing a method at which your opponent is bound to be superior. We must fight with those weapons that are stronger than theirs – the weapons of morality and Truth.'

Put like that it might sound a little woolly-headed, I know, Ganapathi, but don't forget it had worked at Motihari. The hope that it might work again elsewhere, and the knowledge that nothing else could defeat the might of the Empire on which the sun never set, were what made us flock to Gangaji. In a very real sense Hastinapur gave him the leadership of the national movement.

And what of Colonel Rudyard, the great British hero of Bibigarh? His superiors in Whitehall were embarrassed by his effectiveness: there is such a thing, after all, as being too efficient. Rudyard was prematurely retired, though on a full pension. Not that he needed it; for across the length and breadth of the Raj, in planters' clubs and Empire associations, at ladies' tea parties and cantonment socials, funds were raised in tribute by patriotic pink-skins outraged by the slight to a man who had so magnificently done his duty and put the insolent natives in their place. The collections, put together and presented to the departing Colonel at a moving ceremony attended by the best and the whitest, amounted to a quarter of a million pounds, yes, Ganapathi, 250,000, two and a half lakhs of pounds sterling, which even at today's depreciated exchange rate is forty lakhs of rupees, an amount it would take the President of India thirty-five years to earn. It took Rudyard less than thirty-five minutes, much less. The gift, which his Government did not tax, brought him more than £160 per Indian dead or wounded, as one pillar of the Establishment was heard to murmur when the figures were announced, 'I didn't think a native was worth as much as that.'

In some ways this gesture did even more than the Massacre itself to make any prospect of Indian reconciliation to British rule impossible. It convinced Gangaji, who derived his morals as much from the teachings of Christianity as from any other source, that the Raj was not just evil, but satanic. The Massacre and its reward made Indians of us all, Ganapathi. It turned loyalists into nationalists and constitutionalists into revolutionaries, led a Nobel Prize-winning poet to return his knighthood – and achieved Gangaji's absolute conversion to the cause of freedom. He now saw freedom as indivisible from Truth, and he never wavered again in his commitment to ridding India of the evil Empire. There was to be no compromise, no pussyfooting, no sell-out on the way. He would think of the phrase only years later but his message to the British from then on was clear: Quit India.

Rudyard retired to a country home in England. I wonder whether he was ever troubled by the knowledge of how much he was reviled and hated in the country he had just left. Or by the fact that so many hot-headed young men had sworn, at public meetings, in innumerable temples and mosques and *gurudwaras*, to exact revenge for his deed in blood. I like to think that Rudyard spent many a sleepless night agonising if a stray shadow on the blind was of an assassin, starting at each unexpected sound in fear that it might be his personal messenger from Yama. But I am not sure he did, Ganapathi, because he knew, just as Ganga did, the limitations of our people in the domain of violence. The young men who swore undying revenge did not know how to go about exacting it, or even where. Only two of them finally had the intelligence and the resources to cross the seas in quest of their quarry. And when they got to Blighty, and made inquiries about an old India hand with an unsavoury Hastinapur connection, they found their man and, with great éclat and much gore, blew him to pieces.

Do not rejoice, Ganapathi, for it was not Rudyard whose brains they spattered over High Street, Kensington. No, not Rudyard, but a simple case of mistaken identity; to a sturdy Punjabi one British name is much like another, the people they questioned were themselves easily confused, and it was not Rudyard, but Kipling they killed. Yes, Kipling; the same Professor Kipling who had been careless enough to allude to the canine qualities of the Indian people, and who, for that indiscretion, had already been struck by my pale, my rash son Pandu. It makes you wonder, does it not, Ganapathi, about the inscrutability of Providence, the sense of justice of our Divinity. Our two young men went proudly to the gallows, a nationalist slogan choking on their lips as the noose tightened, blissfully unaware that they had won their martyrdom for killing the wrong man. Or perhaps he was not the wrong man: perhaps Fate had intended all along that Kipling be punished for his contempt; perhaps the Great Magistrate had decreed that the sentence of death fall not on the man who had ordered his soldiers to fire on an unarmed assembly but on he who had so vilely insulted an entire nation. It does not matter, Ganapathi; in the eyes of history all that matters is that we finally had our revenge.

Sara Suleri

MEATLESS DAYS

I HAD STRONGLY HOPED that they would say sweetbreads instead of testicles, but I was wrong. The only reason it had become a question in my mind was Tillat's fault, of course: she had come visiting from Kuwait one summer, arriving in New Haven with her three children, all of them designed to constitute a large surprise. As a surprise it worked wonderfully, leaving me reeling with the shock of generation that attends on infants and all the detail they manage to accrue. But the end of the day would come at last, and when the rhythm of their sleep sat like heavy peace upon a room, then Tillat and I could talk. Our conversations were meals, delectable, but fraught with a sense of prior copyright, because each of us was obliged to talk too much about what the other did not already know. Speaking over and across the separation of our lives, we discovered that there was an internal revenue involved in so much talking, so much listening. One evening my sister suddenly remembered to give me a piece of information that she had been storing up, like a squirrel, through the long desert months of the previous year. Tillat at twenty-seven had arrived at womanhood with comparatively little fuss – or so her aspect says – and her astonishing recall of my mother's face had always seemed to owe more to faithfulness than to the accident of physiognomy. 'Sara,' said Tillat, her voice deep with the promise of surprise, 'do you know what *kapura* are?' I was cooking and a little cross. 'Of

Extract from the memoir *Meatless Days*.

course I do,' I answered with some affront. 'They're sweet-breads, and they're cooked with kidneys, and they're very good.' Natives should always be natives, exactly what they are, and I felt irked to be so probed around the issue of my own nativity. But Tillat's face was kindly with superior knowledge. 'Not sweetbread,' she gently said. 'They're testi-cles, that's what *kapura* really are.' Of course I refused to believe her, went on cooking, and that was the end of that.

The babies left, and I with a sudden spasm of free time watched that organic issue resurface in my head – something that had once sat quite simply inside its own definition was declaring independence from its name and nature, claiming a perplexity that I did not like. And, too, I needed different ways to be still thinking about Tillat, who had gone as com-pletely as she had arrived, and deserved to be reproached for being such an unreliable informant. So, the next time I was in the taut companionship of Pakistanis in New York, I made a point of inquiring into the exact status of *kapura* and the physiological location of its secret, first in the animal and then in the meal. Expatriates are adamant, entirely passionate about such matters as the eating habits of the motherland. Accordingly, even though I was made to feel that it was wrong to strip a food of its sauce and put it back into its bodily belonging, I certainly received an unequivocal response: *kapura*, as naked meat, equals a testicle. Better, it is tanta-mount to a testicle neatly sliced into halves, just as we make no bones about asking the butcher to split chicken breasts in two. 'But,' and here I rummaged for the sweet realm of nomenclature, 'couldn't *kapura* on a lazy occasion also accommodate something like sweetbreads, which is just a nice way of saying that pancreas is not a pleasant word to eat?' No one, however, was interested in this finesse. 'Balls, darling, balls,' someone drawled, and I knew I had to let go of the sub-ject.

Yet I was shocked. It was my mother, after all, who had told me that sweetbreads are sweetbreads, and if she were wrong on that score, then how many other simple equations had I now to doubt? The second possibility that occurred to me was even more unsettling: maybe my mother knew that sweetbreads are testicles but had cunningly devised a ruse to make me consume as many parts of the world as she could before she set me loose in it. The thought appalled me. It was almost as bad as attempting to imagine what the slippage was that took me from nipple to bottle and away from the great let-down that signifies lactation. What a falling off! How much I must have suffered when so handed over to the shoddy metaphors of Ostermilk and Babyflo. Gosh, I thought, to think that my mother could do that to me. For of course she must have known, in her Welsh way, that sweetbreads could never be simply sweetbreads in Pakistan. It made me stop and hold my head over that curious possibility: what else have I eaten on her behalf?

I mulled over that question for days, since it wantonly refused to disappear after it had been posed: instead, it settled in my head and insisted on being reformulated, with all the tenacity of a query that actually expects to be met with a reply. My only recourse was to make lists, cramped and strictly alphabetical catalogues of all the gastronomic wrongs I could blame on my mother; but somehow by the time I reached *T* and 'tripe', I was always interrupted and had to begin again. Finally it began to strike me as a rather unseemly activity for one who had always enjoyed a measure of daughterly propriety, and I decided that the game was not to be played again but discarded like table scraps. For a brief span of time I felt free, until some trivial occasion – a dinner, where chicken had been cleverly cooked to resemble veal – caused me to remind my friends of that obsolete little phrase, 'mutton dressed up as lamb', which had been such a favourite of my mother's. Another was 'neither flesh nor fowl', and as I chatted about the curiousness of those phrases, I suddenly realised that my friends had fallen away and my only audience was the question itself, heaving up its head again and examining me with reproach and some scorn. I sensed that it would be unwise to offer another list to this triumphant interlocutor, so I bowed my head and knew what I had to do. In order to submit even the most imperfect answer, I had to go back to where I belonged and – past a thousand different mealtimes – try to reconstruct the parable of the *kapura*.

Tillat was not around to hear me sigh and wonder where I should possibly begin. The breast would be too flagrant and would make me too tongue-tied, so I decided instead to approach the *kapura* in a mildly devious way, by getting at it through its mate. To the best of my knowledge I had never seen *kapura* cooked outside the company of kidney, and so for Tillat's edification alone I tried to begin with the story of the kidney, which I should have remembered long ago, not twenty-five years after its occurrence. We were living in Lahore, in the 9-T Gulberg house, and in those days our cook was Qayuum. He had a son and two daughters with whom we were occasionally allowed to play: his little girl Munni I specially remember because I liked the way her hair curled and because of all the times that she was such a perfect recipient of fake *pan*. *Pan*, an adult delicacy of betel leaf and nut, can be quite convincingly replicated by a mango leaf stuffed with stones: Ifat, my older sister, would fold such beautifully simulated *pan* triangles that Munni would thrust them into her mouth each time – and then burst into tears. I find it odd today to imagine how that game of guile and trust could have survived even a single repetition, but I recollect it distinctly as a weekly ritual, with us waiting in fascination for Munni to get streetwise, which she never did. Instead, she cried with her mouth wide open and would run off to her mother with little pebbles falling out of her mouth, like someone in a fairy tale.

Those stones get linked to kidneys in my head, as part of the chain through which Munni got the better of me and anticipated the story I really intend to tell. It was an evil day that led her father Qayuum to buy two water buffalo, tethering them at the far end of the garden and making my mother beam at the prospect of such fresh milk. My older brother Shahid liked pets and convinced me that we should beam too, until he and I were handed our first overpowering glasses of buffalo milk. Of milks it is certainly the most oceanic, with archipelagoes and gulf streams of cream emitting a pungent, grassy odour. Trebly strong is that smell at milking-time, which my mother beamingly suggested we attend. She kept away herself, of course, so she never saw the big black cows, with their ominous glassy eyes, as they shifted from foot to foot. Qayuum pulled and pulled at their white udders and, in a festive mood, called up the children one by one to squirt a steaming jet of milk into their mouths. When my turn came, my mother, not being there, did not see me run as fast as I could away from the cows and the cook, past the vegetable garden and the goldfish pond, down to the farthermost wall, where I lay down in the grass and tried to faint, but couldn't.

I knew the spot from prior humiliations, I admit. It was where I had hidden twice in the week when I was caught eating cauliflower and was made to eat kidney. The cauliflower came first – it emerged as a fragrant little head in the vegetable garden, a bumpy vegetable brain that looked innocent and edible enough to make me a perfect victim when it called. In that era my greatest illicit joy was hastily chawing off the top of each new cauliflower when no one else was looking. The early morning was my favourite time, because then those flowers felt firm and crisp with dew. I would go to the vegetable patch and squat over the cauliflowers as they came out one by one, hold them between my knees, and chew as many craters as I could into their jaunty tightness. Qayuum was crushed. 'There is an animal, Begum Sahib,' he mourned to my mother, 'like a savage in my garden. *Maro! Maro!*' To hear him made me nervous, so the following morning I tried to deflect attention from the cauliflowers by quickly pulling out all the little radishes while they were still pencil-thin: they lay on the soil like a pathetic accumulation of red herrings. That was when Munni caught me. '*Abba Ji!*' she screamed for her father like a train engine. Everybody came running, and for a while my squat felt frozen to the ground as I looked up at an overabundance of astonished adult faces. 'What are you doing, Sara *Bibi*?' the driver finally and gently asked. 'Smelling the radishes,' I said in a baby and desperate defiance, 'so that the animal can't find the cauliflower.' 'Which one?' 'The new cauliflower.' 'Which animal, *bibi ji*, you naughty girl?' 'The one that likes to eat the cauliflower that I like to smell.' And when they laughed at me, I did not know where to put my face for shame.

They caught me out that week, two times over, because after I had been exposed as the cauliflower despoiler and had to enter a new phase of penitence, Qayuum the cook insisted on making me eat kidney. '*Kirrnee*,' he would call it with a glint in his eye, '*kirrnee*.' My mother quite agreed that I should learn such discipline, and the complicated ritual of endurance they imposed did make me teach myself to take a kidney taste without dwelling too long on the peculiarities of kidney texture. I tried to be unsurprised by the mushroom pleats that constitute a kidney's underbelly and by the knot of membrane that holds those kidney folds in place. One day Qayuum insisted that only kidneys could sit on my plate, mimicking legumes and ignoring their thin and bloody juices. Wicked Ifat came into the room and waited till I had started eating; then she intervened. 'Sara,' said Ifat, her eyes brimming over with wonderful malice, 'do you know what kidneys do?' I aged, and my meal regressed, back to its vital belonging in the world of function. 'Kidneys make pee, Sara,' Ifat told me. 'That's what they do, they make pee.' And she looked so pleased to be able to tell me that; it made her feel so full of information. Betrayed by food, I let her go, and wept some watery tears into the kidney juice, which was designed anyway to evade cohesion, being thin and in its nature inexact. Then I ran out to the farthermost corner of the garden, where I would later go to hide my shame of milking-time in a retch that refused to materialise.

Born the following year, Tillat would not know that cautionary tale. Nor would she know what Ifat did when my father called from Lady Willingdon Hospital in Lahore to repeat that old phrase, 'It is a girl.' 'It's a girl!' Ifat shouted, as though simply clinching for the world the overwhelming triumph of her will. Shahid, a year my senior, was found half an hour later sobbing next to the goldfish pond near the vegetable garden, for he had been banking on the diluting arrival of a brother. He must have been upset, because when we were taken to visit my mother, he left his penguin – a favourite toy – among the old trees of the hospital garden, where we had been sent to play. I was still uncertain about my relation to the status of this new baby: my sister was glad that it was a girl, and my brother was sad that it wasn't a boy, but we all stood together when penguiny was lost.

It is to my discredit that I forgot this story, both of what the kidney said and what it could have told to my still germinating sister. Had I borne something of those lessons in mind, it would have been less of a shock to have to reconceive the *kapura* parable; perhaps I'd have been prepared for more scepticism about the connection between kidneys and sweetbreads – after all, they fall into no logical category of togetherness. The culinary humour of kidneys and testicles stewing in one another's juices is, on the other hand, very fine: I wish I had had the imagination to intuit all the unwonted jokes people tell when they start cooking food. I should have remembered all those nervously comic edges, and the pangs, that constitute most poignancies of nourishment. And so, as an older mind, I fault myself for not having the wits to recognise what I already knew. I must have always known exactly what *kapura* are, because the conversation they provoked came accompanied with shocks of familiarity that typically attend a trade of solid information. What I had really wanted to reply, first to Tillat and then to my Pakistani friends, was: yes, of course, who do you think I am, what else could they *possibly be*? Anyone with discrimination could immediately discern the connection between *kapura* and their namesake: the shape is right, given that we are now talking about goats; the texture involves a bit of bounce, which works; and the taste is altogether too exactly what it is. So I should have kept in mind that, alas, we know the flavour of each part of the anatomy: that much imagination belongs to everyone's palate. Once, when my sisters and I were sitting in a sunny winter garden, Tillat began examining some ants that were tumbling about the blades of grass next to her chair. She looked acute and then suddenly said, 'How very sour those little ants must be.' Ifat declared that she had always thought the same herself, and though I never found out how they arrived at this discovery, I was impressed by it, their ability to take the world on their tongues.

So poor Irfani, how much his infant taste buds must have coloured his perception of the grimness of each day. Irfan was born in London, finally another boy, but long after Shahid had ceased looking for playmates in the home. It now strikes me as peculiar that my parents should choose to move back to Pakistan when Farni was barely a year old, and to decide on June, that most pitiless month, in which to return to Lahore. The heat shrivelled the baby, giving his face an expression of slow and bewildered shock, which was compounded by the fact that for the next year there was very little that the child could eat. Water boiled ten times over would still retain virulence enough to send his body into derangements, and goat's milk, cow's milk, everything liquid seemed to convey malevolence to his minuscule gut. We used to scour the city for ageing jars of imported baby-food; these, at least, he would eat, though with a look of profound mistrust – but even so, he spent most of the next year with his body in violent rebellion against the idea of food. It gave his eyes a gravity they have never lost.

Youngster he was, learning lessons from an infant's intuition to fear food, and to some degree all of us were equally watchful for hidden trickeries in the scheme of nourishment, for the way in which things would always be missing or out of place in Pakistan's erratic emotional market. Items of security – such as flour or butter or cigarettes or tea – were always vanishing, or returning in such dubiously shiny attire that we could barely stand to look at them. We lived in the expectation of threatening surprise: a crow had drowned in the water tank on the roof, so for a week we had been drinking dead-crow water and couldn't understand why we felt so ill; the milkman had accidentally diluted our supply of milk with paraffin instead of water; and those were not pistachios, at all, in a tub of Hico's green ice-cream. Our days and our newspapers were equally full of disquieting tales about adulterated foods and the preternaturally keen eye that the nation kept on such promiscuous blendings. I can understand it, the fear that food will not stay discrete but will instead defy our categories of expectation in what can only be described as a manner of extreme belligerence. I like order to a plate, and know the great sense of failure that attends a moment when what is potato to the fork is turnip to the mouth. It's hard, when such things happen.

So, long before the *kapura* made its comeback in my life, we in Pakistan were bedmates with betrayal and learned how to take grim satisfaction from assessing the water table of our outrage. There were both lean times and meaty times, however; occasionally, body and food would sit happily at the same side of the conference table. Take, for example, Ramzan, the Muslim month of fasting, often recollected as the season of perfect meals. Ramzan, a lunar thing, never arrives at the same point of time each year, coming instead with an aura of slight and pleasing dislocation. Somehow it always took us by surprise: new moons are startling to see, even by accident, and Ramzan's moon betokened a month of exquisite precision about the way we were to parcel out our time. On the appointed evenings we would rake the twilight for that possible sliver, and it made the city and body both shudder with expectation to spot that little slip of a moon that signified Ramzan and made the sky historical. How busy Lahore would get! Its minarets hummed, its municipalities pulled out their old air-raid sirens to make the city noisily cognisant: the moon had been sighted, and the fast begun.

I liked it, the waking up an hour before dawn to eat the pre-fast meal and chat in whispers. For three wintry seasons I would wake up with Dadi, my grandmother, and Ifat and Shahid: we sat around for hours making jokes in the dark, generating a discourse of unholy comradeship. The food itself, designed to keep the penitent sustained from dawn till dusk, was insistent in its richness and intensity, with bread dripping clarified butter, and curried brains, and cumin eggs, and a peculiarly potent vermicelli, soaked overnight in sugar and fatted milk. And if I liked the getting up at dawn, then Dadi completely adored the eating of it all. I think she fasted only because she so enjoyed the *sehri* meal and that mammoth infusion of food at such an extraordinary hour. At three in the morning the rest of us felt squeamish about linking the deep sleep dreams we had just conducted and so much grease – we asked instead for porridge – but Dadi's eating was a sight to behold and admire. She hooted when the city's sirens sounded to tell us that we should stop eating and that the fast had now begun: she enjoyed a more direct relation with God than did petty municipal authorities and was fond of declaiming what Muhammad himself had said in her defence. He apparently told one of his contemporaries that *sehri* did not end until a white thread of light described the horizon and separated the landscape from the sky. In Dadi's book that thread could open into quite an active loom of dawning: the world made waking sounds, the birds and milkmen all resumed their proper functions, but Dadi's regal mastication – on the last brain now – declared it still was night.

I stopped that early rising years before *kapura* and Irfan were old enough to join us, before Ifat ran away to get married, and before my father returned to ritual and overtook his son Shahid's absent place. So my memories of it are scant, the fast of the faithful. But I never lost my affection for the twilight meal, the dusky *iftar* that ended the fast after the mosques had lustily rung with the call for the *maghrib* prayer. We'd start eating dates, of course, in order to mimic Muhammad, but then with what glad eyes we'd welcome the grilled liver and the tang of pepper in the orange juice. We were happy to see the spinach leaves and their fantastical shapes, deftly fried in the lightest chick-pea batter, along with the tenderness of fresh fruit, most touching to the palate. There was a curious invitation about the occasion, converting what began as an act of penance into a godly and obligatory cocktail hour that provided a fine excuse for company and affability. When we lived in Pakistan, that little swerve from severity into celebration happened often. It certainly was true of meatless days.

The country was made in 1947, and shortly thereafter the Government decided that two days out of each week would be designated as meatless days, in order to conserve the national supply of goats and cattle. Every Tuesday and Wednesday the butchers' shops would stay firmly closed, without a single carcass dangling from the huge metal hooks that lined the canopies under which the butchers squatted, selling meat, and without the open drains at the side of their narrow street ever running with a trace of blood. On days of normal trade, blood would briskly flow, carrying with it flotillas of chicken feathers, and little bits of sinew and entrail, or a bladder full and yellow that a butcher had just bounced deftly into the drain. On meatless days that world emptied into a skeletal remain: the hot sun came to scorch away all the odours and liquids of slaughter and shrivelled on the chopping blocks the last curlicues of anything organic, making them look both vacant and precise.

As a principle of hygiene I suppose it was a good idea although it really had very little to do with conservation: the people who could afford to buy meat, after all, were those who could afford refrigeration, so the only thing the Government accomplished was to make some people's Mondays very busy indeed. The Begums had to remember to give the cooks thrice as much money; the butchers had to produce thrice as much meat; the cooks had to buy enough flesh and fowl and other sundry organs to keep an averagely carnivorous household eating for three days. A favourite meatless day breakfast, for example, consisted of goat's head and feet cooked with spices into a rich and ungual sauce – remarkable, the things that people eat. And so, instead of creating an atmosphere of abstention in the city, the institution of meatless days rapidly came to signify the imperative behind the acquisition of all things fleshly. We thought about beef, which is called 'big meat', and we thought about mutton, 'little meat', and then we collectively thought about chicken, the most coveted of them all.

But here I must forget my American sojourn, which has taught me to look on chicken as a notably undignified bird, with pimply skin and pockets of fat tucked into peculiar places and unnecessarily meaty breasts. Those meatless day fowls, on the other hand, were a thing apart. Small, not much bigger than the average quail, they had a skin that cooked to the texture of rice paper, breaking even over the most fragrant limbs and wings. Naturally we cherished them and lavished much care on trying to obtain the freshest of the crop. Once I was in Karachi with my sister Nuz when the thought that she had to engage in the social ferocity of buying chickens was making her quite depressed. We went anyway, with Nuz assuming an alacrity that had nothing to do with efficiency and everything to do with desperation. Nuz stood small and dark in the chicken-monger's shop, ordered her birds, paid for them, and then suddenly remembered her housewifely duty. 'Are they fresh?' she squawked, clutching at them. 'Can you promise me they're fresh?' The chicken-monger looked at her with some perplexity. 'But Begum Sahib,' he said gently, 'they're alive.'

'Oh,' said Nuz, 'so they are,' and calmed down immediately. I have always admired her capacity to be reassured by the world and take without a jot of embarrassment any comfort it is prepared to offer. So I thought she had forgotten about the issue of freshness as we drove home (with the dejected chickens tied up in a rope basket on the back seat) and the Karachi traffic grew lunchtime crazed. But 'Oh,' she said again, half an hour later, 'so a fresh chicken is a dead chicken.' 'Not too dead,' I replied. It made us think of meatless days as some vast funeral game, where Monday's frenetic creation of fresh things beckoned in the burial meals of Tuesday and Wednesday. 'Food,' Nuz said with disgust – 'it's what you bury in your body.' To make her feel less alone, we stopped at Shezan's on the way home, to get her an adequate supply of marzipan; for she eats nothing but sweet things. Food she'll cook – wonderful *Sindi* tastes, exotic to my palate – but sugar is the only thing Nuz actually wants to taste.

Irfan was the same about birds. He preferred to grow them rather than eat them. There was a time when he had a hundred doves on the roof of the Khurshid Alam Road house, which was quite a feat, considering that they'd had to be kept a strict secret from my father. Papa hated doves, associating them with the effete gambling of Deccan princedoms or with

313

Trafalgar Square and his great distaste of the English ability to combine rain and pigeon droppings. So Irfan built dovecote after dovecote on our roof, while Papa had no idea of the commerce and exchange beneath which he was living. When he stayed at home to write, every sound would send him snarling, so then he heard with passionate hatred the long and low dove murmurings. He groaned and pulled his hair to think that his rooftop could actually be hospitable to pigeons: every evening he would dispatch Irfan to stand on the flat brick roof that was designed for summer sleep beneath the stars, so that he could shoo the birds away before they even dreamed of cooing. Since twilight was the hour when Farni preferred to feed the doves, life between him and Papa was perfect for a while. But then things fell apart. One afternoon Papa suddenly remembered that Irfan was at school and felt it incumbent on himself to gather as much information as he could about the academic progress of his youngest child, the renegade. In the evenings two tutors would come to coach Irfan in Urdu and math, and to them my father turned for an assessment of his son. 'Too unhappy!' wailed the math master. 'Today just too sad!' Papa bridled with defensiveness, asking for more specific fact. 'Cat, sir, cat,' mourned the Urdu teacher, 'cat has eaten up his fifty doves.' The math master shook his head in commiseration, and Papa later liked to claim that his mind went from 'bats in the belfry' through every possible idiomatic permutation he could give to cats and doves, until – only just realising he had heard a literal truth – he stared from one face to the next, like a man aghast with knowledge.

Am I wrong, then, to say that my parable has to do with nothing less than the imaginative extravagance of food and all the transmogrifications of which it is capable? Food certainly gave us a way not simply of ordering a week or a day but of living inside history, measuring everything we remembered against a chronology of cooks. Just as Papa had his own yard-stick – a word he loved – with which to measure history and would talk about the Ayub era, or the second martial law, or the Bhutto regime, so my sisters and I would place ourselves in time by remembering and naming cooks. 'In the Qayuum days,' we'd say, to give a distinctive flavour to a particular anecdote, or 'in the Allah Ditta era'. And our evocations only get more passionate now that cooks are a dying breed in Pakistan and have left us for the more ample kitchens of the Gulf states and the more cramped but lucrative spaces of the Curries in a Hurry at Manchester and Leeds. There is something nourishing about the memory of all those shadow dynasties: we do not have to subsist only on the litany that begins, 'After General Ayub came General Yahya; after the Bhutto years came General Zulu Haq,' but can also add: 'Qayuum begat Shorty and his wife; and they begat the Punjabi poet only called Khansama; he begat Ramzan and Karam Dad the bearer; Ramzan begat Tassi-Passi, and he begat Allah Ditta, meanest of them all.'

We were always waiting for Allah Ditta to die. He was a good cook and a mean man who announced the imminence of his death for years, though he ended up surviving nearly half of the family. Still, he was useful. My mother was a nervous cook – probably because her mother had been a stern woman about such decorum – and was glad to be able to turn everything over to Allah Ditta and take refuge instead in the university. It is odd to recall that her precise mind could see a kitchen as an empty space; I think she had given suck so many times and had engaged in so many umbilical connections that eating had become syncopated in her head to that miraculous shorthand. Not that pregnancy was a mystical term in her lexicon: on the contrary, the idea would make her assume a fastidious and pained expression. So she absolutely understood when Ifat, large with Ayesha this time, wafted into the house and murmured, 'Do you know what it is like to have something kicking at you all the time and realise that you can never kick it back?' Mamma, never one to state the obvious, would look up pleadingly at that, as though the obvious was so much with us anyway that we all deserved to be spared its articulation. Or she would utter one of her curious archaisms: 'Don't fret, child,' she'd say, 'don't fret.'

But Ifat was good at fretting, apt at creating an aura of

comfort by being able to characterise precisely the details of anything that could be discomforting to her. And so the state of pregnancy could on occasion make her eyes abstract, as she looked down at herself and vaguely said, 'I've eaten too much, I've eaten too much.' 'There's too much body about the business,' she once told me, 'and too much of it is your own.' Later, when Ayesha was born, a girl with blue unfurling fingers, the baby still would not permit my sister to empty into peace. She refused to eat enough, bloating her mother's breasts into helpless engorgement. So Ifat lay in bed, surrounded by such instruments of torture as breast pumps and expressers and her great facility for imprecation. Expressing letters rather than breasts was my normal ken, and it hurt to watch the meticulousness with which she set about relieving her body of that extraneous liquid. It was worse than a dentist, and for hours we implored her to take respite, but Ifat would not stop until her ferocious fever turned to sweat and her face was as white as in labour. Then she slept, waking once out of a dream like a beautiful gaunt owl to look at me oddly and say, 'Mamma fed me once.' In the morning the infant ate, and when Ifat's breasts lost their raging heat, it was as though stiffness could leave the entire household, erect as we had been to her distress. 'Ordinary pumps again,' she breathed, 'they're mine again, at last.' We smiled at that. Hard to believe, today, that those machines are gone for good.

For Ifat always was a fine source of stories about the peculiarities of food, particularly on the points of congruence between the condition of pregnancy and the circumstances of cooking, since both teeter precariously between the anxieties of being overdone and being underdone. When I left Pakistan, I had to learn how to cook – or, better – how to conceive of a kitchen as a place where I actually could be private. Now I like to cook, although I remain fascinated by my deep-seated inability to boil an egg exactly to the point that I would like to see it boiled, which seems like such an easy accomplishment of the efficient. I have finally come to the realisation that I must feel slightly peculiar about eggs, because I am uneasy until they have been opened up and the flagrant separation between yolk and egg can be whisked into some yellow harmony. When I simply try to boil an egg, I've noticed, I am sure to give it an unconsciously advertent crack, so that the humming water suddenly swirls with something viscous, and then I have to eat my eggs with gills and frills. Not that I very frequently boil an egg: once in five years, perhaps. I can distinctly remember the last occasion: it was when I was about to be visited by the tallest man in my acquaintance, in the days when I still used to tolerate such things.

He was a curious chap, whose bodily discomfort with the world was most frequently expressed in two refrains: one was 'Not enough food!' and the second, 'Too much food!' During the era of our association, I rapidly learned that the one intimacy we had to eschew above all others was the act of making meals and eating them alone. We could eat in restaurants and public places, surrounded by the buffer of other tables and strangers' voices, but for the two of us to be making and taking a meal on our own was such a fearful thought that the physical largesse at my side would break into a myriad of tiny quakes. It was revelatory for me, who had never before watched someone for whom a dining table was so markedly more of a loaded domestic space than was a bed, but I was not totally averse to this new logic. It exercised my imagination to devise oblique methods of introducing food into my house, free-floating and aimless items that could find their way into anyone's mouth with such studied carelessness that they could do no damage to the integrity of a flea. I felt as though I were still in Sussex, putting out a saucer of milk and goodwill for the hedgehogs in the garden and then discreetly vanishing before they froze into prickles of shyness and self-dismay. 'What is it, after all, between food and the body?' I asked one day in an exasperation of pain, and never got an answer in reply.

Tom and Tillat tried to behave like friends; they cooked together in a way I liked – but with me the man was so large that he could conceive of himself only in bits, always conscious of how segments in his body could go wandering off, tarsals and metatarsals heedlessly autonomous. Such dissipation made him single-minded. He never worried about the top of his head, because he had put it behind him. His mother chose his glasses for him. His desires made him merely material: he looked at himself just as a woman looks when her infant takes its first tremulous step into the upright world, melting her into a modesty of consternation and pride. And his left hand could never see what his right hand was doing, for they were too far apart, occupying as they did remote hemispheres of control. Perhaps I should have been able to bring those bits together, but such a narrative was not available to me, not after what I knew of story-telling. Instead, we watched the twist through which food became our staple metaphor, suggesting that something of the entire event had – against our will – to do with hunger. 'You do not have the backbone of a shrimp,' I mourned, gazing up at the spread-sheet of that man mountain. 'You have a head the size of a bowl of porridge and a brain the size of a pea.' This was in a restaurant. I was surprised beyond measure when that big head bent back and wept, a quick summer shower of tears. By the time he left, all surfaces were absolutely dry.

In any event, rain in America has never felt to me like a condition of glad necessity, and Tom and I will never know the conversations that we might have had on something like the twelfth of August in Lahore, for nothing can approximate what the monsoons make available in happy possibility. I think it was the smell that so intoxicated us after those dreary months of nostril-scorching heat, the smell of dust hissing at the touch of rain and then settling down, damply placid on the ground. People could think of eating again: after the first rains, in July, they gave themselves over to a study of mangoes, savouring in high seriousness the hundred varieties of that fruit. When it rained in the afternoons, children were allowed to eat their mangoes in the garden, stripped naked and dancing about, first getting sticky with mango juice and then getting slippery with rain. In our time such games drove Ifat and Shahid and me quite manic in our merriment, while

Mamma sat reading on a nearby monsoon veranda to censor us if we transgressed too far. Years later, Tillat and I served a similar function when Ifat left her children with us – we sat on the veranda, letting them play in the rain. Ifat would have rushed off to shop or to do something equally important, while her children would long for Irfan, whom they loved boisterously, to come back from school. Mamma, on such afternoons, would not be there. It returns as a poignancy to me, that I have forgotten where Mamma could possibly be on such an occasion.

She was not there on the afternoon when, after the rains had whetted our appetites, I went out with my old friends Nuzhat Ahmad and Ayla, as the three of us often did, in a comradeship of girlhood. We went driving to Bagh-e-Jinnah, formerly known as Lawrence Gardens, located opposite the Governor's House along the Mall in Lahore. We were trying to locate the best *gol guppa* vendor in town and stopped by to test the new stand in Lawrence Gardens. *Gol guppas* are a strange food: I have never located an equivalent to them or their culinary situation. They are an outdoor food, a passing whim, and no one would dream of recreating their frivolity inside her own kitchen. A *gol guppa* is a small hollow oval of the lightest pastry that is dipped into a fiery liquid sauce made of tamarind and cayenne and lemon and cold water. It is evidently a food invented as a joke, in a moment of good humour. We stopped the car next to some tall jaman trees (which many years before Shahid and I loved to climb) and enjoyed ourselves a great deal, until a friendly elbow knocked the bowl of *gol guppa* sauce all over my lap. It gave me a new respect for foodstuffs, for never has desire brought me to quite such an instantaneous effect. My groin's surprise called attention to passageways that as a rule I am only theoretically aware of owning, all of which folded up like a concertina in protest against such an explosive aeration. For days after, my pupils stayed dilated, while my interiors felt gaunt and hollow-eyed.

I retold this ten-year-old episode to Tillat when she came visiting, shortly after she had hit me over the head with her testicles-equal-*kapura* tale. I was trying to cheer her up and distract her from the rather obvious fact that, once again, her children were refusing to eat. 'Do you know how much happier my life would be if my children would eat?' Tillat wailed, and there was little I could say to deny it. 'It's your fault, Tatty,' I said consolingly, 'your body manufactured chocolate milk.' Certainly those children had a powerful impulse toward chocolate: it was deranging, to pull out the Cadbury's for breakfast. It gave Tillat a rather peculiar relation to food: it made her a good cook but a somewhat stern one, as though she were always waiting for her meals to undergo a certain neurotic collapse. One day she turned quite tragic, cooking for some visitors of mine, when the *shami kebabs* she was frying obstinately refused to cohere into their traditional shape. I did not expect Tillat's moon-face to look so wracked, as though the secret of all things lay in that which made the *shami* cling to the *kebab*. 'Never mind, Tillat, We'll just call them Kuwaiti *kebabs* and then no one will know they look peculiar.' Of course I was right, and the meal was most satisfactory.

I missed Tillat's children when they left. There are too many of them, of course – all of my siblings have had too many. Each year I resolve afresh that my quota of aunt-hood is full, that I no longer am going to clutter my head with new names, new birthdays. But then something happens, like finding in the mail another photograph of a new baby, and against my will they draw me in again. I did not see Ifat's children for four years after she died, and when Tillat and I visited them in Rawalpindi, in the pink house on the hill, Ayesha, the youngest, whispered to her paternal grandmother, 'My aunts smell like my mother.' When she repeated that to me, it made me tired and grave. Tillat and I slept for ten hours that night, drowning in a sleep we could not forestall, attempting to waken and then falling back exhausted into another dreamless hour.

I described that sleep to Shahid, wondering about it, during one of our rare encounters. I was trying to imagine what it would be like not to meet his children again, since in those days he had lost them. We talked about that, he and I, walking through the benign winter of a London afternoon, while the light was failing in irregular slashes. I always feel quiet to be walking at his side, glad to notice all the ways his face has taken age and yet remains the same. That face and I occupied the same play-pen, ate sand out of the same sand-box together. I had not seen him for two years, which made me tender when we met, talking about how we could not see Surraya and Karim, his children. 'I'll tell you what it's like, Sara,' Shahid said. Then he stopped still and looked at me. 'It's like the thing that a lush forgets, which is the absence of extremity.'

All at once I felt relieved my mother was not there to over-hear such conversation. I was glad that I had never seen, could no longer see, the cast her face would surely have taken hearing that sentence from her son. I wanted her to be put where she should be put, away from all of this, back in a bed where she need not have to know the desperate sleep Tillat and I had slept, hour after hour of reaching for the shoreline only to be pulled back into unending night. It was almost her reproach that I wished to be spared, the quiet voice that would look up and say, 'Honestly, you children.' I was afraid she would tell us that we were just as careless with our children as we had been with our books or our toys or our clothes, and I did not want to hear her proven right. The chagrin of the thought perplexed me as Shahid and I walked on, until I suddenly remembered the chagrin on Barkat the washerman's face when he was three days late in bringing back our school uniforms. Mamma's Urdu was an erratic thing, with sudden moments of access into idioms whose implications would throw her audience into gasps of surprise. When Barkat's recalcitrance kept her children denuded of clean white starched shirts and dresses to wear to school each day, Mamma's Urdu took a deep breath and opened the nearest idiomatic door, which sent her unknow-ing into the great precisions of classic amorous discourse. Barkat did not know where to look in his chagrin when Mamma gazed at him and said, her reproach as clear as a

bell, 'Barkat, how could you cause me such exquisite pain?'
I reminded Shahid of that story. It made us laugh from
Connaught Court to Edgware Road.

Tillat has three children, none of whom my mother ever
saw, and I missed them after they left New Haven. I could not
forget the way Tillat's three-year-old and only daughter,
called Heba, broke my heart when she refused to swallow
food. She sat at a table putting food in her mouth and growing chipmunk cheeks: we would try to ignore them as long as
we could, but Heba knew how nervous we were getting, that
we would soon break down and let her spit her mouthfuls
out, whereupon she could resume her lovely jabber as though
no grief had transpired at all. She ravaged me, but somehow
it was consoling to be so readily available to pain and to
observe in her manner and her face some ancient lineaments
of my own. One day she startled me by confidentially saying
that her brother Omi has a penis, but she has blood. When I
asked her what she meant, 'I looked inside to see,' she
answered, and glanced at me pragmatically. It made me glad
for her that she had had such introspective courage to knock
at the door of her body and insist it let her in. Heba has large
eyes, as black as grapes, and hands that she wields like an
Indian dancer. 'Why don't you like me, Omi?' she would ask
relentlessly. 'I'm nice, too.' It drove her elder brother into
furies of rage. 'I don't like you! I don't!' Omi shouted, while
Heba looked at him with curiosity. Watching over her baby
patience, I realised I need not worry about her, that child who
was busy adding herself to the world and would not rest until
it had made her properly welcome, long after she had forgotten me.

It reminds me that I am glad to have washed my hands of
my sister Ifat's death and can think of her now as a house I
once rented but which is presently inhabited by people I do
not know. I miss her body, of course, and how tall she was,
with the skull of a leopard and the manner of a hawk. But
that's aesthetic, and aside from it, Ifat is just a repository of
anecdotes for me, something I carry around without noticing,
like lymph. One morning last year I woke myself up at dawn

to escape the involutions of a dream that held me like a tax collector in a place where I did not want to be. For a moment I could not remember what city I was in, or what bedroom, until everything became lucid as I realised that Ifat was dead at last. 'Darling, what a nosebleed,' I found myself saying before I slept again and paid my dues.

Thus Nuz was right, absolutely right, when she wrote to me in her sprawling handwriting that looks so much like Karachi and said indignantly, 'Of course my hair is going to fall out, what do you expect, when life is so full of stress? Now I wear a wig and look smarter than ever.' Then she added, with the uncanny knowledge only Nuz can muster, 'People are only good for light conversation.' I liked the way that phrase lingered, born as it was from Nuzzi's unwitting capacity for the lingering phrase. The last time I was in London, I never saw Shahid's face light up so brightly as when he showed me a card that read, in florid script, 'Greetings from Pakistan', beneath the image of some bustling Pathan dancers. Inside it Nuz had written, 'Dearest Shahid, I am so sorry to hear of your divorce, my mother has had a brain hemorrhage and I am completely shattered, Merry Christmas and Happy New Year. Love, Nuz.' Nuzzi's mother was my father's first wife, and also his cousin, so I suppose she can count as a relative of ours although we have never met. Luckily she made a miraculous recovery before Nuz went completely bald.

My own mother would hate it that we could laugh at such a tale. Such merriment made her look at her progeny with suspicion, unable to accept that she could ever whelp this mordant laughter. When Ifat was pregnant with Alia, I remember how worried Mamma looked one day when she came across Ifat's first child, little Tunsi-boy, telling his nurse that Ama had eaten another baby so he'd have a brother or a sister soon. 'So they think you eat them up!' I was full of exclamation when Ifat told me this story, which made us laugh in poignant glee. Mamma came into the room and looked at us in a growing recognition of dismay. 'Perhaps you do,' she quietly said.

Five years later, I wish I had understood and remembered my mother's reprimand during the week she finally died. Sitting in the American Midwest, I thought of all my brothers and sisters, who watched my mother die in the jaunty dawn of a March day and who – fatigued and uncaring of the delicious respite of the dateline – gave me eight hours when Mamma was still historically alive. In a Lahore dawn on the ninth of March my mother's body failed to register on the hospital's grey screens; I in America was informed on the eighth, so technically I had a few more hours of my mother's life to savour before I needed to consign her into the ground. It made me secretly angry that such a reticent woman could choose to do something so rash and declarative as to die in such a double-handed way.

And then, when I was trying to move away from the raw irritability of grief, I dreamed a dream that left me reeling. It put me in London, on the pavement of some unlovely street, an attempted crescent of vagrant houses. A blue van drove up: I noticed it was a refrigerated car and my father was inside it. He came to tell me that we must put my mother in her coffin, and he opened the blue hatch of the van to make me reach inside, where it was very cold. What I found were hunks of meat wrapped in cellophane, and each of them felt like Mamma, in some odd way. It was my task to carry those flanks across the street and to fit them into the coffin at the other side of the road, like pieces in a jigsaw puzzle. Although my dream will not let me recall how many trips I made, I know my hands felt cold. Then, when my father's back was turned, I found myself engaged in rapid theft – for the sake of Ifat and Shahid and Tillat and all of us, I stole away a portion of that body. It was a piece of her foot I found, a small bone like a knuckle, which I quickly hid inside my mouth, under my tongue. Then I and the dream dissolved, into an extremity of tenderness.

It is hard to believe today that I thought the dream too harsh a thing. As parable, the *kapura* does not dare to look much further. It wishes to take the taste of my imagination only quite so far and, like my mother, makes me trebly entranced; had I really been perplexed at such a simple thing? Or perhaps my mind had designed me to feel rudely tender. I had eaten, that was all, and woken to a world of meatless days.

Firdaus Kanga

TRYING TO GROW

'IT WAS HER eyes that did it,' said Defarge, twisting the end of her sari into little bandages around her fingers.

'I can't believe it,' whispered Sera, 'because I've always had such a strong mind, such *will*-power.'

'Yes, but we didn't know what she was trying. Otherwise,' said Defarge, lifting her head, 'even I wouldn't have been tricked. And this son of yours – what was he doing sitting like a statue?'

'Don't you blame him, Defarge. He warned us loud enough – my clever baby.'

God knows, I did. Of course, it was rationing that was the culprit. All of us got a ration of rice from the Government shops, a quota of low-price, low-quality rice. 'Such as we wouldn't even feed our dogs,' Sera used to say. Everyone was on the lookout for the rice-ladies, tribals from Gujarat clad in blouseless saris, their heads crowned with sackfuls of long-grained rice that made every housewife reach for her purse.

That morning, one such raven-haired, green-eyed woman rang our doorbell. Defarge was at our place bursting with some news that she promptly forgot at the sight of the rice, white and thin like tiny needles. 'Look,' intoned the rice-woman, her voice deep as a man's, 'look at the rice in my hand and say how much you will buy.' They looked. Bending over her proffered hand they were bewitched by the rice-spell she had cast. 'How much will you take?' the woman purred.

Extract from the novel *Trying to Grow*.

326

'All, all,' they sighed languidly, 'every grain you have.'

'What about the price?' I shouted from my bedroom, interrupting a *mala* that I'd now have to start all over again. But Defarge would normally ask for the price before she knew what was selling. This was very strange.

'What does it matter?' asked Sera weakly. 'We want the rice.'

'At any cost,' giggled Defarge.

I wheeled myself to the drawing-room but I couldn't see the rice-lady; Sera and Defarge were in the way. They were counting the measures that she was pouring into Sera's giant rice-bin. 'Ten, eleven, twenty . . .'

'What are you doing?' I cried. 'What will we do with all that rice?'

'Eat it, silly boy!' giggled Defarge.

'That will be one hundred and fifty rupees,' throated the lady.

Sera got up to fetch the money. 'Don't worry,' said Defarge, tucking her hand inside her petticoat, producing two crisp notes from some concealed pocket. 'You can pay me back later.'

'Okay!' said Sera cheerfully. 'And do give her a tip, dear Defarge.'

The moment the door shut on the rice-lady, the rice-spell cracked. And what a noise it made. 'Look at that,' said Defarge, going so pale you couldn't see where her face ended and her hair began.

'Come on!' said Sera indulgently. 'You've hidden it somewhere.'

'Hidden rice? In my clothes?' said Defarge. 'Do you think I'm so dirty?'

'Any anyway,' I said watching her big tummy, 'where's the room?'

'Where is the rice?' said Sera, ignoring me. 'I don't have it, you don't have it; the bin is almost empty.'

'Just a fistful of rice,' said Defarge, mournfully running it through her fingers.

'We've been cheated,' said Sera flatly. 'I'm phoning Sam at his office.'

'Is he going to chase the two-rupee harlot through the streets?'

'Don't use such language,' said Sera crossly. 'My child is here.'

'Child! Huh! Soon he'll be shaving and still you will call him baby, baby!'

'Do you think,' I said hastily, 'that the rice-lady was a hypnotist?'

'What's that?' said Defarge.

'Mesmeriser,' said Sera impatiently. 'That's right, Brit. It was the rice in her hand that did the trick.'

'Like Mandrake the Magician,' said Defarge, nodding.

'Not so benevolent,' said Sera.

'Oh, my!' Defarge began wailing. 'What will we do now? My hundred and fifty rupees.'

'Don't worry,' said Sera, putting an arm around her, which was easy since Defarge only came up to her shoulders. 'I'll pay you half like I was supposed to.'

Defarge threw her arm off. 'Why only half?' she said angrily. 'Have I got even a grain of rice that I should pay half? It was your house, your idea to buy the rice.'

'I like that!' said Sera. 'My house and my idea. Suppose the rice-bin were full of slender, fragrant grains, would it still be my house and my idea that counted? Would it? Answer me. Why are you silent, you sly cat?'

The doorbell rang. 'The rice-lady!' the quarrelling women gasped. 'I'll pay half,' said Defarge hastily.

I opened the door and smiled. Standing there was this six-feet-tall guy, about as young as I was, his sloping eyebrows knitted into the most comical, doleful look.

Defarge shrieked, 'Cyrus! I forgot! Forgive me! Sera, I came to tell you before that thief knocked at the door. Oh! I should've been home – you are early.' She embraced his waist with her fat brown arms. He patted the back of her white blouse abstractedly all the while staring at me over her head with a speculative eye. I turned my chair so he wouldn't be able to see my legs.

'Do I live here?' he asked gently.

'You live with me!' said Defarge proudly. 'Not here –
there!' She pointed at her flat through our open door. 'This is
Cyrus,' she said, 'my cousin-brother's son: he's come to stay
with me. His father has been transferred to Delhi.'

'New Delhi,' I said.

'I say,' said Cyrus, suddenly crouching in front of me,
'could you lend me a large safety-pin?' His face was brown,
not brown like Defarge who was born that way but the sort
of golden-brown that pale skins turn in the sun. 'It's my fly,'
he said. His mouth drooped at the corners trying to resist a
smile that would not quit.

'I think I can find one,' I said. 'You'll come in?'

He nodded and held the curtain open for me to wheel
through. 'Phew!' he whistled. 'I'm glad Coomi didn't notice.'
He pulled his thumb out of his waistband. It was red and
creased.

'Who's Coomi?'

'My aunt.' He jerked his red thumb at the drawing-room.

'You mean Defarge's real name is Coomi?'

'You call her Defarge?'

'Everyone does.'

'Cy-coo,' cooed Defarge, 'have you brought an envelope
from your pappa?'

'It's in my bag. I'll give you the money as soon as I unpack,
Defarge.'

'Why're you calling me Defarge? Am I as beautiful as that
French master-knitter?'

'Exactly the same,' said Cyrus, letting himself smile with
every sturdy white tooth in his mouth. I saw my lantern-jawed
grin in the mirror and turned it off.

'The pin,' he said, pleading with his eyebrows.

'Oh, yes! The pin.' I managed to drag out Dolly's massive
dressing-table drawer. There was a twinkle of tiny pins but
only one large one that Dolly used to keep her sari pleats in
place. I picked it up and gave it to him.

'What are you two doing inside?' shouted Defarge. 'Come
on, Cy-coo, I've made yum-yum *dhansak* and big-big kebabs
for you.'

'Yuck-yuck,' said Cyrus through his teeth, forcing the pin through the thick blue denim of his jeans. He clicked it shut; we went out of the room. 'Thanks a lot,' he said. 'By the way, what's your name?'

'Uh-hm – Daryus.'

'We call him Brit,' said Defarge. 'Brit is short for his brittle bones. Poor, handicapped boy . . .'

'That's what you think, Defarge,' said Cyrus, smiling easily.

'At least,' Defarge went on, 'now he'll have a friend next door.'

That night I just didn't feel like making mantra *malas*. But I knew that would be like pulling out my finger from that hole in the dyke. So I broke out in a sweat though it was December and my room faced north. And like the hippie I'd once seen in a lane behind the Taj Mahal Hotel, injecting dope into his bloodless arm with a blood-encrusted needle, I began muttering.

The next morning I sort of hoped Cyrus would drop in. He didn't so I started a new *mala* to make him my friend.

That evening I was listening to *Saturday Date* on the radio when the doorbell clanged.

'Don't open it, pussy,' shouted Sera from her room down the passage. 'Must be a thief.'

'He wouldn't ring,' said Sam. 'It's probably Dolly.'

'Before midnight? Are you crazy?'

'Well, she's forgotten the latch-key; she's back early.'

'Don't be too sure. Brit! You wait near the phone to dial the police. I can't see you. Are you there?'

I unglued myself from the radio and took my post.

'I wish,' said Sera, 'I could come out and face him. But one of my nightie buttons is missing.'

'There's someone who says he knew you, Brit,' said Sam from the door.

I went out grinning. Then I thought of the crumpled cotton shirt and washed-out grey shorts I was wearing and I stopped grinning.

'Hi!' said Cyrus. 'We go for a walk?'

'Brit, it's late,' said Sam.

'Oh, that's my father,' I said, hoping he'd shut up. 'And this is Cyrus; he's staying with Defarge next door. I'll come,' I said.

'Brit, it's late,' said Sam. 'You've got to look after your health.'

'I'm fine,' I said. Sam nodded and left the room. I loved him. 'I'll – I'll just go and change,' I said.

'Change?' asked Cyrus, wrinkling his smooth straight nose. 'What for?'

'I can't go out like this – in shorts.' I had a thing about going out in shorts: people stared.

'What d'you think *I'm* wearing?'

'That's different,' I said, looking at his light-brown, muscled thighs.

'To hell with the difference,' he said. 'Why the fuck should you bother? Let's go.'

The fuck made up my mind for me. I snatched my latchkey; he took over my chair and began pushing. 'Where would you like to go?' he asked.

'Wherever,' I replied. I didn't know where you went for a walk around midnight.

'Okay,' said Cyrus. 'We'll go to Apollo – have it all to ourselves, for once. Want a cigarette?'

'I wouldn't mind,' I said, sounding as casual as a chain-smoker.

'Light one for me,' I said, not too sure about which end I should set on fire.

How flimsy the little white stick felt in my fingers. I put it in my mouth and sucked like I imagined I would on Raquel Welch's nipple. Suddenly there was a gas chamber in my chest and the taste of burnt chicken in my mouth. For the first time in my life I saw stars.

'Breathe,' said Cyrus. 'Breathe deeply. Fucking shit! I didn't know this was your first time.'

I relaxed. My ribs were aching but not enough to go home. 'Now I know,' I said, 'why good Parsees don't smoke.'

Cyrus laughed, his teeth white in the night. 'Serves you right for fooling me,' he said. We raced through the shadowed streets. 'Whoo! this is like driving a Ferrari,' yelled Cyrus. 'Boy! Does your chair move!'

'It's Swiss,' I said. 'The one I use at home is Italian.'

'God! Don't tell me you're one of those –'

'What?'

'The kind who have Kraft cheese for breakfast. Plumrose sausages for lunch, whoop it up in their imitation Dior clothes, end the day on caviare and champagne – all imported, of course. They don't enjoy anything Indian.'

'I think that's the kind of life I'd like,' I said.

'You're a fool if you lean on that sort of thing to have fun. I'd choose a moonlit walk and good company over all the caviare in the world.'

'So would I!' I shouted.

'Good!' said Cyrus. 'How d'you like that whore?' I saw a small woman in a white dress: her face might have been Tina's.

'My cousin is one,' I said.

'Really? You mean for fun?'

'Not really,' I sighed.

'Tell me about her.'

I told him. It was the first time I'd told anyone.

'So that's that,' I said and turned to see if he was yawning. He was trying to erase a tear with the back of his hand. I didn't know what to do. 'It's not so bad for me any more,' I said.

He said, 'I suppose not. But it's worse than ever for her. You know what? My pals and I used to get this great kick, driving through the red light areas, laughing our heads off at the whores, and the men with their tongues hanging out. Can you imagine? I was laughing at someone like Tina . . . It embarrassed you that I cried, didn't it?'

'I shouldn't have seen you.'

'You mean grown men can cry as long as they aren't caught at it?'

'You've said it.'

'You're an ass. Grown men don't care who sees them cry. You ever cry at the movies?'

'No; I'm afraid I'll make too much noise.'

'So you blink and stretch your eyes wide open to make more room for the tears?'

'Ya,' I said. That's exactly what I did. 'But I cry,' I said, 'when I read poetry.'

'Poetry? What sort of weirdo are you?'

'What!'

'Poetry is false, like a painted mouth.'

'False?' I squeaked. 'Are you crazy? It's like distilled water – the closest you ever come to purity.'

'You can't drink distilled water. You know what poets do? They drag their feelings up a hill and let go. What you read is the crash.'

'That's because they live on the mountain-tops. When you live at that altitude you're bound to have accidents.'

'You can't live on a peak; life is here on the plains.'

'So what are you studying?' I asked, feeling curious.

'Law; I'm going to be a solicitor.'

'And earn fat fees.'

'So what's wrong with earning?'

'I'm not going to earn much: I'm going to be a writer.'

'That's nothing to be proud of – not earning much, I mean. If you're going to write, you'd better plan to write well and become rich.'

'Struggling writer in a garret – it's an honourable life,' I said, as a sort of insurance, thinking of yellowed unpublished manuscripts.

'Nothing noble about being unsuccessful,' he said, shaking his head, and his silky hair went flip-flop. 'Just means you aren't good enough.'

'Mozart was poor; you can't say he wasn't good enough.'

'He lived in a world of feudal intrigues, not in Bombay today.'

'I guess it's no use arguing with you,' I said, thrilled with my defeat. I was tired of being the smartest kid around, especially when I knew I wasn't a genius. And Ruby and Tina and Dolly

– I wouldn't have exchanged them for a new pair of legs, but I couldn't have talked to them like I'd talked to Cyrus who'd just out-talked me.

'What's the time?' he asked.

'A little past midnight,' I said, looking at the hands saying five to one.

'Shall we go home?'

'Whatever you like,' I said. 'Actually, you're the first person who's ever asked me. When I'm out with my parents or my sister or my friends they turn back when they want to.'

He chuckled. 'I might do that myself when our walks become a daily affair.' My heart jumped, as if I'd entered a bookshop.

'Why,' I said, breathing slowly, 'why did you stay on in Bombay? Didn't you want to go to New Delhi, be with your parents?'

'What sensible man would leave Bombay? You know what New Delhi's like? It's monstrous. If you aren't a minister or a diplomat or a judge you're a ghost. Hell! You can be anyone in Bombay; as long as you've got brains and bluster, you've got it made. And then New Delhi's got the muddy Jamuna. Bombay's got the sea.'

'You like the sea?' I said, vaguely disappointed. 'I'm afraid of it; imagine getting lost in the endless grey.'

'Shall we try?' He laughed, swooping my chair through the break in the sea wall.

I screamed; I was sliding straight into the sea.

'Don't panic,' said Cyrus, his voice strong. 'There's a ramp here for people to walk on. It's cent per cent safe.'

'I don't believe in percentages; can we go back?'

'We're too far gone to turn,' he chuckled. 'Look! put on your brakes – we can sit here.'

'Here!' I squeaked. 'On the landing-stage for the boats?'

'Sure. And if we're lucky –'

A wave roared into my face, like a giant's sneeze. I howled, 'Save me – f-a-a-s-t!'

Cyrus sat cross-legged on the concrete, laughing, his shoulders moving up and down. 'You think you're going to

drown? I said if we were lucky we'd get some sea-spray.
That's what we're here for.'

'I haven't come here,' I said, trying to wipe my face with my
handkerchief. A wave jumped and snatched it out of my hand.
I had to laugh. 'D'you think it's okay to swallow this water?'
I said, thinking of how Sera boiled and filtered our drinking
supplies back home.

'Of course it's okay. It has all the shit and piss in Colaba
pouring into it by the minute.'

I pretended to retch on him. 'I don't mind,' he said.
'Couldn't be much worse than this.' He got a smack from the
sea in reply.

Riding my rocking-chair hard and crazy, I was thinking of all
the things Cyrus and I would do. They included such improb-
ables as comparing jerking-off techniques and taking a joint
trip to the moon which I could see hard and bright as a gold
sovereign above the sleeping Causeway.

For three hours that street where I lived was the Vatican
and I was the Pope. I surveyed it: Transport House from
where the huge red buses lumbered out like blushing elephants every morning; Electric House where irate customers
lined up to complain every time their electricity bills surprised
them; and opposite me the giant cream archway to the Parsee
Colony, whose red-tiled roofs shone in the moonlight – a
whole town with its own fire-temple and shops and school
and playing-fields where I would be living like most Parsees
this end of town did, if my grandmother had not bought a
love-nest for her British lover.

I scowled at the first milkman who stomped his heavy-
footed way into my kingdom. If I had Swiss Guards I
would've had him thrown out; but I didn't so I decided to go
to bed. I discovered there was no way I could get into my
wheelchair – it had rolled five feet away, further than my long
arms could reach.

It didn't matter a blink. I rocked myself to sleep.

The next day, when Sam found me huddled in the rocking-
chair, he carried me to my bed as fast as he could, before Sera

had a scales-attack. I woke up grinning like Heathcliff. I'd missed a nightful of mantras and nothing had gone wrong.

I stopped reading poetry. There wasn't any point going crazy over beautiful stanzas if I couldn't share them with Cyrus. Five days later, I packed away my art books. I couldn't draw if you offered me a streak of grand slams at bridge but I loved pictures. And Sera and Sam had bought me shelves of books.

'After all,' Sam had once said, 'he never wears out his shoes.'

'Yes,' said Sera, 'he hardly ever outgrows his clothes. We might as well spend on dressing up his mind.'

So every time they saw a book on the Ajanta paintings or Raphael or Amrita Sher-Gil they plonked down the rupees and bought it for me; and I spent more hours with it than there were paise in the price. Cyrus couldn't tell Michelangelo from Modigliani, so I packed away all the artists who came before, in between and after into the top shelf of my bookcase in the drawing-room where they looked lovely and where I couldn't reach them.

Cyrus was mind-deep in politics and economics and, of all things, science. When he talked about swirling nebulae and black holes, cosmic rays and circuits complex as a man's brains, I listened like I used to listen to Dylan Thomas.

That was to come. That day I waited for the night. Defarge came to see us – she came for a cup of Nescafé every morning at eleven – and she couldn't talk of anything but Cyrus whose father paid her a thousand rupees every month to keep him in comfort. 'But I,' she cackled gleefully, 'can make three, four hundred profit from that.'

'That's what you think,' said Sera darkly. 'You don't know how much growing boys eat.'

'Neither do you,' said Defarge, looking meaningfully at me.

'I'm glad I don't,' said Sera. 'My Brit has never been a burden to me.'

'You are forgetting the doctor's bills,' said Defarge. 'It's a long time since your son has broken a leg.'

'Touch wood!' said Sera, hastily looking around for some, tapping her head as a last resort.

'The best thing is that Cyrus is out the whole day – I don't have to give him lunch or snacks in between. He comes home at nine o'clock, goes out all evening with his friends.'

That meant I had to wait till after dinner to see him. But after dinner I had a date with my mantras. The day before I'd forgotten to chant them. Today I had no excuse; and if I didn't say them today all the charms would break. Of that I was as certain as I was of being Sera's son. I didn't know what to do.

So I made two slips of paper, wrote 'C' on one and 'M' on the other, folded them identically and picked one. It said, 'M'. Whoever decides things this way is an ass, I decided. That was really the end for the mantra.

'I'm going next door,' I said, opening the door quietly. It was about ten at night.

'At this time?' shouted Sera. 'Nothing doing! Yesterday you managed to give me the slip but you're not going out tonight.'

'Dolly does – whenever she wants.'

'Dolly's different.'

'You don't have to remind me,' I said, hoping that would paralyse her.

'Oh, yes, I do,' said Sera. 'And don't you start pitying yourself. You're delicate, you've got to be careful.'

'I agree,' said Sam. 'You aren't as strong as Dolly is. You've got to try and understand. Remember I told you once life wasn't going to be easy?'

'You were talking about girls,' I wailed.

'Oh, God!' Sam whispered and I felt awful. He bent down and hugged me like a bandage to his wounds. 'Try to understand,' he said, stroking my hair.

'There's nothing wrong with me.' I was trying so hard not to cry I thought my teeth would break against each other. 'As long as I don't fall I'm safe. I'm not delicate at all, at at all.'

'I thought you were proud of your English,' smiled Sam.

'Let me go,' I whispered. 'I'll come back before midnight, I promise.'

'Let him go,' said Sam, looking at Sera.

'Just because . . .' she answered, her eyes angry.

'No,' said Sam. 'Not because – We live with that like we live with each other. It's something else.'

'What?' asked Sera slowly, worried I'd hear something I shouldn't.

'We must let him go, darling. We're so scared for him we're shutting out his air and light. School, college, friends, picnics. He's hardly had any of those. Think what we got out of it all when we were his age.'

'Nonsense!' said Sera loudly. 'He has so much we didn't. Books and music, and we didn't play bridge when we were teenagers.'

'It's not the same, darling. Books and bridge aren't people.'

'Why are you doing this,' she said, 'making him discontented? Teach him to be happy with what he's got.'

'That doesn't mean he doesn't want more. Let him go, and to hell with his legs.'

'And when he's laid up in plaster like a mummy, are you going to look after him?' she said, muffling the last words with a hand to her mouth.

'I know it's been tough for you, my love. More than for any of us. But d'you remember that morning he was born? How brave you were? You said he was going to grow up like any other boy.'

'I wonder what I'll cook tomorrow,' said Sera. 'I've told the butcher to get me some chops – maybe I'll roast them.' She walked away slowly to her bedroom, old as her fifty-nine years.

Sam smiled his rueful smile. 'Off with you,' he said. 'It's not much longer till midnight.'

I crossed the lobby and rang the bell, stretching my arm to reach it. Defarge opened the door. 'Cy-Cy-Cyrus? Is he here?'

'He's busy,' said Defarge, touching her scarf to say she was praying and wouldn't talk any more. Defarge at the end of the rainbow was too much to take. I wanted to scream so loud it would shatter the half-moon reading spectacles on her Parsee nose. Instead I gasped. Behind Defarge, Cyrus was making

338

funny faces. He was naked as low as I could see. Defarge saw me grinning and turned her head. 'Oh, my!' she said, clutching the end of her sari to her face; I knew the georgetta was transparent. She stood there sucking in Cyrus's biceps, smooth like a statue's, his wide chest silky with hair and the nipples large and crimson. I followed her eyes through the makeshift veil as they made their way down Cyrus's tanned tummy, flat and sinewy, to his blue jockey-underpants, which seemed a size too small for his cock which curved between his thighs, shadowy with small dark curls.

'I'm glad you came,' said Cyrus. 'Mind if we sit and listen to music? I'm too pooped to walk.'

'Perfect,' I said sincerely.

Defarge tore her eyes away. 'Get dressed,' she said.

'I am dressed, Defarge. This is how I sleep every night.'

'I see,' she said, nodding understandingly and patting his head, letting a little finger wander to his neck.

'Hey! You're tickling me,' said Cyrus, ducking.

Defarge laughed flirtatiously, swishing her sari. 'Good night, boys!' she sang, and left.

'D'you think she has the hots for me?' whispered Cyrus, and I laughed so loud he had to jump up and shut the drawing-room door. He slipped a cassette into a gleaming tape machine and switched off the lights. His body vanished and a Chopin waltz took over.

'Gorgeous,' I breathed.

'Shsh! You don't talk when Chopin's talking.'

'Oh!' At home we talked through Chopin, Mozart and everyone else. Sera even sang along. I shut my eyes.

When the tape clicked he jumped up and slipped another one in. Sounds twanged out, groaning and creaking and wailing. 'My God!' I moaned. 'What's this rubbish?'

'Rubbish? You crazy or something? You know who's playing?'

'I don't care. I never listen to Indian classical stuff. Makes me want to puke.'

'Go ahead; you know where the bathroom is. By the way, that's Ravi Shankar.'

'Oh!' I paused, thinking of the blonde lovelies from London and Paris and Washington DC who screamed in ecstasy every time they heard Shankar's sitar. 'Giving it a fair chance,' I said, 'it does sound beautiful.'

'Really?' Cyrus's voice grinned in the dark.

'No, I said that because I felt like an ass wanting to puke at Shankar.'

'If nothing else,' he said, 'your books will be remembered for their startling honesty.'

'It's midnight,' I said. 'I've got to go.' He opened his mouth. 'No,' I said, 'don't say Cinderella.'

He came closer and stood next to me smelling of Pears soap. I looked at his dark thighs and thought of Wagh Baba. He sat down cross-legged on the floor in front of me so, so close I could see a tiny pimple below his left nostril. 'Don't go now,' he said. 'We'll listen to Mozart.'

'I've promised,' I said. I told him why I'd promised.

'Okay,' he said, pulling his lower lip into his mouth. 'I'll take you home.'

We crossed the lobby. The moon held him in a spotlight.

'You look like you're made of gold,' I said.

He struck a pose. 'There's a statue like that somewhere, isn't there?'

'Michelangelo's David,' I said.

He laughed and turned away, throwing a whistle over his shoulder.

I didn't reply; I was watching the muscled hollow of his spine.

A couple of nights later Cyrus had gone to a party and I was lying in bed with nothing to do but jerk-off. Minutes of heavy breathing later, I realised something funny. I wasn't watching Marilyn Monroe surge and shudder. I was staring at a man, his mouth hungry and gasping, nostrils dilated like a dancer's, a tiny pimple staring back at me. I'd never come with such a bang.

Then it all happened like Barbara Cartland says it does. I woke up, saw a triangular cone of blue sky and watched it shimmer like the surface of an enamel vase. I took a bath and the water felt like satin on my skin. The toast I ate for breakfast melted in my mouth; the words of the newspaper sang to my eyes. I breathed mentholated oxygen.

I waited for Sera to go shopping, then I shouted, not squeaked or squawked, but roared from deep inside the cave my pigeon-chest made, 'This is love! The divine love!'

It might sound like lust, but lust is as much part of love as cream is of milk. A square inch of Cyrus was enough for me – an earlobe that curved towards his cheek, a finger of hair that tickled his neck, the white underside of his arm when he lifted it, chapped lips, the bend of his waist, the nostrils that flared when he laughed . . .

We became partners in what Cyrus called 'the serious business of living'. We took in every play that hit the boards, laughing ourselves breathless at the pseudo-Yankee accents of a misplanted Broadway comedy, sniffing and blinking when Anne Frank, writing her diary by lamplight, said, 'I want to live even after I'm dead.' We went to concerts and took bets on whether the audience would applaud between the movements.

We ate out; one evening at the Rooftop Rendezvous, the swankiest restaurant in the Taj. Walls of glass, the city and the harbour glistening at our feet like a movie-shot. 'So romantic,' said Cyrus. 'And here I am –'

'Stuck with me.'

He laughed. 'Oh, well, you're better company than a gaggle of girls.'

'And boys?'

'Oh! Definitely. Men . . .' He grimaced. 'Most men can't talk about anything but their last fuck or the next smoke. Girls, they're fine, but as soon as you're alone with them, they touch their hair and simper and say, "Tell me something nice."'

'And you do.'

'Sometimes,' he grinned. 'You're different, Brit. You can talk about more than Screwdrivers and who's an easy lay. Talking to you is like talking to a very intelligent woman.'

341

'Thanks very much.'

He brushed the hair out of his eyes with the back of his hand. 'I'm not the wordsmith, you know that.'

'Stop acting and say what you meant.'

'Come on! You know you don't think or talk like most men do.'

'Depends on the men you choose.'

'Okay, but you've got your eyeballs trained on different things. You notice stuff I wouldn't.'

'Like?'

'Like I see a girl and think she's stacked, has the face of an angel. You see her and think she's lovely but cold, maybe because she's scared guys want her for her boobs – you understand?'

'What's that got to do with talking like a woman?'

'That's how women think. They never see an envelope without wondering what's inside. You do that too, right?'

I nodded stiffly.

'God! I don't mean you're a fairy or something.'

'I should think not.' I took a deep breath and rumbled out a manly laugh hoping that my blush, hotter than the Charlemagne Châteaubriand in my plate, was invisible by candlelight.

In May Cyrus took his first-year law exams, and I sat my last BA papers at the same time. We used to study together for a week or so, until I realised all I was learning was the shape of his head. (I sat behind him so we wouldn't be tempted to talk.) Now I finished my portion for the day earlier and spent the time till midnight with a book, thirstily watching the sweat-drops on Cyrus's tensed neck muscles.

'We'll go to the Cricket Club for a swim after the exams,' said Cyrus one evening.

'I won't swim,' I said.

'I'll teach you, Brit. You'll be able to. I'm sure.'

'That's not the point.' The blush was gone. 'I . . . I can't . . . I can't share a pool with so many people – it's filthy.'

'Fucking shit! The water's purified and everyone takes a shower before, even after.'

'I don't think that's enough. Now, if I had a pool to myself . . .'

'You're mad.'

I smiled. 'I think it's time you returned to the Indian Contract Act.'

'God! It's midnight. I'd better get going before Sera roars out.'

I nodded. 'See you tomorrow.' The door shut and I threw my arms over my head with relief. It was ridiculous, but it was the only thing I could think of. I was sure he didn't believe me: no one would.

I couldn't tell him the truth. I couldn't say, Look, Cyrus. Look at my body. Picture it in nothing but swimming trunks – osteo-warped.

I fought myself all night and the next evening I agreed to swim once the exams were over.

There, in the changing rooms, Cyrus took off his clothes with the speed of an anxious bather when the tap is running dry. I watched and smiled and smiled.

'What are you smiling at?'

'I was thinking.'

'Of?'

'Of how quickly it's grown.'

'Brit! Are you being funny?' Cyrus looked down at his big dark cock, swinging in a devilishly languid arc.

'I didn't,' I gasped, 'mean that. I was talking about our friendship.'

'Oh! That! God! I'm crazy to think what I did. I'm afraid I'm getting a bit of a complex about this.' He pointed downwards.

'You should be glad. It's a huge turn-on – for the ladies.'

'Which one are you, Masters or Johnson? I keep forgetting who's the man.'

'To complain about a thing like that!' I said, dying to continue the conversation.

'It's embarrassing,' he said, shaking his wet head. 'People think you've got a perpetual hard-on.'

'That would be gigantic,' I said.

343

'It isn't, I assure you,' he laughed.

'Don't pretend.'

'Okay. See for yourself.' I didn't know what to do. Because watching him grow like the magic beanstalk was making me do the same. I turned my chair around, ever so slowly, until my back was turned to him. 'Saw that?' he said. 'If you call that gigantic, you've never seen a blue movie.'

'I haven't.' Was he tall enough to see me over the chair's back? I was shivering so much, I was terrified I'd dislocate a joint.

'Now to get it down,' he said, and I knew I was going to get a stroke. He turned around and I came in a mushroom cloud of semen. The first atomic orgasm in history, I thought, and no one to record it. That made me laugh so much. I went down quicker than ever before so that, when Cyrus turned with his black trunks on, I smiled, serene as a celibate.

When we went to the pool and he lifted me gently into the shock-cold water, I stifled a squeak and looked round. There were half a dozen people sitting under flowering yellow sun-umbrellas. But I couldn't see if they were watching me. I'd known I was short-sighted for a long time, because I could never read the Censor Board's certificate that flashed on the movie screen before every trailer and film – Dolly had to tell me what I was going to see next. I didn't want specs because they'd hide my eyelashes which were the better part of my face. I'd kept my secret and now it was paying off a bonus. I paddled in bliss and the whole of Bombay could have stared for all I cared.

My glee wasn't a day old when Sera smashed it. 'Brit,' she said, mopping the dining table after breakfast, 'last night I heard you and Cyrus talking about a telescope.'

'Ya. We're going to make one and share the cost.'

'What's the use, Brit? You won't be able to see anything through it.'

'Why ever not?'

'You squint at the calendar on the kitchen wall, you hold the book you're reading six inches away, you stare through people you meet in the Causeway and you're trying to fool me that you can see fine?'

'Well, maybe not so fine. But I bet I'll be able to see the moon through a telescope.' I laughed and wheeled off to my room.

'Not so fast, Brit,' said Sera, her voice glinty as the chromium on my wheelchair. 'You're going to see an oculist today. Did you hear me?'

'Yes, Sera. Fucking shit,' I added softly.

I went with Sam. The oculist was a funny, jerky little man with a grin full of plastic teeth. 'Oh, my!' he said, shining a light in my eye. 'Blue sclerae, how pretty! Now what do blue sclerae indicate?'

'*Osteogenesis imperfecta*,' I said helpfully.

'Oh! Yes, yes, yes!' He giggled. 'It's been forty years since medical college. I forget things. Well, do you want to hide that lovely blue and those long eyelashes with which you must be winking at all the girls under thick glasses?'

'No! Of course not.'

'Then contact lenses are the answer,' he said, sounding so much like the commercials on TV that Sam automatically replied, 'No, that's out of the question for him. Cleaning and all that wouldn't be easy.'

'Very well, then,' said the oculist, straightening up.

I read the chart, the few lines that I could. 'Minus six,' said the oculist, twitching out for a pen.

'Six!' said Sam. 'It can't be. This is his first pair.'

'But it is, it is,' said the oculist gleefully. 'A rather thick pair of glasses. Since contact lenses are out –'

'And so is blackmail,' I shouted.

The oculist glared at me, his mouth doing a jig. 'I know why you are this way,' he said, his eyes joining the dance. 'You are a wicked boy and God has punished you.'

'Balls!' I hit him in his blinking eye. 'God is dead, or haven't you heard?' Then I saw Sam's face, white as cottage cheese, and thought he'd have a heart attack; I'd be stuck with this puppet till Dolly or someone arrived. I shut up.

'You mustn't get so aggressive,' said Sam in the taxi home.

'I know it was awful of the doctor to talk like that but *you* were rude first.'

'I wanted to be.'

'Oh, dear. But that's never any use, is it?'

'It is. Makes me feel better.'

'You need to be rude to people to feel good about yourself?'

'Of course not,' I said impatiently. 'But when someone's trying to make you feel rotten and you give it back to him, you feel good.

'You shouldn't care. It doesn't really matter what people say when they're cross.'

'It does to me.'

'I say,' said Sam, 'when are you going to start writing? I mean, really writing every day for six hours like a professional.'

'Writing? Who said I was going to write? It's a lousy profession – you don't make any money.'

'We don't expect you to.'

'That's terrible,' I shouted. The taxi-driver turned to smile indulgently. 'Why don't you expect me to earn? That's unfair!'

'Unfair?' said Sam. 'I thought it was rather fair not to make demands on you. Considering we didn't make you right.'

'I'm right to myself,' I shouted. 'And it's awful of you to go on thinking I'm not. How would you have felt if Sera had said to you when you got married, Darling, I don't expect you to earn a living? You would have felt terrible, as if you – you – you –'

'Yes?'

'As if you had no business being alive.'

Sam sat with his head thrown back against the seat. His eyebrows trudged into his forehead and his eyes tried to focus on something. 'I'm sorry,' he said. 'It's been so difficult. Trying to know what we should do. You don't know what it was like, Brit, when you were born.'

'Tough, very tough,' I said, wishing I hadn't started all this.

'Not tough. Just strange. So unimaginable –'

'You had to grope your way forward.'

'Yes. And every time we stumbled we kicked you.'

'You didn't. Or I wouldn't have turned out so well,' I winked.

Sam put his hand on my head. 'I love you,' he said, his throat hardly bobbing. I wanted to say, Same to you, but I thought he'd feel I was poking fun.

In the lift, he asked me, 'So what's going to take the place of writing?'

'Law,' I said. 'I'll probably be a solicitor, which means I can work from an office.'

'What made you choose law?'

'I don't know,' I said, so quickly he probably knew I didn't want to tell him.

'He says he wants to read law,' he yelled as soon as he heard Sera singing 'This is the Army, Mr Jones' in the kitchen.

'Who says?'

'Brit, darling; who else?'

'Brit wants to study law?' Sera came out, her hands dripping from the tap. 'You mean you want to become a lawyer?'

'A solicitor, he says!' Sam was trying to divert the oncoming storm away from his head.

Suddenly my face and neck and hair were wet, though not with water, as Sera hugged me, crying, 'Oh, Brit, lovey, darling, sweetie –'

I put my arms around her neck and squeezed as tight as I could. For once, I knew she was glad to have me.

'Let's celebrate,' said Sera, her face glistening.

'Oh, yes!' said Sam, 'and we can call over the boy next door. He's been taking Brit out almost every day.'

'So what? He's my friend.'

'His name is Cyrus. You aren't going to call him the boy next door, Sam – Cyrus. Remember, Cyrus.'

'Don't worry,' said Sam, chucking my chin. 'I won't embarrass you. Don't you think we should call Ruby, too?'

'No,' I said. I knew what a pretty girl would do to Cyrus – take his mind right off me.

'Of course we should,' said Sera. 'Suppose she comes over and finds out we haven't asked her, how bad it will look!'

'How awful she'll feel,' said Sam.

Ruby came first. 'You devil, you serpent, Brit. It's taken you six months to introduce me to your dishy friend. I could kill you –'

'He wants to keep him for himself,' said Dolly, who was home early for once. 'Don't you know he's gay?' I felt my ears redden though I knew she was joking.

'I've always suspected that,' laughed Ruby, looking so sensual in the sheer pink dress that licked her body, I felt a huge thrust of lust.

Cyrus came, looking sleek as a fox, his eyes long-lashed. He was laughing. 'To my colleague at the bar,' he said, giving me a box of chocolates, so heavy my hands fell to my lap.

'Swiss!' said Dolly, relieving me of the chocolates. 'Where did you get these?'

'I made them,' said Cyrus with a grin, 'and put them in the box.'

'You mean you can cook?' said Ruby, looking at him as if he were the Prophet Zoroaster himself.

'Oh! Just a little – chocolates, cakes, stuff like that.'

'You must teach me,' said Dolly. 'My cooking's hopeless. Sera says my husband will starve to death.'

Cyrus cocked his head. 'That would be a bit hard, wouldn't it? With someone who looks like you.'

I hooted. Dolly smoothed her black velvet dress over her knees and smiled. She was almost thirty but she didn't look any less lovely than Ruby.

Sera and Sam made their grand entrance, arm in arm. 'So glad you could come,' they said, ending in perfect unison.

'So glad to be here,' said Ruby and Cyrus together.

'Make a wish,' said Ruby, 'quick! Or the magic goes. You did? Okay.' She stood up and kissed Cyrus on his left cheek. 'Do the same to me – Oh, quickly!' Cyrus rubbed his nose and kissed her behind her right ear, making her glow like an apple.

'Ruby, you're marvellously inventive,' I said. She put a

hand on my neck, smiled sweetly and pinched me hard.

'Aren't you going to offer us those chocolates, Brit?' said Sera.

'Have one, do.'

'Like a dream,' breathed Ruby.

'Cyrus or the chocolates?' I asked.

'Shut up,' said Cyrus. Which was about the last thing he said to me for the rest of the evening. He was too busy with the three ladies. Reminded me of those Russian chess players who play any number of games simultaneously.

Sera almost beat Ruby in her enthusiasm. 'Cyrus, have some more *patrani machchi*. You said you liked it.'

'I think I will, thank you.'

'Wait a moment!' Sera unrolled the steaming fish from the plantain leaf in which it was cooked. 'There! Whenever Defarge starves you, come straight over. The way Brit eats, there's always enough for a guest.'

'You too, Ruby,' said Sam. 'You're always welcome.'

'And have been for the last twenty years,' giggled Ruby.

Dolly was strangely quiet. I made a face at her, rolling my eyes in Cyrus's direction, but she smiled and shook her head.

'There's one last bit of chocolate mousse,' said Sera, 'and it's for our chocolate prince.' She plopped it into Cyrus's plate.

'You know what, Sera?' said Cyrus. 'If I were you, I'd stop cooking for them and join the Taj as chief chef.'

Sera tucked her hair behind her ears, tilted her head and smiled wistfully at Cyrus. I wondered if she was thinking how grand it would be if he were her son.

Cyrus was looking around a bit desperately. He caught my eye and held a cigarette made of air between his fingers. I nodded. 'D'you think I might have a smoke?' he said, looking so lost I wanted to lunge over the forks, glasses, spoons and napkins and slip a cigarette between his drooping lips.

'You don't have to ask,' said Sera gaily. 'In fact, I think I'll have one too.'

'Darling!'

'Sam, you don't know this but I used to smoke when I was

at college. Don't look so shocked. That was thirty –'

'Forty,' said Dolly cruelly.

'Years ago,' finished Sera.

'The things you discover,' said Sam to Cyrus, who nodded, smiling distractedly, puffing at his Triple Five. Poor Sam, I thought, bumped into the same boat as me.

'But I warn you,' said Sera, 'if you make my Brit a smoker, I'll never make *patrani machchi* for you again. Keep Brit away from cigarettes.'

'And girls,' said Dolly, perking up.

'You don't have to bother about that,' said Ruby, 'he prefers boys.'

'Oh, my God!' said Cyrus, rolling his eyes into his brows. 'Why didn't you tell me earlier? Sorry, Brit, I'm just not inclined.'

Sam coughed. I wanted to wax Ruby's silky brown waves off her scalp. The embarrassment was okay: what I couldn't take was the way Cyrus had buried my hopes, without a moment's thought. 'I'm just not inclined!' What sort of funeral oration was that? Now, if he'd said I'd love to, but –

'I think,' said Sam, 'Brit has had a tiring day.'

'Hint! Hint!' cried Ruby.

Sam smiled and stood up. 'Actually, I'm the one who's tired. You youngsters can carry on. Good night!'

'Good night!' said Sera, ever loyal. She went to the window where Cyrus was sending smoke rings into the Causeway. 'Thank you, Cyrus,' she said.

'Oh! That's nothing. I'll make you another batch – with brandy.'

'Thank you,' said Sera. 'But I wasn't talking about the chocolates. It's nice of you to be Brit's friend.'

'The pleasure's mine,' said Cyrus, bowing over her extended hand.

'Yes,' said Sam, 'till you came along Brit didn't have a single friend.'

'I like that!' said Ruby.

'I was talking about boys. Before you all his friends were girls –'

'Lucky guy,' said Cyrus, sucking in his cheeks.

'I'd better be going,' said Ruby. 'My parents are home tonight – for once.'

'You mean you normally have your place to yourself?' asked Cyrus.

'Ya,' said Ruby sadly. 'It gets awfully lonely. I mean, how many mags can you read? How many tapes can you hear? How many day-dreams can you dream?' Which was about as big a lie as Santa Claus because Ruby was hardly ever home. 'I say,' she went on, 'why don't you come down and see me some time?'

I roared. 'Mae West redux!'

'He's crazy,' said Ruby, drawing circles at her curl-obscured temple.

'I absolutely agree,' said Cyrus, trying not to smile.

'Tell Brit to bring you over some time,' said Ruby, shutting the door.

'Who needs Brit?' said Cyrus through the closing door.

Ruby tossed her most ravishing smile, white and pink, over her shoulder and left.

'Good night,' said Dolly. 'If I weren't dead beat –'

'Dead beat?' I said, wrinkling my nose. 'Where did you pick that up?' I was surprised to see her blush for the first time in her life – or at least in mine.

'He's such a –' Cyrus shook his head. 'Embarrassing you like that.' Dolly smiled like a beauty and walked away.

'I wonder why she blushed,' I murmured.

'What a stupid question; obviously it's familial. And by the way, I'm sorry.'

'What for?'

'For ignoring you all evening. But you know – you're like – like a brother, I suppose, and when there are people around you don't spend all your time with your brother.'

'I know.' I felt as gracious as the Nizam with a courtier. 'And you don't ever have to be sorry with me. Because I –' The breath went out of me.

'Yes?'

'I guess I love you.'

'You know, one of the best things about you – or at least what I like best – is that you always say what you feel. Even when it's not easy. That's something I can never do. Never.'

'But, why?'

'Perhaps it's got something to do with the kind of families we've got. You know how envious I felt –'

'Of whom?'

'You, dummy. Oh! I know you consider yourself quite unenviable –'

'I don't, other people do.'

'I don't. You know why? Because you've got Sera and Sam and such a lot of noise and giggles and fights.'

'That's how it always is at home.'

'Not at mine. You must remember I come from an aristo family – at least my mother does. When we want to say something to each other we make an appointment in the morning. Will you be free for a little while after dinner?'

I laughed and braked. 'You're serious?'

'Yes!'

'But that's abnormal.'

'Not for my family.'

'But why? Can't you change things?'

'I'm not sure I want to – any more. Brit, why the sudden taste for law?'

I had rehearsed this exactly sixteen times. 'Law's going to let me roll in rupees.'

'If you wanted to write, you must have had something to say. What happens to all that?'

'I leave it unsaid.'

'What if you choke on unsaid words?'

'You sound like a play.'

'But it might be true.'

'I don't care. Because I'm happy. Sam's delighted. Sera's delirious.'

'That's something else I envy you for. When I told my parents I wanted to read law –'

'What happened?'

'My mother fell ill. She missed three mah-jong evenings in

a row, not to mention a charity première – I even remember the film, *Chariots of Fire*.'

'But I thought law was a good solid profession.'

'Are you mad? When her son could've been a concert violinist?'

'What!'

'My *dark secret*.'

Cyrus grinned but his eyes didn't join in. 'Why am I talking like this? God – it's all dead.'

'Never mind. I'd like to know.'

'I was pretty good at the violin. I used to spend every moment I could snatch from homework and school practising. And I was taking exams – you know, the usual Royal Academy ones. And in my last year I won a gold medal.'

'You were the best student.'

He sighed. 'Explicit language! Anyway, I won a scholarship to the Menuhin School in London.'

'My God! And you threw that over? If I were your mother I would never have played mah-jong again in my life.'

'I didn't throw it over; I thought fighting cases would satisfy my brain more than making music. It sounds insensitive but that's how I felt.'

'Didn't you adore your music?'

'I did. But it wasn't enough. It was an unhealthy kind of passion.'

'Music? Unhealthy?'

'Sure. I was using it to push away everyone, to drown the anger, you know – that's no good. It's like building up your body at the cost of your brain.'

'What?'

'I don't mean that, but something similar – I might have been a fantastic violinist on stage and a crackpot off it. That wasn't the kind of person I wanted to be.'

'You mean you had to put away your violin if you were going to grow.'

'That's about the closest anyone has come to understanding what I felt.'

So this, I thought, sitting in the centre of my mind's

polished stage, is what a writer means when he writes, '. . . and I thought my heart was going to burst.' But I said, 'Did you explain things so clearly to your mother?'

'What did she care? She lost the best piece in her show-case.'

'Don't sound so bitter, Cy,' I said, manoeuvring my chair next to the end of the sofa where he was sitting, patting the back of his head, trying to keep things as brotherly as I could. His hair was like soft warm air in my fingers.

'Don't call my Cy,' he said. 'That's what my mother calls me in front of other people – she thinks it sounds English or American or whatever. "Cy, why don't you play something for Lady Manekbai?" Can you believe there are still people who call themselves Lady or Sir?'

'Well, they can't help it if they're titled,' I said, trying to concentrate on his words instead of the tensed muscle and smooth skin under my fingers.

'Fucking shit! They can fling back their titles from where they came – Rabindranath Tagore did it. And the worst thing was I knew what they liked so I'd play a Kreisler trifle and Lady Manekbai would say, "How pretty! But far too short, Cy. Give us something long and brilliant." So I'd start on something like Bach's E major *Partita*. Soon as the first few bars were over they'd settle down to a disgusting conversation about whether you got a better steak at the Taj or the Oberoi, and how their hairstylist was getting quite unreasonable – what if she'd worked with Sassoon – sixty rupees for a cut was daylight robbery.' He relaxed; the muscles under my hand disappeared. He smiled ruefully. 'What a long story.'

'Thank you for telling me.'

He shrugged and swallowed. Then he said, 'It's so crazy Sera and your father and you all thinking me like this. And all along, I've been so glad you became my friend.' He put his hand on my shoulder, almost touching my right cheek. I could see the fine hair on his wrist swaying under my breath like wheat in a field. He stood up. 'See you tomorrow. Will you come over? We'll make the telescope.'

'Oh, yes! That would be great.'

'Bye – and thanks for the neck massage.' He shut the door and I didn't know what to do. I wheeled over to the door and kissed the grainy, polished board. I heard his door shut behind him. Just a gender away.

I wanted Cyrus: his mocking mouth, his quiet eyes, his thighs and hair and cock. Now, if he were someone else, someone who thought life was the food you ate and the movies you saw and not the winds that blew inside your head; or someone who got out of a taxi without thanking the driver; or someone who blew his nose into his hand instead of his hanky, then I wouldn't have given a damn if he looked like Shashi Kapoor or Sean Connery or whoever; not if he had a cock that would've made him a blue movie star.

What if it were the other way around? If he were as perfect as he seemed to me but he looked like Walter Matthau? I wanted to believe it wouldn't matter a thought. But that wasn't true. Because I thought about it for a million minutes and this was what I was sure of – I just didn't know.

Anjana Appachana

SHARMAJI

SHARMA WAS LATE for work. When he signed his name in the attendance register, the clerk in the personnel department shook his head disapprovingly.

'Very bad, very bad, Sharmaji,' he said, clicking his tongue. 'This is the fourteenth time you are late this month.'

Sharma's brow darkened. 'You keep quiet, Mahesh,' he replied. 'Who are you to tell me I'm late? You are a clerk, I am a clerk. You don't have the authority to tell me anything. Understood?'

Mahesh retreated behind his desk. He said, 'What I am telling you, I am telling you for your own good. Why you must take it in the wrong spirit I do not understand.'

'You don't tell me what is good for me,' Sharma said. He raised his voice. 'I am twenty-five years older than you.'

He had an audience by now. The other latecomers and those working in the personnel department were watching with intense interest.

Sharma continued, 'I have been in this company for twenty-five years. At that time you were in your mother's womb.' He surveyed his delighted audience. 'He thinks that after reading our personal files he has power over us.' He snapped his fingers in front of Mahesh's face. 'I can show you how much power you have! What can a pipsqueak like you teach me! It is for *me* to teach *you*!'

'Sharmaji,' said Mahesh, folding his hands, 'I take back my words. Now please leave me alone. And I beg of you, do not shout in the personnel department. It sounds very bad.'

Sharma chuckled. He raised his voice. 'Shouting? I am not shouting. I am talking to you. Is it forbidden to talk in the personnel department? Is this an office or a school?' He smiled again at his audience. Everyone was spellbound. He said, 'So Mahesh, you now think you can tell me how to behave. Very good. What else can you teach me?'

'Yes, Mahesh, tell him,' urged Gupta, the clerk from the accounts department. He was also late, but only for the ninth time in the month.

Mahesh looked harassed. 'You keep out of this, Gupta. This is not your business.'

'Mahesh,' said Gupta. 'You are in the wrong profession. You should have been a teacher, a professor. Join Delhi University. We will all give you recommendations!'

Everyone roared with laughter. Mohan, the peon, was the loudest. 'Today we are having fun,' he said between guffaws. 'Oh, this is wonderful!'

'What is wonderful, Mohan?'

It was the personnel officer, Miss Das. A sudden silence fell in the room. Everyone looked away. She glanced at her watch and then at the silent group. 'What is happening?' she asked. 'Why is there this *mela* here?'

'Madam, we came to sign the attendance register,' Sharma said.

Gupta slid out of the room.

She looked pointedly at her watch. 'The register should have been signed forty-five minutes ago.'

Sharma looked her straight in the eyes. 'Madam,' he said, 'what to do, my daughter has a temperature. I had to take her to the clinic so I got a little late.'

'Did you inform your manager that you would be late?'

'I don't have a phone at home, madam.'

'Why didn't you inform him yesterday?'

'Madam, I did not know yesterday. My daughter fell ill this morning.'

She looked at the register. 'Has your daughter been ill fourteen days of the month?'

Mahesh smirked.

'Oh, madam,' said Sharma, 'that was my other daughter. You know this virus, madam. All my daughters have been falling ill, one after the other. I have three.'

'Fourteen days,' she repeated, shaking her head.

'Yes madam, three daughters with this virus. Well, madam, I should be getting along.' He sauntered out of the room.

In the corridor he bumped into Gupta smoking a cigarette. 'What Gupta,' he said, 'you left me alone to face her.'

'What to do?' said Gupta. 'She has already told me off twice. She thinks it is still Indiraji's raj. Cigarette?'

'Might as well,' said Sharma, and took one. 'So, how are things with you?'

Gupta lit his cigarette. 'All right, so so.' He gave a bashful smile. 'My parents are searching for a girl for me. I have to get married before December. The astrologer has said that the two years after December will be very inauspicious for marriage.'

'Are you looking for a working girl, or what?'

'Yes. We think that might be preferable. How can we manage on my salary? But they bring less dowry. And my sister has to be married off next month. It is very difficult.'

'So, anything fixed up yet?'

'No, I have seen four girls so far. All dark.'

'Do not worry, Gupta. You will surely find a fair bride. Now, how about some chai?'

'Good idea.'

They strolled to the canteen and ordered tea. It arrived, steaming hot, and they drank it with satisfaction. 'Terrible tea,' said Sharma. 'This company has no care for its employees. They are stingy even in the tea they give us – no milk, or sugar. This tea is worth ten paisa. They charge us fifty paisa. Then they say it is subsidised. Ha! Subsidised!'

'Why should they care?' said Gupta. 'They only want to make money. Profit, profit, profit. That is all they care about. We are the ones who do all the work and they are the ones who benefit. This is life.'

Sharma sighed. 'Yes, this is life,' he echoed. 'Give me another cigarette, Gupta. After tea a cigarette is a must.'

They both had another.

'How is your Mrs?' asked Gupta.

Sharma grinned self-consciously. 'She is going to become a mother.'

'Arre!' exclaimed Gupta. 'What are you doing, Sharmaji? You already have three and the Government says one or two, bas.'

'They are all girls, Gupta. Who will look after us in our old age?'

'Forgive me, Sharmaji,' Gupta said, clicking his tongue, 'but I am talking to you as old friend. You already have three daughters. You will have to spend all your money marrying them off. And now one more is coming. Suppose that too is a girl?'

Sharma sighed heavily. 'That is in God's hands. After all, it is fate. I have to suffer in this life for the sins I have committed in my previous life.' He sighed again. 'Gupta, yar, it is so difficult to manage these days. Since my daughters were born I have been putting aside fifty rupees every month for their marriages. Even then it will not be enough to marry them off.'

Gupta patted Sharma. 'Why worry about the future? Deal with things as they come. Think yourself fortunate that at least you are in the purchase department.'

'That is true, that is true,' agreed Sharma. 'Where would a mere clerk's salary take me?'

They ordered some more tea and smoked another cigarette. For some time there was an amiable silence. Then Gupta leaned towards Sharma confidentially. 'Have you heard the latest?'

'What?'

'You don't know?'

'No – what?'

'You won't believe it.'

'Arre, tell me Gupta.'

'Miss Das smokes.'

'Impossible!'

'Yes, yes, she smokes. Rahul saw her smoking.'

'Where?'

'In a restaurant in Connaught Place.'

'Alone?'

'No, not alone. She was sitting with a man and smoking. And when she saw Rahul, she stubbed it out.'

'I cannot believe it.'

'Even I find it difficult to believe.'

'She has a boyfriend?'

'Must be having a boyfriend.'

'Is she engaged?'

'Don't know. She's a quiet one.'

Sharma considered the news. 'Rahul is a great gossip. He talks too much. One never knows how much truth there is in what he says. He does no work, have you noticed? All he does is gossip.'

'Then you think it is not true?'

'I did not say that. It could be true. It could be untrue. Myself, I feel it is not true. Miss Das does not look the smoking kind. She appears to be a good girl.'

'But why should Rahul make it up? What does he have against her?'

'Yes, yes, you have a point. Truly, this is disturbing. But she must be engaged. She does not seem to be the kind to go around with men.'

'Maybe. Maybe not.'

Sharma chewed his lips. He shook his head. 'I will find out.'

Gupta looked at his watch. He got up. 'Sharmaji, it is already 11.30. We had better go to our departments.'

Sharma pulled him down. 'Stop acting so conscientious. No one will miss us. Lunchtime is at 12.30. We might as well stay here till lunch is over.'

Gupta looked worried. 'I am not conscientious,' he disclaimed. 'It is just that my boss has been after my life these days. If he knows I'm here he'll again say that I don't work.'

'Oh, *sit* down,' said Sharma. 'Even my boss is after my life. They are all like that, these managers. They think that only they work. Just because they stay here after office hours they expect people to believe that they work. Ha! All that is to impress the general manager. How else can they get their promotions? All maska.'

Gupta sat down.

'Jagdish,' called Sharma. 'More chai.'

The third round of tea arrived.

The electricity went off.

'Bas,' said Sharma. 'Now who can work? These power cuts will kill us all.' He sat back in his chair.

'My boss says that it is no excuse,' said Gupta gloomily. 'He says that if a power cut lasts three hours it doesn't mean that we don't work for three hours. He says that we are here to work.'

'He can keep saying that,' said Sharma contemptuously. 'Does he think we're animals? They all think that we have no feelings. Work all day, work when the electricity goes off, work without increments, work without promotions, work, work, work. That is all they care about. No concern for us as human beings.'

'Hai Ram,' Gupta whispered. 'Don't look behind you. She's here.'

'Who?'

'Miss Das. She's seen us.'

'So what if she's seen us?'

'She'll tell our managers.'

'Let her tell them.'

'Sharmaji, I have already been warned.'

'Nothing to worry about. What can he do to you? The union will support you.'

'Sharmaji, it will be in my records if they give me a warning letter.'

'So let it be in your records, Gupta. Anyway you are in their bad books.'

'Suppose they give me a charge-sheet?'

'Now you are panicking. Relax. Nothing can happen. Now we have a union.'

'She's gone. Sharmaji, I'm going back to the department.'

'Arre, Gupta, sit down. Just half an hour for the lunch break. We will both go back to our departments after lunch.'

'No, no, I am going now. Excuse me, Sharmaji, see you

later.' He rushed out.

Sharma shook his head. Everyone was scared. That was the problem. He opened the newspaper lying on the table and read for some time. The same news. Nothing changed. He yawned.

'There you are, Sharmaji.' It was Harish, the peon from the purchase department. 'Borwankar Sahib is calling you to his office.' He chuckled. 'He is in a bad temper. There will be fire-works today!'

Sharma looked at him unsmilingly. 'It is lunchtime. Tell him I will come after lunch.'

'Sharmaji, you had better go now. He is in a very bad temper.'

'You don't tell me what to do. You have given me the message. Now go.'

Harish smacked his forehead in despair. 'All right, all right, I will go. Don't tell me later that I did not warn you.' He left.

Sharma curled his lips contemptuously. He leaned further against his chair. He scratched an unshaven cheek. From his pocket he took out a paan wrapped in a piece of paper and put it in his mouth. Contemplatively, he chewed.

'Should we eat, Sharmaji?' It was Gupta.

'Back so soon?' asked Sharma, surprised.

'Yes, it is 12.30 – lunchtime,' Gupta said happily.

'I haven't got my lunch,' said Sharma sadly. 'Last week my wife left for her mother's with the girls for a month. I have no time to cook.'

'Why didn't you tell me earlier, Sharmaji?' exclaimed Gupta. 'You mustn't keep such problems from old friends. From tomorrow, till your wife comes home, I will ask my mother to pack extra lunch. It will be enough for both of us.'

'Gupta,' said Sharma emotionally, 'you are a true friend.'

'It is nothing.'

They shared Gupta's lunch. Then they went down to the dhaba opposite the building. There they ordered puri-aloo. It was a wonderful meal. Then they each had a large glass of lassi. After it was over they sat back, replete, content, drowsy.

'Gupta,' said Sharma, rubbing his stomach, 'I am falling asleep.'

'Me too,' groaned Gupta. 'I cannot keep my eyes open. Hai Ram.'

The heat, their meal and the lassi were having their effect. They could barely keep awake. Sleep . . . wonderful sleep.

'They should have a rest room in the office where we could take a short nap after lunch,' said Gupta. 'Then we would be ready to work, refreshed.'

'Yes,' sighed Sharma. 'In the summer especially, one cannot keep awake after lunch.'

'Sharmaji, it is already half an hour past lunchtime. Let us go back.'

Reluctantly, Sharma rose. He blinked his eyes against the afternoon sun. This was torture. Slowly, they began walking back to the building.

Suddenly Sharma stopped. 'Paan,' he said. 'I must have a paan. Let us go to the paan shop.'

Gupta hesitated. 'All right,' he said, 'but let us hurry.'

At the paan shop they bought four paans, ate one each and had the other two wrapped up. When they reached the office building they found that the electricity had not returned. They could not take the lift.

'I will die,' said Sharma. 'I cannot climb up four floors after a meal like that.' He sat down on the steps.

Mohan passed him on the way upstairs. He hooted with laughter. 'Sharmaji, everyone does it, why can't you? Kaamchor!' He bounded up the stairs before Sharma could respond.

'Haramzada,' muttered Sharma. 'Even the peons in the personnel department are getting too big for their boots.' He got up and slowly began climbing up the stairs with Gupta. 'And they expect us to work in these conditions,' he said. 'They think we are animals.'

Gupta clicked his tongue in sympathy.

On the third floor Sharma said, 'If I don't have some tea I will collapse.'

'In this heat, Sharmaji?'

'I am tired, I am sleepy. Only tea will do the job. Chalo, let us go to the canteen.'

'Sharmaji, you go. My boss has been taking rounds of our office.'

'Sharma, could you please come to my office?' It was Mr Borwankar, Sharma's boss.

Gupta slid away to his department.

Sharma sighed. 'Yes, Borwankar Sahib. I will come.'

He followed his manager to his office.

'Sit down.'

Sharma sighed and sat.

'I had called you to my office more than an hour ago.'

'It was lunchtime, sir.'

'Indeed.'

'Yes, sir.'

'What happened after lunch?'

'I am here sir, after lunch.'

'It is forty-five minutes past lunchtime.'

'I went to the dhaba to eat, sir. There was a long queue there, so I was delayed, sir. All this was because my daughters have been getting the virus, sir, and my wife has no time to pack lunch for me, sir. I am sure you understand, sir. After all, how can I work on an empty stomach? I feel so weak these days sir, so tired. I think I am also getting the virus.'

'Where have you been all morning?'

'Here, sir.'

'Here – where?'

'In the department, sir.'

'You were not at your desk all morning.'

'Sir, what are you saying? I must have gone down to the personnel department or the accounts department for some work.'

'What work?'

Sharma was silent. He shook his head. He looked sadly at Mr Borwankar. He said, 'Borwankar sahib, why are you taking this tone with me? You ask me questions as though you have no faith in me. This is not a detective agency. Why must you interrogate me in this manner? All right, I was not in my department, but that was because I had work in other departments. Still, if it is your wish, I will not go to other departments even if I have work there. I will sit at my desk and work only at my desk. Yes, yes, I will do that. The company does not want me to consult other departments. All right, I will not consult other departments. You will see, work will suffer, but why should I care when you do not? I have been in this company for twenty-five years, but no one cares. For twenty-five years the company has bled me, sucked me dry. What do you know? You have been here only two years. You know nothing. Twenty-five years ago I joined as a clerk. Today I am still a clerk. Why should I work?'

His outburst had touched something raw in him. Overwhelmed and defiant, he glared at Mr Borwankar.

'Sharma, you still haven't answered my question.'

Sharma shrugged his shoulders. 'Borwankar sahib, what is the point of answering? Even if I answer, you will not believe me.' He reflected and said sadly, 'No, there is no point telling you anything. What can you understand?'

Mr Borwankar said dryly, 'I understand that you haven't been at your desk all morning. You were seen loitering in the corridor and drinking tea in the canteen. Presumably that is what you did all morning. And that is what you have been doing virtually every day. In addition, you never come to work on time. Today you were half-an-hour late. This is your fourteenth late arrival this month. Last month you were late twenty days and the previous month, fifteen days. What do you have to say for yourself?'

'What can I say? This is the only work the personnel department has. Every day they sit and count how many late arrivals there are. For that they get paid. Even I can count.'

'Sharma, you are evading all my questions. I have already warned you three times. Each time you gave me to understand that things would change. Nothing has changed. Your work output is zero. Your attitude leaves much to be desired.'

There was a knock at the door and the personnel officer entered. She sat next to Sharma. Mr Borwankar said, 'Under the circumstances I have no alternative but to give you this.' He gave Sharma a typed sheet of paper.

Sharma read it slowly. It was a charge-sheet accusing him

of being absent from his workplace all morning and of coming late to work on specified days. If he did not answer in twenty-four hours it would be presumed that he had accepted the charges.

His hands trembled. So. After twenty-five years – this.

He tossed the paper back to Mr Borwankar and got up. He said, 'You can keep your piece of paper.'

'Sharmaji,' said Miss Das, 'please accept it. Not accepting a charge-sheet is a very serious offence.'

Sharma replied, 'I will do nothing without consulting the general secretary of the workers' union.'

He walked out of the room.

Sharma found Adesh Singh, general secretary of the workers' union, on the production floor, listlessly assembling some components. He walked up to him and said, 'I want to talk to you, come to the canteen.'

Adesh's supervisor looked up from the end of the table. Adesh went up to her. 'Madam,' he said, 'please excuse me for ten minutes. Something serious has come up.'

She replied, 'Adesh, you know I cannot permit time for union activities during office hours. Go in the tea break.'

Adesh continued standing before her. After some time he said, 'Madam, may I go to the canteen to drink some water?'

'You are not thirsty.'

He looked at her in amazement. He said, 'Who are you to say that I am not thirsty? Madam, you surprise me. You permit everyone to go the bathroom or to the canteen for a drink of water. In fact, they do not even ask your permission to go. Why do you make an exception in my case? Is it because I am the general secretary of the union? Does the general secretary have no right to be thirsty? Have things come to such a pass that a worker is denied *water*? Is this the management's new rule?'

'Go, please go.'

'Yes, madam, I will go. I do not need permission from you to quench my thirst. There has been no electricity most of this morning. And yet you deny me water.'

The other workers listened, rapt.

With his hand on his chest, Adesh said, 'Madam, what you have said has hurt me here . . . right here.' He drew a shuddering breath. 'You think we have no feelings, no hearts. You think that only officers have feelings. But madam, believe me, our hearts are more vulnerable than yours. We feel . . . we feel. Sharmaji, chalo.'

With dignity, he walked out of the production floor, Sharma trailing behind him. In the canteen, Adesh wiped his brow. 'Yes, Sharmaji. Now what has happened?'

'What can I tell you? They have given me a charge-sheet.'

'What does it say?'

'That I haven't been in my office all morning and that I don't come to work on time.'

'Is that true?'

'What does that matter? What truth is there in this world?'

Adesh picked his teeth reflectively. 'So, what do you want me to do?'

'You tell me.'

'Accept the charge-sheet. Deny the charges. What else?'

'Then they'll institute an inquiry.'

'Let them. They need witnesses for that. No worker will be a witness.'

'The officers will. Mr Borwankar will. Miss Das will. And those latecomings are on record.'

'Then accept the charges. They'll let you off with a warning letter.'

'How can you say that?'

'I'll see to that.'

'All right. But you come with me to Borwankar sahib.'

They both meditated for some time.

'Some chai?' asked Adesh.

'Yes, of course.'

They ordered tea. Sharma lit a cigarette and smoked sadly.

'Sharmaji,' said Adesh deliberately, 'you had better mend your ways. I can't help you out next time.'

The tea arrived.

'What do you mean, mend my ways?' asked Sharma sulkily.

'You know what I mean. You don't seem to know your limits.'

'Don't lecture me. You are the general secretary of the union. Your duty is to get me out of this, not give me speeches.'

'You keep quiet. If you want me to help you, hold your tongue.'

Sharma simmered. Again, insults from someone so much younger. They finished their tea. 'Chalo,' said Adesh. They went to Mr Borwankar's office and knocked on the door.

'Come in.' They entered. He was talking to the personnel officer. 'Please sit down.' They sat.

'Please show me the charge-sheet,' said Adesh.

'Why are you here, Adesh?' asked Mr Borwankar.

'Why not? You have the personnel officer as your witness. Sharmaji has me as his. Who knows what false accusations the management is making against the poor man.'

Mr Borwankar handed the charge-sheet to Sharma. Adesh took it from Sharma and read it. He looked up, shock registering on his face. 'What is all this, Borwankar sahib? Madam, what does this mean?'

'Isn't that evident?' replied Mr Borwankar.

'No, it isn't. Sharmaji was at his desk all morning. I saw him there.'

'And what, pray, were you doing in the purchase department all morning?'

'Borwankar sahib, you cannot intimidate me. I do not work under you. If anyone can question me, it is my supervisor. She had sent me there on some work. I had to check up on some material. You are not the only person who has work outside your room. We all do. There are other workers who saw Sharmaji at his desk. You will get proof. I can get any number of workers to give it in writing that Sharmaji was at his desk all morning.'

'Indeed. Go ahead. All that can be investigated when there is an inquiry. Sharma, will you please sign the copy and accept the charge-sheet? Enough time has been wasted.'

Sharma and Adesh exchanged glances.

'Sign it,' said Adesh.

Sharma took the letter and signed the copy. He got up. He said, 'Madam, advise the company to change its attitude to workers. Giving charge-sheets left and right is not the answer.' He left.

Adesh looked accusingly at Mr Borwankar. 'Sir,' he said. 'Do you know what you are doing to that man? You have broken him. You have betrayed him.'

'Adesh,' said Mr Borwankar wearily. 'Please spare me the dramatics.'

'Ask him to speak to me,' said Miss Das.

Adesh nodded. 'All right, I'll do that. Tell me, do you intend to hold an inquiry?'

'That depends on whether he accepts the charges, doesn't it?'

'Sir, I request you to let him off with a warning letter this time. I will talk to him. I will din some sense into his thick head. I will see to it that he changes his ways. His wife and children are away these days. He is lonely. He is unwell.'

Miss Das said, 'I thought his daughter was ill and that was why he was late today?'

'That is true. His family left this afternoon. From today he is all alone. He is lost. Madam, why are you asking questions? You as a personnel officer should understand.'

She smiled faintly. 'I do,' she said. 'Ask him to speak to me.'

Adesh said, 'So there will be no inquiry?'

There was a pause. Miss Das said, 'He must accept the charges and apologise in writing.'

Adesh shook his head. 'Yes, yes, you must have your pound of flesh. Yes, I will tell him.' He rose wearily.

Miss Das was in her office when Sharma entered.

'Come in, Sharmaji, please sit down.'

Sharma sighed and sat. He passed his hand over his brow. 'It is so hot,' he said. 'How do you expect us to work with these power cuts, Miss Das?'

'What to do, Sharmaji? That is how life is in Delhi. Would you like a glass of cold water?'

'Certainly.' He gulped down the water. 'What advantages there are to being an officer! You have flasks of cold water in your room. We poor workers have to go to the canteen to drink water. And when we go there and someone sees that we are not at our workplace, we are accused of shirking work.' He returned the glass. 'Thank you, madam.'

'You're welcome.'

There was a short silence and then she said, 'Sharmaji, it seems that you are greatly distressed. What is the matter?'

Sharma gave a short laugh. 'What a question to ask! You give me a charge-sheet and then you ask me why I am distressed. What, madam, does the personnel department not know even this much?'

'I'm sorry, that's not what I meant. I meant that you have been looking run down and depressed for the last few days.'

Sharma looked at her in wonder. 'So,' he said, '*someone* has noticed. Yes, madam, I have been run down and depressed the last few days. I have been run down and depressed the last few months, the last several years. I do not remember what happiness is, madam . . . I cannot remember. And if I do remember, it is so distant a fragment of the past that I feel . . . maybe it never was. The future stretches before me like the night. Ah, madam, what can I tell you? What do you know of life? You are still young, you are not even married. Make the most of this time, madam, it will never return. With marriage, children and careers – much is lost madam, much is lost. You know nothing yet, nothing. When you were sitting there with Borwankar sahib, I thought, poor Miss Das, already she is so involved in office politics. Soon even she will be corrupted. She sees that I, an employee twenty-five years in the company, is given a charge-sheet. I, who have given my best years to the company. She sees. Does she feel anything? Does she care? If she feels, she cannot show it. But maybe she does feel. Maybe her heart goes out to this man. She has to do her duty. She has to be there. But maybe she asks herself, what is happening? Should this be happening? And maybe, something deep within her answers, no it should not. Maybe her heart beats in silent sympathy for this man so completely broken by the company's cruel policies. But she can say nothing. She is after all, in the personnel department. And the personnel department has to be diplomatic. It sees and hears all, it can say nothing. I understand. I do not blame you. But madam, beware. You know nothing of the evils surrounding you. You are too innocent. You do not know what people say, the rumours they spread. Look at me. You must have heard how people talk about me. They make me out to be sometimes a rakshash, sometimes a Harijan. They say I am a bad influence on people. They say I do not work. They say people should not mix with me. I, who was one of the first people to join the company twenty-five years ago. If I did not work, why did the company give me a special award for excellent work twenty years ago? You look surprised. You do not know. Of course, they will not tell you. They know you are intelligent. They know you will ask, what has happened to this man? You wish to know madam, yes?

'Madam, what can I tell you? Where can I begin? What was I then? What am I now! That Mahesh in your department, I was his age when I joined this company. Look at him. He is too big for his boots. He tells me I'm late. He flaunts his power just because he is in the personnel department. Madam, keep an eye on him. He is dangerous. He will alienate everyone from the personnel department if he continues this way. Let me tell you something. He does no work. He sits with his register and pretends he is filling it in. Actually he is doing nothing of the sort. He is planning wicked schemes. He is counting how many times Gupta and I are late. Madam, do you know how often other people are late? No you do not. That is because Mahesh does not give you their names. He gives names of only some people. I happen to be one of those unfortunate few. Madam, keep an eye on him. He is crooked. He will only give you the information that suits him. He will let you down, madam. You are too trusting. That is good. That is also bad. People will take advantage of you. Like they took advantage of me. Once, many years ago, even I was like you; trusting and innocent. I believed everything I was told. I worked hard. Not once was I late. And people said, look at

Sharma, he is our best worker. I got an award. And after that – nothing. Other people rose. Other people got increments. Other people got promotions. Poor Sharma got left behind. Other people buttered their bosses. And I, fool that I was, I believed that only hard work succeeds. Did Srivastava become purchase officer through hard work? Was Tiwari promoted from peon to clerk because he worked hard? No, they all did maska. They accompanied their managers to their homes. They ran personal errands for them. They did jobs for their bosses' wives. Hah! I know how they got their promotions. I refused. I was idealistic. I had principles. And here I am, still a clerk. Now *those* men order me around, tell me, Sharma do this, Sharma do that. And Sharma does it, even though inside, his heart is breaking. Madam, some more water, if I may.'

She gave him another glass of water. She said, 'Sharmaji, I did not know all this.'

He drank the water and wiped his mouth. 'Madam, you know nothing. Even now, you know nothing. You don't know what goes on in this place.'

'What?'

He looked behind him at the door. He got up and opened it. No one. He sat at his chair and leaned forward. In hushed tones, he said, 'Dhanda of girls.'

'I don't understand.'

'Madam, forgive me, you are too innocent. I will keep quiet. I should not have mentioned it.' He looked behind him again. He paused. He whispered. 'When girls are recruited in this company, they have to perform certain favours for certain men for having got in.'

'Oh.'

'I have shocked you, madam. Forgive me. But it is true.' He leaned closer to the desk. He said, 'These men are still working here. These girls are still working here. So much dirt, madam. What can you understand of these things?'

'Who are these men?'

He leaned back. 'I cannot reveal their names, madam.'

'Why not? You can help me remove this dirt.'

'Oh no, madam, no, no.'

'Why not, Sharmaji?'

'No, madam, no. Do not ask me why.'

'But if you don't tell me, Sharmaji, it will continue.'

Sharma smiled gently. 'But you see, it is not happening now. It is a thing of the past. Since you joined the company such things have stopped. People are scared. They say that a woman has come to the personnel department and that this woman is honest. She will protect our girls. Now there is nothing to worry about. Rest assured, madam. All is well, now that you are here.'

'All is not well, Sharmaji. How can all be well when you continue coming late to work every other day and are never at your workplace?'

'Madam, madam, madam.' Sharma wagged an admonishing finger at her. 'You are very persistent. That is your job. You are personnel officer. That is your duty. Good. That is good.'

'So, Sharmaji, what happened today?'

'What can I say, madam? Sometimes I curse fate for bringing me into this world, for flinging me amid such people. Often I ask myself – what sins did I commit in my last birth to suffer so in this one? There is no answer. God has his own ways, madam, who knows why, who knows how?

'I see you are smiling, madam? I know what you are thinking. You are thinking – this Sharma talks too much. Why is Sharma saying all this? Sharma has not answered my question. But I have, madam, I have. Reflect carefully over all that I have told you. You will find the answers. There are no simple answers to simple questions. I read a poem once, an English poem that was translated into Hindi. Somewhere it said:

> There are no small questions for small men
> All men are Hamlet on an empty street
> Or a windy quay
> All men are Lear in the market
> When the tradesmen have gone.

'Madam, if he had not written the poem, I would have written it. Even here someone has done it before me. Can you understand what he is saying, madam? You nod your head. Then you understand me. Your questions are answered, madam. Madam, some more water, please.'

She poured out another glass of water. He drank it thirstily. 'Sharmaji, may I make a request?'

'Madam, any request.'

'From tomorrow you will make an effort to come to work on time?'

'Of course, madam, of course.'

'And I don't want to see you in the canteen or corridors during office hours.'

'Whatever you say, madam, whatever you say.'

'Thank you.'

Sharma gazed at her fondly. 'Do not thank me, madam. Why are you thanking me?' He paused. He said, 'Madam, you have made a request. I agreed. Now may I make one?'

'Certainly.'

'Put in a word for me to Borwankar sahib, madam. In his mind it is set that Sharma is bad. Once such an impression is made, it does not change. In this company especially. Tell Borwankar sahib, Sharma once got a special award. Tell him, his promotion is long overdue. Tell him, is it fair that Sharma remains a clerk for twenty-five years? You have influence, madam. You are personnel officer. If you tell Borwankar sahib, Borwankar sahib will listen.'

'Sharmaji, now everything depends on you. I can do nothing.'

Sharma sighed. 'Yes, that is what they all say. Well, you have been kind, madam. You have patiently listened to me. Madam, do you like cosmetics . . . lipsticks?'

'Like what, Sharmaji?'

'I can get these things very cheap, madam, even free. After all I am in the purchase department. I can get you imported scents and lipsticks, electronic items, cassettes.'

'How?'

'Oh, come, come, madam. What can I get you?'

'Nothing, thank you, Sharmaji.'

Sharma nodded his head seriously. 'You are absolutely right in refusing. Even I refuse. They keep telling me, Sharmaji, please take this, Sharmaji, please take that. They say, you place such large orders for your company; let us give you some gifts to show you our appreciation. But I say, no. No. I am not like the rest. I will not give to anyone, I will not take from anyone. For that they respect me. After all, if there is no self-respect, then what is there?

'Well, madam, I must leave. Here is my answer to the charge-sheet.' He handed the paper to Miss Das.

She read it. She said, 'So, you have denied being absent from the workplace, saying that your manager is victimising you. You have accepted coming late to work, saying that your children have been ill. And you have apologised if this has caused any misunderstanding, Sharmaji!'

'Madam, madam, let us not argue any more. You asked me to apologise. I have apologised. Now let bygones be bygones. Let a new chapter begin.'

Miss Das put the paper away. 'Some more water, Sharmaji?'

'No, madam, thank you.' He rose from his chair. 'I must be leaving.'

'Don't hesitate to come to me if you have any problems.'

'Madam, I do not have any problems. Borwankar sahib has problems. Mahesh has problems. Even your peon Mohan has problems. Yes, if they continue to have problems, I will come to you.'

He got up and was about to leave the room when a thought seemed to strike him. He appeared to hesitate, and then spoke. 'Madam, before I leave, I must ask you a question of a rather personal nature. As a brother, I would like to ask you. Please do not mind.'

'Yes?'

'Madam, you have a good job, you are young. Like an elder brother, let me give you some advice. You must not postpone marriage, no woman should be alone in this world. I am speaking out of concern for you. Maybe, you are already engaged?'

'I am married.'

Sharma reeled. 'Madam!'

She began to laugh.

'But madam, you are *Miss* Das.'

'Yes, I've retained my maiden name.'

'Why?'

'Why not?'

Sharma considered. 'A woman goes into another family. She must take the name of the family.'

'I have not gone into any family. My husband and I are both working.'

Sharma stared at her. 'You are very modern.'

'And that is bad?'

He reflected. 'Maybe not. I cannot say. When did this take place, madam?'

'Two months ago.'

'Madam, forgive me for saying this, but this is very bad, very very bad. You did not tell any of us. You did not distribute any sweets. I am greatly offended. This is a cause for celebration, not secrecy.'

'It was no secret, Sharmaji.'

'Oh well.' He surveyed her. 'You don't even look married. No sindoor, no mangalsutra, no jewellery. What is this, madam?'

'No need for all that, Sharmaji.'

Sharma shook his head in despair. 'What can I say? I suppose things are changing. I would like to meet your husband, madam. Is he also good and kind like you?'

She looked confused. 'You will certainly meet him one day.'

'Good. Very good. Well, madam, I will go. From my side, please say namaste to your husband.'

'Certainly.'

With great dignity he sailed out of the room. A minute later he returned. 'Madam,' he said with a slight shrug, 'I was wondering, you wouldn't be interested in reading some of my poetry would you?'

'I would very much like to.'

Sharma smiled. He nodded. 'I will get them tomorrow.

Madam, I wrote these poems many, many years ago. Since then I have written nothing, nothing at all. Still . . . they are very philosophical, very deep, very complex. Tomorrow, at 9 a.m. I will share them with you.'

She replied, 'In the lunch break.'

He frowned. 'There will be another power cut in the afternoon. How can I read my poetry to you, drenched in sweat?' He considered.

She smiled.

He capitulated. 'If you insist, then, the lunch break.'

Outside the office, Sharma looked at his watch. It was already 5 p.m., just half an hour left for office to get over. Slowly he walked down the corridor, softly humming an old love song to himself. Suddenly he was flooded with memories. Once . . . years ago, he had loved, loved madly, crazily. Her large kajal-filled eyes had haunted him, bewitched him. Those eyes . . . those eyes. He would have gladly died for her. Shy, smitten, he had said nothing. She had never known. Sharma stopped and swallowed. He felt his heart would burst. Twenty-five years.

'Sharmaji, coming to the canteen?' It was Gupta, bounding down the stairs, two at a time.

Sharma smiled indulgently. 'Not scared of your boss now?'

'He has gone out of the office on some work. Chalo, let us have some chai, Sharmaji.'

Gently, Sharma shook his head. 'I have some work.' He patted Gupta. 'You go.'

Gupta stared at him, open-mouthed.

'Gupta,' said Sharma, 'Miss Das does not have a boyfriend. She is married. People in this office are always spreading dirty rumours. Do not listen to them.'

He gave Gupta a final pat and walked to his department, still humming. When he entered the room his fellow clerks grinned.

'You are an elusive man, Sharmaji,' said Rahul. 'Everyone has been looking for you today. Where were you?'

Sharma shrugged his shoulders modestly. 'There were

377

things to do, many things to do. And there is still so much to be done. Rahul, life is very brief, very fleeting.'

Rahul chuckled. 'All right, Sharmaji, I will leave you to your considerations.' He went back to his typing.

Sharma sat on his desk. He took the paan out of his pocket and carefully removed its wrapping. He put it in his mouth. Chewing, he opened his drawer and took out a sheet of paper. Lovingly, he placed it on his desk, licked his pencil and began a new poem.

Amit Chaudhuri

SANDEEP'S VISIT

HE SAW THE lane. Small houses, unlovely and unremark-
able, stood face to face with each other. Chhotomama's house
had a pomelo tree in its tiny courtyard and madhavi creepers
by its windows. A boy stood clinging to the rusting iron gate,
while another boy pushed it backwards and forwards. As he
did so, the first boy travelled in a small arc through space.
When the taxi stopped in front of the house, they stared at it
with great dignity for a few moments, then ran off in terror,
leaving the gate swinging mildly and illegally. A window
opened above (it was so silent for a second that Sandeep could
hear someone unlocking it) and Babla's face appeared behind
the mullions.

Chhotomama and Saraswati, the maidservant, came down
and helped them with their bags. Sandeep ran up the stairs with
his cousins, not looking back. There was a thrilled impatience
about his movements, as if he either wanted to finish or begin
something quickly. His aunt, by contrast, stood at the head of
the stairs, in a place that was half-sunlit and half-shadowy,
with immaculate serenity, seemingly not having moved from
where she had said goodbye to him about a year ago; she said:

'How have you been, Mona?'

When she saw Sandeep's mother, she went down the stairs
and grasped her hand in a relaxed way; all the excitement
shone in her eyes.

'Didi . . .' she said.

Extracts from the novella *A Strange and Sublime Address*.

They went up in a procession, Abhi, Babla, Sandeep, his mother, his uncle, his aunt, as if they were going up to a shrine on pilgrimage. Later, they sat on a wide bed beneath an ancient fan which, as it rotated, moved unreliably from side to side, like a great bird trying to fly. The holiday-mood transported them with its poetry; they could have been anywhere – on a hillside on the Western Ghats or in a cave in Kanheri. Sandeep's mother now opened a suitcase and distributed gifts she had bought from Bombay.

Gleaming objects, clothes, perfumes, emerged from the suitcase.

'And here are saris for you,' she said to Sandeep's aunt. 'Though Calcutta saris are the loveliest.'

'Oh but these are beautiful,' replied Mamima, unravelling a sari, which broke out into a galaxy of hand-woven stars, a cosmos of streaking comets and symbolic blue horizons.

'She's right,' said Chhotomama. 'Calcutta saris *are* the loveliest. Though this is nice,' he said grudgingly, touching the cloth.

Near them, Sandeep and Abhi silently wrestled with each other, looking vaguely like the two angry, rumpled pillows at the head of the bed. The grown-ups, who made a little shifting arena around their bodies, paid them scarcely more attention than they paid the pillows. Both arms pinned down, Abhi stared into Sandeep's eyes in mock exhaustion and with a distant affection.

'Give up?' cried Sandeep.

'No,' whispered Abhi. 'No I don't give up.'

Irreconcilable as two conflicting principles, they fell to struggling again. It was, actually, an excuse for embracing, touching, exploring each other's presence; not having met for a year, they, great friends, wanted to do these things, and fighting seemed the only acceptable way towards intimacy. Babla, meanwhile, sat listening to the adults talking; his eyes darted from one face to the other, then back again, as if he were following a game of tennis, as if he could see questions and answers, like white balls being tossed from one end of the court to another.

The morning passed in a wave of words. Sandeep's mother talked about Bombay, about Sandeep's father's responsibilities in 'the company', about how he worked too hard, and how he never had time to go anywhere. Chhotomama, whose problems were more ordinary and also more difficult to solve, loved listening to the remote complaints of his sister's life, objecting to or agreeing with, now and then, a phrase. Sandeep, an only child, felt the shared background of brother and brother, and brother and sister, throw upon him a shade as that of the cool, expansive branches of a rooted banyan tree. He wandered in the shade, forgetting it was temporary. Mamima brought his mother and Chhotomama cups of tea, which they stirred thoughtfully in the middle of a discussion; Saraswati went to the market and returned with a large, dark boal fish for lunch. The grown-ups never fell short of subjects for discussion; in the kitchen, as Saraswati worked, the pots and pans also held a different, but no less urgent, dialogue. Sandeep, doing something or the other with his cousins, gradually adjusted his senses to Chhotomama's house, to the pale walls, the spider-webs in the corners, the tranquil bedsheets on the old beds, the portraits of grandfathers and grandmothers, the fans that swung drunkenly from side to side – all so different from the quiet and perfected apartment he lived in in Bombay.

After they had exhausted all their games, they had a bath. They stood naked in front of the bathroom; their clothes lay in a heap at their feet; their testicles hung silently and insignificantly like small, unplucked fruit. Babla's penis was hardly visible, a sleeping beetle everyone had forgotten to notice. He wasn't aware that anything unusual had happened; having spent only six years on this planet, clothes were still a relatively puzzling and uncomfortable phenomenon to him.

Mamima now kneaded Abhi's and Babla's bodies with mustard-oil. She twisted them, took them apart, put them together; they surrendered to her as plasticine surrenders its infinite forms to a child's fingers. When she rubbed an arm or leg, it appeared to detach itself from the body, with a wonderful absence of pain, and come into her skilful hands, a live, grotesque appendage. She would oil it till it shone, and then fix it, with a grim, satisfied smile, where it belonged.

A sharp aura of mustard-oil flowered, giving Sandeep's nostrils a faraway sentient pleasure – it wasn't a sweet smell, but there was a harsh unexpectedness about it he liked. It reminded him of sunlight. In Bengal, both tamarind and babies are soaked in mustard-oil, and then left upon a mat on the terrace to absorb the morning sun. The tamarind is left out till it dries up and shrivels into an inimitable flavour and a ripe old age; but the babies are brought in before it gets too hot, and then bathed in cool water. With their frantic miniature limbs and their brown, shining bodies, they look like little koi fish caught from the Hooghly river, struggling into life.

The bathroom was a small square room, with a basin on one side, and a window on the right. The windowsill was cluttered with shampoos and soaps and unguents. On the other side of the closed window, pigeons sat through their afternoons with a serene lack of urgency, and sometimes shifted to look in uncuriously at a nude bather. One could hear mynahs and shaliks singing outside, though one could hear their fragmentary chorus more clearly from the toilet, which was next to the bath. An obsessive, busy music repeated itself behind the frosted glass. Sometimes, one heard the shrill cries of their young, and felt surrounded and safe.

There was a tap in the middle; at the top, a round eye sprinkled with orifices protruded from a pipe that was bent downwards like the neck of a tired giraffe; this was the shower. There was no hot water and no bathtub, but no one seemed to miss what was not there. Sometimes, in the afternoon, Saraswati would wash saris and sheets, tedious yards of cloth, beneath the running tap, sitting fixedly on her haunches, rubbing the clothes, banging them repeatedly with a loud watery 'pluff' on the floor. As she banged them, the bathroom echoed with a strange rhythm. Later, she would wring the saris into long, exhausted pythons of cloth. She would notice the boys observing her with dark, inquisitive eyes from behind the door, and she would say:

'What are you looking at, you hooligans?'

When they had had their bath, they trooped out like naked ruffians on an island, spattering the floor with their wet foot-prints. Later they went down to have lunch in the dining-room; they dangled their feet ferociously from chairs round a large, shabby table with pots thronging in the centre.

Pieces of boal fish, cooked in turmeric, red chilli paste, onions and garlic, lay in a red, fiery sauce in a flat pan; rice, packed into an even white cake, had a spade-like spoon embedded in it; slices of fried aubergine were arranged on a white dish; dal was served from another pan with a drooping ladle; long, complex filaments of banana-flower, exotic, botanical, lay in yet another pan in a dark sauce; each plate had a heap of salt on one side, a green-chilli, and a slice of sweet-smelling lemon. The grown-ups snapped the chillies (each made a sound terse as a satirical retort), and scattered the tiny, deadly seeds in their food. If any of the boys were ever brave or foolish enough to bite a chilli, their eyes filled tragically with tears, and they longed to drown in a cool, clear lake. Though Chhotomama was far from affluent, they ate well, especially on Sundays, caressing the rice and the sauces on their plates with attentive, sensuous fingers, fingers which performed a practised and graceful ballet on the plate till it was quite empty.

Later, after washing their hands, they went up to the second and topmost storey of the house. Sandeep's mother and Mamima reclined on the large bed. Their conversation was a transparent stream that occasionally trickled into desert patches of silence. Chhotomama turned on the radio, which began to babble immediately like the local idiot:

'Both grandson and grandfather love eating Thin Arrowroot Biscuits.'

'Nothing's as kind to your skin as Boroline Antiseptic Cream.'

He lay back on the small bed, secure as a soldier in his trench, with the newspaper in his hands; he folded it several ways and made it crackle festively. His face and his arms drowned in the black and white ocean of the newspaper, surfacing intermittently. Sighing regretfully, Chhotomama fell asleep, the newspaper covering his face. When the breath came up from h. .ostrils, the newspaper rose and fell lightly, as if it were breathing as well. On the big bed, Mamima and Sandeep's mother began to dream, sprawled in vivid crab-like postures. His aunt lay on her stomach, her arms bent as if she were swimming to the edge of a lake; his mother lay on her back, her feet (one of which had a scar on it) arranged in the joyous pose of a dancer.

A mournful song now came on the radio. It was an old radio, a wedding-gift, shaped like a box, with outdated knobs and dials. When Sandeep was younger, he had thought there were little men, talented homunculi, inside the box of the radio, who performed those songs. But that seemed long ago. Beside the radio, there was a clock with a white face which always ran ten minutes fast. Every night, the time was re-adjusted, and every morning, with great accuracy, it had gained ten minutes. At about half-past four, when the clock said twenty to five, the grown-ups woke and stretched their arms like reluctant children. The Sunday lunch, then the Sunday nap – and the thought of Monday, that difficult day, was aborted. The radio crackled with the nervous, breathless sound of football commentary; dust had settled on the floor and furniture of the house.

Calcutta is a city of dust. If one walks down the street, one sees mounds of dust like sand-dunes on the pavements, on which children and dogs sit doing nothing, while sweating labourers dig into the macadam with spades and drills. The roads are always being dug up, partly to construct the new underground railway system, or perhaps for some other obscure reason, such as replacing a pipe that doesn't work with another pipe that doesn't work. At such times, Calcutta is like a work of modern art that neither makes sense nor has utility, but exists for some esoteric aesthetic reason. Trenches and mounds of dust everywhere give the city a strange bombed-out look. The old houses, with their reposeful walls, are crumbling to slow dust, their once-gleaming gates are rusting. Dust flakes off the ceilings in offices; the buildings are becoming dust, the roads are becoming dust. At the same time, dust is constantly raised into startling new shapes and unexpected forms by the arbitrary workings of the wind, forms on which dogs and children sit doing nothing. Daily, Calcutta disintegrates, unwhispering, into dust, and daily it rises from dust again.

A house in Calcutta must be swept and scrubbed at least twice a day. Once, in the morning, Saraswati polished the floor with a moist rag, and Mamima religiously dusted the tables and chairs. The dust rose in the air in breathless clouds and seemed to evaporate and disappear. But by evening, it would condense, like moisture, and resettle on the surfaces of things. A little before sunset, a woman called Chhaya came to clean the house a second time, smiling at the boys as they waited impatiently for her to finish. She had a serious cultured face with a serious smile, the face of a kindly and under-standing teacher; it was hard to believe she lived across the railway-lines, in the clump of huts called the basti, from which whiffs of excrement rose on windy days.

She would sweep the floor – unending expanses, acres and acres of floor – with a short broom called the jhadu, swiping away the dust in an arc with its long tail, which reminded one of the drooping tail of some nameless, exotic bird. She would collect the dust in a corner, and here there would be an accu-mulation of unlikely treasure that had blown in from outside or had gathered, unnoticed, inside: a single elegant pigeon's feather, a page lost from a book, a dead spider which ants had forgotten to carry off, the long, black, tender loops of Mamima's and Sandeep's mother's hair.

Then she would dip a grey rag into a pail, and sit on her haunches at one end of the room, and swish the rag around the floor. Carefully, deliberately, she would begin to advance to the other end of the room, swiping the floor with the moist rag, her right arm moving regularly and automatically, like a fin, till she had reached the other end. Her odd movement forward on her haunches had an amphibian quality, half-human and half of another world. It was laborious, and yet had the simplicity and poise of a tortoise's amble; when she finished, hardly a speck remained, the floor was bright as a mirror or a lake on a calm day. Then, at last, she would unbend her body and straighten her back. Most of the time she worked, her body was slightly bent, as if in obeisance to an invisible god.

There were two rooms on the second and topmost storey. The first was the large one facing the road; here, Sandeep and his cousins slept and woke, and here they wrote and rewrote themselves into their imaginary expeditions and adventures. There were two beds, one big and one small, on which they voyaged daily into nowhere. The cupboards rose like ugly reefs from a fictional ocean, casting long, rectangular shadows in the evening. At one end of the room, there was a mirror and a dressing-table; the mirror imaged the room and gave it a sense of extra space. Next to it, there was a wooden clothes-horse, with several horizontal bars running parallel to, and on top of, each other. One would have expected to find it in a gymnasium, but here it was – it was called an alna, and all kinds of clothes and garments hung from its ribs. A lizard lived behind it.

The other room, facing the backyard, a few palm trees, a field and a professor's house, was much smaller, with one double bed in it. Near the window, there was an ungainly study-table, with Abhi's text-books on it, and metal boxes that contained pencils, rulers and erasers. But no one who studied at this table would ever read more than a page because, just by the open window, almost at arm's length, was a palm tree wearing its rings of coconuts like jewellery, balancing a crow on its broad, fan-tail leaf, and behind the palm tree was the professor's house, with two daughters always getting in each other's way, a rooster, an educated-looking dog and a cat without a conscience, and the professor's son, who performed such enviably intricate exercises in the morning. You just had to watch that window.

Within this room there was another room, hidden away in the corner. Three steps rose to it; it was a world within a world; a world, in fact, more richly inhabited than the sparse outer husk in which it was enclosed. If you sat at the study-table, it was just on your left. It was the prayer-room. Different gods and goddesses reclined or stood in various postures within. Krishna was there with his flute, his peacock-plume, and his mildly flirtatious smile; Saraswati sat thoughtfully upon her swan, playing her veena endlessly and attentively; Lakshmi was accompanied by her mascot, the white owl; Ganesh, with his humorous elephant-head, had been afforded a place as well, with his unlikely mascot, the giant rodent. Durga, the mother-goddess, had been given a slightly more prominent place than the rest. Elegant and self-contained, she rode a fierce lion. Of all the gods, Sandeep liked Ganesh the best, because he seemed so content with his own appearance.

After her bath, Sandeep's aunt would wrap a sari around herself, not wearing the blouse as yet, so that her bare shoulders showed above the borders of her sari, gleaming, a little moist. She would not approach the gods until she had bathed; then she must rub Jabakusum oil vigorously into her hair, till the black hair reflected the sunlight, and turned almost silvery. It was a sweet-smelling oil, dark-red and rich, like wine.

She entered the prayer-room and lit two incense sticks, then stuck them, like slim pencils, into a perforated brass stand. She arranged slices of cucumber and oranges and sweet white batashas on three brass plates and placed them in front of the gods. The gods too are hungry, she said, they too need nourishment. Sandeep smiled politely but contemptuously when he heard this. But when do they eat? he inquired patiently. She muttered something incoherently – not an answer, but a mantra she had begun to repeat to herself as soon as she sat upon the shatranji on the floor.

Sometimes it was a mantra; sometimes it was a long incantation about the exploits of a god or a goddess – how, for instance, a demon had been outwitted, or a demon's sister been embarrassed. Or it was a description of a divine wedding; how a god had won an earthmaiden, or how a goddess had been won by a mortal king after a prolonged and wasteful courtship. They were an irresponsible lot, jealous of each other, doing silly, petty things at times and silly, spectacular things at others – not unlike Sandeep and his cousins.

Sandeep himself did not believe in God, much less in gods. Like most children, he was the opposite of innocent: he was sceptical but tolerant of other creeds. What he enjoyed about the act of worship had little to do with belief or disbelief in divinity; it was the smell of sandalwood incense, the low hum of his aunt's voice, the bell ringing at the end of the ceremony, the white batashas, clean as washed pebbles, taken out of a bottle hidden in a small cupboard, the cool taste of the offerings that were distributed after the prayer, in fact, the general, dignified uselessness of the whole enterprise. And he liked the sight of his aunt surrounded by her gods in that tiny room, like a child in a great doll-house, blowing the conch eloquently; it was a strange sight, to watch a grown-up at play. Prayer-time was when adults became children again.

At lunchtime, at the dining-table, Sandeep asked his aunt:

'Mamima, what did you pray for today?'

Separating some tiny and particularly persistent bones from the fish, she replied:

'Oh I prayed the car would start in the mornings.'

'Didn't you pray for a new car?' asked Abhi, a high-pitched inflection of disappointment in his voice.

They went on eating, inspecting the fish, searching for the fishbones, the tiny, tiny fishbones. Babla sat with his mouth open, into which his mother put little balls of fish and rice. What you prayed for mattered least in the prayer-room; all that mattered was the vivid entertainment of the instant. The gods, in their supreme, all-seeing inadvertence, forgot to answer the prayers, and the devotees didn't care. All that was important to the gods and the mortals was the creation of that rich and endlessly diverting moment in the small chamber, that moment of secret, almost illicit, communion, when both the one who prayed and the one who was prayed to were released from the irksome responsibility of the world. Oranges, white batashas, cucumbers.

On Saturday, a cool breeze surprised them. It smelled of wet earth, sodden leaves. It had rained somewhere in the villages, in groves and fields, and the breeze had travelled to this lane, bringing news of rain from the far-off place of its beginnings. They had congregated after lunch on the double bed on the second storey, when it ran its fingers down their backs, making them break out in goose-flesh. There was something erotic about the first breeze that brought the monsoons.

'Did you feel that?' asked Mamima.

'Yes,' said Sandeep's mother.

'And that smell . . .' said Chhotomama, breathing in deeply.

He had never known any smell like that of wet earth, her own sweet odour, earth-musk. The most natural and unpretentious fragrance.

A few days later, there was the first kal-baisakhi storm. A layer of grey clouds covered the sky, inverting it like a bowl, shutting out sunlight. Dead leaves and old newspapers streamed through the lane like a procession of protest-marchers. Someone cried out from a balcony. A woman's voice. 'Ratna! Ratna, come in this instant!' The wind blew silent and straight. A woman walking alone on the road was teased by the wind; the loose end of her sari, the aanchal, flew helplessly, a lost fragment of colour; it was the most beautiful movement seen on this rainy day. Crows hopped alertly. They sensed a presence, powerful and dangerous, though they could see nothing and no one. The nervous, toy-like city was set against the dignified advance of the clouds, as if two worlds were colliding. There was an end-of-the-world atmosphere. Then, lightning, sometimes a single, bright scar that flashed on a cloud's black face and was gone, and sometimes filling the grey space with light. A moment's heavy silence; then the thunder spoke –

guruguruguru

In obedience, the leaves began to tremble, and the branches moved uniformly, disciplined as a battalion doing exercises – Bend! Rise! Bend! Rise! And, slam! a door or a window banged shut without warning; ghosts and spirits were abroad, making mischief, distracting the servants, knocking at the windows. Only the children had time to investigate or smile at the spirits, because the grown-ups were busy, panicky. Saraswati bundled the clothes left to dry on the terrace, and brought them in before they got wet – with the wrinkled clothes in her arms, she looked like Mother Teresa carrying the light, wispy bodies of dying children. Mamima rushed to shut the windows, which were banging their wooden heads in a religious frenzy. She just managed to lock the last one in time. As if by common consent, it began to rain with a steady sibilant sound. They sat in the room with the windows closed, listening to the sound of the rain beating against the windows and falling on the tin roof of the next house. The children talked to each other, but sometimes they stopped and became attentive, listening, for no apparent reason, to that sound. The room became cool; the beds and floors became cool. When they opened the taps, the water sparkled. They rinsed their mouths with the water. Sometimes, Sandeep and Abhi opened a shutter and stared out into a world where arrows of rain fell continually. They stretched out their hands. They allowed the round, orb-like raindrops to settle on the back of their hands like dewy insects, though the drops lost shape as soon as they touched the flesh. Running to the smaller room at the back, Sandeep glanced out of the window and saw the palm tree dancing by itself, to itself. A silent wave of delight passed over him as he watched it dance.

So another season had come. In another corner of the world

lay the great continent called Australia, an immense unwieldy mass of land floating on the ocean like a giant makeshift raft on water. Who had been set afloat on that raft? Kangaroos, aborigines and cricketers. And India was touring Australia, and there was a test-match being played between the two teams at Sydney. So Chhotomama would wake up at five o'clock in the morning and try to catch Sydney on the radio. He would spin the rapid knobs, and after an incoherent period of time, when the radio cackled in an evil witch-like way, the voice of the Australian commentator would come through, loud and urgent one moment, weak and distant the other, as if a few words were being carried off, on their passage towards India, by a cormorant crossing the ocean.

The room would echo with a strange Australian accent, and an odd and vivid pronunciation of vowels. Everyone would be sleeping, of course, muffled heads and breathing bundles of bodies, because the rains had made the nights cool and relaxed. Abhi, Babla and Sandeep slept like primeval creatures huddled on the island of the bed, close to the horizon, out-waiting the dawn that would bring the first thought to their heads. Their bodies slept with a pure detached love for every moment of sleep.

Into the midst of this delicate surface world of slumber, which could be burst like a bubble so easily, and yet miraculously escaped being burst for around eight hours, Chhotomama trod heavily at five o'clock in the morning.

Twiddling the radio knobs, fiddling with this, dislodging that, coughing, laughing, yawning, he disgusted everyone with his obstreperousness, his clumsiness. The amazing thing was, *he* did not think he was making any noise; he thought that as long as he did not actually utter a word, he disturbed no one. Whatever mischief his hands and legs did, as far as he was concerned, was not his responsibility. Anyway, Sandeep and Abhi had decided that one had to simply and unquestioningly tolerate the grown-ups. One had constantly to see the comic aspects of their characters to remain sane.

The test-match came to an end. India did the one honourable

thing: it lost. How could Gandhi's country bear to win? With the test-match, the sense of expectation died out temporarily. For a few days, the rains fell heavily – continuous white screens blotted out landscapes and landmarks: the main road with its tramlines, its lampposts, its old medicine shop, and then the park; these melted before Sandeep's eyes, while he watched, a little amazed that he too did not melt away.

The gutters in the lane overflowed with an odd, languid grace. Water filled the lane; rose from ankle-deep to knee-deep. Insects swam in circles. Urchins splashed about haphazardly, while Saraswati returned from market with a shopping-bag in her hands; insects swam away to avoid this clumsy giant. Her wet footprints printing the floor of the house were as rich with possibility as the first footprint Crusoe found on his island.

Chhotomama had not gone to work; his car had failed him. The car usually became temperamental during monsoons. It was also temperamental in the winter and the spring and the summer, but Chhotomama said it was especially temperamental in the monsoons. He did not blame the car, he blamed its maker, whoever he was.

He did some work at home, rummaging through files. Then he scanned the newspaper, *The Statesman*, reading the editorial four times, shaking his head and laughing abrasively. 'The man is a fool,' he said quietly. 'I must write to the paper . . .' He took a foolscap sheet and began to write. He scribbled 'Dear Sir', and paused and then crossed out 'Dear'. The letter began 'Sir . . .' He was very angry with the editor.

After the letter was written, he relaxed on the bed, lying on his stomach. Whenever he relaxed, he remembered he had a terrible backache.

'Abhi!' he called. 'Come and press my back.'

Abhi came and put his fingers, gentle as a faithhealer's, on his father's vertebrae.

'Oooh . . . oooh . . .' said Chhotomama, a noise like a wind blowing through an aperture. It conveyed, at once, pain and pleasure.

'A little above,' he said, navigating Abhi's fingers.

The fingers moved a little above.

'A little – a fraction – to the left.'

The fingers shifted a fraction to the left.

'Another fraction left.'

Another fraction.

Searching for that exact spot of pain was a delicate matter, a life or several lives might depend on it; it was like trying to detect a mine in a minefield, or a vein of oil in a desert.

'Yes, yes!' said Chhotomama. '*There*. Press it *there*.'

'Baba . . .' said Abhi, his fingers poised, a master-pianist about to embark on the opening phrase of his sonata, while the audience waits, breathless.

'*Press!*' said Chhotomama, drowning, his voice a choked bubble. 'Oh *what* is it, Abhi?'

'Baba, the cricket bat we had talked about . . .'

'It's yours,' cried Chhotomama, giving in to blackmail and letting the world know about it. 'It's yours! Now press *there*.'

Smiling, Abhi began to play his sonata. The notes rose, lovely and exultant. Chhotomama closed his eyes and sighed, intoxicated by music no one else could hear.

Fifteen minutes later, Chhotomama asked Babla to stand on his back. He was small and would be able to balance himself; he was light enough to stamp out the pain without hurting him.

'I'll fall, Baba,' said Babla, who was not a brave boy.

'Of course you won't,' said Chhotomama. 'Come, only for a few minutes.'

Babla climbed on the bed. He put one leg on his father's back. It was like the picture of Edmund Hillary on Mount Everest. All that was needed was a flag. Then he put both his feet on his father's back.

'Walk,' said Chhotomama. 'Stay in the same place, but walk.'

It was a contradictory demand. Babla tried it. He smiled; he seemed to like the idea of staying in one place and walking at the same time. He did not know legs could do such things. It looked like the reverse of the Shiv Tandav. (The Shiv Tandav:

in the last phase of the universe, when the world is old and corrupt, Shiv wakes from his trance, and sets about destroying everything. With giant strides, he stamps out life. This is the Tandav, the terrifying, cosmological dance of destruction. The sculptors traditionally represent this with Shiv dancing, arms gracefully apart, one leg raised, the other foot on a helpless child lying on his stomach: the latter probably symbolises the innocent life which is crushed as a part of the dance. And the Shiv Tandav was reversed when Babla, the child, danced on Chhotomama's back, while the latter lay on his stomach and made noises.)

Mamima was about to enter a competition held by a famous coffee-making company. She was filling out the entry form with an intent face. 'Mona,' she said to Sandeep, 'give me a good English slogan about coffee.' Sandeep, the boy from Bombay, who wrote poems and stories, was supposed to have a good vocabulary in this idiotic foreign language which no one, especially coffee companies, could apparently do without. Already, he used words like 'tentative' and 'gingerly' and 'enthusiastic'. Would he help his aunt, whose command over English was imperfect, and who cared little about this, with a dignified nonchalance some Indian women have, would he help her win two air-tickets to Kashmir? 'I'll think about it, Mamima,' he said indifferently. Yet he was moved, watching her on the bed, hunched and cutting out the entry-coupon meticulously with her scissors.

Till it was lunchtime, the boys played their energetic 'pretend' games. It was good that it was raining, because they discovered they had stopped sweating. Chhotomama, out of bed, found them in the corridor.

'What are you playing?' he asked, smiling indulgently.

'We're playing freedom-fighters,' said Abhi. 'We're killing the British. We're cutting the British to pieces.'

'And who are you?' asked Chhotomama tenderly, bending low to Babla. 'Are you cutting the British to pieces as well?'

'I'm Subhas Chandra Bose,' said Babla, standing at attention and looking undauntedly into his father's eyes.

'No, I'm Subhas Chandra Bose,' said Abhi. 'Babla, shut up.'

'Abhi, shut up,' replied Babla, still at attention.

'What did you say?' asked Abhi in a mafioso voice. 'Repeat that.'

'And you?' Chhotomama asked, turning finally to Sandeep. 'Who are you?'

'I'm Mahatma Gandhi,' he said, and realised he had made a mistake.

Chhotomama was taken aback momentarily. A contemptuous smile asserted itself on his face.

'Gandhi! Gandhi was no freedom-fighter! He was a sham yogi who knew no economics!'

Sandeep did not know what 'economics' meant; he knew that the girls in his school had a class called Home Economics. 'He's the Father of the Nation,' he replied naively, repeating what he had learnt at school; he saw that, once more, he had committed an error.

Eyes burning, Chhotomama began to lecture them on pre-independence Indian history, quoting several historians of several nationalities. As he spoke to the children, he behaved like a scholar at a seminar addressing a group of inimical scholars who had views hostile to his own. By a magical suspension of disbelief, he forgot he was talking to Sandeep and Abhi and Babla; he saw, in front of him, three conservative, pro-Congress intellectuals.

He began to revile Gandhi, the Father of the Nation, the bald anorexic with the grandmother's smile.

'That man!' he said. 'That man in his obscene loincloth, his ribs sticking out!'

He began to deify Subhas Bose, the brilliant, side-tracked Bengali. He radiated with irritable energy, argumentativeness, obstinacy, a remarkable unwillingness to give in. He spoke with true pride of Subhas Bose, pride shone in his eyes, the pride a son feels when he remembers a calumniated father. The boys, following him as he lectured excitedly and paced from room to room, forgot to finish their game, which remained at a promising, preliminary stage; the British would live to fight another day.

In the afternoon, it stopped raining. It was cloudy, humid and hot. Chhordimoni, Sandeep's great-aunt, who had come early that morning, and had stayed back, had spent the morning making little pyramids out of betel-leaves, stuffing them with betel-nuts (the betel-nuts were round as planets and hard as rocks; she broke them into halves and quarters with a sharp and dangerous implement), smearing them with choona. She chewed on one for hours, her jaws moving imperceptibly. It was a strong and hardy jaw; it was never exhausted. In the afternoon, everyone slept, and nothing moved in the world but Chhordimoni's jaws, with a stubborn, grinding motion that defied logic, with a subtle rhythm, taking utmost pleasure in the betel-leaf.

Chhotomama was asleep, with a half-open book by his side. Sandeep glanced through its pages; it was a novel by Sarat Chandra Chatterjee. Chhotomama's shelves were full of these books; Sarat Chandra, Bibhuti Bhushan, Tarashanker, Rabindranath; like the names of wines, the names of these authors; an entire generation had been drunk with these names.

Sandeep could hardly read Bengali. He could hardly write it. Brought up in Bombay, away from his own province, Bengal, he was one of the innumerable language-orphans of modern India. He was as illiterate in his language as . . . as Chhaya and Saraswati. But he liked opening these classics and looking at the letters while, outside, new rain-bearing clouds moved in the sky. He saw the letters as characters, 'characters' in both senses of the word: এ was a fat man standing straight with his belly sticking out, ঞ was the fat man scratching his back, ৭ was an adolescent, lately grown tall and awkward, his head bent forward shyly, স was a dancer, his right leg forever lifted in a self-consciously statuesque pose. The letters were intimate, quirky, ancient, graceful, comic, just as he imagined the people of Bengal to be.

It was a time of many insects. The skies were prolific with tiny, beating creatures. In the evening, there would be a tribe of insects of arbitrary sizes and origins by the fluorescent lamp on the wall. This made the lizard happy. When it saw an insect minding its own business by a corner of the wall, its body ticked urgently and accurately, like the hand of a clock that never runs faster or slower than the exact time. It would turn and stop and advance with staccato, morse-code-like movements – dot-dot-dash-dot-dot – glide forward in a way that was both jerky and streamlined, and seize and swallow the little insect if it was lucky: if the lizard was lucky, that is. One could never manage to see that precise instant, that half-instant, when it actually grasped the insect with its mouth and swallowed it. Now the insect was here, part of the world of creation, and now it was gone, into the underworld of the lizard's belly.

Once, an insect wandered into Babla's ear. Babla, who had dozed off at seven o'clock in the evening, woke with a start and began to cry loudly. The cry turned into the high-pitched wail of the tragedian trying his best to move his audience. Upon anxious interrogation, he refused to answer, but cried and pointed to his left ear, but not too noticeably, as if he were afraid the insect might take offence and enter his brain.

'It makes a noise,' he wept. 'It crackles.'

Mamima made him lie down. Wave after wave of tears followed; something sad and irreversible seemed to have happened in the house, and only Babla, the youngest child, gave it a voice and expression. Saraswati heated a bowl of oil, Mamima dipped her little finger in it, and holding it an inch away from the earhole, let a drop of oil fall into the dark tunnel. Then another, and another.

'Close your eyes,' she said. 'Don't be a little coward. The insect is more afraid than you are.'

Babla was not convinced. He could not bear the thought of a living creature wandering inside another living creature, himself. He lived alone inside his body; he did not want to share it with an insect. A short while later, a flying-ant came out from the darkness of the tunnel into the dazzling, lighted space of the room. Its wings were sticky with oil, and it stumbled onto the pillow. It seemed overwhelmed by what it had seen in Babla's ear. Mamima killed it swiftly with a magazine, and it appeared quite ready to die, as if its mission in life were now complete.

Sometime during the rains, Abhi's and Babla's school started again. The last week of Sandeep's summer holidays was spent alone in the daytime, with the house and its uninhabited spaces all to himself. Of course, his mother and his aunt were present, but they were more like the furniture in the house that would always be there and which comforted by their presence – they were more like beds to lie in or chairs to sit safely in rather than companions to conspire with; they would always be there.

With the coming of the rains, Saraswati caught a cold, and her coughs got worse and worse. Without Abhi and Babla around, Sandeep began to see Saraswati as an individual rather than a mythical figure, which was a mildly disturbing experience. When she got fever, she went up to the terrace and lay upon a mattress beneath the sun. When it rained, she came in. 'Hai hai! O misery!' she exclaimed. She wanted to work, but Mamima had commanded her to rest. 'O misery, misery!' she said. Why did she want to work? Shivering at the same time? It was not because she was good or wonder-ful (imagine Saraswati being good or wonderful), but because she was frightened of not being needed. Sandeep pitied her, and it hurt him to feel an emotion as elevated as pity for such a crumpled, ugly woman, who could not even talk proper Bengali, who only spoke in a crude village dialect which was a huge source of amusement to the children, and who ate puffed rice soaked in water in the afternoon. Once, when asked to write her name, her fingers, shy and tortured, had scrawled something painful on a piece of paper. There was a fixed smile on Saraswati's face as, far away, her fingers took several minutes to accomplish their task. 'What is this?' they asked mockingly, pointing to the stillborn, deformed word on the paper. 'Who knows?' she replied. 'I could never write. Besides, an old woman can't write.' 'How old are you, Saraswati?' they asked her. 'Forty or fifty,' she said. 'I'm not sure.' Forty years for her was a long time, as was fifty years; they were both nearly an eternity but a little less than a lifetime, and she liked both numbers equally. The sense of time had bypassed her, like a gentle breeze, without disturbing her. What an ignorant woman! Pratap, who got the lowest marks in class, was less ignorant. And now that she was ill, Sandeep pitied her, albeit with difficulty, for he usually reserved emotions like pity for beautiful orphan girls in stories or films. 'Hai hai!' she said. She would not take medicines. Stubborn, pigheaded, stupid woman. Instead, she ate the bitter tulsi leaves of the tulsi plants that grew in pots on the terrace. Bitter, bitter leaves. She too was like the furniture in the house; many, many people had rested in her without knowing it. Old, decaying piece of furniture, never to be removed, giving rest again and again.

At four o'clock each day, the magic moment, Abhi and Babla came back home from school. Sandeep watched them silently from the upper window, his face pressed against the mullions, his hands clutching the long, cold mullions. He felt a light twinge of envy as he watched the porter help them off the schoolbus. When they glanced up and saw him, they waved, and he waved back. This was his way of welcoming them back to the shadowy world of the holidays.

But when they came up, they were full of what they had done at school, what this or that teacher had said, what mischief a friend had been up to. They flung their bags on to the bed. The bags, made of khaki cloth, were stuffed with textbooks and ragged exercise books that had names and classes written neatly on their brown-paper covers. In some of Abhi's books, Sandeep found the following written on the first page:

Abhijit Das,
17 Vivekananda Road,
Calcutta (South),
West Bengal,
India,

    Asia,
    Earth,
    The Solar System,
    The Universe.

It was a strange and sublime address.

Now, ripping the shoes off their feet, they roared to Saraswati for food, and began talking about the school play. Sandeep told them in hushed tones, as if he knew what he was about to say was inconceivable:

'Saraswati's not well.'

'Ooof!' said Abhi. 'Why did she have to fall ill *now*?'

Their faces glowed with sweat and the radiance of another excitement. It gave Sandeep a sense of the other world to which they belonged and in which he played no part; it made his afternoon games with them seem small and temporary. He felt the shadowy, secret life of the holidays, the vivid underground existence during those long afternoons in the house while their parents slept calmly, slip out of his grasp. Yet the three of them, Abhi, Babla and Sandeep, sprawled on the great bed together, and talked and talked, reliving the illusion of togetherness. By simply talking, by simply never ceasing these long, meaningless conversations, Sandeep felt he could buy time and keep the holidays from ending.

It rained during the day, and the old, mysterious sound of thunder rang in the sky. With Abhi and Babla at school, Sandeep lounged in the upper room, lying on his stomach upon the bed, haltingly reading Bengali sentences in a children's magazine, cautiously looking at the pictures. He sometimes found, to his surprise, that it took him a minute to read a single short line of Bengali. He would stare at a difficult word uncomprehendingly for what seemed like hours. How slowly time passed in the last, empty moments of the holidays! The thunder echoed in the sky again, and he was impatient for Abhi to return, so that he could discuss the sound of the thunder with him. He peered at the magazine, and found that it gave him a strange comfort to read these Bengali riddles, limericks, jokes; to hear, through the riddles, limericks and jokes, the language speaking to him. A fly settled near his hand. Looking up, he saw the lizard motionless upon the wall. By accident, he saw himself in the mirror, lying on the bed, his body relaxed and his face serious. He heard his aunt blowing the conch and ringing the bell in the prayer-room. He wished he could live in the mirror, always, the way he saw himself now, a lazy, motionless image, with the fly and the lizard, the sound of the conch and the rain, the jokes and rhymes in his mother-tongue upon his lips.

In these last days, he grew used to the company of women. He eavesdropped on their conversations; he asked them questions to which only a woman would know the answer. He wandered at large among these slow, motherly figures, these timeless busybodies and humorous samaritans, who went around the world in their long, flowing saris like priests in their robes. To be in this old house in the daytime with his aunt, his mother, Chhordimoni and Saraswati was to see women assume life with an unimpedable vegetable dignity.

When Chhordimoni spent a few days with them, it was a great pleasure for Sandeep to watch her briskly and fiercely ordering the rest of the world about, for she was convinced of its insignificance, as she got a special meal prepared for the evening. 'Duffer!' she would say to his aunt. 'Is that the way to peel a banana-flower? Give it to me!' She would proceed with trembling hands to peel it, and fail, because she was so old and unsure of her own movements, though her intellect was clear and frustrated with the ageing body it lived in. Often, Sandeep's mother had told him what Chhordimoni was like in her younger days, a portrait of a majestic and imperious woman, whom servants and children were afraid of, grudgingly taken by men as an equal, one of the first women graduates. And now this. 'Here! Take it! Do you think I have time for these things?' she would say, roughly pushing the vegetable back. She would call the washerwoman a fool for putting too much starch in her sari; she would call the vegetable-seller an ass for bringing such sickly-looking aubergines; she would call Saraswati an imbecile for refusing to take medicine. The air rang out with expletives, intense names as untranslatable as poetry: 'Duffer! Crow-face! Retarded child! She-goat! Cow-eyed imbecile!' Sometimes, in a fit of calculated irony and sarcasm, she produced the opposite range of words: 'O genius! O wonder-worker! O helpless child!' When she fell silent, the inspiration seemed to go out of the air, and a great calm settled upon everything.

In one of these serene and silent moments in the afternoon, Sandeep asked her:

'Chhordimoni, how old were you when you got married?'

She was lying on the bed, scarcely listening. From the well of her subconscious, a voice replied:

'I was twenty.'

'Was that a long time ago, Chhordimoni?'

'Yes. Fifty years.' She counted silently to herself. 'Fifty-two years ago.'

'That's a long time,' said Sandeep.

'Yes.'

He paused to think. Then he asked:

'Did you see the Romans, Chhordimoni?'

'No.'

'Did people say "thee" and "thou", Chhordimoni? Did you ever hear them say that?'

'I don't think I did, Mona.'

There was a brief, thoughtful silence. Then:

'When did Chhordamoni die, Chhordimoni?'

'When I was twenty-five, I think.'

'Why did he die, Chhordimoni?'

'He was not well, Mona.'

'Not well like Saraswati?'

'More not-well than Saraswati, Mona.'

Sandeep paused. He could not picture his not-well granduncle.

'Did Chhordamoni have a moustache, Chhordimoni?'

'He had a big moustache.'

'Did you have Rabimama and Jatinmama after Chhordamoni died or before he died, Chhordimoni?'

His great-aunt stared thoughtfully at him for a moment.

'Before he died, Mona.'

'Did he play with Rabimama and Jatinmama?'

'There was not much time, Mona. But he did play with them, and he took them out on the horse-carriage . . . though he had a bad temper, sometimes.'

'As bad as yours, Chhordimoni?'

She stared at him with tragic, bewildered eyes.

'I don't have a bad temper, Mona.'

'But sometimes you do, Chhordimoni. Not always, but just sometimes-sometimes.'

'It's only when people are stupid. Now go and bother your aunt and let me sleep.'

She turned over on her side, cracked all her knuckles meticulously, and began to snore almost instantaneously. After regarding the wrinkles on her face and hands for a while, Sandeep crawled over her body to the other side of the bed, where his aunt lay reading the health page of a magazine. He loved crawling like a clumsy, four-legged beast across and over the bodies of the grown-ups, these warm figures in cool saris, and then curl up between them like a mountain-cat among huge, sheltering boulders.

He nudged his aunt, who lifted an arm and placed it on her forehead, making her bangles sing as she did so.

'Mamima,' he asked, 'when were you married?'

'Why are you interested in our marriages today?' she said without turning her head.

'No, tell me, Mamima, tell me when you got married.'

'I've forgotten.'

'You've not forgotten, Mamima! How can you forget?'

'I tell you I've forgotten.'

'All right, then tell me *where* you got married.'

'I was married here in Calcutta. Your Chhotomama came in a car. He was wearing a white dhuti and a silk panjabi with gold buttons, and a topor on his head. I, of course, didn't see him till later. But my cousin, Beena, saw them coming and she rushed into our room and told me. She said: The bridegroom's come.'

'What did you say?'

'I couldn't say anything, because they were putting chandan and sindoor on my face, and kaajal around my eyes. I wasn't allowed to move.'

'Not even talk?'

'Well, I could talk, but since they were drawing such beautiful patterns on my forehead, I didn't want to spoil it by talking about the bridegroom. Who wants to know about the bridegroom?'

'Weren't you interested?'

'Not in the bridegroom.'

'Had you ever seen him before?' In Sandeep's mind, it was no longer Chhotomama, but some other man who was about to get married to Mamima, who was no longer Mamima, but some other woman.

'Only in a photograph.'

'Did you like him?'

'Not a bit. He had much too big a nose for me. Also, Shampa, my little cousin, who was the only one from our family who had come with them in the car – she was a small, lively girl then, and she wore a blue frock that day – told me that he had argued with the driver all the way about which was the shorter route to Boubazaar.'

'Why did you marry him, then, Mamima?'

'O I liked your mother and Chhordimoni. When I met them, I thought, They're nice people. So, because I wanted to know your mother and Chhordimoni better, I married him.'

'Do you like him now?'

She wrinkled her nose: 'Not at all. He's such a busybody.'

'Why didn't you . . .' he paused emphatically.

'Why didn't I what?'

'Why didn't you have a love-marriage?'

She wrinkled her nose a little more.

'Of course not. How boring!' She was silent, and then said, 'Not knowing the person makes it so much more exciting! It's such a great adventure . . .'

In the course of the conversation, it was divulged that, on the first night, he had asked whether she liked cricket, to which she had replied, No. They had both agreed that they loved Tagore songs and Sachin Deb Burman's voice. He had asked her if she could sing, and she had said no again. So it was he who had sung a song for her, which she found very funny because of the seriousness of his face, though she had to admit that he sang very well. First she had Abhi, the dark one with large eyes, and they named him Abhijit, another name for Vega, the bright star, and called him Abhi for short. Then they had Babla, the fair one, who looked more like his father, and they named him Surajit, which means the One Who Has Mastered Music, partly because it rhymed with Abhijit, and partly because Chhotomama wanted a son who could sing. Abhijit and Surajit, two brothers, rhyming names, always arguing with each other. O I remember when Babla was born, said Sandeep. I remember going in the car, which was not so old and run-down then, with Saraswati and Abhi and Ma. I remember the nurses and the doctors with masks on their faces. Do you? asked Mamima, surprised. Yes, I often remember that scene, though I didn't know it was Babla's birth until now. Saraswati loved the child, said Mamima, and then she said conspiratorially, she even nursed him to keep him quiet. Sandeep thought of Saraswati's small, wrinkled breasts. They talked until his aunt was tired and wanted to sleep.

'But what shall I do, Mamima?' Sandeep asked.

'Well, go to the terrace,' she said in a sleep-heavy voice. 'I planted some chilli-plants in a pot. See if the chillies are growing, and guard them from bulbuls and parrots.'

So he went upstairs to the terrace to watch the chillies growing.

Saraswati was sleeping on the terrace, a small, huddled figure. The sun was high and scorching, and it was uncomfortably hot, as it always is between rains. Next to her there was a potted tulsi plant, and next to that, two chilli plants. The chilli blossoms were like little lavender stars; the chillies grew from their centre, fierce pointed clots of purple, each a tiny phallus. Sandeep shooed away two crows that were hopping around the plants with a sly and tactful curiosity; they flew to the terrace of the neighbouring house, and from there to the next house, and then to the next. At each house, they paused like burglars and darted around guiltily, as if they were perpetually on the verge of breaking some law, perpetual trespassers in God's world. Then, quite suddenly, in a fit of candour, they hoarsely declared 'Ka! Ka!' in the reverie of the afternoon. No one woke.

Between two and four o'clock, a golden stupor descended upon the city. Sandeep loved these two hours when it was too hot to move, when the eddying waves of people disappeared and a low tide came upon everything, leaving lane after lane like gullies in the sand and house after house like sandcastles upon an empty beach, when the splendid arguments in the tea-shops came to a brief conclusion, and everyone agreed with everyone and fell silent.

Clothes hung from clotheslines in the terrace, and undulated like many-coloured waves, all at once, when a breeze blew from the direction of the railway lines. They were happy, cheerful flags that signified life in a house. There were trousers, shirts, petticoats, blouses, and magnificent lengths of saris, each with a different and striking motif, each a small waterfall of life and colour, unravelled to dry. Sandeep had often seen Saraswati unfolding these sinuous boa-constrictors of cloth (how wrinkled they looked, then, bad-tempered and wrinkled, and how rejuvenated they would look tomorrow, when they were ironed and given their customary face-lift), beating them against the air with a single electric movement to rid them of the last drops of water, then clipping them, her arms wide-apart, as if outstretched in a deep and satisfying yawn.

A mist of drowsiness hung over the lanes. In the still houses, families had eaten their lunch of rice, dal and fish and fallen asleep. Afternoon was a time of digestion, a time of fullness and contentment, full bellies and closed eyes. In all the shadowy houses of Calcutta at this moment, the gastric juices were solemnly at work. There was not a movement in the corridors, no noise; yet if you put an ear against the belly of one of these sleepers, you would probably hear a rich gurgling sound.

Not everyone was asleep. People who had had a meal less substantial dotted the lane perfunctorily. Sometimes, a girl came to a terrace, ostensibly to hang, let us say, a sari on a clothesline; at the same time, a young man appeared on the terrace three houses away, apparently to inspect a water-tank. They glanced at each other, then fumbled with their work, then glanced at each other, then fumbled, then glanced – such shy, piercing glances exchanged in the heat of the afternoon! How straight and undeflected the man's glance travelled, how swift and disguised the woman's answering glance! What rhythm the moment possessed!

Near a derelict tea-shop, a rickshawalla lay slouched in the shade of his rickshaw. Idly, he clapped his hands in the air. After a moment, Sandeep realised he was killing mosquitoes. Clap . . . clap . . . clap . . . clap . . . Four mosquitoes. Clap . . . clap . . . Two more mosquitoes. One was reminded of the joke in which a man whose neck was aching stopped for a minute on the street and turned his head up to ease the pain. People who had been walking past noticed him, and thought that he was watching something terribly interesting and important in the sky. One by one, they stopped beside him and stared up with deep attention. Meanwhile, the first man, feeling somewhat better, continued his journey, leaving everyone else still gazing thoughtfully at the sky. This is what must have happened to Calcutta in the afternoon; the first man had casually walked away; the rest of Calcutta was still staring at that fascinating, non-existent point in the emptiness, waiting for the revelation.

He heard car-horns blowing in the distance. He heard shouts – a taxi-driver must be insulting a bus-driver. It was the first traffic-jam of the evening, punctual, ceremonial and glorious.

The two hours of golden stillness had ended. The cars and crowded buses were on the roads again; Abhi and Babla would come back home from school; pigeons flapped their wings and rose above rooftops, a clean universe of rooftops and terraces. Tomorrow, Sandeep remembered, he would return with his mother to Bombay. He saw Chhaya at the turning of the lane, walking in the direction of the house. It was time – it must be – to sweep the dust from the floors.

Amitav Ghosh

NASHAWY

USING HIS POWERS, 'Amm Taha foretold the events of Nabeel's brother's wedding ceremony the morning before it was held. There would be lots of young people around their house, he said: all the young, unmarried boys and girls of the village, singing and dancing without a care in the world. But the supper would be a small affair, attended mainly by relatives and guests from other villages. Old Idris, Nabeel's father, had invited a lot of people from Nashawy too, for their family was overjoyed about the marriage and wanted to celebrate it as best they could. But many of the people he had invited wouldn't go, out of consideration for the old man, to cut down his expenses – everyone knew their family couldn't really afford a big wedding. Their young friends and relatives would drop by during the day and then again in the evening, mainly to dance and sing. They would be outside in the lanes; they wouldn't go into the house with the guests – the supper was only for elders and responsible, grown-up men.

'They'll start arriving in the morning, insha'allah,' said 'Amm Taha, 'and by the time you get there they'll all be sitting in the guest-room. They'll want to talk to you, for none of them will ever have met an Indian before.'

My heart sank when I realised that for me the evening would mean a prolonged incarceration in a small, crowded room. 'I would rather be outside,' I said, 'watching the singing and dancing.'

Extract from *In an Antique Land*.

'Amm Taha laughed with a hint of malign pleasure, as though he had already glimpsed a wealth of discomfiture lying in wait for me in his divinations of the evening ahead. 'They won't let you stay outside,' he said. 'You're a kind of effendi, so they'll make you go in and sit with the elders and all the other guests.'

I tried to prove him wrong when I went to Nabeel's house that evening, and for a short while, at the beginning, I actually thought I'd succeeded.

By the time I made my way there, a large crowd had gathered in the lane outside and I merged gratefully into its fringes. There were some forty or fifty boys and girls there, packed in a tight semi-circle in front of the bride and groom. The newly married couple were sitting on raised chairs, enthroned with their backs against the house, while their friends and relatives danced in front of them. The groom, 'Ali, was dressed in a new jallabeyya of brown wool, a dark, sturdily built young man, with a generous, open smile and a cleft in his chin. His bride and cousin, Fawzia, was wearing a white gown, with a frill of lace and a little gauzy veil. Her face had been carefully and evenly painted, so that her lips, cheeks, and ears were all exactly the same shade of iridescent pink. The flatness of the paint had created a curious effect, turning her face into a pallid, spectral mask: I was astonished to discover later that she was in fact a cheerful, good-looking woman, with a warm smile and a welcoming manner.

A boy was kneeling beside her chair, pounding out a deafening, fast-paced rhythm upon a tin wash-basin that was propped against his leg. Someone was dancing in front of him, but the crowd was so thick around them that from where I stood I could see little more than the bobbing of the dancer's head. Bracing myself against a wall, I rose on tiptoe and saw that the dancer was a boy, one of Nabeel's cousins; he was dancing bawdily, jerking his hips in front of the girls, while some of his friends reached out to slap him on his buttocks, doubling over with laughter at his coquettish twitching.

All around me voices were chanting the words of a refrain that invoked the voluptuous fruitfulness of pomegranates –

'*Ya rummân, ya rummân*' – and with every word, dozens of hands came crashing together, clapping in unison, in perfect time with the beat. The spectators were jostling for a better view now, the boys balancing on each others' shoulders, the girls climbing upon the window-sills. The dance was approaching its climax when Nabeel appeared at my side, followed by his father. After a hurried exchange of greetings, they put their arms through mine and led me firmly back towards their house.

The moment I stepped into their smoky, crowded guest-room, I knew that I was in for a long interrogation: I had a premonition of its coming in the strained boredom on the faces of the men who were assembled there, in the restlessness of their fidgeting fingers and their tapping toes, as they sat in silence in that hot, sweaty room, while the lanes around them resounded with the clamour of celebration. They turned to face me as I walked in, all of them together, some fifteen or twenty men, grateful for the distraction, for the temporary rupture with the uncomfortably intimate world evoked by the songs outside, the half-forgotten longings and reawakened desires, the memories of fingers locking in secret and hands brushing against hips in the surging crowd – all the village's young and unmarried, boys and girls together, thronging around the dancers, clapping and chanting, intoxicated with the heightened eroticism of the wedding night, that feverish air whose mysteries I had just begun to sense when Nabeel and his father spotted me in the crowd and led me away to face this contingent of fidgeting, middle-aged men sitting in their guest-room.

I looked around quickly, searching for a familiar face, but to my dismay I discovered that they were all outsiders, from other villages, and that I knew no one there, no one at all, since Nabeel and his father had gone back to their post outside to receive their guests. There were a few moments of silent scrutiny and then the man beside me cleared his throat and asked whether I was the doctor who had recently been posted to the Government clinic.

A look of extreme suspicion came into his eyes when I

explained my situation, and as soon as I had finished he began to fire off a series of questions – about how I had learnt Arabic, and who had brought me to Nashawy, and whether I had permission from the Government of Egypt. No sooner had I given him the answers than he demanded to see my identity card, and when I explained that I did not have a card, but I did indeed have an official letter from the Ministry of the Interior which I would gladly show him if he would accompany me to my room, his face took on an expression of portentous seriousness and he began to mutter direly about spies and impostors and a possible report to the Mukhabbarât, the intelligence wing of the police.

He was quickly elbowed away however, for there were many others around him who were impatient now, brimming with questions of their own. Within moments a dozen or so people had crowded around me, and I was busy affirming that yes, in my country there were indeed crops like rice and wheat, and yes, in India too, there were peasants like the fellaheen of Egypt, who lived in adobe villages and turned the earth with cattle-drawn ploughs. The questions came ever faster, even as I was speaking: 'Are most of your houses still built of mud-brick as they are here?' and 'Do your people cook on gas stoves or do they still burn wood and straw as we do?'

I grew increasingly puzzled as I tried to deal with this barrage of inquiries, first, by the part the word 'still' played in their questions, and secondly by the masks of incredulity that seemed to fall on their faces as I affirmed, over and over again, that yes, in India too people used cattle-drawn ploughs and not tractors; water-wheels and not pumps; donkey-carts, not trucks, and yes, in India too there were many, many people who were very poor, indeed there were millions whose poverty they would scarcely have been able to imagine. But to my utter bewilderment, the more I insisted, the more sceptical they seemed to become, until at last I realised, with an overwhelming sense of shock, that the simple truth was that they did not believe what I was saying.

I later came to understand that their disbelief had little or

nothing to do with what I had said; rather, they had con-
structed a certain ladder of 'Development' in their minds, and
because all their images of material life were of those who
stood in the rungs above, the circumstances of those below
had become more or less unimaginable. I had an inkling then
of the real and desperate seriousness of their engagement with
modernism, because I realised that the fellaheen saw the
material circumstances of their lives in exactly the same way
that a university economist would: as a situation that was
shamefully anachronistic, a warp upon time; I understood
that their relationships with the objects of their everyday lives
was never innocent of the knowledge that there were other
places, other countries which did not have mud-walled houses
and cattle-drawn ploughs, so that those objects, those houses
and ploughs, were insubstantial things, ghosts displaced in
time, waiting to be exorcised and laid to rest. It was thus that
I had my first suspicion of what it might mean to belong to a
'historical civilisation', and it left me bewildered because, for
my own part, it was precisely the absoluteness of time and the
discreteness of epochs that I always had trouble in imagining.

The supper was a quick affair; about ten of us were taken
to another room, at the back, where we helped ourselves to
lamb, rice and sweetmeats standing around a table, and as
soon as we had eaten, we were led out again and another lot
of guests was brought in. I decided to take advantage of the
bustle, and while Nabeel and his father were busy leading
their guests back and forth, I slipped out of the guest-room
and back into the lane.

It was long past sunset now, and the faces around the bridal
couple were glowing under a dome of dust that had turned
golden in the light of a single kerosene lamp. The drum-beat
on the wash-basin was a measured, gentle one and when I
pushed my way into the centre of the crowd I saw that the
dancer was a young girl, dressed in a simple, printed cotton
dress, with a long scarf tied around her waist. Both her hands
were on her hips, and she was dancing with her eyes fixed on
the ground in front of her, moving her hips with a slow, languid grace, backwards and forwards while the rest of her

body stayed still, almost immobile, except for the quick, circular motion of her feet. Then gradually, almost imperceptibly, the tempo of the beat quickened, and somebody called out the first line of a chant, *khadnâha min wasat al'dâr*, 'we took her from her father's house,' and the crowd shouted back, *wa abûha gâ'id za'alân*, 'while her father sat there bereft.' Then the single voice again, *khadnâha bi al-saif al-mâdî*, 'we took her with a sharpened sword,' followed by the massed refrain, *wa abûha, makânsh râdî*, 'because her father wouldn't consent'.

The crowd pressed closer with the quickening of the beat, and as the voices and the clapping grew louder, the girl, in response, raised an arm and flexed it above her head in a graceful arc. Her body was turning now, rotating slowly in the same place, her hips moving faster while the crowd around her clapped and stamped, roaring their approval at the tops of their voices. Gradually, the beat grew quicker, blurring into a tattoo of drumbeats, and in response her torso froze into stillness, while her hips and her waist moved ever faster, in exact counterpoint, in a pattern of movement that became a perfect abstraction of eroticism, a figurative geometry of love-making, pounding back and forth at a dizzying speed until at last the final beat rang out and she escaped into the crowd, laughing.

'Where have you been all this while?' a voice cried out behind me. 'We have been looking everywhere for you – there's so much still to ask.'

Turning around I came face to face with the man who had demanded to see my identity card. Nabeel was following close behind, and between the two of them they led me back, remonstrating gently with me for having left the guest-room without warning.

There was a thick fog of smoke in the room when we went back in, for the wedding guests had lit cigarettes and shushas now and settled back on the divans to rest after the supper. Nabeel's father handed me a shusha of my own, and while I was trying to coax my coal into life, my interlocutors gathered around me again, and the questions began to flow once more.

'Tell us then,' said someone, 'in your country, amongst your people, what do you do with your dead?'

'They are burned,' I said, puffing stoically on my shusha as they recoiled in shock.

'And the ashes?' another voice asked. 'Do you at least save the ashes so that you can remember them by something?'

'No,' I said. 'No: even the ashes are scattered in the rivers.'

There was a long silence for it took a while before they could overcome their revulsion far enough to speak. 'So are they all unbelievers in your country?' someone asked at last. 'Is there no Law or Morality: can everyone do as they please – take a woman off the streets or sleep with another man's wife?'

'No,' I began, but before I could complete my answer I was cut short.

'So what about circumcision?' a voice demanded, and was followed immediately by another, even louder one, which wanted to know whether women in my country were 'purified' as they were in Egypt.

The word 'to purify' makes a verbal equation between male circumcision and clitoridectomy, being the same in both cases, but the latter is an infinitely more dangerous operation, since it requires the complete excision of the clitoris. Clitoridectomy is, in fact, hideously painful and was declared illegal after the Revolution, although it still continues to be widely practised, by Christian and Muslim fellaheen alike.

'No,' I said, 'women are not "purified" in my country.' But my questioner, convinced that I had not understood what he had asked, repeated his words again, slowly.

The faces around me grew blank with astonishment as I said 'no' once again. 'So you mean you let the clitoris just grow and grow?' a man asked, hoarse-voiced.

I began to correct him, but he was absorbed in his own amazement, and in the meanwhile someone else interrupted, with a sudden shout: 'And boys?' he cried, 'what about boys, are they not purified either?'

'And you, ya doktór?'

'What about you . . .?'

I looked at the eyes around me, alternately curious and hor-
rified, and I knew that I would not be able to answer. My
limbs seemed to have passed beyond my volition as I rose
from the divan, knocking over my shusha. I pushed my way
out, and before anyone could react, I was past the crowd,
walking quickly back to my room.

I was almost there, when I heard footsteps close behind me.
It was Nabeel, looking puzzled and a little out of breath.

'What happened?' he said. 'Why did you leave so suddenly?'

I kept walking for I could think of no answer.

'They were only asking questions,' he said, 'just like you do;
they didn't mean any harm. Why do you let this talk of cows
and burning and circumcision worry you so much? These are
just customs; it's natural that people should be curious. These
are not things to be upset about.'

I sometimes wished I had told Nabeel a story.

When I was a child we lived in a place that was destined to
fall out of the world's atlas like a page ripped in the press: it
was East Pakistan, which, after its creation in 1947, survived
only a bare twenty-five years before becoming a new nation,
Bangladesh. No one regretted its passing; if it still possesses a
life in my memory it is largely by accident, because my father
happened to be seconded to the Indian diplomatic mission in
Dhaka when I was about six years old.

There was an element of irony in our living in Dhaka as
'foreigners', for Dhaka was in fact our ancestral city: both my
parents were from families which belonged to the middle-class
Hindu community that had once flourished there. But long
before the Muslim-majority state of Pakistan was created my
ancestors had moved westwards, and thanks to their wander-
lust we were Indians now, and Dhaka was foreign territory to
us although we spoke its dialect and still had several relatives
living in the old Hindu neighbourhoods in the heart of the city.

The house we had moved into was in a new residential suburb on the outskirts of the city. The area had only recently been developed and when we moved there it still looked like a version of a planner's blueprint, with sketchy lots and lightly pencilled roads. Our house was spanking new; it was one of the first to be built in the area. It had a large garden, and high walls ran all the way around it, separating the compound from an expanse of excavated construction sites. There was only one other house near by; the others were all at the end of the road, telescopically small, visible only with shaded eyes and a squint. To me they seemed remote enough for our house to be a desert island, with walls instead of cliffs.

At times, unaccountably, the house would fill up with strangers. The garden, usually empty except for dragonflies and grasshoppers, would be festooned with saris drying in the breeze, and there would be large groups of men, women and children sitting on the grass, with little bundles of clothes and pots and pans spread out beside them. To me, a child of seven or eight, there always seemed to be an air of something akin to light-heartedness about those people, something like relief perhaps; they would wave to me when I went down to the garden and sometimes the women would reach into their bundles and find me sweets. In the evenings, large fires would be lit in the driveway and my mother and her friends would stand behind huge cooking-pots, ladles in hand, the ends of their saris tucked in purposefully at the waist, serving out large helpings of food. We would all eat together, sitting around the garden as though it were a picnic, and afterwards we, the children, would play football and hide-and-seek. Then after a day or two everyone would be gone, the garden would be reclaimed by dragonflies and grasshoppers and peace would descend once more upon my island.

I was never surprised or put out by these visitations. To me they seemed like festive occasions, especially since we ate out of green banana leaves, just as we did at weddings and other celebrations. No one ever explained to me what those groups of people were doing in our house and I was too young to work out for myself that they were refugees, fleeing from mobs, and that they had taken shelter in our garden because ours was the only 'Hindu' house near by that happened to have high walls.

On one particular day (a day in January 1964, I was to discover many years later) more people than ever before appeared in the garden, suddenly and without warning. They began to pour in early in the morning, in small knots, carrying bundles and other odds and ends, and as the day wore on the heavy steel gates of the house were opened time and time again to let more people in. By evening the garden was packed with people, some squatting in silent groups and others leaning against the walls, as though in wait.

Just after sunset, our cook came looking for me in the garden, and led me away, past the families that were huddled on the staircase and in the corridors, to my parents' bedroom, upstairs. By the time we got to the room, the shutters of all the windows had been closed, and my father was pacing the floor, waiting for me. He made me sit down, and then, speaking in a voice that could not be argued with, he told me to stay where I was. I was not to leave the bedroom on any account, he said, until he came back to fetch me. To make sure, he left our cook sitting by the door, with strict instructions not to leave his post.

As a rule I would have been perfectly happy to stay there with our cook, for he was a wonderful story-teller and often kept me entranced for hours on end, spinning out fables in the dialect of his region – long, epic stories about ghosts and ghouls and faraway lands where people ate children. He was from one of the maritime districts of East Pakistan and he had come to work with us because he had lost most of his family in the riots that followed Partition and now wanted to emigrate to India. He had learnt to cook on the river-steamers of his region, which were famous throughout Bengal for the quality of their cooking. After his coming the food in our house had become legendary amongst our family's friends. As for me, I regarded him with an equal mixture of fear and fascination, for although he was a small wiry man, he seemed bigger than he was because he had large, curling moustaches which made him somehow mysterious and menacing. When I tried to imagine the ghouls and spirits of his stories, they usually looked very much like him.

But today he had no stories to tell; he could hardly keep still and every so often he would go to the windows and look outside, prising the shutters open. Soon, his curiosity got the better of him and, after telling me to stay where I was, he slipped out of the room, forgetting to shut the door behind him. I waited a few minutes, and when he didn't come back, I ran out of the bedroom to a balcony which looked out over the garden and the lane.

My memories of what I saw are very vivid, but at the same time oddly out of synch, like a sloppily edited film. A large crowd is thronging around our house, a mob of hundreds of men, their faces shining red in the light of the burning torches in their hands, rags tied on sticks, whose flames seem to be swirling against our walls in waves of fire. As I watch, the flames begin to dance around the house, and while they circle the walls the people gathered inside mill around the garden, cower in huddles and cover their faces. I can see the enraged mob and the dancing flames with a vivid, burning clarity, yet all of it happens in utter silence; my memory, in an act of benign protection, has excised every single sound.

I do not know how long I stood there, but suddenly our cook rushed in and dragged me away, back to my parents' bedroom. He was shaken now, for he had seen the mob too, and he began to walk back and forth across the room, covering his face and tugging at his moustache.

In frustration at my imprisonment in that room, I began to disarrange the bedclothes. I pulled off the covers and began to tug at the sheets, when suddenly my father's pillow fell over, revealing a dark, metallic object. It was small, no larger than a toy pistol but much heavier, and I had to use both my hands to lift it. I pointed it at the wall, as I would my own water-pistol, and curling a finger around the trigger I squeezed as hard as I could. But nothing happened, there was no sound and the trigger wouldn't move. I tried once more, and again nothing happened. I turned it over in my hands, wondering what made it work, but then the door flew open and my father came into the room. He crossed the floor with a couple of strides, and snatched the revolver out of my hands. Without another word, he slipped it into his pocket and went racing out of the room.

It was then that I realised he was afraid we might be killed that night, and that he had sent me to the bedroom so I would be the last to be found if the gates gave way and the mob succeeded in breaking in.

But nothing did happen. The police arrived at just the right moment, alerted by some of my parents' Muslim friends, and drove the mob away. Next morning, when I looked out over the balcony, the garden was strewn with bricks and rubble, but the refugees who had gathered there were sitting peacefully in the sun, calm, though thoroughly subdued.

Our cook, on the other hand, was in a mood of great elation that morning, and when we went downstairs he joked cheerfully with the people in the garden, laughing, and asking how they happened to be there. Later, we squatted in a corner and he whispered in my ear, pointing at the knots of people around us, and told me their stories. I was to recognise those stories years later, when reading through a collection of old newspapers, I discovered that on the very night when I'd seen those flames dancing around the walls of our house, there had been a riot in Calcutta too, similar in every respect except that there it was Muslims who had been attacked by Hindus. But equally, in both cities – and this must be said, it must always be said, for it is the incantation that redeems our sanity – in both Dhaka and Calcutta, there were exactly mirrored stories of Hindus and Muslims coming to each others' rescue, so that many more people were saved than killed.

The stories of those riots are always the same: tales that grow out of an explosive barrier of symbols – of cities going up in flames because of a cow found dead in a temple or a pig in a mosque; of people killed for wearing a lungi or a dhoti, depending on where they find themselves; of women disembowelled for wearing veils or vermilion, of men dismembered for the state of their foreskins.

But I was never able to explain very much of this to Nabeel

or anyone else in Nashawy. The fact was that despite the occasional storms and turbulence their country had seen, despite even the wars that some of them had fought in, theirs was a world that was far gentler, far less violent, very much more humane and innocent than mine.

I could not have expected them to understand an Indian's terror of symbols.

Githa Hariharan

THE REMAINS OF THE FEAST

THE ROOM STILL smells of her. Not as she did when she was dying, an overripe smell that clung to everything that had touched her, sheets, saris, hands. She had been in the nursing home for only ten days but a bedsore grew like an angry red welt on her back. Her neck was a big hump, and she lay in bed like a moody camel that would snap or bite at unpredictable intervals. The goitred lump, the familiar swelling I had seen on her neck all my life, that I had stroked and teasingly pinched as a child, was now a cancer that spread like fire down the old body, licking clean everything in its way.

The room now smells like a pressed, faded rose. A dry, elusive smell. Burnt, a candle put out.

We were not exactly room-mates, but we shared two rooms, one corner of the old ancestral house, all my twenty-year-old life.

She was Rukmini, my great-grandmother. She was ninety when she died last month, out-living by ten years her only son and daughter-in-law. I don't know how she felt then, but later she seemed to find something slightly hilarious about it all. That she, an ignorant village-bred woman, who signed the papers my father brought her with a thumb print, should survive; while they, city-bred, ambitious, should collapse of weak hearts and arthritic knees at the first sign of old age.

Her sense of humour was always quaint. It could also be embarrassing. She would sit in her corner, her round plump face reddening, giggling like a little girl. I knew better than ask her why, I was a teenager by then. But some uninitiated friend

would be unable to resist, and would go up to my great-grandmother and ask her why she was laughing. This, I knew, would
send her into uncontrollable peals. The tears would flow down
her cheeks, and finally, catching her breath, still weak with
laughter, she would confess. She could fart exactly like a train
whistling its way out of the station, and it gave her as much joy
as a child would get when she saw, or heard, a train.

So perhaps it is not all that surprising that she could be flip-
pant about her only child's death, especially since ten years
had passed.

'Yes, Ratna, you study hard and become a big doctor,
madam,' she would chuckle when I kept the lights on all night
and paced up and down the room, reading to myself.

'The last time I saw a doctor, I was thirty years old. Your
grandfather was in the hospital for three months. He would
faint every time he saw his own blood.'

And, as if that summed up the progress made between two
generations, she would pull her blanket over her head and
begin snoring almost immediately.

I have two rooms, the entire downstairs, to myself now
since my great-grandmother died. I begin my course at medical college next month, and I am afraid to be here alone at
night.

I have to live up to the gold medal I won last year. I keep
late hours, reading my anatomy text-book before the course
begins. The body is a solid, reliable thing. It is a wonderful,
resilient machine. I hold on to the thick, hardbound book and
flip through the new-smelling pages greedily. I stop every time
I find an illustration and look at it closely. It reduces us to
pink, blue and white colour-coded, labelled parts. Muscles,
veins, tendons. Everything has a name. Everything is linked,
one with the other, all parts of a functioning whole.

It is poor consolation for the nights I have spent in her
warm bed, surrounded by that safe, familiar, musty smell.

She was cheerful and never sick. But she was also undeniably old, and so it was no great surprise to us when she suddenly took to lying in bed all day a few weeks before her
ninetieth birthday.

She had been lying in bed for close to two months, ignoring concern, advice, scolding, and then she suddenly gave up. She agreed to see a doctor.

The young doctor came out of her room, his face puzzled and angry. My father begged him to sit down and drink a cup of hot coffee.

'She will need all kinds of tests,' he announced. 'How long has she had that lump on her neck? Have you had it checked?'

My father shifted uneasily in his cane chair. He is a cadaverous-looking man, prone to nervousness and sweating. He keeps a big jar of antacids on his office desk. He has a nine-to-five accountant's job in a Government-owned company, the kind that never fires its employees.

My father pulled out the small towel he uses in place of a handkerchief. Wiping his forehead, he mumbled, 'You know how these old women are. Impossible to argue with them.'

'The neck,' the doctor said, more gently. I could see he pitied my father.

'I think it was examined once, long ago. My father was alive then. There was supposed to have been an operation, I think. But you know what they thought in those days. An operation meant an unnatural death. All the relatives came over to scare her, advise her with horror stories. So she said no. You know how it is. And she was already a widow then, my father was the head of the household. How could he, a fourteen-year-old, take the responsibility?'

'Well,' said the doctor. He shrugged his shoulders. 'Let me know when you want to admit her in my nursing home. But I suppose it's best to let her die at home.'

When the doctor left, we looked at each other, the three of us, like shifty accomplices. My mother, practical as always, broke the silence and said, 'Let's not tell her anything. Why worry her? And then we'll have all kinds of difficult old aunts and cousins visiting, it will be such a nuisance. How will Ratna study in the middle of all that chaos?'

But when I went to our room that night, my great-grandmother had a sly look on her face. 'Come here, Ratna,' she said. 'Come here, my darling little gem.'

I went, my heart quaking at the thought of telling her.

She held my hand and kissed each finger, her half-closed eyes almost flirtatious. 'Tell me something, Ratna,' she began in a wheedling voice.

'I don't know, I don't know anything about it,' I said quickly.

'Of course you do.' She was surprised, a little annoyed. 'Those small cakes you got from the Christian shop that day. Do they have eggs in them?'

'Do they?' she persisted. 'Will you,' and her eyes narrowed with cunning, 'will you get one for me?'

So we began a strange partnership, my great-grandmother and I. I smuggled cakes and ice cream, biscuits and samosas, made by non-Brahmin hands, into a vegetarian invalid's room. To the deathbed of a Brahmin widow who had never eaten anything but pure, home-cooked food for almost a century.

She would grab it from my hand, late at night after my parents had gone to sleep. She would hold the pastry in her fingers, turn it round and round, as if on the verge of an earth-shaking discovery.

'And does it really have an egg in it?' she would ask again, as if she needed the password for her to bite into it with her gums.

'Yes, yes,' I would say, a little tired of midnight feasts by then. The pastries were a cheap yellow colour, topped by white frosting with hard grey pearls.

'Lots and lots of eggs,' I would say, wanting her to hurry up and put it in her mouth. 'And the bakery is owned by a Christian. I think he hires Muslim cooks too.'

'Ooooh,' she would moan. Her little pink tongue darted out and licked the frosting. Her toothless mouth worked its way steadily, munching, making happy sucking noises.

Our secret was safe for about a week. Then she became bold. She was bored with the cakes, she said. They gave her heartburn. She became a little more adventurous every day. Her cravings were various and unpredictable. Laughable and always urgent.

'I'm thirsty,' she moaned, when my mother asked her if she wanted anything. 'No, no, I don't want water, I don't want juice.' She stopped the moaning and looked at my mother's patient, exasperated face. 'I'll tell you what I want,' she whined. 'Get me a glass of that brown drink Ratna bought in the bottle. The kind that bubbles and makes a popping sound when you open the bottle. The one with the fizzy noise when you pour it out.'

'A Coca-Cola?' said my mother, shocked. 'Don't be silly, it will make you sick.'

'I don't care what it is called,' my great-grandmother said and started moaning again. 'I want it.'

So she got it and my mother poured out a small glassful, tight-lipped, and gave it to her without a word. She was always a dutiful grand-daughter-in-law.

'Ah,' sighed my great-grandmother, propped up against her pillows, the steel tumbler lifted high over her lips. The lump on her neck moved in little gurgles as she drank. Then she burped a loud, contented burp and asked, as if she had just thought of it, 'Do you think there is something in it? You know, alcohol?'

A month later, we had got used to her new, unexpected, inappropriate demands. She had tasted, by now, lemon tarts, garlic, three types of aereated drinks, fruit cake laced with brandy, bhel-puri from the fly-infested bazaar near by.

'There's going to be trouble,' my mother kept muttering under her breath. 'She's losing her mind, she is going to be a lot of trouble.'

And she was right, of course. My great-grandmother could no longer swallow very well. She would pour the Coke into her mouth and half of it would trickle out of her nostrils, thick, brown, nauseating.

'It burns, it burns,' she would yell then, but she pursed her lips tightly together when my mother spooned a thin gruel into her mouth. 'No, no,' she screamed deliriously. 'Get me something from the bazaar. Raw onions. Fried bread. Chickens and goats.'

Then we knew she was lost to us. She was dying.

She was in the nursing home for ten whole days. My mother and I took turns sitting by her, sleeping on the floor by the hospital cot.

She lay there quietly, the pendulous neck almost as big as her face. But she would not let the nurses near her bed. She would squirm and wriggle like a big fish that refused to be caught. The sheets smelled, and the young doctor shook his head. 'Not much to be done now,' he said. 'The cancer has left nothing intact.'

The day she died, she kept searching the room with her eyes. Her arms were held down by the tubes and needles, criss-cross, in, out. The glucose dripped into her veins but her nose still ran, the clear, thin liquid trickling down like dribble on to her chin. Her hands clenched and unclenched with the effort and she whispered, like a miracle, 'Ratna.'

My mother and I rushed to her bedside. Tears streaming down her face, my mother bent her head before her and pleaded, 'Give me your blessings, Pati. Bless me before you go.'

My great-grandmother looked at her for a minute, her lips working furiously, noiselessly. For the first time in my life I saw a fine veil of perspiration on her face. The muscles on her face twitched in mad, frenzied jerks. Then she pulled one arm free of the tubes, in a sudden, crazy spurt of strength, and the IV pole crashed to the floor.

'Bring me a red sari,' she screamed. 'A red one with a big wide border of gold. And,' her voice cracked, 'bring me peanuts with chilli powder from the corner shop. Onion and green chilli bondas deep-fried in oil.'

Then the voice gurgled and gurgled, her face and neck swayed, rocked like a boat lost in a stormy sea. She retched, and as the vomit flew out of her mouth, her nose, thick like the milkshakes she had drunk, brown like the alcoholic Coke, her head slumped forwards, her rounded chin buried in the cancerous neck.

When we brought the body home – I am not yet a doctor and already I can call her that – I helped my mother to wipe her clean with a wet, soft cloth. We wiped away the smells,

427

the smell of the hospital bed, the smell of an old woman's juices drying. Her skin was dry and papery. The stubble on her head – she had refused to shave her head once she got sick – had grown, like the soft, white bristles of a hairbrush.

She had had only one child though she had lived so long. But the skin on her stomach was like crumpled, frayed velvet, the creases running to and fro in fine, silvery rivulets.

'Bring her sari,' my mother whispered, as if my great-grandmother could still hear her.

I looked at the stiff, cold body that I was seeing naked for the first time. She was asleep at last, quiet at last. I had learnt, in the last month or two, to expect the unexpected from her. I waited, in case she changed her mind and sat up, remembering one more taboo food to be tasted.

'Bring me your eyebrow tweezers,' I heard her say. 'Bring me that hair-removing cream. I have a moustache and I don't want to be an ugly old woman.'

But she lay still, the wads of cotton in her nostrils and ears shutting us out. Shutting out her belated ardour.

I ran to my cupboard and brought her the brightest, reddest sari I could find: last year's Divali sari, my first silk. I unfolded it, ignoring my mother's eyes which were turning aghast. I covered her naked body lovingly. The red silk glittered like her childish laughter.

'Have you gone mad?' my mother whispered furiously. 'She was a sick old woman, she didn't know what she was saying.' She rolled up the sari and flung it aside, as if it had been polluted. She wiped the body again to free it from foolish, trivial desires.

They burnt her in a pale brown sari, her widow's weeds. The prayer beads I had never seen touch her encircled the bulging, obscene neck.

I am still a novice at anatomy. I hover just over the body, I am just beneath the skin. I have yet to look at the insides, the entrails of memories she told me nothing about, the pain congealing into a cancer.

She has left me behind with nothing but a smell, a legacy that grows fainter every day. I haunt the dirtiest bakeries and tea-stalls I can find every evening. I search for her, my sweet great-grandmother, in plate after plate of stale confections, in needle-sharp green chillies deep-fried in rancid oil. I plot her revenge for her, I give myself diarrhoea for a week.

Then I open all the windows and her cupboard and air the room. I tear her dirty grey saris to shreds. I line the shelves of her empty cupboard with my thick, newly bought, glossy-jacketed texts, one next to the other. They stand straight and solid, row after row of armed soldiers. They fill up the small cupboard in minutes.

Gita Mehta

THE TEACHER'S STORY

MASTER MOHAN WAS not a bitter man. Although he led an unhappy life, his gentle nature disposed him to small acts of kindness – helping a stranger to dismount from a rickshaw, reaching into his pockets to find a boiled sweet for a child – and when he walked down the narrow streets leading to the avenue where he boarded the tram that took him to his music students, he was greeted warmly by the neighbours sitting on their tiny verandas to catch the breeze.

'Good evening, Master Mohan.'

'A late class tonight?'

'Walk under the streetlights coming home, Master Mohan. These days one must be careful.'

Near the tram stop, the paanwallah smearing lime paste on to his paan leaves always shouted from inside his wooden stall, 'Master! Master! Let me give you a paan. A little betel leaf will help you through the pain of hearing your students sing.'

Even though it meant losing his place on the queue, Master Mohan stopped to talk to the paanwallah and listen to his gossip of the comings and goings in the quarter. And so he was the first to learn the great Quawwali singers from Nizamuddin were coming to Calcutta.

'You should ask Mohammed sahib to go with you. You are a teacher of music, he is a lover of poetry. And they are singing so close, in that mosque on the other side of the bazaar.'

Extract from *A River Sutra*.

'But my wife will not go even that far to hear —'

'Wives! Don't talk to me of wives. I never take mine anywhere. Nothing destroys a man's pleasure like a wife.'

Master Mohan knew the paanwallah was being kind. His wife's contempt for him was no secret on their street. The small houses were built on top of each other, and his wife never bothered to lower her voice. Everyone knew she had come from a wealthier family than his and could barely survive on the money he brought back from his music lessons.

'What sins did I commit in my last life that I should be yoked to this apology for a man? See how you are still called Master Mohan as if you were only ten years old. Gupta sahib you should be called. But who respects you enough to make even that small effort!'

Her taunts reopened a wound that might have healed if only Master Mohan's wife had left him alone. The music teacher had acquired the name of a child singer when he had filled concert halls with admirers applauding the purity of his voice. His father, himself a music teacher, had saved every paisa from his earnings to spend on Master Mohan's training, praying his son's future would be secured with a recording contract.

But it takes a very long time for a poor music teacher to cultivate connections with the owners of recording studios. For four years Master Mohan's father had pleaded for assistance from the wealthy families at whose houses his son sang on the occasion of a wedding or a birthday. For four years he had stood outside recording studios, muffling his coughs as tuberculosis ate away at his lungs, willing himself to stay alive until his son's talent was recognised, urging the boy to practice for that first record which would surely astonish the world.

When the recording contract was finally offered, only weeks before the record was to be made, Master Mohan's voice had broken.

Every day his wife reminded him how his voice had not mellowed in the years that followed. 'Your family has the evil eye. Whatever you touch is cursed, whatever you are given you lose.'

Sometimes Master Mohan tried to escape his wife's taunts by reminding himself of those four years of happiness that had preceded the moment when the golden bowl of his voice had shattered and with it his life. As her shrill insults went on and on, drilling into his brain, he found himself only able to remember his father's anguish that his son would have to abandon a great career as a singer, becoming just another music teacher like himself.

Master Mohan's father had made one last effort to help his son by engaging him in marriage to the daughter of a rich village landowner who loved music. He had lived long enough to see the marriage performed but not long enough to celebrate the birth of his two grandchildren, or to witness the avarice of his daughter-in-law when her own father died and her brothers took the family wealth, leaving her dependent on Master Mohan's earnings.

Prevented by pride from criticising her family, Master Mohan's wife had held her husband responsible for the treachery of her brothers, raising their children to believe it was only Master Mohan's weakness and stupidity that had robbed them of the servants, the cars, the fancy clothes from foreign countries that should have been their right.

'How can I ever forgive myself for burdening you with this sorry creature for a father? Come, Babloo, come, Dolly. Have some fruit. Let him make his own tea.'

With such exactitude had she perfected her cruelty that Master Mohan's children despised their father's music as they despised him, allying themselves with their mother's neglect.

After giving music lessons all day Master Mohan was left to cook a meagre meal for himself, which he took up to the small roof terrace of the house to escape his household's contempt. But he could not escape the blaring film music from the radio, or the loud noise of the gramophone echoing up the narrow stone stairwell leading to the terrace. It set him coughing, sometimes so loudly that his wife, or his daughter and son, would run up the stairs yelling at him to be quiet. Though he tried, Master Mohan could not stop coughing. It was a nervous reaction to his family's ability to silence the music he heard in his own head.

So when the paanwallah told him about the Quawwali singers, Master Mohan found himself day-dreaming on the tram. He had never heard the singers from Nizamuddin where Quawwali music had been born seven hundred years ago. But he knew Nizamuddin had been the fountain from which the poems and songs of the great Sufi mystics had flowed throughout India, and that even today its teachers still trained the finest Quawwali musicians in the country. He could not believe his good fortune – seven nights spent away from his wife and children listening to their music. And what is more, the music could be heard free.

On his way home that evening he stopped outside Mohammed sahib's house. Finding him on his veranda, Master Mohan asked shyly if he would be listening to the Quawwali singers.

'Only if you accompany me. I am a poor fool who never knows what he is hearing unless it is explained to him.'

So it was settled, and the next week Master Mohan hardly heard his wife and children shouting at him as he cooked himself a simple meal, relishing the taste of it while they listened to their noisy film music.

'Make sure you do not wake up the whole house when you return!' his wife shouted behind him as he slipped into the street.

By the time Master Mohan and Mohammed sahib reached the tent tethered to one side of the mosque, the singing had begun and curious bazaar children crowded at the entrances.

Mohammed sahib peered over their heads in disappointment. 'We are too late. There is nowhere for us to sit.'

Master Mohan refused to give up so easily. He squeezed past the children to look for a vacant place in the tent filled with people listening in rapt attention to the passionate devotional music breaking in waves over their heads.

He felt a familiar excitement as he led his friend to a small gap between the rows of people crushed against each other on the floor. The fluorescent lights winking from the struts supporting the tent, the musty odour of the cotton carpets covering the ground brought back the concerts of his childhood, and a constriction inside himself began to loosen.

On the podium nine performers sat cross-legged in a semicircle around a harmonium and a pair of tablas. An old sheikh from Nizamuddin sat to one side, his white beard disappearing into the loose robes flowing around him. Every now and then a spectator, moved by the music, handed the sheikh money, which he received as an offering to God before placing it near the tabla drums sending their throbbing beat into the night.

The more the singers were carried away by their music, the more Master Mohan felt the weight that burdened him lighten, as if the ecstasy of the song being relayed from one throat to another was lifting him into a long-forgotten ecstasy himself.

Twice Mohammed sahib got up to place money at the sheikh's feet. Master Mohan watched him stepping over crossed legs as he made his way to stage, ashamed his own poverty prevented him from expressing gratitude to the singers for reviving emotions that he had thought dead.

After two hours Mohammed sahib's funds and patience were exhausted, and he went home. Gradually the tent began to empty until only a few beggar children remained, asleep on the cotton carpets. Master Mohan looked at his watch. It was three o'clock in the morning.

In front of Master Mohan a young woman holding the hand of a child suddenly approached the podium to whisper to the sheikh. The sheikh leaned across to the singers wiping perspiration from their forehead.

The lead singer nodded wearily and the young woman pulled the child behind her up the stairs. The boy stumbled twice, struggling to recover his balance. Then he was on the podium, both hands stretched in front of him. Master Mohan realised the boy was blind as the woman pushed him down next to the singers.

The lead singer sang a verse. The other singers took up the chorus. The lead singer sang another verse, his arm extended to the boy who could not see him. The singers prodded him and the startled child entered the song two octaves above the others.

> *I prostrate my head to the blade of Your sword.*
> *O, the wonder of my submission.*
> *O, the wonder of Your protection.*

It was a sound Master Mohan had only heard in his dreams.

> *In the very spasm of death I see Your face.*
> *O, the wonder of Your protection.*
> *O, the wonder of my submission.*

Until this moment he had believed such purity of tone was something that could only be imagined but never realised by the human voice.

He crept forward until he was sitting by the young woman. 'Who is that child?' he asked.

The young woman turned a pleasant face pinched by worry to him. 'My brother, Imrat. This is the first song my father taught Imrat – the song of the children of the Nizamuddin Quawwali.'

Tears glistened in the large eyes. Under the fluorescent lights Master Mohan thought they magnified her eyes into immense pearls. 'Last year I brought Imrat with me to Calcutta to sell my embroidery. While we were here, terrible floods swept our village away. Our father, my husband, everybody was killed.'

Master Mohan glanced at the stage. The singers were already intoxicated by the power of their combined voices, unable to distinguish the singular voice of the child from all the other voices praising God.

> *Do not reveal the Truth in a world where blasphemy*
> *prevails.*
> *O wondrous Source of Mystery.*
> *O Knower of Secrets.*

The woman covered her face with her hands. 'I have been promised a job as a maidservant with a family who are leaving for the north of India, but I cannot take my brother because he is blind. I hope the sheikh will take Imrat to Nizamuddin until I can earn enough to send for him.'

Master Mohan felt tears welling in his own eyes as he heard the high voice sing.

> *I prostrate my head to the blade of Your sword.*
> *O, the wonder of your guidance.*
> *O, the wonder of my submission.*

The next evening Mohammed sahib confessed, 'I am not as musical as you, Master. God will forgive me for not accompanying you tonight.'

So Master Mohan went alone to hear the Quawwali singers. The young woman and the blind child were sitting under the podium, still there when the other spectators had gone.

He waited all evening, hoping to hear the child's pure voice again, but that night the boy did not join the singers on the stage. The following night and the next, Master Mohan was disappointed to see the young woman and her brother were not present at the Quawwali.

On the fourth night Master Mohan found himself the last listener to leave the tent. As he hurried through the deserted alleys of the dark bazaar, he heard someone calling behind him, 'Sahib, wait. For the love of Allah, listen to us.'

He turned under the solitary street lamp at the end of the bazaar. The woman was pulling the child past the shuttered shops towards him.

'Please, sahib. The Quawwali singers are travelling around India. They cannot take my brother with them, and in two days I must start work or lose my job. You have a kind face, sahib. Can you keep Imrat? He is a willing worker. He will do the sweeping or chop your vegetables. Just feed him and give him a place to sleep until I can send for him.'

A drunk stumbled towards the street lamp. 'What's the

woman's price, pimp? Offer me a bargain. She won't find another customer tonight.'

The woman shrank into the darkness clutching the child in her arms. 'For the love of Allah, sahib. Help us. We have nowhere to turn.'

To his astonishment Master Mohan heard himself saying, 'I am a music teacher. I will take your brother as my pupil. Now you must return to the safety of the mosque.'

The woman turned obediently into the dark alley. Master Mohan was grateful she could not see the expression on his face, or she must surely have recognised his fear at the offer he had made.

At the entrance to the tent he said, 'I will come tomorrow evening to fetch the child.'

The woman turned her face away to hide her gratitude, whispering, 'Please, sahib, I have a last request. See my brother follows the practices of Islam.'

The next morning Master Mohan went to the corner of the avenue to consult the paanwallah.

'You did what, Master? Do you know what your wife and children will do to that poor boy?'

'They would not harm a defenceless child!'

'Your wife will never permit you to keep the boy. Make some excuse to the sister. Get out of it somehow.'

As they argued Mohammed sahib joined them.

'I couldn't help myself,' Master Mohan pleaded. 'The girl was crying. If she loses her job, how will she feed herself and a blind brother? This is no city for a young woman alone.'

Mohammed sahib pulled at his moustache. 'You have done a very fine thing, my friend. Prohibit your wife from interfering in your affairs. It is you who feed and clothe your family and put a roof over their heads. Your decision as to who shall share that roof is final and irreversible.' He slapped Master Mohan on the back and turned towards the tram stop.

The paanwallah shook his head. 'That fellow is as puffed up as a peacock. It is easy for him to give advice when it costs him nothing. Don't go back for the child, Master.'

But Master Mohan could not betray the young woman's

trust, even when he returned to the tent that night and saw the sobbing boy clinging to his sister's legs. Master Mohan lifted the weeping child in his arms as the sister consoled her brother. 'I'll write often. Study hard with your kind teacher until I send for you. You'll hardly notice the time until we are together again.'

The child was asleep by the time Master Mohan reached his silent household. He crept up the stone stairs to the terrace and laid Imrat on the cloth mattress, pleased when the child rolled over on to his torn shawl and continued sleeping.

Well, you can imagine how his wife shrieked the next morning when she discovered what Master Mohan had done. As the days passed her rage did not diminish. In fact, it got worse. Each day Master Mohan returned from giving his music lessons in the city to find his wife waiting for him on the doorstep with fresh accusations about the blind boy's insolence, his clumsiness, his greed. She carried her attack into the kitchen when Master Mohan was trying to cook food for himself and Imrat, chasing behind him up the narrow stairwell so that everyone could hear her abuse raging over the rooftops.

When Master Mohan continued to refuse her demand that Imrat be thrown out into the street, Dolly and Babloo triumphantly joined in their mother's battle, complaining they no longer got enough to eat with another mouth sharing their food. In the evenings they placed their gramophone on the very top step of the stone staircase just outside the terrace, so the child could not hear the fragile drone of Master Mohan's tanpura strings giving the key for Imrat's music lesson. They teased Imrat by withholding his sister's letters, sometimes even tearing them up before Master Mohan had returned to the house and was able to read them to the waiting child.

Somehow Master Mohan discovered a strength in himself equal to the family's cruelty to Imrat. He arranged for the child's letters to be left with the paanwallah, and on the rare occasion when he entered the house and found his family gone to visit friends, he gently encouraged Imrat to stop cowering against the walls and become a child again. He would cook some special dish, letting the boy join in the preparations, encouraging him to eat his fill. Then he would take the child onto the roof terrace. After allowing his fingers to play over the strings of his tanpura until he found the note best suited to the boy's range, Master Mohan would ask Imrat to sing.

Hearing the clear notes pierce the night, Master Mohan knew he had been made guardian of something rare, as if his own life until now had only been a purification to ready him for the task of tending this voice for the world.

Then one day the music teacher returned late from giving a music lesson and found his daughter holding Imrat down while his son tried to force pork into the child's mouth. The child's sightless eyes were wide open, tears streaming down his cheeks. For the first time in his life Master Mohan struck his children. 'He's only nine years old. How can you torture a child so much younger than yourselves! Get out of this house until you learn civilised behaviour!'

With those words war was declared in Master Mohan's household. His wife accused Master Mohan of striking his own children out of preference for a blind beggar, unleashing such furious threats at the child that Master Mohan was worried Imrat would run away.

Mohammed-sahib would not agree to let Imrat live in his house, despite the music teacher's eloquent pleading. As he listened to Mohammed sahib's elaborate excuses, Master Mohan realised his friend wished to avoid the unpleasantness of dealing with his wife.

'I warned you, Master,' the paanwallah said with satisfaction when he heard of Mohammed sahib's response. 'That man is just good for free advice. Now there is only one thing to do. Go to the park in the early mornings. Only goats and shepherds will disturb you there. Don't give up, Master. After all, there is a whole world in which to practise, away from the distractions of your house.'

So the music teacher woke his young charge before dawn and they boarded the first tram of the morning to reach the great park that is the centre of Calcutta city.

When they arrived at the park, Master Mohan led Imrat by the hand between the homeless men and women wrapped in tattered cloths asleep under the great English oaks turning red each time the neon signs flashed, past the goatherds gossiping by their aluminium canisters until it was time to milk the goats grazing on the grass, toward the white balustrades that enclosed the marble mausoleum of the Victoria Memorial.

The music teacher lowered his cane mat and his tanpura over the side of the balustrade before gently lifting Imrat on to the wall. After climbing over himself, he lifted the child down, both so silent in the dark the guard asleep in his sentry box was left undisturbed.

With a swishing sound Master Mohan unrolled his cane mat, still smelling of green fields, and seated Imrat next to him.

Then he played the first notes of the morning raga on his tanpura. To his delight, Imrat repeated the scale faultlessly.

Master Mohan explained the significance of the raga, initiating Imrat into the mystery of the world's rebirth, when light disperses darkness and Vishnu rises from his slumbers to re-dream the universe.

Again Imrat sang the scale, but there was a new resonance in his voice. He could not see the faint blur of the picket fences ringing the race course in the distance, or the summit of Ochterlony's Needle breaking through the smoke from the illegal fires built by the street hawkers around the base of the obelisk. He could not even see the guard looking through his sentry box, his hand half-raised to expel them from the gardens, frozen in that gesture by the boy's voice. He only saw the power of the morning raga and, dreaming visions of light, he pushed his voice towards them, believing sight was only a half-tone away.

Afraid the raga would strain the child's voice, Master Mohan asked Imrat to sing a devotional song. The boy obediently turned his head towards the warmth of the sun's first rays and sang,

> *The heat of Your presence*
>   *Blinds my eyes.*
>   *Blisters my skin.*
>   *Shrivels my flesh.*
>
> *Do not turn in loathing from me.*
>   *O Beloved, can You not see*
>   *Only Love disfigures me?*

Master Mohan patted Imrat's head. 'That is a beautiful prayer. Where did you learn such a song?'

Tears clouded the clouded eyes. 'It is a poem by Amir Rumi. My father said that one day he and I would sing it at Amir Rumi's tomb together.'

The music teacher took the child in his arms. 'You will still sing at Amir Rumi's tomb, I promise you. And your father will hear your voice from heaven. Come, sing it once more so I can listen properly.'

The child blew his nose and again shocked the music teacher with power of his voice.

> *Do not turn in loathing from me.*
>   *O Beloved, can You not see*
>   *Only Love disfigures me?*

At that moment a sudden belief took root in Master Mohan's mind. He was convinced God was giving him a second voice, greater than he had ever heard, greater than his own could ever have been. He was certain such a voice must only be used to praise God, lest fate exact a second revenge by robbing him of it.

Sure of his purpose as a teacher at last, Master Mohan asked the boy, 'Did your father ever teach you the prayers of Kabir? Do you know this hymn?'

He played some notes on his tanpura and Imrat responded with excitement, opening his throat full to contain the mystic's joy.

> *O servant, where do you seek Me?*
> *You will not find Me in temple or mosque,*
> *In Kaaba or in Kailash,*
> *In yoga or renunciation.*
> *Sings Kabir, 'O seeker, find God*
> *In the breath of all breathing.'*

And now a most extraordinary thing happened. Someone threw a coin over the wall, and it fell on the grass in front of Master Mohan. The music teacher stood up. On the other side of the balustrades, just visible in the first light of dawn, he saw a group of goatherds leaning on the wall.

By the next morning people were already waiting for them, and the guard waved Master Mohan and Imrat benevolently through the gate. Word had spread in the park that a blind boy with the voice of an angel was singing in the gardens of the Victoria Memorial. In the darkness goatherds, street hawkers, refugees with children huddled to their bodies, waited patiently for Imrat to practise the scales of the morning raga before Master Mohan permitted him to sing the devotional songs that would give them the endurance to confront the indignities of their lives for another day.

Morning after morning they listened to the music teacher instruct Imrat in the songs of Kabir and Mirabai, of Khusrau and Tulsidas, of Chisti and Chandidas, the wandering poets and mystics who had made India's soul visible to herself. Sometimes they even asked the boy to repeat a song, and Master Mohan could see them responding to the purity of the lyrics translated with such innocence by Imrat's voice.

To show their gratitude they began to leave small offerings on the wall above the balustrade: fruit, coins, a few crumpled rupees. And when the morning lesson ended, the street vendors crowded around Master Mohan and Imrat to offer a glass of steaming sweet tea or a hot samosa straight off a scalding iron pan.

Within a week Imrat's audience had expanded. Wealthy people on their morning walks stopped at the balustrade, drawn by the beauty of Imrat singing.

Some seek God in Mecca.
Some seek God in Benares.
 Each finds his own path and the focus of his worship.

Some worship Him in Mecca.
Some in Benares.
 But I centre my worship on the eyebrow of my Beloved.

Over the weeks more and more people made the balustrade part of their morning routines, until Master Mohan was able to recognise many faces at the wall, and every day he smiled at a young woman who folded a ten-rupee note, placing it in a crevice in the parapet.

When they dismounted from the tram, the paanwallah shouted his congratulations to fortify them against the raging wife waiting at the music teacher's house.

'Well, little Master Imrat. Your fame is spreading throughout Calcutta. Soon you will be rich. How much money did you make today?'

'Thirteen rupees.' Imrat pulled the music teacher towards the sound of the paanwallah's voice. 'How much have we got now?'

'Still a long way to go, Master Imrat. But here is another letter from your sister.'

The paanwallah kept Imrat's money so Master Mohan's wife would not take it. It was Imrat's dream to earn enough money by his singing to live with his sister again, and each time she wrote he sang with renewed force.

Perhaps it was the fervour in Imrat's voice the morning after he had received another letter from his sister that made the miracle happen.

As Imrat was ending his song a man in blazer shouted, 'Come on, come on, my good fellow. I haven't got all morning. Do you read English?'

The music teacher put down his tanpura and walked to the balustrade. The man handed him a paper without even looking at him, turning to the woman at his side. 'Does the boy have a name or not? Can't sign a recording contract without a name.'

Master Mohan pulled himself to his full height in defence of the child's dignity although the man in the blazer had his back to him. 'He is blind and cannot read or write. But I am his guardian. I can sign for him.'

'Jolly good. Turn up at the studio this afternoon so the engineers can do a preliminary test. That's what you want isn't it, Neena?'

His companion lifted her face and Master Mohan saw she was the woman who left ten rupees on the wall every day.

She smiled at Master Mohan's recognition. 'Is this gifted child your son?'

Master Mohan shyly told her the story of Imrat, suppressing anything that might reflect well on himself, only praising the boy's talent. He could see the interest in her eyes, but the man was pulling at her elbow. 'Fascinating, fascinating. Well, be sure to be at the studio at four o'clock. The address is on the contract.'

Master Mohan studied the paper. 'It says nothing here about payment.'

'Payment?' For the first time the man in the blazer looked at him. 'Singing for coppers in the park and you dare ask for payment?'

'We are not beggars.' Master Mohan could not believe his own temerity. 'I am a music teacher. I give the boy his lessons here so as not to disturb our household.'

The woman laid her hand on the man's arm. 'Don't be such a bully, Ranjit. Offer him a thousand rupees. You'll see it is a good investment.'

The man laughed indulgently. 'You are the most demanding sister a man ever had. Here, give me that paper.' He pulled a pen from his blazer and scribbled down the sum, signing his name after it.

Master Mohan folded the paper and put it carefully in his pocket. When he looked up he saw two men watching him from the other side of the wall. Their oiled hair and stained teeth frightened him, bringing back memories of the musicians who had waited outside the great houses where he had sung as a child, until the menfolk sent for the dancing girls who often did not even dance before musicians such as these led them to the bedrooms.

On their way home Imrat lifted his blind eyes to his teacher and whispered, 'But how much money is a thousand rupees? Enough to find somewhere to live with you and my sister?'

The music teacher hugged the child. 'If the record is a success you can be together with your sister. Now try and rest. This afternoon you must not be tired.'

As they dismounted from the tram the paanwallah shouted, 'Last night two musicians were asking about you, Master. Did they come to hear Imrat today?'

Imrat interrupted the paanwallah. 'We are going to make a record and get lots of money.'

'A record, Master Imrat! Be sure you sing well. Then I will buy a gramophone to listen to you.'

It was no surprise to Master Mohan that Imrat sang as he did that afternoon. The child could not see the microphone dangling from the wire covered with flies or the bored faces watching him behind the glass panel. He only saw himself in his sister's embrace, and when the recording engineer ordered him to sing the studio reverberated with his joy.

'The boy has recording genius,' an engineer admitted reluctantly as Imrat ended his song. 'His timing is so exact we can print these as they are.'

His colleague switched off the microphone. 'Ranjit-sahib will be very pleased. I'll call him.'

A few minutes later the man in the blazer strode into the office followed by his engineers. 'Well done, young man. Now my sister will give me some peace at last. She has done nothing but talk about you since she first heard you sing.'

He patted Imrat's head. 'Come back in ten days. If the engineers are right and we do not have to make another recording, I will give you a thousand rupees. What will a little chap like you do with so much money?'

But he was gone before Imrat could reply.

Master Mohan dared not hope for anything until the record was made. To prevent the child from believing too fervently that he would soon be reunited with his sister, the music teacher continued Imrat's lessons in the park, trying not to feel alarm when he saw the same two men always at the balustrade, smiling at him, nodding their heads in appreciation of Imrat's phrasing.

One day the men followed Master Mohan and Imrat to the tram, waiting until they were alone before approaching the music teacher with their offer.

'A great sahib wants to hear the boy sing.'

'No, no. We are too busy.' Master Mohan pushed Imrat before him. 'The boy is making his first record. He must practise.'

'Don't be a fool,' brother. The sahib will pay handsomely to listen to his voice.'

'Five thousand rupees, brother. Think of it.'

'But your sahib can hear the child free every morning in the park.'

They laughed and Master Mohan felt the old fear when he saw their betel-stained teeth. 'Great men do not stand in a crowd, snatching their pleasure from the breeze, brother. They indulge their pleasures in the privacy of palaces.'

'He must finish his recording first.'

'Naturally. But after that . . .'

'We will be here every morning, Master.'

'You will not escape us.'

To Master Mohan's dismay the men waited each day at the park, leaning against the parapet until Imrat's small crowd of admirers had dispersed before edging up to the blind boy.

'Please, little Master Imrat, take pity on a man who worships music.'

'The sahib's responsibilities prevented him from following his own calling as a singer.'

'He could have been a great singer like you, Master Imrat, if he had not been forced to take care of his family business.'

Master Mohan could see the smirking expressions on the faces of the two men as they tried to ingratiate themselves with Imrat.

'To hear you sing will relieve the pain of his own heart, denied what he has most loved in his life.'

'If you sing well he will give you leaves from Tansen's

tamarind tree to make your voice as immortal as Tansen's.'

Master Mohan knew these men had once learned music as Imrat was doing now, until poverty had reduced them to pandering to the vices and whims of wealthy men. Even as he despised them he was relieved that Imrat's record would save him from such a life.

Now they turned their attention on Master Mohan.

'We have told the great sahib this boy has a voice that is heard only once in five hundred years.'

'The sahib is a man of influence, brother. Perhaps he can arrange to have the boy invited to the Calcutta Music Festival.'

The music teacher felt dizzy even imagining that his blind charge, who had been no better than a beggar only eight months ago, might be invited to sing in the company of India's maestros. The great singing teachers always attended the festival. One might even offer to train Imrat's pure voice, taking it to a perfection that had not been heard since Tansen himself sang before the Great Moghul. He nearly agreed but controlled himself enough to say again, 'You must wait until the boy completes his recording.'

Fortunately he did not have to think long about the temptation offered by the two men.

On the day he took Imrat back to the recording studio, the young woman was also present in the office, seated on an armchair opposite her brother's desk.

'I played this record for the director of the radio station. He thinks Master Imrat has great promise, and must be taught by the best teachers available. A talent like his should not be exposed to the dust and germs in the park. There are empty rooms above one of our garages. He must live there.'

The woman put her arm around the boy. 'Wouldn't you like to stay with me? Your sister could work in my house and your teacher would come to see you every day.'

The boy nodded happily, and she handed two copies of the record and an envelope of money to Master Mohan. 'So it is settled. As soon as his sister reaches Calcutta they will both move into my house.'

Master Mohan took the records but left the envelope of money in the woman's hand for Imrat's sister.

'Are we to be given nothing for feeding and clothing this changeling you brought into our home?' Master Mohan's wife screamed when she learned her husband had left the boy's money with the studio owner. 'What about the whole year we have kept him, restricting our own lives so he could become rich? Are your own children to receive nothing out of this, only blows and abuses?'

Her fury increased when Imrat's record was released and proved immediately popular.

In the weeks that followed, the record was played over and over again on the radio by enthusiastic programmers. While Imrat waited for his sister to send news of her arrival in Calcutta, Master Mohan was informed by the recording studio that Imrat's record was disappearing from the record shops as fast as new copies could be printed.

Now his wife's rage was inflamed by jealousy. She could hear Imrat's record being played everywhere in the bazaars. Even the paanwallah had brought a gramophone to his stall, storing it behind the piles of wet leaves at his side. Each time a customer bought a paan the paanwallah cranked the machine and placed the record on the turntable, boasting, 'I advised the music teacher to adopt the child. Even though he was only a blind beggar, I was able to recognise the purity of his voice immediately.'

A week before Imrat's sister was due to arrive in Calcutta, the music teacher's wife learned from Mohammed sahib that her husband had refused to let Imrat perform at the home of a great sahib.

'And he was offering the sum of five thousand rupees to listen to the blind boy,' Mohammed sahib said in awe.

'Five thousand rupees!' Master Mohan's wife shrieked. 'He turned down five thousand rupees when his own children do not have enough to eat and nothing to wear! Where can I find those men?'

That night the music teacher helped Imrat into the house. To his distress, he found his wife entertaining the two men who had come so often to the park.

She waved a sheaf of notes in Master Mohan's face. 'I have agreed the brat will sing before the sahib tonight. See, they have already paid me. Five thousand rupees will cover a little of what I have spent on this blind beggar over the last year.'

The music teacher tried to object but Imrat intruded on his argument. 'I am not tired, Master sahib.'

'Waited on hand and foot by our entire household! Why should you be tired?' She grabbed the boy's arm. 'I'm coming myself to make sure you sing properly to pay for all the meals you have eaten at our table.'

The two men smiled victoriously at the music teacher. 'Our rickshaws are waiting at the corner of the street.'

As they rode to the great sahib's house, Master Mohan felt tears on his cheeks. In a week Imrat would be gone, leaving him imprisoned again in his hateful household. He hugged Imrat to his chest, his sighs lost in the rasping breath of the man straining between the wooden shafts of the rickshaw.

At the high iron gates of a mansion the rickshaws halted. A guard opened the gates and Master Mohan's wife seized Imrat's arm, pulling him roughly behind her as servants ushered them through a series of dimly lit chambers into a dark room empty of furniture.

Wooden shutters sealed the French doors on either side of the room, and large patches of paint peeled from the walls. The floor was covered by a Persian carpet that extended from the door to a raised platform. Above the platform two unused chandeliers hung from the ceiling, shrouded in muslin-like corpses.

A man sat on the platform, his size exaggerated by the candles burning on either side of him. The musicians bowed to him obsequiously. The sahib ignored them. Still smiling, the musicians climbed on to the platform where a harmonium and drums were placed in readiness for the concert.

'Come here, little master,' the great sahib said. 'I am told you have a voice such as India has not heard for hundreds of years.'

Master Mohan's wife released her hold on the boy, and the

music teacher led him to the platform, grateful that Imrat could not see this empty room with its sealed wooden shutters and the shadows flickering on the peeling walls.

As he helped him up the stairs, the music teacher whispered in Imrat's ear, 'Only sing the two songs from your record. Then we can go home.'

'Soon I will be with my sister again,' Imrat answered in a whisper as Master Mohan gently pushed him down in front of the two musicians. 'Tonight I must thank Allah for his kindness.'

For a few minutes only the music of the harmonium echoed through the heavy shadows of the room, and Master Mohan could feel his wife shifting restlessly from foot to foot at his side. Then Imrat's clear voice pierced the darkness.

> *I prostrate my head to Your drawn sword.*
> *O, the wonder of Your kindness.*
> *O, the wonder of my submission.*

> *Do not reveal the Truth in a world where*
> *blasphemy prevails.*
> *O wondrous Source of Mystery.*
> *O Knower of Secrets.*

The boy's sightless eyes seemed fixed on infinity, and it seemed to Master Mohan that the candles in the shrouded chandeliers were leaping into flame, ignited by Imrat's innocent devotion as he sang.

> *In the very spasm of death I see Your face.*
> *O, the wonder of my submission.*
> *O, the wonder of Your protection.*

Listening to the purity of each note, Master Mohan felt himself being lifted into another dimension, into the mystic raptures of the Sufis who were sometimes moved to dance by such music. For the first time he understood why the Sufis believed that once a man began to dance in the transport of his ecstasy, the singers must continue until the man stopped dancing lest the sudden breaking of the dancer's trance should kill him.

> *The heat of Your presence*
>   *Blinds my eyes.*
>   *Blisters my skin.*
>   *Shrivels my flesh.*

The great sahib rose to his feet. Master Mohan wondered if the great sahib was about to dance as music poured out of that young throat which carried in it too great a knowledge of the world.

> *The heat of Your presence*
>   *Blinds my eyes.*
>   *Blisters my skin.*
>
> *Do not turn in loathing from me.*
> *O Beloved, can You not see*
> *Only Love disfigures me.*

In the flickering light of the candles Master Mohan thought he saw something glint in the sahib's hand. The musicians were smiling ingratiatingly, waiting for the great sahib to circle the boy's head with money before flinging it to them. Now Master Mohan could not see Imrat, dwarfed by the shadow of the man standing in front of him as he sang again,

> *I prostrate my head to Your drawn sword.*
>   *O, the wonder of Your kindness.*
>   *O, the wonder of my submission.*
>
> *Do not reveal the Truth in a world where*
>   *blasphemy prevails.*
> *O wondrous Source of Mystery.*
> *O Knower of Secrets.*

The great sahib turned around and Master Mohan thought

451

he saw tears on his cheeks. 'Such a voice is not human. What will happen to music if this is the standard by which God judges us?'

Imrat was not listening, intoxicated by the power issuing from his own throat.

> *In the very spasm of death I see Your face.*
> *O, the wonder of my submission.*
> *O, the wonder of Your protection . . .*

Master Mohan could hear his wife cursing. He did not know his own screams echoed the blind boy's as he screamed and screamed and screamed.

Vikram Seth

A SUITABLE BOY

LATA ARRIVED AT 20 Hastings Road at five o'clock the next day. She had finished her last paper that morning. She was convinced she had not done well in it, but when she started to feel upset, she thought of Kabir and instantly cheered up. Now she looked around for him among the group of about fifteen men and women who were sitting in old Mr Nowrojee's drawing-room – the room in which the weekly meetings of the Brahmpur Literary Society had been held from as far back as anyone could remember. But either Kabir had not yet arrived or else he had changed his mind about coming.

The room was full of stuffed chairs with flowery prints and overstuffed cushions with flowery prints.

Mr Nowrojee, a thin, short and gentle man, with an immaculate white goatee beard and an immaculate light grey suit, presided over the occasion. Noticing that Lata was a new face, he introduced himself and made her feel welcome. The others, who were sitting or standing in small groups, paid no attention to her. Feeling awkward at first, she walked over to a window and gazed out towards a small, well-tended garden with a sundial in the middle. She was looking forward so much to seeing him that she vehemently pushed aside the thought that he might not turn up.

'Good afternoon, Kabir.'

'Good afternoon, Mr Nowrojee.'

Lata turned around at the mention of Kabir's name and the

Extracts from the novel *A Suitable Boy*.

sound of his low, pleasant voice, and gave him such a happy smile that he put his hand to his forehead and staggered back a few steps.

Lata did not know what to make of his buffoonery, which luckily no one had noticed. Mr Nowrojee was now seated at the oblong table at the end of the room and was coughing mildly for attention. Lata and Kabir sat down on an empty sofa near the wall farthest from the table. Before they could say anything to each other, a middle-aged man with a plump, bright-eyed, cheerful face handed them each a sheaf of carbon copies which appeared to be covered with poetry.

'Makhijani,' he said mysteriously as he passed.

Mr Nowrojee took a sip of water from one of the three glasses in front of him. 'Fellow members of the Brahmpur Literary Society – and friends,' he said in a voice that barely carried to where Lata and Kabir were sitting, 'we have gathered here for the 1,698th meeting of our society. I now declare the meeting open.'

He looked wistfully out of the window, and rubbed his glasses with a handkerchief. Then he continued: 'I remember when Edmund Blunden addressed us. He said – and I remember his words to this very day – he said –'

Mr Nowrojee stopped, coughed, and looked down at the sheet of paper in front of him. His skin itself appeared to be as thin as paper.

He went on: '1,698th meeting. Poetry recitation of their own poetry by members of the society. Copies, I see, have been handed out. Next week Professor O. P. Mishra of the English Department will present to us a paper on the subject: "Eliot: Whither?"'

Lata, who enjoyed Professor Mishra's lectures despite the pinkness with which he was now invested in her mind, looked interested, though the title was a bit mystifying.

'Three poets will be reading from their own work today,' continued Mr Nowrojee, 'following which I hope you will join us for tea. I am sorry to see that my young friend Mr Sorabjee has not been able to make the time to come,' he added in tones of gentle rebuke.

Mr Sorabjee, fifty-seven years old, and – like Mr Nowrojee himself – a Parsi, was the Proctor of Brahmpur University. He rarely missed a meeting of the literary societies of either the university or the town. But he always managed to avoid meetings where members read out their own literary efforts.

Mr Nowrojee smiled indecisively. 'The poets reading today are Dr Vikas Makhijani, Mrs Supriya Joshi –'

'Shrimati Supriya Joshi,' said a booming female voice. The broad-bosomed Mrs Joshi had stood up to make the correction.

'Er, yes, our, er, talented poetess Shrimati Supriya Joshi – and, of course, myself, Mr R. P. Nowrojee. As I am already seated at the table I will avail myself of the chairman's prerogative of reading my own poems first – by way of an apéritif to the more substantial fare that is to follow. *Bon appétit.*' He allowed himself a sad, rather wintry, chuckle before clearing his throat and taking another sip of water.

'The first poem that I would like to read is entitled "Haunting Passion",' said Mr Nowrojee primly. And he read the following poem:

> I'm haunted by a tender passion,
>> The ghost of which will never die.
> The leaves of autumn have grown ashen:
> I'm haunted by a tender passion.
> And spring-time too, in its own fashion,
>> Burns me with love's sweet song – so I –
> I'm haunted by a tender passion,
>> The ghost of which will never die.

As Mr Nowrojee completed his poem, he seemed to be manfully holding back his tears. He looked out towards the garden, towards the sundial, and, pulling himself together, said: 'That is a triolet. Now I will read you a ballade. It is called "Buried Flames".'

After he had read this and three other poems in a similar vein with diminishing vigour, he stopped, spent of all emotion. He then got up like one who had completed an infinitely distant and exhausting journey, and sat down on a stuffed chair not far from the speaker's table.

In the brief interval between him and the next reader Kabir looked inquiringly at Lata and she looked quizzically back at him. They were both trying to control their laughter, and looking at each other was not helping them do this.

Luckily, the happy, plump-faced man who had handed them the poems that he planned to read now rushed forward energetically to the speaker's table and, before sitting down, said the single word: 'Makhijani.'

After he had announced his name, he looked even more delighted than before. He riffled through his sheaf of papers with an expression of intense and pleasurable concentration, then smiled at Mr Nowrojee, who shrank in his chair like a sparrow cowering in a niche before a gale. Mr Nowrojee had tried at one stage to dissuade Dr Makhijani from reading, but had met with such good-natured outrage that he had had to give in. But having read a copy of the poems earlier in the day, he could not help wishing that the banquet had ended with the apéritif.

'A Hymn to Mother India,' said Dr Makhijani sententiously, then beamed at his audience. He leaned forward with the concentration of a burly blacksmith and read his poem through, including the stanza numbers, which he hammered out like horseshoes.

1. Who a child has not seen drinking milk
    At bright breasts of Mother, rags she wears or silks?
    Love of mild Mother like rain-racked gift of cloud.
    In poet's words, Mother to thee I bow.

2. What poor gift when doctor patient treats.
    Hearts he hears but so much his heart bleats?
    Where is doctor that can cure my pains?
    Why suffers Mother? Where to base the blame?

3. Her raiments rain-drenched with May or Monsoon,
    Like Savitri sweet she wins from Yama her sons,
    Cheating death with millions of population,
    Leading to chaste and virtuous nation.

4. From shore of Kanyakumari to Kashmir,
   From tiger of Assam to rampant beast of Gir,
   Freedom's dawn now bathing, laving her face,
   Tremble of jetty locks is Ganga's grace.

5. How to describe bondage of Mother pure
   By pervert punies chained through shackles of law?
   British cut-throat, Indian smiling and slave:
   Such shame will not dispense till a sweating grave.

While reading the above stanza, Dr Makhijani became highly
agitated, but he was restored to equanimity by the next one:

6. Let me recall history of heroes proud,
   Mother-milk fed their breasts, who did not bow.
   Fought they fiercely, carrying worlds of weight,
   Establishing firm foundation of Indian state.

Nodding at the nervous Mr Nowrojee, Dr Makhijani now
lauded his namesake, one of the fathers of the Indian freedom
movement:

7. Dadabhai Naoroji entered Parliament,
   As MP from Finsbury, grace was heaven-scent.
   But he forgot not Mother's plumpy breasts:
   Dreams were of India, living in the West.

Lata and Kabir looked at each other in mingled delight and
horror.

8. B. G. Tilak from Maharashtra hailed.
   'Swaraj my birthright is' he ever wailed.
   But cruel captors sent him to the sweltry jail
   In Forts of Mandalay, a six-year sail.

9. Shame of the Mother bold Bengal reviled.
   Terrorist pistol in hand of the Kali child.
   Draupadi's sari twirling off and off –
   White Duryodhanas laugh to scorn and scoff.

Dr Makhijani's voice trembled with belligerence at these vivid lines. Several stanzas later he descended on figures of the immediate past and present:

26. Mahatma came to us like summer 'andhi',
    Sweeping the dungs and dirt, was M. K. Gandhi.
    Murder has mayhemed peace beyond understanding.
    Respect and sorrow leave me soiled and standing.

At this point Dr Makhijani stood up as a mark of veneration, and remained standing for the final three stanzas:

27. Then when the British left after all,
    We had as PM our own Jawahar Lal.
    Like rosy shimmers to the throne he came,
    And gave to our India a glorious name.

28. Muslim, Hindu, Sikh, Christian, revere him.
    Parsis, Jains, Buddhists also endear him.
    Cynosure of eyes, he stalks with regal mien
    Breathing spirit of a splendid scene.

29. We are all masters, each a Raja or Rani.
    No slave, or high or low, says Makhijani.
    Liberty equality fraternity justice as in Constitution.
    In homage of Mother we will find all solutions.

In the tradition of Urdu or Hindi poetry, the bard had imbedded his own name in the last stanza. He now sat down, wiping the sweat from his forehead, and beaming.

Kabir had been scribbling a note. He passed it on to Lata; their hands touched accidentally. Though she was in pain with her attempt to suppress her laughter, she felt a shock of excitement at his touch. It was he who, after a few seconds, moved his hand away, and she saw what he had written:

Prompt escape from 20 Hastings Road
Is my desire, although prized poets' abode.
Desert not friendship. Renegade with me
From raptured realm of Mr Nowrojee.

It was not quite up to Dr Makhijani's efforts, but it got its point across. Lata and Kabir, as if at a signal, got up quickly and, before they could be intercepted by a cheated Dr Makhijani, got to the front door.

Out on the sober street they laughed delightedly for a few minutes, quoting back at each other bits of Dr Makhijani's patriotic hymn. When the laughter had died down, Kabir said to her: 'How about a coffee? We could go the Blue Danube.'

Lata, worried that she might meet someone she knew and, already thinking of Mrs Rupa Mehra, said, 'No, I really can't. I have to go back home. To my mother,' she added mischievously.

Kabir could not take his eyes off her.

'But your exams are over,' he said. 'You should be celebrating. It's I who have two papers left.'

'I wish I could. But meeting you here has been a pretty bold step for me.'

'Well, won't we at least meet here again next week? For "Eliot: Whither?"' Kabir made an airy gesture, rather like a foppish courtier, and Lata smiled.

'But are you going to be in Brahmpur next Friday?' she asked. 'The holidays . . .'

'Oh yes,' said Kabir. 'I live here.'

He was unwilling to say goodbye, but did so at last.

'See you next Friday then – or before,' he said, getting onto his bike. 'Are you sure I can't drop you anywhere – on my bicycle made for two? Smudged or unsmudged, you do look beautiful.'

Lata looked around, blushing.

'No, I'm sure. Goodbye,' she said. 'And – well – thank you.'

When Lata got home she avoided her mother and sister and went straight to the bedroom. She lay on her bed and stared at the ceiling just as, a few days before, she had lain on the grass and stared at the sky through the jacaranda branches. The accidental touch of his hand as he had passed her the note was what she most wanted to recall.

Later, during dinner, the phone rang. Lata, sitting closest to the telephone, went to pick up the receiver.

'Hello?' said Lata.

'Hello – Lata?' said Malati.

'Yes,' said Lata happily.

'I've found out a couple of things. I'm going away tonight for a fortnight, so I thought I'd better tell you at once. Are you by yourself?' Malati added cautiously.

'No,' said Lata.

'Will you be by yourself within the next half-hour or so?'

'No, I don't think so,' said Lata.

'It isn't good news, Lata,' said Malati, seriously. 'You had better drop him.'

Lata said nothing.

'Are you still there?' asked Malati, concerned.

'Yes,' said Lata, glancing at the other three seated around the dining table. 'Go on.'

'Well, he's on the university cricket team,' said Malati, reluctant to break the ultimate bad news to her friend. 'There's a photograph of the team in the university magazine.'

'Yes?' said Lata, puzzled. 'But what –'

'Lata,' said Malati, unable to beat about the bush any further. 'His surname is Durrani.'

So what? thought Lata. What does that make him? Is he a Sindhi or something? Like – well – Chetwani or Advani – or . . . Makhijani?

'He's a Muslim,' said Malati, cutting into her thoughts. 'Are you still there?'

Lata was staring straight ahead. Savita put down her knife and fork, and looked anxiously at her sister.

Malati continued: 'You haven't a chance. Your family will be dead set against him. Forget him. Put it down to experience. And always find out the last name of anyone with an ambiguous first name . . . Why don't you say something? Are you listening?'

'Yes,' said Lata, her heart in turmoil.

She had a hundred questions, and more than ever she

needed her friend's advice and sympathy and help. She said, slowly and evenly, 'I'd better go now. We're in the middle of dinner.'

Malati said, 'It didn't occur to me – it just didn't occur to me – but didn't it occur to you either? With a name like that – though all the Kabirs I know are Hindu – Kabir Bhandare, Kabir Sondhi –'

'It didn't occur to me,' said Lata. 'Thanks, Malu,' she added, using the form of Malati's name she sometimes used out of affection. 'Thank you for – well –'

'I'm so sorry. Poor Lata.'

'No. See you when you return.'

'Read a P. G. Wodehouse or two,' said Malati by way of parting advice. 'Bye.'

'Bye,' said Lata and put down the receiver carefully.

She returned to the table but she could not eat. Mrs Rupa Mehra immediately tried to find out what the matter was. Savita decided not to say anything at all for the moment. Pran looked on, puzzled.

'It's nothing,' Lata said, looking at her mother's anxious face.

After dinner, she went to the bedroom. She couldn't bear to talk with the family or listen to the late news on the radio. She lay face down on her bed and burst into tears – as quietly as she could – repeating his name with love and with angry reproach.

Mrs Rupa Mehra came breathlessly through the door.

She had been crying in the tonga. The tonga-wallah, concerned that such a decently dressed lady should be weeping so openly, had tried to keep up a monologue in order to pretend that he hadn't noticed, but she had now gone through not only her embroidered handkerchief but her reserve handkerchief as well.

'Oh my daughter!' she said, 'oh, my daughter.'

Savita said, 'Yes, Ma?' She was shocked to see her mother's tear-streaked face.

'Not you,' said Mrs Rupa Mehra. 'Where is that shameless Lata?'

Savita sensed that their mother had discovered something. But what? And how much? She moved instinctively towards her mother to calm her down.

'Ma, sit down, calm down, have some tea,' said Savita, guiding Mrs Rupa Mehra, who seemed quite distracted, to her favourite armchair.

'Tea! Tea! More and more tea!' said Mrs Rupa Mehra in resistant misery.

Savita went and told Mateen to get some tea for the two of them.

'Where is she? What will become of us all? Who will marry her now?'

'Ma, don't over-dramatise things,' said Savita soothingly. 'It will blow over.'

Mrs Rupa Mehra sat up abruptly. 'So you knew! You knew! And you didn't tell me. And I had to learn this from strangers.' This new betrayal engendered a new bout of sobbing. Savita squeezed her mother's shoulders, and offered her another handkerchief. After a few minutes of this, Savita said:

'Don't cry, Ma, don't cry. What did you hear?'

'Oh, my poor Lata – is he from a good family? I had a sense something was going on. Oh God! What would her father have said if he had been alive? Oh, my daughter.'

'Ma, his father teaches mathematics at the university. He's a decent boy. And Lata's a sensible girl.'

Mateen brought the tea in, registered the scene with deferential interest, and went back towards the kitchen.

Lata walked in a few seconds later. She had taken a book to the banyan grove, where she had sat down undisturbed for a while, lost in Wodehouse and her own enchanted thoughts. Two more days, one more day, and she would see Kabir again.

She was unprepared for the scene before her, and stopped in the doorway.

'Where have you been, young lady?' demanded Mrs Rupa Mehra, her voice quivering with anger.

'For a walk,' faltered Lata.

'Walk? Walk?' Mrs Rupa Mehra's voice rose to a crescendo. 'I'll give you walk.'

Lata's mouth flew open, and she looked at Savita. Savita shook both her head and her right hand slightly, as if to say that it was not she who had given her away.

'Who is he?' demanded Mrs Rupa Mehra. 'Come here. Come here at once.'

Lata looked at Savita. Savita nodded.

'Just a friend,' said Lata, approaching her mother.

'Just a friend! A friend! And friends are for holding hands with? Is this what I brought you up for? All of you – and is this –'

'Ma, sit down,' said Savita, for Mrs Rupa Mehra had half risen out of her chair.

'Who told you?' asked Lata. 'Hema's Taiji?'

'Hema's Taiji? Hema's Taiji? Is she in this too?' exclaimed Mrs Rupa Mehra with new indignation. 'She lets those girls run around all over the place with flowers in their hair in the evening. Who told me? The wretched girl asks me who told me. No one told me. It's the talk of the town, everyone knows about it. Everyone thought you were a good girl with a good reputation – and now it is too late. Too late,' she sobbed.

'Ma, you always say Malati is such a nice girl,' said Lata by way of self-defence. 'And she has friends like that – you know that – everyone knows that.'

'Be quiet! Don't answer me back! I'll give you two tight slaps. Roaming around shamelessly near the dhobi-ghat and having a gala time.'

'But Malati –'

'Malati! Malati! I'm talking about you, not about Malati. Studying medicine and cutting up frogs –' Mrs Rupa Mehra's voice rose once more. 'Do you want to be like her? And lying to your mother. I'll never let you go for a walk again. You'll stay in this house, do you hear? Do you hear?' Mrs Rupa Mehra had stood up.

'Yes, Ma,' said Lata, remembering with a twinge of shame that she had had to lie to her mother in order to meet Kabir.

The enchantment was being torn apart; she felt alarmed and miserable.

'What's his name?'

'Kabir,' said Lata, growing pale.

'Kabir what?'

Lata stood still and didn't answer. A tear rolled down her cheek.

Mrs Rupa Mehra was in no mood for sympathy. What were all these ridiculous tears? She caught hold of Lata's ear and twisted it. Lata gasped.

'He has a name, doesn't he? What is he – Kabir Lal, Kabir Mehra – or what? Are you waiting for the tea to get cold? Or have you forgotten?'

Lata closed her eyes.

'Kabir Durrani,' she said, and waited for the house to come tumbling down.

The three deadly syllables had their effect. Mrs Rupa Mehra clutched at her heart, opened her mouth in silent horror, looked unseeingly around the room, and sat down.

Savita rushed to her immediately. Her own heart was beating far too fast.

One last faint possibility struck Mrs Rupa Mehra. 'Is he a Parsi?' she asked weakly, almost pleadingly. The thought was odious but not so calamitously horrifying. But a look at Savita's face told her the truth.

'A Muslim!' said Mrs Rupa Mehra more to herself now than to anyone else. 'What did I do in my past life that I have brought this upon my beloved daughter?'

Savita was standing near her and held her hand. Mrs Rupa Mehra's hand was inert as she stared in front of her. Suddenly she became aware of the gentle curve of Savita's stomach, and fresh horrors came to her mind.

She stood up again. 'Never, never, never –' she said.

By now Lata, having conjured up the image of Kabir in her mind, had gained a little strength. She opened her eyes. Her tears had stopped and there was a defiant set to her mouth.

'Never, never, absolutely not – dirty, violent, cruel, lecherous –'

'Like Talat Khala?' demanded Lata. 'Like Uncle Shafi? Like the Nawab Sahib of Baitar? Like Firoz and Imtiaz?'

'Do you want to marry him?' cried Mrs Rupa Mehra in a fury.

'Yes!' said Lata, carried away, and angrier by the second.

'He'll marry you – and next year he'll say "Talaq talaq talaq" and you'll be out on the streets. You obstinate, stupid girl! You should drown yourself in a handful of water for sheer shame.'

'I *will* marry him,' said Lata, unilaterally.

'I'll lock you up. Like when you said you wanted to become a nun.'

Savita tried to intercede.

'You go to your room!' said Mrs Rupa Mehra. 'This isn't good for you.' She pointed her finger, and Savita, not used to being ordered about in her own home, meekly complied.

'I wish I had become a nun,' said Lata. 'I remember Daddy used to tell us we should follow our own hearts.'

'Still answering back?' said Mrs Rupa Mehra, infuriated by the mention of Daddy. 'I'll give you two tight slaps.'

She slapped her daughter hard, twice, and instantly burst into tears.

Mrs Rupa Mehra was not more prejudiced against Muslims than most upper-caste Hindu women of her age and background. As Lata had inopportunely pointed out, she even had friends who were Muslims, though almost all of them were not orthodox at all. The Nawab Sahib was, perhaps, quite orthodox, but then he was, for Mrs Rupa Mehra, more a social acquaintance than a friend.

The more Mrs Rupa Mehra thought, the more agitated she became. Even marrying a non-khatri Hindu was bad enough. But this was unspeakable. It was one thing to mix socially with Muslims, entirely another to dream of polluting one's blood and sacrificing one's daughter.

Whom could she turn to in her hour of darkness? When

Pran came home for lunch and heard the story, he suggested mildly that they meet the boy. Mrs Rupa Mehra threw another fit. It was utterly out of the question. Pran then decided to stay out of things and to let them die down. He had not been hurt when he realised that Savita had kept her sister's confidence from him, and Savita loved him still more for that. She tried to calm her mother down, console Lata, and keep them in separate rooms – at least during the day.

Lata looked around the bedroom and wondered what she was doing in this house with her mother when her heart was entirely elsewhere, anywhere but here – a boat, a cricket field, a concert, a banyan grove, a cottage in the hills, Blandings Castle, anywhere, anywhere, so long as she was with Kabir. No matter what happened, she would meet him as planned, tomorrow. She told herself again and again that the path of true love never did run smooth.

Mrs Rupa Mehra wrote a letter on an inland form to Arun in Calcutta. Her tears fell on the letter and blotched the ink. She added: 'P.S. My tears have fallen on this letter, but what to do? My heart is broken and only God will show a way out. But His will be done.' Because the postage had just gone up she had to stick an extra stamp on the prepaid form.

In much bitterness of spirit, she went to see her father. It would be a humiliating visit. She would have to brave his temper in order to get his advice. Her father may have married a crass woman half his age, but that was a heaven-made match compared to what Lata was threatened with.

As expected, Dr Kishen Chand Seth rebuked Mrs Rupa Mehra roundly in front of the dreadful Parvati and told her what a useless mother she was. But then, he added, everyone seemed to be brainless these days. Just last week he had told a patient whom he had seen at the hospital: 'You are a stupid man. In ten to fifteen days you will be dead. Throw away money if you want to on an operation, it'll only kill you quicker.' The stupid patient had been quite upset. It was clear that no one knew how to take or to give advice these days. And no one knew how to discipline their children; that was where all the trouble in the world sprang from.

'Look at Mahesh Kapoor!' he added with satisfaction.

Mrs Rupa Mehra nodded.

'And you are worse.'

Mrs Rupa Mehra sobbed.

'You spoiled the eldest' – he chuckled at the memory of Arun's jaunt in his car – 'and now you have spoiled the youngest, and you have only yourself to blame. And you come to me for advice when it is too late.'

His daughter said nothing.

'And your beloved Chatterjis are just the same,' he added with relish. 'I hear from Calcutta circles that they have no control over their children. None.' This thought gave him an idea.

Mrs Rupa Mehra was now satisfactorily in tears, so he gave her some advice and told her to put it into effect immediately.

Mrs Rupa Mehra went home, got out some money, and went straight to the Brahmpur Junction Railway Station. She bought two tickets for Calcutta by the next evening's train.

Instead of posting her letter to Arun, she sent him a telegram.

Savita tried to dissuade her mother but to no effect. 'At least wait till the beginning of May when the exam results come out,' she said. 'Lata will be needlessly worried about them.'

Mrs Rupa Mehra told Savita that exam results meant nothing if a girl's character was ruined, and that they could be transmitted by mail. She knew what Lata was worried about all right. She then turned the emotional tables on Savita by saying that any scenes between Lata and herself should take place elsewhere, not within earshot of Savita. Savita was pregnant and should stay calm. 'Calm, that's the word,' repeated Mrs Rupa Mehra forcefully.

As for Lata, she said nothing to her mother, simply remaining tight-lipped when she was told to pack her things for the journey. 'We are going to Calcutta tomorrow evening by the 6.22 train – and that is that. Don't you dare say anything,' said Mrs Rupa Mehra.

Lata did not say anything. She refused to show any emotion to her mother. She packed carefully. She even ate something for dinner. The image of Kabir kept her company.

After dinner she sat on the roof, thinking. When she came to bed, she did not say goodnight to Mrs Rupa Mehra, who was lying sleeplessly in the next bed. Mrs Rupa Mehra was heartbroken, but Lata was not feeling very charitable. She went to sleep quite soon, and dreamed, among other things, of a washerwoman's donkey with the face of Dr Makhijani, chewing up Mrs Rupa Mehra's black handbag and all her little silver stars.

Vikram Chandra

SHAKTI

WE HAD BEEN talking about Bombay that evening. Somebody, I think it was Khanna, was telling us about Bahadur
Shah, who gave the island to the Portuguese for their help
against the Moghuls. 'At the beginning of everything great
and monstrous,' said Khanna, 'is politics.'

'You're forgetting the other half,' Subramanium said.
'Remember, the Portuguese gave the island to the British as
part of Catherine of Braganza's dowry.'

'Meaning what?' I said.

'Meaning this,' said Subramanium. 'That the beginning and
end of everything is a marriage.'

What you must understand about Sheila Bijlani is that she
was always glamorous. Even nowadays, when in the corners
of parties you hear the kind of jealous bitching that goes on
and they say there was a day when she was nothing but the
daughter of a common chemist-type shopkeeper growing up
amongst potions and medicines, you must never forget that
the shop was just below Kemp's Corner. What I mean is that
she was a shopkeeper's daughter, all right, but after all, she
saw the glittering women who went in and out of the shop,
sometimes for aspirin, sometimes for lipstick, and Sheila
watched and learned a thing or two. So even when you see
those early photographs from the Walsingham School –
where she was, yes, the poor girl – what you should notice is
the artistic arrangement of the hair, which she did herself, and
the shortness of the grey skirt, which she achieved every

morning with safety pins when she reached school. Even in those days there was no argument that Sheila had the best legs at Walsingham, and so when she finished with college and next we heard that she was going to be a hostess with Air France, it all made sense, I mean who else would you imagine pouring champagne for a movie star in some Frenchly elegant first-class cabin or running down the steps of the Eiffel Tower, holding her white stilettos in one tiny and graceful hand – it had to be Sheila.

Air hostessing in those times didn't mean tossing dinners at drunks on the way back from Dubai or the smell of a Boeing bathroom after a sixteen-hour one-stop from New York. Remember, travelling abroad was rare then, and so all the air hostesses were killingly beautiful and St Xavier's graduates, and they all had this perfume of foreign airs which they wafted about wherever they went, and Sheila was the most chic of them all. It could break your heart, the way she smoked a True, placing it ever so delicately between her lips and leaving just a touch of deep deep red on the very tip. And the men came around, the princes and the *jamsahebs* in their convertibles, promising adventure, the cricketing knights in their blue blazers of glory, the actors' sons offering dreams of immortality. We used to see Sheila then in a flash as a car roared around the curve on Teen Batti, and we would sigh because somewhere there was a life that was perfect and wonderful.

So we were expecting a prince for Sheila – at least, a flashing star of some sort – but she disappointed us all when she married Bijlani. He was USA-returned and all, but from some place called Utah and what was electrical engineering anyway when you had Oxford cricketing royalty on the phone – but Sheila liked Bijlani and nobody knew why. He was square and, later, fat and mostly quiet and he told everyone he wanted to make appliances, which was all very well and good, but four-speed electric mixes weren't exactly dashing, dammit. They met at a party at Cyrus Readymoney's and Bijlani was sitting quiet in a corner looking uncomfortable, and Sheila watched him for a long time, and when she asked,

Readymoney said, 'That's Bijlani, he used to be in school with us but nobody knows his first name. He wants to make mixies.' Then Readymoney, who was dressed in black, snapped his fingers and said, 'Let's boogie, baby,' but Sheila looked up her nose at him – what I mean is she was a foot shorter than him but she somehow managed to look him up and down like he was a worm – and she said, 'Why don't you go into a corner and squeeze your pimples, Cyrus?' and then she went and took charge of Bijlani. Now, you must understand that when nowadays you see old Bijlani looking hugely regal in a black silk jacket it all started that night when Sheila took him out of his corner and tucked in his shirt at the back and took him around, never mind his sweating, and kept him by her side the whole evening. I don't think he ever tried to understand the whats and whys of what happened, I think Bijlani just took his blessings gratefully into his bosom and built mixies for Sheila. Everyone made fun of him at the start, but they went and got married, and people rolled their eyes, and a year passed and then another and another, and then they suddenly reappeared with an enormous flat on Malabar Hill, and there was a huge intake of breath clear down to Bandra, and now the story was that she had married him for his money. If you tried to tell someone that the first mixie was built with Sheila's money from a thousand trips up and down an Air France aisle, the next thing you heard was that she was paying you in cash and kind, and more, to say nice things about her. Her success drew out the venom up and down the coast of Bombay, let me tell you, it's a wonder the sea didn't curdle and turn yellow.

So now Sheila was on the hill, not quite on the top but not quite at the bottom either, and from this base camp she began her steady ascent, not quickly; she had patience and steadiness. It was done over years, it cost money, and the hill resisted, it fought back right from the start. In that first year Sheila threw cocktail parties and lunches and Derby breakfasts, and it became clear to her that the top of the hill was the Boatwalla mansion, which stood on a ridge surrounded by

crumbling walls, overlooked by the frame of a new apartment
building coming up just above. The mansion wasn't really on
top of the hill, and it was dingy and damp, but Sheila knew it
was where she had to go to get to the real top, the only one
that mattered. For that first year Sheila sent invitations to
Dolly Boatwalla every other week and received typed regrets
one after the other, she saw Dolly Boatwalla at parties, and
finally she was introduced under an enormous chandelier at a
plastics tycoon's birthday party. Dolly Boatwalla was long
and horsy-looking, she looked down an enormous nose and
murmured, '*Ha-aaloo*,' and looked away into the middle distance. Sheila understood that this was part of the rules of current diplomacy and was happy all the same, and even when
the next weekend at the race-course somebody by mistake
introduced them again and Dolly said '*Ha-aaloo*' as if for the
first time, Sheila didn't mind a bit and took it as part of her
education. Sheila smiled and said, 'You look wonderful, what
a lovely scarf.' She was willing to let Dolly have her way, and
if Dolly had been a little less Boatwalla and a little more saga-
cious, she could have adopted Sheila and taught her and
patronised her in a thousand little ways, but Dolly saw only a
little upstart, which Sheila was, Dolly didn't see the ferocious
political will, that hidden glint. This is how wars start.

How it all really began was this: finally Dolly accepted one
of Sheila's invitations. Actually she had no choice but to
accept, which may be why she went from being coolly conde-
scending to openly sarcastic. And it started. What happened
was that Sheila had finally been able to join the Lunch Club.
Not many people in Bombay knew that the Lunch Club
existed. Most of the people who knew what it was also knew
that they couldn't be in it. The women in the lunch club met
once a month for lunch at one of the members' houses. After
lunch they played cards. Then they had tea and went home.
That was it, nothing very exciting on the face of it, but if you
knew anything you knew that that was where marriages were
arranged and sometimes destroyed, deals were made, casually
business was felt out, talk went on about this minister in Delhi
and So-and-So's son who was school captain at Mayo. It was

the real stuff, you know, *masala*-grinding, how the world works. So Sheila's name came up, naturally, several times, and, every time, Dolly sniffed and said, Not our type, really, and that finished off Sheila's chances. But then Sheila made friends, fast ones, and they pushed it, they liked her, for her money, for her nippy wit, for her snap, and maybe it was also that some of them were tired of Dolly, of her Boatwalla sandwiches served soggy but with absolute confidence, of her pronouncements and the delicate way she patted her pursed lips with a napkin after she ate pastries. So they insisted, and it was clear there would be either agreement or a direct struggle, and Dolly decided that it wasn't worth risking defeat, so finally she flung an eyebrow towards the roof, sighed, and said, 'All right, if you must, can we talk about something else, this is really so boring.'

So this was how they all gathered at Sheila's home. Her new house, that is. It was a white two-storeyed mansion, really, with a bit of lawn in front and a little behind, and of course even though it was big money for the time it was nothing on the sprawling Boatwalla jungles from colonial times, when you could buy land on the hill for nothing. Still, a house was something, actually it was a lot, and the Lunch Club oohed and exclaimed as they came up the short flight of stairs and into the front room, Sheila had it absolutely right, there were the big double doors inlaid with brass and then a carved wooden elephant's foot with walking sticks in it and a Ganesha that was chipped and old and grey stone and it had to be some major antique, two huge plants on either side, and a diffused white gleam through a skylight, and in the halo, changeless and eternal as the day that Bijlani threw his future kingdom at her feet, was Sheila, her skin glowing, her hair as dark as a Malabar wave on a moonless night. She welcomed them silently, smiling as they chattered around her, she led them through a long hall, past a study with a huge brown desk and a brass lamp, past a room full of leather-bound books and brown-and-red Kashmiri rugs, and finally into the dining-room, where on a stone-topped dining table gleamed twelve place settings in silver. Here, finally, Sheila spoke her first words of the afternoon, 'My son,' because a young boy was standing near the table peering at the fantastic ikebana flower arrangement at its centre. Sheila ruffled his hair, and he turned his head to look at her, and the ladies murmured. He was certainly very good-looking. Bijlani's stolid bulk had passed into a sort of slow, unblinking expressiveness in his eyes, a kind of silence, and he had Sheila's sharp features. 'Say hello,' Sheila said, and he did, shaking hands with each one of them. Mani Mennon laughed over her shoulder as he gravely bowed over her hand, and she said, 'Better watch out for this one.' Meanwhile Sheila leaned into the corridor and called, 'Ganga! Take Sanjeev to his room, will you?'

Ganga came in, a short wiry woman with her hands still wet from dishes. She had her red sari pulled between her legs and she pushed back a strand of loose hair with one hand. As Sheila walked Sanjeev to the door, Ganga took his other hand, and they smiled at each other over his head. 'Isn't he so cute?' Mani Mennon said, and as she did, Sheila turned and saw the look on Dolly's face, a kind of absurd pursing of the nostrils, an unmistakable look of offence, as if she had just begun to smell something bad. As everyone went towards the table, Mani Mennon hung back and whispered at Sheila, 'She has *French* maids.' It was true. They weren't actually French, usually Keralans, but all the same the petits fours at the Boatwalla Mansion were served by maids in black dresses and those frilly things around their heads. Mani Mennon rolled her eyes. She was Sheila's main supporter in the Lunch Club, her sponsor, and she hated Dolly Boatwalla but was absolutely silenced by her, robbed of speech and presence of mind by Dolly's height and ruthlessness and way of commanding a room. Mani Mennon was short and funny and plump and couldn't think of any reasons why she should be silenced by Dolly, but always was anyway. 'Boatwalla bitch,' Mani Mennon hissed. Sheila shrugged and took her calmly by the elbow and led her to the others.

'Have some quail,' she said. The food was unusual, small and spicy, made by a Lucknow cook from a Nawabi family. The tastes were light and chased each other across their palates with such foreign essences that they had to exclaim that it was all perfect, because they had never tasted anything like it before. Dolly held a silver fork at an angle and sawed at a tiny wing, and even she was puzzled and pleased, you could see that. Afterwards they sat on the sofas, luxuriously sunk in the pillows and lingering over the sweet dish, a concoction of almonds and cream so light you barely felt it on the tongue. Dolly began to be funny. She sat on a couch by herself, one leg bent over the other, in her cream pants suit, all long lines from the silk sheen of her leg to the nose, which was a little bony but very elegant. She told cruel little stories about people they all knew. All the stories were about people doing silly things or embarrassing themselves or just being stupid and not knowing about something that everybody knew. Dolly had a great sense of timing and was a good mimic and it was impossible not to laugh at her stories. The women sat in a little semi-circle around her and laughed. Sheila laughed, and Mani Mennon laughed. Mani Mennon whispered to Sheila, 'She must tell stories about me, too,' and then she laughed at a story about a Punjabi woman at the club who pronounced *pizza* the way it was written and who dressed her daughters in too much gold.

Finally everyone grew quiet in an afternoon haze of contentment. There was no doubt it had been an enormously successful lunch, and Dolly had been allowed to dominate it completely. Now it was almost over, and there was a quietness in the air as everyone relaxed with the thought that it would actually finish without any horrendous tension, and as they walked toward the front door everyone was exhausted from the relief and strange disappointment of it all. Then Mani Mennon startled everyone by squeaking, 'Hussain!' They were passing by the room with the bookshelves, and what Mani Mennon had noticed on the wall opposite the hallway was a large canvas, the chariot of the sun, gold and red. She went fluttering into the room with her arms held out, and stood swaying in front of the painting. It was quite overwhelming, with its rich swirl of colour and the horses as if they would burst from the canvas, and everyone clustered in front of it. Dolly hung back in the hallway, but then everyone crowded forwards and she was alone, so she came forwards reluctantly and stood behind them all. 'It's your second one, isn't it, Sheila?' said Mani Mennon. 'It's wonderful. Look at those yellows.' And then, seeing Dolly behind the others, she said, smiling, 'It's a Hussain, Dolly.'

Dolly tilted her head back. 'Is it?' she said. Her head tilted further. 'Oh. Is that what it is?' She smiled. 'Freddie has a few of those at his office.'

Sheila was standing next to her. Without a word, Sheila turned and walked back into the hallway. They followed her, and she walked to the door, opened it, and held it open. They walked past, saying thank yous, and she smiled, but her eyes were opaque and she never took her hand off the doorknob. Dolly walked past and murmured, 'Thank you so much, darling.' Sheila shut the door and the click was very firm and crisp and everyone knew then that something had started.

Sheila sat in her office among the books and tried to think about what she had felt in that moment. It hadn't been anger, more a kind of recognition. In that instant she had felt suddenly outside of her body, standing somewhere else and looking at both of them. What she had seen was that she was herself perfect – she was petite, she had an acute sense of colour and line and so her clothes fell on her exactly and well, her features were small and sharp, her hair was thick, and her vivacity came from her intelligence. Dolly was not perfect, she was long everywhere, she was sallow, she wore old jewellery sometimes missing a link here and there, today she wore a tatty green scarf over her shirt, and that was just it. Sheila was perfect, and she knew that however hard she tried she could never achieve the level of careless imperfection that Dolly flaunted. It had nothing to do with perseverance or intelligence and it took generations. It couldn't be learned, only grown with the bone. It was absolutely confident and sure of itself and easy. Dolly had it and she didn't: looking at it honestly, Sheila knew this. She knew it and she was absolutely determined that if it took her the rest of her life she would defeat Dolly. That it had come to open conflict she knew, and she would not stand losing.

'*Memsahib*.' Ganga was standing in the doorway, leaning against the side, a hand cocked on her hip. She was wearing a dark-red sari with a gold-stamped border. Ganga was dark and very thin, she flung herself at her work with such velocity that it was necessary to put the glassware by the side of the wash-basin – otherwise, as she sped through the plates, crystal would inevitably crunch somewhere in the pile. Ganga had been recommended by Sheila's next-door neighbour. She worked, as nearly as Sheila could tell, in another dozen houses up and down the hill, and she sped from one to another without a pause the entire day, after which she stood in a local train for an hour and fifteen minutes to get out to Andheri, where she lived. It had taken Sheila six months to get her to eat lunch, which she did squatting in a corner of the kitchen and holding a plate directly in front of her for greater efficiency.

'It was a good lunch?' Ganga said.

'Yes,' Sheila said. For the first year they had known each other, Ganga had been courteous but dry, her face always expressionless and impossible to read. Then one day, on her way out, seeing Sheila sitting at her desk in the study as usual, she paused in the hallway, her whole body still pointed at the front door, to ask, What do you do in here? Accounts, Sheila had said, for our business, pointing at the ledgers piled up and the sheets of paper that folded out to cover half the room. Ganga had nodded silently and gone on her way, back up to her normal speed with the first step, but since then, she would stop in the doorway, one foot in front of the other, leaning sideways, one elbow angled out, and they would talk for a few minutes.

'Well,' Sheila said. 'It went well.'

Then they talked about their children. Ganga had a daughter named Asha. Then Ganga tightened her *dupatta* about her waist and it was time for her to leave. 'Going,' she said, clipping the word now, and she went.

*

When Ganga got home it was seven-thirty. She put down a small packet of *jira* and set about making dinner. There was a single light bulb in the single room, and Asha was sitting under it studying, or at least flipping the pages of a book. Asha was dressed in a flowered shirt and a skirt that reached to her ankles. Her hair was pulled back and neatly oiled, and around her plait she wore a single string of white *mogra* flowers. She was sitting cross-legged with her spelling book in her lap, her chin in her hands, and now she darted a quick look from huge brown eyes at her mother.

'All right, all right,' Ganga said. 'Come eat.'

They sat near the doorway and ate from brass plates, which were old but shiny. Outside, people were still passing, and occasionally somebody would say something to Ganga. The lane was narrow, and whoever walked by had to brush close to the door. Across the lane, there was a narrow gutter which flooded in the rains, and behind that more shacks made of wood, cloth, cardboard, and tin. Later, when it was dark, Ganga would sit in the doorway and talk to her neighbours. Most of them were from the same village in the Ghats near Poona, but to the left, where the lane curved, it became a mostly Malayalee locality. Today they mostly talked about a man in their own community who drank so much that he finally lost his watchman job. 'He's a fool,' Ganga said. 'You always knew that.' It was true. They had all known him and they had always known that.

Ganga had arrived in Bombay eleven years before with her husband, who had come back to his village to marry, and since then she had lived in the same place. Ramesh, the husband, had been a mill-worker in the days before the labour disputes and the big lockouts. He was a Marxist, and he was killed, stabbed, in a quarrel with another union the year after Asha was born. Ganga remembered him mostly as a melancholy sort of man who seemed to cultivate his own sadness. It was only in the month after his funeral that she found out that he was said to have killed two men himself in the same union fight. But anyway, now the mills were closed and the years had passed. Now it seemed that Ganga was going to move, and this was the news she had to give to her neighbours. Two stops up on the Kurla line she had found an empty plot, and she planned to build her *kholi* there.

'*Pukka?*' said Meenu, her neighbour, her voice a little breathless, because brick would cost more, and everyone knew that Ganga worked so much that she must have money, but nobody knew how much.

'Yes,' Ganga said. 'Ten thousand for the land, five for the construction.'

'Fifteen,' Meenu said.

'Yes,' Ganga said. 'I don't have it.'

'How will you manage?'

Ganga shrugged. She didn't tell them what she planned, because she wasn't sure she would get the money and she didn't want to sound sure before she was. That afternoon it had occurred to her to ask Sheila for a loan. Sheila had said that the lunch had gone well, but the concentrated expression on her face, the set of her shoulders as she sat among her books was not that of a happy woman. Looking at her then, Ganga had realised that this was after all a woman of business, somebody who wanted things from the world, and had realised that she should ask Sheila for the money. She wanted to wait a few days, let the thought sit in her stomach, because she had learned from the world to be careful when one could, since often there was no time for care. Now she had a month from the owner of the plot to come up with the money, and so she waited for a week. It still made sense, so one day after lunch she asked Sheila, and Sheila said, 'Of course,' went into the bedroom for a few minutes and came back with a stack of notes. It was no fuss. They talked terms, and it was decided that Ganga was to pay it back monthly over six years.

But leaving was a fuss. They had lived in that nameless lane for a long time, Asha since she was born, and Meenu organised the people up and down the street to give them a send-off. They rented a television set and a video player and they watched films all night long, and it was very very late when Asha finally fell asleep with her head in her mother's lap. Ganga sat in the darkness, an arm over her daughter, and felt the loss as a tightness in the stomach, a kind of relentless wrenching, and the coloured light from the screen flickered on her face as she wept. But the next day, when they loaded up their belongings into a handcart, she was crisp and organised, and she led the way, holding Asha with one hand a bundle with the other and tireless in her stride, until the men pushing the handcart leaned against it and begged for mercy.

Their new *kholi* was small, but during the rains it was dry, and Ganga kept it in good repair. There were some two-storeyed houses on their street, built very narrow on tiny plots, and at the end of the lane there was a grocery shop built like a cupboard into a gap between two walls. Also there was a *pan* seller who sold cigarettes and matches and played a radio from morning till night. Their years in this street were ordinary, and Ganga continued her work as before, coming and going with a regularity that her neighbours began to depend on.

Finally, what disturbed their life was Asha's beauty. When she was fifteen a local bootlegging *tapori* fell in love with her. He was at least ten years older than she was, a grown man with some reputation in his chosen trade of gangsterism and with some style, he wore tailored black shirts always, and he fell in love with her ripeness. She was not tall, but there was a certain weight about her body, a youthful heaviness that she made a great show of hiding. She was a student of the movies, and always had flowers in her hair, white or yellow ones. His name was Girish, and he fell in love with a glance that she threw at him coming out of a morning show of 'Coolie'. After that he spent his time sitting on the raised platform at the end of their lane, waiting for her to pass, polishing his dark glasses on his shirt. When she did, she never looked at him, but the force of his yearning caused her to duck her head down and blush darkly, amazed and a little frightened and feeling something that was not quite happiness.

Ganga knew nothing about this until the neighbours told her. She had seen him sitting on the platform, spreading out a handkerchief before he sat down, but she had paid no attention, because it had nothing to do with her. The evening when she found out, she sat in her doorway for a long time. When she shut the door, she came in and found Asha sitting on her charpoy, reading a film magazine. As she watched, a wisp of hair fell across Asha's cheek, and the girl pushed it back behind her ear, only to have it fall forwards again. Idly, Asha flicked it away, the hair was heavy and thick and dark brown, and as Ganga watched her daughter's fingers move across her cheek and linger, the danger of it all pressed her heart like a sudden weight. She knew instantly and completely the violent allure of the black glasses, the coiled stance that projected danger, the infinitely dark and attractive air of tragedy.

'Tomorrow I will take you to your grandfather's,' Ganga said, louder than she had intended.

'What?' Asha said. 'In the village?'

'Don't argue,' Ganga said. 'You're going.'

But Asha wasn't arguing, she was silent, caught somewhere between heartbreak and relief. Her sobs that night in her bed weren't full of grief, or even of sorrow, but of the tension of weeks. She left quietly and obediently with her mother, and in the train she smiled at the mountains and the zigzagging ascent of the tracks and the birds floating in the valley below. But in the village – called Asan – she grew sulky at the endless quiet of the long afternoon. Ganga was in no mood for sulks, having spent an unexpected two hundred rupees on the tickets, and she put Asha to work straightaway, in the kitchen and with the cows in the back. Ganga's father was small and very lean, as if every last superfluity of flesh had been burned away by season after season of a farmer's sun. She had brought him two shirts from Bombay, which he would wear on very special occasions. She spent two days in the village, straightening out the house and seeing to the repair of a waterway that came down the hill into their land. When she left, she hugged Asha briefly, and she felt the youthful sigh more than she heard it. 'Don't be silly,' Ganga said. 'What have you seen of suffering yet?'

It was afternoon when she opened her door in Bombay. She went in and put down her bundle, smoothed her hair once in a single movement, tucking back and tightening all at once, and then she reached forward for the *jhadoo*. She was sweeping under the bed with it when she heard the voice: 'What have you done with her?'

When she turned he was looming in the doorway, tall and silhouetted. The sunlight was blinding him, and she could see the glint of the perpetual dark glasses at the sides of his face.

'What –' she began, and then her throat closed up from the fear. She stood holding the *jhadoo* in front of her with both hands, handle up, clutching it.

'If you married her to someone else,' he said hoarsely. 'If you married her.' He moved in the doorway slightly and Ganga's head reeled, her eyes dazzled. 'If you married her I'll kill you and her. And myself.'

He came in, closer to her, and now she could see him clearly. 'Where is she?' he said. 'Where?' But his head was moving from side to side and she understood that it was very dark in the *kholi* for him. He reached up and took off the glasses and she saw his eyes, red-rimmed. He was very young, and under the sleeve of his black shirt his wrist was thin and bony.

She spoke: 'Don't you have a mother?'

A tear formed slowly and inexorably on his eyelid and rolled down his cheek, and she knew he could do exactly what he had said. She looked at him, into his eyes, and the seconds passed.

'Go home,' she said.

Another moment, and then he turned and stumbled out of the doorway. She stood still, holding her *jhadoo*, for a long time, looking towards the door, until the light changed outside and evening came.

On the hill, it was generally agreed that the Shanghai Club was Sheila's masterstroke. There was a whole faction that insisted that Mr Fong was only a front man, that the money behind Shanghai was actually some of the Bijlanis' industrial lucre, that, having diversified from mixies into plastics and transportation and pharmaceuticals, they had resources to spare. Of course, there was no proof for any of this, but what was clear and needed no proof was that the whole thing started when the Bijlanis were blackballed at the Malabar Gym. Sheila and Dolly had conducted a ruthless but fiercely polite war for years, in which the victories were counted in receptions given and famous writers annexed and huge sums collected for causes, and the casualties were the bruised egos of the partisans of either side, who cut each other in Derby boxes and flicked razor-sharp looks over shoulders at openings. But there were some rules, a certain code of conduct that kept it all civilised until the incident of the blackball.

The Bijlanis had applied for membership to the Malabar Gymkhana, a little belatedly but they were busy people, this was understood, and their son was now old enough to want to play tennis and rugby at the Gym, and the passing of the application was a foregone conclusion. And then came the blackball, which was actually not a black ball but a little slip of blue paper at the quarterly meeting of the membership committee, and the blue paper had on it the single word 'No.' Everyone looked at each other, astounded, but they all avoided looking at Freddie Boatwalla, because the process was of course anonymous but of course who could it be but him? There was nothing to be done about it, the rules were clear and ancient and unamendable, a blackball was a blackball, if you weren't in you were out, there was no middle ground. The chairman burnt the slips according to rule, but those who saw that one said the letters were blocked out and firm, and even before the meeting was over the members were talking about the indisputable fact that Freddie had after twenty years of membership suddenly put himself up for the committee – why now unless there was a plot, a plan – and that this was an unprecedented escalation. Freddie left the meeting without talking to anyone and afterwards he was seen drinking a stiff whisky-and-soda downstairs in the Jockey Bar. The bartender said he had come in and made a phone call first and then asked for his drink. Sitting outside on the long patio with the lazy ceiling fans and the field beyond, the commentators related this and said no more, the implications were clear.

Now everyone waited for the inevitable response from Sheila, and nothing happened. It was unbelievable that she had accepted defeat, and yet this was what some believed, and others insisted that it was merely a tactical feint, this doing nothing, watch and wait. The months passed, and in the fullness of time a Mr Fong announced that he was going to start a place called the Shanghai Club, and nobody noticed. No one knew who Mr Fong was, and there was no reason for anyone to ask, and nobody was interested in his club. Then it was known – nobody knew where this came from – that the Shanghai Club would admit only women as members, and furthermore only by invitation. That to do the inviting there was a committee of ten prominent women who were to remain anonymous – and suddenly the phones started ringing all over Bombay. Who was the committee? Nobody knew. Then the first invitation arrived, in a plain white envelope without a stamp, hand delivered at the house of Bubbles Kapadia, of the Ganesha Mills Kapadias. 'We are pleased to offer you a charter subscription to the Shanghai Club,' it said. 'We request the pleasure of your company at the opening on January 26th.' At about the same time, in what must have been a sublimely managed leak, it became known – seemingly in the exact same minute – from Nepean Sea Road to Bandra that Sheila Bijlani and Mani Mennon were one-fifth of the committee, and that only a hundred memberships were to be offered. Now there was wild conjecture, endless lists were drawn up and debated, memories were searched for histories of friendship and betrayal, and suddenly that plain white envelope was the most coveted thing in the city. Mr Fong received so many calls that he changed his home number seven times, and still he was woken up in the middle of the night by desperate pleas from councilmen and captains of commerce. 'I'm afraid I can't do anything about it,' was his standard reply. 'I don't control the committee. They tell me what to do.' The Chief Minister himself made a resigned call to Mr Fong on behalf of the Storrow toothpaste heiress, who sent a hundred and fourteen baskets of fruit to various houses in a scattershot attempt to flush out the committee. Nothing worked.

The white envelopes came in a trickle through October and November, and nobody could tell where one would show up next, and the exact count was tabulated and maintained with increasing tension as the months passed. Those who got one let it slip casually: 'Oh, guess what was under the door today?' And those who didn't affected not to care: 'I can't believe everyone's so crazy about this stupid Mr Fong's club.' Some pretended to sniff at the kind of people who were getting invitations: a policewoman – an inspector, but still; a documentary film-maker; several journalists, some of them of the television variety. And when Ramani Ranjan Das, the erotic poetess, was invited, a whole faction of the Gym set, at the very north of the patio, declared very dramatically and at great length that they were withdrawing from the Shanghai race, until Bubbles Kapadia asked how they knew they were in it. In the dead silence that followed, Bubbles flicked her ashes on to the table, drew long and at great leisure on her green cigarette holder, then got up and turned and disappeared in a great white cloud of triumphant smoke.

Of course Dolly behaved as if the Shanghai Club did not exist and never would. It was at the Gym, at lunch, that somebody first brought up the subject in front of her. The words dropped, and suddenly silence spread around the table like a ripple. Everyone waited, but Dolly was staring into the middle distance, her eyes calm and genial, absolutely imperturbable, as if she were suddenly a stone-deaf idol, elegantly dressed. She had not heard it, even though the softly spoken words were heard from one end of the oak table to the other. After a while she picked up her knife and fork and cut a tiny little piece of quiche and ate it slowly and with pleasure. As the weeks passed and the hysteria mounted and the rumours flew and everyone talked about nothing but the Shanghai Club, she continued not to hear anything. She was absolute and unshakable. The commentators argued: she must really be upset, some said, she must go home and cry in the bathroom. Nonsense, said the other, stronger, school of thought, it is all truly beneath her, she doesn't care a whit. As January 26th drew nearer, she grew more and more to resemble a kind of stately ship in sail, constant and beautiful, unmoved by choppy waters, and her supporters grew delirious with admiration. It was true: she was magnificent in her dignity. One of the north-patio commentators said, in a tone that mingled exactly equal amounts of envy and quiet pride, 'After all, she *is* a Boatwalla.'

All this was true until the evening of January the fifteenth. Bijlani came home, drew Sheila into their bedroom, locked the door, and related a strange and wondrous tale. He had been sitting, as was his custom, on the balcony of the Napier Bar above the Dolphin Club swimming pool, sipping at his nightly Martini. He did this every evening after his fifteen laps and massage, with the cane chair creaking gently under his bulk and the breeze in his hair. On this evening, he was startled out of his meditation by a man's voice: 'Hello, T.T.' Bijlani had acquired, over the years, with his increasing financial weight, with his famous and many-faceted magnitude, a name and a dense, magisterial composure. So his quick turn of the head, his spilling of his drink, was unprecedented but understandable – the man who stood uncomfortably over him, shifting from leg to leg, was Freddie Boatwalla.

Bijlani waved him into a chair, and when he sat Bijlani could see his face clearly in the light from the door. Freddie had always been thin, but now, in the single light against the darkness, he looked like a paper cut-out, one of those black shadow figures from another century, nineteenth or maybe eighteenth or something. Bijlani knew the Boatwalla shipping company had been through some ups and downs, but who hadn't, it was no cause for this kind of deterioration. Bijlani waved to a bearer. 'Drink?' Bijlani said.

'Thanks, old boy,' Freddie said. 'Gin-and-tonic.' He crossed his legs, and Bijlani had a moment of hideous, bile-like envy: Freddie's crease above the knee was absolute straight, without needing a tuck or pull or even a pat. The white pants fell just so, like everything else. His name was actually Faredoon Rustam Jamshed Dara Boatwalla, but he had always been Freddie, son of Percy Boatwalla, grandson of Billy. There had been a great-grandfather, whose name Bijlani could never remember but who stood in full life-size glory in a niche near Crawford Market, haughtily ignoring the pigeons swarming around his feet.

'Nice evening, isn't it?' Freddie said.

'Very.' Bijlani was remembering the story about Freddie that everyone told again and again, that he had in the golden days of his youth bowled out Tiger Pataudi twice in two consecutive innings during a match at Cambridge.

'Heard about your pharmaceutical deal with the French. Good show,' Freddie said.

'Thanks.'

'We've been thinking in that direction ourselves. International hook-ups. Collaborations.'

'Yes.'

'Negotiating with an American party, ourselves. Difficult.'

'Really?'

'Oh, very. Arrogant sods. Full of themselves. But really it's the only way.'

'I'm sure.'

'Change, you know. Adaptation.'

'Absolutely.'

Freddie's drink came and they sipped in a silence that was not exactly companionable but at least business-like. Above them the lights of the tall buildings made a rising mosaic, and a swimmer's slow splashing in the pool beat a sleepy rhythm to and fro. Freddie put his glass down.

'Thanks for the drink. Have to be getting along. Dinner, you know.' He stood up. 'Can't stay away. Family. You know how these women are.' He laughed.

Bijlani tilted his head back, but Freddie was against the door now and it was hard to make out his face. 'Family,' Bijlani said. 'Of course.'

'You know, old boy, you ought to re-submit.'

'What's that?'

'Your application, I mean,' Freddie said. 'At the Gym. I'm sure that whole business was a mistake. Error. Lapse. Awful. Happens. Re-submit. We'll take care of it.' And with that he was gone.

When Bijlani told Sheila about this conversation, she sat very still for a moment, so immobile that she might have been frozen. Then only her eyes moved, and she looked up at Bijlani. 'How interesting,' she said at last. 'Let's go down to dinner.'

That Freddie and T.T. had talked was known by everyone half an hour after it happened, and there was much speculation about what had actually been said. It was clear that some sort of deal had been made, that negotiations had happened, and now Dolly-watching took on a strange, fresh piquancy. When she received her white envelope, what would she do? Would she say something casually about the Shanghai Club at a lunch? Would she now hear the words that had rendered her deaf and blind? Everyone wanted to be there at the event itself, whatever and whenever it was, because it was completely unprecedented and sure to be delicious in many ways. But nothing happened. Dolly remained casually unaware and went about her business, and the days passed. It was now awfully close to the Shanghai opening and everybody was wound tight, what with fittings and appointments and plans. In those last few days you only had to say to someone, 'Has anything happened?' and they'd know what you were talking about.

But of course nothing did happen. Sheila told no one anything either, she was infuriatingly and politely private and unrelenting. Only Mani Mennon knew, because she had been there on the afternoon of the twenty-third, in Sheila's study, looking through a list as Sheila worked with a calculator and her endless files. '*Memsahib*.' Ganga came in, picked up her half-pay from the desk, and paused long enough to watch Sheila make a notation in a long list of her instalments. As Ganga left, Sheila smiled at her. The phone rang, and Sheila picked it up and said, as she had many times that afternoon, 'Sheila Bijlani.' Then there was a moment of silence, and Sheila stared at the receiver as the silence went on, from awkwardness into significance, and she looked at Mani Mennon and both of them knew instantly who it was.

'Hello,' the phone finally said, a little static-y and hissy.

'This is Dolly Boatwalla.'

'How are you, Dolly?'

'Very well, thank you. How are you?'

'I'm fine.'

There was another little moment there, and then Dolly cleared her throat. 'I've been very busy, what with the children being at home. Trying to keep them amused is so trying. Freddie told me he saw T.T. at the pool.'

'Did he? Yes, he did.'

'Keeping fit, that's good. I have to practically send Freddie out with his clubs. Listen,' now a little laugh, 'have you heard anything about this Shanghai affair?'

Sheila took a deep breath. One by one, she relaxed her fingers on the receiver and settled back into her big leather chair. She wriggled her shoulders a little. Then, completely calm, she slowly said the words she had been saving for so long: 'No.'

'Ah.'

Mani Mennon began to laugh into a pillow, holding it to her chest and shaking violently.

'Well, it was nice talking to you,' Dolly said. 'I hear the children coming in. I should go.'

'It was nice,' Sheila said. '*Namaste.*'

Mr Fong stood at the door of the Shanghai Club in a dinner jacket and bow tie, his hair solid black and with a sheen, looking dashing and mysterious and exactly right. Inside, if you looked closely, you could see that the club was really a little too small, that the tables were the same kind that Bhendi Bazaar furniture-makers copied from Danish catalogues, that the drinks were a little diminutive for so much money, that everything was quite ordinary. But it was all transformed that night by an extraordinary electricity, a current of excitement that made everyone beautiful, a kind of light that came not from the dim lamps but from the air itself. Ramani Ranjan Das wore all white, white *mogra* in her hair and a white *garara* suit and a silver nose ring, and she came with a film director twenty years younger. The police inspector wore slacks and turned out to be quite charmingly shy. Sheila wore a green sari and came a little late. She and T.T. sat in the middle of the crowded, smoky room and the air was filled with a pleasant chatter against the faint strains of music, and though it was photographed and written about, nothing ever really caught that feeling. It felt new, as if something was starting, and it was somehow oddly sexy, at least six new affairs and two engagements started that night, but that wasn't all of it. It was the certainty of it, the feeling that for a few hours there was nowhere else in the world to be and nothing else to do, it was that cusping of time and place and history and power and effort that lifted the Shanghai Club that night into romance and made it unutterably golden.

We thought then that Sheila was invincible, but we had forgotten that even the strongest will in the world is easily defeated by its own progeny. Inevitably, Sheila's son came back to Bombay a poet. Sanjeev had been gone a long time, first to school at Doon and then to the States – he went not to his father's college but to Yale, where he took many classes in photography and art history, and broke many hearts with a dark curl of hair on his forehead that gave him a look of sad nostalgia. He had learned to ski, and had an easy physical grace that was quite different from his mother's nervous energy, her focus, and his father's thumping walk. He was indolent and he had a little smile just a little tinged with arrogance, but we all forgave him that because he wrote such lovely poetry. Mani Mennon was the first one outside the family to meet him that summer, and she watched him for a long time, and then she said to nobody in particular, in a tone of wonder, 'You know he looks always like he's just gotten off a horse.' When she said that, she had said everything. Bijlani said to Sheila, 'I don't know what to say to him, and he's not quite what I expected, but he's very wonderful.' Sheila nodded, overwhelmed by her love. She treated her son like a jewel, standing between him and the world, willing not only to give him anything but to take whatever he wanted to give, a poem if that was it. She already understood that getting what you wanted from the world meant that your own struggles became grubby and irrelevant to your children, which was as it was, that was after all why you gave them what you didn't have. But like all parents she never really believed he would fall in love.

This is how it happened. A week after coming home, Sanjeev wandered away from the house, feeling rested in the body but exhausted by loneliness. He said later that he was discovering the strange terror of coming back to a familiar city and not knowing anyone, and he thought that seeing the playing fields of his childhood, the streets and the corners, would fill the gap in his heart. So he wandered off the hill and down to Pastry Palace, and as he crossed the fly-over bridge he was trying to recall the excitement that once had really made the place a palace, that teenage feeling of seeing a cluster of friends and knowing that everything was possible. But now it just looked ordinary. It was disappointment that made him trudge on into the Palace, a bitter determination to see it all through.

So there are opinions and opinions about what happened next. Some say it was just this – that he needed a way to reconnect, you see, to hold on to something. Others contend contemptuously that it was just the narrative force of history that pushed them into their headlong affair, that it was the ferocity of the feud that made them long for each other. 'What a bloody cliché,' we heard on the balcony of the Gym. 'What atrocious taste to allow ourselves.' The best of us believe that it was merely love. But, of course, nobody really knows what happened, except the essential facts, and they tell us precisely nothing: That afternoon, seated at Pastry Palace with her friends, was Dolly's daughter Roxanne, eighteen years old, finishing at Cathedral that year. She was a fair girl, with that milky Boatwalla complexion, dark straight hair, dark eyes, a little plump, sweet and quiet and a little shy, very charming but nothing spectacular, you understand. She and Sanjeev had known each other by sight before, but the last time he had seen her was when she had just turned thirteen. They talked, we know this for certain, but nobody knows what happened next – did they meet again at Pastry, how did they call each other, was it at a friend's house, what exactly went on? Certainly Sheila didn't know. What she did know was that three months later, at the end of the summer, Sanjeev told her that he wanted to marry.

When she heard who it was, Sheila didn't flinch. She asked calmly, 'Did Roxanne tell her mother yet?'

'Yes,' Sanjeev said. 'We thought she should.'

Looking at his face, Sheila suddenly felt old. He was confident of the future. He knew there was a problem, but of course he had the essential belief that the wars of the past were fought because of benighted ignorance, that good sense would after all prevail. She wanted to tell him that the past was responsible for him, for his beauty, but of course there was nothing to say, no possible way to explain. After a few minutes of her silence, he asked, 'Are you angry?'

'No,' she said. It was true; she was baffled. She had no idea what to do next. But as the afternoon passed, as she and Sanjeev sat together in her office, she couldn't endure doing nothing. She picked up her phone and began to make calls. After the first few it became clear that Dolly did know what to do: she had left the city with Roxanne. They had left by the four-o'clock flight for London. They had been seen being driven to the airport, and the report was that Roxanne had looked tearfully out of the window all the way, but this, Sheila was sure, was dramatic value added on as the story passed from phone to phone. In any case, they were gone.

Now Sanjeev looked stunned and wanted to go to London. 'Don't be silly,' Sheila said. 'How do you know you'll find them there? And what'll you do when you find them, tear her away?' Dolly had two other daughters, one married in London, one in Chicago – Roxanne could be anywhere in the world.

So they waited. Sheila was sure that Dolly wouldn't leave Freddie alone for too long, not at this time, she would return soon. Sheila had no idea what she would do when Dolly did return, she thought about it often but could come up with no satisfactory plan. In the meantime she looked after Sanjeev, who was causing havoc as he suffered. He grew thinner, and, with the dark circles under his eyes, his forelock of hair was completely irresistible, women old and young pined after him, they left him notes and waited for him in the pubs he was known to frequent, and they pursued convoluted paths to introductions to him, but it was all useless, he forgot them a minute after meeting them. He saw nothing and heard nothing except the memory of his Roxanne. Sheila understood that every minute he spent apart from Roxanne bound him more irrevocably to her, and she also understood that if she as a mother told him to forget her, Roxanne would become as unforgettable to him as her own childhood. Sheila had to keep quiet. It was a trap finely honed for her by the years of victory. Even now she had to appreciate the justice of its bitterness.

After sixty days, Dolly returned. Bijlani had friends at customs, so they knew even before she was through the green channel that she was back, that she had come alone on a Pan Am flight from Frankfurt. Sheila let forty-eight hours pass, and then on a Saturday afternoon she asked for the car. She sat by herself in the back as it went through a couple of turns, up a long slope to the left, and arrived at the Boatwalla mansion. She could have walked in about ten minutes, but in all the years they had lived so close to each other, she had never actually seen the mansion. The lane that ran up to the gate was shadowed with branches that came over high walls, so that when you actually got to the gate you were surprised by the expanse of lawn beyond. The gate itself was wrought iron, with some kind of coat of arms at the centre, but Sheila noticed with a quick forward leaning of surprise that the marble on the left gatepost was unmistakably cracked. The car went by the gateman, who saluted the Mercedes and let it through without question, and as it swept around the circular drive she was the whole place clearly for the first time – the white columns, the ornate windows, the façade with its grand curls and flourishes, all of it stained and patchy. The front door was opened, incredibly, by a maid in a black uniform, and suddenly Sheila had to hold back a laugh, but then she noticed that the woman had a head of white, very fine white hair, and that she was peering at her with a concentration that was absolute and unwavering.

'Please tell Mrs Boatwalla that Mrs Bijlani is here,' Sheila said, stepping past her. The woman's stare held for a moment, her hand still on the doorknob, and then she turned and shuffled away. 'Mrs Bijlani,' Sheila called after her curved shoulders, but the maid did not turn her head. The only light came through the open front door, catching a myriad of motes that barely moved. In the dim dark, Sheila could see two ottomans against the wall, under a picture of workmen toiling on a dock. The carpet was worn and, near the door, stained with patches of deep brown. There was a very slight smell of damp. There was no light switch that Sheila could see, and so she waited near the door. Finally a sibilant scraping came close and the maid appeared out of the darkness.

'Madame is not in.'

'It's very important,' Sheila said. 'Tell her that it's very important.'

'Madame is not in.'

The woman was saying it without impatience, standing with her hands loosely holding each other in front of her white apron. Sheila had no doubt she would say it again. Sheila nodded and turned away. She heard the door click gently before she was halfway down the steps. As the car pulled away she looked back at the house, but there was no sign of life in any of the windows. Before the car went through the gate her strategy was clear in her head, fully formed. The thought came to her that way, precise and whole. She was going to buy the mansion. She would buy them out complete: lock, stock, ship, and house. Finally it came down to this vulgarity – that they had the pride and she had the money. She sat alertly in the back of the car that she had earned, paralysed no more, her mind moving quickly. It was, after all, she thought, only inevitable. It was time and history.

Sheila and T.T. sat together late that night, figuring the exact liquidity of their cash. That had always struck her as a strange phrase, because money was, if anything, hard, impersonal. But now she saw how it could be like a stream, unpredictable and underground, and she was going to turn it into a torrent that would flow up the hill instead of down, crumbling the bloody Boatwalla gate like paper. It was going to burst out of the hillside under the mansion like a fountain from the interior rock – surprise, surprise. It was two o'clock when they stared down at a figure at the bottom of a white pad, at the long string of zeros they had spent a lifetime accumulating.

'Is it enough?' Bijlani said, rubbing his eyes. 'Is it enough?'

'It's enough,' Sheila said. 'Let's sleep.' They went up the stairs to the bedroom, and Sanjeev's light was on under his door. She resisted the impulse to knock and went on, but when the lights were off she couldn't sleep. She could see the shapes of the companies they owned, how they fit together, and she moved the segments against one another like the pieces on a chessboard, looking for the nuance that would give them the edge four moves down. She got up once to drink water and was shocked by the hour gleaming at her from the bedside table. Again she tried to sleep, but now it was only the zeros that spun before her, symmetrical and unchanging. *Shunya shunya shunya*, the words came to her in her father's high voice teaching her some forgotten childhood lesson: *shunya* is zero and zero is *shunya*. She felt very tired.

The exhaustion passed, but something else remained. As they began their bid, which Sheila insisted was not hostile but necessary, as they began their slow and audacious assault on Boatwalla Shipping International & Co (since 1757), she found that all the pleasure was gone. The take-over was the most complicated puzzle that she had ever faced, and she was perfection itself, her memory was prodigious, her stamina unquenchable, and her charm of course was gleaming and soft and unstoppable. But she felt the gears grinding inside her. She told herself to remember whom she was doing it for, after all; she looked at her son's face and remembered the way he had learned to walk by clinging precariously to her sari and his jerky little steps, but still every morning she lay awake in bed gathering the vitality, a little from here a little from there, for the great effort to get up and war with the day. But the only true thing was that her taste for the game in itself was gone. Suddenly it felt like work, but even when it was over for the day she could only sit silently, staring sometimes at the television, feeling lost. She tried to hide it, and Sanjeev, who had begun to write page after page of poetry, never noticed, but T.T. was uneasy. He said nothing but he looked wary, as if he had smelled something dangerous in the shifting air but wasn't quite sure what it was, where it came from, what it meant.

It was now, in this, Sheila's time of ashes, that Ganga came to her one Sunday. She was wearing a new, bright-blue sari, and with her was Asha, also in a sari, a green one. It was a formal call: they stood in Sheila's study, the mother a little in front.

'How pretty you look, Asha,' Sheila said.

As the girl blushed, Ganga spoke. 'She finished her nurse training last week.'

'Very good, Asha!' Sheila said, touching her on the shoulder.

'She's getting married next month,' Ganga said. 'We came to give you the card. He's a schoolteacher.'

Sheila took the envelope, which was huge, a foot square. Inside, the card was red, with a gold vine that went around the borders. It invited the reader to a ceremony and reception at the Vivekananda School Hall, Andheri.

'Will you come?' Ganga said.

Sheila was looking at Asha. For some reason, she was thinking suddenly about her first flight on an Air France plane, the leap of her stomach when the machine had escaped the ground. 'Yes,' Sheila said. 'Of course.'

'Bring Sanjeev Baba, too.'

'Yes, I will.' Sanjeev hadn't left the house for days, even weeks now, and Sheila was sure she couldn't get him to come out of the edifice of his grief, she had already stopped asking him, but she said, 'We'll all come.'

Ganga nodded. 'Come,' she said to Asha, who smiled over her shoulder at Sheila. She ran down the hall to keep up with her mother, the silver *payals* at her ankles tinkling with every step. Sheila sat down slowly at her desk. The girl's eagerness hurt her, the small musical sound pressed against her abdomen and gave her a feeling of discovering a new emptiness. She remembered – remembered driving in a bus with the other hostesses in the early morning, to the airport, the red lights far away in the cool blue dawn, a plane thundering overhead with its running lights twinkling, and the glad feeling that it was all an invitation, a promise. They used to sing together, sometimes, Hindi film songs, from Marine Drive to Bandra, and sometimes in Paris on the road to Orly, with the French drivers smiling at them.

Now Sheila waited, with her hand on the phone, collecting herself before the next call. There were a lot of calls to make. The take-over was not going as planned. The Boatwallas had conducted the sort of political manoeuvring that had been expected, and that was easily countered – in fact it was welcome, because it revealed their connections and their understanding of their own predicament. It had become clear as the weeks passed that Boatwalla International was even more overextended than T.T. and she had thought. The interest on their debt alone was barely within the Boatwallas' means. But when it seemed that they must surrender or be reduced, there had come a sudden influx of cash. Like a transfusion, it had revitalised them, fleshed them out and made them capable of resistance: Freddie appeared on 'Business Plus', pink and ruddy under the studio lights, and declared that it was all over, they were safe. Sheila knew they had borrowed money, lots of it at unheard-of rates of interest, but when she tried to find out who had lent it there was no answer. Her intelligence sources all over Bombay and beyond dried up like the city reservoirs in May, there was no information to be had. She and T.T. called in their favours and doled out some more, but still, nothing. If they could get a name, everything would be possible: politics could be made to interfere with the vital flow of money, fine legal quibbles could bring down the whole ponderous sickly white elephant. Once in a similar situation they had even purchased outright and cleanly the entire lend-ing corporation. But without a name, without that vital secret, they could do nothing, everything was meaningless.

So now she picked up the phone and looked at it, at the numbers on the key-pad. There was a time when she had handled it like a fine instrument, her fingers used to fly over the keys without her looking, it had been her delight, her sitar and her stiletto. Now she just stared at it. I can't remember people's numbers any more, she noted with a kind of dull surprise. Then she opened her book and began dialling.

When they drove out to the Vivekananda School Hall a month later, the problem was still with them. Boatwalla International stayed perversely healthy, like a patient sprung from the deathbed and made up with rouge. And for Sheila and T.T. the outcome was not quite a draw. In the eyes of the market, the stalemate was their defeat. It was not only for this that Bijlani was silent and distraught; his uneasiness was the trouble of a man whose life has lost its accustomed centre. Sheila knew that her own doldrums becalmed him even more than her, but her best attempts at revitalisation seemed false to her. She could feel the muscles of her mouth when she smiled. There seemed to be no way out, so she endured from day to day, and he with her. Now they sat, apart, in the back seat behind the driver, Gurinder Singh, who besides having been with them for a long time was also a friend of Ganga's.

When the car drew up outside the Vivekananda School, Ganga was waiting outside for them. She welcomed them in the midst of a jostling crowd. As they walked in, a pack of children in their shiny best raced around them, staring unabashedly. The hall had been done up with ribbons, and there was a *mandap* at the middle, with chairs arranged in untidy rows around it. 'Sanjeev was busy,' Sheila was saying as they walked up to two ornate chairs, thrones of a sort, really, all gilt and huge armrests, that had been placed in front of the *mandap*. They sat down and Ganga took her place by her daughter, who was sitting cross-legged next to the man who was becoming her husband. The priests were chanting one by one and in chorus, and throwing handfuls of rice into the fire. Asha smiled up at them with her head down, looking somehow very pretty and plump and satisfied. Sheila nodded at her, thinking of Sanjeev. He was not at all busy, in fact he had been sitting on their roof with his feet up on a table, but he had said he was tired.

It was the first time that Sheila had ever seen Ganga sitting absolutely still. She seemed at rest, her knees drawn up and her hands held in front of her. The priest droned on. Meanwhile, nobody paid attention to the ceremony at all. Children ran about in all directions. Their parents sat in the chairs around the *mandap* and talked, nodding and laughing. Occasionally somebody would come and stand in front of the thrones and stare frankly at Sheila and T.T., whispering to friends. Sheila had her chin in one hand and she was lost in the fire and the chant. Then suddenly the ceremony was over and the couple were sitting on a dais at the end of the hall, on thrones of exactly the same magnificence as those provided for the Bijlanis. Sheila and T.T. were first to go through the reception line, and Sheila hugged Asha, and T.T. shook hands with her husband, whose name was Ramesh. Then Sheila and T.T. sat on their thrones, which had been moved to face the dais, and food was served. Everyone was eating around them. Sheila ate the *puri bhaji* and the *biryani* and the sticky *jalebis*, and watched as Ganga moved among her seated guests, serving them herself from trays carried by her relatives behind her. She gave Sheila and T.T. huge second helpings, and they ate it all.

After the food, Ganga gave gifts to the women at the wedding. She walked around again and gave saris to her nieces and aunts and other relatives. She came up to Sheila, who said without thinking, 'Ganga, you don't have to give me anything.'

Ganga looked at her, her face expressionless. 'It is our custom,' she said. Sheila blushed and reached up quickly and took the sari. She held it on her lap with both hands, her throat tight. She felt perilously close to tears. But there were two girls, sisters, seven and eight, leaning on her knees, looking up at her. She talked to them and it passed, and finally she was sitting on one side of the room, away from the lights, not on a throne but on a folding chair, tired and pleasantly sleepy. T.T. was on the other side of the room, talking about the stock-market scandals with a circle of men. Ganga's father sat beside him, quiet but listening intently. Sheila thought drowsily that T.T. looked animated for the first time in months.

Then Ganga walked up. She paused for a moment and then sat beside Sheila, on a brown chair. They looked at each other frankly. They had known each other for a long time and they liked each other well enough, but between them there was no question of love or hate.

'How did you manage this, Ganga?'

'I sold my *kholi*.'

'You sold it?'

'For thirty thousand rupees.'

Sheila looked around the hall. A song was ringing out, and a group of children were dancing, holding their arms up like Amitabh Bachchan as 'Muqaddar ka Sikandar'.

'Thank you,' Sheila said in English, gesturing awkwardly at the sari that she held in her lap.

For a moment there was no reaction, and then Ganga smiled with a flash of very white teeth. 'We got them at whole-sale,' she said. 'I know someone.' She pointed with her chin at a man Sheila had noticed earlier bustling about, herding people from here to there. 'Him.'

'That's good,' Sheila said.

'You speak English well,' Ganga said.

'I learned it as a child.'

Ganga settled herself in her chair with the motion of someone who is very tired. 'I have heard that Boatwalla speak English.'

'You work for her, too?'

'For longer than for you.'

'I didn't know. I didn't ask.'

'I didn't tell you. I wash dishes and clean the kitchen. Their other people don't do that. I never see her.'

'I see.'

'Except now and then, once or twice every year, when she comes into the kitchen for something.'

'Yes.'

'But she never sees me.'

'You mean you're hiding?'

'No, I'm right there in front of her.'

'Then what do you mean?'

'I mean that she doesn't see me. If she's talking to someone she keeps on talking. To such high people the rest of the world is invisible. People like me she cannot see. It's not that she is being rude. It's just that she cannot see me. So she keeps on talking about things that she would never talk about in front of you or somebody else. Once she saw me, but it was because she wanted to get water from the fridge and I was mopping the floor and she had to step over my hand.'

Ganga's voice was steady, even. Sheila shifted the packet on her lap a little.

'Even then she kept on talking. Once, I heard her say bad things about her elder daughter, the London one.'

'Ganga, do you . . .' Sheila stopped.

'Understand English? A little, I think. I've worked for you for twenty years, haven't I?'

'You have indeed.'

'Last week, she came in to shout at the cook about the bowls he used for the sweet after lunch. Her husband lagging behind her. These people, she said. She sent the cook to get all the bowls in the house. She said something about meetings, and her husband wrote down something on a piece of paper. How she talks in English, chutter-chutter-chutter, like she's everybody's grandmother in the world, she asked something about the American business, then she said something about a Hong Kong bank, all the time going here and there in the kitchen.'

'Bank?' said Sheila.

Ganga straightened up at the sound of Sheila's voice.

'Yes. Bank.'

'In Hong Kong?' Ganga said nothing in the face of Sheila's sudden needle-sharp focus. 'Ganga. Did she say the name of the bank?'

'Maybe.'

'Do you remember it?'

'Is it important?'

'Yes. Very.'

Ganga threw back her head and laughed, and two children running by stopped to gawk at her. 'It was Fugai Bank. Foo Ga. Foo Quay.'

In the car, Sheila reached out and took T.T.'s hand. She said nothing and looked out of the window as they went down the length of the city. Gurinder was playing cassettes of old songs, he was humming along with the music, his mood lightened by the food and the amiable chaos of the wedding. Bombay's night hadn't yet quieted down, and everywhere there were people, and at some intersections the cars and scooters honked at each other madly. As the car came around a curve, Sheila saw a family sitting by the side of the road, father and mother and two children around a small fire. There was a pot on the fire, and the flames lit up their faces as they looked up at the car going by.

At home, Sheila walked ahead as T.T. gave Gurinder a couple of notes. She could hear their voices murmuring behind her, a cricket chirping and the rustle of the wind in leaves. She had said nothing to T.T., and the name of the bank balanced precariously in her stomach, not unpleasant but not quite welcome, there was something moving in her, something not fully born yet and still unknown. The anticipation kept her awake, and finally, much later, she left her bed and went up to the roof. Now everything was dark, it was a moonless night, and the scrape of her *chappals* against the cement was loud. She found a garden chair and sat in it, her hands held together in her lap. Sometimes a freshness billowed up against her face, barely a breeze but cool and moist. It came again, and she was remembering her father. She remembered him as a small, balding man with a pot-belly, dressed always in *chappals* and black pants and a bush shirt in white or brown. He kept the shop open till late in the evening and opened it early, so that Sheila saw him usually at night, when he ate his dinner alone.

When she was growing up she had always thought he was a simple man. But once a year he liked to take his family away from the city, to a resort or a hill station, for a week, two weeks. She remembered waking once while it was still dark. She was ten or eleven, they were in some place on the banks of a river, a small hotel, she couldn't remember the name of the river. But she remembered the cold lifting off the water when she went outside and saw her father sitting in the sand on the river edge below. In the dark, she could see the white of his *kurta* and his head shining above. She walked through a garden with flowers and down the steps that led to the river, and sat beside him, her leg resting on his knee. He smiled at her, then looked away, across the river where the water melted into mist. She shivered a little. There was white speckled into his stubble, which she knew he would shave later with a Parkinson razor. His name was Kishen Chand, and he was a small man. Later, after he was dead and she was older, she would remember his gaze over the water and think that nothing and nobody was simple. Later, she would remember the old story of schisms and horrors, how he had left half his family murdered in Lahore, two brothers, a sister, a father. They had a shop, which was burned. Partition threw him on to the streets of Bombay but he still spoke of his Lahore, his beautiful Lahore. It was something of a family joke. She huddled beside him as the river emerged from the grey light. She remembered her geography lesson and whispered to her father, Is this a sacred river? It must be, he said. It is, he said. What is that smell? she said. He said, Wood smoke. She asked, Smoke? He said, Fire. What fire? she said. He said, Cooking fires, hearth fires, hay fires. Funeral fires. Ceremonial fires. Even the firing of refuse, of things that are thrown away. Home fires and factory fires. It's starting to be day and there are fires everywhere. And she saw the white smoke drifting slowly across the surface of the water.

Sheila heard a footstep and lifted a hand to her face. It was wet with tears. She wiped it with her sleeve and when she looked up she saw that the sea, far below, was gold. She stood up and felt the light hot on her face. Sanjeev came up beside her and subsided lankily into the chair. She smiled down at him. He had a book in his hand and looked very handsome in a kind of tragic way.

'You were out late last night,' he said.

'Yes.'

'You went on to one of your parties?' His mouth was pouty with disdain.

Sheila laughed. As she looked down she could see on his T-shirt a blond, scruffy-looking man and the single word 'Nirvana'. She said, 'Sanju, you're my son, but it would take a lifetime, two lifetimes, to tell you all the things you don't know about the world.' As she walked away, she ruffled his hair.

In her bedroom, she laughed to see the mountainous bulk of her husband under the bedclothes. She pulled at his toe. 'Come on. We have work to do.' He followed her down the stairs, rubbing his eyes, to the office. He sat in front of her as she leaned back in her chair and picked up the phone.

'What are we doing?' he said.

She put her feet in his lap. He rubbed them, smiling, because in her flowered nightgown and with her hair pulled back she looked like a child, and she looked at him sideways from lowered eyes, naughty and a little dangerous. Her fingers moved so quickly over the keys of the telephone that the beep-ings came out as a kind of music. She grinned. 'Ah,' she said. 'I thought we might make a few calls to Hong Kong.'

What we remembered from the wedding was not the scale of it and not the celebration, not even how beautiful the couple was or the speculations about their honeymoon in France. It wasn't even the sight of Sheila and Dolly walking hand in hand into the reception. It wasn't the sight of Tiger Pataudi and a very boozy Freddie recreating their second innings so that T.T. and Mani Mennon could judge whether there had indeed been a flannelled Pataudi leg before the wicket. It wasn't at all the news that Ganga had bought a large shed in Dharavi, where she was going to put in a cloth-reclamation factory. After it was all over, what stayed in the mind was a strange moment, before the double ceremony (one for each religion), when the two families had moved into the centre of the huge *shamiana*. On one side we could see Sheila's aunts, large women in pink and red saris with bands of diamonds around their wrists and necks, and, on the other, Dolly's relatives, in particular one frail, tall old lady in a white sari and a pair of pince-nez glasses, with pearls at her neck, and all these people looking at each other. Then all the talking died away, there was a curious moment of silence, it was absolute and total, even the birds stopped chirping in the trees. Then two of the children ran through the *shamiana*, it was Roxanne's second cousin who was chasing Sheila's niece, both squealing, and the moment was broken and everyone was talking. Yet there had been that strange silence, maybe it was just that nobody knew what to do with each other. But I think of that moment of silence whenever I realise how much changed because of that marriage. What I mean is the formation of the Bijlani-Boatwalla Bombay International Trading Group, then the Agarwal loan scandal, the successes of the BBBI, the fall of the Yashwant Rao Ghatge Government, and the meteoric rise of Gagganbhai Patel, and what happened after that we all know. But that's another story. Maybe I'll tell you about that another evening.

Ardashir Vakil

UNFORCED ERRORS

MY LIFE WAS all balls. The cricket ball, the dog's hard ball, the squash ball, the croquet ball, the football, the rubber-solution ball – but most of all, the tennis ball. The tennis ball is versatile like no other. With it you can play cricket, hockey, pat ball, catch-monkey, donkey in the middle, football, french cricket, basketball, water polo, even volleyball. We were a family obsessed with tennis. All of us, my father apart, played every day of the week except Sunday. There wasn't a club in the city whose courts we did not know: the Khar Gym, the Bandra Gym, the Bombay Gym, the Willingdon Club, the Cricket Club of India and the Maharashtra State Lawn Tennis Association, where I learnt the basics of the game. My mother and I watched, followed and played in tournaments all around the country. We scanned the sports pages of the *Times of India* for news from the grand-slam tournaments around the world. During Wimbledon we were glued to the radio following the progress of Margaret Court, Billie Jean King, Rod Laver, John Newcombe, Stan Smith and Ilie Nastase. My favourite showing-off story was how Newcombe had once visited our house for a beer. Being sixteen at the time, he had to hide behind the curtains to drink it.

In her younger days, my mother had trained at the Queen's Club in London to try and qualify to play at Wimbledon. She was seeded second in the All India rankings of the day. But her training was cut short when the drizzling grey and cold of an

Extract from the novel *Beach Boy*.

Earl's Court bedsit, and the separation from her two-year-old son, got the better of her ambition.

So much in our family revolved around the game. My mother's life, her relationship with my father, and her relationship with me, all these could be decoded and deciphered through backhands, forehands, volleys, lobs and serves. Particular shots decided the fate of future relationships, long and bitter debates ensued about who was better than who: matches that were won left one with a high for weeks to come; matches lost were cause for days of introspection and post-mortem depression.

On a hot afternoon in April, about two-thirty, earlier than normal for tennis, I was due to play Sandeep Gupta in the first round of the Maharashtra Open, Under 12 Competition. He was seeded one, I was an outsider. The Gupta brothers, Sandeep and Sanjay, were of Kashmiri origin and lived in Bandra. Sandeep was ten, Sanjay eleven. Their father, who was also their coach, was a serene-faced doctor. Pale Kashmiri skin and unusual green eyes. His sons had something green, something blue, something slanted in their eyes. They could easily be mistaken for twins. They were a spindly limbed, resilient and cunning duo. Onto their grasshopper bodies were attached these two huge globes for heads – round and smiling. The two boys were well-known protégés of the Bandra Gymkhana. I had seen them play a couple of times and I knew in my gut that I had the beating of them.

On the afternoon of the match, my mother and I drove from our house in Juhu to the suburb of Bandra. I was dressed in my Fred Perry white shorts and shirt, my mother in a dazzling blue dress. On the road, my mother coached me on the art of match play.

'Now, Cyrus, listen to me. When you are practising shots before the match, what you have to do is play a few strokes to both sides, especially his backhand, and see which is the weaker side.'

'Yes, but what if he doesn't play any backhands?'

'He has to play one or two,' she said, tutting irritably.

'What I mean is, most players at your level have a weaker backhand. Even at Wimbledon in 1964, Rod Laver attacked Pancho Gonzalez's backhand. So you see . . . and then when you're playing him, don't start hitting everything to one side. Unless it's very weak: then you just attack . . . from the word go . . . and then he's finished.' My mother was given to not finishing her sentences. Impatience was one of her chief characteristics. She spoke in half-sentences because she didn't think it necessary to complete a sentence once its meaning had been conveyed, because she couldn't wait to make her next point and, most important, because she didn't want to leave a gap in which to be interrupted. I was trying to keep my mind on what she was saying when two women in saris suddenly walked in front of the car as if it didn't exist. Luckily we were not travelling fast. My mother jammed on the brakes and leant her hand on the horn. Most drivers would have shouted at the pedestrians. My mother carried on as if nothing had happened.

'Yah, but then what will Sandeep Gupta do? Are you paying attention or not? What do you think he will do when you play on his backhand? What he will do is run round his backhand,' she said, answering her own question. I was watching a man dragging along a huge ice-block with a hook, his vest drenched in sweat. The block of ice skated meltingly along the baking tarmac.

'What d'you mean "run round"?'

'Don't be silly now, Cyrus. You know what "run round" is. If he is standing here,' my mother let go of the steering-wheel with one hand to give her demonstration, 'and you hit the ball here, to his left,' she pointed with the other finger, 'to his backhand, he runs further to his left and plays it with his forehand. Therefore running round . . .' By the end of these heated gesticulations both her hands were off the steering-wheel and the turquoise Fiat we were in careered towards the pavement. A swerving cyclist shouted an insult through the window.

'Hey, akal ka dushman, jara dekh ke chalao gadi.'

'Oh, shut up, you bloody fool!' my mother replied under her breath. Hardly stopping to take another, she continued,

'So, then, what do you do then? If he runs and tries to play it like that, on his forehead, what do you do?'

Everything was always a test with my mother. Have you heard of . . .? Do you know how . . .? Can you tell me . . .? I was terrible at tests. I always came thirty-ninth out of forty in my class at St Mary's. There was little chance of me coming up with the right answer. At that moment, I would have given anything for John Newcombe to come and whisper it in my ear. I said, 'You keep on playing on his backhand.'

'Nooooooo! Oh, my God! How can you go on playing on his backhand! Cyrus, after all these years . . .' And here she let her hands rise from the steering-wheel and dropped them down again with a sigh and a wry twist of the mouth. Then she went back to her explaining mode. 'If he keeps on running to the left and covering his backhand, then what happens is the right-hand side of the court is left gaping open. Obviously, his forehead side gets left open. So what do you do? Naturally, you play to his forehead. Either you will hit a winner or when he rushes back across the court then you have enough time to play to his backhand. Do you understand now?'

I nodded. I had the feeling that before our journey was up I would hear the explanation again. My mother was fond of repeating herself. It was part of her teaching technique. Drumming it in. I'm still not sure as to the effectiveness of such a method. Did it make me wilfully deaf to her advice or did my pretending not to listen signify an acute subconscious absorption?

'But you must be patient. Wait for the ball . . . George says you've got good shots. But sometimes you try to hurry them . . . you hit them too hard, hit them out . . . You know which turning it is? You mustn't make unforced errors. Never mind if you don't hit winning shots. You mustn't make any,' she stopped to gather up her energy for the emphatic repetition, 'unforced errors.'

I was sitting in the corner of the front seat, wedged between the door and the back rest, like the taxi-drivers, with their elbows leaning out of the window. 'Can one make an unforced error if one isn't playing tennis?' I wondered. 'Are unforced errors a problem in other areas of life?' I was having difficulty concentrating on my mother's voice. Being in a state of nervous excitement, I wanted to spend these last moments before the match quietly, letting my mind wander to anything but the game in front of me. I thought of the Chinese meal my mother had promised to take me to if I won. I thought of both of us returning to our glass house when everything was over, turning into the lane, past Laloo Prasad in his cubby-hole, past the Krishnans' gate with its black and white notice, 'Beware of Dog', glimpsing the coconut seller on the beach, running up the spiral staircase to my bedroom.

Through the car window, I looked out at the tall neon sign for Caesar's Palace. I'd never been into that hotel even though we must have passed it a hundred times. A little further on, the post-box red of the Frankie stall caught my eye. Mr Tibbs's original creation: the nan and egg roll filled with delicious mutton curry. Even my father, who was not one for roadside food, liked them. What was that playing at Bandra Talkies? Oh, *Mere Apne*. I hadn't seen that one. Shatrugan Sinha, trying to be a hero instead of a villain. 'Meena Kumari at her very best!' the poster said proudly. I wanted these familiar signposts *en route* to go on for eternity. I didn't want us ever to get to the Bandra Gymkhana tennis courts, brown and hard in the blinding sun. I wanted to blink and be back in the lane outside our house, the tennis match over, whatever the result. Or back in my bed, where I was lying an hour ago reading my James Hadley Chase novel.

We were stalled in a traffic jam on Linking Road. My mother's voice reached out and grabbed me by the elbow. 'Don't be too confident, huh, Cyrus. Sandeep is meant to be very good.'

'But Sanjay is meant to be better than Sandeep.'

'Yes. But you shouldn't think of that now. Both are very good. Now, c'mon, just grit your teeth. Even if you lose the first few games, don't just give up and start hitting the ball wildly. Be determined, clench your fist, like Billie Jean.'

I thought of my mother's pearly teeth. She was always telling us how her dentist said she had such a perfect set. I recalled a match she'd played in last year, in the final round of the Western India Championships. Her opponent was Neeru Seth, a short, dark, dogged-looking woman from the armed forces. I was sitting watching from a round-backed cane chair in the corner behind the baseline. Absorbing the weight of every ball she hit, every forehand she guided over the net, every backhand she speared to the far corner of her opponent's court. Watching her little pattering footsteps as she frisked from side to side. Her eyes bulging as she swung a forehand winner down the lane. The drop of her head and the swing of her arms to and fro like a clock, while she changed ends. The occasional smile slung to the corner where I was sitting.

And my mother. I should be watching her play, but I couldn't bear to. When she caught my eye, she didn't smile, her mind hot with the strain of thinking about the next few points. I remember, after the match, how upset she was to be beaten by Neeru Seth, who later became the governor of India's most notorious women's jail. Tears mixed in with sweat dripped like melting fat down her arms and neck; her voice cracked as she spoke to the local coach. 'But she behaved very badly, George. She can't behave like that, shouting and grunting and . . . I had three set points, three times I played to the backhand but she got it back. She kept on moving her feet when I was about to serve my second serve, moving her feet like this, pit pit pit, I don't know, maybe that shouldn't be allowed. Are you allowed to distract your opponent like that?' George didn't speak, he just looked at her soothingly through his horn-rimmed spectacles. Impassive as ever. And all through that game I had been thinking, 'She's going to lose the match, she's never going to make it.'

We turned right at Dawood Interiors and into the main streets of Bandra. There was little time left for idle thoughts. The past couldn't come and rescue me now. But my mother still had her favourite story left to tell. 'Don't forget, I've told you so many times about that time in the Davis Cup when Krishnan was 3–5 and two sets to love down, and Koch from Australia was serving. Naresh Kumar, who was the commen-

tator, said, "What a shame India is going to lose the tie."
People were walking away and going home. Everyone had
given up. But then Krishnan broke serve and won the next
game and you could see him talking to himself and saying,
"C'mon, Krish, you can do it," gritting his teeth and clenching his fist. He won that set and then the whole match. I was
fixed to my seat for three hours, I missed all my appointments,
the match was so enthralling. What delicate shots Krish
played! What guts he showed! What determination! Really
he's an all-round player. At the end, Koch was finished, a
broken man, completely finished. The people in the audience
gave them both a five-minute standing ovation.'

I loved this story but I wanted to know more details. I
wanted her to relive the match so I could see it as if it were a
film. My mother was more interested in the moral. As we
approached the Bandra Gym, she spun it out. 'So you see, it
shows you, if you really want to win something badly enough,
even if you're love–five down, if you fight back, you can do it.
Of course, Krishnan was a great player. Okay, now we're
there, have you got everything?'

Mine was the first match of the day on the sun-baked cow-
dung court. My mother strode up to some loitering boys, asking questions and demanding service. This was not her
territory, but she was someone who could command attention
on the North Pole. One of the Gupta brothers trotted over to
me, a smile on his globe.

'Are you Cyrus Readymoney?'

'Yup.' I smiled back. Was I meant to hate this boy? I rather
wanted to be friends with him.

'My brother's just coming. I'm Sanjay,' he said shaking my
hand, 'I think we're playing a match tomorrow in the Under
Tens.'

'That's at the Khar Gym, isn't it?'

'Where is he? Where is Sandeep Gupta?' my mother
boomed. 'They should start now, it's already two-forty-five!'
Two of the boys hanging around the edge of the court, I think
they were going to be linesmen, ran off towards the clubhouse
as if struck by lightning.

'Sandeep's just coming, Aunty,' said Sanjay. 'Just wait one minute.'

'I hope he's hurrying up. Otherwise what was the point of us coming so early? I have to be in town by five o'clock and your father said two-thirty sharp.'

Sandeep arrived, running along the side of the court, grinning like a goblin. His father followed after him, tall, avuncular and bald. He bade my mother welcome and offered her a drink. Sandeep clutched his wooden Maxply. We shook hands and tossed for service. While we were knocking I noticed Dr Gupta chatting happily with my mum. I had borrowed my mother's racquet, a Wilson T2000, the same kind Jimmy Connors played with. It was warm and springy in my hand. Sandeep's shots were steady but weak. I responded with some hard-hit drives on both sides. The balls were falling in. After the long car journey, I felt a certain lightness, a pleasant breeze, a relaxation of being. I opened my shoulders and stroked through the ball, watching it closely on to my racquet. I was lost in the effortless of this hitting. I didn't have to look, I could feel the balls were landing in. I threw myself into the air and scythed through a smash, punched a few volleys. My backhand felt particularly strong. I looked over at Sandeep when we were practising our serves. He seemed shaky, like a rickety chair. His serves were dropping in the middle of the box, where I could eat them up for breakfast.

Sandeep won the toss and elected to serve. I remembered too late my mother's advice to observe his shots during our knock-up. But she was right about his backhand – it was weak. He couldn't find enough power in his chopstick frame to hit the ball flat and was slicing it short. I exploited his tentative replies with surgical severity, sailing ahead to 5–1 in the first set. It was all so easy. I allowed myself a smile of triumph. I was serving more accurately than ever, lunging for volleys on my forehand and hitting smashes into the backhand corner of the court. And Sandeep obligingly made some terrible mistakes. Out of the corner of my eye I could see my mother conversing with the doctor, though I could tell they were both following the score and occasionally watching a rally.

513

There is almost nothing equal to the feeling of bliss when you are on top of a game, playing well and beating your opponent. Your shots get better, the ball speeds to the appointed corner, or depth, or stops dead where you want it to. Your serves come effortlessly: ball, body and racquet all swinging in one harmonious motion. Your volleys dip and angle and slide away from the reach of your flailing rival. If you miss a first serve, you can afford to take a chance and hit the second one. It tends to fall in. When your adversary finds a good stroke you reply with an inspirational one. Great players talk of playing out of yourself, as if the weight of your body floats away and you are left with an ethereal essence of stroke, hand and eye. You move fast, you see things early, reaching balls generally unreachable. It's like passing the fifty mark in a game of cricket: you bid goodbye to caution and a full-length ball on your middle stump is nonchalantly half-volleyed to the boundary. You can be polite, langorous, even slipshod. When the tide is swimming for you, you can be sure your opponent will be floundering in the waves.

Having won the first set by three-fifteen, I was in a buoyant state of exuberance on court five of the Bandra Gymkhana, humming my favourite Elton John song from the album *Goodbye Yellow Brick Road*.

Hello, baby, hello, haven't seen your face in a while . . .
Harmony and me, we're pretty good company
Looking for an island in a boat upon the sea.

The second set resumed where the first had left off. I was three games to love up, strolling around the court like someone on holiday, thinking of the Chinese dinner my mother had promised she would take me to, sprinkling the green chilies on the sweet corn and chicken soup. Already counting on trouncing the elder Gupta brother in tomorrow's match. Going up to the podium to collect the Under 10 and Under 12 winners' trophies. I was four–love up in the second set, receiving serve and Sandeep was 15–40 down. I hit a couple of overambitious forehand returns, one even bounced on to the bamboo-and-rattan backing behind the baseline. From deuce, Sandeep managed to claw back the game. I heard my mother's voice from behind me. She was sitting at the back of the court.

'Now, don't fool around, hah, Cyrus. You can lose the match from anywhere.'

'Quit worrying, Mom,' I thought to myself, pretending I was Jimmy Connors. I smacked the aluminium frame against my calves, I fingered the strings of my racquet, I looked at the crowd and snarled. I lost the next game.

'Oh, for God's sake, get on with it,' I snapped, as Sandeep bounced the ball in front of him for the umpteenth time before serving. Impatience overcame me. I tried to force a couple of backhands down the line. One hit the tape at the top of the net, the other missed the sideline by a fraction. I stared hard at the umpire, as if I were Ilie Nastase. In the next game I had a point to go 5–3 up and I made a double fault. I crashed my racquet to the floor. It was a hallmark of my game that I never committed a double fault. I couldn't believe what was happening.

My mother's voice grew urgent. 'C'mon Cyrus, you can lose a match from anywhere,' she hissed. 'Stop fooling around. Pancho Seguira had nine match points against Pancho Gonzalez and he still lost. The main thing is . . .'

I couldn't believe she was telling me a story in the middle of a game. What would the people think? I turned to her and said, 'Be quiet please, Mummy. There's no problem. I'm fine.'

I sauntered back across the court and thought through my position. I must turn the heat on his backhand. I must focus on each point. Keep the ball in play. The set was now at four–all. The ninth game went to plan. I didn't try anything special, just keeping the ball deep on his backhand. It wasn't easy. His game seemed to have improved and my shots had to be more accurate to prevent him from running round and hitting them with his hungry forehead. In the tenth game he made a couple of nervous errors and that was enough to give me two match points. Fifteen–forty, on his serve. A smile escaped my lips.

'Oh, please shut up, Mummy,' I said under my breath. I

could see her clenching her fists, urging me on to win the next point. Sandeep served to my backhand. I sliced it low across the court to his backhand and rushed up to the net. I saw him struggling with the shot. I've seen it a hundred times after that. A pathetic half-lob floating pitifully towards where I was waiting at the net. The easiest shot in the game to play. I could have closed my eyes and hit a winner ten times over, in twenty different ways. I swung at the ball with all my strength, there was a strange tinny vibration in my hand, I saw the ball fly out of the court, I saw Sandeep Jain looking at me with his mouth open, I saw sadness and pain stretching out in front of me for the rest of my life. The ball had hit the rim of the racquet and flown over the baseline. Any other day, a mis-hit smash would land on the line or on some awkward part of the court. I couldn't bear to look in the direction of my mother.

While I watched Sandeep lunge hopelessly at my vicious slice, I'm sure I had a vision of shaking his hand across the net and saying, 'Well done.' After that squandered match point, Sandeep Jain also had a vision, a vision of winning the match. From that moment onwards he fought like Arjun in the *Mahabharata*, not just with strength but with a force of mind that ran from his head to the steady bend of his elbow as he rained down arrows of woe onto the army of his helpless cousins.

When competition is fierce between two rivals the winner is the person with the greater control over his or her emotions. The blood must remain cool; the hand must keep its balance; something at the centre, perhaps even on the edge, in the ball of one's foot or the lobe of one's ear, must nurse a cruel quietness, a consciousness of the life that exists outside the terrible struggle.

After that dreadful smash, Sandeep managed to win three games in a row and stole the second set. At the start of the third set his eyes had acquired a reddish tinge like someone drunk with longing. We exchanged a couple of games. One all. Then his forehand started to flow. It was a lovely cross-court shot that came from nowhere and disappeared before you had time to take a step towards it. Where had he been hiding it all this time? Having found his rhythm on that shot, the harder I tried to play to his backhand the easier he found it to run round and hit a winner with his forehand. My mother was all passion overflowing onto the court. Haranguing me with different bits of advice, cheering when I made a good shot, desolate when my opponent sent another ball whizzing by me. I could feel her voice as if it were some-one shaking me. I flung my racquet on the floor in disgust when Sandeep went 4–1 up. 'I don't care,' I thought. 'I'm going to lose now.' I just couldn't get the match points I'd lost out of my head. The picture of that missed overhead haunted me through every point of the final set. I stopped listening to my mother. 'C'mon Cyrus! Don't give up now. Show some determination.'

I had lost my will to win or to fight. My opponent swal-lowed the points like a caterpillar. Larger and larger morsels. As the afternoon wore on to evening he became more vora-cious. My mother's voice was hoarse by now. I had points to reduce his lead from 5–3 to 5–4. Endless deuces. My spirits revived momentarily when it was my advantage, but he never lost his lean and predatory look. We had been playing for two and a half hours in sunstroke heat but only in the last game did I feel fatigued. The lifeblood had left my game. My mother had gone suddenly silent with resignation and shame. At the end, when we shook hands, I was still half-thinking of the vision in which I had won the match after putting away that simple smash. I almost thought Sandeep was going to walk over to me and say, 'You won the match really – this rest was just a joke, a bad dream.'

My mother and I didn't speak to one another. I should have said sorry or something like that. Normally she would have been analysing the game by now, telling me what I had done wrong. She bought me a drink. It was cold, but I didn't enjoy it. On the way home, in the car, my mother laid open the corpse of the lost match. Post-mortem, she called it.

'The problem with you, Cyrus, is the same in tennis as with other things in your life. You just don't have the staying power, the perseverance. One minute you want this, then you don't like it and you want something else. You thought you had won when you had that match point. You didn't concentrate and then see what happens, you missed the easy smash. I told you in the car before the match, don't be over-confident, but you never listen properly. Your teachers say the same thing . . .' And I salivated with anguish at the thought of a lost banquet of fried rice and sweet and sour pork, of king-size prawns and Singapore noodles, of beef with chillies and lychees with ice-cream.

Mukul Kesavan

ONE AND A HALF

HE DREAMT OF lepers for years afterwards, but the first time
was after the Gupta wedding. The usual things: rotting fingers
and flattened noses, humanoids with bandaged hands and feet
marooned on the traffic islands of an alien planet. Then him
in jail with them, shaking the bars and shouting for water
while the lepers watched silently; he was their representative,
their shaker-of-bars because they couldn't – they didn't have
the knuckles to go round. He came awake scared, and every
dread, every undone thing, every foreboding, past, present or
imagined, stampeded through his mind. Some of these fears
were obsolete, like being caned by Martin in the fourth period
because he hadn't parsed twenty sentences for English homework, but his mind, still pickling in the sour juices of the leper
dream, wasn't up to sorting panic out by date.

Through the barred window, sunlight was being hosed into
his bedroom by a pre-monsoon sun – flat, malignant brilliance
that washed out the colours inside, that leached, even as it lit
up, the scarlet and brown from the batik bedcover lying anyhow on the floor. He lay still and didn't allow his mind to
graze on the previous night's embarrassment, but the fungus
on the webbing of his left foot wouldn't stop itching and the
sun just carried on. He would have to see about curtains; winter was still five months away and he no longer felt he could
hold out till then. He disliked Delhi. It made him wish he was
married.

Second chapter from a work in progress.

It was a red-letter day. He had an office calendar where Government holidays were marked in red. It was a Second Saturday morning, the best day in the month, a day not just written in red, but spelt like a proper noun inside his head. He had a special routine for this monthly holiday: he got up at the usual weekday time and brushed his teeth and bathed, and then, after Brylcreeming and combing his hair, he surprised himself by not shaving. He changed the blade in his old Gillette and put it away unused. Stepping into his white cotton trousers he noted again that the orange rust mark, near the metal clip that fastened the waist band, grew bigger with every dhobi wash. He was nearly forty, so perhaps this was a sign. At ten o'clock exactly, he left the house and began walking down Rowse Avenue towards Minto Bridge.

He carried the *Statesman* with him, rolled up and rubber-banded. He would read it over coffee in either the United Coffee House or Bankura, depending on where his mood took him. Halfway up the Minto Road slope he decided on Bankura because he wanted bustle, and he liked the sight of tourists struggling out of the Cottage Industries Emporium next door, weighed down by noisy brown paper parcels. Before walking diagonally across the three concentric circles of Connaught Circus, he stopped as he always did at the little rank of shoe-shine boys opposite Empire Stores to have his Peshawari sandals polished. Only today there was just one person there and he wasn't a boy, he was a man. Standing with one foot on the shoe-shine box Hiren felt like Hillary striking an attitude on Everest. The man polishing his sandals wasn't old; he was probably the same age as him, likely younger, but he looked worn out. The skin on the back of his hands and forearms, as he worked the long flat brush around the sandals, was shiny and cracked. He was wearing a sleeveless vest so Hiren could see that he had no biceps at all – his upper arm was just bone and skin and stringy muscle. He wasn't wizened, or shrunk – just eroded. In Iowa he hadn't been able to tell the poor from the rest because the poor weren't smaller there. Also, they weren't poor. They wore the

520

same clothes as everyone else or nearly because a new pair of jeans with seven pockets cost a dollar. The shoe-shine man tapped the side of the box with his brush and Hiren changed feet.

Here the poor were a different species with shorter life-spans, faster clocks. They live dog years, thought Hiren. Not seven years to the human one, but at least two. The man had finished applying polish and cream and was buffing the leather with a strip of cloth, his hands moving so fast that they blurred. Perhaps it was Hiren's eyes that were slow. Maybe for the shoe-shine man it was the lives of ordinary, well-fed, unpoor people that were sluggishly lived, in baffling slow-motion.

He gave him eight annas when the job was done: four annas for the cream polish and four more for using him as an aid to thought. He decided to take the long way round to Janpath because he wanted to walk in the shade of the circular colon-nade. Most of the shops were still shut or half-open; the lepers, the legless, the armless, the elephantiasis victims, the able-bodied unemployed, the un-maimed sick, the ordinarily destitute, the people who moved in when the shoppers left, were still there, rimming the corridor as it curved, gathering the strength to move to daylight stations. But even as he sorted the poor into the improvised categories of a walk-by census, he couldn't help wondering about the shoe-shine's teeth: they were white and regular, and they made him harder to classify.

As he passed Volga, the door of the restaurant opened and exhaled the magical smell of vanilla ice-cream, air-condition-ing and cigarette smoke. The restaurants in Connaught Place's inner circle opened before most of the shops. Grindlays Bank had started doing business, and so had the two Chinese shoe makers adjacent to it. Cheap Jainy's was open too. Walking past the United Coffee House he paused, because the day was suddenly still, overcast and very sticky – the UCH was air-con-ditioned, while Bankura made do with large pedestal fans that sometimes blew the food off customers' plates. He was won-dering whether to change his mind when there was a quick roll of muffled explosions, like a distant cannonade, and it began raining. In five minutes the sky was a dark, worsted grey and it was raining so hard that the cars circling the central roundabout had become dim shapes gliding silently by because the roar of the raindrops drowned out traffic sounds. He smiled in a reflex of childhood. Rain took him back. It was the only way he knew to relive Sylhet and it was the one season in the year when Delhi felt like home.

Someone was tapping his knee. He looked down and saw that a trolleyman had pulled up next to him. Like most trolleymen he didn't have legs, only this one barely had stumps. He had been severed so far up that he was nearly all torso. He was wearing nothing except for a loincloth and an amulet round his neck. He held out an enamel mug with a tin cut-out of Shani inside it. 'Shani Maharaj,' he said. Hiren shook his head vigorously and stepped back. A woman screamed – he had stepped on her foot. He apologised irritably, his pleasure in the rain gone. The passage was full of people sheltering from the downpour and the romantic smell of wet earth had been replaced by the odour of hot, damp bodies packed together. He closed his eyes and listened to the steady rhubarb drone from which the odd lucid phrase broke free, like '. . . due last week of June' and, more often, 'pre-monsoon shower'. Then he opened them. Everyone was still looking out, watching the first rains of the season with the intelligent alertness that they would normally have given to a road accident. The decision about where to eat had been taken for him: this morning's *Statesman* was destined to be read in the United Coffee House. Wary of potential embarrassment, Hiren took out his wallet to make sure he had enough money because this place was more expensive than Bankura. Counting his eight-anna coins he had twenty-seven rupees, so he was all right for coffee and sandwiches. The trolleyman, mistaking his reason for taking out the wallet, pushed with his hands and came sliding up. Embarrassed, Hiren shook his head again, this time so hard that he felt his jowls swing and then quickly pushed the swing door open and walked into the United Coffee House.

Why couldn't he just beg? Those missing legs were reason enough, why bring the god thing in? He always gave, on the simple calculation that no matter how shallow or escapist or bourgeois-guilt-ridden his motives were, the money meant more to them than it did to him – also he didn't have children and curtains and related expenses so there was always enough to give and he resented it when he couldn't. Couldn't – not wouldn't, because once Shani and company were dragged in, some Pavlovian reflex froze his hand. When he was younger and more recently returned from his American university, saying no to god-infected beggars had been easier. It had been a refusal of unreason. Now every time he shook his head, he felt cruel and dogmatic because a godling's name didn't change that halved beggar's need for his change, or even his rupee notes (in small denominations).

He was talking to himself when the waiter turned up with the menu. Without looking at it, he ordered chicken sandwiches and coffee and went back to shaking his head and arguing. Now he said no out of loyalty to a phantom, to that younger version of himself which had been superseded by a later, wiser model, but still lurked somewhere, convinced that saying no was just one part of a large, rational project to repair Indian lives. Hiren didn't know if he believed that any more but he didn't feel he could formally stop believing it either. He was too young . . . not even forty. Maybe he'd keep saying no for the next nine months till his fortieth birthday and then – if it was a Saturday – he could start handing out change to Shani-powered beggars.

He smelt talcum powder and looked up from his paper: it was the girl from last night, who had helped him right the Vice-President. She wasn't in a sari and she looked younger and less pretty in the tight yellow-green kameez she had on, but the intricate henna work on her palms helped him place her. Also she was in the company of the bull-necked man with the shaving shadow who had been keen to breathe life into the Vice-President.

'Hello Uncle,' she said, smiling, as her hands came together in a namaste. 'Can we join you?'

Hiren glanced at the other tables and saw they were all taken; the place had filled up in less than half an hour. He nodded, unamused by the uncle. He was just thirty-nine with no grey hair. They sat down and ordered cold coffees with ice-cream.

'Were you from the boy's side yesterday?' she asked, looking curious in a friendly sort of way.

Hiren noticed her escort hunch forwards alertly. He answered with a very small non-committal nod, that could have been mistaken for a yes.

'Babli Mausi asked me to take Ratan Bhaiya shopping because there aren't any proper shops in Kohima where he is posted. He wants to buy suede shoes but Bata hasn't opened yet. What do you do, uncle?'

Hiren looked at her hard and though her expression was the same, he knew there was more than just curiosity behind that abrupt, apropos-of-nothing question.

'I'm a scientist,' he said briefly, and looked down at the paper, because it wasn't true. It was true in a generic sense; he had trained as one and was employed as one; formally in fact, he was a Scientist with a capital S because that was his official designation in the Council of Scientific and Industrial Research. Scientist.

'A scientist!' she exclaimed. 'Do you know Ratan Bhaiya thought you were a Chinese spy?' She peeped sideways at her companion with demure malice who looked surly but unembarrassed by this indiscretion. 'But I thought you were the Japanese Ambassador because you were sitting on the red VIP sofa next to the Vice-President.'

Hiren didn't know how to respond so he took a huge bite from his sandwich and then sucked up some coffee to soften the breaded mass inside his mouth. How could she say all this? It wasn't as simple as her being young – she looked nineteen – and therefore without self-consciousness, because some of this was clearly intended to make Ratan Bhaiya uncomfortable, including the Bhaiya in Ratan Bhaiya because he'd noticed that the soldier didn't like being her honorary brother any more than Hiren liked being uncle. If she was getting at him, she couldn't be an innocent.

'I stopped doing science in Class VIII,' she volunteered. 'Actually I gave up three years before that when I realised I was no good at maths. Mrs Sundaram, our maths teacher, asked us how long would it take for a bathtub to fill if water was flowed into it at one rate and flowed out of it's bung-hole at another. I just kept thinking, why don't they plug the hole first? The more they made the sums like stories, the more confused I got. I knew science was full of maths so when we had to choose between Science and Arts in Class IX, I did Arts. I'm doing history in college.' She grinned. 'More names than numbers: Tudors, Stuarts, Mauryas, Guptas, Mughals. I mean there are numbers but they're fixed.' The cold coffee arrived and she stopped talking and began spooning the ice-cream floating on top of the tall glass into her mouth. A fuzzy white moustache overlay the down on her upper lip. 'You don't have to do anything with them . . . except remember them like 1526, the coming of the Mughals or 1931, the Civil Disobedience movement . . .'

'1930,' said Hiren, automatically.

She paused. 'Did you ever do history?' she asked him.

Hiren averted his eyes, conscious that he had been staring at her mouth.

'No,' he said with unnecessary emphasis, 'no, never.' Abruptly he wanted to leave, so he looked at his watch, excused himself and walked up to the cash desk to pay his bill there.

Pushing through the swing doors he thought of the two half-truths he had told her. He wasn't a scientist and he did do history. He did history all the time. Some people kept diaries; his great ambition was to devise a formal concordance of history and his personal life in three columns. There would be a public chronology on the right and a private one on the left. In the middle would be the entries that marked the convergence of the two chronologies, when the two worlds touched. There would be fewer entries in the middle column. Meeting the Vice-President the night before was a minor convergence but it qualified. Meeting VIPs was not the only way of getting in. Acting in a great film like *Sahib, Bibi Aur Ghulam*, even as an extra, would count, as would winning the Nobel Prize. When he was writing his doctoral thesis on the sitology of corn in Iowa, he used to dream of a bold-face middle-column entry: a corn hybrid that would do for Indian corn farming what dwarf wheat had done for the Green Revolution in the Punjab. An entry where his science would make a green revolution in the food crops of the poor. An entry in red capitals marking the year when his life made history. Once it was all he ever thought of; now it didn't fill his day but his day-dreams still drifted down that middle column.

He was still in front of the United Coffee House though he had been walking for a while now. He had gone round the inner circle without noticing. He was wet – it was still raining and each time he left the shelter of the colonnade to cross the radial roads that cut through the circles of Connaught Circus like spokes, he got wetter. The poor were still in their places, trapped by the rain. They were trying to beg but no one seemed to be dropping any money. People were meaner indoors. They gave at crossings, outside temples, by river-banks, on pavements, but not in covered corridors or verandas – casual charity was an outdoor sport.

The beggars were the problem, them and the poor generally. It was hard to be properly historical with them around. If history meant change and change meant more than simply growing older, the beggars needed to disappear or at least grow scarcer. Here they were always there like trees or hedges, as durable as the landscape, as uniform as traffic lights, a permanent context for everything. Until that changed there could be no real history for him or any other Indian, no bold-face entries in the middle column.

Janpath, like the other radial roads, was an ankle-deep river in spate. He stepped off the pavement to cross it and nearly disappeared. Someone had taken the lid off a man-hole to let rainwater drain and the resulting hole in the ground was perfectly invisible. Luckily the toe of his sandal landed on the rim of the hole and he had enough purchases to fall forwards. His white trousers, already grey with water, were now brown with churned-up dirt. But he got up and kept walking.

America was the place for history. Even Ames, which wasn't New York. It wasn't even Des Moines which could claim to be Iowa's capital. No; even in Ames which was less than a hundred years old when he was a student there, he had always felt he was riding the crest of world history. It was the kind of country where history could happen to anyone like it had happened to him when Dwight Eisenhower shook his hand. It happened in 1952 during the run-up to the presidential elections when Eisenhower spoke at an election meeting near Ames Station, standing on a platform hung with blue, white and red bunting. There was red-white-and-blue flying in the background . . . he remembered it perfectly because it had also been matriculation day and he had been taking pictures with his new Argus C-3. In them Eisenhower's hair was white. After the meeting was over, Ike shook hands with him. He singled him out; Hiren still didn't know why – maybe he was stalking the Chinese vote. Whatever the reason, in his prime, age twenty-six, weight one hundred and seventy pounds, wearing a matriculation costume with an enveloping cape that made him look like an early drawing for Superman, Hiren shook hands with the man who would preside over the USA's post-war pomp. That's how close he came to living America's golden age. He was even offered a post-doctoral job in Boston . . . but he didn't take it because he wanted to go home.

So shaking hands with Eisenhower couldn't figure in Hiren's middle-column in the way that meeting the Vice-President did because that date was part of a foreign history to which he didn't belong. Or maybe he could put it in as an honorary entry, but in italics to distinguish it from the real ones. The last Eisenhower picture Hiren had, was taken quickly, at an angle to the frame of the camera. It was a close, top-down shot of the cab of an open-top limo. It was a lovely picture, full of rush: the men at the edges of the cab had blurred heads. But Ike's head was in sharp focus.

Eisenhower in his car, surrounded by secret service men, driving away. He took America – and history – away with him.

That same Matriculation Day Hiren took a picture of his Major professor in his office. The professor was an alert-looking man in wire glasses and in the picture he was talking to a great-looking graduate student: dark, lean, Gregory Peck-like, dressed in a boxy suit, not a hair out of place. The colours of the picture glowed – the skin, the hair, the wood of the desk. It didn't look like a snapshot: it looked like a publicity still for a Bogart film because the cubicle they were sitting in had ground-glass partitions and reverse-lettering. Every American slide he had looked like that, each thing he had taken a picture of had a this-must-be-the-American-Dream quality to it – his landlady's backyard with rose trellises, birdbaths, and vaguely classical alabaster garden ornaments, Ames Campanile rising out of trees and carpet lawn, the world all green and gold because the colours of his slides had endured.

Once, in a letter home, to his mother, he spoke of the sharpness, cleanness, hardness, smoothness of American buildings, sidewalks, post boxes, and wrote that it was as if they were immune to time and use, like new things wrapped in cellophane. He contrasted it with the worn-ness, the clutter, the used-ness, the crumbling edges of home. Even as he wrote that he realised that this was evasive and defensive. America wasn't strange and different; home wasn't untidy and comfortable: American was better, India was worse. That was the truth and all the irony in the world couldn't change it. Irony was a defensive reflex, just a posher brand of knowingness. If Americans seemed literal it was because progress happened to them in an obvious way. For almost everyone he met in his time there, the world was visibly getting better. It was easy for them to believe in history.

But in India he needed newspapers and the daily reassurance of changing headlines because beyond the potted world of newsprint, nothing ever changed. And he left his copy of the *Statesman* in the United Coffee House in his hurry to quit the restaurant which meant that he would have to go halfway round the inner circle again. He didn't really mind because he was wet already and having gone round and round, another half-circuit wouldn't kill him. As he approached the restaurant, the door opened and the girl and Ratan Bhaiya emerged. They didn't see him because they turned left and began walking away. Hiren went in and recovered his newspaper. By the time he came out, they were preparing to brave the rain and cross Janpath. Ratan Bhaiya had unfurled a small bright-blue parasol and was holding it intimately over the girl's head. Hiren suddenly remembered the manhole but before he could shout they had stepped off the pavement. The man disappeared with his parasol. The girl remained in view.

Babboo was batting when the ambulance brought Ratan Bhaiya home. Ranga, who bowled very fast with a javelin thrower's action, had switched from throwing bouncers to chucking invisibly quick, crotch-high full-tosses. Everyone knew he chuckled, but he was too big to be told, so as soon as Babboo saw the ambulance he dropped his bat and announced that he had to go home.

'Scared?' sneered Ranga. 'For you I'll bowl underarm, come.'

'It's not that, yaar,' said Babboo with dignity, unbuckling the pad on his left leg. 'Someone's come home. He's dead.'

His sister had telephoned before lunch and lots of the grown-ups had rushed to the Casualty Ward of the All-India Institute of Medical Sciences where she had taken Ratan Bhaiya after he had been dragged out of the manhole. Babli Mausi had brought Meenakshi home immediately. They hadn't actually told Babboo but he guessed that Ratan Bhaiya was dead when he overheard Babli Mausi say that his father was making arrangements to shift the body.

The first thing his sister did after getting home was bathe for two hours. She came out and took less than a minute telling everyone how he had died of a broken neck and not from drowning even though he had fallen into a sewer, and then went on about how dirty she felt when they pulled him out and she had to feel his chest through the black sewer slime to check if he was alive because everyone was looking at her expectantly . . . they thought she was his wife.

'Rama, by-god, I can't tell you . . . I just kept thinking, what am I going to tell Babli Mausi? He was her husband's brother and she had brought him all the way from Jaipur just for the marriage.'

Till then her sister had been as grave as everyone else in the house; now she glanced at Arshi who glanced at her and then both of them covered their mouths with their hands and began heaving. Rama buried her face in a pillow; Arshi straightened hers for long enough to say, 'Sh-she didn't br-ring him j-j-just for the marriage,' and then burst into neighing, wriggling laughter.

Meenakshi looked at the two of them giggling about a freshly dead man she had seen die at first hand, but oddly, all her outraged mind could produce was a close-up of Ratan Bhaiya's bulge and a voice-over memory of Rama claiming that he built it up with socks. Arshi was reading her mind.

'D-did he die with his s-socks on?' she asked and collapsed on the bed, drumming her heels and crying with laughter.

Fed up with the giggling and disappointed by Meenujiji's vagueness on exactly how he died and the total absence of any detailed action – did his neck make a noise when it broke, did he die right off or twitch for a while, were his eyes open when he went, had he been bleeding from anywhere, did the blood trickle like water or glue – Babboo left the bedroom and slipped out of the house to play cricket.

When he returned to the house after the ambulance arrived, everyone was looking solemn again, except his mother, who was looking grim. Ratan Bhaiya had been taken inside. Outside, in the garden, he heard his mother ask his father why he had brought the body home. His father, wrung out by the ordeal of recovering Ratan Bhaiya, was annoyed by the question. 'I told you before leaving for the hospital that I was going to make arrangements to move him from the morgue.'

'But not here!' shouted his mother in a whisper. 'I thought you were planning to send it to his family in Jaipur. What are we going to do with it? Him.'

'Send him to Jaipur?' repeated his father, hissing with incredulousness. 'How? As unaccompanied baggage? By registered post? You think he's a parcel? He was our guest, Mohini. Chunni's called his parents; they said they'd catch the Rajasthan Roadways bus and be here by seven.'

'And then?'

'Then what?' snapped his father. 'He's their son. They'll take charge of him.'

'They'll get to the bus terminus by seven if the bus isn't late which means they'll get here by seven-thirty. It will be dark, they will be hungry, so the first thing they'll do, of course, is to take charge of their dead son. I hope that means they'll wake him up and take him home. Because I don't want him spending the night here. It's bad enough that someone dies the day after my brother's daughter's marriage, but imagine what Bitti's in-laws will think if we have a dead body living in the same house she got married from. When Kiki Babhi was ill I promised her that I'd marry Bitti off so she'd be proud . . .' She broke off holding the corner of her palloo to her quivering lips. 'Oh, why didn't you just leave him in the morgue?'

At nine, with no sign of the Goyals, his mother told Bhagwan Singh to take the twin beds out of the master bedroom and replace them with one of the cots that Babboo and the other children used to sleep on the roof. Since servants weren't allowed to operate electrical devices, she sent Rama up separately to switch on the airconditioner. 'Set it on Hi-Cool,' she called after her. Then she turned to Babboo's father.

'We need three blocks of ice,' she said.

'It's nine-thirty, Mohini. Who will sell me blocks of ice?'

'This may be a vegetarian house,' said his mother in a dangerously even tone, 'but even I know that dead bodies have to be refrigerated. Since we can't put Ratan into the Frigidaire we need to put him on ice. Thanks to you, I am having to get a bed made up for a dead man. So please don't just sit there, get me some ice.'

His father left, but before he returned with the ice, his

mother forced them up to the roof to sleep. He and Tara had to share a cot since they were one short because of Ratan Bhaiya. Tara hugged his arm and went to sleep. He lay awake a long time, looking at the stars through the fine mesh of the mosquito net, wondering what Ratan Bhaiya would be in his next life. Not a human. Babboo had noticed the way he had trailed Meenujiji and tried to touch her. An octopus, he decided; eight arms to touch with but doomed to feel and suck and fart his life away at the bottom of the sea. The cruelty of the thought shocked him. Poor Ratan Bhaiya was dead. *Requiescat in pace*, he made himself think. Father Romeiro had just taught them that in Moral Science class. *Ad Dei gloriam* surfaced sleepily in the same corner of his mind. Carefully, so that he didn't squash Tara, he turned on his side. As he closed his eyes, a last involuntary thought feathered through his head. *Quod erat demonstrandum . . .*

In the middle of the night he came awake. He could hear the shrill whirring of a cricket but he had been woken by something else. Tara was asleep. He looked around and saw that three of the beds were empty: he could tell because there was enough moonlight to see that the mosquito nets weren't properly tucked in under the mattress. Rama, Arshi and Meenakshi were missing. He slid out of bed and carefully tucked in the edges of the net to keep Tara from being bitten. Then, clutching the bannister, he felt his way down the moonless stairs. He knew where they'd be; he had known from the moment he saw that they weren't in bed. So he turned right where the steps ended and crept to the doors of the master bedroom. He edged the doors open and slipped in. The room was incredibly cold. 'I dare you,' rasped someone in a whisper. By the erratic light of a single torch held by one of them he could make out the body shrouded like a mummy lying on a shiny, silver mattress. Meenakshi was nearest the door. The other two were standing close to each other by the foot of the body. Arshi was holding the torch.

'I dare you!' hissed Rana, her plain face ugly with excitement.

'Shut up!' said Arshi, wiping her upper lip.

The torch's beam jagged through the room, bouncing off the dressing table's invisible mirror.

'What's this dare business. I've dissected dead bodies for a whole year. I'm doing this for you. You're the one who was dying to see it.'

'Arshi, no!' pleaded Meenakshi, hoarse with fear. 'Switch the torch off and let's go up. You two are mad! If Maji comes in . . .'

'I dare you,' whispered Rana for the third time.

Arshi fumbled for endless seconds then whipped the sheet off Ratan Bhaiya's legs and pointed the torch. Suddenly there were two spot-lit groins in the room: one in the mirror, one outside it. Babboo thought it looked like a small blind vulture: a long naked neck with a ruff of black feathers where it ended. There was breathless silence in the room and then inky blackness as Arshi switched off the torch without warning. Taking advantage of the darkness, Babboo slipped out and raced upstairs. He climbed into bed, tidied up the mosquito net behind him and was shamming sleep by the time the other three climbed the stairs. He heard cots creak as they climbed in. Someone walked up to his cot.

'I saw you downstairs.' It was Rama. 'If Maji gets to hear a word of this, I'll bury you alive. You hear?'

Babboo bobbed his head without looking up. She walked away.

Some time passed. Babboo felt hugely alert. He thought he could hear bat-wings flap across the night sky. He heard a far-away flush being pulled, the cistern emptying then filling. He wondered if he would ever sleep again. A cot rocked noisily. He looked around and saw Meenakshi's mosquito net billow as she pushed off her bed and ran to the drain grate by the parapet. She doubled up over it and he heard horrible retching sounds as she vomited. He half-sat up and then lay down again when he saw the other two climb out of bed. One put her arm around Meenakshi and the other poured water from the surahi into a glass and gave it to her to drink. They were murmuring to her but she didn't want to talk. She drank the water and went back to bed, sniffing a little. Much later, in the early morning when he got out of bed to piss, he walked up to the drain where she had thrown up. Spreading his legs, he trained his stream on the vomit and hosed it down the drain. He wanted to help his sister forget the strangeness of yesterday.

Arundhati Roy

ABHILASH TALKIES

ABHILASH TALKIES ADVERTISED itself as the first cinema hall in Kerala with a 70mm CinemaScope screen. To drive home the point, its facade had been designed as a cement replica of a curved CinemaScope screen. On top (cement writing, neon lighting) it said *Abhilash Talkies* in English and Malayalam.

The toilets were called HIS and HERS. HERS for Ammu, Rahel and Baby Kochamma. HIS for Estha alone, because Chacko had gone to see about the bookings at the Hotel Sea Queen.

'Will you be okay?' Ammu said, worried.

Estha nodded.

Through the red formica door that closed slowly on its own, Rahel followed Ammu and Baby Kochamma into HERS. She turned to wave across the slipperoily marble floor at Estha Alone (with a comb), in his beige and pointy shoes. Estha waited in the dirty marble lobby with the lonely, watching mirrors till the red door took his sister away. Then he turned and padded off to HIS.

In HERS, Ammu suggested that Rahel balance in the air to piss. She said that Public Pots were Dirty. Like Money was. You never knew who'd touched it. Lepers. Butchers. Car Mechanics. (Pus. Blood. Grease.)

Once when Kochu Maria took her to the butcher's shop, Rahel noticed that the green five-rupee note that he gave them

Extract from the novel *The God of Small Things*.

535

had a tiny blob of red meat on it. Kochu Maria wiped the meat blob away with her thumb. The juice left a red smear. She put the money into her bodice. Meat-smelling blood money.

Rahel was too short to balance in the air above the pot, so Ammu and Baby Kochamma held her up, her legs hooked over their arms. Her feet pigeon-toed in Bata sandals. High in the air with her knickers down. For a moment nothing happened, and Rahel looked up at her mother and baby grand-aunt with naughty (now what?) question marks in her eyes.

'Come on,' Ammu said. 'Sssss . . .'

Sssss for the sound of Soo-soo. Mmmmm for the Sound of Myooozick.

Rahel giggled. Ammu giggled. Baby Kochamma giggled. When the trickle started they adjusted her aerial position. Rahel was unembarrassed. She finished and Ammu had the toilet paper.

'Shall you or shall I?' Baby Kochamma said to Ammu.

'Either way,' Ammu said. 'Go ahead. You.'

Rahel held her handbag. Baby Kochamma lifted her rumpled sari. Rahel studied her baby grand-aunt's enormous legs. (Years later during a history lesson being read out in school – *The Emperor Babur had a wheatish complexion and pillar-like thighs* – this scene would flash before her. Baby Kochamma balanced like a big bird over a public pot. Blue veins like lumpy knitting running up her translucent shins. Fat knees dimpled. Hair on them. Poor little tiny feet to carry such a load!) Baby Kochamma waited for half of half a moment. Head thrust forwards. Silly smile. Bosom swinging low. Melons in a blouse. Bottom up and out. When the gurgling, bubbling sound came, she listened with her eyes. A yellow brook burbled through a mountain pass.

Rahel liked all this. Holding the handbag. Everyone pissing in front of everyone. Like friends. She knew nothing then, of how precious a feeling this was. *Like friends* . . . They would never be together like this again. Ammu, Baby Kochamma and she.

When Baby Kochamma finished, Rahel looked at her watch.

'So long you took, Baby Kochamma,' she said. 'It's ten to two.'

> *Rubadub dub* [Rahel thought]
> *Three women in a tub*
> *Tarry a while said Slow*

She thought of Slow being a person. Slow Kurien. Slow Kutty. Slow Mol. Slow Kochamma.

Slow Kutty. Fast Verghese. And Kuriakose. Three brothers with dandruff.

Ammu did hers in a whisper. Against the side of the pot so you couldn't hear. Her father's hardness had left her eyes and they were Ammu-eyes again. She had deep dimples in her smile and didn't seem angry any more. About Velutha or the spit-bubble.

That was a Good Sign.

Estha Alone in HIS had to piss on to naphthalene balls and cigarette stubs in the urinal. To piss in the pot would be Defeat. To piss in the urinal, he was too short. He needed Height. He searched for Height, and in a corner of HIS, he found it. A dirty broom, a squash bottle half-full of a milky liquid (phenyl) with floaty black things in it. A limp floor-swab, and two rusty tin cans of nothing. They could have been Paradise Pickle products. Pineapple chunks in syrup. Or slices. Pineapple slices. His honour redeemed by his grand-mother's cans. Estha Alone organised the rusty cans of nothing in front of the urinal. He stood on them, one foot on each, and pissed carefully, with minimal wobble. Like a Man. The cigarette stubs, soggy then, were wet now, and swirly. Hard to light. When he finished, Estha moved the cans to the basin in front of the mirror. He washed his hands and wet his hair. Then, dwarfed by the size of Ammu's comb that was too big for him, he reconstructed his puff carefully. Slicked back, then pushed forwards and swivelled sideways at the very end. He returned the comb to his pocket, stepped off the tins and put them back with the bottle and swab and broom. He bowed to them all. The whole shooting match. The bottle, the broom, the cans, the limp floorswab.

'Bow,' he said, and smiled, because when he was younger, he had been under the impression that you had to say 'Bow' when you bowed. That you had to *say* it to do it.

'Bow Estha,' they'd say. And he'd bow and say 'Bow', and they'd look at each other and laugh, and he'd worry.

Estha Alone of the uneven teeth.

Outside, he waited for his mother, his sister and his baby grand-aunt. When they came out, Ammu said, 'Okay Esthappen?'

Estha said 'Okay,' and shook his head carefully to preserve his puff.

Okay? Okay? He put the comb back into her handbag. Ammu felt a sudden clutch of love for her reserved, dignified little son in his beige and pointy shoes, who had just completed his first adult assignment. She ran loving fingers through his hair. She spoilt his puff.

The Man with the steel Ever Ready Torch said that the picture had started, so to hurry. They had to rush up the red steps with the old red carpet. Red staircase with red spit stains in the red corner. The Man with the Torch scrunched up his mundu and held it tucked under his balls, in his left hand. As he climbed, his calf muscles hardened under his climbing skin like hairy cannon balls. He held the torch in his right hand. He hurried with his mind.

'It started long ago,' he said.

So they'd missed the beginning. Missed the rippled velvet curtain going up, with light bulbs in the clustered yellow tassels. Slowly up, and the music would have been *Baby Elephant Walk* from *Hatari*. Or *Colonel Bogey's March*.

Ammu held Estha's hand. Baby Kochamma, heaving up the steps, Rahel's. Baby Kochamma, weighed down by her melons, would not admit to herself that she was looking forward to the picture. She preferred to feel that she was only doing it for the children's sake. In her mind she kept an organised, careful account of Things She'd Done For People, and

Things People Hadn't Done For Her.

She liked the early nun-bits best, and hoped they hadn't missed them. Ammu explained to Estha and Rahel that people always loved best what they *Identified* most with. Rahel supposed she Identified most with Christopher Plummer who acted as Captain von Trapp. Chacko didn't Identify with him at all and called him Captain von Clapp Trapp.

Rahel was like an excited mosquito on a leash. Flying. Weightless. Up two steps. Down two. Up one. She climbed five flights of red stairs for Baby Kochamma's one.

> *I'm Popeye the sailor man* dum dum
> *I live in a cara-van* dum dum
> *I op-en the door*
> *And Fall-on the floor*
> *I'm Popeye the sailor man* dum dum

Up two. Down two. Up one. Jump jump.

'Rahel,' Ammu said. 'you haven't learnt your Lesson yet. Have you?'

Rahel had: *Excitement Always Leads to Tears.* Dum dum.

They arrived at the Princess Circle lobby. They walked past the Refreshment Counter where the orangedrinks were waiting. And the lemondrinks were waiting. The orange too orange. The lemon too lemon. The chocolates too melty.

The Torch Man opened the heavy Princess Circle door into the fan-whirring, peanut-crunching darkness. It smelled of breathing people and hair oil. And old carpets. A magical, *Sound of Music* smell that Rahel remembered and treasured. Smells, like music, hold memories. She breathed deep, and bottled it up for posterity.

Estha had the tickets. Little Man. He lived in a cara-van. Dum dum.

The Torch Man shone his light on the pink tickets. Row J. Numbers 17, 18, 19, 20. Estha, Ammu, Rahel, Baby Kochamma. They squeezed past irritated people who moved their legs this way and that to make space. The seats of the chairs had to be pulled down. Baby Kochamma held Rahel's seat down while she climbed on. She wasn't heavy enough so the chair folded her into itself like sandwich stuffing, and she watched from between her knees. Two knees and a fountain. Estha, with more dignity than that, sat on the edge of his chair.

The shadows of the fans were on the sides of the screen where the picture wasn't.

Off with the torch. On with the World Hit.

The camera soared up in the sky-blue (car-coloured) Austrian sky with the clear, sad sound of church bells.

Far below, on the ground, in the courtyard of the abbey, the cobblestones were shining. Nuns walked across it. Like slow cigars. Quiet nuns clustered quietly around their Reverend Mother who never read their letters. They gathered like ants around a crumb of toast. Cigars around a Queen Cigar. No hair on their knees. No melons in their blouses. And their breath like peppermint. They had complaints to make to their Reverend Mother. Sweet-singing complaints. About Julie Andrews who was still up in the hills, singing *The Hills Are Alive* and was, once again, late for Mass.

> *She climbs a tree and scrapes her knee*

The nuns sneaked musically.

> *Her dress has got a tear*
> *She waltzes on her way to Mass*
> *And whistles on the stair . . .*

People in the audience were turning around.
'Shhh!' they said.
'Shh! Shh! Shh!

> *And underneath her wimple -*
> *She's got curlers in her hair!*

There was a voice from outside the picture. It was clear and true, cutting through the fan whirring, peanut-crunching darkness. There was a nun in the audience. Heads in the audience twisted around like bottle caps. Black-haired backs of heads became faces with mouths and moustaches. Hissing mouths with teeth like sharks. Many of them. Like stickers on a card.

'Shhhh!' they said together.

It was Estha who was singing. A nun with a puff. An Elvis Pelvis nun. He couldn't help it.

'Get him out of here!' the Audience said, when they found him.

Shutup or Getout. Getout or Shutup.

The audience was a Big Man. Estha was a Little Man, with the tickets.

'Estha for heavens' sake, shut UP!!' Ammu's fierce whisper said.

So Estha shut UP. The mouths and moustaches turned away. But then, without warning, the song came back, and Estha couldn't stop it.

'Ammu, can I go and sing it outside?' Estha said (before Ammu smacked him). 'I'll come back after the song?'

'But don't ever expect me to bring you out again,' Ammu said. 'You're embarrassing *all* of us.'

But Estha couldn't help it. He got up to go. Past angry Ammu. Past Rahel concentrating through her knees. Past Baby Kochamma. Past the Audience that had to move its legs again. Thiswayandthat. The red sign over the door said EXIT in a red light. Estha EXITed.

In the lobby, the orangedrinks were waiting. The lemondrinks were waiting. The melty chocolates were waiting. The electric blue foam-leather car-sofas were waiting. The *Coming-Soon!* posters were waiting.

Estha Alone sat on the electric blue foam-leather car-sofa, in the Abhilash Talkies Princess Circle lobby, and sang. In a nun's voice, as clear as clean water.

> *But how d'you make her stay?*
> *And listen to all you say?*

The man behind the Refreshments Counter, who'd been asleep on a row of stools, waiting for the interval, woke up. He saw, with gummy eyes, Estha Alone in his beige and pointy shoes. And his spoiled puff. The Man wiped his marble counter with a dirt-coloured rag. And he waited. And waiting he wiped. And wiping he waited. And watched Estha sing.

> *How do you keep a wave upon the sand?*
> *Ohhh how do you solve a problem like Maree . . . yah?*

'Ay! *Eda cherukka*!' the Orangedrink Lemondrink Man said, in a gravelly voice thick with sleep. 'What the hell d'you think you're doing?'

> *How do you hold a*
> *moonbeam*
> *in your hand?*

Estha sang.

'Ay!' the Orangedrink Lemondrink Man said. 'Look, this is my resting time. Soon I'll have to wake up and work. So I can't have you singing English songs here. Stop it.' His gold wristwatch was almost hidden by his curly forearm hair. His gold chain was almost hidden by his chest hair. His white Terylene shirt was unbuttoned to where the swell of his belly began. He looked like an unfriendly, jewelled bear. Behind him there were mirrors for people to look at themselves while they bought cold drinks and refreshments. To reorganise their puffs and settle their buns. The mirrors watched Estha.

'I could file a Written Complaint against you,' the man said to Estha. 'How would you like that? A Written Complaint?'

Estha stopped singing and got up to go back in.

'Now that I'm up,' the Orangedrink Lemondrink Man said. 'Now that you've woken me up from my Resting Time, now that you've *disturbed* me, at least come and have a drink. It's the least you can do.'

He had an unshaven, jowly face. His teeth, like yellow piano keys, watched little Elvis the Pelvis.

'No thank you,' Elvis said politely. 'My family will be expecting me. And I've finished my pocket money.'

'*Porketmunny?*' The Orangedrink Lemondrink Man said with his teeth still watching. 'First English songs, and now *porketmunny!* Where d'you live? On the moon?'

Estha turned to go.

'Wait a minute!' The Orangedrink Lemondrink Man said sharply. 'Just a minute!' he said again, more gently. 'I thought I asked you a question.'

His yellow teeth were magnets. They saw, they smiled, they sang, they smelled, they moved. They mesmerised.

'I asked you where you lived,' he said, spinning his nasty web.

'Ayemenem,' Estha said. 'I live in Ayemenem. My grandmother owns Paradise Pickles & Preserves. She's the Sleeping Partner.'

'Is she, now?' the Orangedrink Lemondrink Man said. 'And who does she sleep with?'

He laughed a nasty laugh that Estha couldn't understand. 'Never mind. You wouldn't understand.'

'Come and have a drink,' he said. 'A Free Cold Drink. Come. Come here and tell me all about your grandmother.'

Estha went. Drawn by yellow teeth.

'Here. Behind the counter,' the Orangedrink Lemondrink Man said. He dropped his voice to a whisper. 'It has to be a secret, because drinks are not allowed before the interval. It's a Theatre Offence.'

'Cognizable,' he added after a pause.

Estha went behind the Refreshments Counter for his free cold drink. He saw the three high stools arranged in a row for the Orangedrink Lemondrink Man to sleep on. The wood shiny from his sitting.

'Now if you'll kindly hold this for me,' the Orangedrink Lemondrink Man said, handing Estha his penis through his soft white muslin dhoti. 'I'll get you your drink. Orange? Lemon?'

Estha held it because he had to.

'Orange? Lemon?' the man said. 'Lemonorange?'

'Lemon please,' Estha said politely.

He got a cold bottle and a straw. So he held a bottle in one hand and a penis in the other. Hard. Hot, veiny. Not a moonbeam.

The Orangedrink Lemondrink Man's hand closed over Estha's. His thumbnail was long like a woman's. He moved Estha's hand up and down. First slowly. Then fast.

The lemondrink was cold and sweet. The penis hot and hard.

The piano keys were watching.

'So your grandmother runs a factory?' the Orangedrink Lemondrink Man said. 'What kind of factory?'

'Many products,' Estha said, not looking, with the straw in his mouth. 'Squashes, pickles, jams, curry powders. Pineapple slices.'

'Good,' the Orangedrink Lemondrink Man said. 'Excellent.'

His hand closed tighter over Estha's. Tight and sweaty. And faster still.

> Fast faster fest
> Never let it rest
> Until the fast is faster,
> And the faster's fest.

Through the soggy paper straw (almost flattened with spit and fear), the liquid lemon sweetness rose. Blowing through the straw (while his other hand moved), Estha blew bubbles into the bottle. Stickysweet lemon bubbles of the drink he couldn't drink. In his head he listed his grandmother's produce.

544

PICKLES	SQUASHES	JAMS
Mango	*Orange*	*Banana*
Green pepper	*Grape*	*Mixed fruit*
Bitter gourd	*Pineapple*	*Grapefruit marmalade*
Garlic	*Mango*	
Salted lime		

Then the gristly-bristly face contorted, and Estha's hand
was wet and hot and sticky. It had egg-white on it. White egg-
white. Quarter-boiled.

The lemondrink was cold and sweet. The penis was soft
and shrivelled like an empty leather change-purse. With his
dirt-coloured rag, the man wiped Estha's other hand.

'Now finish your drink,' he said, and affectionately
squished a cheek of Estha's bottom. Tight plums in drain-
pipes. And beige and pointy shoes.

'You mustn't waste it,' he said. 'Think of all the poor
people who have nothing to eat or drink. You're a lucky rich
boy, with *porketmunny* and a grandmother's factory to
inherit. You should Thank God that you have no worries.
Now finish your drink.'

And so, behind the Refreshments Counter, in the Abhilash
Talkies Princess Circle lobby, in the hall with Kerala's first
70mm CinemaScope screen, Esthappen Yako finished his free
bottle of fizzed, lemon-flavoured fear. His lemontoolemon too
cold. Too sweet. The fizz came up his nose. He would be given
another bottle soon (free, fizzed fear). But he didn't know that
yet. He held his sticky Other Hand away from his body.

It wasn't supposed to touch anything.

When Estha finished his drink, the Orangedrink
Lemondrink Man said, 'Finished? Goodboy.'

He took the empty bottle and the flattened straw, and sent
Estha back into *The Sound of Music*.

Back inside the hair-oil darkness, Estha held his Other
Hand carefully (upwards, as though he was holding an imagined orange). He slid past the audience (their legs moving
thiswayandthat), past Baby Kochamma, past Rahel (still tilted
back), past Ammu (still annoyed). Estha sat down, still hold-

ing his sticky orange.

And there was Captain von Clapp Trapp. Christopher Plummer. Arrogant. Hard-hearted. With a mouth like a slit. And a steelshrill police whistle. A Captain with seven children. Clean children, like a packet of peppermints. He pretended not to love them, but he did. He loved them. He loved her (Julie Andrews), she loved him, they loved the children, the children loved them. They all loved each other. They were clean, white children, and their beds were soft with Ei. Der. Downs.

The house they lived in had a lake and gardens, a wide staircase, white doors and windows, and curtains with flowers.

The clean white children, even the big ones, were scared of thunder. To comfort them, Julie Andrews put them all into her clean bed, and sang them a clean song about a few of her favourite things. These were a few of her favourite things.

1. Girls in white dresses with blue satin sashes.
2. Wild geese that flew with the moon on their wings.
3. Bright copper kettles.
4. Doorbells and sleighbells and schnitzel with noodles.
5. Etc.

And then, in the minds of certain two-egg twin members of the audience in Abhilash Talkies, some questions arose, that needed answers, ie:

(a). *Did Captain von Clapp Trapp shiver his leg?*
He did not.
(b). *Did Captain von Clapp Trapp blow spit bubbles? Did he?*
He did most certainly not.
(c). *Did he gobble?*
He did not.

Oh Captain von Trapp, Captain von Trapp, could you love the little fellow with the orange in the smelly auditorium?

He's just held the Orangedrink Lemondrink Man's soo-soo

in his hand, but could you love him still?

And his twin sister? Tilting upwards with her fountain in a Love-in-Tokyo? Could you love her too?

Captain von Trapp had some questions of his own.

(a). *Are they clean white children?*
     No. (*But Sophie Mol is.*)
(b). *Do they blow spit bubbles?*
     Yes. (*But Sophie Mol doesn't.*)
(c). *Do they shiver their legs? Like clerks?*
     Yes. (*But Sophie Mol doesn't.*)
(d). *Have they, either or both, ever held strangers' soo-soos?*
     N . . . Nyes. (*But Sophie Mol hasn't.*)

'Then I'm sorry,' Captain von Clapp Trapp said. 'It's out of the question. I cannot love them. I cannot be their Baba. Oh no.'

Captain von Clapp Trapp couldn't.

Estha put his head in his lap.

'What's the matter?' Ammu said. 'If you're sulking again, I'm taking you straight home. Sit up please. And watch. That's what you've been brought here for.'

Finish the drink.

Watch the picture.

Think of all the poor people.

Lucky rich boy with porketmunny. No worries.

Estha sat up and watched. His stomach heaved. He had a greenwavy, thick-watery, lumpy, sea-weedy, floaty, bottom-less-bottomful feeling.

'Ammu?' he said.

'Now WHAT?' The WHAT snapped, barked, spat out.

'Feeling vomity,' Estha said.

'Just feeling or d'you want to?' Ammu's voice was worried. 'Don't know.'

'Shall we go and try?' Ammu said. 'It'll make you feel better.'

'Okay,' Estha said.

547

Okay? Okay.

'Where're you going?' Baby Kochamma wanted to know.

'Estha's going to try and vomit,' Ammu said.

'Where're you going?' Rahel asked.

'Feeling vomity,' Estha said.

'Can I come and watch?'

'No,' Ammu said.

Past the audience again (legs thiswayandthat). Last time to sing. This time to try and vomit. Exit through the EXIT. Outside in the marble lobby, the Orangedrink Lemondrink Man was eating a sweet. His cheek was bulging with a moving sweet. He made soft, sucking sounds like water draining from a basin. There was a green Parry's wrapper on the counter. Sweets were free for this man. He had a row of free sweets in dim bottles. He wiped the marble counter with his dirt-coloured rag that he held in his hairy watch arm. When he saw the luminous woman with polished shoulders and the little boy, a shadow slipped across his face. Then he smiled his portable piano smile.

'Out again so soon?' he said.

Estha was already retching. Ammu moon-walked him to the Princess Circle bathroom. HERS.

He was held up, wedged between the not-clean basin and Ammu's body. Legs dangling. The basin had steel taps, and rust stains. And a brown-webbed mesh of hairline cracks, like the road map of some great, intricate city.

Estha convulsed, but nothing came. Just thoughts. And they floated out and floated back in. Ammu couldn't see them. They hovered like storm clouds over the Basin City. But the basin men and basin women went about their usual basin business. Basin cars, and basin buses, still whizzed around. Basin life went on.

'No?' Ammu said.

'No,' Estha said.

No? No.

'Then wash your face,' Ammu said. 'Water always helps. Wash your face and let's go and have a fizzy lemondrink.'

Estha washed his face and hands and face and hands. His

eyelashes were wet and bunched together.

The Orangedrink Lemondrink Man folded the green sweet wrapper and fixed the fold with his painted thumbnail. He stunned a fly with a rolled magazine. Delicately, he flicked it over the edge of the counter on to the floor. It lay on its back and waved its feeble legs.

'Sweetboy this,' he said to Ammu. 'Sings nicely.'

'He's my son,' Ammu said.

'Really?' the Orangedrink Lemondrink Man said, and looked at Ammu with his teeth. 'Really? You don't look old enough!'

'He's not feeling well,' Ammu said. 'I thought a cold drink would make him feel better.'

'Of course,' the man said. 'Ofcourseofcourse. Orange-lemon? Lemonorange?'

Dreadful, dreaded question.

'No thankyou,' Estha looked at Ammu. Greenwavy, sea-weedy, bottomless-bottomful.

'What about you?' the Orangedrink Lemondrink Man asked Ammu.

'CocacolaFanta? IcecreamRosemilk?'

'No. Not for me. Thankyou,' Ammu said. Deep-dimpled, luminous woman.

'Here,' the man said, with a fistful of sweets, like a generous air hostess. 'These are for your little Mon.'

'No. Thankyou,' Estha said, looking at Ammu.

'Take them Estha,' Ammu said. 'Don't be rude.'

Estha took them.

'Say Thankyou,' Ammu said.

'Thankyou,' Estha said. (For the sweets, for the white egg-white.)

'No mention,' the Orangedrink Lemondrink Man said in English.

'So!' he said. 'Mon says you're from Ayemenem?'

'Yes,' Ammu said.

'I come there often,' the Orangedrink Lemondrink Man said. 'My wife's people are Ayemenem people. I know where your factory is. Paradise Pickles isn't it? He told me. Your mon.'

He knew where to find Estha. That was what he was trying to say. It was a warning.

Ammu saw her son's bright fever-button eyes.

'We must go,' she said. 'Mustn't risk a fever. Their cousin is coming tomorrow.' She explained to Uncle. And then, added casually, 'From London.'

'From London?' A new respect gleamed in Uncle's eyes. For a family with London connections.

'Estha you stay here with Uncle. I'll get Baby Kochamma and Rahel,' Ammu said.

'Come,' Uncle said. 'Come and sit with me on a high stool.'

'No Ammu! No, Ammu, no! I want to come with you!'

Ammu, surprised at the unusually shrill insistence from her usually quiet son, apologised to the Orangedrink Lemondrink Uncle.

'He's not usually like this. Come on then, Esthappen.'

The back-inside smell. Fan shadows. Backs of heads. Necks. Collars. Hair. Buns. Plaits. Ponytails.

A fountain in a Love-in-Tokyo. A little girl and an ex-nun.

Captain von Trapp's seven peppermint children had had their peppermint baths, and were standing in a peppermint line with their hair slicked down, singing in obedient peppermint voices to the woman the Captain nearly married. The blonde Baroness who shone like a diamond.

> *The hills are alive*
> *with the Sound of Music*

'We have to go,' Ammu said to Baby Kochamma and Rahel.

'But Ammu!' Rahel said. 'The Main Things haven't even happened yet! He hasn't even *kissed* her! He hasn't even torn up the Hitler flat yet! They haven't even been *betrayed* by Rolf the Postman!'

'Estha's sick,' Ammu said. 'Come on!'

'The Nazi soldiers haven't even come!'

'Come on,' Ammu said. 'Get up!'

'They haven't even done *High on a Hill Was a Lonely Goatherd!*'

'Estha has to be well for Sophie Mol, doesn't he?' Baby Kochamma said.

'He doesn't,' Rahel said, but mostly to herself.

'What did you say?' Baby Kochamma said, getting the general drift, but not what was actually said.

'Nothing,' Rahel said.

'I *heard* you,' Baby Kochamma said.

Outside, Uncle was reorganising his dim bottles. Wiping with his dirt-coloured rag the ring-shaped water-stains they had left on his marble Refreshments Counter. Preparing for the interval. He was a clean Orangedrink Lemondrink Uncle. He had an air hostess's heart trapped in a bear's body.

'Going then?' he said.

'Yes,' Ammu said. 'Where can we get a taxi?'

'Out of the gate, up the road, on your left,' he said looking at Rahel. 'You never told me you had a little Mol too.' And holding out another sweet 'Here Mol – for you.'

'Take mine!' Estha said quickly, not wanting Rahel to go near the man.

But Rahel had already started towards him. As she approached him, he smiled at her and something about that portable piano smile, something about the steady gaze in which he held her, made her shrink from him. It was the most hideous thing she had ever seen. She spun around to look at Estha.

She backed away from the hairy man.

Estha pressed his Parry's sweets into her hand and she felt his fever-hot fingers whose tips were as cold as death.

' 'Bye Mon,' Uncle said to Estha. 'I'll see you in Ayemenem sometime.'

So, the red steps once again. This time Rahel lagging. Slow. No I don't want to go. A ton of bricks on a leash.

'Sweet chap, that Orangedrink Lemondrink fellow,' Ammu said.

'Chhi!' Baby Kochamma said.

'He doesn't look it, but he was surprisingly sweet with Estha,' Ammu said.

'So why don't you marry him then?' Rahel said petulantly.

Time stopped on the red staircase. Estha stopped. Baby Kochamma stopped.

'Rahel,' Ammu said.

Rahel froze. She was desperately sorry for what she had said. She didn't know where those words had come from. She didn't know that she'd had them in her. But they were out now, and wouldn't go back in. They hung about that red staircase like clerks in a Government office. Some stood, some sat and shivered their legs.

'Rahel,' Ammu said. 'Do you realise what you have just done?'

Frightened eyes and a fountain looked back at Ammu.

'It's all right. Don't be scared,' Ammu said. 'Just answer me. Do you?'

'What?' Rahel said in the smallest voice she had.

'Realise what you've just done?' Ammu said.

Frightened eyes and a fountain looked back at Ammu.

'D'you know what happens when you hurt people?' Ammu said. 'When you hurt people, they begin to love you less. That's what careless words do,' Ammu said. 'They make people love you a little less.'

A cold moth with unusually dense dorsal tufts landed lightly on Rahel's heart. Where its icy legs touched her, she got goose bumps. Six goose bumps on her careless heart.

A little less her Ammu loved her.

And so, out the gate, up the road, and to the left. The taxi stand. A hurt mother, an ex-nun, a hot child and a cold one. Six goose bumps and a moth.

The taxi smelled of sleep. Old clothes rolled up. Damp towels. Armpits. It was, after all, the taxi-driver's home. He lived in it. It was the only place he had to store his smells. The seats had been killed. Ripped. A swathe of dirty yellow sponge spilled out and shivered on the back seat like an immense jaundiced liver. The driver had the ferrety alertness of a small rodent. He had a hooked, Roman nose and a Little Richard moustache. He was so small that he watched the road through the steering wheel. To passing traffic it looked like a taxi with passengers but no driver. He drove fast, pugnaciously, darting into empty spaces, nudging other cars out of their lanes. Accelerating at zebra crossings. Jumping lights.

'Why not use a cushion or a pillow or something?' Baby Kochamma suggested in her friendly voice. 'You'll be able to see better.'

'Why not mind your own business, sister?' the driver suggested in his unfriendly one.

Driving past the inky sea, Estha put his head out of the window. He could taste the hot, salt breeze on his mouth. He could feel it lift his hair. He knew that if Ammu found out about what he had done with the Orangedrink Lemondrink Man, she'd love him less as well. Very much less. He felt the shaming churning heaving turning sickness in his stomach. He longed for the river. Because water always helps.

The sticky neon night rushed past the taxi window. It was hot inside the taxi, and quiet. Baby Kochamma looked flushed and excited. She loved not being the cause of ill-feeling. Every time a pye-dog strayed on to the road, the driver made a sincere effort to kill it.

The moth on Rahel's heart spread its velvet wings, and the chill crept into her bones.

In the Hotel Sea Queen car park, the sky-blue Plymouth gossiped with other, smaller cars. *Hslip Hslip Hsnooh-snah*. A big lady at a small ladies' party. Tailfins aflutter.

'Room numbers three hundred and thirteen and three hundred and twenty-seven,' the man at the reception said. 'Non airconditioned. Twin beds. Lift is closed for repair.'

The bellboy who took them up wasn't a boy and hadn't a bell. He had dim eyes and two buttons missing on his frayed maroon coat. His greyed undershirt showed. He had to wear his silly bellhop's cap tilted sideways with its tight plastic strap sunk into his sagging dewlap. It seemed unnecessarily cruel to make an old man wear a cap sideways like that and arbitrarily reorder the way in which age chose to hang from his chin.

There were more red steps to climb. The same red carpet from the cinema hall was following them around. Magic flying carpet.

Chacko was in his room. Caught feasting. Roast chicken, finger chips, sweetcorn and chicken soup, two parathas and vanilla ice-cream with chocolate sauce. Sauce in a sauceboat. Chacko often said that his ambition was to die of overeating. Mammachi said it was a sure sign of suppressed unhappiness. Chacko said it was no such thing. He said it was Sheer Greed.

Chacko was puzzled to see everybody back so early, but pretended otherwise. He kept eating.

The original plan had been that Estha would sleep with Chacko, and Rahel with Ammu and Baby Kochamma. But now that Estha wasn't well and Love had been reapportioned (Ammu loved her a little less), Rahel would have to sleep with Chacko, and Estha with Ammu and Baby Kochamma.

Ammu took Rahel's pyjamas and toothbrush out of the suitcase and put them on the bed.

'Here,' Ammu said.

Two clicks to close the suitcase.

Click. And click.

'Ammu,' Rahel said. 'Shall I miss dinner as my punishment?'

She was keen to exchange punishments. No dinner, in exchange for Ammu loving her the same as before.

'As you please,' Ammu said. 'But I advise you to eat. If you want to grow, that is. Maybe you could share some of Chacko's chicken.'

'Maybe and maybe not,' Chacko said.

'But what about my punishment?' Rahel said. 'You haven't given me my punishment!'

'Some things come with their own punishments,' Baby Kochamma said. As though she was explaining a sum that Rahel couldn't understand.

Some things come with their own punishments. Like bedrooms with built-in cupboards. They would all learn more about punishments soon. That they came in different sizes. That some were so big they were like cupboards with built-in bedrooms. You could spend your whole life in them, wandering through dark shelving.

Baby Kochamma's goodnight kiss left a little spit on Rahel's cheek. She wiped it off with her shoulder.

'Goodnight Godbless,' Ammu said. But she said it with her back. She was already gone.

'Goodnight,' Estha said, too sick to love his sister.

Rahel Alone watched them walk down the hotel corridor like silent but substantial ghosts. Two big, one small, in beige and pointy shoes. The red carpet took away their feet sounds.

Rahel stood in the hotel room doorway, full of sadness.

She had in her the sadness of Sophie Mol coming. The sadness of Ammu's loving her a little less. And the sadness of whatever the Orangedrink Lemondrink Man had done to Estha in Abhilash Talkies.

A stinging wind blew across her dry, aching eyes.

Chacko put a leg of chicken and some finger chips on to a quarter plate for Rahel.

'No thankyou,' Rahel said, hoping that if she could somehow effect her own punishment, Ammu would rescind hers.

'What about some ice-cream with chocolate sauce?' Chacko said.

'No thankyou,' Rahel said.

'Fine,' Chacko said. 'But you don't know what you're missing.'

He finished all the chicken and then all the ice-cream.

Rahel changed into her pyjamas.

'Please don't tell me what it is that you're being punished for,' Chacko said. 'I can't bear to hear about it.' He was mopping the last of the chocolate sauce from the sauceboat with a piece of paratha. His disgusting, after-sweet sweet. 'What was it? Scratching your mosquito bites till they bled? Not saying "Thankyou" to the taxi-driver?'

'Something much worse than that,' Rahel said, loyal to Ammu.

'Don't tell me,' Chacko said. 'I don't want to know.'

He rang for room service and a tired bearer came to take away the plates and bones. He tried to catch the dinner smells, but they escaped and climbed into the limp, brown hotel curtains.

A dinnerless niece and her dinnerfull uncle brushed their teeth together in the Hotel Sea Queen bathroom. She, a forlorn, stubby convict in striped pyjamas and a Fountain in a Love-in-Tokyo. He, in his cotton vest and underpants. His vest, taut and stretched over his round stomach like a second skin, went slack over the depression of his belly-button.

When Rahel held her frothing toothbrush still and moved her teeth instead, he didn't say she mustn't.

He wasn't a Fascist.

They took it in turns to spit. Rahel examined her white Binaca froth that dribbled down the side of the basin carefully, to see what she could see.

What colours and strange creatures had been ejected from the spaces between her teeth?

None tonight. Nothing unusual. Just Binaca bubbles.

Chacko put off the big light.

In bed, Rahel took off her Love-in-Tokyo and put it by her sunglasses. Her fountain slumped a little, but stayed standing.

Chacko lay in bed in the pool of light from his bedside lamp. A fat man on a dark stage. He reached over to his shirt lying crumpled at the foot of his bed. He took his wallet out of the pocket and looked at the photograph of Sophie Mol that Margaret Kochamma had sent him two years ago.

Rahel watched him and her cold moth spread its wings again. Slow out. Slow in. A predator's lazy blink.

The sheets were coarse, but clean.

Chacko closed his wallet and put out the light. Into the night he lit a red-tipped Charminar and wondered what his daughter looked like now. Nine years old. Last seen when she was red and wrinkled. Barely human. Three weeks later, Margaret his wife, his only love, had cried and told him about Joe.

Margaret told Chacko that she couldn't live with him any more. She told him that she needed her own space. As though Chacko had been using *her* shelves for *his* clothes. Which, knowing him, he probably had.

She asked him for a divorce.

Those last few tortured nights before he left her, Chacko would slip out of bed with a torch and look at his sleeping child. To learn her. Imprint her on his memory. To ensure that when he thought of her, the child that he invoked would be accurate. He memorised the brown down on her soft skull. The shape of her puckered, constantly moving mouth. The spaces between her toes. The suggestion of a mole. And then without meaning to, he found himself searching his baby for signs of Joe. The baby clutched his index finger while he conducted his insane, broken, envious, torchlit study. Her belly button protruded from her satiated satin stomach like a domed monument on a hill. Chacko laid his ear against it and listened with wonder at the rumblings from within. Messages being sent from here to there. New organs getting used to each other. A new Government setting up its systems. Organising the division of labour, deciding who would do what.

She smelled of milk and urine. Chacko marvelled at how someone so small and undefined, so vague in her resemblances, could so completely command the attention, the love, the *sanity*, of a grown man.

When he left, he felt that something had been torn out of him. Something big.

But Joe was dead now. Killed in a car crash. Dead as a door knob. A Joe-shaped Hole in the Universe.

In Chacko's photograph, Sophie Mol was seven years old. White and blue. Rose-lipped, and Syrian Christian nowhere. Though Mammachi peering at the photographs, insisted she had Pappachi's nose.

'Chacko?' Rahel said, from her darkened bed. 'Can I ask you a question?'

'Ask me two,' Chacko said.

'Chacko do you love Sophie Mol Most in the world?'

'She's my daughter,' Chacko said.

Rahel considered this.

'Chacko? Is it *necessary* that people HAVE to love their own children most in the world?'

'There are no rules,' Chacko said. 'But people usually do.'

'Chacko, for example,' Rahel said. 'Just for *example*, is it possible that Ammu can love Sophie Mol more than me and Estha? Or for you to love me more than Sophie Mol for *example*?'

'Anything's possible in Human Nature,' Chacko said in his Reading Aloud voice. Talking to the darkness now, suddenly insensitive to his little fountain-haired niece.

'Love. Madness. Hope. Infinite joy.'

Of the four things that were Possible in Human Nature, Rahel thought that *Infinnate Joy* sounded the saddest. Perhaps because of the way Chacko said it.

Infinnate Joy. With a church sound to it. Like a sad fish with fins all over.

A cold moth lifted a cold leg.

The cigarette smoke curled into the night. And the fat man and the little girl lay awake in silence.

Kiran Desai

STRANGE HAPPENINGS IN THE GUAVA ORCHARD

THAT SUMMER THE heat had enveloped the whole of Shahkot in a murky yellow haze. The clutter of rooftops and washing lines that usually stretched all the way to the foothills at the horizon, grew blurred and merged with the sky before the end, sometimes, of even a neighbourhood street.

'Problems have been located in the cumulus that have become overly heated,' read Mr Chawla from the newspaper. 'It is all a result of volcanic ash thrown up in the latest spurt of activity in Tierra del Fuego.'

And a little later, he reported, to whomever might be listening: 'The problem lies in the currents off the West African coastline and the unexplained molecular movement observed in the polar ice caps.'

And: 'Iraq attempts to steal monsoon by deliberately creating low pressure over desert provinces and deflecting winds from India.'

And even: 'Hungarian musician offers to draw rain clouds from Europe to India via the music of his flute.'

Shahkot itself boasted some of the highest temperatures in the country, and here, there were dozens of monsoon-inducing proposals. Mr Chawla himself submitted a proposal to the forestry department for the cutting and growing of vegetation in elaborate patterns, the army proposed the scattering and driving of clouds by jet planes flying in a special geometric formation, the police a frog wedding to be performed by temple

Extract from the novel *Strange Happenings in the Guava Orchard*.

priests. Vermaji of the university invented a giant fan which he hoped would attract the southern monsoon clouds by creating a wind tunnel moving north towards the Himalayas, and he petitioned the Electricity Supply Board for enough power to test it. Amateur scientists from Mr Barnala of Tailor Gully to Miss Raina from the Sainik Farms area attended trade fairs where they displayed instruments that emitted magnetic rays and loud buzzing sounds. Everyone in the town was worried. The mercury in the police station thermometer had shot far past the gradations Kapoor & Sons Happy Weather Company had seen fit to establish; it had leapt beyond memory and imagination, and outdone the predictions of even Mr Chawla's mother, Ammaji, who liked to think she knew in advance exactly what would happen in the future.

It was a summer that sent the dizzy pulse of fever into the sky, in which even rules and laws that usually stood straight and purposeful, grew limp like plants exposed to the afternoon sun, and weak. The heat softened and spread the roads into sticky pools of pitch and melted the grease in the army major's moustache so it drooped and uncurled, casting shadows on his fine, crisp presence. It burned the Malhotra's daughter far too dark for a decent marriage and caused the water, if it came at all, to spurt, scalding, from the taps. The policemen slept all day in the banana grove; the local judge gave his property away in bribes and left to join his brother in Copenhagen. Foreigners in their tour buses turned and went home while Shahkotians migrated in groups from fan to fan, arguing for spots directly below, leaving only for minutes if absolutely necessary and hurrying back. In the market-place, they raided the shops for palm-leaf fans and bought grey blocks of ice, smoking like small fires. They rested their heads against the coolness of melons before cutting into them, held glasses against cheeks and against foreheads between sips, fanned themselves at the stove with bunches of spinach before letting go reluctantly, for the sake of the evening meal.

The weeks passed, but the monsoon did not arrive. And by the time it was September, they had given up hope.

*

It was this year, the year of 1964, that Sampath Chawla was born to his mother Kulfi. She was twenty-one years old, newly married to Mr Chawla, and pregnant. By late September the heat and lack of rain had combined to produce terrible conditions of drought. She grew bigger, and the drought got to be so bad, famine relief camps were set up by the Red Cross to the west of Shahkot. The supply planes flew right over the bazaar; and Shahkotians watching with their heads tilted back, couldn't for the life of them understand why they didn't stop for them as well, for surely they were suffering quite enough to warrant the same attention and care being so assiduously delivered elsewhere. The ration shop was rationing out rice and lentils in smaller and smaller portions all the time. There was no fruit to be found anywhere and hardly any vegetables. Prices had become so high, nobody would buy the scraggly chickens sitting in cages outside the meat shop; finally the poor butcher had to eat them himself, and after he had eaten the last one, he was forced to turn vegetarian like the rest of the town.

Kulfi, in these months, was so enormously large, she seemed to be claiming all the earth's energy for herself, sapping it dry, leaving it withered, shrivelled and yellow. People stopped short in amazement as she walked down the street. How big she was! They forgot their dealings over the almost empty shelves in the market. They teetered on their bicycles as they looked around for just another sight of that stomach extending improbably before her like a huge growth upon a slender tree. Her eyes were so dark, so sooty and vehement though, these people who turned their heads to stare turned quickly away again, ill at ease for some reason, and unsettled. Not noticing them, she passed by as if they weren't there at all. On her face, about her mouth and in the set of her chin, was an expression, intent and determined, but yet faraway and distant as if all her thoughts were concentrated upon a point invisible to everybody but herself. She walked through Shahkot like this, as distracted as this, as strange as this.

'What do you expect?' asked Ammaji, her mother-in-law, making excuses when curious neighbours asked about Kulfi's state of mind. 'What do you expect from a woman with a baby in her belly like a little fish?'

But Kulfi was not thinking of the baby in her belly like a little fish. She was thinking of fish themselves. Of fish in many forms. Of fish big enough and good enough to feed the hunger that had overtaken her in the past months like a wave. She thought of vegetable curries and mutton kebabs. Of food that is abundant in all its many incarnations. Mangoes and coconuts and custard apples. Of mushrooms sprouting like umbrellas in the monsoon season. Of nuts, wrinkled in their shells, brown skinned, milky-fleshed.

The house was small for her big desire. She walked from the tiny blue bedroom to the kitchen thick with the smell of kerosene, around the table and chairs, up and down the balcony, then around the jamun tree in the middle of the courtyard. Meal after meal of just rice and lentils could not begin to satisfy the hunger that grew big inside her, and she bribed the vegetable sellers and the fruit sellers and the butcher with squares of silk, with embroidery, a satin petticoat, an earring set in gold, a silver nutcracker taken from her mother-in-law's trunk kept in a corner of the bedroom. She bribed them until they had nothing left to give her anyway. By then, her hunger was so fierce, it was like a big, prowling animal. In her mind, eggplant grew large and purple and crisp, and then, in a pan, turned tender and melting. Lady-fingers were flavoured with tamarind and coriander. Chicken became fragrant with cloves and cardamom. She thought of chopping and bubbling, of frying, slicing, stirring, grating.

'What on earth is she doing?' shouted Mr Chawla as he watched his wife disappear down the road to the market-place again and again, as he surveyed the empty cupboards in the house, the missing items, the gaps upon the shelves. 'What have you married me to, Amma?' he demanded ferociously of his mother who looked worried as well, but since she was responsible for the marriage, she put her worry as far from herself as possible, clucked her tongue and said soothingly: 'She is at a very delicate stage. Wait a little and maybe she will come out of it.'

'Come out of it,' he snorted. 'She is not going to come out of it. And if the baby takes after her, we are really in for trouble.'

Oddness, like aches and pains, fits of tears and lethargy always made him uneasy and he had a fear of these uncontrollable, messy puddles of life, the sticky humanness of things. He intended to keep his own involvement with such matters to the minimum, making, instead, firm progress in the direction of cleanliness and order. He went to the public library to look for books about babies and waited in line outside the Mission School to enrol the baby in school for he knew how long the waiting lists were. He collected vitamins from the Government clinic and when Kulfi refused to accompany him; he brought the poor clinic doctor home on the back of his motor scooter to give her the injections she required.

'You must take care to boil your drinking water for twenty minutes.' He followed her about the house reading aloud from his library book even though she wasn't listening to a word he said. He held one of his fingers up in the air. Despite his young age and slight build, he felt a powerful claim to authority. 'You must sit down and rest after any exercise,' he advised, and 'You must stand up and exercise regularly and diligently.' 'Don't eat raw fruit any more,' and 'Don't sing songs and tire yourself out. Don't drink tea on an empty stomach. Keep yourself extra clean. Wash your hair, take a nap, put your legs up in the air and do bicycling exercises.'

Behind him followed Ammaji. She fussed with pillows and herbs, with hair brushes and bottles of strong-scented oil for massages. 'Sing songs to improve the baby's mood,' she advised. 'Go to the temple. Say the right prayers. Make sure the baby is healthy. Make sure the planetary configurations are good. Make sure you have no lice. Make sure you smell nice, and the baby will smell nice too.'

Everywhere there was the feeling of a breath being drawn in and held as if it wouldn't be let free again until the baby was born and it could be released – released happy and full of relief if the baby was a boy; released full of disappointment and resentment if it wasn't.

In Kulfi's stomach Sampath was at first quiet, as if he wasn't there at all. Then, as if excited, he grew bolder and more full of life, until he kicked and turned and even leapt. Kulfi paced up and down, up and down with her hands upon her belly and thought she might soon begin to scream, and that, whether she wanted to or not, she might continue to scream all the way up until the birth and maybe even after. Her stomach grew larger. Her dreams of eating more extravagant. The house seemed to shrink. All about her the summer stretched white-hot into an infinite distance. Finally, in desperation for another landscape, she found a box of old crayons in the back of a cupboard and, with a feeling bordering on hysteria, she began to draw on the dirty, stained walls of the house. She drew around the pictures of babies Ammaji had put up. Babies eating porridge, posing with dolls and fluffy yellow chicks, attempting somersaults. Babies fat and fair and male, that she hoped would somehow, through some mysterious osmotic process, influence the formation of her grandchild. Kulfi drew a pond, dark, but leaping with colourful fish. A field of bright pineapples and pale, dangling snakegourd. Big lumbering jackfruit in a jackfruit tree and a scratching bunch of chickens. As her husband and mother-in-law retreated in horror, not daring to upset her or the baby still inside her, she drew a parade of cooks beheading goats. Others running to a market-place overflowing with things to haggle over. Some standing over steaming pots with ladles or pounding whole spices on a grinding stone. She drew creepers and vines that climbed in at the window and spilled a wilderness of leaves upon the walls. She began to draw fruit she did not know; spices yet to be discovered in strange pods or sequestered in the heart of unknown flowers. She drew dishes that she had never eaten. A black buck suspended over a fire with a row of ingredients destined to transform it into magnificence; a peacock cavorting among cloves of garlic; a boar entangled in a jungle of papaya trees; onions grew large beneath her feet; creepers burst from the floorboards; fish swam beneath the doors.

In the next room was the sound of Mr Chawla pacing up

and down. 'What have we gotten ourselves into?' The sound of Ammaji whispering, 'Just wait a little, son, wait and see.' Outside, in the barren sky, the drone of the Red Cross planes.

When there was almost no space left to draw on any more, and the walls, floor and ceiling were full, packed tight to the point of bursting, Sampath was born. And he was born in such remarkable circumstances, they were remembered for ever afterwards by the people of Shahkot as outdoing even the remarkableness of his mother's pregnancy.

One day, as Kulfi sat at the bedroom window looking at the street, prepared to sit through another seemingly endless stretch of time until Ammaji finally cooked and served her dinner, all of a sudden, a shadow fell across the sun and, magically, as quickly as a winter's day tumbles into a smoky evening and then into night, the white-lit afternoon deepened into the colour of old parchment as the sky darkened.

Rain! It couldn't be, could it? After they had tried so many things to bring on the monsoon and none of them had worked?

But it was!

Who knew whether it came because of the giant fan, the wedding of frogs, the pied piper, because of mercurial powers or magician's marvels? Who knew? And in the end, who cared! The rain had come to Shahkot. The monsoon was in town. Kulfi watched with unbelieving elation as the approaching smell of rain spiked the air like a flower, as the clouds shifted in from the east, reached the trees at the town's edge, and moved in. Curtains billowed white out of every window. Bits of newspaper and old plastic bags turned cartwheels in the indigo streets. The air thinned and stirred in a breeze that brought goose bumps out upon her arms. 'Look,' she shouted, 'here comes the rain.'

Outside, she could hear the sound of cheering from the bazaar. 'Rain, rain, rain, rain.' And in the streets, she watched the children leap like frogs, unable to keep still in their excitement. 'It's getting cold,' they shouted and pretended to shake. 'It's going to rain.' They wrestled and tousled each other in an exuberance of spirit while the grown-ups hurried, in this shifting, shadowed light, to get to the market and back, to bring in washing, to carry in string cots. They raised their hands in greeting to each other. 'At last!!'

In the Chawla household, Mr Chawla bustled about with plastic sheeting, while Ammaji placed buckets outside to catch the rain water and brought out candles and kerosene lanterns in preparation for the inevitable breakdown of electricity. They paused, though, to test the growing strength of the wind against their cheeks; looked up to check the progress of the clouds. When they were finally prepared for the downpour, they watched from the windows like Kulfi and the rest of Shahkot's residents leaning from balconies and verandas, from beneath the flaps of scooter rickshaws and buses; the entire town with anxious, upturned eyes until an especially strong gust sent the leaves flying like birds before gunshot and brought the first drops of water to sound loud against the parched earth.

Kulfi watched the rain come down. It came down fast and then faster yet. It filled up every bit of sky. It was like no other sound on earth and nothing that was ever suggested by the thin trickles from Shahkot faucets. It came down black with dust from the sky and dirt on the trees, and then clear. But always louder. She stretched out her hands to feel the weight of the drops on her flat palms, and then put her face out too: holding it out, luminous, pale, in this city enclosed within the dark heart of the monsoon.

As she did so, she felt Sampath kicking inside her stomach. She felt her heart jump from the rhythm. He kicked harder and harder. The jamun tree in the courtyard thrashed and creaked. The rain streamed down Kulfi's hair and washed over her face. Her husband shouted, 'Get away from the open window,' but she paid no attention. He wrapped her in a square of plastic, but she shrugged it off. The rain descended in great sweeping sheets. The neighbours withdrew in quick sharp movements, slammed their windows, barred their doors, but Kulfi stretched out further still, further and further until the rain took up all the space inside her head. It seized her brain, massaged and incorporated her into the watery sounds until she felt that she herself might turn to storm and disappear in this blowing, this growling, this lightning flutter quick as a moth's wing. If she would only let go of the metal window frame, she herself could take all those tedious days of summer and crash them to the ground, transform them into water and wind and pounding.

How the baby leapt! She felt all her muscles contract as a clap of thunder echoed about her. Again, the thunder roared. Kulfi, soaking wet, opened her mouth wide and roared back. Below her, the ground had disappeared. Ponds formed, joined to make lakes, and ran down streets to make rivers. Rivers took the place of roads.

A mere two hours later, as Mr Chawla and Ammaji ran back and forth between Kulfi and the telephone that had gone dead making it impossible to reach the doctor, the storm still raging, rain pouring through the windows that would not stay closed and flooding in beneath the doors, – Sampath was born. As his face with a small brown birthmark upon one cheek appeared to the cheers of his family, there was a roaring overhead that almost split their ear-drums, followed by a vast crash in the street outside.

'What was that?' said Mr Chawla nervously, as the ground shuddered. Could it be that his son's birth had coincided with the end of the world? Leaving the side of Kulfi and the new baby, he and Ammaji ran to the window to investigate, and discovered that far from being the end of things, it was more like the beginning.

Split over their old jamun tree, they found a crate of Red Cross supplies dropped by a Swedish relief plane befuddled by the storm in an accident that must surely have been planned by the Gods above. The departing plane rose up high into the sky and vanished among the swirling clouds, unmoved apparently by the townspeople jumping and waving down below as they ran out despite the downpour to greet this unexpected largesse. Draped in the foliage of the ruined jamun, they discovered bags full of sugar and tea, of rehydration mixes, dried-milk powder, raisins and digestive biscuits. There were unidentifiable powders in boxes covered with pictures of smiling foreign women. There were nuts, chocolates, and baby-food tins galore. Filling their arms with their part of this booty they ran up and down with umbrellas.

Climbing high into the tree, the street urchins tossed down what they found lodged in the broken branches. Mr Chawla ran back and forth like a silly chicken filling a shopping bag with supplies, while Ammaji alerted the neighbours of the birth by shouting out of the window near Kulfi's bedside. Soon the house was full of well wishers, chattering excitedly, not knowing whether to talk of the baby or the rain or the food. 'Wonderful,' they kept exclaiming. 'What a beautiful baby . . . and can you believe the monsoon? Oh and the food! . . . What a baby!'

Only Kulfi was quiet and turned her head when Mr Chawla offered her a digestive biscuit. Soon the storm would end and the world would grow silent and fragrant; the air weathered soft as the hour of sleep. Soon, the winged ants would be flying, and lizards would grow fat on dozens of multiplying insects. The water would turn muddy and soft. Doors would swell, and it would be impossible to close them once opened, or to open them once closed. Fungus and mould would sprout green and voluptuous and strange mushrooms would be discovered in the cupboard under the sink.

Attempting to include Kulfi in their high spirits, they assured her Sampath was destined for greatness. 'Let's name him Sampath,' they said. 'Good fortune.' For though he might not be very plump or very fair, he was triumphantly and indisputably male. In great good humour, chewing on famine relief, they joked by the light of a roomful of candles (for the electricity had gone, of course), that the world, large and mysterious beyond Shahkot, had taken notice of him: 'Look! Even people in Sweden have remembered to send a birthday present.'

BIOGRAPHICAL NOTES

Mulk Raj Anand was born in 1905 and began writing in Mahatma Gandhi's retreat in Ahmedabad in 1927. He was awarded the International Peace Prize of the World Peace Council in 1950. His novels include *Untouchable*, *Coolie*, *Seven Summers*, *Morning Face*, *Confessions of a Lover* and *The Bubble*. He lives in Bombay.

Anjana Appachana's first book, *Incantations and Other Stories*, was published in England, the USA and India, and has also been translated into German. One of her short stories in the collection won an O. Henry Festival prize. In 1993 she was a Hawthornden Fellow at Hawthornden Castle, Scotland. She received the National Endowment for the Arts Creative Writing Fellowship for the year 1995-96. Anjana Appachana's novel, *Listening Now*, will be published by Random House in early 1998.

Vikram Chandra was born in New Delhi in 1961. He is the author of *Red Earth and Pouring Rain* (1995), which was awarded the David Higham Prize for Fiction and the Commonwealth Writers Prize for Best First Book, and *Love and Longing in Bombay* (1997). He lives in Washington, DC and Bombay.

Upamanyu Chatterjee was born in 1959. He is the author of two novels, *English August: An Indian Story* (1988) and *The Last Burden* (1993). He lives in Bombay.

Amit Chaudhuri was born in Calcutta in 1962 and brought up in Bombay. He is a graduate of University College, London, and was a research student at Balliol College, Oxford. He is now Creative Arts Fellow at Wolfson College, Oxford, and has received the Harper Wood Studentship for English Literature and Poetry from St John's College, Cambridge. His first novel, *A Strange and Sublime Address*, won first prize in the 1991 Betty Trask Awards, the 1992 Commonwealth Writers Prize for Best First Book and a runner-up award for the 1991 *Guardian* Fiction Prize. His second novel, *Afternoon Raag*, won the 1993 Southern Arts Literature Prize, the Encore Award and a runner-up award for the 1993 *Guardian* Fiction Prize. His next novel, *Freedom Song*, will be published by Picador.

Nirad Chaudhuri was born in rural Bengal in 1897. He has lived in England since 1970. His books include *The Autobiography of an Unknown Indian* (1951), *A Passage to England* (1959), *The Continent of Circe* (1965), *Hinduism* (1979) and *Thy Hand, Great Anarch* (1987). He lives in Oxford.

Anita Desai was born in 1937 and educated in Delhi. Her published work includes *Clear Light of Day*, which was shortlisted for the 1980 Booker Prize, *Fire on the Mountain*, for which she won the Royal Society of Literature's Winifred Holtby Memorial Prize and the 1978 National Academy of Letters Award, *In Custody*, which was shortlisted for the 1984 Booker Prize and was filmed by Merchant Ivory, and, most recently, *Journey to Ithaca*. She is a member of the Advisory Board for English of the National Assembly of Letters in Delhi and a Fellow of the Royal Society for Literature. She is married, with four children and divides her time between the UK and the United States, where she teaches.

Kiran Desai was born in India. Her first novel, *Strange Happenings in the Guava Orchard*, will be published by

Faber and Faber.

G.V.Desani was born in 1909 in Nairobi and educated in England. His novel *All About H.Hatterr* was published in 1948.

Amitav Ghosh was born in Calcutta in 1956. He is the author of two novels, *The Circle of Reason* and *The Shadow Lines*, and a work of non-fiction, *In an Antique Land*.

Githa Hariharan was born in 1954 and educated in Bombay, Manila and the United States. She is the author of two novels, *The Thousand Faces of the Night* (1992), which won the Commonwealth Writers Prize for Best First Book, and *The Ghosts of Vasu Master* (1994), and a collection of stories, *The Art of Dying* (1993). She has also edited *A Southern Harvest*, a volume of stories in English translation from four major South Indian languages. She lives in New Delhi where she works as a freelance editor.

Ruth Prawer Jhabvala was born in Germany of Polish parents and came to England at the age of twelve. She graduated from Queen Mary College, London University, and married an Indian architect. They lived in Delhi from 1951 to 1975. Since then they have divided their time between Delhi, New York and London. Her published work includes the story collection *Out of India* and the novels *To Whom She Will, The Nature of Passion, Esmond in India, The Householder, Get Ready for Battle, A Backward Place, A New Dominion, Heat and Dust* (which won the 1975 Booker Prize), *In Search of Love and Beauty, Three Continents* and *Poet and Dancer*. In collaboration with James Ivory and Ismail Merchant she has written scripts for film and television, including *A Room with a View*, which won an Academy Award in 1987, and *Howard's End*, winner of an Academy Award in 1993. She won the Neil Gunn International Fellowship in 1978 and the MacArthur Foundation Award in 1984.

Firdaus Kanga was born in Bombay in 1959. He graduated in history at the University of Bombay and came to England in 1989. He is the author of *Trying to Grow* (1990), *Heaven on Wheels* (1991) and the play *A Kind of Immigrant* (1992). He has also written and presented programmes for television. His film adaptation of *Trying to Grow*, in which he stars himself, is in post-production with the BFI/BBC.

Mukul Kesavan was born and raised in Delhi. He was educated at Delhi University and Trinity Hall, Cambridge. His first novel, *Looking through Glass*, was published in 1995. He teaches history at Jamia Millia University in Delhi, where he lives with his wife and children.

Saadat Hasan Manto was born in Sambrala in Punjab in 1912. In a literary and journalistic career spanning more than two decades, he wrote over 200 short stories and scores of plays and essays. He died in Lahore, Pakistan, in 1955.

Kamala Markandaya was born and educated in India. She settled in Britain in the early 1960s. Her work includes *A Silence of Desire* (1960), *Possession* (1963), *A Handful of Rice* (1966), *The Coffer Dams* (1969), *The Nowhere Man* (1972), *Two Virgins* (1973), *The Golden Honeycomb* (1977), *Nectar in a Sieve* (1982) and *Pleasure City* (1982).

Gita Mehta is the author of the novels *Raj* and *A River Sutra*, and two non-fiction works, *Karma Cola* and *Snakes and Ladders*. She is married, with one son, and divides her time among the United States, England and India.

Ved Mehta was born in Lahore in 1934. He was educated at the Arkansas School for the Blind, at Pomona College, at Balliol College, Oxford, and at Harvard. His first book, *Face to Face*, was published in 1957. Since then he has written many autobiographical works, including *Vedi*, *The Ledge Between the Streams* and *Sound Shadows of the New World*. He has received two extended Ford Foundation grants and held two Guggenheim Fellowships. In 1982 he was selected as a MacArthur Prize Fellow.

Rohinton Mistry was born in Bombay in 1952, and has lived in Canada since 1975. He is the author of a collection of short stories, *Tales from Firozsha Baag*, and two novels: *Such a Long Journey*, which was shortlisted for the Booker Prize and won the Commonwealth Writers Prize for Best First Book, the Governor General's Award and the W.H.Smith/Books in Canada First Novel Award; and *A Fine Balance*, which was shortlisted for the Booker Prize and the IMPAC Dublin Literary Award and won the Commonwealth Writers Prize for Best Book.

R.K.Narayan was born in Madras in 1906. The first of his twenty-nine books, *Swami and Friends*, was published in 1935. His subsequent novels include *The English Teacher* (1945), *Waiting for the Mahatma* (1955) and *The Painter of Signs* (1977). His novel *The Guide* (1958) won him the National Prize of the Indian Literary Academy, his country's highest literary honour. In 1980 he was awarded the A.C.Benson Medal by the Royal Society of Literature, and in 1982 he was made an Honorary Member of the American Academy and Institute of Arts and Letters. He is currently working on the sequel to *The World of Nagaraj* (1990). He lives in Madras.

Jawaharlal Nehru was born in 1889. He became India's first Prime Minister in 1947. He died in 1964.

Padma Perera, who has also written under the name of Padma Hejmadi, was born in Madras and educated in India and the United States. She is the author of two collections of short stories, *Coigns of Vantage* and *Doctor Salaam and Other Stories*, and a series of volumes of non-fiction, *Sumi Spaces*. She teaches at the University of Colorado in Boulder.

Satyajit Ray, India's premier film-maker, was born in

Calcutta in 1921. His films include *Pather Panchali* (1955), *Aparajito* (1956), *The World of Apu* (1959), *Kanchanjangha* (1962), *The Adversary* (1971), *The Home and the World* (1984) and *Enemy of the People* (1984). He died in 1992.

Arundhati Roy was trained as an architect. She has worked as a production designer and written the screenplay for two films. Her first novel, *The God of Small Things*, will be published by Flamingo. She lives in New Delhi.

Nayantara Sahgal was born in 1927. A novelist and author of numerous articles and short stories, her publications include *Prison and Chocolate Cake*, *A Time to Be Happy* and *Rich Like Us*.

I.Allan Sealy was born in Allahabad, and has taught at universities in the USA, Australia and Canada. He is the author of *The Trotter-Nama*, which won Best First Book (Eurasia) of the 1989 Commonwealth Writers Prize, *Hero* (1992) and a travel book, *From Yukon to Yucatan* (1994). He divides his time between India and New Zealand.

Vikram Seth was born in 1952. He trained as an economist and has lived for several years each in the UK, California, China and India. He is the author of *The Golden Gate: A Novel in Verse*, *A Suitable Boy*, *From Heaven Lake: Travels through Sinkiang and Tibet*, and four volumes of poetry.

Bapsi Sidhwa was born in Karachi and brought up in Lahore. An active social worker among Asian women, she represented Pakistan at the Asian Women's Congress in 1975. Her novels include *The Crow Eaters*, *The Bride* and *Ice-Candy-Man*. She now lives in the United States.

Sara Suleri was educated in Pakistan, England and the United States. She is currently Associate Professor of English at Yale University. She is the author of *Meatless Days* and *The Rhetoric of English India*.

Shashi Tharoor was born in 1956 and grew up in Bombay and Calcutta. He is the author of *The Great Indian Novel*, *Show Business* and a collection of stories, *The Five-Dollar Smile*. His most recent book is a work of non-fiction, *From Midnight to Millennium*. He lives in New York and works for the United Nations.

Ardashir Vakil was born in Bombay in 1962. He lives in London with his wife and daughter and teaches English at Pimlico Comprehensive School. *Beach Boy*, his first novel, is published by Hamish Hamilton.

ACKNOWLEDGEMENTS

The editors and publishers gratefully acknowledge permission from the following to reprint stories or extracts from works in copyright:

Mulk Raj Anand for 'Liar' by Mulk Raj Anand from *Contemporary Indian Short Stories in English*, edited by Shiv K. Kumar, published by Sahitya Akademi, India (1991); the author c/o Arcadia for 'Sharmaji' from *Incantations and Other Stories* © Anjana Appachana, published by Virago (1991); Faber & Faber and Little, Brown and Company for 'Shakti' from *Love and Longing in Bombay* © Vikram Chandra 1997; the author c/o A. M. Heath & Co. Ltd for 'The Assassination of Indira Gandhi' by Upamanyu Chatterjee from *Best Short Stories 1986*, edited by Giles Gordon and David Hughes, published by Oxford University Press; William Heinemann Ltd for the extract 'Sandeep's Visit' from *A Strange and Sublime Address* © Amit Chaudhuri 1991; Chatto & Windus Ltd. for the extract 'My Birthplace' from *The Autobiography of an Unknown Indian* © Nirad C. Chaudhuri 1987; the author c/o Rogers, Coleridge & White Ltd for 'Games At Twilight' from *Games at Twilight* © Anita Desai 1978, published by Penguin; the author c/o the Watkins Loomis Agency for the extract from *Strange Happenings in the Guava Orchard* © Kiran Desai 1997; Penguin Books for 'Nashawy' from *In an Antique Land* © Amitav Ghosh 1992; the author c/o the David Godwin Agency for 'The Remains of the Feast' from *The Art of Dying*